Mencken

H. L. Mencken, 1926. Photograph by Edward Steichen. Reprinted with permission of Joanna T. Steichen.

Mencken

The American Iconoclast

MARION ELIZABETH RODGERS

OXFORD

UNIVERSITY PRESS

2005

OXFORD
UNIVERSITY PRESS

Oxford University Press, Inc., publishes works that further
Oxford University's objective of excellence
in research, scholarship, and education.

Oxford   New York
Auckland   Cape Town   Dar es Salaam   Hong Kong   Karachi
Kuala Lumpur   Madrid   Melbourne   Mexico City   Nairobi
New Delhi   Shanghai   Taipei   Toronto

With offices in
Argentina   Austria   Brazil   Chile   Czech Republic   France   Greece
Guatemala   Hungary   Italy   Japan   Poland   Portugal   Singapore
South Korea   Switzerland   Thailand   Turkey   Ukraine   Vietnam

Copyright © 2005 by Marion Elizabeth Rodgers

Published by Oxford University Press, Inc.
198 Madison Avenue, New York, NY 10016
www.oup.com

Oxford is a registered trademark of Oxford University Press

Library of Congress Cataloging-in-Publication Data
Rodgers, Marion Elizabeth.
Mencken : the American iconoclast / Marion Elizabeth Rodgers.
p.   cm.
Includes bibliographical references and index.
ISBN-13: 978-0-19-507238-9
ISBN-10: 0-19-507238-3
1. Mencken, H. L. (Henry Louis), 1880–1956.
2. Authors, American—20th century—Biography.
3. Journalists—United States—Biography.
4. Editors—United States—Biography. I. Title
PS3525.E43Z79   2005
818'.5209—dc22   [B]
2005047786

*Permission to quote H. L. Mencken has been granted by the Enoch Pratt Free Library,
Baltimore, in accordance with the terms of the bequest of H. L. Mencken.*

1 3 5 7 9 8 6 4 2

Printed in the United States of America
on acid-free paper

To Leon Livingstone
and
Jules Witcover

THE ICONOCLAST: The liberation of the human mind has been best furthered by . . . fellows who heaved dead cats into sanctuaries.

—H. L. Mencken

Fifty years ago I spent my mornings reading to an old man who suffered, as I now suffer, from a series of strokes. He was a writer. He was H. L. Mencken. I have never known a kinder man. But when he unsheathed his typewriter and sharpened its keys, his prose was anything but kind. It was rollicking and it was ferocious. Witty, intellectual polemicists are a vanishing breed today. Their role has been usurped by television boobs whose IQs measure just below their body temperatures. Some journalism schools even warn their students to shun words that may hurt. But sometimes words should hurt. That is why they are in the language. When terrorists slaughter innocents, when corporation executives betray the trust of shareholders, when lewd priests betray the trust of little children, it is time to mobilize the language and send it into battle.

When Mencken died in January 1956, he was cremated. That was a mistake. He should have been "rolled in malleable gold and polished to blind the cosmos." I still miss him. America misses him more.

—William Manchester (1922–2004)

CONTENTS

Contents

"Mencken was our god." Holding the Maryland flag aloft with cheering students at Harvard University, 1926. H. L. Mencken Collection, Enoch Pratt Free Library.

Prologue

BOSTON, 1926

On the morning of April 5, 1926, a multitude of Harvard and Boston University undergraduates, reporters, and the curious gathered at Brimstone Corner in Boston. Students, many of them clutching magazines, awaited the Baltimore journalist and editor H. L. Mencken.

Boston newspapers had already announced his impending fate. One headline blared:

FAMOUS EDITOR DEFIES POLICE: WANTS TO MAKE TEST CASE IN COURTS

Another said:

MENCKEN, READY FOR JAIL, SELLING MAGAZINES HERE

From curb to curb, the crowd awaited the man who had famously derided Puritanism as "the haunting fear that someone, somewhere, may be happy." For more than a quarter of a century, he had assaulted it in a variety of publications, from the *Baltimore Herald* and the *Baltimore Sunpapers* to his popular magazines, the *Smart Set* and the *American Mercury*, in his forty books, and in his defense of such authors as Theodore Dreiser. Along the way, he had battled the mentality that had caused *Huckleberry Finn* to be banned from local libraries.[1]

Mencken was a believer in liberty "in its wildest and imaginable sense," as he put it, "liberty up to the extreme limits of the feasible and tolerable." It was Mencken who had convinced Clarence Darrow to defend John Scopes in the infamous Monkey Trial the previous hot summer. At issue was not simply Darwin's theory of evolution but freedom of speech itself, a matter of concern to no one more than Henry Mencken. In a long and varied career as reporter, columnist, author, and literary and social critic, his very existence was committed to the free expression of ideas, no matter how controversial and unpopular. "The two main ideas that run through all my writing," he explained, "whether it be literary criticism or political polemic, are these: I am strongly in favor of liberty and I hate fraud."

Freedom had always been an issue with Mencken: first, at an early age, freedom from his father's choice of a career; later, as he began to develop as a critic, from the Victorian Puritanism that stifled literature and every aspect of American life; then, from governmental laws that violated civil liberties for whites and blacks; finally, during the two world wars, from censorship of the press. The Constitution and the Bill of Rights, Mencken believed, were sacred documents that set up clear lines of demarcation that no government should trespass.

Now Mencken, as editor of the *American Mercury*, was embarking on another battle against censorship in a challenge to freedom of speech that the *New York Times* had likened to a second Scopes Trial. Accompanied by Arthur Garfield Hays, counsel to the American Civil Liberties Union, and with a peddler's license in his pocket, Mencken was about to do battle with the Reverend J. Franklin Chase, secretary of the New England Watch & Ward Society, over one particular article in his magazine.

Since its earliest days Boston had had a history of literary bigotry. Items that Chase censored from Massachusetts readers included Boccaccio's *Decameron*, Sterne's *Tristram Shandy*, even lyrics by John Dryden. Among modern publications, they included works by Eugene O'Neill, Theodore Dreiser, and Sherwood Anderson. As Chase said, "A whole high school class of unwedded mothers may be the result of a lascivious book."

Chase's tyranny and oppression were indomitable. He seldom appeared in public, simply notifying his committee that he believed certain passages in a given magazine or book were illegal. His influence over the local courts had saved him from ever having to name the offending passages. Consequently, hundreds of volumes were shelved, their authors never given the opportunity to be heard in court. Chase became so adept in his tactics that merchants obeyed the Watch & Ward Society with scarcely a question; the press did not dare criticize the censor.

Chase now focused his ammunition on an innocuous but true story that appeared in the April 1926 issue of the *American Mercury*, written by Herbert Asbury. It told the tale of a prostitute called "Hatrack" from Farmington, Missouri. Its theme was Christian hypocrisy. Each Sunday night Hatrack would attend church, hoping to be treated as a Christian lady; each Sunday she would be spurned. After church she then would take customers to one of the two town cemeteries—the Protestants to the Catholic cemetery and the Catholics to the Masonic burial ground. Chase found the *American Mercury* so immoral as to be unfit to read. Notwithstanding the warning, a newsdealer at Harvard did sell a copy of the censored magazine and was now being confronted with a possible prison sentence.

Mencken jumped into the fray with relish. "Every censorship, however good its intent, degenerates inevitably into the sort of tyranny that the Watch & Ward fanatics so long exercised in Boston," he reasoned. If Chase were permitted to get away with this assault, others would follow. Mencken decided to come to Boston and offer himself as a substitute defendant. He would deliberately try to sell a copy of the banned magazine directly to Frank Chase himself in the Boston Common, thereby forcing the reverend to meet the editor in open court. Now it was up to the courts to grapple with the question as to whether a private individual in society could dictate to the public what it should or should not read.

Mencken knew the risks he was exposed to. "By the time you get this I may be in jail," he hastily communicated to one of his girlfriends before leaving Baltimore. Yet he maintained his position resolutely: "I believe that any man accused of circulating indecent literature should have his day in open court, and until he gets it he should be unmolested by any sort of intimidation."[2]

The editors of the *Boston Herald* were not amused. Under the headline "MR. MENCKEN CRAVES ARREST," they had written: "When an editor broadcasts to the world at large via Associated Press his intention to get arrested, two theories of his conduct are deductible. He may intend to vindicate a great moral principle. Or he may intend to put over a clever publicity stunt. He will avow the former, of course."[3]

HARVARD AND THE BOSTON COLLEGIATE COMMUNITY were not alone in their enthusiasm for the outspoken editor from Baltimore. "You have no idea the enormous vogue Mencken has among students," wrote one university president. The *American Mercury* ranked first among magazines sold in the Harvard University bookstore, at Columbia University, and other campuses across the country, surpassing *Harper's* and the *Atlantic*. The college students who formed a part of this audience flaunted the magazine in class to irritate their instructors; if a lecture was too dull, copies of the magazine were held up in protest. No one had done more to change the attitude toward conventions and affect the literary tastes of an entire generation. As one critic put it, the *American Mercury* was one of the loudest voices whose noise combined to make the Roaring Twenties roar.[4]

BY EARLY AFTERNOON on this spring day, the crowd had grown so large that some viewers climbed trees; others clung precariously to the sides of buildings for a closer look. Just before two o'clock, a taxicab drew up to the curb and Mencken sprang out, carrying under his arm several of the green-colored magazines. In an instant, he and Hays were surrounded by a swarm of men and women, waving dollar bills in their hands, bawling for copies of the banned publication. The throng pressed so close that the two men were literally swept off their feet. Police

Spreading terror among enemies: Arthur Garfield Hays brandishes the *American Mercury*.
H. L. Mencken Collection, Enoch Pratt Free Library.

tried to break up the jam, and finally, by threats of wholesale arrests, induced the petitioners to move on. Laughing, spectators relocated across the street to the Common, where, in front of the subway entrance, thousands more waited.

For many of the college students, the arrest at Brimstone Corner would be their first opportunity to see Mencken in the flesh. News photographers had a little difficulty in picking him out from the sea of fedoras. He was only five feet eight inches tall, and his stockiness made him look shorter.

Physically his weight and pug nose made his appearance unimposing. One photographer compared Mencken unflatteringly to "a brewer's son." Yet this same photographer labeled his obvious energy as "supercharged." In fact, all of his life Mencken had the buoyancy of a naughty boy.

On this April day in particular, in anticipation of Mencken's arrival, many Harvard undergraduates, among them reporters for the *Harvard Crimson*, had run to the local kiosk at dawn to buy remaining issues of the magazine. That same day, the last copy in the public library was stolen. Such activity was justified, one student said, with this excuse: "The *American Mercury* was our Bible, and Mencken our god."[5]

THE MOB WAS NOW getting larger and uncontrollably restless. "Where's Chase?" voices cried.

"Yes, where's Chase?" Mencken echoed.

Finally, from the crowd's outer edge, came a shout. "Here he is!"

The chief of the Boston Vice Squad and a young officer pushed their way through the onlookers, as Rev. J. Franklin Chase grimly approached Mencken. The secretary of the Watch & Ward Society was known to be a man of quick temper who had, on occasion, punched attorneys for men against whom he appeared in court. Along the route, the secretary was greeted with jeers. "Is this a free country or not?" yelled one student. "Why did we fight the revolution?" called another.

At last Chase was face to face with the editor of the magazine he claimed was corrupting the morals of America's youth.

"Are you Chase?" Mencken asked.

"I am," glared the crusader. He pointed to the bundle of magazines in Mencken's hand. "Will you sell me a copy?"

"I will," replied Mencken. "I will, indeed."

Mencken gave a polite little bow and handed Chase a copy of the *Mercury*. When Chase offered him a fifty-cent piece, Mencken's entire face lit up. To the delight of the crowd, Mencken suddenly bit the coin in an exaggerated, dramatic way so that everyone could see him checking on its authenticity. There was a wild cheer as Mencken innocently handed over a copy of the magazine to the reverend.

Chase pointed a quivering finger at Mencken. "Arrest that man!" But by then, the catcalls were so loud that he could hardly be heard.[6]

Before Mencken could be hustled away, he tossed the remaining copies of the *Mercury* into the air. Immediately there was a mad scramble. Police darted after them, but they were too late. In the near-riot, one of the periodicals was torn to pieces; pages were pocketed as souvenirs. The students hailed Mencken and booed the police.

Meanwhile there was no doubt the arrested man was enjoying himself. With his hat pulled low, he gestured with a cigar in his left hand, swiveling his head to take in the spectacle he had created as he was being led off. Police headquarters were a mere four blocks away, but the crowd was so dense that progress was slow. Men and women were told to stand back; instead, they followed the prisoner almost into the building.

"Why, he's much smaller than I thought," murmured one woman to her companion. The most remarkable thing, commented another, was the editor's undistinguished taste in clothes; she, along with many others, had expected America's most famous critic to be wearing spats.[7]

Inside headquarters, Mencken was surrounded by guards and newsmen as he spent an hour in custody. He was in a frisky mood, maintaining a cheerful attitude as a desk clerk filed the preliminary paperwork. Birthplace? "Baltimore." Occupation? "Editor and clergyman," Mencken winked—but asked that the latter be off the record.

Mencken being led to court, Boston, 1926. H. L. Mencken Collection, Enoch Pratt Free Library.

To the assembled members of the press, Mencken looked like an earnest schoolboy as he stood before the bench, his eyes fixed uneasily upon the judge. All parties connected with the arrest had been told to speak in an undertone, so the details of the case would not corrupt anyone else in the room. Reporters now pressed forward toward the rail, straining to hear what was being said.

Chase's attorney, "a tall, gaunt, seedy-looking fellow," held a handwritten brief that "had plainly seen much service." He began by denouncing Mencken in furious whispers. The *American Mercury*, he said, was obscene, indecent, and impure. A copy, underlined in red ink, was handed to the judge, along with the half dollar that had been paid for it and willingly surrendered by Mencken.

Soon it was Mencken's turn.

Any idea of youthful demeanor was put to rest as soon as he pleaded not guilty and argumentatively made his case. He resented, he said, any suggestion that his magazine was salacious. Contributors to the *American Mercury* included a bishop and a United States senator. He then attacked the mistaken orientation of the prosecution. If anyone should be prosecuted, he boomed, it should be the responsible editor or publisher, not some hapless newsdealer. "I am the editor of the magazine and I want to accept the responsibility."

"This case involves the principles of American liberty," claimed Mencken's lawyer, Arthur Garfield Hays, *sotto voce.* "There is a spirit throughout this country of minorities imposing their ideas upon the majorities," Hays continued. His voice grew louder. "I was in the Scopes case in Tennessee. Those people were just as intent down there that their children should be saved as Mr. Chase here is that the point of view of this society shall be forced upon the public."

The judge decided to read the magazine for himself before replying. He adjourned the trial overnight and took it home.

"It's a cinch," said one Boston reporter. "Chase always wins."[8]

THE NEXT MORNING, Mencken was called back to the bar. The minutes ticked by. Then, amid a rustle of cloaks, the judge entered the room and took his seat. A copy of the *American Mercury* lay on his desk. Mencken braced himself for the worst. After the requisite hush, the judge began disposing of Chase's contentions one by one, then handed down his decision: Mencken had committed no offense; the *American Mercury* was not obscene and in no way violated the law. The complaint was dismissed.

The victory was both unexpected and overwhelming.

"We all stood silent for a moment," Mencken recalled, with the lawyers blinking and swallowing incredulously. A clutch of newspapermen immediately surrounded the Baltimorean, congratulating him. Clearly, Mencken had scored a legal triumph. What the country needed, he told the assembled press, was criticism to sting it to thought. Scribbling into his notepad, a reporter turned to the editor. "Then you believe it is a useful thing to keep the animals stirred up?"

Mencken grinned. "Of course," he answered. "What could be more useful?"

A moment later, dashing for his coat, Mencken left the building, exiting to a round of applause.[9]

WHEN NEWS of Mencken's impending arrival reached Harvard, it struck the campus like a surge of electricity. Hundreds of pupils slammed down their books and ran to Union Hall. In less than an hour, it was jammed. Luncheon had been prepared for two hundred, but more than 2,000 stood among the tables and at every spot in between; others on the outside craned their necks through the open windows. They did not know that Mencken had been acquitted.

When Mencken entered the hall, preceded by professors Felix Frankfurter and Zechariah Chafee of the Law School, all present leaped to their feet.

Deafening cheers swelled; it was some minutes before Frankfurter, champion of civil liberties, could make himself heard.

"We had assembled to console with a martyr," he said. "We did not hope to greet the martyr vindicated." There was a great whoop. "Mr. Mencken has done a dreadful and brave thing," Frankfurter continued. "His was the courage to resist brutality."

The applause of hundreds of youthful undergraduates momentarily made Mencken feel shy. He began with a joke, apologizing that he wasn't much of a speech giver. "Pursuing such business gives me a lot of fun," Mencken confessed. The hall was still; one boy leaned over a balcony for a closer look.

"But this affair was something more than fun," Mencken continued, looking out over the eager faces. "I did not intend to go to jail while I was here," Mencken added, smiling at the crowd.

"But all joking aside, I came to make these people accuse a man openly in the courts, by laws which are the same for all and known to all. . . . That was the sole purpose." Mencken's eyes scanned the hall.

"This sort of thing," he intoned, "is going on all over America at present. One advantage it has is that it will put well-disposed liberty-loving men on notice. The worst thing in the state, though, is the indolence in the face of such outrages. Nine-tenths of the people when confronted by this sort of thing won't fight. Yet it *can* be done and *ought* to be done."

Mencken lifted from a chair beside him the flag of Maryland and unfurled it. "I want to give you something that I know you will appreciate, thinking as you do," he said. "This is the flag of the Free State of Maryland, of which I have the honor to be a citizen."[10]

The erupting ovation lasted for more than two minutes. The room, the *Boston Post* noted, "sounded like the Harvard stadium on a Saturday afternoon in November, as it reverberated and re-echoed with a long football cheer for 'MENCKEN!'" All at once listeners surged from their seats and surrounded the editor, thrusting forward their copies of the *American Mercury*, eagerly clamoring for his autograph, their hands reaching across to shake his.

"It was sheer pleasure, and heartening pleasure, to have witnessed that fine outpour of youth to celebrate your fight," Frankfurter would later write to Mencken. A small number of alumni of the college, after hearing a church sermon chastising Harvard for inviting "a certain individual of a vulgar publication," wrote President Lawrence Lowell of Harvard, asking for his opinion. "I do feel that the students have received no permanent harm," replied Lowell, "and that our habit of allowing them to ask to address whom they please tends, in the long run, to sound and healthy principles."[11]

In the months to follow, Mencken would be recognized as having won a major victory. His was the most significant effort against censorship in Massachusetts; others would follow throughout the nation. For ten years after 1926, no such trial would take place in the United States without some reference

to the *American Mercury*. Mencken's name would become internationally identified with freedom of speech. It would be the mantra of his life.

"There was no chance given to me but to fight," Mencken told the group of
young admirers surrounding him that day. "The best thing about liberty is that it
is such a charming thing to fight for."[12]

Part One
1880–1914

Advertisement for August Mencken & Bro. H. L. Mencken Collection, Enoch Pratt Free Library.

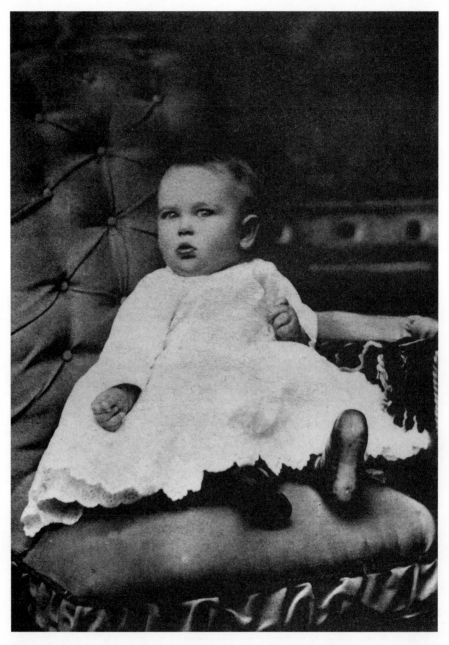

"I'd have butchered beautifully." Mencken as an infant. H. L. Mencken Collection, Enoch Pratt Free Library.

1

THE CITIZEN OF BALTIMORE

H IS OWN FAMILY CALLED HIM *HARRY*, newspapermen *Hank*, occasional friends *Henry*, and New Yorkers *Menck*. But his trademark was H. L. Mencken.

There was H. L. Mencken, the public figure, noisy iconoclast and national wag; there was also Henry Mencken, the citizen of Baltimore and sentimentalist: the emotionally Victorian, earthy romancer of various women, and kindly, generous visitor to the sick, who shared his gusto for music and food among a small circle of loyal and devoted friends. "He was fully aware of this distinction and drew it sharply himself," a colleague observed. "As far as he could, he screened Henry Mencken from the observation of press and public, while thrusting H. L. Mencken to the fore."

It was the citizen of Baltimore whom very few were to come to know.[1]

HENRY LOUIS MENCKEN came into this world in the age of horses, before Buffalo Bill organized his Wild West Show and when settlers were still staking out territory in the West. He left it when military jets were crossing the breadth of the United States in three hours. When he was a child, typewriters were a novelty. He lived to see the beginning of television, though he thought its future uncertain, and he would not have imagined (but would not have been surprised) that "video verbiage" would replace reading. When he was a boy, Civil War veterans still marched in parades; by the time Mencken departed this earth, men had returned from the Korean War.

For seventy-five years, Mencken lived in Baltimore, a conservative city criticized for being too slow to change. Yet this man, who in thought and action seemed so modern and who instilled a liberating spirit in the cultural fabric of his own century, refused to live anywhere else.

Infancy, that nonage Mencken defined as that larval stage of his life, began for him on September 12, 1880. Of his earliest years nothing more need be said. Years later, when a suffragette accused him of suffering from "the dread disease known as babyophobia," he observed: "I have long advocated the segregation of all babies upon remote and well-guarded farms from birth until the age of 3 years."[2]

Indeed, his first memories of Baltimore were formed at age three, while staring from the ledge of the second-story window of his father's cigar factory at 368 Baltimore Street. The time was the day after his third birthday; the occasion was the Summer Night's Carnival of the Order of the Orioles, one of the city's more curious parades which made its final appearance that year. From above the sign August Mencken & Bro., sitting on his mother's lap, little Harry saw unfolding the greatest spectacle the town had ever witnessed.

The parade had begun a few blocks away at the harbor, where fireworks cascaded in showers of red, blue, and green. Yellow torches of flaring gas made Baltimore Street blaze with a hard light, "as bright as day," according to the *Sun*. Passing by August Mencken's factory, a costumed Lord Baltimore sat atop a float festooned with oysters, representing the riches of the Chesapeake Bay that gave the city its reputation for unsurpassed dining.

These marvels were lost on one of its youngest spectators. But even from that admittedly nebulous stage of childhood, he recalled the lights with the greatest clarity for the rest of his life, and "the world I had just burst into seemed very brilliant." More than half a century later, a contemporary remarked that this first recollection was significant: "He has been blinking at lights ever since, staring them down."[3]

During those first months after the parade, Baltimore for young Mencken was limited to what he could see from the second-story window of his house at 1524 Hollins Street. He watched the lamplighters make their rounds outside at Union Square while his mother read aloud the tale of Simple Simon. To the boy, the story seemed a perfect comic situation, leading him, as an adult, to reflect that "my lifelong view of the American yokel was generated by poor Simon." It was here that he had his introduction to the world of letters, where Anna guided her son's stubby fingers across the page with a pencil to spell out his name.

Through the windows he could hear the music of the street: the sounds of pianos coming from nearly every house, the loud clattering of the milk wagon, the freight train of the B&O railroad that ran only a few blocks away, the bells of St. Martin's Church, the oyster man making his rounds, the organ grinder and the one-man band. At an early age, the boy's ears were already attuned to melody; soon he would be decorating his composition books with tiny musical notes.[4]

The row house at 1524 Hollins Street was like its neighbors, spacious with a side garden shaded by trees, a home of new red brick with gleaming white marble steps facing the square. Distinguishing one from another could be a challenge, Mencken later quipped, if you were not coming home sober. Behind the house were alleys. Their gutters were perfect for floating miniature toy boats, and a dead cat or two sometimes could be found for the Hollins Street Gang to grab for ammunition and fling over a wall.

The alley, he recalled, was the home to black workmen, "great shiny fellows with immense knots of muscles in their legs and arms. In summer they liked to work bare-chested, swarming up ladders in long files, each with a load of bricks on his shoulder." Watching, the boy fancied them descended in a direct line from the Nubians who endured the burden and heat of the day when Cheops built his pyramid. Here, too, was a favorite preaching place for black evangelists, whose sermons he enjoyed while perched on top of the pony's stable in the garden. Mencken later said he picked up a great deal of useful information from them about the geography, dimensions, temperature, and social life of hell.[5]

Hollins Street, Baltimore. The similarities of the rowhouses could pose a dilemma, if you were not coming home sober. H. L. Mencken Collection, Enoch Pratt Free Library.

Farther afield from Hollins Street was the bluff that began at Baltimore Street and Fulton Avenue. The walls to Steuart's Hill were scarcely more than twenty feet at their highest point, but made sharp, jagged edges, and from the bottom seemed to a small boy like the Grand Canyon of the Colorado. "The tin can was its adornment," wrote Mencken years later, along with the "melancholy half brick." Paths wound in every direction—paths worn hard by a youthful army. In these enchanted Badlands, Indians came thundering down the plain, where wealthy cattlemen were regularly assassinated. Hordes of bandits roamed the hill, armed with table knives from their mothers' kitchens, and highway robberies of the utmost bold and desperate sort were committed within the shadow of St. Martin's steeple, where a grunting horse struggled to pull a Red-line trolley not fifty yards away.

For Henry Louis Mencken, the first memories of life were here, in what he would call the well-fed if somewhat frowsy Baltimore of the 1880s and 1890s. He attached himself fondly to these childhood memories of Hollins Street and vicinity: to the servant girl who let him and his little brother Charlie eat blackberry jam warm from the pan, and who the brothers plagued by smiling at her through blackened teeth; to the pony, Frank, who they happily fed gobs of ice cream through the dining-room window; to the livery stable, where T. E. Reveilles took care of his father's buggy and the men plaited the tails of horses. Above all, there were Papa, strong and genial, and Mama, fragile and beautiful. Together, husband and wife presided over their growing brood of four children with devotion and affection, enveloping each with a sense of security and love, so that all were kept, by their own admission, fat, saucy, and contented.[6]

THE FAMILIES WHO LIVED ON HOLLINS STREET appreciated their neighborhood as unlike any other section of the city. It was a composed and pleasant place of cool greenness and relaxing quiet; no trolley car lines intruded on its brief length. There were many German families in a neighborhood that was sufficient unto itself. "It had its own stores and society . . . its own great men," noted the *Baltimore Sun*. The grocers "vended delicacies of purely local acclaim. . . . There were people who lived for years within its bounds and knew no yearning to venture beyond them." It was a decade of intense German Americanism, with an exclusive Germanic club of drinking and choral groups. German Americans made up one-fourth of the total Baltimore population and the German American heritage was more firmly established than in any other port on the Atlantic seaboard. They had their own newspapers, labor unions, public schools, and churches.

The boy's father, August, was Baltimore-born and of this heritage, but he belonged to none of the groups commonly joined by German Americans. He was proud of his lineage, emblazing the family crest on his stickpins and on the labels of the cigar boxes that left his factory, but he did not feel bound to Germany by sentimental ties. If anything, it was the Abhau clan, on the maternal side of the family, who had entered fully into the life of the German American community. Harry's paternal grandfather, Burkhardt Ludwig, regaled the young fellow with the past glories of the Mencken family in far-off Oldenberg and Leipzig, and his mother, Anna Abhau, peppered her speech with German, but Harry did not pay much attention to his background during these early years. When, in his boyhood, he pasted together a booklet of "Great Men" and included a portrait of Bismarck, it was an example of his respect for Germany's rich culture during that part of the century, not just the fact that the Mencken family had been distantly related to the Iron Chancellor.[7]

Life was pleasant for these upper-middle-class families as they moved with assurance during the Gilded Age, removed from the discomforts that many other Baltimoreans faced, and satisfied with living arrangements common to their time. In a more reflective moment, Mencken wondered what the American of the future would find in his childhood that would amuse or disgust him.

Only Philadelphia had more residents living in individual houses than did Baltimore. "This feeling for the hearth" that Mencken repeatedly praised was the aspect that would most impress visitors to the city. To Mencken, it was the primary reason the city was so special, so different from, say, New York.

> A Baltimorean is not merely John Doe, an isolated individual of *Homo sapiens*, exactly like every other John Doe. He is John Doe *of* a certain place—of Baltimore, of a definite *house* in Baltimore. It is not by accident that all the peoples of Europe, very early in their history, distinguished their best men by adding of this or that place to their names.

Save for the years of his marriage, Harry Mencken would grow up, live, and die at 1524 Hollins Street. "It is," he said simply, "as much a part of me as my two hands."[8]

AT A VERY EARLY AGE, Harry dimly began to acquire a sense that his family was different, set apart from others. "It was believed by every boy of that era," he later wrote, "that Chinamen ate rats and were all opium addicts." In the neighborhood, it was not unusual for Harry Mencken to play run-a-mile with the black children of the alley, but when he came inside to play the piano from a popular music book sold during that time, he might play a tune called "Ten Little Niggers." In his Baltimore of the 1880s, he confessed "We kids knew only the following words for 'Dixie' ":

> *Way down South where the corn grows bigger,*
> *Whitewash nigger, whitewash nigger,*
> *Look away! Look away! Look away! Look away!*[9]

Many of his classmates at school were the sons and daughters of Jewish businessmen, but his mother forbade him to play in an unkempt store down the street, kept, according to her, by a "twenty-dollar Jew." There was an understanding in the Mencken household that there existed "crooked Jews" of the type his father railed against and with whom he refused to trade. "We are not *Jews*," August Mencken made sure to emphasize in his business letters.

Such remarks were common parlance in America during that time, spoken with far less reserve than they might be today, a reflection of the social milieu and environment in which Mencken grew up. But this prejudice was not limited to blacks or Jews. "The immigrant Germans whom I saw at home as a boy all affected a certain aloof superiority toward Americans and everything American," Mencken recalled. His family pride implied the notion that heredity made some nationalities or races superior to others. Both Anna and August regarded the habits of the Americans then living in Baltimore and their neighborhood, many of whom who hailed from the southern counties of Maryland, with amusement and even contempt. "To say that anything was American, in my family circle, was to hint that it was cheap and trashy," Mencken later wrote. "The Germans owned their own homes and paid their way. The Americans were renters and made a hollow show. I here speak, of course, of majorities. There were German deadbeats and there were competent and honorable Americans—but not too many." Mencken summed it up: "I inherited a bias against the rabble. I come of a family that has thought very well of itself for 300 years, and with some reason."[10]

In the Mencken family, arrogance was intertwined with the pruderies and class distinctions of that era. His grandfather Burkhardt Ludwig was the undisputed head of the entire clan. His decisions ranged from patterns of wallpaper to a baby's name, indeed, to all minutiae in family affairs: from how a grandson's hair was trimmed to whom he might marry. His authority could be dictatorial. When a nephew boldly rebelled and married a singer—an act considered, in those far-off times, as brazen as marrying a prostitute—he and his bride were banished. The nephew eventually perished in barren mining country in Idaho, and when the singer, now turned housewife, returned to Baltimore with their children, the youngsters were promptly taken away from her. Despondent over this turn in her fortune, she eventually committed suicide. As for the children, they had already been placed in the care of an uncle, under whom they were said to have suffered harsh abuse. One of them ran away from home and later moved to Florida, determined to have nothing to do with the family again.

It was a story apparently never fully discussed in the Mencken family. In any case, to anyone considering marriage, a partner's social standing seems to have been emphasized, with the example of the nephew and his singer serving as an unspoken lesson. "I have always wondered something about that family," mused the Baltimorean writer James Cain, who questioned, along with some of Mencken's other friends, why so many of the siblings remained unmarried. Henry Mencken knew of this family history; his cousin Conrad years later helped him with the details of the family tree.[11]

ABOUT THE TIME HARRY TURNED SIX, in 1886, he attended F. Knapp's Institute, a German school downtown. Now, the boy's horizons expanded from the furthest reaches of West Baltimore to what later became City Hall Plaza. The mile-and-a-half ride by horsecar from his house was a journey of infinite pleasure to him. Near his school, his father's cigar factory offered endless interest: the heady romantic smells of tobacco from distant places; trash baskets full of discarded cigar bands and paper clips; even the stripper boys peeling tobacco leaf were objects of fascination and envy.

With a population of less than 500,000, Baltimore was then enjoying its golden age. During the 1880s, the city rivaled New York as the chief shipping port on the East Coast. Among its major exports, as young Harry Mencken recorded in his school notebook, were "oysters (for which the city is famed)." In the quiet hours of dawn and dusk one could hear the whistles of the steamboats entering and leaving the bay, or the deeper horn of an ocean freighter docking. It was a maritime city, where seagulls swooped and gusts of air from the harbor carried the tang and promise of adventures in lands far away. Each morning, at the waterfront, trucks jammed its narrow streets waiting to load the bay boats, and horsecarts staggered with goods from its leading industries—clothing, canning, and tobacco.[12]

But unlike New York, whose tall buildings seemed to sprout from its harbor, Baltimore in the 1880s had a hunched skyline, its buildings crowded against the wharves, rarely rising more than three stories. Its center was marked by the Washington Monument, the second oldest in the country, completed in 1829. From its top, on a clear day, Harry would have been able to see downriver the smokestacks of the Maryland Steel Company at Sparrow's Point. Cutting diagonally through the city from the north and passing east of the monument was the malodorous Jones Falls, more than four miles of slow-moving, slimy, dark green mud carrying refuse from the city. Across was East Baltimore, the largest working-class section of the city, home of Johns Hopkins Hospital and the tenements of newly arrived immigrants. North of East Baltimore were the rural towns of Hampden, and beyond them the Arcadian woods and morning-glories that would later become the suburb called Roland Park. West of the heart of the city lived one-third of the city's African Americans. Due west were the finer row houses including the Mencken family's, and south of this neighborhood sprawled the yards of the Baltimore and Ohio railroad.

From this vantage point, the city of Mencken's boyhood was a collection of crowded rooftops with curling smoke. Throughout this low horizon were endless crooked alleys; St. Paul Street was so narrow a boy could jump across it. On some avenues, only one carriage and few pedestrians could be seen. Compared to its bustling rival, New York, Baltimore had an unhurried pace. Visiting the city twenty years later, Henry James wrote of its relative solitude: "It affected me as a sort of perversely cheerful little city of the dead."[13]

Many Baltimoreans of that era, however, took a defiant pride in its bucolic aspect. At East Mount Vernon Place, the traffic was so light a clump of alfalfa grew. Transportation service was good, but one New Englander remarked, "No streetcar in the North would be permitted to be detained fifteen or twenty minutes while wagons are unloading coal." When the circus came to town as it did once a year, preceded by gaudy, painted handbills plastered on street corners, Baltimore came to a standstill. It was, a young Harry Mencken observed, "as if some plague had struck the town—something—measles, or the mumps." Despite the saloons on every corner, by one a.m. the streets were pitch dark. The most excitement the townspeople might experience was a runaway horse thundering straight into a man's store; in typical Baltimore fashion, the man would refuse to move.

It was, the boy later recalled, the era of the Latrobe stove, horsehair furniture, seashells on the mantel, square pianos, and universal tobacco chewing; when men still wore boiled shirts, stiff as boards, or detachable cuffs "as large as stove-pipes," which they fastened with "flat, square cuff-buttons as big as postage stamps." But even here the new century was making itself felt, and by the time Harry was six, rapid transit was becoming the daily slogan; anyone suggesting Baltimore was behind the times would have been hotly contradicted by one of the city's most loyal defenders. Slow, creeping horsecars were being replaced by fast trolley cars whose knots of wires crisscrossed high above Baltimore streets, a tangle of lines that hummed with a low, steady metallic whistle. In his walks to school, Harry might loiter to watch the sparks fly from anvils, as blacksmiths hammered at new steel beams and hauled them into place, lifting the skyline for the new Equitable Building, its girders supposedly imperious to any fire.

This was the Baltimore of Mencken's childhood. A sense of self-assurance by its natives accompanied the pace of this city. "In every instance," another tourist remarked, "they would say to me, just as though they were of heaven-born, 'I am a Baltimorean.' . . . To them Baltimore is Baltimore, and every outsider is to be pitied for not having been born here." Its people were proud of their initiative, having been leaders in the building of railways, the introduction of the telegraph, the use of steam for transatlantic transportation, and the production of the linotype machine—all momentous innovations that had profoundly modified modern life.[14]

Though ready to welcome useful changes, the city had never broken with its past. In its very placidity, there was a vast charm. In the era before Jim Crow laws, race relations were fluid and permissive. Baltimore's population, regardless of class or color, mingled in the countless parks that graced the town, enjoying simple pleasures of food, drink, and music. As a little boy, Harry Mencken was already praising its terrapin, "none which can equal those caught along the shores of the Chesapeake," and the canvasback duck his mother served on holidays that "cannot be excelled." Families like his relaxed in beer gardens, men lifting schooners while children chased each other and a band played Sousa. The city was noted throughout the North for its beautiful women and for its manners; men removed their hats when ladies entered a streetcar; everyone seemed courteous and hospitable.[15]

THE BALTIMORE OF MENCKEN'S CHILDHOOD had little to do with the one that Mencken would discover in his newspaper days—the Baltimore of crowded tenements, unsanitary food, and disease. Until the first years of the new century, Baltimore was the largest unsewered city in the country. A visitor could see water running down the gutters at the sides of streets even if there had been not a drop of rain the day before. The streets were paved with cobblestones that were noisy, bumpy, and unclean, with gaping holes dangerous to the limbs of man or beast. "It is the easiest thing in the world for a horse to break his leg in such a place," stated an editorial in a liberal labor paper of the time, "and the jolting and rebounding of the springs of a vehicle may be the means of scattering the brains of its occupant on the street." The school system was one of the worst in the country, yet another example of mediocrity in Baltimore's mismanaged government of that period.

Baltimore had one of the largest urban black communities in the United States; it trebled Philadelphia's and was more than six times that of New York and Boston. Opportunity for African Americans was limited, their jobs menial. Racially mixed neighborhoods had been one of the most impressive aspects of the population in Baltimore, though in the better sections of the city, as on Hollins Street, blacks lived in alleys, in tiny brick houses with wooden steps, their backyards festooned with flowers. The new immigrants pouring into the city during the next ten years were predominantly impoverished Russian Jews, living in conditions described in the labor papers of that time as "dilapidated," "deplorable," and "wretched."

From within the warm comfort of 1524 Hollins Street the discord of the underclass could hardly be fathomed. The six-year-old therein became dimly aware of it only on certain evenings upon hearing his father's reactions to the newspaper, which duly reported the depressing litany of agitators and Knights of Labor. Throughout the spring of 1886, as Harry bent over his homework, August broke the silence by rustling his paper, growling that anarchists were threatening to send the world to hell.[16]

For August Mencken, humanity was divided into two segments: those who paid their bills and those who did not. As for the city, it had its patricians and its poor. But mostly it was a small metropolis of comfortable middle-class citizens. Of these, businessmen outnumbered the clergy, lawyers, or doctors. A glance at any leading local newspaper of this period would reveal the city's great popular interest in the prominent men of commerce. The papers were full of their vacations and their travels.

August Mencken was part of this merchant class. When Harry was born, August was 26 and already the successful proprietor of the cigar factory that bore his name. Started with only 35 dollars, August Mencken & Bro. by 1886 was considered one of the best cigar-makers in the southeast. The cigar-makers union, however, was a repeated annoyance to him. When men demonstrated for an eight-hour day in April 1886, August had to close up his shop. Thousands of tobacco workers, cigar-makers, and Knights of Labor carried banners in a parade through Baltimore, threatening to disrupt the way of life he had so successfully nurtured.

Harry was inadvertently drawn into his father's world of class and politics. In a piping voice, he started chanting a slogan he had learned that day from a teacher in school:

> *Eight hours for work*
> *Eight hours for sleep*
> *Eight hours for what you will.*

The recital caused such an uproar that August threatened to rush to the school "and have the Red fired," until Anna calmed him down. Already, in those early days, Harry Mencken was beginning to grasp that there might be another side to Baltimore, with needs far different from those he encountered within the enclave of his home. "I came out of school convinced that [an eight-hour day] was reasonable, and was glad when it began to be generally adopted." Such radicalism, however, the boy learned to keep to himself; "it was thus only natural I should grow up full of suspicions of democratic sentimentality."[17]

HARRY WAS BEGINNING TO OBSERVE, even then, that his father was a strong, high-tariff Republican. The fight for the eight-hour day marked only the beginning of the bitter struggle between August Mencken and the labor movement. The manufacture of August Mencken's biggest-selling cigar, named after local baseball hero Matt Kilroy, temporarily ceased one summer because of union threats. When a cigar-makers' strike threatened to interfere again, August devised a ruse to eliminate union workers from the city by bankrupting their funds, until the labor paper reported that the union had resolved "to declare amnesty to all cigar-makers in the city."[18]

So dominating a man, to the eyes of the small boy, seemed the ideal of strength and masculine appeal. "There was never an instant in my childhood when I doubted my father's capacity to resolve any difficulty that menaced me, or to beat off any danger."

In all respects, August was totally individualistic. Like his father before him, he had developed his own code of ethics. He was an agnostic, belonging to the minority of skeptical German Americans who disliked conventional religion, though he sent his children to Sunday school (if only to get some sleep). Unlike many of the Baltimore business elite, he had an aversion for most associations, yet he belonged to the Freemasons. As part owner of the Washington Baseball Club, he summoned the ball players to his home (especially when they had the impudence to ask for more money), to the delight of the neighborhood children who crowded at the back gate to get a peek at their heroes. He loved good jokes, some of which, his son later said, could be idiotic, and he invented a mythical brother named Fred, who was supposed to have created a family scandal by becoming a bishop. (Years later, when one of his father's friends stopped Henry on the street to inquire after his uncle, "it seemed time to end it. I told them that Fred had been murdered in Abyssinia.")

Gus, as the father was known to his friends, was a popular figure in Baltimore; his wife never knew when to expect him home for meals. It didn't matter whether

"The ideal of strength and masculine appeal." August Mencken Senior. Photo taken by H. L. Mencken. H. L. Mencken Collection, Enoch Pratt Free Library.

he was visiting tobacco fields in Cuba or Ohio, his stores in Washington and Baltimore, conferring with his fellow Shriners at King David's Lodge, or cheering Matt Kilroy at Oriole Park. Young Mencken did not approve of his father's lack of consideration in this regard, saying later: "Even then that sort of thing seemed to me to be unjust and unnecessary." Such indignities to his wife and family, however, were borne in silence; fathers, in that bygone era, were the heads of the house. Even the youngest member of the family knew a small boy was supposed to "keep in the clear."[19]

BY CONTRAST, HARRY'S MOTHER WAS A GENTLE WOMAN whose femininity still clung long after her four children had reached adulthood. "She was one of the most beautiful women I had ever met in my life," marveled writer James Cain. "Stunning. And with a tremendous presence. Here was a woman to look up to, to admire, to love, and in some part, to be possessed by."

With her slight frame, she looked younger than her years. The earliest photograph of Mencken himself is at five months old, clothed in a white lace dress of the Victorian era, a corpulent baby with intense, intelligent eyes. The bonnet and dress survive to this day; his mother had crocheted the bonnet extra large to accommodate an oversized round head. "If cannibalism had not been abolished in Maryland some years before my birth," Mencken wrote, "I'd have butchered beautifully." As it was, his large bulk attracted notice when the infant was seen with his tiny young mother. "Good God, girl," an old man inquired, "is that baby *yours?*" As homemaker, Anna did everything, from managing instructions to the hired girls to coaxing pears from the large tree in her garden. Her home, patterned from the engravings she admired in *Ladies' Home Journal*, was constantly being polished, the larder scrupulously well stocked.

Between those chores, she sang songs and read stories, and knelt at eye-level to the children on the parlor floor to play games. To visitors and family alike, she made sure no one was less comfortable than herself. In private, her son reflected, she was of "a jittery disposition, rushing throughout the house, violently shutting the windows whenever she heard the faintest peal of thunder, worrying and making everyone else suffer" with fear of every imaginable catastrophe that might befall her loved ones. Her appearance, combined with her fragile outlook, elicited a sense of protectiveness, most especially from her eldest son. Moreover, she suffered from a chronic cough, probably asthmatic, but for years it was suspected she had tuberculosis. A neighbor remembered Anna Mencken as having "that lovely quality that made her appear to be not exactly incompetent, but—just helpless."

For all of her delicacy, neighbors recognized that Anna dominated the household: "She had that family right under her thumb." Her children later recalled that Mama was a person not to be trifled with. Yet discipline was rarely achieved through punishments. It was solicited through rewards for good conduct—extra rations of animal crackers—and an untiring daily dose of homilies from Anna, a repertoire that was large and frequently cited: "Lazy people take the most pains." "What is worth doing at all is worth doing well."

How much discipline Harry endured can be inferred from an essay in his school composition book, in which he cites a Mother Goose rhyme as "rather an insult to good breeding than a rule of etiquette." Mercifully, a reprieve from homilies came when Anna was confined to her bedroom upon the birth of Gertrude, and later of little August, and a nurse was put in charge of running the house. That hapless woman had the responsibility of policing the energy of Harry and his younger brother Charlie, with the result that both boys admittedly had a grand time of it.

August and Anna could not have been more different in appearance. "As I remember it," Mencken wrote as a teenager, "she was rather small, of light and fair complexion, with a hair of gleaming yellow and eyes of blue," compared to his father, "who was tall and swarthy." This difference extended to their character, also, even to their manner of speech. "My father had a house language of his own, and it seemed very amusing to my brother Charlie and me," recalled Mencken. When bedtime came, he would say, "It's time to go to roost." Baby August was referred to as "the little bugger"; clothes were "duds." Anna avoided all kinds of slang; you would never hear her speak of a "cop" or "hayseed." Like his own father before him, August was negligent in grammar: "As I got on in school," Mencken said, "I was outraged by his occasional use of 'I seen' and other similar barbarisms. . . . But my mother always spoke precisely correct English." Nonetheless, it dawned on the boy that the language spoken by average Americans was quite different from the formal text he was forced to memorize in class.[20]

BOTH PARENTS LAVISHED ON HARRY the adoration that an elder child could normally expect. He grew up a lively boy, and no doubt August Mencken had already concluded that such high energy would serve the family business well. Consequently he began gently to harness the yoke of August Mencken & Bro. at an early age. Businessmen in Baltimore during the 1880s conformed to a similar path. No matter what their occupational experience, an overwhelming proportion of the city's businessmen expected their sons to start in the family business as they had—from the bottom. To this tradition Harry Mencken was born, and throughout his youth it was generally understood within the household that he was to follow in his father's footsteps.

August had introduced his son by the age of six to a different education than could be gained at Knapp's. Every Friday the father rode to Washington, D.C., to the branch of August Mencken & Bro., his "seegar" store at 7th and G Streets, N.W. August would hoist his small son on the train, and together they would journey to the Capitol, a mecca for smokers, where it was not an uncommon to see congressmen puffing cigars during sessions and peering through wreaths of smoke, as ladies in the galleries grew sick from the smell.

The memory lingered for Harry of the cigar store bell sounding a musical "*clang!*" as father and son entered the world of spittoons and six for a quarter. On these trips they lunched in cool marble-floored saloons on Pennsylvania Avenue with men who spoke endlessly about baseball players and political gossip, oblivious to the little boy who steadily consumed pretzels and sarsaparilla.[21]

Washington fascinated the boy, and its curiosities later became subjects for his school compositions. But Harry was not yet an avid reader—until late one summer afternoon, when he took a copy of the *Chatterbox* magazine and sat with it, on his lap, on the front steps of his house. He had done little with the magazine except to emboss "Harry" in orange pencil and paste his father's advertisement, "Smoke La Mencken Cigar," on its front cover. Yet from the first moment he began to read "The Moosehunters," he discovered a new world.

No one, especially not those who grew up with and cherish books, can ever forget the electric epiphany of the event, that moment when mysterious black shapes, so small they appear like ants on a page, suddenly and miraculously are transformed into words with meaning. Dimly, Harry could hear his mother's warnings that reading by dusk would ruin his eyes; more dimly still came his companion's shouts to join them in run-a-mile. All these sounds faded into the Baltimore twilight; what were any of these compared to the adventures of the self-made man fighting the savage Canucks on the Little Magalloway River? "The story was written in the best journalese of the era," he recalled; even better, the sixteen-year-old heroes were treated as if they were grown men.[22]

"LITERARY FANS OF THE YOUNGEST BRACKETS," Mencken noted, however, "do their reading slowly and painfully and like to come up frequently for air." No sooner had Harry finished "The Moosehunters" than August bundled his family into his carriage for the bumpy ride to Ellicott City. The countryside, however, did more for Harry than introduce him to cows and poison oak. "It also determined the whole course of my life. For it was by gaping into the window of the old Ellicott City *Times* office that I got my first itch for journalism, and into that sad but gaudy trade all my days have been devoted."

In the gloomy *Times* office Harry watched, entranced, while John Lynch, the muscular pressman, hollered and rolled papers off the press. Lynch hardly noticed the thin, staring boy, whose bare legs were criss-crossed with bramble scratches, except to give him a glare now and then while he halted the press and took a chew of tobacco. Years later, Lynch would become assistant foreman of the *Baltimore Herald's* composing room, and Mencken would be his managing editor. All other ambitions dissolved. Then and there, the small boy decided he would join that fraternity of men who inhale the intoxicating smell of printer's ink.[23]

The press retained its fascination for Harry long after they returned to Baltimore. Months passed. The days grew shorter, and the long boredom of winter set in. With it came a succession of female music teachers who taught compositions of such homely tastes ("Nearer, My God, To Thee") that it would take years before the boy's interest in music would revive. There was nothing else to do but restlessly explore the house for another story as engaging as "The

"I got the smell of printer's ink up my nose at the tender age of eight, and it has been swirling through my sinuses ever since." Courtesy Jack Sanders.

Moosehunters." He bypassed the old black family Bible that stood on the table in the parlor ("No one, so far as I can recall, ever opened it"). Harry struggled through *Grimm's Fairy Tales*, flipped through his mother's copies of *Ladies' Home Journal*, even the hired girl's *Fireside Companion*. With his brother Charlie he roamed the house in search of adventure. By Thanksgiving their investigations accomplished at least something: in a cupboard he found, tucked away in a corner for Christmas, a tiny toy printing press: the marvelous Self-Inker!

From that moment on, Christmas could not arrive soon enough for Harry. At last, holly stuck out in sprigs from horse's collars. From the upper window in every home on Hollins Street hung turkeys and geese for seasoning. Inside 1524, a smell of spices from the kitchen promised to produce a generous supply of raisins and ginger cakes, later to be grabbed by the handful.

There was a security and comfort to the holidays during those early years of Harry's childhood. But nothing could compare to the Christmas of 1888, when he and his brother came leaping downstairs in their flannel nightgowns and beheld a pile of gifts under a dazzling tree. Beneath the gilded pine cones were books, including *The Life and Battle of Napoleon Bonaparte in Words of One Syllable*—babyish after "The Moosehunters" and whose sole use appears to have been for painting a stick figure of a man with a set of Christmas watercolors. Still less attention was paid to *Children's Thoughts in Song and Story* given to him by his music teacher. To this day the jacket is crisp, unspoiled by a single mark, its pages uncut.[24]

Throughout that holiday season, long after Harry's younger siblings may have blasted their Christmas horns and beaten toy drums into a pulp, the delights of the Self-Inker retained their hold. While the Hollins Street Gang may have tried to entice him to enjoy the unusually balmy weather outside in Union Square, Harry struggled to print his own newspaper, copied from the telegraphic bulletins in the *Baltimore Sun*. By then he was able to advertise himself on cards, which he sold to his father. "My change to H. L. was not due to any feeling that the form became the dignity of a businessman but simply to the fact that my father, in the course of his Christmas morning gaucheries, had smashed all my black letter lower-case *r*'s."[25]

When he was not printing, Harry searched the house for another book to read. In the parlor, a secretary beckoned with books, with deadly and repelling titles. Standing on top of a chair, he pulled down a green quarto written by a man named Mark Twain. "I had heard my father mention this gentleman once or twice in talking to my mother, but I had no idea who he was or what he had done: he might have been, for all I knew, a bartender, a baseball player, or one of the boozy politicos my father was always meeting in Washington." Sneaking the book upstairs, he stretched out on his bed.

> If I undertook to tell you the effect it had upon me my talk would sound frantic, and even delirious. Its impact was genuinely terrific. I had not gone further than the first incomparable chapter before I realized, child though I was, that I had

entered a domain of new and gorgeous wonders, and thereafter I pressed on steadily to the last word. . . . As the blurbs on the slip-covers of murder mysteries say, I simply couldn't put the book down.

As Mencken looked back on his life, he could see Mark Twain had influenced him constantly, as a boy and as a grown man. From Twain, Mencken learned the tools of a humorist: how to cast, as Alistair Cooke put it, "a deadly, sensible eye on the behavior of the human animal." Long before the novel was assigned as mandatory reading to students, Mencken was among the first critics to hail *Huckleberry Finn* as distinctly American, worth more than the complete works of Poe, Hawthorne, Cooper, and James.[26]

The discovery of Mark Twain prompted another visit to the secretary and a systematic exploration of its volumes. *A Tramp Abroad* baffled him at this early stage, but other publications did not. *Chamber's Encyclopaedia* became well worn with use; *Our Living World* helped to identify all of the animals when the circus visited Baltimore. At the library of his Sunday school, he borrowed his first travel book. *The Florence Stories: Excursions to the Orkney Islands* by Jacob Abbott, was different from the common run of boys' books, and he happily followed the adventures on the Cunard steamship as it rocked drearily across the waves. "Years later it still stuck in my memory," he recalled, when he saw the desolate islands himself in 1917. Near his home was the newly opened branch of the Enoch Pratt Free Library, and with his own card he visited its stacks again. In short order, "I began to inhabit a world that was two-thirds letterpress and only one-third trees, fields, streets and people."[27]

As Harry's reading abilities developed, a love of language began to form. In the valley behind the house he found his African American friend "old Wesley" and "sought to floor him with 'phthisic,' then all the rage at my school." Wesley repeated it without a second's hesitation and even offered to pronounce it backward. In one of his notebooks, Harry wrote down a list of words that attracted his attention, filling two pages: *chalybeate, maudlin, victuals, hemorrhage, pythoness,* and *labyrinth*, which, he noted, "may or may not say something to psychoanalysts." His teachers at Knapp's not only appreciated his lists but also his compositions, which by 1892 were earning him exemplary marks.

"The mother of such a prodigy is proud of its attainments, and feels a glow when bored friends hypocritically marvel," advised the adult Mencken decades later in his anonymous publication *What You Ought to Know About Your Baby*. "Later on she will wonder why her child has watery eyes, constant colds or round shoulders." Such a boy, he advised, should be taken out of school and turned out to grass, to breathe pure air "and make acquaintance with splinters, bruises and sunburn."

The opportunity for such a change came when his Grandfather Abhau invited Harry to accompany him to visit his cousin's farm in Ohio. Hauling wood and feasting on doughnuts left Harry little time for writing. "I am glad you are not homesick," wrote his mother. She ended her letter on a more plaintive note; even in these early years it is obvious the adored older son was the center of the family's life: "Papa asked every time he came home if we had a letter from you ... I think we are all a little homesick for you."[28]

IT WAS NOT LONG BEFORE SPRING ARRIVED, and with it the first evidence of summer: the aroma of sewage from Jones Falls. Before this could radiate over downtown, August Mencken led his family, in the custom of the period, to the cool sanctity of the hills ten miles from the city. In the meantime, with the increasing success of August Mencken & Bro., he had purchased a permanent summer home in Mount Washington—for twice the amount he had paid for the one on Hollins Street. From 1890 to 1898, and for untold years beyond, the house became known as Pig Hill—a hoax August played on his horrified neighbors, who believed his invention that he intended to use the land as a place to breed hogs.

Today, what Mencken called the "remote and beautiful place" of his child-hood overlooks the roar of traffic along Interstate 83. In those days its windows opened to the stars and moonlit landscape of the valley. "From our veranda," he recalled, "we could look up country ten or twelve miles. On some nights we could see lightning as far as Pennsylvania."

That summer when the shadows grew long and cool, and fireflies blinked their way through the humid air, they would be joined by Frank Cross of the Washington cigar office. The men would hold mint juleps cool in their hands and gaze out over the wooden veranda, as Frank spoke glowingly of Washington newspapermen. Hearing such open admiration for members of the press was enough to make young Harry, sitting nearby, listen and remember.

He had already begun observing the world about him. On winter days, in old age, he would revive those summers of long ago from scrapbooks of faded drawings and photographs carefully bound. With the camera his father had given him, young Harry recorded the sights of Mount Washington through a lens: the heat of summer seethes into each portrait. More might have been taken—Anna allowed Harry to convert the tower on the corner of the house into a darkroom—but in the July temperature all of Harry's films melted off his dry plates. So, taking his notebooks and paints, he instead plunged into the half mile of shady paths of leafy woodland and hidden streams. A pencil sketch, labeled in juvenile hand "Scenes on the Upper Pataspco" is simple and effective, the line firm and economical. A picture of Jones Falls, with water gushing over rocks, decorated his office wall for the next forty years. Sketching, he could sit under the large trees, lean his head against a tree trunk, and look up through the branches at the sky. "If I had nothing else to do," he wrote years later to a friend, "I'd buy a place consisting wholly of woods."[29]

Behind the stretch of trees near their house was an immense field, sloping down toward Baltimore but relatively flat on top. Until fairly recently it was part of the Baltimore Country Club, dotted with golfers, practicing their sport (to

Mencken, golf and idiocy were the same word). During the 1890s the field was devoted to baseball. Here, summer and fall, Sundays and weeknights, a boy could be found with a mitt made of one of his father's old kid gloves, chewing shavings of licorice root (pretending it was Fine Cut), spitting promiscuously in manly imitation of every Oriole who played at Union Park. An enthusiastic shortstop and a good base runner, Harry was, however, a poor hitter and a bad pitcher. That notwithstanding, he swung, bunted, and slid until dark, finally stumbling home, admittedly full of aches.

With his brother Charlie and the neighboring boys, Harry roved the wooded hills for many contented summers. "Those long walks of long ago," remembered Otto Schoenrich, one of his childhood companions, "the happy days of Mt. Washington, your kind mother and your father's watch" were things of tender memory and delight. "Whenever I drive over Belvedere Avenue bridge, I recall once when we boys went swimming in Jones Falls under the bridge, and your toes gave rise to an anatomical discussion."

Looking back to a sentimental hour when he was a boy himself, Mencken admitted he was happy to be one of *these* boys, "from his frowsy head to his stubbed toe, from his felonious mind to his insatiable stomach, from his loose incisor to the scab on his shin"—part of the whole gallery of the young male of the human species, "and every one of them alive, human, and irresistible." A good many of Harry's activities during this period could be traced to *Boys' Useful Pastimes*, by Prof. Robert Griffith, the only other book, in his mind, comparable to *Huckleberry Finn*. A chapter on "How To Tie Knots" was scrupulously studied, judging by the ink smudges on its pages. But Harry had no more mechanical ability than his father, and into even adulthood he required outside assistance to help knot his ties.

What served a larger purpose, unbeknown to him, had nothing to do with how to construct a fake mouse or how to build a table. Instead, the book had one other function: for years Mencken believed "My apparent interest may have been responsible for my father's decision to transfer me from F. Knapp's Institute to the Baltimore Polytechnic in 1892."

Mencken, in his late sixties when he wrote this sentence, went to his grave believing this was indeed so. More likely, August, alarmed by the repeated strikes of the cigar-makers union and the inroads the Knights of Labor were beginning to establish in public German American schools, decided to pull his son from such influences to a different environment that prepared him for a career in a trade. Whatever the reason, "it did me an evil service in the end," Mencken recalled, "for my native incapacity for mechanics made my studies at the Polytechnic a sheer waste of time, though I managed somehow to pass the examinations, even in such abysmal subjects as steam engineering."[30]

The brilliant summer days were over. In that excited autumn of 1892, while Baltimore and the rest of the nation were about to plunge into a major economic depression, Harry headed toward the most difficult years of his young life.

2

THE ETERNAL BOY

THE SCHOOL WHERE HARRY MENCKEN began his preparation for a career in letters could not have been less inviting. When he entered the Polytechnic on September 5, 1892, it was located, according to its newest student, in "an extraordinarily hideous building." The poor sanitary conditions were a matter of concern to the faculty. One winter the pipes froze; another, the building became so cold that the protesting students built a fire on the hard basement floor. The outside needed painting; the bathrooms were in such a state of decay that the stench was deemed injurious to students. Long after Mencken graduated, he wrote that "this monstrosity was turned over to the city health department."

The aim of the school was not merely to teach trades or manual arts, but to lay the foundation for other professions: law, medicine, and—critically for Mencken—literature. The discipline was stern, the curriculum inflexible, with a military drill once a week. The lunch break was only twenty minutes long. Among the equipment the school boasted was a chemistry lab. By 1892 its course methods and materials were being adopted by other schools around the country and attendance had increased. The faculty members were congratulating each other on the improved class of boys now attending.

For young Harry, to survive what he considered the imbecilities at the Polytechnic was to be capable of surviving anything. "It doesn't take a bright boy long to discover that most of what is rammed into him is nonsense," he wrote later, "and that no one really cares very much whether he learns it or not." Indeed, "all I learned at the Polytechnic was forgotten a year after my graduation. I can't imagine a more useless education than I received there."

The lectures on machinery, he said, almost put him to sleep. The teacher of electricity affected an English accent: "All I remember of his teaching is a formula $1/2$ ev $= 0$." No one could understand the German instructor's explanation of grammar, so much of the time in class was devoted in stuffing bits of paper in the speaking tubes that connected to the president's office, undoubtedly to prevent his coming to the rescue of the instructor (which he invariably and frequently was called upon to do). The students considered most of the teachers incompetent and rewarded these unfortunates by bombarding them with all of the classic weapons of the day: live rats, hydrogen sulfide, and once, an ear from a cadaver, borrowed from a medical student and stuffed into a teacher's inkwell.

Of the 28 boys in Harry's class, 20 graduated. With the support of Richard Henry Uhrbock, a teacher of mathematics and algebra, Mencken progressed so well that in three weeks of steady work after school he was promoted. Moreover, not all of his classes were as useless as Mencken made them out to be, particularly the history of English. It was from the German classes, however, that Mencken said he learned the nuances of language.[1]

In writing of his own early adolescence, Mencken described a classic American boyhood in a Baltimore aglow in its gilded age. Then, in 1893, came an economic convulsion that had been festering the previous winter and would wrench American society.

Each copy of the newspaper brought more information of the crisis as firms went under. In Baltimore, even the most conservative estimates placed the number of unemployed at 30,000—almost one half of all workers in the city, overwhelming every institution. "I saw poor people plodding through the snow—barefoot," Mencken wrote years later. On winter evenings they would knock on the door at Hollins Street, asking for something to cover their feet. "There was no public fund to relieve them. Nobody in Baltimore had any money. The whole town was flat on its back. Those who could not find shelter from the cold simply froze. And the hungry actually starved."[2]

In the nation, more than 600 banks and other financial institutions had gone bankrupt, as had 32 unions and steel companies, and one railroad in every six. The slide of the southern states—the largest source of revenue for August Mencken & Bro.—threatened to ruin the Mencken business. The financial crisis wrecked the territory of one of August Mencken's most successful salesmen, in South Carolina, Georgia, Alabama, and Mississippi. Adding to August's woes was a fire that same year. Suddenly, as he was closing shop, a wall of the adjoining building crashed into the room, flames poured in, and as August made his hurried exit, the ceiling collapsed, leaving the place where he had stood a pile of bricks and mortar. In less than half an hour, more than \$25,000 worth of tobacco cases, cigars, and machinery had gone up in smoke.

Such dramatic episodes were missing when Harry later wrote his autobiography. Of the time, he would only reflect about his father: "I never saw him in a place of disadvantage or embarrassment," even though the catastrophe of the fire threatened to annihilate his family's security. Only a few days after, August, undaunted, was already supervising the construction of a new warehouse. A few weeks later he was sailing for Cuba to replenish his stock of tobacco. In the depression of 1893, Harry was able to continue the placid years of his early boyhood, a member, he recognized, of "the comfortable and complacent bourgeoisie."[3]

NONE OF THE CLASSES THAT HARRY ATTENDED at the Polytechnic fanned a desire to follow in his father's footsteps. "I had a desire to write," he told an interviewer years later, "but really I wanted to be a chemist; as a boy that was my work." His camera spurred this interest. For weeks he took photographs of various subjects: his father's office, the dam at Gwynn's Falls, anyone willing to be captured by his lens—his father, the baby Gertrude, little August, even his dog. Pages of his composition books didn't list new words but rather the chemicals he had in stock. The house was awash with the smells of toning solutions as Hollins Street became a laboratory for elaborate experiments in new methods for printing pictures. No less than 72 vials of chemicals crowded the shelves; they survived in the house for more than 30 years, when his marriage necessitated a move to other quarters and his sister, Gertrude, no doubt in some relief, finally threw them out.

His knowledge of chemistry was remarkable. Much of it was acquired through books; far less was gleaned from his teacher, William Hall. Other students in the class began consulting the boy, with the unhappy result that a frustrated Hall had to rap for order and truculently remind his students "Mencken is not the teacher of this class."[4]

The influence of two English teachers in the end caused his interest to shift in favor of belles-lettres. Both had taken their posts to pursue higher studies; both were drinkers and chewed tobacco, traits whose very raffishness made them popular. But most of the students were interested in machinery and not literature, so lectures were accompanied by what one student remembered as the instructor's talent with a blackboard eraser or piece of chalk hurled toward any of those not paying attention. Presumably Mencken escaped such treatment: "When they encountered a boy who showed any taste for reading," Mencken later recalled, "they encouraged it diligently and offered him very intelligent counsel. I was such a boy, so I got a lot out of them." Through them, Harry was introduced to the English classics. Before he was seventeen he had read the entire canon of Thackeray. Methodically, Mencken proceeded through the entire works of Addison, Shakespeare, and Swinburne. "He read like an athlete, in fact," his little brother August observed.

By this time Harry began devouring four or five books a week. When he was not visiting the library, he bought armfuls of magazines popular in the Victorian era. This reading was augmented by his father's subscription to a magazine that brought out a succession of paperback books: the poetry of Tennyson and Justin McCarthy's *A History of Our Times*, of which he read every word. He became a

Kipling fanatic. The bedroom that he shared with his little brother Charlie now was decorated with portraits of his hero.

The difference between the two brothers was now evident. Harry earned some of the higher marks of the school, but Charlie, who had already lost a year, "was a rather wild fellow and the question of his profession had not been settled, nor even seriously discussed," Mencken wrote later. On the other hand, Charlie was physically robust while Harry was sickly, his shoulders so round that at one point he was forced to wear a brace. In a boxing match, Charlie invariably won. Watching them at play, August must have felt bewildered how little his eldest son had inherited of his own sturdy constitution—he easily shook off illness like a horse flicking a fly with its tail.[5]

At age fourteen, Harry was by no means a scholarly recluse. Like every other Baltimore boy of 1894, he was a fan of the local baseball team, the Orioles, and he went to their home games whenever he could raise the quarter it cost to sit and roast in the bleachers. The games started at 4 p.m. He made sure to arrive by 3 to watch the players at practice as they perfected their combination of ferocity and skill that would win them 3 championships. In the following weeks, the thin adolescent with the sloping shoulders could be seen taking pictures of the players, drawing their likenesses in his notebook, visually recording what his latent talent would later put in words.

When the team won the pennant that year, he joined 200,000 others in the general delirium as the mayor greeted "the best baseball team in the world." Buses followed the players in their carriages, with as many small boys and men who could hang on.

From the top of his bus, Harry could see the procession as it uncoiled from Camden Station and moved into Baltimore Street, past familiar landmarks thrillingly lit up in the glare from bursting fireworks. Everybody who could make a noise on anything did; all blending their voices into one vast roar that could be heard a mile away: "*Baltimore champions, Rah! Rah! Rah! Ziss, Ziss, Zam! Ziss, Ziss, Zam!*"

The event was what Mencken later recalled as the great street parade of childhood memory, exemplifying his love for the glorious Baltimore of the Gilded Age. To many left destitute by the depression of 1893, that evening was the high point of the nineteenth century.[6]

MEANWHILE, STRIKES SPREAD to all organized labor, including the Cigar-Makers International Union. Wages fell or jobs disappeared altogether throughout the city. In Baltimore, the total sales of August Mencken & Bro. fell to half by the end of the year. With his business in distress, August was forced to cut costs, sublet his large warehouse, and eventually move to a smaller location. Trips to Holland and Cuba for tobacco leaf were postponed; August paid a visit to tobacco farmers in Ohio instead. Hundreds of letters were dispatched from his office with pleas for clients to pay their debts.

By January of 1895, gold flows out of the United States Treasury totaled a record $43 million. Each week the newspapers continued to report stories of Baltimore workplaces that were insolvent or dissolved. "Business continues to be dull," August wrote a friend that year. He did not expect any improvement until the Republicans were back in power. Of his continuing financial troubles, his family, not even his eventual successor, had a clue. If anything, August was a remote figure to his children.[7]

With the completion of his fifteenth birthday, however, Harry had his own affairs to interest him. When not stretched out on his bed reading or about to smother the entire block of Hollins Street under a cloud of chemicals, he was developing his writing skills. Once a week, as part of the curriculum at the Polytechnic, students had to write and deliver a speech. Mencken's composition, on the theme of George Washington's birthday, was recalled by the other boys many years after their own graduation. In it Harry recounted how he had asked his father for two dollars to buy a hatchet, which he then purchased at a neighboring store for twenty-nine cents, thus making a handsome profit. His humor, high spirits, and elaborate argument were equally praised at a public debate at the Boys' Club of his Sunday school. He showed how the United States had emerged from an agrarian to an urban nation, successfully convincing his audience that purer water and better medical attendance made the city far superior to country living.

With far more frequency Harry began writing verse, his influences ranging from the simple brass-band rhythms of Kipling to romantic French rondels he found in his copies of Victorian magazines. Years later, with nearly forty books to his name, he remained convinced that writing verse was the best preparation for writing prose. "It makes the neophyte look sharply to his words, and improves that sense of rhythm and tone color—in brief, that sense of music—which is at bottom of all sound prose, just as it is at bottom of all sound verse."[8]

Music, in fact, was the center of Harry's creative burst of frenzy. "When we were boys," Charlie recalled, "we had music pounded into us—two lessons a week, whether we liked it or not, until we were old enough to break over the traces." The lessons were taught on a shiny, black Stieff square piano. By age twelve Harry had shaken off the last of the series of lady music teachers; by 1895 Harry had successfully convinced his father that the "infernal scales" of Czerny ("admired only by vinegary little girls who wore tight pigtails with tight pink ribbons") were a disagreeable chore on which he was making little or no progress. More complex melodies could be heard at the Holliday Street Theater or the Academy of Music, when, during the last period of shop work at the Polytechnic, he and a friend would slip out the back door and attend the matinee. In that romantic era of theater and song, it was the ambition of many boys with literary aspirations and a love of music to write comic opera.

In music, Harry found refuge for those emotions that he could not express in any other way: "When I think of anything properly describable as a beautiful idea, it is always in the form of music," he confessed. "If I could write a string quartet,

I'd put things into it that I really feel and I believe in." His first piece, neatly written in ink, was a short "Two Step" for piano. The next, also for piano, was "Tempo di Marchia." Then came a number of waltzes and marches. Each piece was written in a firm, almost professional hand, with a pretty sense of melody according to music critic Isaac Goldberg, later Mencken's first biographer, though Mencken told him only the pianola could do them justice.

He did more than just compose music at home. Right before the school closed for the Christmas holidays, the annual "Poly Follies" was presented. Mencken wrote the score for the musical and launched into a program that kept him on the piano stool. If it was not met with the same degree of enthusiasm by the Polytechnic instructors (the show spoofed most of them), it was at least applauded by family, friends, rivals, and fair ones with rustling skirts.

Here, at last, was an outlet. If the Mencken family was now hearing more harmonies being played at the keyboard downstairs at Hollins Street, in the months to come they might have noticed their son had adopted still another habit: parting his hair stylishly down the middle and plastering it down with military brushes, in the manner of a Victorian dandy.9

HER NAME ESCAPES HISTORIANS; she was a blonde neighbor at Hollins Street, the first of many fair-haired "pink wonders" to whom Mencken was attracted. He had achieved an age when he no longer thought of girls as "catlike creatures with pigtails to be pulled." This was a period when his tastes leaned in the direction of "trig little blondes, stepping like Shetland ponies." Entering his life would be another: "a blonde named Maggie" and quite possibly "the only girl I am sorry I didn't marry." Years later, when running into "the one I truly loved most," he confessed to being quite overcome. Somehow, in this instance, he recognized her instantly, she was so little changed.

As the years went roaring by, the memory of these love affairs faded. Sometimes, he recalled, they survived merely as "perfumes; sometimes as curious, caressing laughs; sometimes as frocks; sometimes as mere details of spacious, blue-sky days." But there was also one who remained the clearest of them all:

> Looking back, it seems almost inconceivable that kissing her could have been the stupendous experience it actually was. Her folks inhabited a suburb and we used to take long walks along the winding roads. She had a way, whenever we came to a favorable spot, of halting suddenly, turning toward me, holding out her arms and closing her eyes. Without a word, I'd solemnly and even reverently enwrap her, and there we'd stand for perhaps a full minute, like prize-fighters in a clinch. Nothing was ever said. As for me, speech was as impossible as flying. The experience was simply colossal, overwhelming. Sometimes, as we resumed our walk, I'd be literally shaky in the knees, like a man just emerging from some shattering shock. But it was very chaste kissing. No vulgar pawing, gurgling, eye-rolling, gasping. [She] scarcely opened her lips. She was a girl intrinsically reserved and virginal. I have never known another woman to kiss so exquisitely. . . . I daresay I loved this [girl]. If so, my detractors should make note of it, for it was a love

infinitely idealistic and sublimated—a passion almost disembodied. It died, I suppose, of mere attenuation—it was too delicate to live.[10]

THAT SPRING, as new shoots of grass were sprouting in Union Square and fruit vendors were strolling on Hollins Street with fresh baskets of produce, Harry Mencken resolved with increasing fervor on the career of a newspaperman. For a young writer coming of age during the 1890s, the daily newspaper could put him in touch with the stirring events of the day, providing a range of experience in a way that no other institution could approach. His part-time work at his father's factory had probably already convinced him of this direction. So, too, had his discovery made the year before, in 1895, of Stephen Crane's *The Red Badge of Courage*. He would recall the blast it had made:

> [It] came like a flash of lightning out of a clear winter sky; it was at once unprecedented and irresistible. . . . The miracle lifted newspaper reporting to the level of a romantic craft, alongside counterfeiting and mining in the Klondike. More, it gave the whole movement of the nineties a sudden direction and a powerful impulse forward.[11]

His school friend Arthur Hawks, the only other member of his set who harbored any literary ambitions, had an older brother, Wells, who was not only a reporter for the *Baltimore Morning Herald* but also wrote comic opera. When one of Wells's stories appeared in a magazine, Harry thought it so well written, he naively thought it would impress his father. It did not exactly elicit the response he desired: August dismissed it with a laugh. As for Harry's own compositions, he resolved to keep them squirreled away in a drawer.

Even if no one from his family saw his purple prose, his determination to be a newspaperman was imbued with the romance of such a prospect. One evening in March he wrote a short story, "Idyl," the tale of two young newspapermen from New York, both of whom are in love with young women.

Such fantasies, however, were put aside in the bright glare of day. Sometime later that spring he headed with his notebook to the bleachers at Union Park to report a baseball game. While legendary Oriole hero John J. McGraw spat, swore, and swung, Harry's pencil recorded the scores. It was his very first attempt at reporting. When he secretly compared his copy to that printed in the *Baltimore News* the next morning, he was thrilled to see that his own amateur scribbling perfectly matched that of a professional. He and Arthur Hawks now conspired about how they would land jobs at a daily metropolitan newspaper once school had ended.[12]

ONE LAST HURDLE REMAINED to be overcome before graduation: a general examination, with a gold medal from the Alumni Association awarded the winner. Hearing that there might be one other student who might pose competition, August offered Harry $100 if he won. By rising early the boy undertook a marathon of study, and it would be safe to say his first thoughts on awakening were verbs, verses, equations, and geography, and that along the road to school he conjugated, memorized, figured, and recited. To engineering alone, the subject he liked least, he devoted seven hours of study.

With fatherly pride August Mencken recorded the final grades in a memorandum book in tiny, careful, neat handwriting. Harry Mencken's average on the final examination was the highest of the Polytechnic up to that time. It was three months before his sixteenth birthday; he was the youngest student at the school.[13]

It was in the midst of this success that Harry announced the startling news that upon graduation he intended to be a newspaper reporter. Added to the undesirability of the boy's choice was the social handicap of the profession. The public position of a journalist, Harry Mencken later acknowledged, "was above that of a street-walker but below that of a police captain."

Young boys harboring that same ambition during the 1890s were encountering similar reasoning from their fathers. It was no small wonder August was outraged. "There was such an explosion, I decided to say no more at present."[14]

On June 23 Ford's Opera House pulsated to the music of Sousa as the Class of 1896 prepared for its graduation. To John Saville, president of the Polytechnic, the highlight of the program was the presentation of the Chicago World's Fair Medal, for which there had been 33 competing schools. For the young graduates fidgeting in their chairs, the best event of the evening was to come later, at Granzhorn's City Hotel, for the banquet of Green Turtle au Madeira and Harlequin Ices.

Before that heady dinner, however, it fell to *Henry* Mencken, as winner of the Alumni Medal, to give the honorary address. Looking out over the plush seats of the opera house, stiff in his rented dress suit and white vest, the eyes of his family, his friends, school officials, and Mayor Latrobe upon him, he admitted later to feeling scared. Sharing the stage was the steam engine to which he and his class had devoted the last seven months. Five pages on its merits had been painfully pounded out by Henry on the typewriter in his father's office; nervously, he now began to stumble his way to the speech's conclusion:

> Our task at times seemed endless. . . . Like the western camp parson of whom Mark Twain wrote, we "done our level best." It is within the power of mortals to command success but it is within the power of all to deserve it. The class of 1896 endeavored to do the latter: whether it has done so or whether it has failed is for you, ladies and gentlemen, to judge.

"That speech must have been a dreadful thing," wrote Mencken years later. "My mother insisted afterward that it had gone off beautifully, but on that point I had my doubts, and it was a long time afterward before I ever undertook public speaking again." As he made his way to his seat amidst the applause, "I was myself too elevated to be conscious of its badness, for my [father's] check for $100 was in the inside pocket of my tailcoat."

"I can't imagine a more useless education . . ." Henry Mencken at his graduation from the Polytechnic. Courtesy Jennifer B. Bodine.

Then a local luminary stepped forward, instructing the graduates to "find out what you are fitted for, and then stick to it." Diplomas were handed out and the Alumni Medal was presented. This young graduate, at least, knew exactly what he was fitted for. But in the weeks to follow, as he obediently entered his father's cigar business, that advice must have seemed a luxury directed to those boys with more freedom in their choice of a career than he could ever hope to possess.[15]

3

AUGUST MENCKEN & BRO.

WHEN HENRY MENCKEN BEGAN WORKING at his father's cigar factory in the summer of 1896, the street sprinklers had commenced their obligatory ritual, shooting jets of water over the cobblestones day and night, settling hot dust from the sultry air. From the window, he was able to watch the horses and the water barrels rumble down Greene and Pratt streets. Soon the sun would soak up any moisture that lay in the hollows of what he called "the merciless cobbles," whose very sound was "a ballad of Baltimore."

It was a dismal scene that he could watch from that same window for another three summers. With each successive year, he grew increasingly bitter at the fate that had brought him to this pass. The years he spent at his father's cigar factory were so unhappy that they went unrecorded in his memoirs. Quite simply, they were "the hardest years of my life."[1]

Immediately upon graduation from the Polytechnic, he was put to work in the factory in the same way as had his father: at the bench, learning the manual art of selecting the leaf fillers, trimming the binder, smoothing the wrapper, and pressing the finished edge of a cigar into shape. At the same time, at the suggestion of August—who reasoned that since Henry was going to spend the rest of his life in the tobacco business, he should learn to appreciate the product—he began to smoke. Henry rolled his own, dipping into the cellar for fragrant quantities of coffee-brown Havana leaf ("My father, of course, assumed I was using far less expensive material").

Days took on a predictable routine. The smell of burnt toast along with the sound of the hired girl scraping it in the kitchen signaled breakfast. Then August

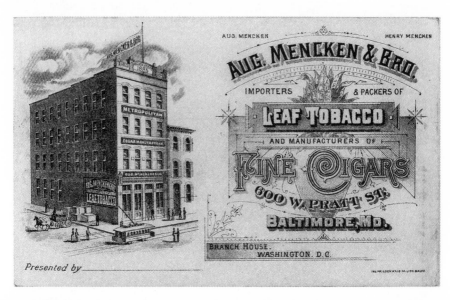

"The hardest years of my life." August Mencken & Bro. H. L. Mencken Collection, Enoch Pratt Free Library.

would put on his hat; by eight o'clock father and son would be at the factory. On a normal morning, all of the finished cigars were waiting for August's inspection, arranged in long rows. "If he found a bad one," his son recalled, "he would take the sick cigar upstairs, holding it at arms length as if it had smallpox," and would reprimand the offending cigar's maker. The cigar would then be dropped into a drawer that supplied complimentary smokes to visitors. The rest of the morning was spent in calculations of rows of tiny numbers. Job complete, this was the last anyone, even the bookkeeper, saw of August's figures. Before one o'clock, August would go to lunch, usually at home, then fall asleep on the lounge in the dining room. After thirty minutes of loud snoring, he would awake with a start, look about him wildly, and race back to the office. Once there, he calmly spent the afternoon reading *Tobacco Leaf* or the *Sporting Times* for baseball news. At five thirty he went home.[2]

August was a shrewd buyer and a competent manager. Most of the cigar-makers he hired were German; August would not permit any women in his factory. He greatly enjoyed bargaining and had negotiations with wrapper salesmen lasting for days; when he completed a deal, they sealed it with a drink. The principal brands from his factory were La Cubana, Havana Rose, and Daisy, which, along with La Mencken Panatela, were considered repeaters in the field. He was a hard trader, paid cash for everything, and never borrowed money. In the field, he advised his team of salesmen to obtain as much information as they could about their customers, and to reject an order if a customer's financial standing was not sound.

Since Henry Mencken's conversation with his father some months before, August Mencken had not given further consideration to his son's desire to become a newspaper reporter. "My father hoped and believed that I would succeed him in the business," Mencken wrote. The drive home from the factory to Mount Washington those summer afternoons was devoted to lectures on the mysteries of tobacco and credit. This monologue was mercifully interrupted when they came to a flat stretch on Falls Road, when Henry gave a touch of the whip to their trotter, and off they went, outrunning all the other buggies in their path.[3]

At first, the tobacco business was not disagreeable to Henry Mencken. He found it romantic to inhale the heady smells, to handle the long, pointy leaves that came from lands far beyond the horizon of the Baltimore harbor. That first summer he ran errands and helped as janitor. Drawing on his love of chemistry, he tried to invent a method in which cheaper Pennsylvania leaf could be moistened with wine to give the aroma of genuine Havana, and to his delight, his prescription was followed. One of his odd jobs was the monotonous pasting up of containers, done by hand, but he failed to successfully design a machine to do the job. He even tried growing his own tobacco leaf in the garden at home (result: tasteless).

But when August Mencken promoted his son from factory hand to office boy, Henry became intensely unhappy. On his first day, he promptly broke the letter press (a cumbersome contraption used to make copies of correspondence on damp tissue paper for the file), but then managed to repair it neatly in the machine shop of his old alma mater. August also insisted on keeping Henry involved in the irksome task of selling cigars to tobacco and grocery stores. "The very idea of selling revolted me," Henry wrote. "I never got over my loathing. . . . I hated to shine up to people and argue with them." The numbers showed it. There were salesmen in the factory who managed to sell as much as $1,000 worth of cigars in four weeks; in the first six months, Mencken squeezed out only $171 in business. During the entire month of August 1896, he made only one sale, for the grand total of $3.50. "In the end," he wrote, "it became apparent, even to my father, that I was hopeless as a salesman."

The episode was only one in a string of dismal failures. At the office, the mystifying tasks of running a business made Henry aware of his incompetence. When he went to the bank to make deposits, he made mistakes; when he made out the bills, he made even more glaring ones. Moreover, he was still required to sell cigars. The winner of the Polytechnic Alumni Medal with the highest grade point average in the history of the school began to sink into self-pity.[4]

His evenings, however, were his own. At the Monumental Theater, Henry paid his 25 cents to sit in the burlesque show gallery. The spectacle of the vaudeville acts and costumed girls came long before the days of the striptease. Here, free from the searching and suspicious eye of his father, Henry could smoke the cigars he had rolled himself and join the newsboys and bootblacks in whistling the chorus of every song, each in itself a history of American language, manners, and absurdities that kept pace with the spirit of the time. Looking back, he recalled that "the chief favorite at that time was 'My Gal's a High-Born Lady.'" It was one of the many popular tunes white Americans used to call "coon songs," and it had taken the entire country by storm:

> My Gal is a high-born lady,
> She's black but none too shady,
> Feathered like a peacock, just as gay,
> She is not colored, she was born that way.
> I'm proud of my black Venus, no coon can come between us,
> 'Long the line, they can't out-shine, this
> High-born gal of mine![5]

On Sundays, Henry took his bicycle and, accompanied by his friend David Orem—the factory bookkeeper, a decent soul who helped prevent him from committing more inept horrors in the factory books—rode up and down Park Heights Avenue, then known as Pimlico Road. The bicycle craze had swept America, and the tortuous country pike had been widened so that wheelmen could race on their favorite speedway in the spacious open air. "On hot summer nights the lights of the bicycle lamps danced upon it like swarms of fireflies," Henry remembered from those evenings. "Standing at the bend just above the park, one could sometimes see fully a thousand of them along the easy grade."

Few boys aspired to much more. Henry did. He had abandoned many other hopes to cling with increasing tenacity to one dominant ambition: to become a writer of distinction. With every day that passed within the confines of his father's factory, he was depressingly aware of what was denied him: the rhythmic *clickety-clack* of the linotype, the aroma of hot molten lead, the bloodcurdling stories of the latest police reports, the rush to meet deadlines, and then sharing the day's work with fellow newspapermen in the cordial air of the saloon. It was a front-row seat at the greatest show on earth. The biggest news that might break after several months in the office of August Mencken & Bro. was which salesman had sold the most boxes of La Cubana.

But Henry was determined that even if his days were choked in tedium, he could at least begin to take some steps toward that career. The Baltimore Orioles were playing again, and on his father's typewriter he tapped out a satirical poem: "Ode to the Pennant on the Centerfield Pole." He submitted it to the *American*, and to his great thrill actually saw his poem in print in the newspaper. It was an awkward effort—it seemed dismal to him years later—but it was his first published work. No one in the Mencken family ever knew of it, for Henry made sure to conceal his achievement.

Much less is known of his relationship with a certain blonde neighbor, except that from 1896 through the following year his poetry hinted that not all was well beneath the stars on either Hollins Street or Mount Washington that summer.[6] Throughout his life, Mencken would take great pains to suppress all references to love affairs—precisely to avoid the "happy hunting ground to quack psycho-logists" he so despised. The few collected poems he did choose to keep for pos-terity were full of laments of a lovesick sixteen-year-old. One poem, entitled "A Song of Advice," warned against marriage; another described love's sorrow: "Ah, it be a bitter payne!"

Behind a swarm of inflamed, agitated poetry was a mixture of romance and an ignorance of sex. Years later, when Mencken stumbled across *The Awakening of Spring* by Frank Wedekind, he pronounced it to be the one book that best described his own adolescence. Its descriptions of a son's arguments with his father and of the yearning to write at a newspaper all struck a chord. Like the hero, he, too, could search *Chambers Encyclopaedia* from A to Z and find nothing but words. The anatomy course at the Polytechnic had taught something; but it could also leave a boy ashamed with qualms of conscience when he dreamed of legs in light blue tights, waking him startled as if by lightning.

Mount Washington and the girls of the surrounding countryside offered better opportunities for dalliance. Unlike city girls, who held strict codes of con-duct, these young women, Mencken found, were looser. There was no effective policing, whether public or parental, for there was too much space, with too many dark spots. He had an introduction to carnality with an older girl at one of the neighboring mill towns: it was best left forgotten, swallowed up in the morass of memory. One day he promised to Tell All. "It is a sad thing, but true, that nearly every man's first taste of pure and refined love is with a slavey," he observed, joking to a friend he should write a book about such things, and with it a chapter called "The Approach to the Servant Girl." To another he confided that although the lady had been a servant, to Mencken "she was really a princess in disguise." When, during the 1930s, he was asked about the morals of the day's flaming youth, he compared his own memories to "the young flappers and sheiks of today."

> Certainly necking is not a new invention. I practiced it in 1895, and on girls who are highly respectable matrons today, and full of horror over the banal deviltries of their daughters. So did every other enterprising young buck of my time. . . . The young of today simply do openly what their elders did furtively. . . . Today they moan over their daughters. Whenever I hear any moaning of unusual horsepower I draw my own quiet conclusions. . . . Here, as in other fields, moral indignation is almost invariably the sign of bad conscience.[7]

THE HOT SUMMER MONTHS dragged on. Street lamps were littered with the shiny corpses of June bugs; at Union Square, dead moths floated in the fountain. After Henry's dreary days at the factory, he kept his bitterness in check by retreating into books. The discovery of Thackeray had completely reorganized his view of literature. The greatest literary influence of them all for him, however, was Thomas Henry Huxley. In clear, lucid prose, the essays gave order and coherence to Henry's own vague ideas of the cosmos. Social Darwinism, as explained by Huxley, revolutionized his own thinking, converting him into a violent agnostic.

Writing of Huxley on the centennial of his birth in 1925, Mencken evoked his own youthful ardor of a quarter-century earlier:

> All of us owe a vast debt to Huxley. . . . All his life long he flung himself upon authority—when it was stupid, ignorant, and tyrannical. He attacked it with every weapon in his rich arsenal—wit, scorn, and above all, superior knowledge. To it he opposed a single thing: the truth as it could be discovered and established—the plain truth that sets men free.[8]

Henry's sense of duty to his father did not deter him from reading all he could lay his hands on about how to become a newspaperman. So, as in the case with photography and chemistry, he visited the Enoch Pratt Free Library to see what he could find on the subject. The most useful resource was Edwin L. Shuman's slim brown volume, *Steps into Journalism: Helps and Hints for Young Writers*. Shuman, then an editorial writer for the *Chicago Tribune*, had written his book "for those only who have the divine call"—"the thousands of young men and women who are trying heroically at home to write for newspapers and magazines and who cannot understand why their manuscripts are rejected with such painful regularity."

Shuman's words encouraged Mencken, who found the book full of useful tips he would use for the rest of his life. The best start for a newspaper career, Shuman advised, was not with formal study—"No school or college can ever teach it"—but to begin at one of the smaller hometown papers: "The boy who dispenses with the college and goes directly to reporting gets far ahead."

It must have seemed to Mencken by 1897, if it had not already been obvious to every workman in the factory, that he simply had no natural ability at August Mencken & Bro. That summer Henry made a renewed effort to explain to August his yearning for a journalistic career. Looking back to that day many years later, Mencken said in characteristic understatement that the discussion between father and son caused such unhappiness on all fronts that he was left with no other recourse but to retreat. While Mencken never believed seriously that he would stick to business, August was determined that any thoughts his son harbored for a newspaper career would have to be postponed, if not abandoned.

The thought of escaping from Baltimore simply did not occur to him. For two weeks, one of his cousins tried to induce him to an expedition to North Dakota to fight Indians. On the block where he lived, at least six boys had run off at one time or another, but nothing came of the trip. "Life to a boy in his teens is certainly not pleasant," Mencken wrote of the incident. "He is always policed, and most of the things he is asked to do are disagreeable to him."

The prospect of continued years at August Mencken & Bro. seemed unendurable. *Gloom, pain, sad, dead, mourn*—these words are repeated throughout his verses. "*How it feels to kill a man. Afterward killed himself*" he jotted as an idea for a future poem in one note. He might have wondered what alternative lay open to him. With the weight of various disappointments pressing upon him, 1898 was, for him, a particularly horrible year. In one of his dark moments of real despair, he wrote later, "I contemplated suicide."[9]

THROUGHOUT 1898, Mencken continued his systematic reading of English literature. When the biographical editions of Thackeray's works, edited by the author's daughter, began to appear that year, Anna gave him each new volume as it was issued. But increasingly Thackeray was replaced by something else. He became aware that around him pulsated the undercurrents of a new literary age, what he later defined as "the mild and *pianissimo* revolt of the middle 90s." The fossil literature he had been taught at the Polytechnic began to give way to the grand sweep of literary currents in the smaller, avant-garde magazines that looked to the Continent, not just England, for inspiration.

One of the liveliest of these was the *Criterion*, a short-lived magazine that was almost as large as a tabloid newspaper. The magazine, a potpourri of dissimilar views and tastes, printed a jumble of articles that ranged from anti-Jewish and anti-black (these appeared with alarming frequency) to reviews of Ibsen and the latest works of Stephen Crane. Across its pages were hints that were to gather into the movements of the 1920s: an iconoclastic reevaluation of American literary heritage. Some librarians refused to stock it on their shelves, so Henry bought a subscription.

"How, as a youngster, I used to lie in wait for *The Criterion* every week," Mencken recalled. Once it was delivered, he was able to exult in its slogan, printed in thick black angular letters: "The New and the Bold," and devour a bohemian world of revolt. Theater and book reviews on not only Ibsen, but also Oscar Wilde and Ambrose Bierce, and even impressionistic reporting of such events as Buffalo Bill's Wild West Show were written by a critic named Percival Pollard. "He knew everything that was going on," Mencken exulted. Oscillating between New York and Paris, London and Berlin, he was "bringing valuable knowledge and enthusiasms to the developing American literature of his time."[10]

One other critic on the *Criterion* stood above the others: he conveyed delight in mocking sacred institutions, combined with what Mencken later called the contagious and inflammatory enthusiasm into the aesthetic values in the arts. This was James Gibbons Huneker. Whether he was writing about music or literature, to Mencken it seemed that "Huneker makes a joyous story of it." Long considered one of America's most authoritative critics, Huneker was being praised on both sides of the Atlantic by those who admired his vivid prose and European outlook that was aimed toward an intelligent minority.

Huneker's influence on Henry Mencken would be profound. It was he who introduced the magic names of George Bernard Shaw and Joseph Conrad, who led the fight for Henrik Ibsen, and steered Mencken toward Friedrich Wilhelm Nietzsche. In sum, Mencken wrote, Huneker "gave some semblance of reality in the United States, after other men had tried and failed, to that great but ill-starred revolt against Victorian pedantry, formalism and sentimentality which began in the early 90s."

The 1890s, Percival Pollard had said, "was a battle for new life in our art." It was a view embraced by our young man in Baltimore. Here were adults who captured the artistic ferment he felt within himself. Pollard's and Huneker's style of writing, he later said, highlighted "the difference between the bombastic half-knowledge of a school teacher," full of "ponderous nothings," and "the discrete and complete knowledge of a man of culture."

Henry Mencken unwittingly was getting closer and closer to this goal. What he could not guess, at this period of loneliness and despair, was that these same men who guided him toward the approaching century on the printed pages of the *Criterion* would, in years to come, be among his friends in real life.[11]

No DOUBT WITH A MOTHER'S INSTINCT, Anna Mencken noticed her son's unhappiness. The little free time Henry had from the factory was being spent in solitary reading. It had been ages since Henry had played the piano in the parlor. More and more, he turned toward that observant, patient woman as she sat quietly in her chair, unburdening his despair. She may have confided Henry's helpless yearning to her brother, because in 1898, Charles Abhau, who was a subscriber to the *Cosmopolitan*, called his nephew's attention to a correspondence school it had organized.

By May Henry had enrolled, and for the next months he mailed his lessons and got them back covered with red ink. His second exercise, a description of an excursion boat in Baltimore, received this chilling admonition: "You seem to have cared more about what you said than how you said it; your description is interesting, but the style is careless. . . . Make it your aim to use simple and direct language." More red marks on the manuscript reinforced the advice: "This sentence might be more concise," "Language is not simple enough," "stilted," "bookish."

By September his writing had improved. "An Alley Case" (later retitled "The Outcast"), about a young man living in Honduras with a rare disease, was submitted on September 4, 1898. The teacher returned it, with this praise: as "excellent a work as we often receive." Its style was far superior to the mawkish, Victorian love stories he had been writing earlier. Buoyed by the critique, Henry began writing day and night.

About the time he turned nineteen, he focused his attention on a new correspondence school, the Associated Newspaper Bureau School of Journalism in New York. On its application sheet, he carefully listed his attainments. When it came to the question, "Do you expect or hope to make journalism or literary work your means of livelihood, or make it a means of general culture?" With fierce determination Mencken answered: "Expect to begin as a reporter & after that trust to hard work and luck for something better."[12]

In the fall of 1898, newspapers burst with reports that Theodore Roosevelt's First U.S. Volunteer Army—soon to be known as Roosevelt's Rough Riders—had made its way up San Juan Hill. For the cigar industry, the problems the conflict presented made business difficult and stressful. August was faced with an inconstant supply of the desirable Cuban tobacco leaf (a problem exacerbated by the inferiority of the local American crop, ruined by a drought) and an increase of taxation and price.

August was additionally confronted with the painful reminder that his son's ambition to become a newspaper writer had not abated in the past year; if anything, it had become more pronounced. During 1898 Henry braced himself for the inevitable. He did not look forward to yet another scene with his father. Disappointing August's long-cherished plans was disturbing, but the alternative was terrifying. One afternoon, when the day had simply been too much, he stormed into his father's office. If Henry was expecting him to flare up in anger, he was surprised to find that he did not protest. Instead, August listened: it was obvious to his son that "he was naturally pretty well dashed."

They resumed their conversation in the buggy ride to their summer home that evening. This time August sought to find a solution to Henry's unhappiness by suggesting various alternatives to a newspaper career. Suppose Henry was to matriculate at the University of Maryland Law School? The knowledge would be useful for whatever career he undertook. The Johns Hopkins undergraduate school could prepare him for further study in Germany. He, too, could join the youths in Heidelberg, sipping their pilsner in the *Schloss* gardens and toting their books, the very picture of students in *A Tramp Abroad*, by their mutual favorite author, Mark Twain.

A melancholy sympathy now overtook the boy as he listened to his father's groping for alternatives. Even then the boy sensed August was making all of these proposals only, as he noted, "half-heartedly." More than once he had overheard his father discussing with his mother plans to ease Uncle Henry out of the family firm. "Those plans, I gathered, were based on the assumption that I would be ready, soon or later, to take his place."

With each bend in the road, August confided more to his son that summer afternoon. He, too, knew the pains of thwarted ambition. There had been a time, he told Henry, when his love of mathematics had made him aspire to another career, as an engineer. But the realities of life had interceded, a more practical activity chosen: he, too, had had a dream, and the dream had to be abandoned.

Under the overhanging branches of Falls Road, father and son had reached an understanding. No more would be said about newspapers, at least for not another year.[13]

MENCKEN'S MISERY LASTED until New Year's Eve. Upstairs, he was lying in bed with influenza, observing the close of the year with the composition of a new poem: "My wants are simpler,—all I ask is Rest." Anna was in the parlor, quietly reading. The gaslight cast a warm glow on August, stretched out on the divan for his usual after-dinner nap. Hearing her husband mumble incoherently, Anna glanced over at him, then continued to read. Outside, a strong wind brushed snow against the window panes and in the distance, the muffled strains of music being played indoors by neighboring revelers may have been heard.

The next time Anna looked over at August, his head had sunk unnaturally on the pillow, his face strangely pale under his closed eyelids. He began to breathe heavily, and almost at once had a brief convulsion and lost consciousness. Alarmed, Anna shouted up the stairs. Racing down to the living room, Henry took one look at his father; that one look confirmed their fears.

There was no telephone in the house, and the family doctor lived eleven blocks up the hill on Carey Street, so Henry had to fetch him by foot. The raw wind hit Henry with a sharp gust as he pushed forward, running past homes where happier families would soon be sending out the old year with joyous blasts on their tin horns.

Shivering outside Dr. Z. K. Wiley's basement office, Henry pulled on the bell and heard it jangle for a minute or two inside. It grew colder. He tried again, rousing the family upstairs. No one knew where the doctor was or when he would return. There was nothing to do but leave a note. Then it was off to the home of Pilson, an eccentric druggist, whose store was on the south side of Baltimore Street, east of Calhoun. "I recall waking up Pilson in the middle of the night. . . . I shivered outside until he came down." Crunching his way back home through drifts of snow, Mencken came to the sudden realization of what his father's illness meant to his future. With each step toward Hollins Street that night, he confessed later, he kept repeating to himself: "If my father dies, I will be free at last. . . . *If my father dies, I will be free at last.*"

Steamboats in the harbor were getting ready to blow their whistles and church bells to chime in the New Year. At Union Square the boozy bellowing of merrymakers disturbed the air, as they prepared to drape themselves out of windows, waving flares, ringing cowbells, and, in Baltimore tradition, shooting guns into the air. But at 1524 Hollins Street, Anna and Henry Mencken stood apprehensively at August's bedside. Dr. Wiley, who had finally come to their aid with the whiff of liquor about him and with one eye on his patient, decided to stretch out on a nearby lounge chair. Even in Henry's stunned state, the sharp eyes of the future newspaperman noticed the huge white patches of dandruff on Dr. Wiley's closely cropped head as it lay on the armrest, and "how obscene he looked," in comparison to his own father—handsome, feverish, pale, lying on his bed, gripped with an illness no one could yet identify.[14]

In such agony the Mencken household greeted 1899.

WITHOUT THE TREATMENT of today's modern drugs that would have cured his kidney infection, August languished, drifting in and out of consciousness. "The story of my father's last illness illustrates the state of medicine in Baltimore at the turn of the century," Mencken later observed. As it was, no one knew what to do. So wife, children, friends, and relations took turns watching August as his body became wracked by a formidable series of convulsions over the next twelve days and nights.

Only Anna could keep up the strain of watching him around the clock. As she nursed her husband nonstop, days and nights blended together. Twenty years earlier, August had wooed her with his clowning and exuberant gaiety. The family recalled how "he struck her as a kind of comic character and [she] laughed at him for some time afterward." Her beauty and femininity had appealed to his protective, masculine nature. To their children, their marriage had been "a love match." Now, her love was not enough to keep her husband alive.[15]

Friday the thirteenth dawned, rainy and bleak. A brisk northeast wind shook the leaves on the trees outside Union Square; the bells of St. Stephen's chimed the quarter hours. For the family, another week of the death watch had begun. Propped against the bed, August Mencken stared at them, unseeing. It seemed incongruous, that the man who had never lost his capacity to beat off any danger, now battled vainly against death. Both Henry and Charlie restrained their father against the fever that repeatedly shook his body before it surrendered, exhausted, into the pillows; the struggle had already lost August twenty pounds.

When the end came at 10:45 that evening, he was in the midst of another convulsion, with the complication of hypostatic pneumonia. Henry had collapsed with exhaustion in an adjacent room and was unaware of his father's agony during his last moments; his uncle's gentle shake broke the news. Years later, when one of his own friends lost his own father, he remarked: "You are lucky to have had your father with you for so long." For years Henry grieved: "I missed him sorely after he was gone."

But there still remained the memory of their struggle and of his first thoughts of liberation when the realization of August's approaching death had first struck him. "If he had lived," Henry reflected afterward to the poet Edgar Lee Masters, "I'd have stuck on in the tobacco business for at least a few years longer, probably to my permanent damage."

In maturity, Henry was able to overcome his feelings of rebellion and objectively credit his own agnosticism, business acumen—indeed, an entire body of ideas—to traits he had inherited from his father. Purged from those adolescent years of brooding resentment at the factory, a nostalgic portrait of August Mencken surfaced throughout Henry's memoirs. Forty-seven years later, long after he had successfully attained his own ambition, Mencken was able to reflect on what his father had actually achieved:

> If he were alive today he would be a member of that class of reactionaries which is execrated by all right-thinking Americans. He worked diligently at his business, kept his family in comfort, and laid by enough to maintain his wife and children indefinitely. I was already 18 . . . and in a little while I was self-sustaining, but Charlie was but 16, Gertie was but 13, and August was but 10. The yield from his estate enabled my mother to bring them all up, and her life was secure and comfortable until she died. . . . The old family home at 1524 Hollins Street, which he bought in 1883, is still in good condition, and August and I still live in it. Such men are not much esteemed these days, but I remain of the conviction that they were good citizens, just as they were good husbands and fathers.[16]

On Monday afternoon, January 16, 1899, a special meeting of the King David Lodge of the Masonic Temple was called to order as the officers recorded in rounded script into their ledger the death of one of its youngest members. Eight carriages from the Masonic Temple slowly clattered to a halt in front of 1524 Hollins Street. Before the funeral could proceed, a bugler on the corner of Hollins and Gilmore tilted his instrument to the sky and trumpeted a fanfare to the heavens.

Shortly after 2:30 p.m. the procession began its long ride up the hill toward Loudon Park Cemetery, where the coffin holding August Mencken was lowered into the ground, facing west toward the setting sun. Family, relatives, and Masons gathered side by side at the top of the small incline. Beyond, toward the east, in the direction of sunrise, lay Baltimore and farther still, the Chesapeake Bay, as Henry Mencken, head of the house, stood facing the city that would be so closely identified with him by an entire generation during the next century.[17]

WHEN MENCKEN CAME TO WRITE his trilogy of memoirs, *Happy Days*, he spoke exuberantly of "a normal, happy childhood," but told his publisher, Alfred Knopf, there would be little public interest in their publishing a book on his adolescence, filled with "the green sickness of youth." Only two or three letters, and then only to the slightest of acquaintances, have survived to testify to the bitterness of those particular years; only one gives a glimpse of the suppressed anger he felt. Sometime before his death, his son wrote, August Mencken employed an artist to paint a florid pastel of him. No sooner had the mourning family returned from August's burial when Henry decisively removed the grotesque portrait of his father from its frame, took it into the yard, and set it afire.

Three decades later, Henry admitted that burning the portrait had been "a foul deed." At the time, Anna made only a brief protest and then withdrew. She seemed to understand her son's anguish even better than he did himself. In the days that followed, when he again broached to her his vow to become a newspaperman, he braced himself for yet another battle of wills. To his amazement, she said she had been well aware of his unhappiness at August Mencken & Bro. Besides, she confided, she had not relished the idea of seeing her son involved with Uncle Henry, of whose business talents she had a very low opinion.

With her son's advice, she sold her shares of stock to her brother-in-law who, with his own son, mismanaged the factory until its inevitable collapse. The cigar industry was changing; the popularity of cigarettes was driving most of the business away. When both uncle and cousin unceremoniously dumped the factory ledgers full of August's careful notations into a trash heap in an alley, Henry Mencken dusted them off and had them bound in blue moroccan leather, a permanent testimony to his father and to his own unhappy adolescence.

Sometime later, Henry crossed the threshold of the *Baltimore Herald* in the heart of downtown Baltimore, free at last to enter "the maddest, gladdest, damnedest existence ever enjoyed by mortal youth."[18]

The Baltimore *Herald*. Courtesy Maryland Department, Enoch Pratt Free Library.

4

BALTIMORE AND BEYOND

THE *HERALD* HAD RECENTLY MOVED to new quarters at the northwest corner of Fayette and St. Paul, where a large arched window dominated its comfortable city room. The paper's staff had abundant opportunities to partake of the city's life and to search out its news. At the turn of the century, the entire staff shared a sense of fellowship and a strong belief in their product. Like the *Sun*, Baltimore's predominant newspaper, or its other rival, the *American*, the *Herald* contained only eight pages. But within them, its reporters strived for the liveliest writing in Maryland.

Shepherding this flock and giving the paper its color and charm was Max Ways, city editor, one of the most popular and respected newspapermen of Baltimore. At 7:30 one evening in January 1899, Ways looked up from his desk and saw standing before him a young boy with outstanding ears, glowing in his Sunday best with ascot cravat, his hair slicked. Staffer Arthur Hawks and his brother, Wells, had recommended him as a worthy fellow with some talent for writing. However, Ways told him, there were no vacancies on the *Herald*. No, he could not promise anything. Well, perhaps the boy could come back another time—maybe something would turn up. Then Ways turned back to his papers.

The next night, at 7:30, the boy showed up again. Still nothing. After a few evenings of this, Max Ways motioned for him to wait while he finished thumbing through a pile of copy, then asked suddenly: "Do you ever read the *Herald*?" When the boy answered yes, he followed with, "What do you think of it?" Years later, Mencken recalled:

"The greatest achievement of modern fireproof construction." The Baltimore *Herald*.
The Maryland Historical Society, Baltimore, Maryland.

This one had all the appearance of a trap, and my heart missed a couple of beats, but the holy saints were with me. "I think," I said, "that it is much better written than the *Sunpaper*." I was to learn later that Max smelled something artful here, but, as always, he held himself well, and all I could observe was a faint flutter of a smile across his face. At length he spoke. "Come back," he said, "tomorrow night."

Mencken did, and the next, and the next—but with each successive visit Ways simply shook his head.[1]

Baltimore's weather throughout February 1899 had been colder than previous years. At first, the light snowfall brought forth high-stepping trotters. Throughout Union Square and outlying areas, the tinkling of bells could be heard as laughing couples, dripping with furs, skimmed over the powdery roads in sleighs. In a matter of days, however, the snow was accompanied by a biting wind that whirled ice from the roofs into the faces of pedestrians. Outside the *Herald* office, the drifts would have been up to Henry's knees.

By the second week the papers reported that the Baltimore weather was the worst since 1873, when record keeping had begun. Navigation had ceased on the bay, except for heavier steamships that could cut through the ice; even the trolleys had a difficult time keeping their schedules, and many of the drivers were suffering from frostbite.

One morning a blizzard hit that broke all records. The mercury sank below zero. Funerals were postponed; trolley services were suspended; businesses closed; mail service stopped. Any right-minded person would have stayed home under such extraordinary circumstances; but in Mencken's version of the story, he was a boy of extraordinary determination. "I hoofed it ever hopefully to the *Herald* office," he wrote, "and then hoofed it sadly home."

Or so the story goes. When Mencken wrote his recollections for public consumption in 1940, he was continuing his lifelong habit of embellishment and exaggeration. In his preface for *Newspaper Days*, he threw himself upon the bosom of friendly readers "who refuse to take everything perversely in the absolute and literal sense." To Mencken what mattered, as he cited Charles Lamb, was "a fair construction, as to an after-dinner conversation."

For those, however, who yearn for absolute accuracy, one must turn to Mencken's first written recollection of the event, which he prepared for his biographer in 1925. The draft he handed to Isaac Goldberg, with its spelling errors, notations, and unedited confessions, was kept by that author until his death; it is not the polished manuscript Mencken would later bequeath with his own papers. Here, in this early draft, can be surmised the more truthful account: that Mencken visited the *Herald* office two weeks after his father's death, then a second time toward the end of February, when Max Ways proposed he come to the office during the evening to try his hand at a few assignments.[2]

So, on February 23, after what seemed like a geological epoch to the boy, Max Ways handed him an assignment. His mission was to collect any bit of news at Govanstown, a detached neighborhood that, during those remote days in Baltimore, made it seem to Mencken, psychologically and physically, as foreign as Cairo. The blizzard had blockaded doors with drifts fifteen feet high, and glaciers of ice covered the roads; nonetheless, Mencken still managed to find an item. Returning to the *Herald* office he took a vacant desk at a far corner, and after several attempts produced his first of two stories.

> A horse, a buggy and several sets of harnesses, valued in all at about $250, were stolen last night from the stable of Howard Quinlan, near Kingsville. The county police are at work on the case, but so far no trace of either thieves or booty has been found.

At midnight an exultant Mencken headed home. He knew that more than writing skills alone and a kind word from Arthur and Wells Hawks to upper management had given him his opportunity. Years later, Mencken advised a hopeful correspondent that there was only one way to break into the newspaper business: to "keep on banging away at city editors until one of them gives you a real chance. They put on a hard front but they are really very sentimental fellows, and in the long run persistence always makes an impression on them. They know very well it is an important qualification for a journalist." Within a few days Mencken was being introduced by Max Ways to a few other reporters as a youngster trying out for a job. " 'My name,' he said, 'was Macon,' " Mencken recalled years later. "They greeted me with considerable reserve."3

FOR THE NEXT FEW MONTHS, "Macon" jumped between two jobs. The daylight hours spent at the cigar factory did not seem as depressing as before, for once twilight fell and the street lamps cast their patches of light on the pavement, Mencken's nocturnal adventures began. Mile by mile he was becoming acquainted with the city and its inhabitants. The waterfront was romantic, with its gloomy sheds and old vessels fresh from journeys from Canton to Manila, down to Valparaiso and back again. Mixed in with the waterfront's salty smell mingled other odors—tar, rum, molasses, and the aromatic scent of freshly hewn timber. Downtown was full of sinister alleys, neglect, and decay. Through all this, Mencken found, "odd fish were washed up by the hundred. Strange marvels unrolled continuously. Above all, there was the pervasive rowdiness and bawdiness of the town—the general air of devil-may-care freedom—the infinite oddity and extravagance of its daily, and especially nightly, life."

Mencken threw himself into his assignments with characteristic vigor. Racial ill feeling and de facto segregation, slowly increasing since 1890, were being felt during the gubernatorial campaign of 1899. The Democratic Party campaigned on the notion that Baltimore was a white man's city, and party members rarely missed the opportunity to remind white voters of Republican reliance on black support. Mencken was assigned to cover their reactions, and he wrote stories on industrial education for blacks and on the meetings of black Republicans, as he listened to their indignation at the Democratic Party's racial pitch. Other subjects for his pen in 1899 were piano recitals, the Huerich brewing company, labor, tobacco, addresses on Americanism, and testimonies of cures made by Christian Scientists. He touched upon the way Germany was portrayed in the "mud-slinging" press and America's role in the Spanish-American War: "a one-sided and almost ridiculous fight between a giant and a pygmy." All these news stories were written perfunctorily, with a simple statement of facts, but in many ways they foreshadowed the subjects he would later address.4

Often Mencken did not get home until the rest of the city had fallen silent, broken by the footsteps of a passing policeman and the occasional clang of the all-night trolley. If Anna Mencken was disturbed about her son's irregular hours, she did not let it show, instead quietly making a plateful of sandwiches for him when he returned home after midnight. When, one evening, Max Ways found the boy dozing off at his desk, he permitted him Sundays off, and Mencken's delight renewed itself tenfold.

Racing up the stairs to the fifth floor city room, his pockets full of notes detailing the latest incident from the crooked streets, Mencken's happiness was complete. So what if some of his assignments had consisted of simply covering an oyster supper or an interview with the town bores just back from Europe? "I was young, goatish and full of an innocent delight in the world," he recalled. As he sat writing copy, pausing to aim a stream of tobacco juice into a handy spittoon (conveniently at every desk), he exchanged the latest office jargon with an older reporter assigned to show the new apprentice around (done, gladly, at the nearest saloon, always at the boy's expense).

Looking back at his early years, Mencken later wrote: "I believe that a young journalist, turned loose in a large city, had more fun a quarter of a century ago than any other man. The Mauve Decade was just ending, and the new era of standardization and efficiency had not come in." The city staff came in at 12:30 p.m. and worked until 11 at night. When a man was sent out on an assignment, he was expected not to return without it.

According to Mencken, there was no hurry to get stories in the paper, and there were no rewrite men. "The modern office, with its clicking typewriters and careful grooming, simply did not exist." There were few typewriters; the machines they had were regarded as effeminate. Only two telephones graced the office: "Paleozoic instruments attached to the wall," Mencken recalled, "and no one ever used them if it could be avoided." Indeed, "the charm of the life, in those remote days, lay in the reporter's freedom. Today he is at the end of a wire, and the city editor can reach him and annoy him in ten minutes."

To Mencken and many of his generation, it was a golden era to be a newspaperman, a period "before newspaper reporters were publicists and confidantes of the eminent." In the saloons they socialized with working men. Beer was five cents a glass, but there were saloon keepers in Baltimore who held reporters in such high esteem they offered it for three. "There weren't any tabloids, there wasn't any news on the air," recalled one contemporary. "Most reporters worked at space rates, and made money without much effort, and they swarmed the sidewalks like the lords of the earth."[5]

Other influences were at work. One of them was George Ade's *Fables in Slang*, humorous sketches published that year, which won attention for its portraits of contemporary Americans and their speech. Ade always maintained that he was not a humorist but a realist, which Mencken immediately recognized after reading his fables and especially his short stories about politicians, women, and bachelors. Other vivid flashes of the national spirit could be found in the fragments of paper left on the telegraph editor's desk; stories from the *New York Sun*, mined regularly for bulletins and tossed, but which Mencken rescued and eagerly studied on the trolley car going home.

"The dull professors who write literary histories never mention the New York *Sun*," he wrote years later, but for "a hopeful young newspaper reporter in the year 1899, the *Sun* was your daily food and drink, your dream and your despair." The creator of that cynical style was Edward M. Kingsbury. From 1881 to 1915 many of the notable articles and casual essays that appeared in the *Sun's* pages were due to him. Its subjects ranged from the tricks and devices of politicians to language, kissing, food, bald heads, and college yells—topics Mencken would borrow much later for his own column. Kingsbury made the editorial page sizzle with humor and originality of ideas and phrase, many of which crept into Mencken's prose.

Other writers, such as Theodore Dreiser, Stephen Crane, and James Huneker, developing independently of each other, were also appearing on the pages of the *New York Sun*. By encouraging originality and discouraging imitations of the English journalistic style (long considered a model), the *Sun* became distinctly American, known for its incisive conversational writing. The end result, Mencken later asserted, made the paper one of the most influential factors in delivering "American literature from its former formalism and hollowness."[6]

The goal Max Ways demanded of each of his reporters on the *Herald* was very much like that asked of reporters on the *New York Sun*: not what is a piece of news worth judged by the conventional standards, but how you can make it interesting. By the end of the summer of 1899, few of Mencken's stories resembled his earlier ponderous format. As he grew in self-confidence, he began to play up stories of human interest. Accompanying health department inspectors on a tour of East Baltimore sweatshops, Mencken observed firsthand the ghettos of the newly arrived Polish and Russian immigrant Jews who formed a large source of cheap labor. "I . . . was appalled by what I saw," he recalled. No one seemed to mind that dirty urchins played in the garbage, constructing a chain of potato peelings. The sight convinced him of the inferiority of the mob and the opinion, expressed when he was an adult, that the bulk of Russian Jews lived in filth.

Years later, looking over these early stories, Mencken felt chagrined about their "shabby writing, full of cliches and banalities." But Max Ways believed the boy's use of the vernacular and the vividness with which he portrayed this area of metropolitan life were nothing less than remarkable.[7]

IF OTHER *HERALD* REPORTERS had eyed Mencken suspiciously at first, they couldn't help overhearing the increasing praise Ways was giving to the new arrival. While others plodded, Mencken dazzled. His enthusiasm to take on new tasks was not unnoticed. By the end of June Mencken's days as a volunteer, writing on space, had ended. On July 2 he was hired at $7 a week—the youngest reporter in the office, and the first cub reporter on the *Herald* to get paid a salary.

Just when Mencken was reveling in his success, his Aunt Pauline alarmed his mother, telling her that all newspapermen were enormous boozers and that large numbers of them died in the gutter. To her credit, Anna checked whatever private fears she held, and Mencken had his future assured.

That summer Max Ways assigned Mencken to the central police district. Mencken later wrote, "I can still smell it. Its odor was a mixture of dissecting-room and brewery." Here he witnessed his first hanging. He admitted that he had been so little affected that he returned to the office with a length of the hangman's rope as a souvenir. Even so, the act of going to a cramped county jail at dawn and seeing a condemned man "trembling and sobbing" before paying the drastic penalty made Mencken think that it was hard-hearted to believe that "murder is the only cure for murder." Eventually Mencken changed his mind. Any "mercy for the merciless" was for "mushheads," he stated. Criminals should be hanged at once, instead of "devouring three hearty meals a day at your expense and mine." He was now experiencing another side to Baltimore, the world of murder and suicide.

In November, Ways assigned Mencken to the presidential election between William Jennings Bryan and William McKinley, to write not only the main story but also the side features. One feature described his own juvenile memories of election bonfires that outshone the electric lights at Baltimore street corners. Still another instructed voters how to fill out their ballots. The new *Herald* reporter doing the teaching was ineligible to vote, being not yet 21 years old.

Mencken's talents were not lost on Max Ways—especially during election night, which in Baltimore, like Christmas Eve, was a carnival. The city editor had the security of knowing he could count on his youngest reporter to keep sober. Dealing with drunken reporters was one of the more annoying tasks with which Ways had to contend. Half the time he had to send Mencken to rouse one from a saloon, dig out his notes from his pocket, and finish writing his story.

In December Mencken's first poem of any importance—a tribute to his hero, Rudyard Kipling—was published in that month's issue of *Bookman*, which he had discovered by flipping through the magazine at a bookstall. "I was enchanted," he recalled later, but "so addled that I was quite unfit for work." Escaping to a burlesque house, he sat in the solitude of the theater, savoring his triumph. Eventually he made his way back to the office, shyly confessing his publication, whereupon congratulations spread through the building.[8]

ON THAT HAPPY NOTE, 1899 drew to a close. From the top of the *Herald* roof Mencken looked over the city, attuned to the sounds below. Just one year before on New Year's Eve, he had been standing at his father's bedside while August hovered between life and death.

Since then, the absence of August Mencken had been keenly felt at 1524 Hollins Street. With his own freedom assured, Mencken found even the commonplace reminders of his father held a special place for him. As for Anna, she seemed to her son to have the wifely devotion of Queen Victoria. She would never marry again.

From near Fort Carroll, the faint shriek of a tugboat whistle could be heard. The year 1900 marked a milestone, an open port toward a new world of opportunity. Suddenly the heavy blast of a steamer's whistle came from the Chesapeake. As the deeper booms of steamers quieted, the church bells of Baltimore could be sharply heard in the crisp air. After the sound of a low-toned bell ceased, the trembling F of a smaller one, somewhere from the eastern part of the city, floated upward to the roof of the *Herald*, as Mencken, his ear always sensitive to melody, listened enraptured. There was no doubt as to the joy this young writer felt. No longer was he a child; at the *Herald*, "I began to be a man."

For Henry Louis Mencken, "The first day of the new year had dawned."[9]

5

TERSE AND TERRIBLE TEXTS

W ITH THE NEW YEAR, the publication of Mencken's short stories had increased his esteem at the *Herald* office, and he learned a truism too little noticed by young journalists: the prestige of a reporter is often more nourished by what he does outside the office than what he does inside. In 1900, workers at the *Herald* office agreed that Mencken was "a genius."

While working twelve hours a day, seven days a week, the ambitious young reporter found time to produce poetry, articles for out-of-town papers, and short stories. None of his fiction had much literary merit, though it was vividly written. Later in life, Mencken would think fiction not worth writing; but even this apprenticeship was valuable in teaching him, by practice, the craft he later assessed as a critic and magazine editor. In a review in the *Smart Set* several years later, he noted: "It seems easy to spin such droll colloquies, to devise such simple plots. But those of us who have poured out our sweat upon the making of short stories know just how much careful planning, just how much effort, goes into every one of them."

Many of the themes of his fiction reflected his reading. He had been buying each new volume of Rudyard Kipling as it appeared; he also gave them as Christmas presents to other Kipling fans such as his friend Arthur Hawks. Now he transferred what he read to his poetry and his own short stories, from the genteel sentimentality of plot and character to the exotic locales, such as Central America and, later, Jamaica. Interspersed were traces of the word-fascination that would become so characteristic of Mencken's literary style. In one story that described dentistry, readers had to cope with such terms as "apocryphal" and "lagniappe."

"I began to be a man." A confident Mencken with fellow reporter Arthur Hawks, Spring 1900. H. L. Mencken Collection, Enoch Pratt Free Library.

Stories that explored the Baltimore waterfront or the crews of a British tramp steamer fared best. He described their characters and settings with realism and humor. The clarity was not so much an influence of Kipling as of Thomas Huxley, who he said later, "greatly influenced my short stories, though he never wrote any of them himself." About 1900, when Mencken began reading Emile Zola, he was excited to find a novelist who recognized the relevance of Darwinism in literature. Zola introduced Mencken to "the conception of man as a mammal —man swayed and fashioned, not by . . . arbitrary gods, but by natural laws, by food and drink, by blood and environment."

At this time Mencken came across a copy of Theodore Dreiser's *Sister Carrie*. Here was a brand-new creation, speaking of a world that had not existed in American fiction of that time. Previous writers had projected morality on the lives they had observed; instead, with a heap of details, Dreiser depicted the life ordinary Americans were living. It made a powerful impression on Mencken.

Meanwhile, he began methodically filling a notebook with incidents, recording scraps of dialogue and slang, columns from the *New York Sun*. He made records of where he had sent his latest story: *Harper's*, *Scribner's*, even the *Smart Set*. On the next lines a few weeks later he recorded their rejections. His steadiest targets were *Short Stories*, *Red Book*, and soon *Frank Leslie's Popular Magazine*.[1]

All this hyperactivity took its toll, and Mencken's chronic bronchitis grew worse. At the turn of the century, such ailments were cause for justifiable concern. To the consternation of Baltimore's medical faculty, including its health commissioner, the death rate in the city had increased; among its leading causes were tuberculosis and pneumonia. The Mencken family physician promptly sent his patient to a specialist, who suggested the young reporter take a trip. At that time most Americans went to Florida, Bermuda, or Europe in search of winter resorts; the only passage available was aboard a British tramp steamer headed to Jamaica to pick up a cargo of bananas. That island still had not been recognized as the new Riviera by Americans, though in travel booklets the British were calling attention to its charms as a cure for consumptives. Mencken took his chances, and in June he boarded the peeling and decrepit *Ely*, determined to write about his experiences for the *Herald*.

The boat gave a blast of its whistle, and with a thrust they were leaving Baltimore and rolling into the Atlantic. As the horizon heaved and dipped, Mencken made repeated visits to the leeward rail, until finally, on the sixth day, he began to feel against his face the narcotic caress of the Caribbean. Great masses of yellow seaweed floated by, and as the east began to show streaks of pink, Mencken got his first sight of the tropics in the vast splendors of dawn, as Jamaica's palm trees bulged out of the sea.

Within moments, the lookout shouted, "Light four points on the starboard bow!" and the little ship docked in the turquoise harbor of Port Antonio. As the *Ely* swung idly from her anchor, Mencken leaned over the side, watching a silvery fish slowly zigzag through the purple coral. Mencken, whose only idea of the ocean had been the murky gray of the Atlantic, could only silently stare at the immeasurable strangeness of it all. For once, language failed him.

When an army of banana handlers surrounded the ship, Mencken for one moment imagined he had landed back at Bowley's Wharf in Baltimore. But when he began to distinguish individual voices from the babble, and heard a black man yell that his "kerridge" goes "pawst the 'otel," he felt like stuffing his copy of Kipling into the galley fire.[2]

On July 11 Mencken arrived in Kingston, and again, any previous notions he had of race outside Baltimore were shattered. Exploring that city, he found himself in the midst of a variegated, cosmopolitan mob, jostling between tall Jamaican girls gracefully balancing baskets of mangos, alongside them a curious mix of Haitians, French, and Spaniards. As in Baltimore, whites and blacks sat side by side. True enough, he reported, "alack, too true!—the colored brother grabs the end seat of a street car, but what of it? What odds?"

"A nigger here, if he is decent, is as good as a white man," he wrote to his family, informing, in colloquial style, "The mayor of Kingston and most of the city council are coons, as are all of the police, post office clerks, custom officers and legislators." The news must have caused the Mencken family some astonishment; in Baltimore, such desired clerical and administrative positions were given only to whites.

When not meeting newspaper editors, Mencken spent his time sitting on the veranda of the hotel, sipping rum punch and listening to Brits spin stories of trading and cannibalism, which he enthusiastically recorded for the *Herald*. For the *Pittsburgh Press* he described a near-crucifixion of an evangelist named George James Cousins who tried to save the souls of his fellow Jamaicans. In his poetry Mencken described the beach of Watling's Island, marking the place where Columbus first landed, and in his stories the curiosities of voodoo. Wherever he went, Mencken became photojournalist, coaxing families to pose for his lens. In between, he bought souvenirs and hired a tailor to fit him with a gleaming suit of white ducks, clothing that, at home, would shine brilliantly under the lights of Electric Park.

By the time Mencken was ready to return home, he had amassed enough experience to enliven his writing. "I'll never forget the sounds and sights of that tropical morning," he reminisced to a friend years later about his first day ashore. In his *Handbook of Jamaica*, he gently pressed several exotic flowers and leaves. In the next few years he would return, once accompanied by his mother and siblings Gertrude and August, another time with his bride, to share with those he loved the sight of blinding green water.

On this trip, however, the tropic sunshine had not worked its cure, and Mencken's chronic bronchitis had not abated by the time Baltimore loomed into view. Before him seemingly lay a choice: a sedentary occupation punctuated by visits to sanitariums, or a short life guaranteed by working strenuously as a journalist. "I then resolved that, inasmuch as I was probably doomed to an early death, I might as well have a good time as I lived," he vowed. "So I plunged into newspaper work and took to drinking beer. Gradually the bronchitis wore off."[3]

BY AUGUST, Mencken's articles had attracted the attention of Charles Grasty's new paper, the *Evening News*. Mencken did not hesitate to advertise that fact to upper management at the *Herald* in an effort to get a raise. In order to keep his best young reporter on his staff, Max Ways increased Mencken's salary for a third time since his brief arrival, now to $14 a week. Moreover, his manner of writing had earned him his own column. "In that remote day columnists were still rare," Mencken recalled, and when the column began running twice a week, it became increasingly hard to fill it. Resorting to his desk drawer full of schoolboy verse, Mencken began loading the newspaper with his poetry, which he renamed "Knocks & Jollies." Then he added another occasional title, "Terse and Terrible Texts," and later "Untold Tales."

In his most significant column, "Baltimore and the Rest of the World," Mencken showed his affection for his city and his agitation for reform of laws that impinged on individual freedom. When the Baltimore police began enforcing Maryland Blue Laws one Sunday in 1900, he ridiculed them in print. He protested the popular belief that regarded Mark Twain as an entertaining buffoon. "Someday," he wrote in one column, "the critics will awaken to the fact that *Huckleberry Finn* is the greatest novel yet produced by an American writer. At present it seems to be regarded as a cross between the Elsie books and the *Fables in Slang*. The penalty of humor is a cruel one."

This penalty, however, would not last long. Between 1900 and 1920 the humorous column of the urban daily would become the most important single medium in revitalizing American literature in the idiom that was the speech of average Americans. Elsewhere, the columns of Eugene Field, Finley Peter Dunne, Don Marquis, and later Ring Lardner brightened the pages of newspapers across the country, anticipating the social criticism Mencken would write in the 1920s.[4]

Autumn had arrived. Emerging from 1524 Hollins Street one morning, Mencken briskly set off for the *Herald*, walking against the exhilarating breeze. He was convinced that no human being had a better time of it than he. At the end of the day, riding home on the trolley after work, the cool air of the early morning ruffling through his hair, Mencken's reflections turned upon the virtues and defects of his trade. Life was arduous, certainly, but also gay and carefree: "The days chased one another like kittens chasing their tails."

With autumn, Max Ways gave Mencken yet another raise and promoted him to City Hall, replacing an older reporter. No doubt Ways, with his practiced eye, had already discerned a bit of himself in the young man. He too had joined the *Herald* shortly after school. Moreover, he seemed to detect in Henry Mencken those same qualities that had led to his own rapid advancement: industriousness, writing ability, an eye for news, and a gift for making a wide circle of friends. If Max Ways ever observed any resentment among the staff toward the talented new recruit, he may have also noticed that the very man Mencken replaced had been charmed by the sheer force of his personality. By February 1, 1901, with barely a year and a half of service behind him, Mencken's salary was increased to $18 a week: he was now the highest paid young reporter on the staff.[5]

Once at City Hall, however, all of Mencken's confidence vanished. Roaming the cavernous halls, he scrambled to find leads, and said one judge, "pestered me with unanswerable questions." Mencken missed the days in the company of friendly policemen whom he had accompanied on their rounds. Now there were days when his deadline approached and he was not able to write anything. One dull Sunday he decided to put the lonely northern district of the city into the news by inventing a wild man who roamed in its woods. "For weeks afterward the children of the neighborhood were kept indoors, and the cops kept on dragging in suspects." Another time, when a City Council member refused to meet with Mencken, he concocted a farcical report of the City Council's meetings, and went on with it thereafter from week to week.

Shortly after its publication, Mencken was told to report to the office of the *Herald's* publisher, Colonel A. B. Cunningham, and explain.

> The Colonel glared at me in silence while I told my halting tale and remained silent for a full minute afterward. Then he suddenly ran both hands through his vast mop of black hair, threw back his head . . . and emitted a whoop that must have been audible in St. Paul Street, five stories below.

Instead of punishing the paper's youngest star for printing falsehoods, he was given the benefit of the doubt. Cunningham's wrath was reserved for the "tin-soldier" who had refused to understand that a *Herald* reporter was as good as any in the world. "In any controversy between a *Herald* reporter and anyone else—and newspaper work is full of rough and bitter controversies," Mencken wrote, Colonel Cunningham "was always with the reporter: first, last, and all the time." It would not be the last time that Mencken faked the news.[6]

BY THIS TIME Max Ways had left the *Herald* for local politics. Overseeing Mencken's work was Dwight Burroughs, a former City Hall reporter himself and alert to any fiction that any young reporter would dare slip into his news stories. From then on, Mencken's reports were carefully written; civic improvements were duly recorded and filed.

The *Herald*, however, now lacked the same humorous irreverence that had prevailed when Mencken first joined the paper. The business of the *Herald* was overseen by Frank Peard, who eventually rose to the position of president and general manager. He was described by Mencken as "a large, handsome pompous fellow, amiable enough, but wholly unfit to run a newspaper." Mencken later satirized him in a short story about newspapermen called "The Bend in the Tube." Years after, Mencken would privately remark: "I have never, in this life, met a worse jackass." With spasmodic persistence, Peard summoned his workers from their labors through a speaking tube, a relic of the old days of hand composition and chalk plates. With each shrill whistle, Mencken knew that he and his colleagues would be subjected to inane questions from "the preposterous Peard," stealing precious time from work at hand.

As the weeks wore on and Mencken sat at his desk, his scissors and paste pot before him, he felt a growing dislike toward the men above him. At the end of such a day, Mencken would bound into what he called "the purgatory of the unregenerate"—some saloon that might lurk in the dark recesses of an inconspicuous side street—to share a beer with Josh Lynch of the printing staff. It had been years since that summer day, long ago in Ellicott City, when a smaller Mencken had peered through the window of the *Times* and watched Josh Lynch roll the paper off the press. Now, as he sat across the table from him, Mencken thought Lynch the only one at the *Herald* who could teach him about his craft.[7]

By the spring of 1901 Mencken made a realistic assessment of the profession that had brought him this far, from the viewpoint of a worker in the ranks. There was, he argued, nothing for an ambitious young man: no guideposts or words of counsel. Visiting the Enoch Pratt Free Library, thumbing through books of advice, he lamented that most had been written by old men who had been in their prime during the 1870s, twenty years before the current revolution in journalism. How to conduct newspaper interviews, pointers about colored supplements and up-to-the-minute extras, the salary question, or the vagaries of city editors— there was nothing of value. A perusal of indexes to the magazines revealed worse: reams upon reams written by "those cheerful do-gooders who waste valuable ink in giving the public information about 'The Mission of the Press' and 'The Future of Journalism.' "

Mencken's palpable need for advice did not diminish for the rest of that year. His short story "The Flight of the Victor," in *Frank Leslie's Popular Monthly Magazine*, brought him an encouraging letter from its editor, Ellery Sedgewick. "My other editors had been polite, but that was all," Mencken recalled. "Sedgewick went further, and I began to glow with the feeling, so pleasant to a young author and so stimulating, that an editor was really interested in me."

Delighted as he was, within a few weeks of its receipt even some of this glow inevitably began to wear off. He measured his progress by meticulously record-ing entries into a notebook that cited the latest rejection of his manuscripts, but he had no one to consult with at the office about his literary aspirations. "To be sure, my occasional appearances brought me considerable *kudos*," he recalled, "but no one else on the staff was going the same way, so I had no one to talk to about my problems and my hopes—an extremely important thing to a youngster."[8]

Meanwhile, he struggled with his poetry and his stories, even buying a book to help him with rhymes. "Such sadness often overcame me in 1901," Mencken admitted years later to his friend, novelist Joseph Hergesheimer. "I was in a low state, full of romance and with a bad cough." Unpublished, his scribbles would have little excuse for being, a depressing circumstance of which he was well aware.

Picking up his pen, he wrote a poem called "Finis," about a man who fights the long and comfortless battle for justice and the writer who fulfills his dream of becoming famous. The last stanza reads:

> *And the end of it all was a hole in the ground*
> *And a scratch on a crumbling stone.*

"When I finished this and read it over," he confessed, "it really scared me."[9]

6

PLAYS AND PLAYERS

INALLY, A REPRIEVE APPEARED for Mencken. Robert I. Carter, the new managing editor of the *Herald*, moved him from City Hall to the role of Sunday
editor, in which he would also serve as drama critic. Since his boyhood,
Mencken had been drawn to the stage. He exulted in the musical overture, the
expectant hush of those first few seconds when the house lights dimmed and the
curtain struggled upward, introducing him to other worlds.

The productions were of the popular variety: comedies and musical pieces
he had been attending since the 1890s. It was the era of music and especially
of vaudeville, with its stereotyping of the ethnic groups flowing into cities like
Baltimore. The immigrants who graced the Baltimore theater stages—Sophie
Tucker, Harry Houdini, Al Jolson—spoke the American English as it was heard
on the streets. Mencken, with an increasing interest in the vernacular, told his
Herald readers that most of the queer words of the American language were
invented by "the authors of popular songs and vaudeville witticisms."

But it was burlesque, with its mixture of parody and pretty girls, that was then
considered family entertainment and, to Mencken, some of the most amusing. It
emphasized comedy; indeed, it provided Broadway with most of its comedians.
Mencken preferred the shows of Sliding Billy Watson: "His 'Beef Trust' was
almost perfect," he later told Robert Carter's widow. "I'll never forget his advertising matter, with the huge legend 'Ten Tons of Women.' In those days the
masculine taste in this great Republic was for bulk and a really Class A burlesque
queen had a backside like a barn door."

On Monday evenings, when the two men returned to the *Herald* after a theater preview, Carter would read Mencken's criticism. One day the older man took him aside and gave him the advice he would value for the rest of his life: "He believed, and taught me, that a dull notice, however profound, was not worth printing."

"Knock somebody in the head everyday," Carter told him. "That is Rule No. 1 of American psychology. . . . You must give a good show to get a crowd, and a good show means one with slaughter in it." This advice kept turning over and over in his memory, Mencken confessed, and went a long way toward explaining the development of his irreverent style.[1]

Although Mencken became widely known as a literary critic, it was as a drama critic at the *Herald* that he honed his craft. Such opportunities to show his mettle, however, were slow in coming. At the turn of the century, the public still saw the theater primarily as a means of escape from everyday life. Farce, insincere melodrama, and historical costume pieces succeeded each other monotonously; critics such as James Huneker were complaining in the *New York Sun* of the "sentimental mush, the pious pap, and the cheap vulgarities of Broadway."[2]

It was not Huneker, however, but Will Page, a talented drama critic from the *Washington Post*, who first led Mencken to recognize the revolutionary realism of the new artists who were about to forge modern American theater.

One evening during the autumn of 1902, Page told him that Mary Shaw, then the undisputed leader of the intellectual faction among American actresses, was searching for a play to show off her talents. During the course of the conversation someone suggested Henrik Ibsen's *Ghosts*. The play had been suppressed in almost every country. Its questioning of the invincibility of marriage and its allusions to venereal disease had forced a recent London production to close. Audiences who attended Ibsen productions had been dismissed by British drama critics as pallid spinsters, sickly youths, and depraved old men. Would the Baltimore public stand for Ibsen? As Mencken recalled, "I was naturally hot for it."

William Winter of the *New York Herald Tribune*, then widely considered the dean of drama critics, was, Mencken well knew, a violent opponent to all novelty in the theater. Erudite, opinionated, and conservative, he labeled Ibsen a menace and George Bernard Shaw a degenerate, and lambasted any drama that smacked of sex. As Mencken wrote later: "If he had lived into the Eugene O'Neill era he'd have suffered so powerfully that his death would have been a kind of capital punishment."

Mencken now challenged Winter and "other dramatic archeologists." Competing for attention were traditional plays starring Mrs. Patrick Campbell and Richard Mansfield. But Mencken asked: "What other event of the year will be of more real interest?" Two columns of the theater page were given to Mary Shaw so that she could elaborate "As to Ibsen and His Play."[3]

When the curtain rose on *Ghosts* on Monday evening, November 12, 1902, it was a performance that would remain long in memory. Ibsen had drawn his characters with merciless realism. Virginia Kline, a young and attractive actress who was making her first appearance with the company, astonished Mencken with her intelligent interpretation of her role, leading him privately to vow that here was someone whose friendship he would like to cultivate.

As the cast delivered its lines, Mencken looked around to see what reaction Ibsen was having on the audience. Baltimore patrons of the theater were notorious for behaving, as one producer later said, "like talking drunks." On that evening, Mencken calculated that half the crowd was composed of smart people; the other half, typical theatergoers, utterly unable to comprehend even the most elementary ideas of the play. The house manager, misunderstanding the bold action of *Ghosts*, rushed out of the theater exclaiming, "We'll all go to jail!"

The next morning, Mencken awoke to find that the reviewers for the local papers, who had previously taken Ibsen to task, were actually favorable. Instead, it was the *audience* who objected to the production. They found it morbid and unpleasant. "Such gruesome plays as those of Ibsen and his cult," complained an irate patron, had been justifiably criticized in a sermon by the rector of a local church in Baltimore. Such reactions led one drama critic from the *Baltimore Evening News* (an old man of the William Winter type, at his best only when Shakespeare was the fare), to conclude that Ibsen was obscene. Confronted by such reaction, George Fawcett withdrew the play from Baltimore.

Instead of giving up on the play, the little company took the work on the road, introducing Ibsen to more than 100,000 Americans. Mary Shaw, Mencken said, was a tradition-smasher after his own heart. By taking *Ghosts* on tour, she had been instrumental in promoting realistic drama in the United States, and its production was an important turning point in Mencken's role as a critic. He had been foremost among the Baltimore theater critics to promote forcibly the works of Ibsen and other realists. As Mencken's stature increased, an idea began to take hold in his mind for a work in which he could visit the subject of George Bernard Shaw and Henrik Ibsen again, and to a much wider public than he had ever reached before.[4]

WHEN CARTER APPOINTED Mencken as Sunday editor, he was still the youngest man at the *Herald*, conspicuous for what one contemporary observed as "his roaring mannerisms, colorful rhetoric, overflowing energy." This energy, indeed, kept his staff running. One of his first tasks as Sunday editor was to downplay the personalities of the actors and focus on the plays themselves. His job was to receive the press agents who traveled ahead of itinerant theatrical groups. "Nine-tenths of these enthusiasts seemed to me very pleasant fellows," he recalled, "but I cannot say I was very generous about giving them space."

In the regular column devoted to "What the Press Agents Say," Mencken strictly admonished the press agents: "Confine your compositions to the English language." Likewise, Mencken improved the art department. In the new century, photographic halftones were gradually replacing line drawings. The new Sunday editor considered illustrations as important as text, and whenever he could convince upper management, they were used.

When Mencken was not inspecting woodcuts and engravings for the *Sunday Herald*, he could be heard bellowing, "Boy, COPY!" The summoned copyboy, after delivering Mencken's story, was often sent scurrying to Pippin's Book Store and—even more frequently—on trips for corncob pipes, Uncle Willie cigars, and Mail Pouch chewing tobacco. Accompanied by printer Josh Lynch, the editor fortified himself throughout these busy days with enormous lunches of what was then called "the working man's friend": a beef stew at fifteen cents, providing maximum nourishment at minimum cost. "By the time we got back to the office," Mencken recalled, "we were ready to either fight or sing."

Mencken's improvements to the Sunday paper did not go unnoticed. Of the eight dailies in Baltimore, a local guidebook to the city commented that year, the *Herald* was most direct in furnishing and analyzing the news, and most attractive in its headlines and display. "These methods, which are being consistently improved upon," it noted, "give the paper warm friends among thousands who favor the style of journalism of which the *Herald* is a key example."[5]

Notwithstanding the pace, Mencken still made ample time for outside writing. He devoted weeks corresponding with an interested publisher about a volume of his short stories—only to abandon this project when he discovered the publisher was a huckster who would only be too glad to bring out the volume for $300. For the next few months Mencken floundered, anxious to see his writing captured between covers and yielding the money and glory he thought his abilities deserved. Finally that opportunity came.

One evening, while he was in a neighboring saloon in the company of artists who illustrated the *Herald*'s Sunday supplement, one of them declared the time was ripe for setting up his own printing office. Within a week, the group of illustrators had rented a small space, put in presses and type, and was soliciting trade. But prospective customers did not want to hear plans; they wanted to see a concrete sample of the firm's work. Charles Gordon remembered: "We asked my boss, who was kind and generous in helping people, to suggest some sort of copy we might make into a little volume." Immediately Mencken suggested a book of his own short stories. But the group objected; 250 pages of text were far too expensive to print. As Mencken later recalled the event:

> Someone, as a way out, suggested that a book of verse be substituted for the short stories—a book of no more than 50 pages, elegantly hand-set by Marshall and decorated by Siegel and Gordon. It seemed a good idea, but I was inclined to balk. Most of my verse, I protested, was poor newspaper stuff; I had written only a few better things for the magazines. But there was plenty of arguments against that. No one read verse anyhow—and certainly not businessmen. The thing would not go any further than Baltimore—and Baltimore had already digested and survived my worst.

For the next few hours, Mencken rescued files of youthful ballads and triolets from his literary potter's field and pasted them together. Then he began putting together the title page. Beside his copyright he issued this warning: "Some are imitations—necessarily weak—of the verse of several men in whose writing he has found a good deal of innocent pleasure."

"I was already a good critic in 1903!" Mencken wryly observed. For good measure, he and the publisher listed the book as the first—and *last*—edition. One hundred copies were printed.

In late April, Gordon showed Mencken the first copy of *Ventures Into Verse* and asked him to autograph it, "When I first saw it," Mencken recalled, "I damn nigh bust with delight." On its cover, printed in a vivid red, were the title and his name. Within, on stiff ivory paper, with green single rules, were his verse and the handsome illustrations of Charles S. Gordon and John Siegel, with text set in Old English and elegant Caslon italics, with plenty of decorations and other designs to satisfy any future client. "At twenty-two," Mencken exulted, "I was to see my first book!"

Of his own copies, several were promptly sent for review, others to libraries. Mencken then subscribed to a clipping service and awaited the results. Meanwhile, he happily autographed copies for family and friends. To the first of his pals to share the lofty ambition of seeing his own poetry in print, he scrawled: "To Arthur W. Hawks, Jr., my old side-partner, in memory of many discussions of art, literature, and immortality."

The seventeen reviews that came in were, for the most part, polite. When they were not hailing Mencken as a "Kiplingite," they praised him for being a genius (albeit an eccentric one). Such reception raised Mencken's status at the office. Within the Mencken family, Charlie joked to his little sister Gertie, "He must be becoming a sport, wearing all those fine clothes."

With Mencken, as with all authors, the reviews that were the most negative were the ones that struck home. The *Nation* magazine, he later recalled, was among those that "told the bitter truth, and in harsh terms," by tartly describing the poet as "Anglicized." Others tired of the poems, finding them "saleable rather than sincere."

Despite Mencken's later embarrassment at what he called his "appalling" verse—"Kipling fermented, ratted and radiating ammonia"—rumors persisted that he bought up all remaining copies of *Ventures Into Verse* and burned them. He admitted, however, to hiding a certain number; later he gave a few to friends. Yet because of its scarcity, this little volume, which was not supposed to go any further than Baltimore, became a collector's item. Within Mencken's lifetime, he saw its price jump from $1 to $275. Today among collectors the volume is worth as much as $15,000, and there may be a day when its value is higher. "Such news naturally caresses an author's gills," Mencken later wrote. "Nevertheless, I find myself somewhat disquieted, for the book, in the main, is dreadful stuff, and any buyer who happens to be a man of taste must needs conclude that he has been rooked, and lay some of the blame for the swindle upon me."[6]

MENCKEN HAD NOT LACKED for female company during his adolescence and did not seem to now. His clothes were noticeably more dapper, his tailoring of finer cut. If he suffered from indifferent health, it did not show on his face. According to one male contemporary, "Mencken was so very handsome. . . . He looked lots like an actor." Moreover, with the sale of his short stories, the checks were now beginning to flow in with pleasant frequency. The appeal of the *Herald* Sunday editor was not lost on females—nor were their charms lost on him.

The truth is, there did not seem to be any lack of opportunity to meet women. When the hot scent of a Baltimore summer grew to be too much, a young man could put on his thinnest coat and lightest straw hat and take the trolley to River View, to promenade along the narrow boardwalk and mingle with proper young ladies dressed in summer frocks and big hats, or help them step lightly into the Venetian gondolas. If he wished to satisfy a baser inclination, then what Mencken called "the pervasive rowdiness and bawdiness of the town" provided it. Either at the dance halls, at the secluded houses at the waterfront, or at the parties held in the fashionable Stafford Hotel, a harem of frisky girls was eager to play with an energetic young newspaper reporter.[7]

The romanticism of his earlier years had not left him, however. In one of Mencken's short stories of the period, he described the allure of a stage actress who was "dark-haired and dark-eyed and graceful and soft-voiced." Sharing those attributes in real life was Virginia Kline, who had played Regina Engstrand in *Ghosts*. Minnie Fiske, a highly admired actress herself, considered Kline one of the best Ibsen interpreters. Kline was also, according to various contemporaneous descriptions, a striking brunette of lithe figure, considered clever by her peers. She was among the first of many slim, literary brunettes possessing talent, looks, and—equally attractive to the musically sensitive Mencken—a melodious voice, whose company he would enjoy.

Virginia Kline differed from most actresses of Mencken's acquaintance. It was not the glitter of the limelight that appealed to her; it was the study of the script. Moreover, she had read Shakespeare at age eleven, Mencken noted, and "her leaning at first was toward writing rather than acting." Readers of the *Sunday Herald* were able to read some of her verses, which the editor was only too happy to print. As for Kline, she wrote into a stage direction those love poems Mencken had written.

But for the most part, Mencken's inclinations were to spend his time in masculine company. A favored group was the Stevedores (so named because they devoted themselves to the unloading of schooners of beer), composed of reporters and musicians of the Holliday Street Theater. Another was a dinner club called the Vagabonds, which included writers, lawyers, doctors, and businessmen who read aloud from works they had written.

By far the most important of these groups met the following year at a building a few blocks south of Johns Hopkins. There, the sound of tuning music could be heard in the night air. Indoors, four men sat in a circle. There was *Herald* copy editor Joseph Callahan, who played a feeble second fiddle. Through Callahan,

"The first of many." Actress Virginia Kline, 1903. The Billy Rose Theatre Collection, New York Public Library.

Mencken met Albert Hildebrandt, a Baltimore violin maker; he was the cellist. Samuel Hamburger, a businessman, played the viola; Mencken played the piano. They called themselves the Saturday Night Club.

Mencken could enjoy the fact that he was "almost my own man." *Almost.* As head of the house, he still had the responsibility of his mother and sister to consider. Nonetheless, he was unfettered and unbound. "I am unmarried," as he often said, "and glad of it."[8]

BY 1903, WITH INCREASING ALARM, Mencken noted the reputation of the *Herald* was suffering but there was little he could do about it. The revolution that had developed in the newspaper world, some of which Mencken had tried to introduce into its pages—extensive advertising, lavish illustrations and photographs, ingenious composition, the demand for foreign news, the advances in printing—had bypassed the *Herald* in the last year. Its owner insisted that the paper print items about himself and his friends. The new business manager had little talent for obtaining advertisements. And managing editor Robert Carter had little interest beyond music and drama. Consequently, the paper suffered under the management of editor-in-chief Dwight Burroughs, who had neither sound news judgment nor an eye for effective writing. Indeed, older reporters had been allowed to fill their stories with purple prose—a radical departure from the sharp wit that Max Ways had always encouraged.

Carter's resignation changed all that. In his place, Lynn R. Meekins arrived. Thin, prissy, scholarly, with the look of a Prohibitionist Methodist clergyman, Meekins would eventually command respect. Encountering an office in chaos, he reorganized the editorial department quickly and effectively. "Of all the older men that I have come into contact in this life," Mencken later recalled, Meekins "had the best influence on me and gave me the greatest service." For it was Meekins "who really 'discovered' me; it was due to him, and to him alone, that I rose so rapidly on the staff." When he died years later, Mencken mourned: "I'll never forget his immense kindness to me."

Meekins, for his part, later said: "Those *Herald* days were about the happiest part of my life. They were low in cash but high in friendships." He saw much promise in Mencken, and shortly after his own arrival made him his new city editor. It was not a job Mencken had consciously sought, and it gave him pause. Such a post, he well knew, required "an incredible amalgam of army officer and literary critic, diplomat and jail warden, psychologist and fortune-teller." He had to be able to "see around corners and through four or five feet of brick," to "hear noises heard normally only to dogs and children," "to know the truth of everyone and everything." In short, he had to possess all the skills, and then some, that he had observed in Max Ways. Extremely unsettling was the task of having to fire many of the older reporters who had once been his superiors. The discomfort it caused him required Mencken to seek long consultations not only with Meekins but also with the one woman who had always been his confidante in times of trouble: his mother, Anna Mencken.

Once Anna helped her son to make up his mind, however, his determination took hold, and several adjustments hit the *Herald* with lightning speed. Mencken interviewed a stream of younger applicants and took in at least two dozen men under the same terms as he had been hired by Max Ways years before. (One, citing his qualifications, told Mencken he had a B.A. degree. Mencken's reply: "Believe Anything, eh?") For the first time in the history of the paper, Mencken hired a female reporter, a young woman whose poetry he had been publishing in the *Herald*. A new typeface was installed and better advertising produced. Improved writing was encouraged, with the *New York Sun* once again held up as the ideal. And—aware of his own youthful capers—Mencken strictly discouraged the fictionalizing of news stories.

The consequence of such modernization was the disappearance of the bohemian spirit of the old *Herald*. In its place was the efficient machinery of a modern newspaper, in keeping with the changes taking place in papers across the country. In less than one month, Mencken established himself and commanded the respect of both Meekins and the staff. Visiting him at the *Herald* office, his childhood friend, Otto Schoenrich, found Mencken "enthroned in dignified majesty" at the city editor's desk.[9]

With his new title came the daily responsibility, long hours, and endless vexations of the executive. The burden of being city editor was so consuming that he was shocked when Arthur Hawks, himself an editor at the *Evening News*, bragged to him how little work he managed to accomplish in his own position. Mencken could testify this was surely no trade for the indolent man, and it made him finally conclude that his boyhood friend was not only extraordinarily lazy but "a little stupid."

The bias against democratic sentimentality that had been forming within Mencken since his childhood now began to harden when he became city editor. Heredity, a tenet of Social Darwinism, was a factor that determined men, Mencken believed. And while he was city editor, he began to observe that there was something more:

> I don't say that these men were to blame for their incompetence—that is, in any moral sense. Many of them did the best they could. They were simply botches. Some of them were also the victims of bad luck. But it seemed to me then, and it seems to me now, to be cowardly to bawl against luck. Every man has both kinds.[10]

For momentary relaxation, Mencken escaped from the battles of the city room and often wallowed in the luxury of a meal eaten in peace at a French restaurant. As the months progressed, his escapes ranged farther out of Baltimore: his excursions went so far as taking a quiet round trip to Washington, dining on the train, resting his eyes on the sight he loved best, the tangle of leafy trees in the woods bridging the two cities.

Near year's end, however, Mencken grew weary of the worsening of the paper under the "imbecile mismanagement" of its general manager, Frank Peard, and the increasing ennui he felt regarding daily journalism. He was torn between writing factual news and fiction, and even then, "I was beginning to realize sadly that fiction was hardly my trade." Now he felt he needed another change, but how to channel it? Mencken's restlessness continued through the New Year.[11]

SATURDAY, FEBRUARY 6, 1904, ended as it had begun: mild and windy. Downtown, the workforce had long since called it a day, and gradually men and women began to leave brightly lit restaurants and head for home. As the city settled for the night, only the newspaper offices were still alight. The whir of their linotypes and the smell of ink and steam escaping from the grates mingled with the sounds and smells of the street outside. There still remained a few more hours before the *Herald* could be put to bed. The news for Sunday's edition was not particularly scintillating: the threat of war between Japan and Russia had been a constant item for the past few weeks; on the national front, the ill senator Mark Hanna was being attended by Dr. William Osler of Johns Hopkins. Poking the last of the stories onto his copyhook, Mencken hurried to join his friends.

As he swung open the door to Frank Junker's saloon, members of the Stevedores Club hailed him; a schooner of beer was put before him. As was his habit, Mencken drank eagerly from the clinging foam, roaring with laughter at all the jokes, sometimes singing. The group that night, he recalled, was in a frolic-some mood, and he did not part from its company until the nighthawk trolley lumbered him back to West Baltimore at 3:30 a.m. At Hollins Street, Anna's customary plateful of sandwiches awaited him. Taking advantage of the quiet stillness of the house, he may have read a few pages from a book. An unforeseen situation was about to overtake Baltimore that would change his life. Right now, the night had suddenly turned colder, and his bed felt warm. It was almost 4 o'clock; tomorrow was Sunday, Mencken's one day to sleep late. With that, he turned down the light.[12]

7

THE GREAT BALTIMORE FIRE

1904

A T ELEVEN O'CLOCK on Sunday morning, the phone rang at 1524 Hollins Street. A fire had broken out in downtown Baltimore. Fifteen minutes later a *Herald* reporter rushed to the house: the fire had grown bigger, and the city editor must accompany him at once.

In newspaper offices it was not unusual for the men to come in late for work. But when Mencken arrived at the office on this particular Sunday, he found most of the *Herald* staff already assembled. From every direction of the city, reporters, editors, and printers were streaming downtown, following the clangor of heavy fire trucks and galloping horses. Churchgoers could see flaming embers wafting like kites into the air.

Immediately Mencken dispatched reporters for the first extra. With bulky cameras and glass-plate films, cameramen dodged flames playing tricks in the wind, keeping clear of fallen electric wires. They graphically recorded the losing battle of the firemen: streams of water being poured on a smoking building, while just a few doors away the fire gutted and collapsed the walls of several others.[1]

Many later surmised that the fire had been caused by a lit cigar or match that had fallen through a sidewalk grate and into the basement of the Hurst Building, where it ignited blankets and cotton goods. But a decisive factor was the weather. Mild temperatures had been replaced with high winds and freezing temperatures. After spreading the fire in one direction for several hours, the wind shifted and carried it into another quarter of the city. All the firemen could hope to do was follow the rear line of the conflagration, although experts agree the fire should have been fought from the front, not from the back. Even so, getting windward of it was difficult because of the smoke. Moreover, there is some doubt as to how effectual a firebreak was created by the use of dynamite. It was placed too near the fire and only helped spread the flames. The eventual devastation covered far more area than city officials had intended.[2]

Only three years earlier, Mencken had written stories on the immense fire losses in Baltimore and the need for more fire department resources. Since the reorganization of the professional department before the Civil War, there had been little new investment beyond the addition of steam engines. The fire department had pleaded with city officials, year after year, for the resources and regulatory powers to cope with the incendiary perils of the downtown area, always to no avail. The fire chief had warned of the danger of closely built warehouses, where kerosene, cotton, chemicals, and grains were stored side by side, alongside lumber and coal yards, and tiers of electric wires. Horses were stored in multistory stables, with hay in their lofts. There were no regulations. It was an accident waiting to happen.

By noon on that Sunday, as the blaze made its way through the downtown area, city officials came to the horrifying realization they were facing a catastrophe.

AT ONE O'CLOCK, Mencken looked out the windows of the *Herald*. "The scene was particularly picturesque," he wrote for the first extra, "and from the beginning it was evident that the fire would be a record-breaking one." Great clouds of smoke hung over the city, while the *Herald* itself was being bombarded by flying brands and sparks, some as large as coconuts. A high wind blew from the southwest, hastening the spread of the flames. Raging below him, through twelve city blocks, the fire was pushing rapidly north, south, and east, taking buildings in a matter of seconds.

Mencken recalled it years later as "a swell day for young journalists, and they enjoyed it immensely." As city editor of the *Herald*, he had been a hard driver to a lethargic staff; now he did not have to urge his reporters. Column after column of interviews with city officials and eyewitnesses were being rapidly compiled. The entire scene, Mencken recalled, "made a grand show, full of catnip for a young city editor."

For the Washington firemen who had just arrived at Camden Station, the scene was anything but grand. Pulling in, they could see the reflection of the conflagration in the sky: "We knew then that we were heading for something big," one of them recalled, "and I think we all got a little scared." They soon discovered they could not connect their hoses to the Baltimore hydrants and had to resort instead to wrapping them with clumsy canvas bandages. The resulting loss of pressure was disastrous; the streams of water were so weak, they evaporated into steam. When a reporter asked one of the firemen about the city's status, his response was simple: "We are in the hands of God."[3]

By four o'clock in the *Herald*, thirty typewriters were banging away at once and Mencken's desk was piling high with copy. Through the *Herald* windows

Mencken could hear the hoarse cries of firemen and the whoosh of the flames, sounding like the steady pounding of an ocean. Mayor Robert M. McClane climbed to the top of the City Hall tower and began ringing its bell, summoning the National Guard. Mencken called home to reassure his mother. From time to time he jumped from his desk to peek outside the window before continuing with his work.

At five o'clock, *Herald* newsboys were hawking their second extra on the streets. "WHOLESALE DISTRICT WRECKED BY GREATEST FIRE IN THE CITY'S HISTORY" shouted the newspaper's mast. Thirty-eight pages described the scenes: a little fox terrier, seen dashing up Baltimore Street; police making their way into buildings, evacuating businessmen at gunpoint when they refused to leave; groups of firemen fighting the brave but hopeless battle. To those family members not busy sweeping cinders from their rooftops, worrying about their loved ones and praying for the fate of their city, the *Herald* provided the latest harrowing details.

No one in the *Herald* office thought evacuation would be necessary. That afternoon, several employees had begun to pack bound volumes of the paper and other valuables, but they did so in a half-hearted way. Several of their colleagues laughed at them; no one wanted to be considered afraid.[4]

As night fell, the glare from the fire grew brighter. Its reflection could be seen fifty miles away, as far as Maryland's Eastern Shore and northern Virginia. Residential areas were still untouched, but as a precaution, a man rode a horse through Federal Hill in the manner of Paul Revere, rapping on doors and yelling for households to turn off the gas. Meanwhile, the downtown area had become an inferno, as wooden Belgian blocks on the pavement caught fire, and blazing embers set flame to horses' tails and manes. Firefighters could be seen in gray silhouette through dense clouds of smoke; to the aid of crews from Baltimore and Washington came others from Wilmington, Philadelphia, and New York.[5]

It may have been after the second extra that Lynn Meekins decided against wasting time and energy on further editions. "The story was too big for such banalities: it seemed like a toy balloon in a hurricane," Mencken wrote years later. Among the major Baltimore papers, the *Sun* was the only one not printing an extra, reserving its space and energy for a final edition. Meekins instructed the *Herald* to close at nine o'clock.

By seven, columns of type were ready and new pictures were coming in from the engraving department. Every fifteen minutes the dull thud of explosions was heard as officials began dynamiting more buildings in an effort to stop the progress of the flames. With a fearful crash the glass in the windows of the upper floors of the *Herald* shattered. Another blast from the dynamite and the floors of the building trembled, as if from an earthquake.

Reporters rushed back to the streets. On the seventh floor, engravers converted cuts into pictures. In the composing room, the linotypes clicked in almost deafening chorus, and forms were hurried into the stereotyping rooms, where plates for the presses were made. Every now and then the electric lights in the building flickered, yellowed by the glare from the bonfire that shot upward nearby and by the spectacular showers of sparks that unceasingly descended on top of the *Herald* building.

From roof to basement Meekins sent the message: "Prepare to leave at a moment's notice."

And from the basement to the roof the collective answer came back: "We will stand by until we are *driven* out."

A valiant little band on the *Herald* roof shut and fastened the big fire shutters on every side of the building, closing every window to keep out the cinders. Inside the offices the air was hot and stifling, but still Mencken and his staff kept working. A big dray, loaded with the *Herald*'s business files and papers dating back to its origin, raced floundering through dimly lit streets amid tangled wires and fallen poles to Lynn Meekins's house for safety. On seeing the wagon, Mrs. Meekins almost fainted. She thought it contained the remains of her husband.[6]

A LITTLE BEFORE NINE that evening, Mencken was supervising the make-up of the front page when two excited policemen rushed in and ordered the staff to bail out; the buildings next door and opposite were to be blown up in the next few minutes. Although a fire was already burning fiercely on the *Herald* roof, Mencken and his staff refused to stop working.

The windows of the composing room smashed. Then came another explosion that sent printers bounding from the linotype machines. Ten minutes later the police returned and again ordered everyone to leave. Mencken tried reasoning with the officers, to no avail. Office boys dashed from the basement to the top floor. Shouts of "All out!" were heard throughout the building. "All out! All out!" Hats and coats were grabbed as every man fled down the long stairways. "Rendezvous at the Lexington!"

Out they went reluctantly, many of them men who had first entered the building as employees when it was erected in 1895, others who had been with the paper all their lives.

The dismal little procession made its way to temporary quarters at the Lexington Hotel, nearby on Holliday Street, opposite City Hall. Each man believed he would be back soon, that the *Herald* building itself would be saved. Before leaving, Joe Bamberger of the composing room, and Joe Callahan, assistant city editor, had stuffed into their overcoat pockets galley proofs and copy not yet set, as well as twelve halftones, a pot of paste, two boxes of pencils, and the assignment book. Mencken recalled: "Meekins and I refused to believe that we were shipwrecked." He was sent back to the *Herald* building, later reporting, "The *Herald* loomed up out of the surrounding flame like a giant sentinel towering over the ruins of its less fortunate mates, which had been consumed by the flames."

As Mencken stood outside, sparks swirled about the city, the marble facade of the courthouse began cracking and fell into the street. Farther along, the

Continental building, at one time touted as the city's first completely fireproof skyscraper, began to burn like a torch, pouring fire skyward from every window. "The flames leaped through as if it had been made of matchwood and drenched with gasoline," Mencken recalled, "and in half a minute were roaring in the air at least 500 feet." Along its front entrance cast-iron mullions were twisting with the heat, melting into the shape of the letter S. Mencken ran from the scene: "I fully expected the whole structure to come crashing down behind me."[7]

Seeing the Continental burn extinguished the spirit of confidence remaining in the city; the stampede was on. In East Baltimore, tenements full of Russians and Poles, who had previously refused to leave their houses, were forced by the National Guard to evacuate, taking their bundles and terrorized children screaming into the streets already crowded with men and carts. Horses were whipped into frenzy as men swore at the immigrants to get out of the way. The activity in the neighborhood, reported the *Afro-American Ledger*, was "so wild as to beggar description." The city had finally reached a common denominator: "In the frantic excitement," stated the paper, "there was no class or creed."

Half aware that he was missing the most melodramatic moments of the fire, Mencken ran on. The air shook as timbers fell. Above, the sky was luminous with raining sparks and bits of coal, but stars eerily shone in a purple atmosphere beyond.[8]

HURRYING THROUGH THE CHAOS to his print shop, six blocks from the *Herald*, Charles Gordon began collecting account ledgers and correspondence files. He had been there only an hour when police ordered him to vacate. The wind had changed and the Telegraph Building was to be blown up by dynamite. "In our rush," he later wrote, "I had to leave behind all our copies of Mencken's little books," the only remaining copies of *Ventures Into Verse*.[9]

RETURNING TO THE LEXINGTON HOTEL, Mencken found the staff huddled in a cramped room, with typewriters balanced on chairs. No one knew where the next issue would be printed, but everyone was certain it *would* be. The *World* office was still safe, and Meekins now ordered the staff to proceed there. Mencken wound his way through the densely packed streets, running a gauntlet of National Guard bayonets. Inside the *World*, it was hot and smoky, and the red windowpanes of the office were cracking. In five minutes, as typewriters were busily clicking, it was decided to dynamite the buildings adjacent to the *World*.

"Back to the Lexington!" Meekins shouted, and back Mencken and his weary reporters marched, hugging their typewriters. Some still hoped that the *Herald* could be saved, but by midnight, sparks shot up St. Paul Street and embers sifted into the *Herald* pressroom. The paper for the Monday morning edition became kindling, and in a few moments the interior of the *Herald* was a seething furnace. When he heard the news, Edmund, the office boy, began to weep. He had lost a pet cat in the fire.

A colleague burst into the Lexington with the news: the wind had shifted, and the *World* was saved. With a rush the staff hurried from the hotel to the *World* a second time. They worked there for an hour, uninterrupted, with their typewriters rattling and the linotype machines clicking as if their lives depended on it.

A few minutes later, told it would be a matter of seconds before the structure would have to be razed, the group, undismayed, trooped once more back to the Lexington Hotel.

"Hurrah for the *Herald*!" cried a man on the street as they passed through the throng. "When will you publish another paper?"

"This morning," was the confident answer.

Meanwhile, with a great roar, the flames grabbed more buildings—the Equitable, then the Calvert, then the Maryland Trust. The sight of all the fireproof symbols of finance and power going up at once jolted the corps of firemen, already exhausted, their eyes red from the smoke, their feet swollen with blisters. For one moment they paused, demoralized. Then, with sodden boots and charred jackets, they grimly moved on. The *Sun*'s iron building, the first of its kind built in the United States, burst into a mass of blue, red, yellow, then white flames. Against such an inferno, hoses were useless. In the terror of the night, it seemed that nothing could be saved.

The city was doomed.[10]

AT THE LEXINGTON, the roof of the hotel was now ablaze. "We are without a home," Meekins told his staff, "and we must, therefore, get a temporary home."

"The city was doomed." The Great Baltimore Fire of 1904. Courtesy Maryland Department, Enoch Pratt Free Library.

Mencken and a small squad of men headed for Camden Station, with Mencken financing the expedition from the ruined city to the nation's capital "in a race," he wrote, "to beat the series of misfortunes that had set so heavily upon the paper."

Arriving in Washington a little after three o'clock in the morning, Mencken observed the moon shining down on the dome of the Capitol, then looked at the horizon. Forty miles away, he could see a blood-red glow from Baltimore.[11]

At 3:20 a.m., Mencken was at the *Washington Post* on Pennsylvania Avenue, working frantically alongside the paper's managing editor. Six columns of *Herald* copy were rushed into the *Post*'s composing room—then twelve, then fifteen. Three halftone cuts, saved before the *Herald* building had been vacated, were clapped into forms. Dawn came as the presses began churning out the new editions of the paper. An eight-column streamer ran across the top: "HEART OF BALTIMORE WRECKED BY GREATEST FIRE IN CITY'S HISTORY."

Great stacks of the newspaper were placed on wagons that rattled through the streets of Washington in the morning sunlight. Thirty thousand copies were loaded onto trains and began their record trip to Baltimore. At 8:45 a.m. they pulled into the station. The *Herald* had been put to flight twice in one night and conducted a retreat that had ended in victory. The *Herald* office boys were waiting at Camden Station.

"I told you we'd get out all right," said one to another.

"Yes," replied the other. "We had to."[12]

When Mencken returned to Baltimore, he found the fire still raging. The waterfront was a mass of billowing pillars of smoke and steam fed by the oils and chemicals stored in warehouses, until the wind dissipated the puffs into a mockingly clear blue sky.

Mencken learned on his return to the city some distressing news: the *Herald*'s chief rival had beaten them on the big story by about four hours. Somehow, even though its own building had burned, the *Sun* had managed to distribute copies before five that very morning. The *Sun* editors assumed mistakenly that theirs had been the only Baltimore paper available that day. In contrast to the *Herald*, the *Sun* staff had saved its energy for its final edition, which had long and vivid accounts of the fire, as well as Associated Press reports on the Russo-Japanese War, including a map showing the countries involved in the dispute. The main story had been written by reporter Frank Kent at the Hotel Lexington bar, with the top editor taking copy, page after page, and the bartender supplying both men with ample amounts of liquor.

The discovery, though dismaying, was not without good news: there was money to be made. Thirty thousand copies of the *Herald*, which normally sold for a penny each, were eagerly being bought at twenty-five cents a copy. Moreover, thousands of firms and individuals who had been burned out were already establishing temporary quarters in residential sections, and all were eager to notify clients of their new addresses through advertisements in the paper. Baltimoreans may have been temporarily set back but were already looking to the future.

Meanwhile, Mencken and Meekins had to decide quickly what to do for the next edition. While they had been in Washington, the fire had destroyed the powerhouse, leaving the city without electricity and telephones. Directing their staff to move to a safer hotel away from the line of the fire, the two men returned to Washington to make another arrangement with the *Post*. If the *Baltimore Herald* wanted to produce its edition the following day, the *Post* informed them, it would have to print it at the one paper that had apparently escaped the flames— the *World*. Mencken could hardly believe it: could it be? Again the men raced back to Baltimore.

The next few hours were torture for Mencken. "The ensuing night gave me the grand migraine of my life, with throbs like the blows of an ax and continuous pinwheels," he recalled later. The *World* was a weekly paper, with an ancient linotype that promptly stalled, its repairs delaying publication by several hours. Adding to the troubles, the *World* only contained enough type in its cases to fill several columns. Within a few hours Mencken found a fresh supply at the *Catholic Mirror*, to which a team of compositors was dispatched to set the copy. Nightfall found Mencken hauling the completed galleys back to the *World* office for printing, in a wagon pulled by a horse that kept slipping and sliding down a steep ice-covered hill.

The fire had finally been brought under control at two o'clock that day, halted by Jones Falls, the slimy stream Baltimoreans regularly denounced but now praised as a barrier to the raging conflagration, after all human opposition had failed. But the stench of burnt wood permeated the city and made eyes ache. After the noise and tumult of the night before, the silence and desolation were almost terrifying. The streets were enveloped in gloom, relieved only by the faint glare of an occasional gas lamp. Dimly lit thoroughfares were haunted by ghostly moving figures who appeared suddenly out of patches of darkness, then vanished again.

Lengths of ruined fire hose and snarls of electric wires—live wires, for all anyone knew—were tangled up in bricks and masonry. Immense high walls swayed like sheets of paper in a stiff wind that swept over the ruins with a faint moaning sound. Water from the fire hoses froze as it cascaded from the burned buildings, making weird formations. Above this pile of debris, reported the *Baltimore Sun*, rearing in a "grotesque shape against the sky," were the "outlines of City Hall, the hands of the illuminated clock on the dome striking mournful notes over its lost city." Making his solitary way through the icy streets at night amid the ruins must have been for Mencken like being in a darkened room with the dead.

By dawn, notwithstanding various breakdowns in the *World* pressroom, the first copy of the *Herald* finally rolled off its rickety press. In the face of hopeless difficulties, Meekins told the staff, they had shown the resourcefulness of Robinson Crusoe. Yet, as the first copies of the *Herald* were waved by newsboys on the streets, along with those of the *Sun*, the *American*, and the *Evening News*,

Meekins's enthusiasm waned. Even Mencken admitted their paper looked "as though it had been set up by country printers locked up in a distillery." Printing another copy of their paper under such conditions, both Meekins and Mencken agreed, "would disgrace us forever."[13]

The pressure for space had now almost doubled, for in addition to copy there was now so much new advertising they could fill more than ten columns, enough to begin offsetting the crippling financial loss the *Herald* had suffered. But where to print the *Herald*? Once again, Meekins won the respect of the staff by finding an available press in Philadelphia, at the *Evening Telegraph*. Mencken met with Oscar G. Murray, president of the B&O railroad, and persuaded him to run a special nonstop express train from Philadelphia to Baltimore, at Mencken's disposal thereafter whenever the *Herald* needed it. As for the cost, the magnanimous Murray graciously waved the city editor away.[14]

Mission accomplished, Mencken rushed downtown to satisfy his curiosity. The city was under martial law and looked like a war zone as troops of cavalry marched through the streets.[15] News photographers had descended like a flock of crows on the ruins, their black coats flapping in the breeze as, from various locations, they took pictures to sell to the highest bidding publication. On the streets, too, they displayed their images of the rubble, calling to curious sightseers to buy their wares.

As Mencken made his way through the devastated area, he supposed the *Herald* building had been burned in its entirety, but was pleased to find that it had valiantly held its own, its very structure putting a halt to the fire and saving the $3 million courthouse across from it.

Mencken picked his way through piles of rubble and bits of glass that partially blocked the *Herald* entrance. Around him, the fireproof shutters of sheet metal that his staff had closed before their departure had burst open with the heat of the fire. Most of them now lay twisted and crooked on the floor, curled by the intensive heat from two nights before. Clambering up the partially destroyed stairs, Mencken surveyed what remained. Cabinets, linotype machines, fifteen thousand cuts of type—one of the largest and best collections in the entire United States—all were gone. In the editorial room, where his desk once stood, he saw through the heap of white dust the frame of the goose-necked lamp that once shone on top of it. Amid the ashes, "twisted as if it had died in agony," he later wrote, was his copyhook—the only souvenir he would take from the fire, it would grace the top of his bookcase at Hollins Sreet for the next half a century. From the arches of the *Herald* window, the view was no less grim: most of downtown Baltimore had been leveled. It looked like Pompeii, with smoke rising from the rubble and bits of ash drifting in the cold winter air.[16]

EARLIER IN NEW YORK, Ellery Sedgewick had written a letter to Mencken. The young city editor had been on his mind a great deal, long before "this hideous catastrophe" had even begun. Now that Baltimore was burned out, the

"... with smoke rising from the rubble ..." Note the *Herald* building, one of the few left after the 1904 fire. J. Adams Photograph, The Maryland Historical Society, Baltimore, Maryland.

reconstruction of the *Herald*'s business inevitable, he advised Mencken "it would be a good time for you to pull up stakes." For a man of Mencken's abilities, a space could be made at *Leslie's* magazine. "I think you would find this office most congenial," wrote Sedgewick. "We are all wrapt in our work. There is no jealousy, nor is there office politics. . . . Write me at once," he concluded, "and tell me . . . what you would consider a fair salary."[17]

FOR NEARLY THREE ENTIRE DAYS Mencken had been working nonstop. At 4 a.m. that Wednesday morning he collapsed into what he described as nightmare sleep. To Meekins's growing concern, he then saw his young city editor resume a schedule that went without pause for fourteen hours a day, with no time for meals until the work was over. The rest of the staff concluded that the vigor of the city editor was nothing less than heroic. As for Mencken, "It was brain-fagging and back-breaking," he recalled years later, "but it was grand beyond compare—an adventure of the first chop, a razzle-dazzle superb and elegant, a circus in forty rings."

For the next five weeks the *Herald* was published in Philadelphia at the *Evening Telegraph*. The first edition, Mencken remembered, "was a gorgeous thing of fourteen pages, with twenty columns of advertising," printed with the neat and graceful head type of the host paper, giving its Baltimore rivals cause for envy. From a newsdealer came word that the *Sun* had taken a decided slump. The

Herald had eclipsed all other newspapers in the city. It was 40 percent larger than the *American*, twice as large as the *Sun*, with 100 columns of advertising. Its advance orders were the largest in the paper's history. When bundles of papers were dropped in one city store in West Virginia, "All clamored for the *Herald*," rejoiced a customer. "I was standing nearby and counted twenty *Heralds* sold, two *Americans*, and not one *Sun*. As I was leaving the store, men were still crowding in, and all of them were calling for the *Herald*."[18]

It was not long before a *Herald* headline was able to proclaim "GREATER BALTIMORE BEGINS TO ARISE FROM THE ASHES." No one knew how citizens would react. The last disaster to cripple Baltimore had been the Civil War. By the end of the week the papers were reporting that the tragedy had turned into triumph. Banks had opened; grain elevators had not been destroyed; the work of clearing the debris was progressing quickly. The Chamber of Commerce had broadcast to Europe that only four days after the fire, Baltimore was now open for trade. As for the damaged *Herald* building, the paper announced that a contract had been signed for its restoration, and that it would be ready for occupancy in sixty days.

Meanwhile, life in Philadelphia began to feel like home to the city editor and those of his staff temporarily in exile—"if," Mencken added, "anybody not born in the town can ever feel at home in Philadelphia." The copyboy assigned to Mencken's beck and call kept racing to and from his desk. "Copy!" Mencken would yell, and to his side came Emmanuel Haldeman Julius, future book publisher, then only fifteen years old. With the help of the telephone, Western Union, and half the staff of Baltimore, Julius later recalled, "the material got to blue-eyed, cigar-chewing, short, snub-nosed grinning Mencken, called 'Macon' by those who didn't know better."

It was evident to all, even the young boy, that the "quick, alert, hard-working editor" managed to get through "a terrific amount of work, but yet had time to josh around with the men, do away with a lot of beer in the bar of the Hotel Green up the street a little, and read books by Bernard Shaw, Ibsen and Nietzsche." In old age, his brother Charlie wrote to Henry: "I can remember how mother worried when you were publishing the paper out of town after the fire." After herding dispersed and bewildered reporters at long distance, by 2 a.m. Mencken was on board one of Murray's special trains, racing back to Baltimore at hair-raising speed. They broke all known records of transportation, said Mencken, "with piles of *Herald*s in the baggage car, thrown helter-skelter on the curves, and the passengers in the coach scared half to death."

Few newspapermen had surmounted greater difficulties. Twice driven into the street the evening of the fire and forced to publish in two cities, the *Herald* had not missed a single issue. Reflecting on Mencken's experience almost forty years later, Samuel G. Blythe, then Washington bureau chief of the *New York World*, wrote, "In my opinion, you have done few things greater than that."[19]

The disaster had stimulated a movement to improve conditions in the rest of the city. For years, streets laid out during the colonial period had obstructed the movement of trucks and caused traffic jams. On February 13, the mayor and City Council decided the intact *Herald* building must come down in order to widen St. Paul and Fayette Streets, opening the front of the courthouse to public view.

The announcement was met with considerable alarm among the staff. The improvement to the streets would take from them the most valuable corner of Baltimore, an ideal newspaper location and one to which the *Herald* was attached by many ties of affection. Immediately, a *Herald* reporter was dispatched to interview an architect who had made an examination of the few remaining buildings left standing. It was the expert's opinion, the paper reported, that the condition of the *Herald*, constituted "the greatest achievement of modern fireproof construction under the severest test to which it could possibly be subjected." However remarkable this feat, plans for a greater Baltimore held firm.[20]

The decision to tear down the intact *Herald* building was only the beginning of Mencken's ire against the boosters and Babbits who promised but failed to deliver, with their grand plans to make the city bigger at the expense of the town he remembered. After years of use as a storage place for old paving stones and sand, decades later the Courthouse Plaza was reduced to a parking lot. "I often wondered in those days," Mencken later wrote, "why the judges did not jail the Mayor and the City Council for obscenity."

Meanwhile, a team worked to take the great sextuple press from the basement of the old *Herald* building. On top of its surface, workers could see the melted plates that had been left in the pressroom from the last extra run just 30 minutes before the fire had caught the building. Huge beams of wood had been made into a gangway, and in the early morning light, while shocks from dynamiting the surrounding carcasses of ruined buildings shook bits of brick upon their backs, workmen slowly skidded the mammoth presses into waiting wagons, the first of many loads to be hauled away before the *Herald* building itself would be torn down. It would have been difficult for any member of the *Herald* staff to watch such progress. "The fate of its old time," the *Herald* bitterly conceded in its editorial, "is out of our hands."[21]

MENCKEN HAD NOT GIVEN much thought to Ellery Sedgewick's generous offer for a position at *Leslie's*. Just the same, he met with the older man, who subsequently proposed Mencken become assistant editor at the tremendous salary of $60 a week, with a guarantee of a round-trip pass to Baltimore once a month.

But as the days passed and Mencken considered Sedgewick's proposal, he saw his duty was to the *Herald*, printing a newspaper 100 miles away from its base—"a feat," he affirmed, "that remains unparalleled in American journalism, as far as I know, to this day." Moreover, "I was disinclined," he reflected years later, "to desert my mother in Baltimore, and the comfortable home she had provided for me, and take up a lonely life in a town I disliked." His answer was a blow to the editor at *Leslie's*. Responding to Mencken's rejection, Sedgewick replied: "It is hard for me to believe that you have chosen wisely."[22]

WHEN THE OUT-OF-TOWN FIREMEN finally left the city, a crowd of grateful Baltimoreans cheered the procession as it made its way to the train station. En route the men were handed flasks of Maryland rye. On top of the New York City fire engine balanced a fox terrier, smudged with smoke and wagging its tail. On its neck was an engraved collar: "Baltimore: A Waif of the Flames."[23]

The Great Baltimore Fire of 1904 ranks with the Chicago fire of 1871 and the San Francisco earthquake of 1906 among the great disasters of American history. It destroyed more than 140 acres, 1,500 buildings, and 4 large lumberyards, leaving more than 35,000 Baltimoreans jobless. Yet very little looting occurred and only one life was lost. Total damages were estimated between 125 and 150 million dollars. President Theodore Roosevelt, when first hearing of the catastrophe, promised the city as much federal aid as it needed. Offers of help from other cities came by the dozens. Local officials expressed their thanks but gently refused. It would rebuild without assistance. In three and half years the mission was accomplished.

Of all the city's industries, contemporary accounts agreed it was the press that had been hurt the most. Nine separate newspapers lost more than half a million dollars in machinery alone—an especially large loss because so many had recently installed new technology. This figure did not include the losses to their buildings, libraries, and cabinets. Yet the papers were the first to recover and face the situation. Baltimore's greatest achievement was the survival and performance of its press. "It is claimed that the *Herald*'s editorial organization is one of the best in the world," *Publisher* magazine noted. "A test of its quality was the big Baltimore fire. The *Herald*'s account . . . was the one telegraphed to the world by the press association."[24]

ADS BECKONED Baltimoreans to Jamaica, enticing them to leave behind devastation and ash, to escape the outbreak of pneumonia that had gripped the city, and to seek the restoration of health under a yellow sun. Once the *Herald* was on an even keel, Mencken packed his mother, sister, and little brother and set sail to the island he now knew so well. Once again he was on a ship headed toward the tropics; once again a warm breeze played on his brow, giving comfort to every aching sinew that marked the toil encountered during those fateful weeks.

Seated in a deck chair, clad in his pajamas, Mencken began reading a volume of stories by a new writer named Joseph Conrad. He found a tale of a young sailor "that struck home to me as the history of Judas must strike home to many a bloated bishop, though the sailor naturally made his odyssey on a ship, not on a newspaper." He began to read: "You fellows know there are those voyages that seem ordered for the illustration of life, that might stand for a symbol of existence."

Eagerly Mencken turned the pages of his book and began devouring each sentence that seemed to describe so vividly his own recent experience. The gale that struck the ship of the hero in Joseph Conrad's story seemed to him very much like the fire that had consumed the *Baltimore Herald*:

It seemed to last for months, for years, for all eternity, as though we had been dead and gone to a hell for sailors. We forgot the day of the week, the name of the month, what year it was, and whether we had ever been ashore. . . . To me [the ship] was the endeavour, the test, the trial of life.[25]

As Mencken's steamer sailed south toward Jamaica, the Baltimore of his childhood, its old familiar haunts, all destroyed forever, would soon recede into the past under the eyes of the very men who set out to rebuild it. True, new buildings were to come, but to many other Baltimoreans "something not built by hands was gone—the spirit of a colorful age, an atmosphere, an attitude to life as it was in the eighties, the nineties and before. All these did not return with reconstruction, nor will they ever come back."[26] Yet enough of the images of the rush and roar of the Great Baltimore Fire survived in the recollections of those reporters who covered it. Its memory shone as brightly as the original flames that consumed it, but never more so than for a certain city editor.

Ahead, Mencken would encounter different challenges that would test him during his life, but in that instance, when the fire flicked its fury upon the walls of the *Herald* building and the streets of his city, he had encountered a moment of strength and romance, an adventure that would bind him even tighter to the place of his birth. It had been an experience that would lead him further from the world of daily journalism and closer to the career he had previously been struggling to define for himself.

It delighted him in his autumnal years to dwell upon the fire, for as he said later, "It reminds me how full of steam and malicious animal magnetism I was when I was young." As the years passed, he, too, would "remember my youth and the feeling that will never come back anymore—the feeling that I could outlast forever, outlast the sea, the earth, and all men . . . Youth! All youth! The silly, charming, beautiful youth!"[27]

8

A MAN OF ABILITY

NORTHERN OR WESTERN CITY devastated by a fire might rebuild more quickly than Baltimore," observed *Harper's Weekly*, "but it could not accept a tragic situation with more philosophy and good humor." Among those the magazine singled out for praise was the *Herald* staff, which had moved from one of the finest newspaper buildings in the country to temporary quarters in a three story, brick car-barn located on South Charles Street, a neighborhood populated by dealers in old clothes and live chickens, one block from the waterfront in the hottest part of Baltimore. A small sign proclaiming "Editorial Offices, Baltimore Morning Herald" and its appearance as the tidiest establishment in the vicinity were the only indications of the paper's location.

Despite efforts Meekins and Mencken had made to improve the building, the new office was so full of vermin that Mrs. Meekins had to disinfect her husband every time he came home. Very few of the other newspapers had fared much better. New quarters had to await financing or further progress by the Mayor's Burnt District Commission to supervise the reconstruction of Baltimore. Meanwhile, debris continued to be hauled away and a light powdery ash fell softly over the city, obliging many men to change their collars twice a day.[1]

As Mencken made his way up the hardwood colonial staircase to his small office, he wondered what might have been the consequence of his accepting Sedgewick's job offer. For a young man as impatient as Mencken, the summer of 1904 could have been one of complete frustration. Instead, other activities engaged him. That June he boarded a train that took him farther West than he had ever been before, to a city he would come to admire for its picturesque adventures.

The Republican National Convention was about to convene in Chicago, to nominate Theodore Roosevelt for the presidency. It would be the first of eleven convention seasons Mencken would cover for the next 44 years, and he could not have been more enchanted. If the theater had fascinated the 24-year-old before, he now encountered a living drama that would outstrip any stage performance.

Mencken was determined to enjoy the experience to the fullest, and his writing, while not fully possessed of the confidence he would show in later years, was exuberant in the attention it paid to human detail and the unmasking of the absurd. Here were the perspiring delegates, with cries that shook the rafters as the Rough Rider was nominated without a dissenting voice; the dingy flag that nearly knocked over one of the main speakers; the oratory—"imbecilities," he would muse, "as even a Methodist conference could not match"—that echoed and re-echoed throughout the hall. So intense were his efforts to capture the show for *Herald* readers, he did not notice until later that a pickpocket had relieved him of his money and his lucky rabbit's foot.

The Democratic National Convention, held two weeks later in St. Louis at the height of the World's Fair, offered more thrills. In the rush of what many observers called the most melodramatic convention in years, Mencken joined 20,000 others as William Jennings Bryan fought his last political fight and went down to defeat with the yells of his enemies ringing in his ears.

No one, least of all Mencken, would ever forget the sight. The *Herald* city editor watched, transfixed, while Bryan, dressed in an alpaca suit and with what looked to be tears glistening in his eyes, arose before the audience and said good-by. Mencken's description of Bryan's farewell as a tragic play was, ironically, the chronicle of a man he would help destroy two decades later, in what would be called the greatest trial of the century. "I was against Bryan the moment I heard of him."[2]

No sooner had Mencken returned from the convention than he noticed that advertising had begun to slacken and the prosperity the *Herald* had enjoyed after the fire had slumped. It was plain that a new beginning had to be made. To increase revenue, an evening paper was added, still a relatively new phenomenon but becoming nationally popular as readers began to demand their news hot off the wire.[3]

Mencken began work early each morning, when telegraph machines were already clicking the main bulk of foreign news from across the ocean. Even within its cramped quarters, the *Herald* continued to set higher standards for newspapers in Baltimore. Typographically it was a handsome paper, with news displayed with high quality photographs ("no black smudges," as its advertisements proclaimed). It printed local, national, and foreign news, and proclaimed it had the best women's page in the United States. "Usually," its ads read, "there are *two* of them." They were geared toward the Baltimore woman of average income. "Why show Paris gowns that would cost $5000 to make?"

Elsewhere the *Herald* advertised "bright, breezy editorials," most of which Mencken wrote in addition to his two columns—"Notes in the Margin" that concerned itself with books and theater and another called "Mere Opinion." The Sunday edition had news, comics, and a magazine bursting with short stories, poems, puzzles, and articles, even a color double-page picture suitable for framing.

Together, Meekins and Mencken had worked very hard to rehabilitate the *Herald*; soon Mencken was promoted to managing editor. "My change of jobs gave me no extra stars and I am responsible for typographical errors and libel suits only when the bosses are away," Mencken wrote to his friend Richard Steuart at the *Sun*. "My official title is 'round sergeant' and I have the rank and pay of a first-class camp follower." Under Mencken's helm, the paper seemed to acquire a new lease on life. It had been known as a Republican newspaper. On the new masthead it now proclaimed it was "an Independent Democratic newspaper." The *Herald* believed "the principles of the Democratic party have in them more *justice*, more COMMON SENSE, more of RIGHT" than principles of any other political party; indeed, the paper proclaimed, the average Democrat of Maryland "is more apt to make a good public official than the average Republican."

Standards that Mencken insisted on in his own writing were also imposed on the *Herald*. Dull padding, stupidity, and verbosity were castigated; dispatches told their stories simply and briefly. The aim of the *Herald* was to "record events as they occur, without fear or favor, and regardless of whether they are creditable or discreditable to any man, high or low"—criteria Mencken would insist upon throughout his career.

The reaction to Mencken's new leadership was positive. It had been expected, the *Typographical Journal* noted, "recognizing the safety of mediocrity," that the *Herald* "would continue to lay before its readers a few lines of local intelligence, a dispatch or two from New York or Washington, and a few namby-pamby editorials. But it is far, far different now." The "enterprising journal" had now "jumped at a bound to be one of the leading positions among the daily papers of Baltimore." Its news features were up-to-the-minute and "as bright as a new silver dollar, and above all, its editorials are fearless and dignified."[4]

Despite the *Herald*'s strict codes of accuracy and truthfulness ("No decent newspaper," Mencken had declared, "runs falsehoods knowingly and willingly"), on May 28, 1905, during the Russo-Japanese War, Mencken abandoned his own principles.

The war had posed new challenges for all the major papers. Japanese censorship was tight. Wireless telegraphy and ocean cables were undependable. Most of the American dailies relied on the Associated Press or another major paper for war news, and few of the top papers, such as the *New York Sun*, the *Los Angeles Times* and the *New York Tribune*—let alone the *Baltimore Herald*—had correspondents or freelance writers in the field. Every newspaper in the country was receiving bulletins on the war that were nothing more than rumors of rumors.

On May 28 the Tokyo Associated Press gave the first clue that a major battle had occurred. The morning papers, including the *New York Times*, reported that details of the day's historic events were being withheld by Japanese authorities. Only one newspaper, the *Los Angeles Times*, came close to printing the true story. With its time zone allowing it several hours of leeway, that paper alone carried an exclusive dispatch from Tokyo. But even so, it could only say, "The world will probably have to wait another day to learn even the skeleton facts of the stupendous drama."

"Like every managing editor of normal appetites I was thrown into a sweat by this uncertainty," Mencken later recalled. He and his news editor stayed late at their posts, "hoping against hope that the story would begin to flow in at any minute, and give us a chance to bring out a hot extra." The hours ticked by, but nothing came in.[5]

Returning to his tiny office, Mencken sat down and typed in a plausible location: "Shanghai, China" for his dateline. His typewriter keys poised over the blank sheet of paper. "After that, I laid it on . . . with a shovel." He rationalized to himself that, in the art of synthesizing the news, he had a conscience. After all, he was hardly manufacturing a story from whole cloth—or so he figured. In this instance, newsmen across the country knew where the battle might be fought and that a Japanese victory was imminent. All that was missing were the details, and all that he had to do was fill them in. Poring over maps, he and the news editor examined lists of commanders, names of ships, and photographs, embellishing what they thought would be a newsbreaking story of a Japanese victory to appear under the banner: "FLYING SHELLS STRIKE ROJESTVENSKY; FIVE OF THE FUGITIVES ELUDE TOGO; SATURDAY'S BIG BATTLE DESCRIBED."

Indeed, the battle was laid out in all its imagined detail. It began: "From Chinese boatmen landing upon the Korean coast comes the first connected story of the great naval battle in the straits of Korea." It had been "a spectacle of extraordinary magnificence." The day, Mencken typed, had been clear; the Russian ships grimy and unkempt; the roar of guns could be heard fifty miles from the scene of battle as the big battleship *Borodino* went down at the hour of noon. Here Mencken paused, adding "or thereabout."

It was the first full story of what they supposed had happened. By 3:30 that afternoon the newsboys were hawking the last edition, proclaiming the headlines of Japan's predicted victory. "Thus," Mencken proudly recalled years later in his reminiscences, "the *Evening Herald* scored a beat on the world, and what is more, a beat that lasted for nearly two weeks, for it took that long for any authentic details of the battle to reach civilization."

It was not enough that as an evening paper, the *Herald* had a ten-hour lead over the morning papers with the same news of the war. "They couldn't help it," boasted one *Herald* notice written by Mencken. "It wasn't their fault. But," here he emphasized, "*it made them look rather foolish, all the same.*"

Privately, Mencken and his news editor searched the cables for days, living in fear they might be wrong and would be found out. To the great relief of both, when authentic news arrived (not two weeks, as Mencken cited, but only two days later), Mencken said he had actually guessed right "in every particular detail of the battle." Decades later, when a firsthand account of the battle was published, he was gratified to note "we were still right."[6]

Mencken never gave any indication as to how outrageous his exercise in manufactured news had been. Instead, all of this made for good material in his memoirs—which, he warned readers, was full of "stretchers." But, contrary to Mencken's claim, not every detail of the battle had been correct, as alert *Herald* readers soon learned. It had been a misty day, not a clear one; the battle did not begin at noon but during the evening; *Borodino* did not fit the description of being unkempt, having recently been repaired.

"How could an editor in Baltimore, 9,000 miles from the Korea strait," Mencken asked in his *Herald* editorial after the event, "differentiate between the true and the false, when all reports came from a source presumably authoritative?" He assured his public that "when a story is received and printed in good faith and afterward found to be 'fake,'" they could be sure there would be "roars of indignation" in the *Herald* office. The truth was that no roar of indignation ever came Mencken's way regarding his fabrication of this story.[7]

Mencken had been criticized before for making up stories when he was a cub reporter. Even then, the paper's youngest star had been given the benefit of the doubt, though it should be noted that by 1905–06 the practice was being condemned with far more vehemence than in 1899. As an editor, Mencken had shown no reluctance to confront such renegade behavior on the part of his staff. But when it came to his own story, and trying to revive the circulation of the ailing *Herald*, Mencken avoided any questions about his actions. Only a year later did he broach some word on the subject. When asked by the *New York Herald* about his views on journalistic responsibility, Mencken said that "there are shams and frauds in the newspaper offices as well as in the legislative halls and corporation offices that newspapers so often turn inside out. Exaggeration and deliberate falsification will have to die."[8]

MENCKEN WELL RECOGNIZED, as he later wrote, that "journalism is a fleeting thing, and the man who devotes his life to it writes his history in water." Throughout the year 1905, Mencken had been working on an entirely new project, larger in scale than any he had undertaken before and in a new field: a book on George Bernard Shaw. It was by no means an easy task. Only fifteen of the British playwright's works had been published; no full length study on him had yet appeared.

As a work of criticism, *George Bernard Shaw* was only adequate, written, as some have noted, in "an earnest, almost a sweating parody" of iconoclasts he admired. But it was inevitable that it should quickly become outdated as Shaw continued to write more plays and others wrote more comprehensive studies of his work. Nevertheless, it was the first analytical study of Shaw to be published in the United States. As one critic points out, it remains today probably far more important in what it says about Mencken than what it says about Shaw.

Like Shaw, Mencken felt theater was a powerful medium in which to scrutinize the beliefs of society. To Mencken, the characters in Shaw's plays fell into two general classes: ordinary people who represented the majority, and the iconoclasts. It was the latter who clearly attracted Mencken; they were the chief agents of human progress. The small minority of fearless truth-seekers, Mencken would assert, constituted the highest caste produced in human society by natural selection. By now, Mencken's literary enthusiasm had moved beyond his youthful preference for Kipling. In Darwin and Huxley, Ibsen and Shaw, he had discovered men with whom he could identify, and he cited his admiration for some of this literature and his feeling that it had permanent relevance.[9]

When the galley proofs of the Shaw book arrived, Meekins was as enchanted with them as Mencken. "If you live to be two hundred years old," he told him, "You will never forget this day." Obeying Meekins's order to take the rest of the day off and correct the galleys, Mencken went into his office, locked the door, and experienced the joy of seeing his first book of prose in type: "I can still remember the unparalleled glow after all these years."

In November 1905, he held the slim blue volume of *George Bernard Shaw: His Plays* in his hands for the first time. Opening its pages, the indefatigable editor in him spotted more typographical errors and dotted the text with his corrections. The reviews mostly denounced Shaw, still a controversial figure in the United States. They were cordial toward Mencken and, in some cases, laudatory, even if one called him "Meneker."

Though the book had been modest in its pretensions, it made Mencken's name known in quarters he had not been heard of before. Sales that fall were steady, much to the satisfaction of writer and publisher alike. News of Mencken's accomplishments were collected by the clipping service to which he had subscribed since *Ventures Into Verse*; now the thick pages of his scrapbook were rapidly being filled. At the same time, Mencken had his short stories bound into one volume. He put them on the shelf and there they remained. In 1905 he decided not to turn to fiction writing again: "In Shaw I found my real vocation."

Shortly before Christmas, Mencken wrapped a copy of his book and sent a letter to Shaw. He then waited for a response. None ever came, though in time, George Bernard Shaw would become one of his fervent admirers and Mencken would be dubbed America's George Bernard Shaw.[10]

WITH THE PUBLICATION of his book on Shaw, Mencken found his literary stature rising, not only in professional circles but also in the office. In the short span of seven years Mencken had reached the pinnacle of his profession. The boy of eighteen who had hesitated by the *Herald*'s door and shyly asked Max Ways for a job was now, at age twenty-five, on top of the world as the youngest managing

"... the hot ichor of youth in his veins ..." Mencken as managing editor of the *Herald*.
H. L. Mencken Collection, Enoch Pratt Free Library.

editor in the country. Colleagues who had been with him in 1899 were still reporters; some were unemployed. "It was a great day," Mencken recalled, "when I overheard an office boy speak of me, to a colleague, as the Old Man."

Breaking precedent, the *Baltimore Sun* printed an editorial observing Mencken's rise to prominence. From New York, Ellery Sedgewick sent his congratulations: "I hesitate to imagine where you will be at fifty if you are where you are at twenty-five."[11]

Mencken's lofty position was not, however, to last long. He was too aware of the *Herald*'s gloomy financial prospects to appreciate fully his rise to fame. Since the summer after the fire, the paper had been in perilous straits. Throughout the spring of 1906, Meekins had been unable to obtain the funds to meet the paper's weekly deficits. The situation, bad as it was, however, did not diminish Mencken's optimism. "I was still only twenty-five—and at twenty-five the hot ichor of youth is still roaring in the veins," Mencken recalled. "I argued, even against the wise Meekins, that the paper could still be saved."

Mencken took on whatever posts needed filling in, sacrificing his usual activities, even his paycheck. He continued to praise the *Herald* in ads, hoping to encourage more subscribers to risk their cent for his newspaper.

But it was not enough. On June 17, 1906, less than five months into Mencken's tenure as editor, the *Sunday Herald* printed its own obituary. Shortly after lunch, Mencken returned to his office and found that the *Herald's* new owners had watchmen standing guard over the editorial office, denying entrance to any members of the staff, including its former editor-in-chief. Mencken's reaction, as one *Herald* staffer described in his diary, was "a great rage to find he was not permitted to go to his desk and retrieve his favorite corncob pipe."[12]

AFTER HIS SPECTACULAR RISE, Mencken suddenly found himself a young editor out of a job.

The first offer of employment came from the owner of the *Evening News.* The affable Charles Grasty was a man Mencken could relate to. Grasty firmly believed the function of a newspaper was to assume the worst of politicians and therefore to hold them up to scrutiny at all times.

Earlier that year, Grasty had confessed he had been struggling with the knotty problems of a daily newspaper office. They were enough to dissuade anyone from taking over the helm, but when Grasty asked Mencken to be his news editor, the young man accepted at once. In less than a few hours after the *Herald's* demise, he was newly employed.[13]

Immediately, Mencken found himself overwhelmed by his new executive duties and the paper's "maniacal system of handling news." It was a thin gruel of telegraphic reports lifted from other papers, Mencken noted, arranged in haphazard fashion. News space was reduced in favor of advertisements. Unlike the *Herald* with its clockwork system of deadlines, the editorial page of the *Evening News* was often late being made up and its writing weak. Mencken daily encountered countless aggravations of concern to no one else at the office—not even to Grasty, who cared little for ordinary news. There must have been times when Mencken's mind reflected on the choices he had made but this one, he found, was simply intolerable.[14]

On July 16, 1906, a special meeting of the *Baltimore Sun's* board of directors was called. Walter Abell, the newly appointed president, sat at a long table, turned his handsome, clean-shaven face to his colleagues, and nominated H. L. Mencken to be the new Sunday editor. No one, not even Abell, could be sure that Mencken would even be interested in the post. Nine days later, the board met again to record that Mencken had been engaged at $40 a week. "Think of it," crowed the *Louisville Courier-Journal.* "The staid old *Baltimore Sun* has got itself a real Whangdoodle."[15]

9

A YOUNG MAN IN A HURRY

B Y THE TIME MENCKEN HUNG HIS HAT in the *Sun* office on July 30, 1906, revolutionary changes were occurring in journalism. The increasing efficiency of linotype and the formidable competition from Charles Grasty's *Evening News* had persuaded Walter Abell to accept that when times changed, traditions had to give way. And so he began overhauling the paper's ancient practices. One of the bolder reforms was to revive the old *Sunday Sun*, with Mencken in charge.

Only once before had the paper had a Sunday edition. Now plans were laid for an ambitious edition of 24 pages. With his eye for printing and display, Mencken revised the make-up, taking out six columns of newsprint to create space for illustrations. On one occasion, when Abell gave his new editor permission to run one illustration the full width of the page, the president's office was jammed with complaints from readers.

Mencken doggedly followed this innovation with others. He reduced an old-fashioned feature on Maryland and Virginia genealogy and dropped a series of travel articles by William Jennings Bryan, then touring Northern Europe, as soon as he returned home; he replaced these with music criticism by John Philip Sousa. He also introduced poetry and serialized the work of popular authors —such as George Ade's revised history of slang and Finley Peter Dunne's "Mr. Dooley" pieces. At the time of the Lincoln centennial, it occurred to Mencken to canvas the South for negative opinions. "I hoped to get some hot stuff," he confessed, but to his surprise "all the Confederates had become convinced the old scoundrel was a saint." He printed a page of their tributes. ("I was probably the only reader of the paper who saw any humor in them.")

A typical Sunday issue included such random articles as saving the buffalo, the letters of Thomas Jefferson, tales of the supernatural, a discussion of the technique of the marriage proposal, and a 24-part medical report on the city's health concerns, including what Baltimore was doing to stamp out tuberculosis. A feature entitled "Here in Baltimore," news about music and theater, cartoons, drawings, puzzles, and pictures comprised one copy, all for the munificent sum of three cents.

Such changes in typography and content triggered hostility from many older subscribers. *Sun* staffers watched as these older men came, demanding to meet with Walter Abell, and left sadly shaking their heads and saying they were sure the paper's founder would turn in his grave. Undeterred, Mencken persisted with the changes and was rewarded for his efforts. In two months under his editorship, circulation for the *Sunday Sun* climbed steeply.[1]

Mencken's days now followed a wholly new routine. At nine he might be seen briskly stepping up the marble stairway of the new *Sun* building, located on the southwest corner of Baltimore and Charles Streets, in the heart of the business district. If no one was present to take down a news tip, he did so himself, and even went out and reported on it. With his prodigious energy, he voluntarily organized the *Sun* library and prodded his staff. "He was an agreeable boss, but a meticulous one," remembered his assistant, Helen Essary. "No excuses were accepted and copy had to be composing-room proof." When Mencken's duties were completed for the Sunday edition, he found ample time for planning his own outside writing. From his polished oak desk he could look out a large window onto Charles Street and a sweeping view of the city. Below him, in the basement of the building, four steel monsters would print more than one hundred thousand copies of the paper, carrying new ideas—*his* ideas—across Baltimore.

When the day's work was over, he traveled the twenty-odd blocks back to Hollins Street and had dinner with his family, before climbing the three flights of stairs to his third floor study for the evening's writing. At ten, through for the night, he would meet for beer with his friends. As was so common with Mencken, he combined work with pleasure. The automobile craze having swept America, Mencken's *Sunday Sun* printed a series of illustrated articles describing the attractions of one-day excursions. As for the Sunday editor himself, he joined in the adventure, bouncing on makeshift roads paved with stone and oyster shell. Saturdays were devoted to music with the Saturday Night Club and Sundays to the Vagabonds.[2]

As satisfying as these activities were, Mencken felt restless; he was anxious to follow his book on Shaw with another volume. To this end he proposed to his book publisher, Harrison Hale Schaff, a digest of criticism of current drama geared to the average playgoer. When Schaff proposed a book on the German philosopher Nietzsche, Mencken responded with uncharacteristic caution. "The task is one for a man of ample leisure and thorough scholarship," Mencken wrote.

With brothers Charles and August. H. L. Mencken Collection, Enoch Pratt Free Library.

"I have little of the former and make no pretense to the latter." However, as more reviews for *George Bernard Shaw: His Plays* continued to fatten his scrapbooks, Mencken's self-confidence was fortified, and in a few days he wrote Schaff that he would accept the challenge.

As Mencken settled in to study Nietzsche, his bookshelves groaned under the weight of the books that would ultimately form part of his comprehensive bibliography. Of these, only a few parts of the eleven-volume English translation of Nietzsche were available. Mencken spent long hours grappling with these texts, many of which he found hopelessly involved and poorly phrased, making his own progress clumsy and exasperating.

In his small hall bedroom on the third floor, his desk and typewriter, as well as his cot, were rammed against the window, so that when it came time to write, he was forced to drag away his cot and then, late at night, drag it back. In such manner was Mencken's nightly progress on his book measured by his family, the sound disturbing not only his mother, who slept in the room directly below, but also the neighbor next door. In these close quarters, Mencken began writing *The Philosophy of Friedrich Nietzsche*, which would earn the distinction of having contributed more to the popular understanding of Nietzsche than any other American publication.

Nietzsche was the ideal subject of study for Mencken. Like so many others of his generation coming of age, he had been brought up with the philosopher in his reading of the avant-garde magazines of the 1890s, such as the *Criterion*. Nietzsche's criticism of civilization had been equated with the wave of scorn that swept against Victorian Puritanism.

Mencken's reading of Nietzsche concentrated on the social and political dimensions of Nietzsche's thought; he chose not to relate it to philosophy (a subject in which his knowledge, he confessed, was very slight) but to life itself. In his examination of marriage, women, government, Christianity, education, and crime in *The Philosophy of Friedrich Nietzsche*, Mencken began exploring the themes that would become his adopted trademark and stay with him until the end of his life. He scorned the mob man or the believer, what he later called the "booboisie," versus the first-rate man of the civilized minority—in other words, the iconoclast, whose mission it was to "attack error wherever he saw it and to proclaim truth wherever he found it. It is only by such iconoclasm and proselytizing that humanity can be helped."

The philosopher served Mencken well by clarifying his notions and providing him with a framework for concepts he had been formulating from an early age. For, as he admitted, "those ideas were plainly *based* on Nietzsche; without him, I'd never have come to them." It was, he said, the iconoclastic spirit that led to progress and freedom. Decades later, when he explained his own ideology to a German publisher, it was the one he had formulated during this time: "My literary theory, like my politics, is based chiefly upon one idea, to wit, the idea of freedom. I am, in belief, a libertarian of the most extreme variety, and can imagine no human right that is half as valuable as the simple right to pursue the truth at discretion and utter it when found."

At the end of his "Introduction" to *The Philosophy of Friedrich Nietzsche*, Mencken indicated what sacrifices iconoclasts must make:

> Error was his enemy and he was ever merciless in combatting it, even when the combat meant a war upon himself. He attacked men, gods and devils, but his purpose was ever the lofty one of discovering the truth. It is the fashion among the adherents of the old order to berate him for his ferocity, and to urge the sorrows of his darkened life against him, but some day, perhaps, the world will learn to give men of his kind the honor that is their due. It is a fine thing to face machine guns for immortality and a medal, but isn't it fine, too, to face calumny, injustice and loneliness for the truth which makes men free?[3]

Calumny, injustice, and loneliness: such was the penalty facing those men— Nietzsche, Darwin, Ibsen, Shaw, and, Mencken would have said, himself.

By summer 1907, Mencken's manuscript on Nietzsche had grown into a satisfying pile on his desk. At the same time, he was keeping a full schedule writing for magazines. With Leonard Hirshberg, a doctor he had met through the Vagabonds Club, he undertook a series of articles on the care and feeding of infants, published in the *Delineator*. As the weeks progressed, the *Delineator* editor found himself increasingly curious about his new contributor. "Be sure, when you come to New York, to come in and see me." The note was signed Theodore Dreiser.[4]

In the meantime, the *Sun* requested that Mencken continue to review plays, a task he did not approach eagerly, for though he enjoyed criticism, his interest in live theater had diminished since his years on the *Herald*. Nonetheless, for the next few years, on Monday evenings Mencken could be found entering a Baltimore theater. There, in the plush splendor of velvet and mahogany, he could focus on the theatrical season in a city that showcased some of the greatest actors of the time.[5]

"It was a happy Monday night that I encountered Forbes Robertson in Shaw's 'Caesar and Cleopatra,'" Mencken recalled. Not every play he reviewed was necessarily of such high caliber. Richard Mansfield, in the title role of *Don Carlos*, showed him "just how dull and flabby it is possible for a fine play to be when it is badly acted." Others failed miserably, with the villain barking about on stage, the hero delivering ponderous banalities, and the heroine just standing still. "It is all vastly in earnest," Mencken concluded after that particular performance, "but somehow it fails to astonish." There was another production, Mencken recalled, "in which the sole virtue was the superb fit of the leading man's pantaloons." Others were simply "painful."

"Baltimore should be thankful for one man at least who comes out in the open with the expressed opinion that all plays are not successes and all stars are not brilliant," one reader wrote the *Sun*. "It is a well known fact that the majority of dramatic criticisms printed in Baltimore are for the most part worthless, since nine times out of ten they are favorable to the actor and the play. Possibly they are written by the office boy." Younger journalists, such as Hamilton Owens, later editor at the *Sunpapers*, attested to having learned from Mencken's example:

> I recall, in some detail, the first time I met him. It was at the performance of one of those well contrived French plays. . . . I was a cub reporter sent to write my first theatrical notice. . . . In my naive way, I thought the play pretty good, but during an intermission I checked with Mencken. . . . In five minutes he pointed out the silliness of its theme and the falsity of its view of life. After that I could hardly fashion a half dozen stumbling sentences about it for my own paper. But the following afternoon . . . he set forth his scorn in words so pungent that I can still quote some of them verbatim. Some day a scholar will dig out those fugitive reviews and republish them. Most drama critics could learn something from them.[6]

Indeed, Mencken's criticism was so highly regarded that after one performance one actress wrote him complaining that he had failed to give her a better review. As for E. H. Sothern, he proposed Mencken become his press agent—an offer Mencken declined. Actors offstage, Mencken had discovered, were "blatant and insufferable pests." No more hideous punishment could be devised, he stated, than that of "locking up an intelligent man in some airtight barroom, with a dozen actors fresh from the road."

With some satisfaction, Mencken noticed theaters were still attracting a larger crowd than the movie houses. "In two or three years," he erroneously predicted, "it seems likely the moving-picture show . . . will be extinct." He continued to celebrate the rough, popular slapstick and praised such Yiddish theater as *The Melting Pot*, which he called "a rare and welcome play."

Authentic drama remained for him a force that liberated society. The fact that Ibsen's *A Doll's House* could be put on by a provincial stock company without scandal proved to him that the world was making progress. George Bernard Shaw's *Man and Superman* convinced him that in the game of love, the woman, not the man, does the pursuing. "If your liking is for seltzer siphons or for platitudes, keep away from it," Mencken told his readers. "But if you have reached that stage of civilization marked by an acceptance of the axiom that what everybody believes is necessarily never true, then you will enjoy *Man and Superman*."[7]

When he was not watching drama, he was going to New York and attending special meetings of the International Society of Dramatic Critics Who Have Never Written a Play, of which he was the founder. Into this group were welcomed such friends as Wells Hawks and Will Page; those who had tried to write theater criticism, such as William Winter, were not. A typical agenda for their evening was:

9:00 P.M. — Procession starts up Broadway from the committee rooms.
9:01   — Drinks.
9:05   — Procession proceeds to Longacre Square and joins Branch No. 7.
9:08   — More drinks.
9:10   — Procession proceeds up Broadway in V-shaped course.
9:11   — More drinks.
9:25   — March to Broadway Theater to amalgamate with Branch No. 17.
After this there will be no regular line of march. Although this is to be no torch-light procession, every participant will be well lit up.

After one such evening, Mencken was found blissfully slumbering in an abandoned traincar, where his well-meaning though silently dazed co-members had carefully deposited him in the belief that they were starting him auspiciously on his way back to Baltimore.[8]

As MENCKEN CONTINUED his involvement with the theater, he began hearing complaints from Ibsen enthusiasts impatient with the schoolmarmish translations made by William Archer. It was an observation Mencken had made ever since he had seen *Ghosts* in Baltimore. Now, he solicited the help of such leading actresses as Mary Shaw, Minnie Fiske, Helen Modjeska, and his old friend Virginia Kline, as well as the linguistic skills of Holger A. Koppel, the Danish consul in Baltimore, and began working on a retranslation of the whole Ibsen canon, to be called *The Player's Ibsen*. With an ear already attuned to the nuances of spoken language, on stage and off, Mencken was the perfect candidate to undertake the job.

After dinner, Mencken would head downtown and meet Koppel at his office. Together, they would pore over several texts. Koppel, who read Danish, would call out the literal translation; Mencken, who read German, would compare it with those; then the collaborators would turn to a French version before drafting their own. Finally, Mencken would smooth out the final copy.

In their first attempt, Mencken and Koppel tackled *A Doll's House*. They sought to convey not only the exact phrases of the original but also those smaller shades of speech that Ibsen employed to throw light on character. As Mencken pointed out, Ibsen had made a deliberate effort to write the way in which language was *spoken*. Correspondingly, in the climactic scene when Nora leaves her husband, William Archer's stilted pronouncements yielded to Mencken's more natural phrases. "I must stand quite alone if I am ever to know myself and my surroundings; so I cannot stay with you," uttered in the heat of passion, is replaced by "*I must stand quite alone—to know myself and the things about me. Therefore, I can't stay with you.*" Archer's "I lay the keys here" becomes Mencken's "*Here are the keys.*" And when Archer's Nora expresses to Helmer the hope "That communion between us shall be a marriage," in Mencken's translation it becomes the simple, poignant wish: "*That life together will be a marriage.*"

If Mencken had expected his painstaking labor to be a sensation, he was bitterly disappointed. When the book was eventually published, the public, still wallowing in the genteel tradition, was not ready to embrace the colloquialisms of the American language. *The Player's Ibsen* "was a complete failure, and I never had a hand in one that got less notice," Mencken groused.[9]

Eventually he began to lose interest in the theater. Writing reviews had become a chore. It wasn't just the smell of perfumes that assailed his nose every time he entered a stuffy auditorium that he found unwelcome; it was the childish playwriting and barnstorm acting that was driving out the intelligent theatergoer and the production of less commercial plays. Theater managers were constantly being forced to manufacture marvels, and the press agents to lift stars to eminence. Some of these had no talent at all, Mencken concluded, but people flocked to see them because of their "horsepower as curiosities." Each time he went, Mencken found himself surrounded by men in dinner coats and women in their finery who insisted on speaking of a *play* as a *show*.

Mencken's assaults on theatrical frauds so offended local managers that they repeatedly complained to Walter Abell, who stood by him. In the end, however, Mencken concluded that the managers were right, that it was a bit unjust of him to treat them so badly. They had to take whatever plays the theatrical syndicate sent them. Ultimately, he decided to abandon theater criticism entirely. He would rather spend his evenings reading a book.[10]

As WITH IBSEN AND SHAW, Mencken was becoming more attuned to language as well as to the feminine point of view. But there were arenas in Baltimore other than the theater that contributed to Mencken's outlook on women. The Sweetair Lyceum in Baltimore County was a place where the literati could gather and debate. One evening, Mencken attended a discussion in which, for an hour and a half, the issue of masculine and feminine intellects was argued.

Previously, in his study of Nietzsche, Mencken had proclaimed that while women were shrewd, they were not strong intellectually. The debate at the Lyceum shattered this presumption by acknowledging the superior intelligence of women lay in their intuition, an insight Mencken now praised in the *Sun* as being "unspeakably acute and unutterably accurate." From then on, Mencken's editorials on women increased. He had discovered a topic that allowed him to peel away another layer of Victorian dogma. Nor would it be the last time in his career that he would tackle the subject of the feminine mind.

Increasingly he had become the bright target of the young wives of his friends, otherwise charming creatures who possessed the nefarious techniques of a matchmaker. Mencken found himself often ambushed as these shameless hostesses led choked conversations to the subject of love:

She makes her husband—poor fellow!—tell his guests how glad he is that he is married. . . . A bachelor guest, under such circumstances, is in the position of a lone warrior ambushed by a superior and desperate force. . . . It is a serious and delicate situation, and unless he takes a good grip upon himself he is lost. The girl is pretty; someone—the hostess?—had let fall a hint that her papa has a bank roll; the lights are pink; the dusk drifts down; the host grunts like a happy dachshund—and may the fates protect the bachelor![11]

Such observations prompted readers to send letters to the *Sunday Sun*. "I have no doubt that the author of your articles is some crazy old bachelor who has been jilted by a woman too sensible to marry him," wrote one. "He drinks, I am sure."

Yet his defense against establishing a lasting relationship with a woman was that creativity and matrimony were incompatible, citing rosters of eminent philosophers, musicians, writers (including Nietzsche), and scientists who had remained bachelors. To Mencken's discomfort, however, his few remaining bachelor friends, even his own brother Charlie, were one by one falling prey to the dreaded institution. With each visit from the postman would come yet another wedding invitation, obliging Mencken to attend a new round of ceremonies, "his cheeks shaven overclose, collar overtight, coat overthick, and countenance frozen into a fixed, mechanical smile." He knew he would be seated to suffocate in an ill-ventilated church while "a bibulous organist fights a program entirely beyond his technique, and a thousand old maids swarm in to get a view of the bride shouting 'I will!' . . . like a delirious auctioneer." Each square, engraved envelope, "horrible in its whiteness," brought with it the memory of "quasi-chicken salads on sticky June afternoons," and the reminder to reach into his wallet to buy a gift.

Worse was the news that his collaborator on Ibsen, Holger Koppel, had deserted the noble brotherhood of bachelors. "Traitor!" Mencken wrote to congratulate him. But then he added prophetically, "Some day, if I have the time, I may do likewise."[12]

The challenge, indeed, was finding the time.

As THE DRIFTS OF RAIN AND SNOW FELL outside on Union Square, *The Philosophy of Friedrich Nietzsche* was finished and reviews were reaching Mencken at Hollins Street. They were tart and scornful. This was certainly discouraging, but as the months progressed more positive reviews began to come in. With *Nietzsche* Mencken had begun to achieve something far more enduring: a style of his own. He had been influenced by the master of aphorism and epigram. "Whatever he had to say," Mencken wrote of the philosopher, "he hammered it with gigantic blows"—a skill he tried to apply to his own work, albeit clumsily.

While later works on Nietzsche would reveal to Mencken the flaws of his book, he continued to read and write about the German philosopher the rest of his life. In the years ahead, he would review English translations and do one of his own, in addition to editing a selection of Nietzsche's aphorisms. Before long, *The Philosophy of Friedrich Nietzsche* went through three American and one English edition, making Mencken the most influential of Nietzsche's popularizers. Gradually, Mencken became alarmed that such reviews threatened to establish him as a philosopher of academic proportions. "This latter prospect," observed his publisher Harrison Hale Schaff, "frightened him nearly to death."[13]

As a result of his successful publication, by spring 1908 Mencken had saved enough money to go to Europe. First, however, he had not forgotten his promise to the editor of the *Delineator*, and before his ship sailed he dropped by his office.

"More than anything else, he reminded me of a spoiled and petted and possibly over-financed brewer's or wholesale grocer's son out for a lark," Theodore Dreiser recalled. The Baltimorean had, in fact, barged into Dreiser's enormous office with a cocky smile and, according to Dreiser, "with the *sang-froid* of a Caesar or a Napoleon" made himself quite comfortable in the largest chair in the room. "Well, well," laughed Dreiser after a moment, "if it isn't Anheuser's own brightest boy out to see the town." Mencken was equal to the occasion. What else did Dreiser expect? His father brewed the best beer in the world. Responding to this engaging insolence, Dreiser resolved that "from then on, I counted him among those whom I most prized."

Dreiser looked and acted much older than Mencken, yet there was only nine years' difference between them. Dreiser gave the appearance of heaviness, from his face, shaped like a solid, square block of granite, to his thick mouth. It seemed incredible that the author of *Sister Carrie* should be the editor of a women's magazine. In the ungainly man before him, Mencken sensed a native genius that would give form to a new movement in American fiction, while Mencken's very confidence solicited Dreiser's admiration.

This increased confidence was due, in part, to the publication of *Nietzsche*. With the good reviews he again found his stature rising. One afternoon he and his newspaper colleagues were surprised to find a notice from the front office announcing that H. L. Mencken had been made the editorial writer. He had been with the *Sun* for only two years. Walter Abell handed the young man a $100 bill toward a trip he had long dreamed about—across the Atlantic to London and then to Germany, with Mark Twain's *A Tramp Abroad* serving as his guidebook. By his own admission later, the highlight of his trip was not his visit to Leipzig, but to London, where he visited the graves of Goldsmith and Thackeray.

As Mencken's ship headed for Europe, his happiness seemed complete. With each accelerating knot, the shore's horizon became more distant, and with it, Mencken's doubts from previous years. There seemed to be nothing he could not do. In the exhilaration of that moment, as the waves churned beneath his ship and he leaned over its rail in the shining, bright spring air, a new serenity filled H. L. Mencken about his future.[14]

En route to Europe, March 1908. H. L. Mencken Collection, Enoch Pratt Free Library.

10

BROADENING HORIZONS

B ACK IN BALTIMORE, Mencken was searching for a new project when a letter from the *Smart Set* arrived. In 1908, the beleaguered journal "by, for and about The Four Hundred" was determined to change its course and become known as "the magazine of cleverness." Would Mr. Mencken, the editor inquired, be at all interested in writing book reviews regularly for the magazine? If so, would he please come to New York to discuss the matter?

Mencken did so, whereupon he was given an armful of publications and the simple mandate from the editor: "Write what you damn well please as long as it's lively and gets attention!" For the next fifteen years, for the *Smart Set*, Mencken would read a novel a day and produce 182 essays in which he reviewed some two thousand books.

It was the era of novels, and regularly they arrived at Hollins Street, some with gilt stamping, shining pink paper, and rainbow illustrations, their covers padded like sofa pillows. Mencken would pile them high in the middle of the floor in four-foot stacks next to his writing table. His Sunday afternoons were now given over to reviewing. Sometimes they were gloomy, soggy afternoons, and in such weather he was able to read two or three books in one day. "Life is short," he remarked, "but the procession of novels is long." At times, when he felt depressed, he looked at the rows and rows now crowding his third floor study, and despite his energy almost balked at the labor that faced him. Then, reaching out for a book from the top of a pile, he would open its pages.

He would set to work with a certain savagery. "In the practice of the gentlemanly art of criticism," Mencken wrote, "one's first impulse, on coming to the end of an elegantly bound romance, is to write 'This author is an ass,' and let it go at that, but the laws of etiquette and libel make necessary a far more subtle and circuitous conveyance of the idea." Sometimes the first words that occurred to him were "fake," "bunk," "lunatic," and—more often than not—"garbage." Even with those books he considered well written, it was a struggle to plow through. To compose a review that avoided platitudes was as impossible, he said, as "a woman trying to recite the Lord's prayer with a mouse nibbling at her ankle."[1]

Although his first review for the *Smart Set* was not to be published until November 1908, even with his allotted lead time Mencken was affected by a certain amount of stage fright: "I still recall with what uneasy painstaking I labored at my first article." Now he was facing a national audience, in a position where he could mold opinion. Eighteen books were tackled under the title "The Good, the Bad, and the Best Sellers." He devoted several pages to Upton Sinclair's *The Moneychangers*, passing sentence with the brief injunction: "Let Mr. Sinclair choose . . . between crusading and writing." The shortest review was a one-line description of a new book called *Views and Reviews*: "Early essays by Henry James—some in the English language."

Mencken stashed the books into two categories—"Those that no one reads, and those that no one ought to read." A Victorian pall was still over American literature. "No novel that told the truth about life as Americans were living it, no poem that departed from the old patterns, no play that had the merest ghost of an idea in it had a chance."

As article followed article, Mencken performed what he called a "barbaric war dance" upon the "mush for the multitudes," but as he did so, the circle of his enemies grew in numbers and virulence. Readers became convinced there was no critic equal to Mencken. He could sell a book by simply denouncing it, so amusing was his invective. Mencken defended his forceful stance. "Criticism," he said, "to be effective, must have a goal, and it must strive for that goal with a certain fine frenzy." Few believed in the principles as passionately as Mencken; few hammered on the anvil quite as hard or as loudly.[2]

IN THE SPRING OF 1909, Mencken met a man who applied these same principles to theater criticism as he had to literature. It would herald the start of one of the most significant friendships in his life. The new member of the staff of the *Smart Set* that May was George Jean Nathan, who had written theater reviews for the *New York Herald* before becoming editor of *Bohemian* and *Outing* magazines. By then, Nathan's drama criticism had already attracted attention. In time he would be called the nation's greatest two-act theatergoer. Unless he considered a play worthwhile, by the second act he could be seen striding toward the exit, to the stares of the audience.

On their first encounter, Mencken was impressed by this dapper man with a sullen mouth, his body as trim as any fencing master's, with the air of a born aristocrat. With inherited wealth produced by the harvest of vineyards in France and coffee plantations in Brazil, and a select education by the best tutors in Europe and at Cornell University—he thought it the American university most closely resembling Heidelberg—Nathan, as one observer put it, had the manner of a man too bored to flick the ashes from his cigarette. In walk, voice, and gesture, he betrayed his spectacular pedigree. When it came to theater, he benefited from the fact his mother was the sister of one of the most important theater magnates of that century; another brother, Charles F. Neidlinger, was one of the founders of the *Criterion* with Huneker and Pollard. Even his dress was singular. "He was an overcoat fanatic," Mencken said. Nathan owned no fewer than 38, including an Inverness cape that he invariably wore to first nights, and a Russian wolfskin coat that, as one actor remarked, he had trained to bite.[3]

Nathan's impression of Mencken was of a stoop-shouldered, "cherub-faced man with golden hair parted in the middle," slicked down in the fashion of the 1890s, "like the actor who plays the heroic lieutenant in the military dramas." The stranger who bounced into the room left little time for observation. In one quick movement he thrust his hand out and exclaimed, "I'm H. L. Mencken from Baltimore and I'm the biggest damned fool in Christendom and I don't want to hear any boastful reply that you claim the honor." Fifteen minutes later they were sharing a cocktail at a café. "What's your attitude toward the world?" Mencken asked, and then continued before Nathan had a chance to open his mouth. "I view it as mess in which the clowns are paid more than they are worth, so I respectfully suggest that, when we get going, we get our full share."

Nathan's view of the world, in fact, was fundamentally similar to Mencken's, although, as time went on, it became more apparent that the two were at opposite poles in temperament and interests. Unlike the disciplinarian Mencken, Nathan cultivated the point of view of an avowed hedonist. "To me, pleasure and my own personal happiness . . . are all I deem worth a hoot," Nathan admitted airily on one occasion, adding, "That I am selfish and to a very considerable degree possibly offensive is thus more or less regrettably obvious." What made for pleasure in life, Nathan declared, were the arts, a moderate but satisfying alcoholic diet, decently prepared food, and "the amiable company of amiable women." As for the cocktail sparkling in his glass: "I drink to make other people interesting."

But on this afternoon, as Nathan sat listening to Mencken, there was no need for any stimulation. From his abrupt gestures to his habit of waving his cigar like a baton in time to his discourse, or the way he would set his seidel down to cock his head as something occurred to him, Mencken was in constant motion. Throughout their meeting, he kept up a steady monologue in a voice that was a bit rough but also raffish, saying the most savage, iconoclastic things with the sunniest innocence. Then, just as suddenly, a Mephisophelian grin would break over Mencken's face, and he would roar with laughter. All this, coupled with mastery of the English language, gave him a magnetism that was utterly irresistible. "Never have I known such a man," Nathan would later remark, "who had so much fun out of life as Mencken had in those years."

As the weeks progressed, Mencken became a favored friend, trooping to sample cocktails in Nathan's small apartment at the Royalton, a stylish hotel on West 44th Street within walking distance of the theaters. Here, Nathan would live for more than fifty years, advising any one who was planning to move into the city that in New York it was important to save on everything except rent: "The location of a literary man made all the difference." In this space, with books piled high amid a clutter of knickknacks and a three-year store of champagne "in case of siege," Nathan wrote his theater reviews in fountain pen on crisp, bond paper, working from one o'clock in the afternoon until four.

In that first meeting in May 1909, Mencken and Nathan immediately understood each other. "We are both essentially foreigners," Mencken later explained to a friend, although Nathan was "more French than anything else, and I am more German than anything else. We work together amicably because we are both lonely, and need some support."[4]

THROUGHOUT THAT SPRING, Mencken once again felt restless. It would not be the first instance he began feeling time was running out for him. He wanted to write a play of his own—a desire, he confessed to Dreiser, that "now encumbers and tortures my system." Eventually he completed *The Artist*, a play greeted with praise for the American satirist who "knows his people better than they know themselves." He had also finished a new book, with Dr. Leonard Hirshberg, on baby care. Nor would this be his last contribution to medical writing. His friendship with Joseph Bloodgood from Johns Hopkins had prompted him to write a series of articles on women and cancer—one of the pioneering works on the subject. He had by this time written, jointly written, edited, or helped to translate seven books, while holding a demanding newspaper job and another with the *Smart Set*.

Overriding all of this activity was a real concern that his comfortable position at the *Sun* might be threatened. He confessed to Dreiser that it "kept me sweating." Only six months after his twenty-ninth birthday, Mencken was again feeling apprehensive about his career. "I am getting along toward thirty and it is time for me to be planning for the future," he wrote Dreiser. "You will understand what a stew I am in." Mencken worked himself into such a state that he began having coughing fits. He went to Hirshberg's office and had his uvula removed. The operation was performed in that doctor's rough-and-ready manner, with a dab of cocaine and a pair of scissors.[5]

The uncertainty of his position at the *Sun* affected not only Mencken. The entire staff was paralyzed with apprehension, especially many of the older reporters, who feared they would lose their jobs. The Abell regime was coming to a close, and Charles Grasty of the competitive *Evening News* was now buying out the *Sun* with the aim of revitalizing the paper. Mencken took it as a matter of course that Grasty would hold it against him for quitting his paper three years before. With some bravado Mencken told himself he hardly cared. He had two books behind him, a third nearly done; for the last two years he had been building a national audience writing articles for the *Smart Set*. "If this was to be the end of my career in newspapers," he thought, "then let it *be* the end, and be damned."

Instead, Grasty confided to Mencken his plans for the *Sun* takeover and promised to put him in an executive position. Mencken raised the fate of the older reporters, many of whom had been with the company all their lives, and persuaded Grasty to keep them. "Never in this life have I felt more like a Boy Scout with a Class A good deed to his credit. In a few minutes the news was spread through the office, and the prevailing glooms vanished," Mencken recalled. "By eleven o'clock I was in a nearby saloon with half a dozen reporters, and we were drinking to the health and prosperity of Grasty. One bold and revolutionary fellow even proposed drinking to the damnation of the Abells."[6]

The next morning Mencken found himself welcomed as the office hero. If he had not been considered a *Sun* man by the staff before, he was sure everyone considered him a *Sun* man now. The irony, of course, is that as one of Grasty's confidants, and later as an instrumental figure of the new *Evening Sun*, Mencken could never be on the same level as a struggling *Sun* reporter. Mencken unwittingly gave a better description of himself in an article he wrote about the profession, published that year. Week by week, he said, the journalist "comes nearer the high estate and dignity of the Olympian gods."[7]

". . . certainly a *Sun* man now." With the staff. To the far right is Charles Grasty; next to him is Paul Patterson. Mencken is in the last row; standing directly in front of Mencken is Frank Kent. H. L. Mencken Collection, Enoch Pratt Free Library.

Seventy thousand copies of the first edition of the *Evening Sun* appeared on April 18, 1910. Many would remain unsold. Comments about the new paper, however, were mostly favorable. Among its merits were its editorials, most of which were written by Mencken. They dealt with such varied topics as Theodore Roosevelt, music, cigarettes, psychotherapy, and race.

RACE WAS ONE OF THE KEY ISSUES that preoccupied Mencken, and his book on Nietzsche had initially helped define it for him. Nietzsche's insistence on dividing men by rank into superior and inferior men was a concept extending back to Aristotle. In his *Nicomachean Ethics* (a work, Mencken later confessed, that made him "feel at home"), Aristotle contended that the division between superior and inferior men was simply a product of nature.

Although *The Philosophy of Friedrich Nietzsche* had played a crucial role in the formation of Mencken's beliefs, nonetheless Mencken acknowledged that it was his preparation of *Men Versus the Man* that clarified his ideas. The issues raised in this book were more than a dialogue between the merits of socialism and individuality, however.

What was singular about this book was Mencken's interest in what he viewed as the inborn differences in the races. Here Mencken spelled out attitudes that, in time, would come to bring some of the heaviest criticism of him in a long career of controversy. For all of its blatant views of racial inferiority, the book failed to generate much discussion. "Curious" was one of the kinder epithets from the reviewers. *Men Versus the Man* "seems to be a failure," Mencken wrote to one of his friends. "During the first month it sold less than 200 copies." This result upset Mencken far less than it did Robert Rives La Monte, his socialist coauthor.[8]

Men Versus the Man, a dialogue between Mencken, the individualist, and La Monte, a socialist, contained the rudiments of Mencken's social philosophy on which he had been ruminating since childhood: the distinction between the superior individual and the inferior mob. Consistent with his views of social Darwinism, Mencken argued that the prime quality of the superior man was "the one whose work in the world increases, to some measureable extent, that ever-widening gap which separates civilized man from the protozoan in the sea ooze. It is possible, you will note, for a man to amass billions, and yet lend no hand in this progress; and it is possible, again, for as man to live in poverty, and yet set the clock ahead a thousand years."

The inferior man, he argued, deserved the place to which he was assigned. "He is forever down-trodden and oppressed. He is forever opposed to a surrender of his immemorial superstitions, prejudices, swinishness, and inertia. He is forever certain that, if only some god would lend him a hand and give him his just rights, he would be rich, happy, and care-free. And he is forever and utterly wrong."

Just who constituted the inferior man? Mencken included all races in the category, as well as the "ignorant and superstitious foreigner." None were to blame for their "poverty and ignorance," for being "lazy and stupid": for "he is a low-caste man and he has a low-caste mind." Moreover, "Castes are not made by man, but by nature."

He cited the prime example of the "peculiarly conspicuous inherited marks of the low-caste man," the blacks who surrounded him in Baltimore.

> The educated Negro of today is a failure, not because he meets insuperable difficulties in life, but because he is a Negro. His brain is not fitted for the higher forms of mental effort; his ideals, no matter how laboriously he is trained and sheltered, remain those of a clown. He is, in brief, a low-caste man, to the manner born, and he will remain inert and inefficient until fifty generations of him have lived in civilization. And even then, the superior white race will be fifty generations ahead of him.

As for the newly arrived immigrants, "the European peasants who are now coming to America—and particularly those from Russia—the same marks are to be seen."9

By 1910, relations between races had deteriorated to such a degree, Baltimore's mayor feared riots and bloodshed. But when it came to finding a solution to the "the race problem," Mencken could find none. Instead, his newspaper editorials called for a discussion about what was, as he put it, "by long odds, the most important" and perhaps "the most depressing of American problems."

At the turn of the century there was a rise in interest in the social significance of hereditary characteristics. Eugenics proved to be one of the most enduring aspects of social Darwinism. Popular credulity about the scope and variety of hereditary traits was almost boundless. The Darwinian mode sustained the belief in white racial superiority. In this, Mencken was no different from what many American thinkers of his time were saying, reflecting basic racist components of American social thought.

He was fascinated by books treating the racial traits of various minority groups. In *Men Versus the Man,* Mencken made his first formal attempt outside of his newspaper columns to wrestle with biological determinism. He also tackled notions about the relationship of genetics, heredity, intelligence, and race being published during the century's first decade and later debated by the eugenicists of the 1920s and 1930s.

Mencken believed he was not a racist in pursuing the discussion, as his life-long championship of the civil rights of African Americans and his later actions in defense of Jews escaping the Holocaust during World War II would argue. In accordance with the spirit of the times, Mencken insisted that science gave him the basis for objectivity, for, as he wrote, "I believe fully only in what may be demonstrated scientifically. The fact that there is sodium chloride in the blood will never be abandoned. It is immutably true." And because science, he argued, provided him with what he believed to be these truths, he felt comfortable stating that he was concerned only with "the world as it is, and not with the world as it might or should be."

As a philosophy, social Darwinism disappeared in America by the end of the First World War. But Mencken would continue to hold fast stubbornly to some of its tenets long afterward, when discussion of racial differences was no longer congenial to the mood of the nation. It was only until eugenics became a world-wide movement during the 1920s, with its planning committees heavily involved in race betterment, that Mencken found much to criticize.[10]

MENCKEN WOULD BE THE FIRST to admit that the period between 1908 and the outbreak of World War I would be one of the most decisive in his career. He had worked out his private philosophy in his books on Nietzsche and in *Men Versus the Man*. Many of his later books had their genesis in his editorials for the *Evening Sun*. Moreover, he had solidified his style of writing with his reviews in the *Smart Set* and laid the basis for his national reputation as a literary critic. But one other key assignment awaited that would prepare him as a social critic and help promote him as one of the most powerful voices of prewar America, one that would gain him a greater sensitivity toward race that he had not demonstrated before.

On April 18, 1911, the staff of the *Evening Sun* celebrated its first anniversary. Much of the evening was spent in praise for their colleague, the "Teutonic prodigy, Henrik Ibsen Manikin." In a private commemorative paper printed for the occasion, the staff marveled at the mental gymnastics that characterized those editorials signed "H.L.M.," and they quoted from Oliver Goldsmith to describe the admiration that so many felt:

> And still they gazed, and still the wonder grew,
> That one small head could carry all he knew.

That same spring, Harry Black, one of the directors of the *Sunpapers*, approached Grasty. The *Evening Sun* should have, in addition to its editorial page, its own columnist who could tackle any subject to unleash the full force of his personality. Grasty asked for suggestions. "Whoever 'H.L.M.' is," was Black's answer. "He can do it."[11]

11

THE BAD BOY OF BALTIMORE

W E HAVE IN BALTIMORE," thundered the weekly issue of the *Merchants'* *and Manufacturers' Journal*, a critic who is "a pusillanimous pest and a damage to the community." Few would have disagreed. Within a month of its appearance, Mencken's daily column, "The Free Lance," was already stirring up controversy, and "Letters from Our Readers" were filled with uncomplimentary comments.

Baltimore had never seen anything like it. First, there was Mencken's choice of vocabulary, the use of such unheard-of terms as "rabble-rouser"—"whatever that may mean," shrugged one reader; another, after closely studying the column, congratulated himself for simply being able to digest it "without due aid from the dictionary." Letters to the editor expressed disgust with the "maniacal ravings" of the new columnist, identified as "an immature and bumptious stripling" who wrote "drivel."

Newspapers were equally loud in their denunciation. "These 'sputterings' of the Free Lance," complained the *Towson Union News*, "show an absolute ignorance of the laws of God and man (and grammar), and utter disregard of morality and decency." The influential *Suffrage News* maintained that Mencken was "debauched," while others reacted negatively to the "flippant, reckless, and even Smart Aleck manner" in which he wrote.

All these reactions were encouraged by the editor of the Letters column—unbeknown to many, Mencken himself—who urged correspondents not to apologize for their views: "This is a place for frank discussion, not for the exchange of polite nothings." Eventually, "Letters from Our Readers" grew to such a volume that Mencken was obliged to move into a new office and call in a carpenter to build cabinets to accommodate his files, bulging with invective. "What are you *doing*, Harry?" his mother finally asked. "I'm stirring up the animals," Mencken gleefully replied.[1]

"MY FREE LANCE JOB was the pleasantest that I had ever had on a newspaper," Mencken later recalled, for he realized full well that his column marked his departure from the world of anonymous opinion. "I'd be glad to work for nothing if I could afford it," the young man told Grasty, and he meant it, "for my daily grind was still more fun than labor." From the moment Mencken entered his office each morning, he arrived at a desk piled high with abusive mail, the source, he recognized, of considerable *Schadenfreude*: "When some virtuosi of virtue has at me in the Letters column, stabbing me with rusty saws, removing my hide by inches . . . —the joy of my friends and acquaintances is enormous and undisguised," he wrote, adding wryly, "Here in the *Evening Sun* office there is the atmosphere of circus day; the whole staff comes in to see how I am taking it. And if, perchance, the murder is done in some other print, then I get from 25 to 200 marked clippings from . . . well wishers."

Mencken did not seem to mind this, for he considered the experience an educational one. Although virtually every statement he made in his column was instantly attacked, the pressure forced him to examine his notions with care. He emerged from the experience very tough minded and with considerable skill at controversy. It also gave him the opportunity to expound on a cherished theory: that people love to read abuse.

That the column produced such a popular, if negative, reaction did not go unnoticed. "I am pleased to see that the circulation of the *Evening Sun* is increasing," wrote one subscriber. "But why go behind the returns? Undoubtedly there are worse papers than the *Evening Sun*, more depraved columns than the Free Lance, and more degenerate individuals than Mr. Mencken." This reached the point that whenever the column was temporarily suspended, as on those occasions when Mencken went on vacation, readers lamented its absence: "O, give us Mencken or give us death!"[2]

INITIALLY, MENCKEN FILLED THE COLUMN with self-professed buffooneries. A dollar-a-day levy on bachelors, for example, was suggested on the ground that it was worth that to be free; a letter from "Satan" expressed the wish for Sundays with virulent Blue Laws that allowed people to play poker, drink alcohol, and beat children, to assure Baltimore "its old representation in Hell." Beneath the light-hearted banter, however, lay a more serious aim—as stated by Mencken: "to combat, chiefly by ridicule, American piety, stupidity, tin-pot morality, cheap chauvinism in all their reforms," that played upon a gullible public.

It was an era of progressive reform in the country as well as in Baltimore. Mencken supported many of the goals dear to the urban progressives, but he was suspicious of many proposed civic improvements. Ambitious plans for the Chesapeake Bay Bridge he dismissed as "a lunacy worthy of Jules Verne" (although he did suggest the city build a subway). To support his views, Mencken cited facts and figures gleaned from various sources. "My daily column," Mencken asserted, "was very carefully put together, and sometimes the preparation of it required a long and hard investigation." In the four and a half years of its existence, "The Free Lance" was never caught out in any factual error of consequence.[3]

Drawing on his fascination with medicine and bacteriology, Mencken beat the drum loudest for change on matters of public health. The city health department was run on older political lines, not according to the scientific principles of the new profession. As American cities began to grow and the flow of immigrants continued, epidemics became ever more acute. Boston and Providence were noted for their public health programs; Baltimore trailed far behind.

To combat such passivity, Mencken regularly scanned Baltimore's *Public Health Reports* as well as those of other cities of approximately the same size, and frequently printed tables attesting to the number of cases of typhoid reported in Baltimore. Then, to the horror of civic leaders, Mencken compared Baltimore's alarming death rate from typhoid cases with that of comparable-size cities abroad. Trying to overcome misunderstanding with statistics, he urged adults and children to submit themselves to vaccinations. In time, typhoid in Baltimore declined. "The Free Lance," Mencken wrote a friend, "was not defeated in all campaigns."

Mencken's other columns dealt with cholera, scarlet fever, diphtheria, tuberculosis, and smallpox. He deplored the fact that Baltimore seemed to be the only city that did not have ambulances and, in outmoded fashion, saw public health as largely a police function. The injured were routinely carted away in patrol wagons, under the care of policemen who could hardly distinguish between a vein and an artery. "All the poor cop can do is drive fast and pay for a new uniform," Mencken observed. "He means well, but he lacks science."[4]

Mencken vigorously denounced the quacks of the time, particularly antivivisectionists and chiropractors. He conducted a campaign to more fully educate the public on the need to detect cancer in its early stages. Likewise, Mencken dismissed the appeal of psychotherapy, "now quite the rage in our fair republic," as the teachings of Christian Science: "Both appeal powerfully to folk whose yearning to say something is unaccompanied by anything to say."

Mencken's interest in public health led him to dwell on the plight of the city's blacks, showing a sensitivity that had not been apparent in his earlier columns or in *Men Versus the Man:* "The black Baltimorean is just as much a Baltimorean as his white brother." In this, he showed himself to be more progressive than many Democratic reformers.

In the zest for reform, Mencken noted, nothing had been done by the local politicians to improve the housing conditions of this large segment of the population. Mencken reminded his white readers that their short-sightedness about the men and women who cooked their food, washed their clothes, and cared for their children would ultimately lead to consequences that would affect them also. "The *tubercule bacillus* is no respecter of persons. Bred in a darky waiter, it may perchance invade and finish a bank president."

As "The Free Lance" continued over the years, Mencken's call for new thinking about this often ignored segment of the population became more persistent. He condemned the various attempts to disenfranchise Maryland blacks and was fully aware that in discussions of public reform not all segments of the community were being represented. As late as 1915, he derided the empty reports of "the usual band of bumptious and bogus experts" about Baltimore's death rate that excluded the blacks from the discussion, despite the fact that they were the most concerned.[5]

As MENCKEN LOOKED BACK on this period, the wars for free speech he engaged in took place especially in Baltimore. "The Free Lance" was a turning point in Mencken's career. "Before it had gone on a year," he noted, "I knew precisely where I was heading." Not only did he begin championing the rights of Baltimore's blacks. In writing about local matters, his curiosity was piqued by the behavior of Americans in general, and he wrote a series on their habits and beliefs. In "The Free Lance" could be seen the blueprint for many of his future books. As early as 1911, he was writing of the need for a new book of quotations; the final product would not begin for another thirty years, but its origins were here, as were those of his series for *Prejudices*, his nostalgic autobiographical works, editorials for his magazines, even his later history of the bathtub.

Here, too, could be seen the development of one of his greatest works. On the Baltimore streetcars, as his nostrils were accosted by the smell of fish baskets, and the legs of his pants invariably swathed from a paperhanger's paste bucket, he overheard snatches of conversation that offered the best varieties of the American language. In his very first column he discussed the language's flexibility; in subsequent pieces he remarked on the use of diphthongs and made observations, like Shaw's Professor Henry Higgins, on the manner in which a chorus girl pronounced "third" as "thoid." "Why doesn't someone write a handbook of American, the mother tongue of millions of free Americans?" he asked. After four years, Mencken was using "The Free Lance" as a forum to solicit material for a proposed study on the language currently spoken in the United States.[6]

Mencken often returned to another subject that fascinated him: women. It was time, he insisted in 1912, to address the question of their rights. There was the matter, for instance, of women smoking, a custom that seemed acceptable to most Europeans, but to the average American indecent and unladylike. "Who the deuce wants to be a lady?" asked Mencken. "Certainly no intelligent and healthy woman in these bouncing times! The essential thing about a lady is the public assumption that she has neither legs nor brains. The nearer she comes to the intellectual and physical vacuity of a wax figure in a Lexington Street shop window, the more she is esteemed. If she bumps her shins and lets loose with a *damn*, then, the argument runs, she ceases to be a lady: for it is the theory of civilization that (*a*) a lady doesn't know the word and (*b*) that she has no shins."

Most important of all was the matter of female suffrage, for whites as well as for "the colored sister," a vote that he thought would most benefit those women who had to work for a living. In this, Mencken tempered his backing with his own particular brand of banter. Once the vote was given to the female sex, he argued, women's superior knowledge would reduce democracy to an absurdity. As for the suffragettes, he advised them against adopting the "shrill-scolding" of the crusader; in fact, they might get better results if they sent a barrel of liquor to the state legislature.

Mencken quickly found that most women were not amused by his teasing—specifically, the movement's most prominent local reformer, Elizabeth King Ellicott of the Towson, Maryland, *Suffrage News*. Meanwhile, he observed, "no other journalist in Baltimore has said a single . . . kind word for the girls." It was enough, Mencken protested, to make any man give up. Nonetheless, "I am still hot for the suffrage." With that, he caught the train to Washington, D.C., and joining the crowds, watched hundreds of females march by, as thousands of yellow streamers marked "Votes for Women" billowed and fluttered in the breeze.

If readers expected insults between the Maryland women's movement and "The Free Lance" to reach a fever pitch once these suffragettes were on the march, they were soon disappointed. One correspondent noted Mencken's increased politeness on the subject of suffrage was linked to the rumor that he had been seen with one attractive protester at one of the local theaters. "I have no defense to make," Mencken answered. "I am not up for trial, but for sentence. What is more, I warn the court frankly that I would do it again." In one afternoon, a pretty girl had accomplished as much, if not more, for the women's movement than all the crusading of what others had previously labeled "the vengeful old maids out at Towson."[7]

During the four and half years that Mencken's column continued, the city made considerable progress in civic improvement—finally completing its sewage system, building a water filtration plant, strengthening child-labor legislation, establishing a Baltimore chapter of the NAACP, and passing education reform. But Maryland's program was admittedly slower than that of other states. The rest of America had spent millions completing a host of necessary improvements a full decade earlier.

The great fire of 1904, Mencken pointed out, had made prominent Baltimoreans by the score. Hundreds of men, hitherto obscure, were appointed to various reconstruction committees. Whenever Mencken read news stories that gave any suggestion of self-congratulation, he penned a new attack. After reading the mayor's budget report that noted that Baltimore had 550.92 miles of street now paved with "various materials," Mencken went on a walk one morning

between Stricker and Gilmore Streets and made a list of 113 "various materials"
that he encountered: among them, dead cats, old horseshoes, slate pencils,
drowned roaches, dogs' ears, dogs' tails, celery tops, cigar stumps, fish heads and
apple cores. "An imaginary, a super-farcical, a fanciful, burlesque list? Not at all,"
said Mencken. "At 8 o'clock this morning, when I left home, fully 40 percent of
them were visible."[8]

For every claim of progress in the city, there were at least ten examples he
could give highlighting the boomers' "noise and nonsense." In what budget
report, for example, were there guidelines for the protection of foodstuffs in the
local markets, which were covered with flies and dust from filthy streets? He then
reviewed the mortality rate for the city and took upon himself the arduous task of
rechecking the figures cited, arguing that they were compounded of half-truths.
And where was the health warden for the investigation of the city dump? On one
sweltering August afternoon, Mencken climbed over its pyramid of garbage.
Where were the boomers now? Looking at the junk heap with dismay, Mencken
knew the answer: they were together that very moment, bawling a new and
improved Baltimore, meetings whose net results he listed as these:

Banquets arranged	46
Flashlight photographs taken	122
Committees appointed	1,284
Prominent Baltimoreans manufactured	116
Proclamations issued	73
Local newspapers denounced for woodpecking (times)	931
New factories brought to Baltimore	0

"I know of no other city in civilization in which empty pretension is received as
seriously as in Baltimore," Mencken declared. As for any discernable difference
between a Prominent Baltimorean and A Very Prominent Baltimorean, Mencken
could find precisely none: as exactly between a stale egg and a very stale egg.

As a crowning insult, Mencken devised a Society for the Suppression of
Prominent Baltimoreans, with a statute requiring the licensing of Uplifters, for
which prizes were offered for the worst public platitude of the week: a can of
oysters or a corncob pipe. Mencken reserved his most biting attack for the
Anti-Saloon League, composed of "militant moralists" who were responsible,
Mencken noted, for a new form of "Puritan snouting" that sought "to make life in
Baltimore as dull and depressing as life in the House of Correction."[9]

While some viewed agitation against alcohol and tobacco a simple nuisance,
Mencken believed such attitudes actually endangered individual liberty. "The
Free Lance" bristled with indignation at the pretensions of a moral mania that
was chipping away at man's basic freedoms; his right to smoke a cigar, for example. A moralist could challenge him to a debate on smoking, he declared, even
denounce him as a sinner, "but when, not content with this, he proceeds to snatch

my cigar out of my mouth, or to belabor me with a club from behind, or to have a law passed condemning me to 30 days in jail, then he goes beyond my rights, and I am fully justified in calling him names, in pulling his whiskers and blacking his eyes. And whether I am justified or not, I am going to do it."

His interest in medicine did not blind him to the overwhelming evidence linking smoking and cancer, but he was not won over by the logic that all smokers are moral lepers, and that a boy who inhaled would be a dope addict at 25. On the contrary, Mencken warned, a fierce crusade against children smoking would only pique their natural curiosity, making the cigarette the "malodorous symbol of the adolescent outlaw." Indeed, "the surest way to make a given action attractive is to prohibit it and put a penalty on it."[10]

Mencken recognized that he was conducting a never-ending campaign against the moralists. To them, "life down here is one darn crusade after another," he confided to a friend. His greatest ire was reserved for the Society for the Suppression of Vice, which he scornfully nicknamed "the Boy Snouts." "Two-thirds of the cat-houses have been closed," he wrote. The Free Lance publicly asked its readers: which was worse, the admitted prostitute or the clandestine one: "Who is the greater menace to public decency and the public health?"

A grand jury was called in to investigate, and the next morning a subpoena summoned the editor of "The Free Lance" to give his view on social evils in Baltimore. As usual, Mencken reveled. "I am having a hot row down here with vice-crusaders and have aroused the good old dears to a state of incandescence," he wrote another friend. "I wish you were nearby to see the fun."[11]

Mencken's attitude provoked the entire city of Baltimore. The head of the Jewish Educational Alliance wrote "The Free Lance" regarding the need to eradicate houses of prostitution where many Russian immigrants lived, saying the state owed a special debt "to those children whose parents are too humble and too obscure to shelter them from such contact." Thereupon the columnist became embroiled in a series of public discussions that made some wonder whether Mencken was, in fact, anti-Semitic.

Quoting from the rabbi's letter, Mencken said

he knows the difference between an immigrant who makes intelligent efforts to help himself and one who sinks supinely into a wallow and calls upon his betters to haul him out. The former deserves all the aid that we can give him, but the latter, I believe, is best assisted by the policeman's club. Let us not fall into the sentimental fallacy of assuming that *all* immigrants are worthy of pity. Some of them are worthy of no pity at all, and the sooner we discover it the better it will be for the decent ones.

This debate went on for days, with the letters becoming increasingly shrill and Mencken increasingly dismissive. As he put it, he refused to be "scared to death" by accusations of racial prejudice and asked his readers to be fair. He had toured the tenements of East Baltimore with health inspectors when he first became a reporter in 1899; and he shared the thought, as many Americans then did, that the immigrants now crowding their cities simply chose to live in squalor. He believed that Baltimore had been ruined by the rise of ghettos. "It was not until the appearance of Russian Jews and Italians that ghettos began to be set off," he later observed. "Their effects upon the town were uniformly deleterious." Earlier he had concluded that the only way in which this new class of citizens could survive in America's great melting pot was to learn its language.[12]

Mencken was annoyed to read an earnest essay in a local publication that chided him for his lack of constructive criticism. Mencken's answer was swift and his anger evident.

> I am a Baltimorean—a Baltimorean of the third generation, born here, living here in great contentment, and hopeful in finding a quiet resting-place, along about 1971 to 1980, in Loudon Park. . . . The one thing we suffer from, at the moment, is a plague of bad advisors, of moral, political, and economic charlatans. . . . It is dangerous to spread the crazy notion that commercial prosperity is the only measure of a city's progress, and it is dangerous to preach the doctrine that evils are best dealt with by denying them.

Such fraud, "The Free Lance" fairly shouted, "makes every true Baltimorean ashamed, at times, of his city, and honestly fearful, at other times, of its future."[13]

"WE HAVE A FELLOW HERE on this paper who conducts a column on our editorial page," Charles Grasty told frequent visitors to the *Sun*, "who writes anything that comes into his mind and frequently he takes sharp issue with me and my editorial staff. I want you to meet him."

A visitor would be led up the stairs into a dark cubbyhole of an office in disarray, with book shelves, files, tobacco jars, and a littered table that was a discomforting reminder that the intruder just might be causing the loss of valuable time to the workman who occupied such a space: a heavy-set, pink-cheeked individual, in shirt sleeves, chewing away on a half-burned cigar, pounding on a typewriter. That, Grasty would point out, was Mr. Mencken.

"I remember how disappointed I was when I first saw him," recalled one journalist. "He was then running the Free Lance . . . and had the town on its ear all the time. I saw this rather pudgy fellow—met him—and thought, 'My God, is that H. L. Mencken?'"

Others who entered Mencken's office had similar reactions. Yet, in each instance, whether they intended to chortle over the latest invective or remonstrate against it, their admiration would increase once Mencken regaled these tourists with his own brand of seductive charm and devastating logic. As one contemporary put it, "the coldest hate thawed before such easy warmth."

> I sat in his room for 30 minutes. During that time he consumed two excellent cigars and a generous pipe of tobacco and a mug of a certain guileless drink. To say that he "consumed" these things is to say too little; he absorbed them. He

does not draw lightly on a cigar; he pulls long and heavily, and the rapidly length-ening ash approaches his face at a quarter of an inch at a clip. . . . And as he talked I sat and grinned with delight—not because I agreed with the things he said, but because I enjoyed his incredible skill with words.[14]

The superintendent of the local Anti-Saloon League could often be seen lunch-ing with the notorious Free Lance (a habit that outraged his Methodist sup-porters). Even Mayor Preston of Baltimore, who had often been pricked into a frantic rage by the Free Lance, admitted that the "divertent little cuss" wrote "quite readable stuff"; the two men often met amicably at beer parties.

For those who could not "come tiptoeing into my cage," as Mencken put it, a curiosity grew. The *Evening Sun* eventually published a cartoon picturing Mencken as a tyrannical German schoolmaster, with bushy hair and wire-rimmed glasses. What delighted the 32-year-old columnist most of all was the assumption, which continued for years, that this was his true likeness.[15]

"What delighted . . . was the assumption that this was his true likeness." The Bad Boy of Baltimore, by McKee Barclay. H. L. Mencken Collection, Enoch Pratt Free Library.

". . . decked out in gaudy festoons." Baltimore during the National Convention of 1912. The Maryland Historical Society, Baltimore, Maryland.

12

OUTSIDE, LOOKING IN

T HE TWO YEARS prior to the outbreak of World War I brought significant alterations in how Mencken looked at his country, at the world, and at himself. The advent of the Progressive era with its reformist zeal spurred his questioning of American attitudes, and several trips to Germany rekindled his deep attachment to the land of his forebears.

The presence of a national political convention in his own hometown, and the emotional appeal of the dynamic if wrong-headed William Jennings Bryan, drew him intellectually toward politics. A further examination of American mores and the role of the press made him a local celebrity in demand as a commentator and critic. At the same time, in these two short years Mencken was obliged to wrestle with an old problem—the survival of the *Smart Set* and his struggle to improve American literature—and to cope with the impending war, which eventually pitted the land of his birth against the land of his cherished heritage.

On April 11, 1912, Mencken sailed for Europe. "Farewell, dear hearts, for a short space," waved the Free Lance; he was heading for Munich, "that damp but salubrious city" from which he would entertain "a fond (if somewhat fatuous) hope of coming back."[1]

LIFE SEEMED VERY GAY in Germany in those years, according to tourists who flocked there. In cafés and public parks, the bands played constantly. The public love-making ("One can see *anything* in the cabs at night," wrote one American tourist to his wife), the confetti and flower-throwing, were like a scene from a Viennese opera.

Now, with a coppery, glinting seidel of Spantenbrau before him in Munich's Hofbrauhaus, Mencken felt in his element. Cheerfully clinking his seidel with a Bavarian seated nearby—"*Gruss Gott!*"—he wondered: "What other land has such a greeting for strangers?" As for the women: "Beware of Munich countesses! There is not a *Kellnerin* in that fair city who does not claim some title or other." And with that the young man would promptly engage these alleged countesses in conversation, making a mental note of the musical sound they made when they walked.

Mencken's consciousness about his German background had been stirred by the critic Percival Pollard. In their long talks, Pollard greatly widened Mencken's understanding of the German character. Mencken had discovered a spiritual kinship to the land of his ancestors that would eventually bind him closer to the country of his birth.

If the foundation for Mencken's dawning ethnic consciousness was laid by Pollard, his reading of I. A. R. Wylie's *The Germans* during this time period convinced him of its dominant ideas. Its descriptions of that empire, its emphasis on individuality and the respect toward work, along with the values placed on freedom, learning, and discipline ("only the fittest survive"), resonated with Mencken. Wylie's chapters on the German attitude toward music—theaters packed with Germans of all social strata, intensely enjoying Bach—reminded Mencken of a conversation he overheard among twenty or more salesmen in Leipzig. He reflected that their American counterparts would have talked about sports. Not the Germans. For half an hour there was a lively discussion about how Beethoven's *Pathétique* in C Minor should be played, who played it best, whether it was opus 22 or 13!

Mencken was not blind to German weaknesses, including, as he put it, their "curious reverence for authority." At the same time, during this period of preliminary rumblings in Anglo-German relations, Mencken was determined to defend the German people against what he called "the ignorant and vicious libels of English propagandists and the ready credulity of American dupes."

RETURNING TO THE UNITED STATES, a nation in the midst of enjoying its industrial wealth, he concluded that his fellow citizens were not the self-reliant individualists of their heritage. They were nameless soldiers in a large army, haunted by fears. The Americans who emerged from his articles in 1913 and 1914 were *homo boobiens*, inferior men herding themselves into large and uniform masses. One of their characteristic manifestations, according to Mencken, was opposition to free thought and free speech. Ruling the nameless mob were Puritan reformers who assaulted individual liberty: "If there is one mental vice, indeed, which sets off the American people," Mencken wrote, "it is that of assuming that every human act must be either right or wrong, and that ninety-nine percent of them are wrong."

It was, as later argued, the cause of the astounding hypocrisy that foreigners saw in Americans, "both when we denounce them and when we seek to court them."

We posture as apostles of fair play, as good sportsmen, as professional knights-errant—and throw beer bottles at the umpire when he refuses to cheat for our side. . . . We save the black-and-tan republics from their native [statesmen]—and flood them with "deserving" democrats of our own. We deafen the world with our whoops for liberty—and submit to laws that destroy our most sacred rights. . . . We play policeman and Sunday-school superintendent to half of Christendom—and lynch a darky every two days in our own backyard.

The observation that "such and such an idea is 'American,' its contrary is full of sin" was a dangerous principle, Mencken argued, since in the long run it would "throttle all intelligence and make for a groveling and ignominious stupidity." Yet Americans seemed content to flaunt their contempt for sound sense before the entire world. "Europe sees Americanism, in brief, as a sort of Philistine uprising against the free spirit of man—as a conspiracy of dull and unimaginative men, fortuitously made powerful, against all the ideas and ideals that seem sound to their betters." Moreover, Mencken argued, "a nation that cherished such notions and feelings, and with the money and men to enforce them, deserved to be watched very carefully."[2]

At no time was mob rule more apparent than at the 1912 Democratic National Convention Mencken, in fact, concluded that mob rule was the chief mark of democracy in the United States.

It would be Mencken's first convention since 1904, and a source of delight. The conservative, genial William Howard Taft was the candidate for the Republicans. The energetic, crusading Theodore Roosevelt, who had split with his former vice president, ran for the Progressives, and Woodrow Wilson for the Democrats. Undeclared but viewed by some as still a possible choice was William Jennings Bryan of Nebraska.

As Bryan began to speak, Mencken observed how a hush fell over the crowd, and how he was cheered and jeered in turn by the excited hall. "He knew that the swift way to get things done in this country was not to argue for an idea, but to arouse a hatred," Mencken wrote later, "and that is exactly what he set out to do, dramatically and ruthlessly. . . . He knew, too, the subtle power of religious reminiscences and suggestions—its power to enchant and to arouse ancient and deep-lying passions, its power to sentimentalize even as dull a thing as a problem in political economy. In a word, he knew how to make the crowd run amuck. . . . The people were not brought in to decide a problem, but merely to slaughter a villain." With some heat, Mencken noted: "Such a mountebank as the Hon. William Jennings Bryan, with his astounding repertoire of bogus remedies, would be almost unimaginable in Germany."[3]

MENCKEN'S CRITICAL THOUGHTS about the United States culminated in a series of articles that ran intermittently in 1913 and 1914, beginning with an introductory essay called "The American" and including "His Morals," "His Language," "His Idea of Beauty," "His Freedom," and "His New Puritanism." Mencken's observations boosted his notoriety, bringing him many requests for speaking appearances, which he politely declined on grounds that

> My stage presence is disgusting.
> I have no voice for public speaking.
> It would take five kegs of beer to neutralize my stage fright.
> I am notoriously no Christian.
> I am ditto unlearned.
> Once they see me they will set the wolf-hounds on me.

Most of the invitations were purely local. Years later, Mencken reflected, "My dislike—perhaps I had better say disdain—of neighborhood celebrity was developed in my earliest newspaper days. I was always fearfully aware of the possibility that I might become a mere local worthy"—a dangerous situation for a man trying to achieve a national reputation.

Thus, on Wednesday afternoons he could be seen boarding a train for New York, to discuss the new direction of the *Smart Set* with George Jean Nathan. Determined to offer "something better than lemonade and macaroons," Mencken, Nathan, and William Huntington Wright, the magazine's new editor, introduced the American readers to such writers as D. H. Lawrence, August Strindberg, William Butler Yeats, and Joseph Conrad, and others whose work had been rejected elsewhere.

With Nathan and Wright, Mencken roamed the city until the small hours of the morning. Invariably, what they called "an intellectual evening" (fooling nobody, least of all Mencken's Baltimore friends with such "rot"), as Wright wrote to his wife, really consisted of "swilling the Hofbrau and gabbling. Saturday night we had a real 'evening,' I winning the beer drinking championship with 12 seidels. Menck ran second with eleven." Not infrequently, after such a wet night, the boss would call a conference at the office the next morning, during which, Mencken later confessed, he sat with only the vaguest notion of what was going on.

Sooner or later, the group wound up at Lüchow's on Fourteenth Street, listening in a sort of fever as the critic James Gibbons Huneker, now in his last years, held forth. "Huneker is a wonder," Wright exulted. "Mencken and I spent eight hours at lunch with him Friday afternoon. We have struck up a great friendship." The feeling was mutual. "After the lunch," Wright added, "he wrote to me saying, 'You and Mencken are the deep-dyed true fellows, rare to meet socially and now almost extinct in print. It has added five years to my life to know that there are still such men in the world.'"

Huneker became a close friend of Mencken, who admitted that the elder man had given him more ideas than any other living critic. Mencken had been avidly following his writing since the 1890s and repeatedly praised him in print. By this time, Huneker knew that his time was on the wane, although whenever he remarked on it, Mencken was the first of the group to protest. Many began to regard Mencken as a critical leader in his own right, as the man best equipped to carry on as a champion of individual freedom with all of Huneker's skill, plus a zest for combat that Huneker never had.

When it came to doing battle, however, before the decade was out, Mencken faced the Puritans head on. In the meantime, Percival Pollard suggested to Mencken that he find "an author who would serve me as a sort of tank in my war upon the frauds and dolts who still reigned in American letters." Such an author, Mencken recognized, was Theodore Dreiser, "who was completely American in his themes and his point of view." He had long admired *Sister Carrie*: now he would praise the much maligned *Jennie Gerhardt* as the finest American novel "with the lonesome but Himalayan exception of 'Huckleberry Finn.'"

Mencken's reviews in the *Smart Set* had caught the eye of a young book editor in New York named Alfred A. Knopf. In 1913, he took a train to Baltimore with the single purpose of visiting Mencken. "As was his habit," Knopf remembered, "he was sitting in his shirt sleeves at his typewriter with his corncob pipe in his mouth and his glasses raised to his forehead." The two men began a lively discussion: "I think we took to each other at once." It seemed to the young man that the critic of the *Smart Set* was the kind of person he wanted to have in his own publishing venture: "I thought of Henry as a likely author to join me." As for Mencken, the young "Noff" (as he nicknamed Knopf privately to friends) seemed to suit his own ambitions exactly, although at first he was somewhat wary of joining him. Nevertheless, he had grown dissatisfied with his book publisher, Harrison Hale Schaff; besides, anyone who shared his passion for Conrad was a friend indeed.[4]

During Wright's one turbulent year as editor, the *Smart Set* had lost money and had been the scene of bitter infighting that Mencken sought to counteract. At issue was a series of stories, "Daughters of Joy" and "White Silk Tights," by Barry Benefield, an author of whom Wright was enamored. As for the publisher, "Thayer is the original bonehead with an old maid's antipathy for such words as *damn* and *God*," Wright complained, "and whenever he sees the word *mistress* in a story, he wants it changed to '*the other woman*.'" As the year went on, Thayer and Wright began disagreeing daily, to the point that the editor finally admitted "I am absolutely at the end of my rope."

Mencken concluded that the best solution was for Wright to be bought out of his contract and thus rid himself of constant rows and turmoil. As for Thayer as publisher, Mencken realized he was wholly unfitted to run such a magazine. "What Thayer is going to do with the *Smart Set* God only knows," Mencken wrote a colleague. Contributors had already pulled out. Mencken's own contract was to end that very year. As for the magazine surviving, he thought it improbable. The entire situation had left Mencken feeling, he confessed, "utterly hopeless."

Meanwhile, Mencken found the fun-loving but irresponsible Wright a job with the *New York Evening Mail*. His proposed book on "The American" had come to a standstill, not progressing beyond the few articles he had already written, and he felt capable of only the most routine assignments. "I am in rotten shape physically and mentally," he wrote to Dreiser in January 1914. "A hell of a world."[5]

IN APRIL 1914, the Free Lance announced his temporary withdrawal from the paper; he had decided to devote himself to "the noble art of idling" with friends on his third vacation to Europe.

His departure provided the occasion for a spirited defense of its star by the *Sun*: "Mr. Mencken's absence gives us a chance to say a word about him which his protests would probably cause not to, were he still in the office."

> That word is that he personally is as virile as his writings, a hater of shams, a mocker of precedents, a provoker of thought, a contender of fallacy, a copious fountain of stimulating wit. He is a companionable associate, a good friend, and a center of radiating cheerfulness. This shop is a less pleasant place to work in while he is away, and none of his readers will welcome his return to this column more than we will welcome his return to the office.

"Mencken is going away," Mayor Preston, who had been a particular target, wrote to a local Baltimorean. "I hope it will be forever."[6]

On a lovely spring day, Mencken's ship landed in Gibraltar, "all in pastel shades," he recalled, "like the backdrop for a musical comedy." On the boat from Naples to Capri, Mencken was captivated by a young German girl. "In such a way does the *vin rouge* of those coasts fire the blood of youth." Besides, Mencken added, she was a brunette: "I wouldn't have you think that I fell for a blonde."

From Rome, Mencken traveled to Florence and Venice, then through central Germany to Munich, the latter journey "all in one day, with the apple trees in bloom." Once again Mencken was seated before an appetizing meal of savory *bifstek*, once again washed down with a seidel of Spantenbrau. At Cafe Luitpold he actually sat in Henrik Ibsen's old chair and pondered the fact that the playwright's best works had been written on that very table, nourished with Lowenbrau. He sent a postcard home: "Ah, what poetry a man might write in such a town as this!" In Innsbruck he bought his little sister Tyrolean silver buttons. His impressions were captured in *Europe After 8:15*. The Germany Mencken had seen on three separate occasions was the land his grandfather, Percival Pollard, and James Huneker had described: a country to which Mencken had pledged his soul, a vision that no despot could ever destroy.[7]

Then, on June 28, 1914, a gunshot in Sarajevo provided a turning point in the history of the twentieth century, and, as it would turn out, in Mencken's own life.

"Once the bands begin to play and the men are on the march," Mencken wrote in "The Free Lance" that August, there would be no more "imbecile following of snide messiahs" such as the William Jennings Bryans and the Billy Sundays. For Mencken, the conflict was a means of regeneration of a United

States that had become too self-indulgent, "brooding over petty wrongs and ills" that the nation's forefather's "never gave a thought to."

Most people believed modern warfare in the twentieth century would be over swiftly. Many at that time, including President Woodrow Wilson, believed war would free Western civilization of the complexities that seemed to plague it. Mencken therefore did not hesitate to declare, in characteristic combative over-statement, that "a war would do us good."

"The outbreak of war in 1914 was destined to interrupt my work for the *Sun*," Mencken reflected years later, "but I didn't know it at the time."[8]

Part Two
1914–1919

Shield for the Saturday Night Club. H. L. Mencken Collection, Enoch Pratt Free Library.

At his desk at the Baltimore *Evening Sun*. H. L. Mencken Collection, Enoch Pratt Free Library.

13

THE HOLY TERROR

A S MENCKEN BECAME MORE AND MORE CONVINCED that he had a responsibility to present the German side of the war, his pro-German essays became dominant in his increasingly controversial "Free Lance" column. "Regardless of your sympathies," one colleague wrote at the time, "writing war stuff is jolly game, and at least in Mr. Mencken's case, it has resulted in as good reading as there is."[1]

Mencken was dismayed at what he called "the influence of deliberate propaganda . . . practically all the news of Europe that came to the United States in those days came through England. That news appeared in the American newspapers as special cablegrams, but I know of my own personal experience that nine-tenths of it was made up of clippings from the English papers." Mencken systematically investigated stories that the *Evening Sun* reprinted from the *London Globe*, and he found repeated examples of bias and even fraud, guaranteed to influence neutral countries, especially the United States. This deliberate battle of hearts and minds, Mencken claimed, was a trap set to catch a gullible American public, succeeding "as such traps always do when the suckers are numerous and eager to be caught."

From a faltering start, beginning with a series of appeals to unite civilians behind the war effort against "the Beast of Berlin," a propaganda machine developed in England that became the envy of the world. Against this, Mencken sought to establish balance. In his scrutiny, he took on the *London Globe*, *Daily Mail*, *Daily Telegraph*, and, in the United States, the *New York Times*, the *New York Herald*, and even the *Sunpapers*. In "The Free Lance" columns during 1914 and

1915, he provided a wealth of primary material for precisely those who he thought could most learn from it: the modern student of history and "youngsters entering journalism."[2]

Daily, Mencken thumbed through the London papers, arguing that all discussions of the war were "pitched in exactly the same, strident, hysterical, preposterous key." In the September 7 issue of the *London Daily Telegraph*, anything but a yellow journal, Mencken cited this remark of a British official: "I regard everyone of German nationality as criminal," and in the *London Weekly Dispatch* of October 25, "Every German, old or young, naturalized or not, is a potential spy. . . . The only safe plan is to arrest or deport every German." It was, Mencken concluded with sarcasm, "new proof of the calm and dignity with which the English are facing the hazards of war!" The rigidity of censorship, Mencken contended, prevented newspapers from giving actual news of the war, but this "home-made product is," if anything, "even worse."[3]

Not only were editorials, headlines, cartoons, or even methods of display misleading, so were the photographs. Until 1916, only two photographers had been assigned to cover the Western Front. Routinely, photos were miscaptioned. In the *Evening Star* Mencken found a six-column photograph labeled "French Troops in the Field Under Fire." Beneath it, text described "mixed infantry," calling attention to "the rolling nature of the country." But, as a matter of fact, Mencken wrote,

> the picture showed *German* infantry and artillery (no cavalry) on the march in Poland, and the country on view, far from being "rolling," was palpably flat. This very picture was printed in the *Hamburger Fremdenblatt* for January 1, page 19, with the correct caption over it.

What angered Mencken most of all were President Wilson's claims of impartiality at the same time that the administration adopted the British point of view as its own. In the first 21 months of so-called neutrality, policies governing peace negotiations, the arming of merchant ships, preparedness, embargo, and loans documented a transition to partnership with and finally to open support of Great Britain and her allies. The idea that America was neutral was a myth.[4]

Fireworks were bursting over Fort McHenry when Mencken celebrated his thirty-fourth birthday in September 1914. During that enthusiastic week of patriotic hymns, he made plans to get away from the star-spangled city. In so doing, he missed Secretary of State William Jennings Bryan's speech to thousands of schoolchildren praising President Wilson for making the conflict the last the world would ever experience. "How do you stand in this war?" Mencken wrote to Dreiser. "As for me, I am for the hellish Deutsche until hell freezes over."[5]

As THE WAR ABROAD PROGRESSED, Mencken reflected that reviewing books for the *Smart Set* "measurably mitigated the horrors of my existence." His nerves were strained by tensions at the *Baltimore Sun*, whose point of view was making his workdays "extraordinarily turbulent." The appreciation of Mencken's columns by Baltimore Germans embarrassed him. Delegations of them arrived at the *Sun* office to shake his hand. "I was, of course, no more a German patriot than I was an American patriot," argued Mencken, "but it was impossible to make them understand and believe it."

To Mencken, the most extreme phase of British propaganda was the campaign against German atrocities in both the British and American press. As he repeatedly pointed out in "The Free Lance," all references to actions by soldiers of Allied countries were censored: "When those airships happen to be English or French, nothing is ever said about the effects of their bombs upon civilians."[6]

Newspapers endlessly reported merciless atrocities. Lord Bryce, a noted historian and former ambassador to the United States, was made chairman of the Committee to Investigate Alleged German Outrages. The result, the Bryce Report, is now generally acknowledged to have been largely a tissue of unsubstantiated observations by unnamed witnesses who had not been put under oath or cross-examined. Moreover, all the documents and reports of the witnesses were destroyed at the end of the war, making it impossible to verify their testimony. Yet, the Bryce Report became the major source for the most gruesome stories of the war, geared to exert the most powerful influence on American opinion.[7]

Among American correspondents who joined Mencken in protesting that such stories were groundless were Irvin Cobb of the *Saturday Evening Post*, Roger Lewis of the Associated Press, Harvey Hansen of the *Chicago Daily News*, and James O'Donnell Bennett of the *Chicago Tribune*. All had spent weeks accompanying German troops and were unable to confirm rumors of brutality.[8]

Mencken cited a journalist in the *London Herald* who commented that "not one solitary case" of infamy could be given "that could survive the easiest scrutiny, and not one will be produced." Mencken's stand provoked violent reactions among British readers, some of whom classified "the Mencken column" as "bosh."

After a German submarine torpedoed the British liner *Lusitania*, on May 7, 1915, Mencken's criticism of the British methods of propaganda took on an even shriller tone. He spared no one, not even his former childhood hero, Rudyard Kipling, who, along with other writers and artists, had joined a nationwide campaign to rally the forces of good against the forces of evil. "There are only two divisions in the world today," Kipling wrote, "human beings and Germans." Mencken called the poet "most pathetic." He advised Americans to learn the reality about the war: "to wit, that the Germans are going to win."

Criticism of "the sauerkraut columns" became more strident. "Oh, you should read the editorials of the Free Lance," commented a reader to the *Sun*, who characterized Mencken in two ways: as having "some brains" and as "a laughing stock."

"Who is Mencken?" one reader questioned. Seeking an answer, this same individual went to the *Sun* office, "but there seemed to be no one willing to talk about H. L. Mencken. Every one whom I apprehended seemed to be anxious to change the subject, and the way they did it looked sort of queer to me."9

"I'D THROW UP MY NEWSPAPER WORK AT ONCE if were not for the war," Mencken confided to Ellery Sedgewick, adding morosely: "A lot of time wasted—but all existence begins to bear an aspect of time wasted." Things were to become worse when the United States entered war, but they were already bad enough. "I had to live among people whose view of the events of the time seemed almost insane to me," Mencken recalled, "and whose concept of honor, whether national or personal, was violently at war with my own." In the months to come, he felt that his colleagues at the *Evening Sun*, "in the traditional Anglo-Saxon manner, took to hitting below the belt," adding to his feelings of despair and disgust with his own newspaper. When "The Free Lance" column was conspicuously absent, surprised readers sent letters asking if the paper's leading luminary had been fired, interned, or buried.

It amazed some of the friends of Van Lear Black, chairman of the *Sunpapers*, that he did not get rid of Mencken. The *Bookman* commented: "Its owners have been repeatedly asked to dismiss him; instead they give him a free hand." According to Mencken, his freedom was never inhibited in the slightest, and when he ultimately did give up "The Free Lance," he insisted it was on his own motion entirely. In his old age, Mencken gave as the reasons for leaving regular journalism the exigencies of his interests in New York and his growing conviction that America would enter the war and he would be forced to retire. "I could not imagine myself either going over to the English side or ceasing, while I had a signed column, to denounce its fraudulence," he wrote. Also, as he put it, "I had probably been on the staff of the *Sun* long enough."

These reasons may easily have been authentic, but considering that they were the recollections of a man writing his memoirs, it would be well to compare them with the other pressures facing Mencken. Managerial criticism focused on falling circulation figures, a hardship then for all American newspapers, but which some readers blamed on Mencken's column. In his unpublished memoir, James Cain said flatly that "Mencken did not quit his column. It was taken away from him." In any event, without explanation, on October 23, 1915, "The Free Lance" made its last appearance. Mencken signed off with "The truth that survives is the lie that it is pleasantest to believe."

Looking back on this unhappy period, Mencken observed that, during war, unless there is tolerance for free speech, "to argue anything in such a time seems to me to be as impossible as to stop a stampede by playing on an E clarinet. It simply can't be done."10

14

MENCKEN, NATHAN, AND GOD

THE WAR IN EUROPE WAS NOT THE ONLY PRESSING MATTER for Mencken
that year, although it overshadowed all else. On August 16, 1914, he and
George Jean Nathan became editors of the *Smart Set*. It was a happy
arrangement for the two friends who had already resigned themselves to ending
their association with the magazine by the end of the year.

Mencken noted to Dreiser that under Thayer's management, the *Smart Set*
had become "as pure as the *Christian Herald*." But Thayer had been hit by the
stock market slump of 1914, the magazine's circulation was down, and he was
tired. He sold it to a new owner: Eugene F. Crowe, a paper manufacturer, and his
associate, Eltinge F. Warner, a young midwestern publisher who had rescued
Field & Stream from oblivion and turned it into a huge success. When Warner
asked Nathan to edit the *Smart Set*, the drama critic consented, but "only if
Mencken comes in with me." The publisher was nonplussed: "Who the hell is
Mencken?" Nathan became senior partner, his name appearing first on the
masthead, with Mencken as co-editor.[1]

Arriving at their offices in the Knox Building on New York's Fifth Avenue,
Mencken would lay out a feast of cold cuts on an alabaster slab taken from a
cemetery. Then he would place beside his desk his paternal grandfather's brass
spittoon, lugged on the train all the way from Baltimore. The fastidious Warner
demanded its removal, but Mencken refused; it was, he argued, for the con-
venience of their friends. (As a concession, he agreed that whenever he held a
conference with a lady author, he would discreetly drape the offensive spittoon
with a tasteful cotton print.)

Thus the *Smart Set* was relaunched by Mencken and Nathan, whose first issue for September 1914 bore the slogan: "One Civilized Reader Is Worth a Thousand Boneheads." They promised from then on that the magazine would be edited "without any other 'policy' in the world than to give its readers a moderately intelligent and awfully good time."[2]

"Nathan and I never took the magazine seriously," Mencken later wrote. "Our main purpose was to have a pleasant time—and we always had it." Visitors to the office gazed at the decorations in amazement. On the wall were signed portraits of William Shakespeare (all dedicated to Mencken, and all forgeries), banners advertising corn cures, a large flag, and a streamer bearing the words "God Bless Our President"; life-size Follies girls gazed down from the wall. These works of art, Mencken and Nathan assured visitors, were not for sale (though portraits of the two editors were). Smoking was permitted, with Mencken generously producing a supply of "Uncle Willies," swearing they were Cuban and making the request to their recipients that when puffing, they "kindly blow on me."

The policy of the *Smart Set*, Mencken confided to his former mentor Ellery Sedgewick, "is to be lively without being nasty. . . . A magazine for civilized adults in their lighter moods. A sort of frivolous sister to the *Atlantic*." Nathan was to perform all the editorial office work, copy-reading the manuscripts and making up the magazine. Mencken's primary task was, as he put it, "to keep on the lookout for good stuff." In the collaboration on the departments "Repetition Generale" and "Clinical Notes," they tackled the ideas that came up during the course of their nightly conversations.[3]

Each Monday and Friday for nine years, Nathan carefully tied brown paper packets containing *Smart Set* manuscripts and sent them to Mencken in Baltimore. If Mencken found one he liked, he marked it "Yes" and returned it to Nathan. If Nathan liked it too, it was set in type at once, and the author's check went out at the end of the week. If Mencken dissented, the manuscript was returned. The procedure also worked in reverse order, Mencken to Nathan. No time was wasted on discussions of manuscripts although brief written comments sometimes were included. The "No" of either was final. "This plan was so simple and so practicable that we often wondered that no other editors had ever thought of it," commented Mencken. Surely, few periodicals had handled the business of selection with greater speed. "Take a look at this," Mencken wrote on top of one letter. "I am in doubt about it, but the author shows promise. Read her letter. I vote for sending it back, but with a polite request for more."

Sometimes a whole packet would be returned to Nathan with brief summaries by Mencken: "A triangle story, but very well done," "A good character sketch of the boob," or "This fellow has good material, but it seems to me that he still uses it ineffectively." And there were letters from Nathan to Mencken: "I am against printing any more so-called poetry by K_____, even if it happens to be good, which is not likely. This K_____ has cheapened himself by becoming a public character down in Greenwich Village."

Each of their rejections was accompanied by a personal remark. To one agent Nathan wrote: "This Danish novel seems to Mencken and myself to be awful stuff. If we are wrong, we offer to present to you gratis the best red flannel lingerie you can buy on Tenth Avenue." To an ambitious young writer, who sent Mencken a poem written on her heavily scented stationery, he returned the verse with the following scrawled across the rejection: "Madam, your poetry is awful, but your perfume is divine." Most authors were able to learn more about what was wrong with a rejected piece in one or two candid sentences than in entire paragraphs from other editors.

As a result of such tutelage, contributors were able to develop their own styles. The important thing to Mencken was to keep a writer encouraged, especially those struggling to establish themselves. "Whenever a volunteer showed the slightest sign of talent," Mencken later recalled, "I wrote to him encouragingly, and kept on blowing his spark as long as the faintest hope remained of fanning it into flame." In literary courses around the country, young scribblers wanted to write for the *Smart Set* just as several decades later they would want to write for the *New Yorker*.

Each issue contained about twenty short stories, ten poems, four articles, one novelette, and one play. Fully three-fourths were by unknowns, many who never became household names. Mencken once confessed that sometimes only a small proportion of the contents of the magazine had been really fit to set before the readers he had in mind. Some of the manuscripts submitted left him "feeling between lukewarm and cold."[5]

At the beginning, the reputation of the *Smart Set* was so poor that many authors were not eager to contribute. Established writers Mencken and Nathan desired—Theodore Dreiser, Joseph Conrad, and Max Beerbohm—were difficult to attract. There were times when the two editors needed sixteen short stories— and had only two weeks to get them. With very little substance available those first years, Mencken and Nathan were forced to include anonymous contributions of their own under such pen names as William Fink, Janet Jefferson, and Robert W. Woodruff.

The discovery of new writers was a specialty of the *Smart Set*, and it included a roster of such impressive names as Thyra Samter Winslow, whose first story appeared in Mencken and Nathan's first number, and Ruth Suckow. Eugene O'Neill's *The Long Voyage Home* was his first published play, later followed by *Ile* and *The Moon of the Caribbees*. Other discoveries of this time included James Branch Cabell, Ben Hecht, and Willa Cather. Edgar Lee Masters, a Chicago lawyer who had once been the partner of Clarence Darrow, was then unknown. Mencken's *Smart Set* review of *The Spoon River Anthology* helped launch the poet's success.

One of the magazine's fairest accomplishments was the publication of F. Scott Fitzgerald. Fitzgerald was then surviving by writing streetcar ads in Manhattan—his most successful was "We Keep You Clean in Muscatine"—

while at night he wrote stories and papered the walls of his room with rejection slips. The only story accepted was "Babes in the Wood," for which Nathan paid Fitzgerald $30 and launched his career. As a regular contributor to the *Smart Set*, Fitzgerald now easily convinced Charles Scribner & Sons to take his novel, *This Side of Paradise*.

Black writers such as W. E. B. Du Bois and Latino writers such as Luis Muñoz Marin (later the first governor of the Commonwealth of Puerto Rico) also made their appearance. Works by recent immigrants from Eastern Europe such as Avram Yarmolinsky were included, as well as many writers who had difficulty in being accepted by mainstream magazines.

Thanks to the editors' broad outlook, American audiences were introduced to the works of Continental writers as well. One of these was suggested to Nathan by his friend, playwright George M. Cohan: the Anglo Irish playwright Lord Dunsany, in vogue during the 1920s and 1930s. From Russia came stories by Count Alexey Tolstoy, and Ezra Pound functioned as their London scout. Pound wrote to James Joyce: "The S.S. is disposed in your favour if you have any sugar tits for 'em," and as a consequence two of Joyce's short stories from *Dubliners* were the first ever to appear in an American magazine. On another occasion, Pound wrote Mencken on behalf of "the last intelligent man I've found, a young American, T. S. Eliot," though Mencken could see nothing in his work but "nonsense. His poetry, in fact, was largely only prose sawed up into lengths."

Mencken and Nathan were rapidly becoming among the foremost iconoclasts in the changing literary and dramatic scene, and they were not unaware of this. A couplet of those days went:

> Mencken and Nathan and
> > God.
> Yes, possibly, possibly
> > God.

The *Smart Set* did miss out on some of the best-remembered writing of the time. The *Dial*, another magazine with different shortcomings, published the novelettes of Thomas Mann and D. H. Lawrence, Sherwood Anderson's "I'm a Fool," and T. S. Eliot's *The Waste Land*. But if the *Smart Set* was not uniformly good, noted one critic, it paved the way for something better. "In a historical sense it deserved great credit," noted Louis Kronenberger in the *New York Times Book Review*. "It was free from the old taboos, it was relatively catholic and it was relatively very discerning."[6]

NEVERTHELESS, BY 1915 THE MAGAZINE was still struggling. Various means of getting out of the red were tried. Cheaper paper was used and the number of pages was cut. It also occurred to the editors that they might make a tidy profit from some of the other material they received, by anonymously publishing by-product magazines. Despite the warnings, they launched *Parisienne*, a magazine intended, as Mencken said, "to turn to advantage the Francophilia prevailing at the time. Now, many aspiring hacks were receiving letters not on the usual *Smart Set* stationery but on mauve paper with pink lettering, with a note from Mencken stating how much they liked their material and that it would appear in their "sister publication." The new magazine was cheap in every sense; locales were changed to the French Riviera and featured wealthy titled heroes and beautiful heroines, illustrated with women clad in transparent pajamas or flimsy bathing costumes. "I had never heard of this sister," recalled the playwright S. N. Behrman, "but I was happy to be admitted to the family."

So great was the magazine's success it aroused the ire of the New York Society for the Prevention of Vice, which claimed that the *Parisienne* was obscene. The New York Post Office threatened to ban it from the mails. That such censorship existed was not unusual; a biography of Oscar Wilde had already been suppressed before its publication. When the resulting case was decided in Mencken's favor, the *Parisienne* was making more money than the *Smart Set*, returning four thousand dollars a month.

Mencken and Nathan repeated the success with another pulp monthly entitled *Saucy Stories*, with an initial circulation of 12,000 per month. Calling itself "America's Most Entertaining Magazine," it featured romantic novelettes and short stories that the editors promised their readers were full of "the drama of poison and jealousy and the triumph of love." When fillers were needed, the poetry and short stories of William Sanford, Lew Tennant, and John Hamilton were featured—all written by Mencken himself, and all invariably poked fun at the war between the sexes. Their success in the "louse magazines," as Mencken called them, produced needed revenue, convincing their publisher that he had a pair of editors of high degree. Encouraged, Mencken and Nathan hatched schemes for more.

One of the ideas considered was a dignified Negro monthly, patterned after the *Crisis*, but instead of covering politics, devoting space to literature and the fine arts. The magazine would have African American editors, contributors, and advertising; an all-black news company in Atlanta would handle circulation. Mencken proposed a department that would deal with African Americans in other countries—Martinique, Panama, and Cuba—with portraits of African American beauties, many of whom Mencken admired in Baltimore. Mencken's idea generated considerable excitement with the circulation manager, but the project was too far ahead of its time and was abandoned.

Shortly thereafter, they made plans for another pulp, made up of thrillers. If, as Mencken and Nathan reasoned, detective stories and those of the occult were successful as bound books, why shouldn't they triumph as a magazine? *Black Mask* was actually the first such publication, and it was quickly making money. Woodrow Wilson, widely known to read murder mysteries, was reported to be one of the first subscribers—not true but, as Mencken commented later, it no doubt helped sell the magazine. In a little while Mencken and Nathan began recruiting authors of skill, including S. Dashiell Hammett, a former Pinkerton Agency detective from Maryland, thereby launching him on his hugely successful career.

In time *Parisienne*, *Saucy Stories*, and *Black Mask* were sold, leaving Mencken and Nathan with more money than they had ever touched before.[7]

MENCKEN'S WORK ON THE *SUNPAPERS* had proven to be less satisfying. As a compromise between Mencken and management, he agreed to write occasional signed articles for the *Evening Sun* editorial page. For the most part, they were limited to his two favorite themes at that time: the influence of Puritanism on all phases of American life, and "the pervasive dishonesty of Woodrow Wilson's course in the war." Avid supporters of the president on the staff were at their wits' end; no doubt they breathed a sigh of relief when, on occasion, Mencken turned to such relatively harmless subjects as Billy Sunday.

Howard Kelly, a renowned doctor at Johns Hopkins and a rabid vice-crusader, had invited Mencken to accompany him to see Sunday preach. Kelly had often gently scolded Mencken, speaking to him of God "rather sugarishly," expressing his hope that he would be able to bring Mencken up to grace. "I bade him to do his damndest," the columnist told him, "but predicted that he would never fetch me."

Nonetheless, for Mencken, a self-described connoisseur of mountebanks and rabble-rousing in all its forms, the invitation to cover Billy Sunday was too good to refuse. He had been well aware of the flamboyant evangelist preacher and the enormous following he had gained. By 1916, Sunday's zealous advocacy of puritanical morality was having considerable effect in rural areas. Thanks to the financial backing of wealthy Marylanders, the fundamentalist could be seen jumping in and out of limousines throughout Baltimore, grasping the hands of hundreds of men and women, urging them to help him make the city a religious center of brotherly love. By the time Sunday left town, Mencken noted, not only was Baltimore full of the spirit of God, but also the preacher had amassed a considerable private fortune.

Joining the crowd at the Baltimore tabernacle for Billy Sunday's first sermon, Mencken watched in delight as deafening applause greeted the evangelist on stage. "I'll bet my life that some of you out there are filled with the devil!" the preacher roared. Unable to contain himself, Mencken glanced at the Children of the Devil seated next to him. "Nearly all looked pitifully poor and wretched and god-forsaken," he observed, more in need of "square meals, less work, and a chance to learn what joy is."

For two hours, Mencken goggled at Billy Sunday. The next day, he described the preacher's skillful litany against scoundrels who would roast in hell forevermore. After reading the column, most *Sun* readers asserted that when it came to choosing between Billy Sunday and Mencken, the latter "is not a rival to the man we all adore." Instead, the more pious of them suggested that Mencken be tarred and feathered, then burned alive. Even the less vociferous seemed to agree that converting H. L. Mencken would be a struggle. With salvation in mind, Dr. Kelly opened a tiny black notebook and fervently penned for himself a "Prayer List" that enumerated the names of twenty-one men.

Topping the chart as the sinner most in need of his attention was H. L. Mencken.[8]

MENCKEN'S PENCHANT for doing battle with reformers did not end with Billy Sunday. His greater interest was taking on would-be reformers in literature, and in this regard his friend Theodore Dreiser would soon provide him with a more serious target. Observing Mencken, one editor later remarked: "There is a tremendous personality, living a most interesting life of doing and saying what he pleases, fighting stupidities, lambasting moral uplifters, showing up charlatans—and having a devil of a time doing it."[9]

15

ROUND ONE!

O NE DAY IN 1916 a man walked into Brentano's bookstore in New York and asked for *The Genius* by Theodore Dreiser. His order was politely declined. *The Genius* had been declared obscene by the New York Society for the Prevention of Vice. All copies had been seized and the publisher had run for cover. No orders could be filled; doing so would result in prosecution. At issue was a long list of profanities (Dreiser had used "Goddamn") and lewd references (such as "kissing"), then considered sexually explicit. Moreover, *The Genius* had brought charges that Dreiser was linked to "the Hun menace." Before any of his books could be sold, shops awaited the decision of the courts.

Mencken considered *The Genius* Dreiser's poorest book but saw the attack as an injustice. He swung into action, generously devoting his time and money, soliciting the help of the Author's League, collecting signatures, and making the case an international cause célèbre. He sent 25 letters a day, more than 100 a week, to Ezra Pound, Jack London, Arnold Bennett, and other authors, launching "A Protest Against the Suppression of Theodore Dreiser's *The Genius*."

The response of nearly 500 signatories was unprecedented in American letters, uniting the literary community behind the principle of opposition to unreasonable censorship. In praising Mencken's defense of the Bill of Rights, Sherwood Anderson declared it to be "the most important matter that has ever come up in America."

When, in the midst of all this, Dreiser insisted on adding the names of other writers, including sexologists, whose books had a great undercover sale, Mencken became enraged. "The old ass is ruining his case by his folly," he griped. To make matters worse, Dreiser now began promoting his new work, *The Hand of the Potter*, a badly executed play that contained scenes of child molestation, incest, and rape. Aside from its lack of artistic merit ("a cheap piece of pornography," in Mencken's judgment), its publication was professionally suicidal and further threatened to undermine all the efforts made to save *The Genius*. It was, Mencken fumed, "almost impossible, in those days, to offer him anything resembling rational advice." Dreiser was simply "a peasant."

While their private quarrels had little outcome in the case of *The Genius*—the publisher had withdrawn the novel—the affair promoted the public view that Mencken and Dreiser were shapers of a major literary revolution. After this, Mencken promised to devote his life to combating "not the Puritan heroes but the laws they hide behind."[1]

MEANWHILE, MENCKEN, TOO, felt the public indignity of censorship. He wrote fewer articles for the *Sun* and derived less satisfaction from his writing. "Conditions at the office, in truth, are so unpleasant that I seldom go there myself," he wrote to Willard Wright; by December 1916 he had retired even his signed editorial. That year, President Wilson was elected for a second term on the slogan "He Kept Us Out of War." What Mencken called "the depressing tramp, tramp, tramp" of preparedness parades—generously funded by the nation's big businessmen—now began. "Forward the Zeppelins!" Mencken told Dreiser. "I am tired waiting."[2]

While Mencken continued on friendly terms with Dreiser, their only real bond in those days was their opposition to the war. In 1916, the two men had reached a turning point in their relations, helped no doubt by the fact that they had mistresses who were sisters. In Mencken's case, he had established a romantic relationship with an attractive woman named Marion Bloom.

He had met her two years before, in 1914, when she had visited the *Baltimore Sun*. During this period, when Mencken's own spirits were at their lowest, he had taken note of Marion's brown hair with reddish glints, the dark eyes that looked up at him in a lively, coquettish way. However, none of those things was what made this particular woman so appealing. "What stands in your mind is [her] vividness," a contemporary remarked. The flirtatious way she glanced, the ease with which she laughed, her playful demeanor when she engaged in gay repartee, or the manner in which she could dramatically swirl an elegant cape around her shoulders: "She had a distinct air about her. If anyone came into the room, you would look at Marion first. You sensed immediately, 'Here is a personality.'"[3]

In the following months, Mencken often found himself heading for her home in Washington, abandoning his favorite saloons in Baltimore in favor of sitting across the table from this delightful young woman. It was the beginning of a passionate love affair that would continue for many years. No other woman would excite Mencken in quite the same way.

"... the air of one who was enjoying life." Marion Bloom. H. L. Mencken Papers, Manuscripts and Archives Division, The New York Public Library, Astor, Lenox and Tilden Foundations.

What chiefly irked Mencken about his relations with Dreiser was his regret in ever having introduced Marion's sister, Estelle, a woman he admired and respected, to a man who, he discovered, was devoting himself "largely to the stud."

Dreiser's claims of bedding four women a day (sometimes between dinner courses) and his transparent cover-ups when sneaking off to one of his many trysts were acts Mencken found of a generally immoral nature. Estelle, who harbored literary ambitions herself, spent countless hours typing Dreiser's manuscripts, even as she recognized that loving a genius who was also a woman-izer was insane. It was not uncommon for her to return to the apartment she shared with Dreiser and find pillows mussed up, a handkerchief lying suggestively on the couch, cups and saucers in the sink, and the teapot still warm. "I can't stand it anymore," she confessed, finally announcing to Dreiser: "I would like an after-noon in which I am not always finding traces of other women."

But nothing changed. Mencken later chided Estelle for wasting her devotion on such a man, telling her, "You have allowed the old boy to make a doormat of you, and yet you have gone back every time." When she declined his offers of money to enable her to leave Dreiser's company, Mencken eventually exploded, classifying Estelle "among the damned fools."[4]

In contrast, Mencken's own relationship with Marion was, as Dreiser observed, that of "a cautious conventionalist." Edwardian in matters of discretion, Mencken was very proper in his desire for decorum in his affair with Marion, while upholding a Victorian code that there were two kinds of women—the first visited in bordellos and the second taken to the altar. Such values made for Mencken's pleasure and guilt in his enjoyment of Marion, and would, in time, cause anguish for both of them. Marriage was constantly discussed, but it was just as constantly evaded. At some level, especially in the years ahead when he was with several women at once, Mencken had to realize his behavior was not that different from Dreiser's.

Both Marion and Estelle belonged to a class of independent women who had moved to the big city sharing a love of books that drew them into the arms of literary giants. Marion was not one to comply with ordinary conventions, whether in the home, at work, or in matters of sex—though when it came to the last, Mencken would have been the first to say that the belief that women were devoid of any sexual instinct was nonsense. Indeed, as he asserted, "Life without sex may be safer, but it would be unbearably dull," reducing human existence "to the prosaic, laborious, boresome, imbecile level of life in an ant hill."

Nonetheless, for all his words, Marion observed in a letter to Estelle: "I'd bet that my lack of virginity is the cause of my trouble with H. He pretty well proves that I'm the kind of woman he would take in marriage, but he can't forget that I leapt the fence. . . . He probably sweats some himself over this problem. I am aware of his psychology but unable to help."

Similarly, although Mencken understood a woman's need for economic security and self-expression, he held to the middle-class tradition that women should leave work upon marriage. Being economically dependent upon a man caused Marion much anxiety, for, as she complained to Estelle, "I suppose I should have to ask a husband for money every time I wanted a roll of toilet paper."[5]

Mencken liked Marion to be stylish, but she saw his standards of dress as Victorian, not only for himself but for the women he courted. Knowing his weakness for "little navy blue coatsuits with lace around the collar," Marion considered buying herself such clothes. As their courtship progressed, she discovered that Mencken's other ideas about women were also quite rigid. After being among the first to celebrate women's right to smoke in public only a few years before, now he protested their "little coffin-nail" cigarettes after dinner, their puffing pipes and even cigars, a phenomenon giving "disquiet to the more austere and forward-looking division of moralists, of whom I have the honor to be one." Added to this was their latest willingness to "swear like pirates."

When it came to those conventional feminine attributes Mencken valued and expected from women in his genteel, middle-class world, Marion seemed to be lacking. She was completely innocent in the details of housekeeping. His premise that this new generation regarded domestic duties as somehow degrading —to call a modern woman a good cook, he found, turned into a sort of libel—led him to the conclusion that men across the country were sitting before meals so vile they would "gag a cat." Prior to one visit to Marion's apartment, he stopped at a store and bought a chicken, anticipating a delicious dinner and her company.

What she set before him, it turned out, was an undercooked bird, raw and inedible. "I was so embarrassed, I thought I'd die of shame," Marion recalled. "He was so noble about it. He said, 'Well, all people make mistakes in cooking. Come on, let's go downtown and have dinner.'" It was an experience that found its way into *In Defense of Women*, in which Mencken observed if the average American middle-class husband wanted a sound meal, he had to go to a restaurant to get it. It certainly convinced Mencken and his girlfriend that, if ever they did marry, they would have to hire a cook.[6]

If Marion lacked domestic skills, what attracted Mencken was not her beauty so much as her vivacity, what he called her "babbling mood." Contemporary accounts all agreed: "Oh, she was a joy! The sweetest thing"; "witty all the time"; "the life of the party." Mencken, however, found that beneath the fun Marion masked variations of mood that swung from exuberance to depression. Mencken became quite expert at exhorting her to get over her blues, "even when you curse God for not making the world as pleasant as a moving picture film."

Some of Marion's melancholia may have stemmed from a social upbringing far different from Mencken's; what Dreiser later portrayed as coming from a family without background or means. Marion's mother was a farmer's daughter, her father a schoolteacher from New Windsor, a small agricultural community forty miles northwest of Baltimore. When Marion was only six, her father committed suicide, leaving a widow who was physically disabled, with six children and no money. They were all put to work in the family dairy and also in a canning factory, giving their mother every nickel they had. Somehow, even though Mrs. Bloom was worn to a frazzle, the children never did without. Their genteel poverty eventually earned the respect of the community, though Marion later admitted that the death of her father was not accepted, let alone understood: more than once the children felt like social outcasts. As soon as she could, Marion joined her independent sister Estelle and moved from New Windsor to Washington, D.C., and later to New York.

The fact that Marion was unconventional and did not come from a respectable family did not initially seem to matter to Mencken. But as Marion was painfully to discover much later, it was certainly a factor in Mencken's growing dissatisfaction with her. Again, what Mencken did appreciate was an excellent mind; he was not one to feel threatened by her intelligence.

In a pattern reminiscent of how he had urged other female admirers to contribute to the *Herald*, Mencken pressed Marion to write epigrams for the *Smart Set*: "You are 80 times as clever as most of the literary wenches who are pictured in the public prints, with long crepes hanging from their nose glasses, and a melancholy, nobody-will-betray-me air about them." Her compositions eventually found their way into Mencken's other magazines, under various noms de plume. A regular feature, "Silhouettes of Stage and Styles" by one Marion Burton was included in *Parisienne*, along with poetry by Marianne du Fleur.

Many of the couple's encounters centered on his tutoring—whether of her reading (he piled on books by Zola) or her writing—or on his subsequent efforts to shake her out of her self-perceived lack of talent. Such phantasms, real or imaginary, he wrote her, "have sharp teeth. I have been bitten by them myself, and more often than I like to think of."

As for Marion, she rejoiced in Mencken's masculinity; to her, he was a "HE man," handsome with his pink face, the "fine bigness he always used in handling money." She asked her sister: "Who ever felt his big free nature pinched inside a sou?" There was comfort in the fact that she could lean on him. "In every crisis, every anguish," she wrote later, "I had comforted myself that Henry could straighten it out." In short, "I admired him in many ways. I liked his amiability, his kisses, and so forth, combined with the tenderness which he as a lover could not conceal when he cared for me." "Tender" was a word she used repeatedly to describe him, so that when it came to parting at the train station, they would be "heaving and longing for each other and he wished he did not have to go."[7]

When they had been dating for a year, Mencken bought a Studebaker with a canvas top and side curtains that could be put on when it rained. Driving with him could be an adventure. "Henry was a sight," Marion attested. "He was totally unfitted for running a car." Mencken spent most of his time at the wheel wildly waving his arms, all the while turning around to speak with his passengers in the back seat, who meanwhile were holding on in terror as they watched approaching vehicles suddenly careen out of their way. In Baltimore, when the summer evenings became too hot, Mencken would take his family for a ride. At thirty miles an hour, the journey provided a refreshing breeze. But the only two who seemed to enjoy these jaunts immensely were Mencken and his little niece Virginia. His own mother was afraid to drive with him; likewise, his siblings found the experience "grueling."

When Marion lived in Washington, Mencken would often drive there on the pretext of having to visit the Library of Congress. She would be waiting, ready to assist him in collecting material on the American language long before he decided what he would do with it. "I don't think I helped much, but he pretended I did," Marion recalled. "I really did very little for him. It was more to be with him."

Mission complete, they would go to the Ebbitt Grill for a steak dinner, where he would gently chide her to eat all of her spinach ("like a good little girl," Marion recalled him saying), which obediently she would do. Then, perhaps not wishing to admit that their day together had come to an end, he would offer, "Would you like to ride over to Baltimore?" "Oh, I'd adore it." Together, they would climb into his Studebaker and bump along the hilly miles toward home. Once they reached Baltimore, Mencken would suddenly decide that Marion's returning to Washington alone just wouldn't do; he had to turn the car around and drive her back the same route. "We'd have a little argument over that, and I'd end up by not letting him do anything like that. But he was concerned." Instead, she would take the train.[8]

Though their courtship initially was happy, Mencken's need to be close to a woman was mired in his own inner conflict—one that Marion subsequently recognized—that a woman could impinge upon his freedom. Ever since his father's death, being head of the household had given Mencken importance as a child and later as an adult. The fact that his mother leaned on her son may have made him feel overwhelmed by women's needs later in life. Consequently, quarrels flared, especially when Marion thought Mencken was avoiding her. "You infuriate me by hiding a tenderness behind your cruelty," Marion chastised him.

Even so, Marion began to realize there was something ominous in Mencken's refusal to introduce her to his family. He rarely spoke of his siblings, especially of Gertrude, leading Marion mistakenly to believe he cared little for his sister. And though they toyed with talk of marriage, it would be years before Mencken even broached the possibility of any kind of introduction to either sister or mother. In all probability, Anna didn't even know of her existence. Intimates such as Dreiser saw Marion as nothing more in Mencken's life than a "social playmate."

But there were suspicions that Mencken must be courting. "Oh, Mr. Mencken," fluttered Miss Stowe, the *Sun*'s society editor, "when are you going to give me a chance to write a notice of your wedding for my society column?" "When that occurs," rasped Henry Mencken, "it will be police news, not society."[9]

IN 1916, DESPITE HIS FLOURISHING ROMANCE with Marion Bloom, Mencken was depressed about the world situation and his own professional future. When it became obvious that the United States would enter the war and that open discussion would soon become impossible, Mencken appeared defeated. "I chafed against the restraints that gradually hedged me in," he said of this period of inner turmoil. "For the first and last time in my life, I suffered from a feeling of bafflement. I knew where I was headed, but I had not yet formulated a definite programme for writing; all I was sure of was that when I came to it eventually it would not be the one I was perforce following." "What's eating you, anyhow?" asked Dreiser. Certainly it was a combination of things, but what exactly, Mencken refused to say.

"Although those who did not know him sometimes mistook Mencken's air of supreme confidence for brag," Nathan reflected, "he often said privately he considered himself a failure." For the past two years, Mencken confessed, "I seemed to be going downhill." As was always the case when Mencken was under stress, he began suffering from daily hypothetical physical agonies that made life as intolerable for him as for fellow hypochondriac Nathan.

Chief among his complaints was hay fever. A cacophony of sneezes seized him each August, his eyes leaking copiously, his head feeling cloudy. He could neither sleep nor work; reading was almost impossible. Submitting to the experiments of Johns Hopkins doctors, he swallowed burning elixirs, snuffled powders,

MoM!

endured probes and needles—all in vain. Hay fever, Mencken announced, "is worse than leprosy. It is unaccompanied by the salve of sympathy. It hasn't even the kindness to kill."

Nor was this the only instance when Mencken found "the Devil teasing me." Throughout these years his health was so aggravated by his nervous excitement over the war that he was obliged to diet. Feasts of crab stew à la Maryland, steamed turkey with oyster sauce, and the daily evening ritual of several seidels of beer had transformed him from "a puny youth into the magnificent specimen of Anglo-Saxon manhood that I am today," but they also had taken their toll. At 198 pounds, Mencken suddenly found that he could no longer climb the stairs to his third floor study at Hollins Street without losing his breath.

From then on he was off liquor, starch, fat, and sugar. The regime seemed to work, for in four weeks he lost eighteen pounds. Although he bragged of his triumph to Marion, it was not long before he was "back in the trenches," drinking pilsner, "praising God from whom all blessings flow," and resolving never to indulge in such idiocy again. "There is only one diet worth a damn," he vowed. "Eat all you please of whatever you like, and wash it down with whatever the good God is decent enough to send you."[10]

HEAPING PLATEFULS OF FOOD, HOWEVER, were still not enough to quell Mencken's frustration. Throughout 1916 he was thinking constantly of Germany, sensing a bond with the highly educated Germans from whom he was descended. "There was a whole century," Mencken once wrote, "when even the most ignorant of my house was at least *Juris utriuesque Doctor*."

He was particularly interested in Otto Mencken and his son Johann Burkhard Mencken. Otto had received his degree from the University of Leipzig at the age of twenty, and after a brilliant lecturing career throughout Germany and Holland, he returned as a professor of morals and politics. In 1682 he founded the *Acta eruditorum*, one of the earliest of learned journals, whose contributors included Sir Isaac Newton, Pascal, Locke, Descartes, and other important intellectual figures.

But it was the son, Johann Burkhard Mencken, who most fascinated this young Baltimore descendant. He had taken his degree at Leipzig at twenty-one and three years later was elected a member of the British Royal Society. In 1713 and again in 1715, he delivered two lectures under the title *The Charlatanry of the Learned.* For a while the book was banned in Leipzig. Nonetheless, it became a sensation, and over the years its Latin was translated into French, Dutch, Spanish, German, and Italian.

Mencken first read this book in 1916 and was astonished by things he himself might have written. "It gave me a great shock," he told a friend. "All my stock in trade was there—loud assertions, heavy buffooneries, slashing attacks on professors. It was really uncanny." Reading it when he did gave Mencken much to ponder, not only about his own intellectual heritage but also about the direction

Johann Burkhard Mencken, ancestor and Leipzig scholar (1674-1732). H. L. Mencken Collection, Enoch Pratt Free Library.

he could be headed. "If I ever get the time I shall translate this seminary bombast into English and publish the book," he promised himself. "But this must wait."

Setting his eyes on Germany, believing that there was still little news coming out of Europe that bore the stamp of credibility, Mencken convinced his friend Paul Patterson of the value of his making a trip and writing his impressions for the *Sunpapers*. The date for his departure was set for December 28.[11]

THE HARBOR WAS HOURS BEHIND HIM, the ship's propeller thumping its way north, when Mencken pulled out his new Corona, balanced it on top of a suitcase, and began to type letters to the two most important women in his life. He calmed any worries his mother might have by reporting the sea had been smooth all the way from New York. He wrote to Marion that he was "more crushed than ever" at leaving her behind, signing for the first time, "with love." The *Oscar II*, he said, was cramped, cold, and depressing. Most of the passengers spent their time gloomily pacing slippery decks, miserably looking over the icicled sides of their ship at the gray mists, and "guzzling liquor day and night, full of resigned belief that a German submarine might fetch them any minute."[12]

Yet even during these uncertain times, crossing the Atlantic was a small price to pay to escape a life that Mencken thought had grown unendurably stagnant. As for reaching the other side, he little knew what awaited him there.

16

BERLIN, 1917

Berlin for American correspondents stationed there in the winter of 1917 was a far different city from the one Mencken had visited only three years before. Heavy clouds loomed over the tall spires of the capital, its broad streets covered in ice. The bleakness of the weather intensified the atmosphere of oppression as an ominous hush hung like a pall over the city. Except for the few military automobiles and the whir of an occasional Zeppelin overhead, little disturbed the silence. Restaurants that once bustled with nightlife were subdued, their liveliest sound the clinking of spoons on plates, scraping up the last rationed drops of sauce and gravy. At ten o'clock the theaters all closed, and at 11:30 so did the cafés. "Berlin, once so full of gaudy night life," Mencken found, "is as quiet as Blue Boston."[1]

It was not quite eleven one morning when Mencken, after picking up his ration cards at the front desk of the Adlon Hotel, set off for the American Embassy to pay his respects to Ambassador Joseph Gerard. The embassy was located in a little square off the Wilhelmstrasse, a convenient block or two from the German Foreign Office. Every morning the newspaper correspondents would enter through its huge double doors and go down a long hall to meet the ambassador. Between eleven o'clock and noon, Gerard would sit at his desk signing papers, seldom looking up at the reporter asking a question and hardly ever making eye contact when replying.

Outwardly, the American correspondents got along well with Gerard, despite the fact that they entertained little regard for his diplomatic skills. In an effort to give history what he called an unvarnished verdict, Gerard's principal aide, Joseph Grew, summed up the ambassador in his diary: "Tact, adaptability, foresight, poise, moderation, unprejudiced judgment, finesse, are totally lacking in his makeup. . . . He made his success in Tammany politics and that is where he should have stayed."

It was an opinion shared by the newspaper correspondents, who privately thought the ambassador would be in a much better position if he were polite to the Germans. President Wilson's most trusted adviser, Colonel Edward M. House, personally had urged Gerard to be more diplomatic, especially after receiving complaints from the German ambassador to Washington, Johann von Bernstorff, that "Gerard was not the most useful man for our good relations."[2]

At his very first meeting with Gerard on this morning, Mencken came to the same conclusion. Gerard's contemptuous attitude was too readily apparent and prevented negotiation with the professionals of the Wilhelmstrasse, who placed great value on formality and courtliness.

Moreover, Mencken observed firsthand that the ambassador's animosity toward the Germans was, he wrote, "apparently limitless." Among Gerard's first words to him was a warning against his having any association with Oswald Schütte, chief of the German office of the *Chicago Daily News*. There is little doubt the ambassador had also already made up his mind about Mencken.

Oswald Schütte had also upset his home office and his publisher, Victor Lawson, with what was perceived as a pro-German partisanship in his cable dispatches about British casualties. Schütte's superiors warned him "to guard against being sympathetic at expense of the facts." Yet when officials in London were forced to acknowledge heavy British losses, Schütte felt vindicated. Schütte redoubled his contacts with German officials, sending back what he believed to be unbiased reporting, only to find that many of his dispatches were being intercepted en route to Chicago. Only a month before Mencken's arrival, Schütte had charged the *London Times*, who shared representation with the *Daily News*, with censoring his stories.

Mencken foresaw the threat of censorship of his own dispatches. Far more troubling to him was the British propaganda in American papers and now, here in Berlin, the hostility with which Schütte, a German American, was viewed. These experiences would color Mencken's attitudes twenty years later, in another visit under strikingly similar circumstances. Now, it alerted Mencken to the new kind of interference he might face with his own paper and with the ambassador. Nevertheless, he was determined to report what he chose, no matter the consequences.[3]

Mencken had been in Germany only a few days when he sent back word to the United States that on the basis of his observations, Herbert Swope's highly touted reports on the state of the nation were "cock-tales." The *Sunday Sun* printed Mencken's first story, which derided the British and American press as exaggerating Germany's food rationing, though he wrote to Marion he hoped its scarcity would reduce his girth and thus make him as slim as a fawn. Here,

Mencken's sympathy toward Germany outweighed his journalistic objectivity. As Mencken well knew, Berlin was highly dependent on imported food. Long lines were common as women waited for the small amounts of meat and vegetables to purchase with their ration cards.

But if Mencken thought he could fool his readers, he was mistaken. Reaction to his articles was mixed. Readers questioned Mencken's impartiality, arguing that Mencken would be able to learn "only what the German authorities want him to see and hear."

The *Sun* defended its star. Foregoing its usual advertisement for Mencken's columns, it boldly announced: "MENCKEN IS NOT NEUTRAL."

> He is pro-German. He has told you so in his first Free Lance column time and again. But this will not prevent him from giving you the . . . "inside story." He will be trusted to give Germany a square deal, and it is believed he will be allowed greater latitude by the censor than almost any other writer.

An Innocent Abroad.

". . . the most important mission of his life." "An Innocent Abroad," *Sun* cartoon by Tom Bee. H. L. Mencken Collection, Enoch Pratt Free Library.

"Whether you damn them or praise them," the *Sun* concluded, the articles were going to be "mighty interesting."[4]

MENCKEN REACHED THE GERMAN LINES along the river Dvina wearing an extra overcoat and a pair of leather boots loaned by war correspondent Raymond Swing of the *Chicago Daily News*. His destination, cryptically disclosed in his dispatches to the *Sun*, was battalion headquarters beyond Novo Aleksandrovsk, where the temperature often dipped to forty degrees below zero. This little town, at the beginning of 1917, "was the spearhead of the great German Vormarsch into Russia," Mencken later reminisced, "and the show it offered was certainly exciting enough to a novice." Mencken arrived at nightfall, when colored sky-rockets heralded a terrible attack by machine guns, shells, and deadly gas. Headquarters was tucked into a tiny protected hollow but was easily reached by shrapnel and shells.

Daylight disclosed gentle rolling country with little hills separated by small creeks and frozen swamps. Beyond the brow of another gulch was the Russian line. Between the German and Russian lines ran a hollow of scrub pines and birch saplings, all beautifully laced with frost.

After hot tea in the dugout, a lieutenant led Mencken on a tour of the trenches. There was a mathematical exactness to their layout, with examples of German precision for directions and warnings: on boxes of hand grenades, Mencken read *Lebensgefuhrlich!* (Dangerous to Life!) "Imagine such a warning in a trench," Mencken wrote in one subsequent dispatch, "with grim death at every hand!" At one lookout he and the lieutenant were interrupted by the watchman, peacefully enjoying a cigar, who invited them to look through the lens of a periscope. Halfway up the Russian hill stood the ruins of a house with huge holes where German shells had hit it days before. It stood horribly silent.

Turning, the men examined the *Horstposten*, a series of advance trenches that ran down the hill in front of the main trench. Narrow, shallow, turning sharply at a 45-degree angle, they were no match for the young lieutenant, who easily loped ahead like a Nordic gray wolf, his body bent double to hide from any Russian sentry. Mencken followed—"I had difficulty getting along, being matronly in habit"—when the familiar *zzzip* of bullets, fired from a few hundred yards away, suddenly passed by his exposed head. For a moment, Mencken recalled over three decades later, "it seemed to me to be all up with Henry." Crouching in the trench, the lieutenant was philosophical. "They'll give it up after a few minutes," he told Mencken, as a hail of gunfire continued to whiz above their heads.

A few minutes later, the guns did, indeed, stop. Unscathed, Mencken passed by two soldiers repairing the walls of one of the trenches: by evening they would be restored.[5]

After Mencken's dispatches about his trip to the front, there could be no doubt among *Sun* readers that "Herr Mencken" not only was impressed by the German army but had also enjoyed himself. Evenings he dined among the generals at the *Offizieresheim*, or Officers Home, in the Gartenstrasse in Novo Aleksandrovsk. Because of the recent Bismarck centennial, the country had been reminded that Bismarck's mother was a Mencken of Leipzig, so, Mencken said, "my name got me extra politeness," and he was duly seated next to the highest ranking general, "despite my assaults upon his politeness with my execrable German." There, he sampled grilled tenderloin and some "capital Moselle." Nor did Mencken dine badly at the front. In Germany during that period, the army came first: every German knew the whole nation depended on it. Food was plentiful and meals were served four or five times a day.

After five days along the German lines, Mencken was ready to return to the capital. Long after the war, he would continue his correspondence with his guide, Captain von Vignau, who would often look back on "the trip we made together that winter to the Dunaberg front." Before leaving Novo Aleksandrovsk, Mencken received a certificate testifying that he was free from any disease. On the railroads near the front were special cars for the *nichtsaniserte*—the undisinfected. More than once, as Mencken wrapped Swing's coat around him, he mentally thanked his colleague for his thoughtfulness. One foot was already frozen, and his nose had turned a bright vermilion. Despite the cold, Mencken was aware he had been a privileged witness to one of the most interesting views behind the German front lines, with the promise of another—a proposed tour of the whole Austrian front, lasting five weeks: "A truly magnificent junket! . . . I had the time of my life."[6]

OUTSIDE THE AMERICAN EMBASSY, Ambassador Gerard took a walk alone through the white streets of Berlin. A few hours earlier, the German Foreign Minister Arthur Zimmermann had handed him a note declaring that unrestricted submarine warfare would begin at midnight. Gerard knew it was only a matter of hours before a break in relations between the United States and Germany. He walked on, lost in thought, as Berlin sank into a quiet, frozen calm.[7]

When Mencken arrived at his office in Unter den Linden with his gift of *Leberwurst*, Raymond Swing was already hammering at a typewriter at his desk, the morning papers piled up around him. "Pack your bags!" said Swing. ". . . This is the end of the comedy."

Whatever fantasies Mencken may have had of additional trips to the Austrian front or of meeting friends in Munich were suddenly over. He was now on the go day and night. As he hurried toward the American Embassy, he passed schoolboys, old men, and women, digging at the frozen snow, clearing paths in the icy streets. The bitter cold of Lithuania seemed to have followed him to Berlin. Horrible blasts of frigid air roared down Unter den Linden, and Mencken's body seemed to swell. He felt stiff in every joint, and the pain in his right foot throbbed as he walked. The cold was far beyond anything in his previous experience; it had an almost solid quality, and at the same time it was "as penetrating as X-rays." For all this, he noted gloomily, it was "an historic and a somewhat feverish day."

At the embassy, Ambassador Gerard warned Mencken to do everything he could to get out of the country. As for himself, he seemed to be in a jovial mood. Less than a few weeks before, the ambassador's letters home contained a phrase that perfectly summed up his feelings about his post: "Rotten weather—sad life." Now it seemed obvious to Mencken, as he visited Gerard at his office, that the ambassador was immensely relieved the long ordeal would soon be over.

When Mencken arrived at the Military Bureau of the Foreign Office, Rittmeister Freiherr von Plettenberg and Captain von Vignau greeted him hospitably, pulling out a jug of Scotch whisky. "Well," said the Rittmeister, "what is it going to be?" Mencken ventured a guess that the finish was now in sight and voiced his pessimism that the United States would stay out of war. The Rittmeister looked thoughtful. "England has escaped too long," he said, lighting a cigarette. "We must give her a taste of steel." He hoped the United States would see Germany's point of view: "We have absolutely no desire to hurt Americans. All we ask is that they keep out of the way while we tackle England. They have done much for the English. Perhaps they'll do as much for us." And if they didn't? The Rittmeister shrugged at Mencken. "We are ready to fight as long as it is necessary."

"You've seen the German army in the field," interrupted Captain von Vignau, looking at Mencken. "Did you find any sign that it was *Kriegsmude*, war weary?"[8]

FOR THE NEXT FEW DAYS, moving through the frozen and cheerless streets of Berlin, his ears growing every more brittle, Mencken pondered the countenance of the Germans around him, and the more bewildered he became. To him and his fellow American correspondents, these were times of uncertainty and suspense, and yet the public received the news of probable war with the United States calmly.

The German population's trust in their leaders was in part responsible for their attitude. If the older Field Marshall von Hindenburg was the national hero, Erich Friedrich Wilhelm Ludendorff, a professional soldier by nature and the idol of the nation's populace, was the brains and hidden factor behind the current U-boat campaign. Poking his head into half a dozen cafes and theaters, Mencken found the usual crowds, the usual stolidity, the usual determined pursuit of recreation, war or no war. "If the Berliners are worried about the situation," Mencken wrote in his diary, "they surely conceal the fact magnificently."

For Mencken's part, his main concern now was "about worry at home." Letters to the United States had been held up at the censor's office for the last ten days; he could only imagine what his mother might be suffering. Indeed, across the miles at that moment, she had already read her copy of the *Sunday Sun* bannered with alarming headlines: "U.S. SEIZES INTERNED GERMAN WARSHIPS AT PHILADELPHIA; AMERICAN SHIPS SUNK BY U-BOAT; BREAK TO BE COMPLETE; AMBASSADOR GERARD AND ALL OF HIS STAFF AND ALL AMERICAN CONSULS HAVE BEEN ORDERED OUT OF GERMANY."

That very same day, in fact, Mencken was making his way to the Foreign Office to see what could be done about his own future. An order had come from the German government changing the rule about when an American correspondent could depart following return from any front. The time had been extended from two to eight weeks. For many of Mencken's own colleagues, the matter was simply academic, as they were on salary and had orders to cover the news until war was declared, which would be shortly. Mencken's date of departure, however, would not be for months. The thought of being marooned in Berlin, with no way of getting in money from the United States and nothing to do all day save to tramp the streets, caused Mencken, with an uneasy smile, to joke to the officer in the Military Bureau of the Foreign Office that he felt like "the darky about to be hanged." Rittmeister Plettenberg responded with a laugh; Mencken, he said, was invited during the months ahead to call on him daily and sample his excellent Scotch.9

MEANWHILE REUTERS, THE ENGLISH NEWS AGENCY, began loading the wires with stories that Mencken felt were designed to provoke the Germans. One stated the United States was raising an army of two million men; another that all wireless stations had been seized, that the whole U.S. Navy was preparing to set sail. In addition, the Germans were inflamed with tales of what was happening in the United States. The noon edition of the *Berliner Zeitung* ran the headline: "GERMAN SHIPS IN AMERICA SEIZED!" Another stated that German crews were being imprisoned in a quarantine station.

The German reaction to the Reuters dispatches from London was swift. At the American Embassy that evening, all of its telephones were disconnected and letters and telegrams were neither received nor delivered. "We were," embassy aide Joseph Grew wrote in his diary, "almost completely cut off from the outside world."10

Visiting the American Embassy the next morning, Mencken encountered crowds of anxious Americans, some quietly weeping, blocking the corridors, seeking renewal of their passports and, above all, available passage back home.

The ambassador greeted the correspondents for their morning meeting in a somber mood. He complained that he was being held hostage, announced that he had heard nothing from Washington and had nothing to communicate to the reporters. He could not even telephone the Foreign Office across the street, finally declaring that he fully expected all American correspondents would be interned in a prison camp, along with other members of the American colony. "You fellows are in for it," he told the correspondents. "You'll all be locked up before it's over."

Mencken realized that "all that is needed to clear up the situation is a little common friendliness and common sense." None, however, seemed forthcoming. For days he and the other correspondents besieged the American ambassador, who continued to fume that he was being held prisoner. Finally, at one morning meeting, impatient with Gerard's lack of diplomacy, Mencken suggested that one of the American correspondents send a cable to the President or to Secretary of State Lansing to clarify matters. His proposal was received in silence.

Even if the American ambassador chose to remain powerless, behind the scenes other correspondents were trying to clear up misunderstandings. Schütte was doing his best to relieve a delicate situation, telling German officials that delaying the departure of Americans was creating a very bad impression. Oscar King Davis, of the *New York Times*, finally brought matters to a head when he received a 200-word dispatch from his managing editor, Carl Van Atta, that scotched all the rumors being printed in Berlin. Van Atta stated the Reuters reports had been "amazingly absurd" and "there's astonishment and indignation that they could be believed in Germany."

Copies of this cablegram were distributed to the Foreign Office and to the German newspapers. Mencken, with his eye forever on history, saved the original for his scrapbook. "After this," he duly noted, "there was no more trouble, and German suspicions were changed to the old cordiality," as Americans were offered friendly assurances and even financial assistance to facilitate their departure.

Thus the air was cleared, not by diplomatic means but by one American newspaper correspondent and his paper, among the very ones whom Ambassador Gerard had professed to despise for giving the Germans a wrong impression of Americans.[11]

THROUGHOUT THE WAR Germans referred bitterly to Reuters as "the fabricator of War Lies" and to the Allies as "All-Lies." Even long-time American residents in Berlin were furious at these British reports devoid of factual and objective news. This phenomenon had an immense impact on Mencken and conditioned him to believe that the worst was coming from the Allied side. It was a conditioning that much later would make him insensitive to the actual atrocities perpetrated by the Nazi regime.

Meanwhile, Mencken's own outlook had improved considerably, and seeing his role as a responsible, fair-minded newspaperman convinced him to stay on in Berlin. He assumed that some of his colleagues felt the same way, but few did.

A number of correspondents, including Carl Ackerman of the United Press, were planning to return home with the ambassador if they could, and most of these, Mencken had found, were strongly anti-German. Others, like Schütte, wanted to stay until war was actually declared. Their role had been one long battle to report the war as they saw it, not as the British, German, or—later—the American censor would have it. Those who proposed to remain in Germany thought it would be a good idea for Mencken to get out, "so that I might counteract the efforts of the German-haters." Schütte told Mencken he was the only American correspondent who could be trusted, on reaching home, to refrain from libeling the Germans with "bogus revelations," or indulging in the story that Gerard and the correspondents had been held hostage.

That evening Mencken renewed his request at the Foreign Office to waive the rule specifying the waiting time before a correspondent might leave Berlin. "The gentlemen there, as always, were charming," Mencken recalled, "but they held up their hands."

"Well, let Ludendorff bestir himself," Mencken later reasoned with characteristic aplomb. With that he went out to dinner with some friends. By evening he was sound asleep, under a stack of feather bedding.[12]

He was hauled out of bed by a call from the Military Bureau. He was free to go or to stay; more, "I was a marked and favored man." It seemed incredible to Mencken that in the midst of the war, Ludendorff, who, common gossip had it, might one day be offered the chancellorship, had found time in the field to revise the rules governing American correspondents, and to hear and decide on an appeal from those rules by the last and least of them. And yet he had, as it turned out, thanks to the intervention of Schütte who had managed to get word to Ludendorff through the Foreign Office about Mencken's case. At the Military Bureau there were handshakes all around, with promises to agree to meet after the war and share a magnum of pilsner. As Mencken left the cavernous stone building for the last time and slipped out of its huge gate, he could not help but reflect: "It is hard to think of them as enemies."

After walking into the chilly, blustery day, the streets ankle-deep in slush, Mencken quickly packed his bags and headed for the train station. There, the flood of Americans trying to leave received studied courtesy from the Germans. At ten after eight the train whistled into the black and rainy night, while someone on the platform called out to the ambassador, "Good-bye, Judge." Gerard stuck his head out of the window and replied: "*Auf Wiedersehen* on Broadway." Within his compartment, the festive sound of champagne corks popping could be heard.

As the train sped toward Zurich, Mencken caught glimpses of the Thuringian Forest, dark masses of fir trees heavy with white snow that gleamed in the moonlight, looking like the ghostly setting of a fairy tale. Lying on the only available space on the floor, he wrapped his fur vest around his Corona typewriter and made it into a pillow. Outside, the moon shone; somehow, as his teeth kept chattering, Mencken managed to fall asleep: "Out of Germany at last."[13]

BACK HOME, THE FRONT PAGE of the *Baltimore Sun* ran the headline "ALL PERFECTLY SAFE, SAYS MENCKEN." His readers, however, were not easily convinced. Among the criticisms heaped on Mencken was a mocking poem, "Take Me Back to Uncle Sam."

> *Little Henry Mencken went to Germany one day,*
> *To show the Kaiser how to win the war the shortest way . . .*
> *And so this brave and true Free Lance sent up a mighty call*
> *And was so anxious to get home he couldn't wait at all . . .*

The *Sun*'s cartoon, showing Mencken sprinting for dear life across the German border, remained popular among Baltimoreans; one recalled that the clipping was kept on her father's desk for months.[14]

The farther the train sped from Germany, the more Mencken became aware of what awaited him back home. In Berne, he spent an hour perusing the past week's Paris editions of the *New York Herald* and *London Daily Mail*, full of inflammatory headlines, particularly one that announced "Mr. Gerard Held Hostage in Berlin." By contrast, throughout his stay in Germany, Mencken had not encountered the slightest hint of anti-American feeling, either in conversation or in print. "The German papers, in the midst of their worst fulminations, always speak of the foe with decency, with none of the opprobrious nicknames the British used for the Germans: Huns, pirates, or Goths." To Mencken, the fact that Americans were using disparaging language in their newspapers put the United States to shame.[15]

It was a relief for Mencken when the sun crept over the hills of southern France, his first glimpse of the country for nearly two months. From the train he could see the blue waters of the Bay of Biscay and a yellow sun beating down—a glorious vision after the dirty grays of the north. Joyfully, he leaned out of his window, soaking up the sun's soothing warmth: "It was like opium after pain."

Mencken had entered a world of light—and peace. After crossing into Spain, in La Coruña, Mencken read news of ships docking at the bay. *La Infanta Isabel*, one of the most beautiful ships in Spain's fleet, was slated to arrive at dawn and carry Ambassador Gerard, embassy staff, and other significant *yanquis* back home through a long but safe route, safely skirting the U-boat zone. Knowing that if he took a different route, he could scoop the rest of the press by writing the truth about Gerard's claim that he was held hostage, Mencken chose a different vessel. Mencken doubted if one American in ten thousand had ever heard of the ship he was sailing on. He managed to convince the American ambassador to Spain to secure him a cabin on the *Alfonso XIII* so that he could get home before any of the other reporters. "The number 13 bemuses me," Mencken wrote to his friend Ernest Boyd. "No doubt it will give encouragement to mines and U-boats."

Aboard the *Alfonso*, he discovered his cabin was below the water line. The air in this dungeon (nicknamed "the Sewer") smelled of garlic and cologne, with a jellylike consistency that clung to his hair. Mencken spent the ensuing week typing his reports in the smoke room, chewing Cuban cigars, and at mealtimes discussing tuberculosis and world events with fellow passenger Dr. Herman Biggs, the Health Commissioner of New York, over Spanish sherry and red wine.

In a few days the air had become warmer, the sea bluer and smoother; great bunches of golden seaweed floated past. By the time they approached Havana, the sea had become slick and oily, and "the Sewer" infernal: "There is such a thing, it would appear, as too much sunlight," Mencken wrote in his diary. "Three weeks ago, in freezing Berlin, I had friendly thoughts of Hell. Now I go back to the usual prejudice."

Yet it all seemed a small sacrifice to pay to get the lead on such a major story. As the *Alfonso* drew near the Bahamas, Mencken drew a sigh of relief: "The retreat from Berlin is over."[16]

A FLYING FISH PLAYFULLY LEAPT into the air, and from far away Mencken could see a lighthouse blinking on the Florida coast. Just when he was luxuriating in his freedom, to his dismay a steward from the ship handed him a yellow slip of paper:

HAVE IMPORTANT CUBA ASSIGNMENT. DO NOT LEAVE. CABLE US ARRIVAL FOR INSTRUCTIONS. THE SUN.

The assignment awaiting him in Cuba could not have been more difficult. President Mario G. Menocal, who in private life had been the manager of sugar estates for American investors, had almost been defeated for a second term by the opposing candidate, José Miguel Gomez. It was believed by most Cubans that the popular Gomez had won by an enormous majority (most regarded Menocal as little more than an American agent), but instead Menocal was counted as the winner. A revolution was on.

As Mencken recalled, "I came in utterly ignorant of the Revolution, and didn't even know the names of the leaders, and had to dig up the whole thing in a few hours notice." A wireless to his old friend, Captain Leonhard of the Munson Line—who long ago had given Mencken passage from Jamaica and who "knew everyone worth knowing in Latin America and thousands who were not"— brought him a quick passage through customs and within a hour, a visit to the Presidential Palace. Then Mencken's new companion from the ship, Dr. Herman Biggs, who knew many Cuban liberal leaders from his large medical consulting practice, whisked the *Sun* correspondent to the secret headquarters of the Revolutionists, where Mencken heard their side of the conflict.

Mencken's dispatch complete, he submitted it to the ever-present censor, who promptly proceeded to cut out everything even remotely resembling a fact. Another quick call to Captain Leonhard, and in ten minutes Mencken was aboard an American ship anchored in the harbor, where he was able to slip his completed news story into the pocket of one of the accommodating and friendly mates. This routine went on for several days. Meantime, at the cable office, other news-papermen were threatening revenge but were never able to get anything through save the official communiqué issued from the palace at hourly intervals.

Hot weather and hard work did not deter him. When Mencken was not working on the intricacies of the Cuban revolution he was sending cables on his adventures in Germany to both the *Sun* and the *New York World*. Within his tiled hotel room, the rattle of his typewriter sounded like the discharge of a machine gun. Enterprise and energy: such attributes were not lost on his paper. Mencken was the first of the Americans from Berlin to reach the other side of the Atlantic and give to the public an uncensored account of events within the American Embassy in Germany and in Cuba.

Mencken found Havana an ideal place from which to cover a revolution. The food and its people delighted him. Nonetheless, as he wormed his way through Havana's narrow streets, he noted with disillusionment that it had, for his taste, even in 1917, too much American influence. Before his fourth day, the opposition leader José Miguel Gomez was captured and the revolution ended. "It took the form of a threat from the late Dr. Lansing, then Secretary of State, that if José Miguel did not give up his evil courses at once American Marines would come in and deal with him," Mencken explained later. "José Miguel had won the election, but Menocal was preferred at Washington."

"The United States in 1899, with a great burst of rhetoric, guaranteed the Cubans free and representative government," Mencken noted with disgust. Each time, however, Cubans were subjected to being under the mercy of some "tin-pot tyrant, supported in his outrages by Washington. This is what *Cuba libre* amounts to . . ." In 1917, another revolution was casting its shadows, but Mencken did not know that then. At the time of his visit, it had been, as Mencken wrote his mother, "a very tame affair." That evening he bought the February number of the *Smart Set* at a local newsstand and read himself to sleep.[17]

Not until six days into his Cuban visit did Mencken finally write to Marion Bloom. At the bottom he signed "H," an intimacy that made its appearance for the first time. As was customary in his letters, he boasted about his work and his triumphs, but it was obvious that he genuinely missed her. Now, for the first time in all those weeks, Marion was within a reasonable distance; he would be able to hold her in his arms that very weekend. Before then, however, he cautioned her, "it is all a matter of getting rid of my job." Even Marion must have realized, as many of Mencken's women were to learn, that when work was involved, business always came before pleasure.[18]

THE BIRDS WERE ALREADY SINGING outside the French doors of his balcony when Mencken arose at 4:30 the next morning to see the *Infanta Isabel* looming out of the morning mist. Climbing on board, he greeted Ambassador Gerard, who was polite but somewhat distant. That changed, however, when they later traveled by train from Florida en route to Washington. Mencken listened as the ambassador resolutely insisted that the Germans had planned to intern all the American correspondents in Berlin, and it had been only thanks to his own diplomacy that they had changed their minds. "His talk was almost idiotic," Mencken recalled. "I knew, of course, that this was buncombe." Moreover, he had already sent in his dispatch, citing the facts, to prove it. Gerard, Mencken concluded, "was an almost fabulous ass." It convinced him that nine times out of ten, the U.S. government consistently sent the least qualified people abroad to represent the American people.

As his train sped north, Mencken had undergone a considerable transition from weeks before, when he had seen the voyage as a magnificent junket. The many examples of censorship, the practice of war news, and the anti-German feeling he had witnessed was the beginning of a compressed process of maturation for Mencken. His experience hardened the ideas he had already formed and provided a host of new evidence about notions he had earlier discussed in print, to little attention.

It was drizzling by the time their train pulled into Washington's Union Station. Gerard was almost swept off his feet by people rushing to shake hands. "I am very, very happy to get back," the ambassador told the crowd, as forty newspaper reporters and photographers pressed close. "*Auf Wiedersehen!*" said Mencken, and they shook hands over someone's shoulder.[19]

A few days later his trip ended in his reunion with Marion, waiting to hear his adventures with an encouraging smile. A woman could experience different kinds of kisses, Marion Bloom later recounted in a poem for the *Smart Set*, written after her meeting with Mencken: "Ah! There *is* a Heaven, after all!"[20]

But the happy reunion with Marion could not dispel the heavy war clouds gathering over their country and over Mencken's personal struggle as an independent and controversial public voice.

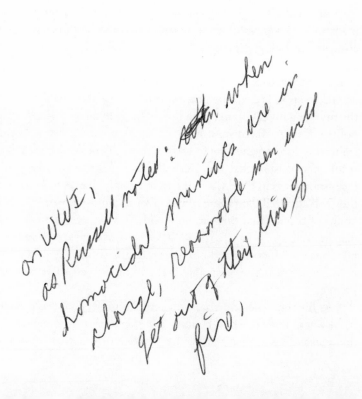

17

THE PREVAILING WINDS

ENCKEN HAD BEEN HOME for less than two weeks when a riot shook the tranquil streets of Baltimore. Nearly a thousand pro-war protesters forced open the heavy bronze doors of the Academy of Music, interrupting the speech of visiting pacifist David Starr Jordan, and with a howl began swinging their fists. Alarmed, the speaker quickly left the stage. The mob then hunted Jordan through the city well into the night, parading through the streets, chanting "We'll hang Dave Jordan to a sour apple tree." Nearly twenty people were injured. One man was beaten so badly he had to be hospitalized.

The violence was enough to convince Mencken to forego a trip to New York. "My mother and sister are here alone, and I don't want to leave them unprotected," he confided to Dreiser. "It is very likely that there will be some smashing of windows and other delicate heroics when war is declared."

The request for a declaration of war came the very next evening, on April 2, 1917, when President Woodrow Wilson told the nation that "the world must be made safe for democracy." Mencken again wrote Dreiser, "Once the world is made safe for democracy, all that will remain will be to make democracy safe for the world."[1]

The American entry into war turned Mencken's life upside down. A target of superpatriots before, he now faced even greater hostility. Within days, supporters of the war lashed out at all who stood in their way. They suggested that pacifists should be silenced, jailed, or even killed. In Baltimore, five boys who refused to salute the flag, including one who left the room during the singing of "The Star-Spangled Banner," were suspended from school and their parents were brought before the school board.

Adding to the hysteria were attacks against immigrants, pacifists, and German Americans. In Baltimore as elsewhere, German-born persons, already suffering from an acute conflict of loyalties, rushed to take out citizenship papers, changing their names from Schmidt to Smith, from Wolfsheimer to Wolf. "All men with names like yours and mine will be jailed before September, 1918," Mencken wrote to Louis Untermeyer.

The teaching of German was eliminated from public schools. German clubs disappeared. Local epidemics were blamed on contamination of the local water supply by German spies. At Baltimore's prestigious Goucher College, President William Westley Guth demanded the resignation of one of the most beloved and respected members of the faculty, Professor Hans Froelicher, on the grounds that, while declaring his complete loyalty to the United States, he had expressed sympathy for the German people. (He was, incidentally, Swiss, without a drop of German blood.)

Freedom Fries!

The hamburger became the liberty sandwich, sauerkraut, the liberty cabbage. In Congress, a resolution was introduced that would eliminate German names from cities. Streets across America were now renamed, including those of Baltimore: German Street to Redwood, while in Mencken's neighborhood, the city council debated long and hard as to whether Hollins Street should be changed to American Street.

Support for the war could be seen everywhere. In Washington, senators began to wear little enameled American flags on their coat lapels. When newspapers began publishing long poems about flags and churches—one of the worst features of the war, according to Mencken—Theodore Dreiser retrieved Mencken's youthful tribute to Rudyard Kipling's "The Orf'cer Boy" previously published in *Ventures Into Verse*, and thanked him for his patriotism.

Not a single newspaper in the whole United States, said Mencken, offered any fair play to its opponents. Instead, the worst curse of the American press was the grand moral tones of its editorials.

> The kinds of courage I really admire are not whooped up in war, but cried down, and indeed become infamous. No one, in such times . . . ever praises the man who stands out against official balderdash, and seeks to restore the national thinking, so called, to a reasonable sanity. On the contrary, he is regarded as a shabby and evil fellow, and there is not much protest when he is punished in a summary and barbaric manner, without any consideration of the evidence against him. It is sufficient that he refuses to sing the hymn currently lined out. That alone is enough to condemn him.[2]

gone padilla 2005

SHORTLY AFTERWARD, on April 9, the John Wheeler syndicate canceled its contract for Mencken's remaining articles from the German front. "In view of the rapid developments of the last few days," John Wheeler wrote, carefully wording his language, this was a time "to adhere closely to pro-Americanism."

That his *Diary of a Retreat* should be met with such censorship was, to Mencken, understandable but not forgivable. Herbert Swope's collection of

all of this buttressed HLM's view of the Booboisie, the imbecilic "Methodist"

"... the grand, gorgeous show." Third Liberty Loan Parade in Baltimore. The Maryland Historical Society, Baltimore, Maryland.

dispatches from Germany, collected in book form bearing the title *Inside the German Empire*, had been published in January to acclaim, earning him the first Pulitzer Prize ever awarded for reporting. Responding to Ellery Sedgewick's offer to find a publisher for his own book, Mencken recognized that "if I print it now I shall have to perfume it, particularly in the parts dealing with Gerard . . . whereas if I hold it until the end of the war I'll be able to tell the truth." Even so, the book was quite harmless—"but in such times as these idiots run the world."

Not wishing to leave anything to chance, Mencken took the diary and other souvenirs of his recent German trip and buried them in a box in the backyard in Hollins Street. For the next two years there they remained, hidden under brick.[3]

HIS PRECAUTIONS PROVED WISE. Only a week later, President Wilson signed an executive order creating the Committee on Public Information, responsible for publicizing the American cause. He put in charge George Creel, a former editor of the *Rocky Mountain News* of Denver, who was known for his bitter personal relations with members of the press. Creel, who had been a close political associate of President Wilson, defined his new task as a "fight for the minds of men." He made imaginative use of advertising, organized successful loan drives, and appointed public speakers. His principal contribution was the introduction of voluntary censorship by the American press.

Most major papers and magazines, such as the *New York Times*, *Los Angeles Times*, and the *Atlanta Constitution*, took a strong nationalistic stand, relaying the propaganda handed to them by Creel's committee as part of their patriotic duty, maligning any opponent of war in their news stories. Now and then Mencken would see these newspapers on the newsstand: "Headlines six inches high," he observed, "brimstone in every line." The *Detroit Free Press* and the *St. Louis Post-Dispatch* were more independent minded, but their failure to comply would be severely tested in the months to come.

Of great support to Creel in his task was the Espionage Act that took effect two months later, containing some of the broadest and most restrictive sanctions against publications in American history. To Mencken, the act was one of the most "outrageous and obviously unconstitutional laws" the nation had ever seen. Harvard lawyer and leading civil rights advocate Zechariah Chafee believed the Espionage Act went "much farther than in any other war, even in the Civil War with the enemy at our gates." The Post Office and the attorney general set the rules, with penalties of $10,000 and twenty years in prison for publishing any negative discussion of the war—including the printing of antiwar cartoons. Creel would pass documents, syndicated editorials, and circulars to the attorney general's office, suggesting that its agents make inquiries.

Within the administration, some officials found the act too drastic, a net that included the innocent as well as the guilty. Nonetheless, two hundred prosecutions resulted for speeches, newspaper articles, magazines, and books. Those who suffered most were the little newspapers and socialist publications, along with the foreign-language press. Among the victims were the *Milwaukee Leader*, the *New York Call*, the *Masses*, and the more conservative *Christian Science Monitor*.

Aiding in silencing opponents of war were such private organizations as the Boy Spies of America, the American Protective League, American Defense Society, Liberty League, All-Allied Anti-German League, Knights of Liberty, and, most repressively, the American Protective League, with units in six hundred cities and an ever-growing membership of volunteers to inform on their fellow citizens. "There must be at least 100,000 detectives in the United States," Mencken guessed, but his assumption was an underestimate: the American Protective League alone boasted a membership of 250,000.

When Mencken suggested casually to John Halsup Adams, editorial writer for the *Sun*, that these new laws were bound to bear heavily on many German Americans who were completely innocent, "his reply startled but did not surprise me. What he said, in brief, was that they deserved it for being Germans. Their sufferings, he told me, did not interest him."[4]

Such bigotry did not deter Mencken from writing for other papers now that the *Sun* was closed to him. That June he was busy writing articles for the *New York Evening Mail*. His articles from Germany had always interested the publisher, who was now pleased to include his column as a regular feature. "No man," publisher Edward Rumley wrote, "was ever selected in the *Mail* because of his pro-German antecedents." They were chosen "because they had background that enabled them to make the kind of paper that I had in mind." What he had in mind was a balanced press organ catering to those readers who had been dissatisfied with the increasingly intolerant trend of the majority of American newspapers.

But with the Espionage Act in effect, Mencken noted, Rumley had hard sledding. It was impossible to write articles about war "save in terms of prevailing blather," so Mencken's arrangement consisted of writing two articles a week with the proviso that they would not discuss the war. "More than one of my articles had to be suppressed," Mencken recalled; all the same, he made sure he was able to "get in a few licks for free speech."

Mencken's topics, in more than 120 pieces, ranged from his admiration for suffragettes and Mark Twain to his observations about food and the language spoken in the trenches. Once, when he was ill and forced to spend time in bed, he spent the week reading back issues of the *Congressional Record* and the debates on war legislation. This inspired him to write a column advising his readers to subscribe to the *Record* to get a literal report about Congress that differed from highly slanted newspaper reports. The column was his first exposure to a newspaper audience outside of Baltimore. More than once, editors refrained from running Mencken at all. One of them confessed to a colleague that his controversial views were considered by other newspapermen to be "a little raw."[5]

THROUGHOUT 1917 AND LATER YEARS, Mencken's attention turned increasingly to racial themes. Nothing could be more ironic than the drafting of blacks to save the world for democracy when they were being denied every vestige of that democracy. Woodrow Wilson had disappointed African American leaders who cared about civil rights; he had instituted segregation in government offices where it had not existed before. The administration began taking steps to silence black dissidents, suppressing African American publications and placing individuals under surveillance. Moreover, lynching had steadily increased in the South, and Washington officials, busy saving the world from the Huns, had little to say about those heinous crimes. The NAACP tried unsuccessfully to have Congress outlaw lynching as a war measure.

Until this point, Mencken had not commented on the civil rights of blacks. But since the beginning of the war, when it began to dawn on him that, as a German American, he was "a member of a race lately in worse odor among 100% Americans than either Jews or Negroes," a new passion for those who were being discriminated against had taken hold of him.

As a German American who felt separated from American society, Mencken began to gain insights toward one group that he had derided years earlier. During these uncertain times, he made friends with James Weldon Johnson, then writing for the *New York Age*. The black social reformer was determined to meet the *Smart Set* editor, for as he said later, "Mencken had made a sharper impression on my mind than any American then writing." When the two finally did meet, Johnson recalled: "I had never been so fascinated at hearing anyone talk. He talked about literature, about Negro literature, the Negro problem, and Negro music." He felt "buoyed up . . . as though I had taken a mental cocktail."

Then and there began a collaboration that would anticipate many of the themes of the later Harlem Renaissance. Johnson told his black readers Mencken was not just "the cleverest writer in America today"—"the best part of Mencken is truth." When a group of black leaders in Maryland sought an interview with the president to discuss race riots, Wilson, apparently, was too busy to receive them, prompting Dr. Kelly Miller of Howard University to write a letter to the White House. Mencken wrote an article, "Negro Spokesman Arises to Voice His Race's Wrongs," calling attention to "the ablest document the war has yet produced in the United States." Mencken felt Miller's letter put the South and all white Anglo-Saxons to shame.

With a sweeping indictment of the beaux arts aptly named "The Sahara of the Bozart," Mencken also cited the demise of a culture that once flourished. He observed: "Once you have counted James Branch Cabell you will not find a single Southern novelist whose work shows any originality or vitality." Writing to Cabell one year later, Burton Rascoe reminisced how, as a newspaper editor, he had the "sudden suspicion that I was endangering my job" if he printed "The Sahara of the Bozart" without his managing editor's approval. He showed it to his boss, "who read it with many chuckles of delight and then asked me to hold it over until he had conferred with the chief editorial writer. Came next day a note saying that he thought I had better not use it."

James Weldon Johnson, on the other hand, was not deterred by Mencken's severity; indeed, he felt Mencken had not gone far enough. Taking his cue from Johnson, Mencken would later revise "The Sahara of the Bozart," going so far as to maintain that hope for Southern literature and culture lay in the hands of black writers. In the columns of the *Evening Mail*, meanwhile, he began exploring the possibility of the Great Negro Novel.[6]

THROUGHOUT 1917 AND 1918, Mencken continued to write on a variety of subjects. As a relief from "the patriotic libido" he saw printed daily in the American press, Mencken wrote a humorous article on the supposed history of the bathtub, "A Neglected Anniversary." The article told how one of those contraptions was first built in Cincinnati during 1842 and was eventually installed in the White House. There was a bit of Peck's Bad Boy in Mencken, who took a certain pride in this burlesque creation: "I had confidence that the customers of the *Evening Mail* would like it."

They liked it too well. Clippings circulated across the country; Mencken's hoax was reprinted in newspapers, magazines, and books. It was alluded to on the floor of Congress, became the subject of talks in weekly luncheons of Kiwanis clubs, and was discussed solemnly in England and on the Continent. As time passed, Mencken's satisfaction turned to consternation, and he appealed to historians to eliminate it from standard works of reference. When it came to his bathtub hoax, Mencken concluded, "there is something in the human mind that turns instinctively to fiction, and that even journalists succumb." What remains to the world, Mencken argued, "is a series of long tested and solidly agreeable lies."

MENCKEN HAD NOT FORGOTTEN HIS SERIOUS WRITING. Returning to his manuscript for *A Book of Prefaces* that spring, he now felt the whole work needed to be rewritten, a Herculean effort and far more labor than he had originally intended. By the time Mencken finished, it was July, and the temperature in his workroom was 98 degrees. "If the book is warped," Mencken said, "blame the gods. It left me old, haggard, and used up. If I die, bury me beneath it."7

Alfred A. Knopf, whom Mencken had met in 1913, received the manuscript. Subsidized by his father, Alfred had started his own firm, working in one room with the assistance of Blanche Wolf, who shortly became his wife and vice president of the firm. Both were diligent students of design. Before long, the Prussian thoroughness and the lavish interest Knopf paid to all the details of his books became a byword in the trade. If the history of publishing was ever written, Mencken once declared, Knopf must have credit in it for what amounted to a revolution.

Samuel Knopf, who had previously regarded his son's activities as distinguished but unprofitable, became the company's treasurer and began devoting most of his time to the business side of the firm. Novelists such as Theodore Dreiser and Ellen Glasgow were under contract with older firms. Nonetheless, authors on their list included best-selling author Joseph Hergesheimer, whose novels made the firm an even greater success, and H. L. Mencken, whose *Book of Prefaces* now bore the Knopf imprint.8

Mencken, for his part, thought *A Book of Prefaces* had been his most important book in its effect on his professional career. Although Mencken said the aim of *Prefaces* was to clear the way for writers of genuine talent, the volume was political as much as it was literary. Its essays on Dreiser, Huneker, and Conrad were familiar material to his readers. Far more important was Mencken's own admittedly "headlong and uncompromising attack upon the American *Kultur* ever made up to that time," an 85-page discussion on "Puritanism as a Literary Force." In it, he attacked the Puritan's "unmatchable intolerance of opposition, his unbreakable belief in his own bleak and narrow views, his savage cruelty of attack, his lust for relentless and barbarous persecution," all of which "have put an almost unbearable burden upon the exchange of ideas in the United States."

Mencken was not surprised to find that the most negative reviews originated in the South, where Mencken's German American background was denigrated. But the review Mencken resented most was written by Stuart Pratt Sherman, an English professor at the University of Illinois. He was among the Puritans, according to Mencken, who "simply wrap the Grand Old Flag around them." Taking advantage of the war hysteria, the unscrupulous Sherman gave force to the rumor that Mencken was engaged in traitorous activities and secretly taking pay from the German government, lumping Mencken in with Dreiser and Alfred Knopf. Such "patriotic piffle," Mencken confided, made Knopf "scared stiff" and prompted him to loudly reaffirm his patriotism by writing a letter of protest to Sherman. "Knopf seems to be a doubly-damned ass," Mencken exploded. "He will get no more books of mine." If free speech was too dangerous to a democracy to be permitted, Mencken vowed to print his books in Zurich or Leipzig. The dispute, albeit temporary, was never acknowledged by either man. In later years, Knopf said he had no recollection of any quarrel.

Meanwhile, at the University of Illinois, students listened to their teacher, Stuart Sherman, vigorously condemning a man whose name they had never heard before. "Many of us got the urge to know more about H. L. Mencken," one said later. "So we became readers of the *Smart Set.*"⁹

Now that America had declared war on Germany, professional patriots who remembered Mencken's denunciations from his columns openly attacked him. In efforts to ascertain if Mencken was a dangerous alien enemy, a flurry of solemn reports were dutifully filed at the Department of Justice.

Not even the Saturday Night Club was immune from scrutiny from the volunteer spy agents. One Baltimore informer was convinced he saw H. L. Mencken and a group of various men (all, he observed, of Teutonic appearance) communicating in German, English, and (most suspicious of all) in sign language. He was quite horrified when his gawking was noticed by one man, who, upon leaving the restaurant, "winked at me."

To assist other agents in the field, a purported sketch of Mencken was sent to the attorney general. Dutifully filed was a cartoon of a bearded German academic —none other than the lampoon drawn in 1913 during Mencken's "Free Lance" days on the *Baltimore Evening Sun*!

Letters from Mencken to his friends arrived opened, with the War Department seal plainly marked; tips reached him that his house on Hollins Street was to be searched. On another occasion, an attempt was made to lure him into a compromising position. One time, Mencken recalled, "a plausible looking young man asked me to take charge of what he said was the manuscript of a book on Nietzsche, allegedly of his composition. He said that he was going to the war, and feared that his poor old mother might read it, and, since she was a pious woman, destroy it."

In an unpublished manuscript, author James Cain wrote:

"That," said Mencken, "was when I woke up. I took him by the lapels, gave him a shake, and told him: 'You're no writer at all—you're a federal agent, aren't you? Sent here to frame me, to send me to prison for the stuff you've got in that briefcase.' The fellow broke down, admitted it, begged me to forget it, and swore he never wanted the assignment in the first place."

There was more to the story that Cain could not recall, "but what lingered with me are the glint in [Mencken's] eye, the edge in his voice, the jerky mode of his teeth as he told that very strange tale. . . . He wouldn't have been human if the whole thing didn't affect him the rest of his life."[10]

No one in America, Mencken told friends abroad, seemed free of persecution by volunteer spies. This was the experience of his former colleague, Willard Huntington Wright, on the staff of the *New York Evening Mail*, annoyed by a stenographer whom he found nosing through his papers. Laying a trap, he dictated a decoy letter full of German names. She called the Secret Service, who rushed to the scene with police and arrested both Wright and the stenographer. The charges were subsequently dropped. Wright later dismissed it all as "a comedy."

When Mencken learned that Wright had given the name of a mutual friend to the stenographer in jest, and that friend was subsequently investigated by the Secret Service, he blamed him for the entire affair. "To put such burdens on innocent friends in crazy days such as these is an unforgivable offense," Mencken wrote his friend Ernest Boyd.

Indeed, Mencken's circle of friends, rapidly widened since 1914, began to narrow. His dissent from the prevailing American opinion about the war, he later reflected, "cut me off from some amusing and perhaps even valuable companionships, and certainly increased my feeling of aloofness from everything American." Those who were put on ice included not only Wright but also German American friends from the *Baltimore Herald*, who denied their German ancestry and professed to be 100 percent American. Among them was his old companion from the *Herald* days, Wells Hawks, who had now joined the hothouse growth of press agents, a group, Mencken thought, infested by bounders.

As he put it, "I simply can't get on with those indifferent to common decency." He so classified Dreiser, though many friends had tried, since their break in 1916, to bring the two back together. "I see no way to avoid it," Mencken remarked on this lifelong penchant for shedding friends—a habit that in the years ahead would also claim George Jean Nathan. "All those men adored Henry yet he washed them down the drain," Marion Bloom later reflected. His lack of constancy toward friends was a side that "made Henry seem mean and nasty."

As cruel as these dismissals may have seemed, Marion also realized they caused Mencken a certain degree of pain and regret. "Whenever somebody goes to the dogs he blares like an old elephant," Marion recalled, one of the few who came closest to breaking his outer shell.

"In brief, I suddenly find myself very lonely in New York," Mencken wrote at the time. On the other hand, many could never forget Mencken's acts of generosity during those years: acquaintances who received comfort in prison; or the soldier, stationed at a military camp, who had been invited to partake in the Saturday Night Club. "Mencken knew I was lonely, and saw to it that I was taken into the bosom of his little musical and beer-drinking group. The man's heart and soul are even bigger than his mind."[11]

DURING THESE TROUBLING DAYS Mencken met Philip Goodman, a Philadelphian who shared his devotion to Germany. Goodman had moved to New York to go into advertising; he soon became one of the highest paid consultants in the country. But he later made his fortune in musicals, introducing W. C. Fields to the world with *Poppy*. Soon, Goodman's *The Five O'Clock Girl* became one of the favorite shows on Broadway.

Mencken and Goodman took to each other on very short acquaintance. Like everything else about him—in size, appetite, and generosity—Goodman thought big. He wore a derby hat slightly cocked, an expensive walrus-skin coat, and was handsome, thick, and stocky, with, as James Cain put it, "a boulevardish air that completely captivated Mencken." In addition, as the product of a German Jewish background, he was in love with all things German. As his daughter Ruth recalled, both men "came together believing that Germany was the most cultured country in Europe and that England consisted of a pile of frauds."[12]

For his part, Goodman looked up to Mencken as someone who had made journalism into a fine art. Functioning briefly as a publisher, he brought out Mencken's next book, *Damn! A Book of Calumny*, for sale at discount in drugstores—an ambitious scheme ahead of its time. The book failed to attract readers, but it did attract publicity.

Most critics seemed to base their reviews on the title, without bothering to read the book, and viewed it as cynical and immoral. "Imagine such hollow platitudes shocking anyone!" commented Mencken. His very first chapter began fairly innocently, or so he thought:

> If George Washington were alive today, what a shining mark he would be for the whole camorra of uplifters, forward-lookers and professional patriots! . . . He was not pious. He drank whisky whenever he felt chilly, and kept a jug of it handy. He knew far more profanity than Scripture, and used it and enjoyed it more. . . . He took no interest in the private morals of his neighbors. Inhabiting These States today, George would be ineligible to any office of honor or profit. The Senate would never dare confirm him; the President would not think of nominating him . . . the Methodists of his native State would be denouncing him (he had a still at Mount Vernon) as a debaucher of youth. . . . And what a chance there would be for that ambitious young district attorney who thought to shadow him on his peregrinations—and grab him under the Mann Act!

Inevitably, a complaint was sent to the Department of Justice. "I came across a vicious and atrocious attack upon George Washington in a book called 'Damn' by one H. L. Menken," wrote one informer, in a letter full of spelling mistakes. Not only was Mencken unpatriotic; he had charged "Washington for being a drunkard."

The American Protective League assigned the matter to one of its members, Eltinge Warner, publisher of the *Smart Set*, who, in great discomfort, showed the letter to its editor. Mencken helped him in composing a reply. Enclosed in his

Philip Goodman. Courtesy Jack Sanders and Judy Sanger.

letter was a direct challenge from Mencken, not one to avoid confrontation with the entire system head on.

Censorship, "with all its usual imbecility," Mencken told Ernest Boyd, had become the fate of *Damn!* "on the ground that it accuses George Washington of fornication, and is hence unpatriotic. The libel is ameliorated in a new edition. I am glad George is not alive. He would probably sue me for making a Methodist of him."[13]

AFTER MENCKEN FINISHED *Damn!*, he turned to another subject: women. In order to avoid irritation of the censor, Mencken was determined this new work would be a simple *"pastiche* of proverbs." That "pastiche," to many of his readers, seemed different from Mencken's earlier style. Others found *In Defense of Women* held greater syntactical percussion, better cadence, and more elegance than his earlier writing. Its language differed from that of his articles in the *Evening Mail*, certainly, but in its device of humor it remained the same.

The argument was one that that Mencken had been formulating for years:

A man's women folk, whatever their outward show of respect for his merit and authority, always regard him secretly as an ass, and with something akin to pity. His most gaudy sayings and doings seldom deceive them; they see the actual man within, and know him for a shallow and pathetic fellow. In this fact, perhaps, lies one of the best proofs of feminine intelligence, or, as the common phrase makes it, feminine intuition. The mark of that so-called intuition is simply a sharp and accurate perception of reality, an habitual immunity to emotional enchantment, a relentless capacity for distinguishing between the appearance and the substance. The appearance, in the normal family circle, is a hero, a magnifico, a demigod. The substance is a poor mountebank.

For too long, Mencken wrote, men had placed women in "preposterous grooves," simply because they were far too vain to admit women's superior attributes. "They are enormously dangerous and hence enormously fascinating," Mencken said; to the average man, they offered "the only grand hazard that he ever encounters. Take them away and his existence would be as flat and secure as that of a milch-cow." They were clearly the thoughts of a young man susceptible to the attractions of "the eternal feminine," a phrase of Goethe's that Mencken now changed to "the infernal feminine." Mencken's own taste in female beauty, as his colleague Nathan had observed, "runs to a slim hussy, not too young, with dark eyes and a relish for wit."[14]

The object of his affection continued throughout this period to be Marion Bloom, though in a letter to Dreiser he marveled that she could even sit on a train with him, "a man so hideous and in such a state of nerves,"—a condition he attributed to the world situation, which "made men jumpy, flighty and violent in their reactions."

By the summer of 1918, events had reached such a pass that Mencken said he felt like "a homesick foreigner." It heightened his desire for music, which, especially now, remained his greatest support and comfort in the attempt to organize the chaos that surrounded him.

Wandering through the house on the eve of the Fourth of July, Mencken was unable to work as neighboring children set off a din of fireworks up and down Hollins Street. In anticipation of the national holiday, President Wilson had approved special parades to which the foreign-born were asked to give 100 percent support to indicate their loyalty. Finding himself at the piano, Mencken began to play a Mozart sonata to escape from the abominable cacophony of the actual world. The man who uses and esteems art most, Mencken reflected, is simply the man who is out of conceit with the life of his race and time. "It is not without reason that the artist, at all times everywhere, has been regarded as malcontent and anti-social by the average respectable citizen."[15]

Only a few days later, when Mencken was back in New York, publisher Edward Rumley was arrested, charged with purchasing the *Evening Mail* with money supplied by the German government and making it a principal outlet for German propaganda in the United States. For four days Mencken was hounded by sleuths on his trail, but, he reflected sourly, "this sort of thing is now usual." Almost immediately, the Committee on Public Information, although admitting the case against Rumley had not been proved in court, sent hundreds of flyers to the national press, suggesting they flash it on their front pages. The case of Rumley, read the flyer, "Preaches to Us a Lesson: *Be on the alert, be on guard, be not deceived!*"

It would be the second time in Mencken's career that the newspaper on which he worked had fallen to pieces: first, it had been the *Herald*. Now, with the *New York Evening Mail* suppressed, "I stopped writing and believed I was done with newspaper work forever."[16]

Mencken still could count on working on the *Smart Set*, but even here he was doubtful about how long the magazine could continue. Like most editors of that time, Mencken and Nathan were encountering almost insurmountable wartime difficulties: loss of circulation, an increase of postal rates, and tremendous costs for paper. That paper was so full of wood pulp that Mencken allowed if readers found fault with it, at least they could chop it up and use it for toothpicks. With so many authors at the front, Mencken found it difficult to put together an issue; he and Nathan were reduced to relying on literary agents even for the most mediocre material, leading Mencken to observe that the trade "is full of dolts who merely collect commissions." Neither Mencken nor Nathan had collected a salary for months.

Mencken and Nathan studiously avoided printing anything about the war in the *Smart Set*. They well knew that even the mildest criticism would be considered subversive, even traitorous. According to Creel, "It is not alone the people of the United States who are on trial, but the press of the United States as well." When Mencken alluded to war at all, it was, he described, "with scarcely concealed derision for the great crusade to save humanity."

To his credit, the publisher of the *Smart Set* did not try to influence Mencken's and Nathan's editorial policy, though Warner insisted on printing patriotic advertisements. The American flag flapped from the office window, and he enjoyed giving notice of the *Smart Set*'s unanimous participation in buying war bonds. Nonetheless, Warner's wartime activities brought Mencken to the unhappy conclusion that he was "something of a bounder." His joining the American Protective League meant he also had a hand in rounding up German nationals. "Warner gloated over it, and once, I remember, he entertained Nathan and me by describing how terrified some of the victims were when he and his gallant associates asked them where they wanted their bodies sent. He was somewhat taken aback when Nathan and I let him understand that we thought such poltrooneries were disgusting."

That fall, the Committee on Public Information decided to take over the *Smart Set*'s building for its New York bureau, forcing the magazine to move. "The thing is very vexing and costly," Mencken complained. "Unless the government reimburses us for our added expenses we'll be in a hell of a hole. We run in bad luck. On all sides are fellows making fortunes out of the war, but to us it is a very heavy financial burden."

Those fortunes, Mencken said, staggered the imagination. Now the loudest patriots rolled up billions. Babbitts had been made overnight. On the train from Baltimore to New York, Mencken overheard the gabble of these types: "Their air was that of men who had struck it rich. They talked in figures and smoked large cigars. . . . They constitute the backbone of the right thinking, conservative *bloc* today, and are unanimously in favor of another war, if necessary, to denounce Bolshevism."[17]

JUST WHEN THE *SMART SET* HAD SETTLED into different quarters, a new development threatened its future. Mencken and Nathan, both young, both bachelors, and thus supremely eligible, were shortly to be drafted into the infantry. Nathan announced that he was studying the piccolo and he would serve as a field musician, aware that the medical board would, as it did, reject him for his poor eyesight. "George is palpably unfit physically," Mencken wrote Boyd, "but I suppose my own gaudy physique will fetch me despite my asthma, piles, tongue trouble, hay fever, alcoholic liver, weak heels, dandruff, etc." After that, "what will follow, God alone knows. If they take me with my asthma, my barks will at least alarm the Hun."

Many of Mencken's friends had been called up much earlier. He had gotten his younger brother and other individuals excused from the draft in a persuasive letter to the secretary of war. As for himself, friends from Johns Hopkins proposed he assemble a medical history of the war. That August, Mencken wrote a letter to officials at the surgeon general's library.

A week later, military officials wrote him that he had "queered" himself for any government job by things he had written. Resigned, Mencken wrote to a friend: "My experience is fine for the medical department, but that is already overcrowded, so, as a bachelor, I'll probably draw the infantry." Though irritated, he was amused by the vision that conjured up. "Picture me, with my weight, digging ditches and learning the goose-step! After all, there are some humors in war."[18]

→ as now: Halliburton, KBR,
    Blackwater

18

OVER HERE

A T SEVEN O'CLOCK IN THE MORNING of September 12, 1918, Baltimore awoke to the sound of the bells of the City Hall booming a hundred times. Factory whistles took up their chorus, calling Maryland's men to join those at the front. "'Twill be a great day!" read the *Sun*'s lead editorial in lofty moral tones that Mencken derided as "mainly idiotic." Only the day before, the *Sun* had printed its daily list of casualties that filled a full page. Other newspapers also exalted the day's significance for the state: "There never was a September 12 like this, there will never be another like it."

All men between the ages of 18 and 45 now had to register for the draft, and failure to do so could lead to imprisonment. As military bands marched through the streets, half of the hundreds enrolling in service fully expected to be toting a gun before Christmas.

Inside a small room, sitting behind a pile of gray-blue cards, a uniformed clerk curtly addressed the next man in line.

"Name in full."

"Henry Louis Mencken."

"Name of nearest relative?"

"Mrs. Anna Mencken."

The clerk perfunctorily jotted down a description of the man in front of him: medium height, brown hair, no physical disability whatsoever to prevent war service.

"Date of birth?"

Only the army's newest registrant could appreciate the irony of the occasion: the day of his signing up, was, in fact, Mencken's thirty-eighth birthday. "Perhaps

"I am for the hellish Deutsche until hell freezes over." Star Spangled Centennial, Howard Street, Baltimore. The Maryland Historical Society, Baltimore, Maryland.

it may be God's will that we meet at the front, and jointly horn the abhorrent Hun," Mencken wrote to Dreiser. "I grow more patriotic every day."[1]

Many of the newspapers agreed with the *Sun* that this was "the real romance of the times," that "soldiers are everywhere." Walking through Baltimore, one could not escape the sight of servicemen and civilians alike saluting each other and repeating "On to Berlin!" To all this the editorial added: "Here's hoping that our bully boys may never stop going until they have burned the Palace at Potsdam and marched down the Unter den Linden singing 'The Star-Spangled Banner.'"

Mencken's focus, however, was not on Potsdam but on a growing situation at home that threatened to undermine civil liberties. "Let the troops come home to beer, not to bootleggers," he stated. Throughout the previous year he had been writing articles observing how Prohibitionists had been "trying to ram their peruna down the national gullet under cover of a great clatter for God and country." Not one congressman, Mencken noted in disgust, had been bold enough to tackle the reformers. It led him to conclude that congressmen were simply "a poor lot of sticks" with "the courage of a cow."

On the subject of Prohibition, Mencken was not an optimist. What awaited him, as well as all those soldiers returning from war, was a future of beverages drunk surreptitiously in the privacy of the garage. Against this dismal eventuality, Mencken had laid in his own stock of liquor provisions, bought with the proceeds from the sale of his Studebaker car some weeks earlier. In the cellar of Hollins Street, hundreds of bottles of good whiskey, prime beer, and Spanish wine glistened on the shelves of a newly built room, which now began to smell sweetly of the grape. On its door, Mencken hung a metal sign:

> THIS VAULT IS PROTECTED BY
> A DEVICE RELEASING CHLORINE
> GAS UNDER 200 POUNDS PRESSURE.
> ENTER IT AT YOUR OWN RISK.

To readers of the *Smart Set* he added the advice:

> Go thou and do likewise. See to your locks and chain-bolts, and get a smallpox sign to hang upon the door. Hire a confirmed diabetic to mount guard. Fill every third bottle with nitroglycerine, that heaven may swiftly welcome any righteous scoundrel who horns in.

The advent of Prohibition was not his only concern. "In the Middle West," he wrote, "there is also a growing movement against tobacco. In a few years you will see a republic that is chemically pure. Pray for the day."[2]

THE SUMMER HEAT HAD NOT YET PASSED, and at Hollins Street the backyard was still in a blaze of sunlight. In the rich beds of the garden, Anna's phlox and zinnias bloomed in abundance, and for many weeks the family was treated to her harvest of tomatoes. Helping her mother was Gertrude, who had begun a flower garden under the shade of the pear tree. In the heat of day, that corner seemed lush and cool with her plantings of ferns and violets.

Earlier Mencken had retrieved a schoolboy textbook from 1892 and had begun studying the number of bricks needed to build a garden wall. He discovered there was more to the ancient handicraft than muscle: he had to deal with hard, immovable lines, precise distances, and mathematical levels. Years later, small crumbs of brick, dirt, and leaves still clung to the pages. Perhaps never before did a former schoolbook occupy Mencken so pleasantly. Later, he built a fountain to entertain his niece.

Meanwhile, in the house, workmen hauled out the old coal furnace and replaced it with one using gas, equipped with a thermostat that Mencken could set at any degree required. It was a memorable day for him, "for it saw me move at one leap from an inferno into a sort of paradise." No longer was he subjected to heaving coal and shifting ashes; no longer was anyone in the family too hot or too cold. The cellar became so roomy that Mencken was able to enlarge his wine room, add a vault for his papers, and even set up a carpenter shop. That such a simple device could bring so much promised relief and comfort made him feel like working.[3]

With this new sense of liberation, Mencken soon took on a subject that would ever after identify him as a uniquely American voice. The *New York Evening Mail* was closed to him and the *Smart Set* was in peril. There seemed only one neutral topic not likely to arouse the hostility of the Espionage Society, yet sufficiently engrossing to appeal to the general public: the American language. Such a work, Mencken felt, would probably be "my swan song." Through the humid months, a shirtless Mencken could be found upstairs on his sleeping porch surrounded by piles of heavy books and dictionaries. There, in the afternoon, he would sweat through each tome, dog-earing the pages and jotting notes, digging out articles he had written for the *Evening Sun*, the *Smart Set*, and the *New York Evening Mail*, and other helpful contributions from American and British friends over the years. From the chaos, the collection fell into a certain order.

The material on hand was not extensive. In 1918, linguistics as a science was hardly recognized at all. In that era of genteel tradition, the concerted aims of educators were to preserve the sanctity of the King's English, with the implicit understanding that American English was inferior to the British variety. On the large and important subject of American pronunciation and spelling, for example, Mencken could find only a few casual essays, and even less on grammar. But the difference between the English and the American language was a subject that had preoccupied America since colonial days. As early as 1789, in a letter to Benjamin Franklin, Noah Webster had foreseen that a new country and its relations with Indian tribes would produce a new vocabulary. Not only in words alone did the two languages differ. Much later, in 1882, Mark Twain remarked that, when he spoke his native tongue in England, an Englishman could hardly understand him.

To this observation Mencken added some of his own. No American, Mencken noted, would think of sounding the Italian "z" sound in "piazza," but an Englishman did. In the same way, Americans transformed "cello" to "shello." At a concert Mencken once heard a man pronounce "scherzo" as if it were spelled "shirtso." Opening the *Congressional Record* at random Mencken was sure to find "He don't." Yet, the bulk of the material Mencken unearthed was devoted "to absurd efforts to prove that no such thing as an American variety of English existed—that the differences I constantly encountered in English and my English friends encountered in American were chiefly imaginary."

"No professional scholar of the time would have dreamed of presenting a discussion of the totality of American English," noted linguist Raven I. McDavid Jr. In this role, Mencken was ideally suited. As one trained to observe the world around him, as a social historian, and as a critic of what he called the *booboisie*, Mencken was able to summarize information in a clear style. By comparison, the writing by linguists seemed dull.

That task, even for a writer as talented as Mencken, was not always easy. "This tome is infinitely laborious and vexatious—a matter of writing and rewriting," Mencken told Ernest Boyd. Nevertheless, after six months work he had typed the last sentence of *The American Language*. "It is anything but an exhaustive treatise upon the subject," he added modestly. "All it pretends to do is to articulate some of those materials—to get some approach to order and coherence into them, and so pave the way for a better work by some more competent man. That work calls for the equipment of a first-rate philologist, which I surely am not." What he called "that damned American language book," Mencken privately described to friends as "a heavy, indigestible piece of cottage cheese." As for pursuing the subject further, Mencken assured them, "Never again! Such professorial jobs are not for me."

Mercifully, a small edition was planned.[4]

THROUGHOUT THE AUTUMN OF 1918, as Mencken was struggling to complete the indexes to *The American Language*, an outbreak of influenza struck the nation. Each day columns of obituaries filled the papers, as many as 1,500 a week. More civilians had died than troops abroad. "All that could be seen from our house were funerals," August Mencken recalled. Outside the window, the mournful sound of wagons could be heard on nearby Lombard Street, carrying the day's dead to outlying cemeteries.

Nathan's brother had died of the flu; so had twenty men and women of Mencken's acquaintance; it was not uncommon for Mencken to see fifty coffins piled in a shed at Union Station in Washington. He continued to plow through his material; throughout he felt in a muggy state, suspecting he might have influenza himself. While the war raged on, and although the air resounded with talk of peace, Mencken's own prognosis was gloomy.

Then, at three o'clock in the morning of November 11, 1918, the siren at the *Sun* office began to blow, joined by one church bell after another. As the sun rose, jubilant Baltimoreans took to the streets. Above them the air was white with fluttering fragments floating from open windows. A band appeared in front of the *Sun* building, and from the center of the city thousands began to sing "The Star-Spangled Banner."

From every street huge army trucks lumbered by, loaded with children beating on metal drums and waving flags. A courtly gentleman embraced a charwoman at Baltimore and Charles Streets: "My son is coming home," she said. "So is mine," he retorted.

The courts, the public schools, the stock exchange closed down; everybody quit work for a municipal holiday. Armistice was signed. The war was over. At Hollins Street, the city's victory jubilee filled the house. It was one constant, heavy, uninterrupted throb, pierced at intervals by yells of joy from outside.

"What thinks the erstwhile Free Lance now?" asked a reader of the *Evening Sun* in a letter to the editor. "Does Mencken still think the same German thoughts, the same German brutalities, the same German bombast and egotism of yore? What a typical German fraud Henry L. Mencken has been!"[5]

Germany was indeed very much on Mencken's mind, and his thoughts now turned to the fate of those men he had befriended in that country during 1917. The scope of their country's defeat came as a tremendous jolt. For years the Germans had been ignorant of the number of their casualties, only to discover that the greatest toll had been nearly two million fatalities.

During the unhappy months spanning the Treaty of Versailles, Mencken flirted again with the idea of moving to Munich or settling near Orkufstein and never coming back to the United States. Sensing a kindred spirit, German Americans living abroad wrote to Mencken telling how bitter they felt. "I left America," one of them commented, "because, less hopeful or perhaps less courageous than yourself, I felt that it was futile to fight against these things. But had I known you in those days . . . I might have remained."[6]

THE WAR'S IMPACT ON FREE SPEECH at home made Mencken realize how dramatically the United States had changed. In the fall of 1919, just six months after the triumphant parades of returning troops, Attorney General Alexander Mitchell Palmer ordered a series of brutal raids on hundreds of suspected radicals. "The whole point of government," Mencken observed, "was concentrated upon throwing the plain people into a panic." Driven by the fierce wave of xenophobia and isolationism, the fear of foreigners increased, causing German Americans to feel even more severely alienated from American society. Mencken was no exception. More than ever before, as he wrote one correspondent, he was "standing on the outside looking in," only this time, the shock of the world war had carried him all the way; he felt purged of any remaining vestiges of patriotism or sentiment towards the United States: "It was a great joy to be thus set free."

Ironically, at this time, Mencken became more involved with his country than ever before, as his passion for the Constitution and the Bill of Rights intensified. The war upon free speech should be the subject for a book, in which the full record "must be printed," Mencken argued. "The whole story will come out one day—but no one will believe it," he wrote to his friend Fielding Garrison, agreeing with Union Army commander George Gordon Meade "that history always lies. You will recall that he refused to write a book on the Civil War on that ground: he said so many lies were already believed in 1866 that it would be hopeless to attempt to blow them up."

Meade's sentiment notwithstanding, Mencken intended to remind Americans, whenever he could, of this period of "complete abandonment of all decency, decorum, and self-respect," simply because "the facts must be remembered with shame by every civilized American." He realized that the American people might never again be able to enjoy the individual freedom to the extent known before the war. After his own experience, Mencken was unrestrained in expressing his opinions, and they helped propel him toward one of his greatest victories.

Before 1919 came to an end, a new kind of audience was ready to follow him into battle.[7]

ONE OF THE FIRST SIGNS of what the upcoming decade held in store for Mencken came that spring, when the reviews of *The American Language* arrived. The book's reception surprised Mencken and Knopf; most of the 1,500 copies printed had quickly sold. Mencken was now being hailed as "the Christopher Columbus of Americanese." Even *Modern Philology*, an academic journal primarily concerned with language studies, found much to commend.

Far from deploring the work, George O. Curme of Northwestern, considered one of the great historical grammarians in the United States, and Brander Matthews of Columbia, a sensitive observer of Americanisms, accepted *The American Language* on its merits: "as a synthesis of available information, in its appeal for more research, and the obvious delight its author took in recording the variegated uses of language." Even the footnotes were as good as his text. "But the truly marvelous thing," commented critic Jacques Barzun, "is that all these facts, which could be as heavy as lead, and as gray, float and sparkle on a vast Mississippi of comment that sweeps us along and puts everything in its place. . . . As such it stands high in the tradition of the great amateurs, from Dr. Johnson himself to Noah Webster."

Mencken recognized that language was a living and developing organism. Within spoken language Mencken could hear new melodies; there was something magnificently fascinating in its color and novelty. His advice to those who "would do honor to our incomparable tongue" was to "listen to it on the street. It is there that it is alive."

Piles of correspondence from readers arrived at Hollins Street, leading Mencken to reconsider the topic. But it had not made him abandon another work in progress. "In order to put an end to this new respectability I shall insert some rat-poison into *Prejudices*," he confided. "It is a slaughterhouse."[8]

Of the 21 chapters of *Prejudices*, 19 were devoted to various forms of literature. For readers accustomed to Mencken's scathing criticism in the *Smart Set*, *Prejudices* only confirmed Mencken's place as the leader against the genteel tradition that had done so much to discourage original American writing. But *Prejudices* was aimed at a much larger audience than the *Smart Set*. What dazzled new readers was Mencken's boldness in disparaging the most widespread of human weaknesses: "intellectual cowardice, the craven appetite for mental ease and security, the fear of thinking things out." This attack was extended to the country as a whole: "We are, in fact, a nation of evangelists; every third American devotes himself to improving and lifting up his fellow-citizens, usually by force; the messianic delusion is our national disease."

Mencken had issued similar assaults before, but the times had changed. Edmund Wilson, who appreciated Mencken's German heritage and the value it brought to American literature, wrote: "I do not see how our literary colonialism could possibly have been blown up at that moment by men of Anglo-Saxon stock. If the rivalry between Germany with England led Mencken to be unfair"—as Edmund Wilson thought he was later toward Franklin D. Roosevelt—"it also counted for something in the boldness with which he met head-on the self-conscious Anglophile culture."

As the critic Burton Rascoe astutely observed, Mencken had come upon the field of criticism in a manner that set him apart from either the cosmopolitan Percival Pollard or James Huneker, both of whom had been his mentors. As a journalist, Mencken was closer to average life than either of them. Pollard was an aesthete, too preoccupied with artistic problems, too reticent to give battle. Huneker, although admired for his versatility, was more enthusiastic than penetrating; at home in the opera houses of Germany, he was only vaguely interested in sociological, political, or general ideas.

Mencken, as Rascoe recognized, was interested in the major problems of human life. As a student of science, theology, and economics, a newspaper reporter who had covered police courts, fires, and political conventions, Mencken had learned a great deal about life as it was lived in the United States. He took that knowledge into his works of criticism. And it was this that has withstood the test of time—what made him, according to Edmund Wilson, a writer of authentic genius.

Contemporary approval was best summed up by James Huneker, who congratulated his young protégé. "You have us *all* lashed to the mast. You are *It* in the American critical circus. All the rest are fading ghosts."

Within weeks, *Prejudices* became a sensation on both sides of the Atlantic. In London, from a country that had been a target of Mencken's strongest attacks, he was praised for being "genuinely American—only out of the States could come that accent, that way of looking at things. He is as peculiarly American as pumpkin pie. . . . In this sense he is the first American critic, except Poe."[9]

Now, on those frequent occasions during the autumn of 1919 when Mencken met with a reporter for yet another interview, he could be seen walking into the lobby of a hotel dressed in a blue serge suit with a high white collar, his right hand swinging a heavy black walking stick, adopting the confident manner of a debonair. Midway through the interview, the journalist assigned to write about Mencken would find himself being asked questions about his *own* writing. By the time the meeting was over, he would be signed up as a new contributor to the *Smart Set*—another convert to the Baltimorean's persuasive charm and to the magazine that was rapidly regaining ground it had lost during the war.

In November, the esteemed London critic Hugh Walpole landed in New York and astonished the country by declaring "I should think that Mencken will do a lot of good for your literature." This news, Mencken wrote his brother August, "will give the patriots pause." In Baltimore the next day, a photographer's flash caught Walpole and Mencken seated side by side, snickering and slightly bleary with drink; as Mencken described the picture to Blanche Knopf, "A Portrait of Two Souses."

"I have discovered something," Alfred Knopf said to him one day. "It is that H. L. Mencken has become a good property."[10]

THE WAR HAD ENDED; a new era had begun, and the nation, as if shaken awake from the moral indignation of the American Protective League, was poised to embrace the iconoclastic opinions of H. L. Mencken. Hoping to forget the war, one segment of Americans headed toward Puritanism and 100 percent Americanism, supporting such movements as Prohibition, the Klan, and censorship. Others rushed hedonistically after amusement and excitement in the decade of jazz, gin, radio. Mencken was never comfortable with the Big Business atmosphere of the Coolidge years, or, like F. Scott Fitzgerald, given over to the excesses of indiscriminate partying. And, certainly unlike the streams of Americans flowing to Europe, he chose to remain in the United States. He was the most outspoken representative for what he considered the civilized minority. As the year came to a close, he was about to become identified as one of the key instigators of the intellectual and artistic revolt gripping the country.

"Henry Mencken . . . could extract energy and encouragement from apparent defeat," the writer Gerald Johnson once observed, and "detect and savor lusty humors in situations which to most men meant only tragedy and despair." If friends thought Mencken indignant over the war, he repeatedly assured them that they were wrong. Besides, as he was quick to point out, "Indignation is the function of impotence, and I am no longer impotent. Think of the noble mark that American *Kultur* offers! My hands itch!"

But even at this stage, beneath the bravado, those who knew Mencken came to suspect that he would never forget how the war had altered everything. The changes ranged from his personal life to the national erosion of freedom of speech that would not be overcome until a decade later. Propaganda and censorship had been used deliberately to fuel patriotism and, Mencken believed, they would be so used again. It was a hint of what was yet to come, in another war, a generation later. For now, "It has been a curious time," he soberly wrote to his old mentor Ellery Sedgewick, "and I think it has changed me a lot."

In 1919, Mencken had finally come to terms with the world he lived in. Now he sought to broaden his horizons. "The wider field of ideas is too alluring," Mencken wrote a friend. "We live, not in a literary age, but in a fiercely political age." Sooner or later, he was convinced, a new magazine had to tell "the *whole* truth." It was a goal shared by Alfred Knopf, and when that same year the publisher toyed with the idea of finding a suitable editor for a monthly review, Knopf knew his man. But postwar conditions made the project too difficult. It was years before such a magazine could be launched.

As was so typical in Mencken's life, another outlet opened. Throughout the war years, Mencken had been meeting with the business manager of the *Baltimore Sun*, Paul Patterson. Now that Patterson had been promoted to president, he asked Mencken to come back and write for the *Sunpapers*.

With these new prospects awaiting him, Mencken went to the backyard of Hollins Street, dug through the brick and unearthed a box from its hiding place. Carefully unwrapping his German diary from 1917, he found that it had survived entombment.[11]

Mencken's hour had struck.

American Protective League — ↔ Like today — would be a "think tank" or Fox news Indignation, the function of Impotence!

19

THE INFERNAL FEMININE

NO ONE SENSED CHANGES in Mencken more poignantly than Marion Bloom. She saw all too clearly how, during the war years, Mencken's private life had undergone its severest test. One year earlier, in 1918, she was one of only a few of Mencken's friends who had not known about his possible draft orders. "I think he was trying to save me from knowing his own service," Marion reflected. That year, with the war still on, she was "tied up in knots" about her own activities, preparing to set sail for France in a new assignment as nurse's aide with the United States Medical Corps. She realized that events had suddenly brought a change in Mencken's attitude toward her, that her imminent departure had "brought his own thinking to a head."

Now that Marion was about to set sail for France, the relationship resumed with Mencken, once again, as master at the art of seduction. With each passing day came renewed promises that he would introduce her to his mother as soon as she returned from the war. He even more seriously discussed marriage. Would she, he asked, be willing to live on the top floor of Hollins Street if he took an office downtown? On second thought, he tried another approach. "I don't think it's fair to ask a young wife to live with her mother-in-law," he told her. "No, that wouldn't do. We will get a place out in Catonsville or somewhere out of the city with a big fence around it, and on the outside of it we'll hang a sign, 'SMALLPOX HERE, DO NOT ENTER.' "

Whenever Mencken painted rosy pictures of their married life (what Marion called his "liquor gabblings"), she confessed to her sister, "my head would swim, and in those moments I supposed I touched the very acme of joy and happiness."

Mencken seemed to be quite in earnest. With their approaching separation, their previous quarrels seemed insignificant. On September 20, 1918, they spent their last night together in New York. Those few hours were all the more precious now that Marion was about to leave, and Mencken's feelings of tenderness overcame him. "I shall not forget, my dear, this last visit, nor any of the others," he wrote to her afterward. "You will believe how much I have loved you when the bad dream is over and we are all secure and happy again."

His letters to her before she left the United States were filled with advice about sailors and seasickness, varying from stern instructions for her to keep a diary to curiosity about how she must look in her new uniform ("trig and tasty," was his guess). His natural optimism convinced him that the war could not last and that soon they would be with each other again. But for all his good spirits, he was assailed by the reminder of her impending absence, and ache and longing permeated all the notes he sent even before her ship set sail. At night he lay awake, tormented with visions of the woman he loved. New York, he told her, "is simply full of you. I'll be seeing your tracks everywhere, and wishing this and that—you know the fancies of a romantic young man." In Baltimore he fared no better: "I am infernally lonesome." When he was not expressing his adoration on paper, he was mentally composing love letters. It was not long before he came to the inevitable conclusion that "Nobody ain't like you, Miss Marion."

These feelings overwhelmed and surprised Mencken. "I'll miss her a great deal, old as I am," he confided to his friend Ernest Boyd. A better ear for what he described as his mooning was Estelle, Marion's sister, whom he met in New York over dinner to discuss his favorite subject. "I miss her very much," he told her. "I have no one to talk to when I feel like blowing or bragging. She had developed a fine technique for concealing mirth. My family simply leaves the room, and George [Jean Nathan] falls asleep." His happiest thoughts were for the day Marion would come back, and, he naively believed, "unchanged." To Estelle, he wrote: "I believe that she is having the time of her life in France."[1]

MARION'S EXPERIENCE IN FRANCE, however, proved to be far less entertaining than Mencken imagined. Throughout those long, freezing marches in mud and rain and the time spent tending hundreds of wounded soldiers, Marion was filled with a sense of desolation that left her exhausted. While other nurses gladly relinquished their shifts, Marion added hours to her own with self-imposed duties that included helping dying men write letters to loved ones back home and stealing sugar from officers' rations to sweeten their last cups of tea. Despite how she might privately feel, nurses and doctors noticed that when it came to cheering up a patient, no one was more devoted than Marion. "A boy came in, his chin dragging to the ground, in complete despair, and she could lift his spirits quicker than anyone I ever saw," one of them recalled. Not until half a century later did one of her nursing colleagues adequately summarize what made Marion so special to that one man waiting for her in Baltimore: "Oh, she was a joy! I am sure it was she who gave him a lift if ever he was down."

The war, however, had taken its toll on Marion herself. By the time she returned in February 1919, Mencken found a pale version of the woman he loved. As soon as he left her company, he wrote her a cheerful note from Baltimore: "Did I impress on you sufficiently that you never looked better?" But he expressed to Boyd his real concern that "the horrors and privations of Brest nearly finished her."

He was, nevertheless, stimulated by her return. "I have been mooning and groaning since September," he confided to her, "but now I somehow feel keen for work again." Leaving Marion in Atlantic City on a fresh spring day, he thought of a new play on the train back to Baltimore. In the next mail, he sent her a copy of his latest book, *In Defense of Women*, with the instructions, "If you don't laugh, then go to hell."

If Marion thought that her absence would spur a further blossoming of those feelings Mencken had so sweetly expressed in verbal bouquets only five months earlier, she was soon sadly disillusioned. Now that she was back, Mencken seemed blissfully indifferent to whatever doubts she may have been entertaining. For her part, through those long months in France her thoughts had been of Mencken, so much so, she had told Boyd, that "except for Henry, I am not at all eager to go home." Now that she was once again in the United States, it seemed as if her sweetheart's resistance to all conventions had renewed itself tenfold, and with each passing day the prospect of marriage seemed dimmer. Her uncertainty about Mencken's feelings could not but increase as she turned each page of *In Defense of Women* and found herself reading that "marriage is a bargain in which [the man] gets the worst of it."[2]

As the weeks went on, without any encouraging signs from Mencken, Marion's discontent grew. Snatching time between the rush of his appointments, Mencken continued to visit her in New York, unaware of her emotional needs and concentrating only on the pleasure of the moment. Then he would leave and return to a routine that did not include her. Their meetings resumed the pattern that had existed before she sailed for France: Mencken, in his role as author and editor, endlessly gabbing on about ideas and projects, and Marion as the loyal mistress, sitting mutely by and dutifully listening. If she would reintroduce the dreaded topic of weddings, Mencken would laugh it off, speaking about his need for a tranquil haven in which to accomplish his work, airily telling Marion that marriage to someone like him was really *her* decision. It flashed over her that it was "wicked for men to put the burden of decisions on women, at least women who are essentially the home-marriage kind like me." It was inevitable that something would give, and finally it did.

In March, Marion wrote Mencken a letter releasing the torrent of agitation and hurt she was feeling:

You talk against the rush of appointments, against train schedules, against work, allowing for so little tranquility, and it is through your talking and my thinking (a kind of crystal ball effect) that I begin to see that I do not want to marry you. It would be a ghastly ambition. I see you a quaking, shaking, mass of rebellion and flesh and there is no romance in the vision. . . . You want to throw all responsibility of a matrimonial decision on me so that I can be blamed if it does not go right. . . . You utterly lack that bravado and deviltry in speaking of marriage, so dear to a woman. . . . You firmly believe that matrimony would interfere with your career, yet you can't stop playing with its charming provocations. You want to be married and you want to be single. You are as capricious as a young gal. . . . You are good enough for a light-hearted weekend, but the old lines probably suit you best, "Down to Gehenna and up to the throne, He travels fastest who travels alone." I don't know. You confuse me with these eternal ponderings—the carefree gesture that is always withdrawn in fear that you *may* be taking a chance.

Such honesty achieved the desired effect. "I wrote a long, long letter to you this morning, but have torn it up. It was too damned abject," a contrite Mencken wrote to Marion, admitting that "you have penetrated to some unbearable truths." On their next visit, he assured her, he wanted to hear her for an hour: "a solo a cappella. That will be either our last real talk—or our first. I am almost beyond intelligible thinking."

As the days grew warmer and the pastels of early spring began to deepen into the darker hues of early summer, there was a suggestion that some sort of harmony had been achieved. Mencken wrote Marion: "We are making good progress."[3]

MENCKEN'S INCREASING FAME in the autumn of 1919 with the publication of *The American Language* and *Prejudices* boosted Marion's own stature. Only in a burst of some funny story with her friends would Mencken's name be mentioned—but it was enough to impress. "I remember him kidding me that I would never love him if he were a truck driver," Marion recalled. "And I said, 'Oh, indeed I would—maybe because you *look* like a jolly truck driver.'" Nonetheless, by November 1919, it was sadly obvious to Marion that her relationship with Mencken was not progressing at all the way she had hoped. They had already broken up once that summer, only to get together with the amazing admission on Mencken's part that "it would be less of a nuisance to go on."

Ignoring Mencken's advice, Marion had given up her nursing job to write, in order, as she explained to Estelle, to show the outside world that she could be proud and strong. Yet inside, she felt so weak it made her sink into "utter despair." Overriding her struggles to produce good prose ("the stuff looks so bad," she wailed), her financial difficulties, and the trauma of what she had witnessed in France was the turmoil about her relations with Mencken. She felt overwhelmed and bewildered about how she was supposed to behave; this, plus her feelings of frustration and of being overpowered by her partner contributed to her feelings of depression. Much of her time was spent doing very little: "I am so unhappy,"

she admitted, "and I seem lifeless." When her friends coaxed her out, they noted
Marion could be "the life of the party," but in general she fell into a cycle of
sadness and lethargy. "Oh," recalled Marion of her heartache over Mencken's
behavior, "if only he had held me close when I was hurt by war and life."

Marion's sentimental patriotism, though sincere, seemed childish to
Mencken, but on this score she was inflexible. "She was so involved with it emotionally," a friend observed. "Mencken could bend her anywhere except on this."
Both of her brothers had been in the war; one of them had died. There was an
additional factor of disagreement. One evening Marion naively confided to him
that her shattered loss in faith for human ways and means had been cured by
Christian Science.

> Henry had kept so silent as I stumbled on that I assumed he was thoughtfully
> absorbing my words. I never made a greater mistake! He turned on me with an
> explosive roar of contempt for the "bilge" and fakery I had doubtless learned
> from one of the C.S. hoodwinkers. It was obvious I was in love with this faker.
> Who was he? How much of this stuff had I actually believed? How could I
> believe such rot after he had shared his own civilized thinking for years; had
> given me the benefit of his teachings? I had no answer. There could have been
> none against his wrath. We spent the following ten years, if not trying to convert
> each other, certainly each to show the other "the light." The rage against
> [founder Mary Baker] Eddy was shocking. Years later, it was suggested that he
> felt I had displaced him as my mentor and was furiously jealous that he now had
> a competitor—and that one a woman!

"You can't rid yourself of the notion that it would be nicer if I had a more intelligent appreciation of Christ," he wrote Marion, presumably after one of these outbursts. Such religious beliefs, he observed, were matched by her dislike of Mark
Twain: "He was the eternal skeptic and you are the eternal believer," and he
warned her not to assume that the only idealism was of one who believes in Jesus.
And yet, to explain the horrors of a war in which her two brothers had fought and
which she had seen firsthand, Christian Science seemed to provide the comfort
and answers Marion was so anxiously groping for. "All my life I have thrown my
faith and strength on my own pitiful resources," she confessed, "and now my back
is free from all those burdens, knowing God is over all and All for me."

This was too much for Mencken. "What is this Christian Science stuff that
Marion is unloading on me by the gallon?" he complained to Estelle during the
autumn of 1919. Although Mencken recognized that Marion's new-found religion "has made her more contented and probably helped her health," he later
wrote Estelle, "it happens to be my pet abomination. All I ask is that no one try to
convert me." And he added," I thought I had a nice girl, but she turns out to be an
evangelist. God help us all."4

As the weeks wore on, Mencken wrote a play called *Heliogabulus: A Buffoonery
in Three Acts*, about the efforts of a beautiful Christian trying to convert the irreverent and disreputable Roman emperor Heliogabulus to her faith. At one point,

the main character threatens his girlfriend: "Either you put that crazy Christian balderdash away or I put *you* away." Justly, Marion complained: "He wrote *Heliogabulus* to ridicule me."

"He had no idea what it meant to her," observed one of Marion's friends. "He didn't know the depth of it." Looking back on their arguments, Marion ruefully recalled she could hardly dismiss Mencken's "fury and vituperations." They were "violent and many. What torment he put me through!"

The struggle went on for months. With her friends, Marion argued a case for having it both ways: it was their private life, why would anyone need to know about her own religious beliefs? Her friends tried to convince her that Mencken —a public figure, after all—with all of his combats with Christian Scientists in Maryland, could not possibly accept this ambivalence. There seemed to be no possible solution. "I bespeak your prayers and advice," Mencken appealed to his friends. Without a clue as to how to handle this emotional woman, he asked Marion in despair, "But what could I have done that I didn't do?"

The truth is the conflict revolved around one central issue that Marion recognized and yet Mencken refused to acknowledge: his lack of commitment. To her, "Hank" lacked guts. "The world knew him as a misogynist, and he was ashamed to be caught getting married like a regular human," she told her sister. "I would not be surprised to hear Mencken virtuously blame [Christian Science] for his attitude toward me from the beginning of our affair, when he wanted to marry me but lacked the courage—long before I had even heard of it."

Mencken attributed the cause of Marion's problems not to any failure on his part but to her propensity to play the victim. To him, her despair was yet another example of "women's delight in martyrdom, the subtle pleasure the female sex seemed to take of being pictured as slaughtered saints." He had described the type clearly through his writing and *In Defense of Women*. It was a viewpoint he maintained steadfastly, complaining to Estelle that Marion was simply "moping . . . she lashes herself into a fury of self-pity and then empties the whole thing on me. I can't stand it any longer."

On the rare instances Marion was able more calmly to assess her situation, she wrote to Mencken. But he no longer had the patience to listen to her. "God knows what to do with her, or about her," was his reaction to one of these "plain and sensible" letters from this "remarkable girl, with an amazing talent for riling me." Such a lack of understanding drove Marion to despair. "Always it is I who must go forth to 'make good,' to prove myself," she railed. "It is a harsh position for a woman."[5]

Then occurred a development most calculated to arouse the jealous fury of any woman. Marion thought she discovered that while Mencken had been courting her, he had simultaneously been seen in the company of another woman, a certain Margaret Lee. "Certainly you know that this is not true," Mencken appealed to Estelle. "I know a lot of women, but seldom see them," he said, joking, "if I take a gal to bed it is chiefly out of politeness."

The key factor in the difficulties their relationship suffered did not go unde-tected by many of his friends: Mencken's respect for class. It meant much more to him than he acknowledged. It was an attribute of the social class order in which he had been brought up, and an indispensable feature of the type of woman his mother had expected him to marry. Moreover, hadn't he proved to himself, and seen demonstrated countless times, that there was no excuse in the United States for men and women of talent not to be able to prosper financially? "To one ineradicable prejudice I freely confess," he wrote in the *Smart Set*, "and that is a prejudice against poverty. I never have anything to do, if it is possible to avoid it, with anyone who is in financial difficulties. . . . Such persons do not excite my compassion; they excite my aversion. . . . The blame, so far as my experience runs, always lies within." Reading it, Marion took these words personally. "It was these very thoughts, uttered," she wrote her sister Estelle, "that caused me in my discouragement to separate from him."

This attitude was confirmed in one of their most unhappy encounters. After spending an "idyllic afternoon," Marion recalled, Mencken had "swatted me cold . . . with the statement that if I had background, financial security, in brief, our affair might have been different." Mencken then "explained this estimate on the ground that he was a high-born German and had it in him to desire his wife make a fine showing before his world."

That evening, Marion recalled, "when he said I was unlucky, unfortunate, and that he couldn't bear unfortunate people—and I struggling like a wounded animal to emerge from the tragic fogs a war had blinded me with overlong—," the break finally occurred. The scene took place in public—the train station—where presumably the matter would be closed as soon as Mencken hopped aboard the vehicle that would conveniently take him away. "Menck's weakness," Marion concluded, "is his intolerance." He was "a shallow man who judges a woman by what she possesses," and she added as a parting shot, "I know that merely writing famous books doesn't make a gentleman in my definition of the word."

There followed what Marion referred to as "his eager and willing absence." Eventually she returned home to her family in Westminster, Maryland. The change was not for the better. Her family's suppressed curiosity and silence, she discovered, was worse than if they had discussed the situation openly. And when her brother, noticing the absence of letters and visits from Hollins Street, jovially bawled out, "Oh, Marion thought she would get him, but she never will," she confided to Estelle: "Jesus, Nellie, I could have sunk through a rat-hole."

IN BALTIMORE, Mencken was also faring badly. He, too, had had his dreams, and his own unhappy state throughout those months, while less emotionally involved than Marion's, asserted itself in various forms of minor illnesses. In addition to feeling constantly in discomfort by heart pains, he mashed his thumb while mixing concrete for the garden's brick wall, an incident indicative of his state, all of which lead him to conclude: "The world is managed by an ass."

Perhaps to blame it all on Christian Science, as Mencken later did, was the simplest excuse for a problematic relationship that was no longer viable. Nevertheless, in the years ahead, Mencken and Marion would continue their union with quarrels, separations, reunions—what Dreiser called "the usual rhythm of desire, frustration, opposition, compromise." But never again would either of them ever feel the same blissful passion they had during those earlier years when everything seemed possible; there had been too much anger, too many tears. As to the love affair, Mencken's friends could only shake their heads. "I know what love can be," Joseph Hergesheimer confided, "in a way that Mencken has yet to realize."[6]

He lashes out at all forms of prejudice and intolerance: The H. L. M. Eyeball cannot see itself. Unhappy because he is intolerant

Part Three
1920–1930

Pillow at 1524 Hollins Street. Photograph by A. Aubrey Bodine. The Maryland Historical Society, Baltimore, Maryland.

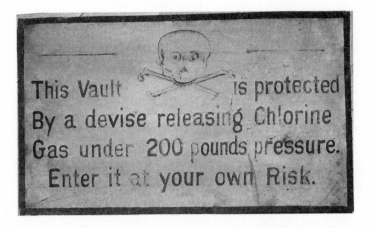

"Fill every third bottle with nitroglycerine, that heaven may swiftly welcome any righteous scoundrel who horns in." Mencken's wine cellar, built at the advent of Prohibition. Photographs by A. Aubrey Bodine. The Maryland Historical Society, Baltimore, Maryland.

20

THE DRY MILLENNIUM DAWNS

J ANUARY 16, 1920: BEFORE MIDNIGHT on that fateful day, serious drinkers lined up at the nation's bars. As the final hour drew near, all partially empty bottles at the saloons were given away. Final toasts were drunk quietly. Prohibition, Mencken warned, "will be enforced with the full military and naval power of the republic," with the appointment of a "full staff of spies," and "the boobs, as usual, will obey."

Shortly thereafter, as Mencken got out of a taxicab at Pennsylvania Station in New York, a redcap greeted him and hauled out his bag. As he lifted it, he suddenly lost his professional smile and looked about him furtively. Mencken asked him what was the matter. The man hesitated a moment and then answered that the bag seemed to be heavy.

MENCKEN: Well, you look like a strong fellow. Can't you carry it?
RED-CAP: Sure, I can carry it. But I was thinking about them detectives.
MENCKEN: Detectives? What have any detectives got to do with it?
RED-CAP: They watch all bags going through.
MENCKEN: What for?
RED-CAP: So as to notice the heavy ones. When a heavy one goes past, they stop and look inside to see if there are any jugs.
MENCKEN: What! Right here in the station?
RED-CAP: No, sir; they take the gentlemen downstairs. They have a room there. And then they search his bag.
MENCKEN: And suppose they find a jug or two?
RED-CAP: Then they lock him up.
MENCKEN: And if they don't?

RED-CAP: Then they let him go, and he can catch his train.
MENCKEN: But suppose he has missed it?
RED-CAP: Then he has to catch the next one.
MENCKEN: Where are those detectives?
RED-CAP: Over yonder is one. (*Indicating a man standing near the Pullman office.*)
MENCKEN: Are there any more?
RED-CAP: Yes, sir. There is one. (*Indicating a second man.*) Two more are out in the train-shed. Another one is down in the washroom.
MENCKEN: Do they do much business?
RED-CAP: Well, this week I seen them nail about thirty gentlemen.
MENCKEN: Do you believe that there is a jug in my bag?
RED-CAP: Yes, sir. Most gentlemen has them. But don't worry. I know how to carry it.
MENCKEN: What do you mean?
RED-CAP: I know how to carry it so's it looks light. Watch me.

"And off he went swinging the heavy bag very gaily," recalled Mencken. "It must have weighed 60 lbs.—it is large double suitcase—but he was a strong Aframerican and knew his business. As he passed close to one of the detectives, he gave it a very effective flourish. I got aboard my train safely. Such is life in our great free Republic!"[1]

For Mencken, Prohibition was the ultimate violation of the individual liberties he cherished. Quite often he wondered what George Washington would have thought of the Eighteenth Amendment—or Jefferson, particularly, for Virginia went dry before the rest of the country. Mencken read reports of officers waking women passengers on sleeping cars and searching their suitcases, pawing through their underwear for contraband liquor. "Imagine it! Virginians doing that! Try to imagine Jefferson's comment on it." Such indignities meant that civilized people had to submit to a form of espionage "by great hordes of shoddy and dubious men, each with full legal right to harass decent citizens." It was one of the most cynical violations of the Bill of Rights he had ever witnessed.

Mencken's hostility to Prohibition also stemmed from his own love of drinking. None of his friends ever saw him drunk, for he adhered strictly to his determination to lead an orderly life, and indeed pitied men who drank to the detriment of their health. Moreover, he kept to his rule, learned during his days on the *Herald*, never to drink a drop, whatever the temptation, until the day's work was done. Nor were his choices limited to beer. Before Prohibition took effect, Mencken equally favored Moselle (or "Mos'l," as he pronounced it) as being the finest of German wines; once Cutty Sark began to flow into Baltimore from the Bahamas, he gradually took to Scotch.

Admittedly, for Mencken alcohol was definitely one of the attractive features of life, "the greatest of all the Devil's inventions," as he put it. "It is my belief that no man ever grows so old that he has got beyond learning something about the art of alcoholic stimulation," a subject in which he considered himself an expert. He noted whiskey was superior in its potency as an aphrodisiac ("Here even amour becomes a chemical matter"). He advised quite blandly that the surest cure for a hangover was simple table salt, and would provide a lot of chemical information about changes in the water content of the large intestine, only to have his listeners follow his suggestion with gruesome results. On those rare occasions when doctors ordered him to go on the wagon, Mencken found the procedure worse than losing a leg.[2]

Mencken's home state was the sixth to ratify the Eighteenth Amendment and the only one that did not pass a local enforcement act, thereby gaining the reputation for being the wettest state in the Union and earning its nickname as "the Maryland Free State." At the beginning, Baltimore did its best to ignore Prohibition, as did almost every other American city. Malt shops sold real malt. When you asked your druggist for drops, he'd give you something to flavor your bathtub gin. Siphons, tongs, and crocks became standard kitchen equipment. In New York, bootleggers toured the office buildings daily, taking orders on a list of wares as long as Mencken's arm.

None of the great benefits expected to follow passage of the Eighteenth Amendment came to pass. There was not less drunkenness, less crime, less cost to government, but actually more, and respect for the law had diminished. As soon as it became illegal, alcohol acquired a new chic. Women began drinking in public, and adolescents also in great numbers.

During the early 1920s, Mencken noted ironically these "accomplishments" of Prohibition: All decent potent beverages became four times more expensive, so the poor could no longer afford to drink them; drinking in restaurants became expensive and unnerving, because a lady was apt to be scared half to death of a possible raid; dining in private was no longer charming—"If drinks are served, one hesitates to gullet them freely. If they are not served, one wishes one's host were in hell." With drinking thus made gloomy in saloons, the home manufacture of beer reached colossal proportions. As Prohibition gathered momentum, so did the force of Mencken's prose as well as his expertise in the making of home brews.

Many of the bottles in Mencken's cellar were provided by his private bootlegger, who regularly made a grand entrance into the *Smart Set* office and was treated like a visiting ambassador. Eventually, Mencken learned how to make his own beer with the best German ingredients he could obtain. "Home-loving" as an epithet that described Mencken now gave place to "home-*brew* loving" for his friends, with whom he shared the fine points of his production. Throughout Hollins Street on Sunday afternoons there was a pleasant smell of malt and hops in the air, with now and then a whiff of something stronger.

At 1524, mother and sister would be shooed out of the kitchen. With an enema tube (handy for bottling), and dried Lowenbrau yeast cultivated in the laboratories of Johns Hopkins' bacteriologists, Mencken would begin the weekly ritual of stirring, boiling, straining, and cooling. He noted the precise measurements of corn sugar and how to darken color with caramel, the results when fermenting in either wood or stone, and the type of spring water used. In due time, Mencken mastered the procedure, and if the product sometimes looked drab or sickly, no one seemed to mind. Occasionally the home brew had a real kick, and members of the Saturday Night Club who dipped into the stock either got sick to their stomachs or cheerfully boiled.

During the thirteen awful years that Prohibition remained in force, Mencken devoted at least 42 newspaper columns to the subject and made innumerable references in his articles and books. When Prohibition began, he received seven cocktail shakers, eight sets of beer or wine glasses, and ten other drinking utensils of one kind or another, sent in recognition and encouragement of the war against Prohibition in which he was the foremost spokesman.[3]

Mencken's battle against Prohibition was accompanied by an earnest effort to reinvigorate the *Sunpapers*. On this topic, both Mencken and Paul Patterson felt passionately. Patterson was cool, calm, and self-assured. If he was "a weird duck" to some (he had an odd stare, caused by myopia), no one could deny his tremendous vitality. This energy spilled over now in Patterson's new role as president of the *Sunpapers*.

Night after night in 1919, when the day's routine was finished, Patterson and Mencken would meet in the home of the chairman, Harry Black, to debate how to inject life into the *Sun* and its evening edition. By the year's end, the outcome was "An Editorial Memorandum," written primarily by Mencken.

It proposed a more diligent coverage of national news with special and early information, presenting it honestly and fairly, and interpreting it with independence. On the latter point Mencken was adamant: despite the *Sun's* commitment to the Democratic Party, the paper must be free from all entanglements.

"*Free*" was the keyword in the memorandum. The newspaper must have "the *freedom* to deal with the Administration honestly and realistically"; it "must be *free* from any suspicion of loyalty to private interest or rigid formulae"; "it must be absolutely *free*" from national and local party loyalties, from foreign interference; *free* even to make its own mistakes. "Here is an opportunity for a great newspaper to lead rather than to follow in politics," Mencken wrote.

In the *Sun* office the memorandum became known as the "White Paper," and there were those who had a low opinion of it. The document remains Mencken's statement of the guiding principles of freedom that were to mark his conduct throughout the rest of his newspaper career. It was a clear demonstration of the high hopes he held not only for the *Sunpapers* but for journalism in general. Only in light of these ideals is it possible to comprehend Mencken's subsequent disillusionment in the years ahead.[4]

As a result of the memorandum, Paul Patterson made practical changes, starting with bringing Mencken back to the paper. His first contribution to the *Evening Sun* editorial page was printed on February 9, 1920, under the title "A

Carnival of Buncombe." It was not only a review of the presidential candidates but also of the continued suppression of civil liberties in America, treated with a realism that the *Sunpapers* had not seen since 1914.

In his column, he described the candidates as "more or less palpable frauds." He denounced Attorney General A. Mitchell Palmer, the architect of the Red Scare of 1919–1920, for his "medieval attempts to get into the White House by pumping the Bolshevik issue." He called President Wilson, felled by a stroke in 1919, simply a "corpse" and a "cadaver." "That's a fine piece of murder," Paul Patterson congratulated Mencken. "I enjoyed it hugely." Local Baltimoreans whistled under their breath; upon reading "A Carnival of Buncombe," they knew instinctively its author was a fish much bigger than Baltimore.

For the next eighteen years, until 1938, Mencken's Monday column became a fixture. It lit up the pages of the *Evening Sun*, dazzling with its brilliant style and virtuosity of language that caused the reader to grope for a dictionary while tears of laughter streamed down his face. The vocabulary of the Monday columns was the same that Mencken had always used—such favorite words as *palpable*, *puerile, puissant, mountebank, hon. gentleman, frauds*. He also invented words: perhaps the most famous of which was *booboisie*. He was most proud of *Bible Belt* (which, he noted, was being used among Southerners, although if they knew Mencken had invented it, "they'd probably be shy of it"). Borrowing from a wide range of languages, the master philologist popularized the British term *flapper* and used German and Yiddish words and phrases. The humorist S. J. Perelman said H. L. Mencken was "the ultimate firework. He loosened up journalism. With his use of the colloquial and the dynamic, the foreign reference, and the bizarre word like *Sitzfleisch*, he brought adrenalin into the gray and pulpy style of the day." Any man who thinks clearly can write clearly, Mencken argued. When asked for his definition of a sound writing style, Mencken equated it with breathing: "The main thing in it is rhythm, but it must always be irregular rhythm, never a steady beat."

The tone and treatment of Mencken's subjects were quite different from the "Free Lance" diatribes with their self-conscious attempts to shock and horrify. Now Mencken did not strain for effect. The ease was all the more incredible when one remembered that reporters and columnists, working against a deadline, had little opportunity to devise the unexpected; more often than not, as Mencken liked to point out, sentences fell on a store of stale cliches acquired as soon as a reporter learned how to make out an expense account: "dash for freedom"; "blood streaming" from wounds; news that "spread like wildfire." Somehow Mencken survived what he called "the crippling strain of the city room" and "the bellicose imbecility of the copyreaders" to achieve an originality of thought and a genuine distinction of style.

Part of it was his facility at turning a phrase by framing an epigram and molding an epithet. "By overstatement to the point of absurd exaggeration, by ridicule, by hyperbole and paradox," wrote one contemporary, "he makes readers gasp with horror or chortle with glee, makes them wonder and revolt, question and even think."

When the *Evening Sun* thumped against their doorsteps, readers immediately turned to Mencken's column. One might announce to his family at the dinner table, "Mencken was great tonight!" while others might slam their fists in anger. Some preferred the columns written in a lighter vein, in which the topics were food, music, and movies; others welcomed the times Mencken's column did not appear at all, his diatribes replaced by a photograph of an attractive chorus girl "Pinch Hitting for Mencken." In admiration, Harry Black coined a new nickname for his *Sunpapers* colleague: "Horrible Henry." Others, much less fondly, said worse. Few could remain indifferent.[5]

AN UNPRECEDENTED LEVEL OF FREEDOM ENABLED Mencken to tackle subjects seldom mentioned in other papers. He pummeled censorship, Prohibition, and hypocritical Puritanism with equal ardor. The defense of individual freedom always brought out the best of his powers, and the suppression of civil liberties became one of his dominant targets, bringing it more fully into the mainstream of public discourse.

In January 1920, when Mencken was about to launch his Monday column, the news allowed him ample opportunity to discuss civil liberties. Many Americans began to blame their current ills on a new bogeyman, the Soviet Bolshevik. That month, federal agents arrested 6,000 alleged Communists in 33 cities around the country; many were picked up without warrants or the right to contact lawyers or families. Throughout the nation, state governments, businesses, private detective agencies, and the American Legion continued antilabor and antiradical activities, much of them directed against the foreign-born. Political protest had been driven underground; the sale of alcohol had been prohibited; and big business was in full ascendance. America was going on "the most expensive orgy in history," but, as F. Scott Fitzgerald wrote, "we didn't remember anything about the Bill of Rights until Mencken began plugging it."

For two and a half years Attorney General Mitchell Palmer had subjected the nation to tyranny, enlisting volunteers to keep foreigners under surveillance and entertaining the country, as Mencken put it, "with gaudy tales of imaginary conspiracies and imbecile boasts of secret and colossal achievements." But in the case of the Wall Street explosion in September 1920, no evidence to support Palmer's accusations that radical anarchists were to blame was ever found. The Justice Department, Mencken maintained, was "a conspiracy against justice, and what is more, against common honesty and common decency."

Mencken was particularly effective in dealing with the denial of individual rights, especially those of radicals. In this matter, he differed from all that had been instilled in him when his father would impatiently swear against the labor leaders he saw as threatening to destroy the comfortable world he knew. William H. A. Williams has pointed out that part of Mencken's value as a social critic in the 1920s was in looking beyond his own political and economic beliefs and judging problems on principle rather than on ideology.

As Mencken looked about the Republic, he saw innocent people being imprisoned or even going to the electric chair. The case against the aliens Nicola Sacco and Bartolomeo Vanzetti was one of the most politically charged of the decade. They had been found guilty of murder in a South Braintree, Massachusetts, payroll robbery. Though the evidence against the self-avowed anarchists was inconclusive, and despite numerous appeals, the two men were sentenced to death. As the debate raged, Mencken was the first literary voice to speak in protest. He devoted five columns to the subject, drawing his readers' attention to an independent study by Felix Frankfurter of the Harvard Law School that criticized the appellate courts for not helping "innocent men beset by perjurers, and facing gallows on false testimony."

In the deportation of radicals after the Red Scare of April 1921, Mencken reminded his readers that "probably two-thirds of those allegedly Reds were wholly innocent, and even the guilty ones were not fairly tried." Though by no means sharing the views of Eugene Debs, Mencken opposed the jailing of the Socialist leader, imprisoned for his Marxist views and for opposing the war. Mencken also corresponded with Emma Goldman, the deported anarchist writer known as "Red Emma." Mencken called on the Bureau of Immigration to allow her to return to America to visit her relatives and then sent the Emma Goldman Recovery Committee a check for $25. "Bless your heart," Goldman wrote to Mencken, "how naive you are to think that you could help change the law in my direction. It is splendid of you to want to attempt it. . . . The fact that you have tried has done me a world of good."

Mencken also examined the 1920 Carlo Tresca case. Tresca was the owner of *Il Martello*, an antifascist New York newspaper. The government suppressed it, arresting Tresca on a trumped-up charge of publishing advertisements for birth control. When Tresca was convicted, Mencken asked in his column: "What becomes of the old notion that the United States is a free country, that it is a refuge for the oppressed of other lands?" The American Civil Liberties Union wrote Mencken that his was the best statement about Tresca.

When the Red Scare died down, the superpatriots shifted their energies to immigration control. Mencken—again in a departure from his early days as the author of *Men Versus the Man*—championed the immigrants for their important contributions to the food, language, and literature of the United States. As for the rising membership of the Ku Klux Klan, Mencken argued that the actions undertaken by the invisible empire were as dishonest, ignorant, unjust, and cowardly as the war the superpatriots had declared against the "Reds."[6]

IT DID NOT TAKE LONG for some of Mencken's *Sunpaper* colleagues to decide that they did not want him to be associated with the paper. Their resentment had been fermenting for a while. According to James Cain, who heard the story from

"A panorama of patriots." The Ku Klux parade in Washington, D.C., during the 1920s. Reproduced from the Collections of the Library of Congress.

Mencken, the leaders in the rebellion were "bent on getting Mencken out, as a pro-German, as an anti-Christian, undesirable Bolshevik." On May 28, 1920, the opportunity for a staff revolt finally came.

Under the title "The Armenian Buncombe," Mencken's Monday column derided a British proposal, supported by the French, to install an American mandate in Armenia to protect Allied interests. Mencken scorned the president's attempts to discuss such issues with the American public by pointing out that Wilson suffered from "a congenital incapacity for telling the truth." As for trusting foreign news from abroad, in what could be construed as a thinly disguised criticism of his *Sunpaper* colleagues, Mencken wrote: "Practically every line that has come to this country since 1914 has come from various press agents. The sort of man who believes whatever he reads is . . . the typical man in a democratic society hammered and herded by dishonest newspapers."

As soon as the *Evening Sun* hit the stands, the ensuing negative public reaction created a dilemma for Paul Patterson at the onset of his new administration. Arthur O. Lovejoy, a celebrated professor of philosophy at Johns Hopkins, delivered a diatribe that covered two columns of the paper. He raised the specter of Mencken's allegiance to Germany.

author of "The great chain of Being

But the most heated reaction was within the *Sun* itself. Woodrow Wilson had been a hero to the *Sun's* editorial writers, among them John Halsup Adams, who demanded that Mencken be dismissed. If this were not done, Adams said, he himself would resign, for he could not in good conscience work on a paper that allowed a member of the staff to question the veracity of the president of the United States. Frank Kent and several others signed a petition in support of Adams.

It was an uncomfortable situation, but Patterson faced it with his usual aplomb. He argued for a middle ground: perhaps Mencken had been too harsh; then again, maybe Adams had been too ardent in his support of Wilson. When Mencken was called into the office, he immediately offered his resignation, but all such talk was rejected. Patterson quietly began instituting reforms. He relieved Adams and Kent of their responsibilities at the *Evening Sun*, making the *Sun* and *Evening Sun* completely independent of each other. In 1922 Patterson adroitly pacified Kent by giving him a page-one daily column—"too fat a plum to be declined," according to Cain, "and an assignment that would take the sore spot out of the office and permit things to go on." The new column, titled "The Great Game of Politics," launched Kent's career as a columnist.

Patterson then hired as editor of the *Evening Sun* a young Baltimorean, Hamilton Owens. From then on, Mencken would come to the *Sunpapers* building on Monday afternoons for the news and editorial conferences. "Very frequently these Monday meetings turned into Menckenian monologues," Owens recalled. "He would have read something in the paper, either on the editorial page or in the news columns, of which he disapproved, and he would give us all a stern lecture on newspaper ethics and morals and so on—always humorously, and have us in stitches most of the time—but there would always be that essential bold integrity that was a part of Mencken." Patterson and Harry Black would always support Mencken, although Owens observed that "sometimes it seemed to me that he was asking an impossible ideal, and I'd venture to argue with him. I didn't often get anywhere."

Their conversations would continue late into the night over mugs of beer. During the day, a wave of correspondence poured over Owens's desk, for Mencken's fertile mind allowed no detail to escape that might prove useful to the editor of the paper, whether it was about typos, punctuation, letters, editorials, or the hiring of new talent. The ultraconservative editorial page of the war years became transformed, said Owens, into one that was "at worst, smart-alecky, and, at its best, witty and pungent. Most of it was due to Mencken."

Before long, students and teachers in Baltimore were systematically visiting the paper, shuffling through the lobby and then trooping downstairs, deafened by the roar of the huge cylindrical presses. The *Nation* praised the revitalization of the *Sunpapers* as one of the bravest newspapers in America; it was the only paper the president read in the morning.

Mencken continued to be Patterson's fair-haired boy. According to Cain, Patterson "was aware that as a setpiece in the show window, Mencken was worth more than all the rest put together. Anyhow, partly as an intellectual, partly as a court jester, partly as an honestly liked friend, Mencken was kept on. Patterson basked in reflected glory, and Mencken basked in the admiration of an eminent, to say nothing of powerful, stooge."

Had Adams, Kent, and other *Sun* staffers succeeded with their petition, James Cain argued, "Mencken's life might have been different."[7]

21

OF POLITICS AND PROSE

OW THAT THE *SUN* HAD BECOME a leading chronicler of national
news, Paul Patterson assigned eight top reporters to cover the 1920
Republican and Democratic national conventions. Seated on the train
to Chicago with Mencken for the GOP affair were the very men who had sought
to oust him from the paper. To smooth the journey, Patterson had packed a case
of 100-proof whiskey. When the train arrived, all members of the party burst into
song, proof of one of Mencken's favorite doctrines, that "the whole world would
be better if the human race was kept gently stewed."[1]

However, in Chicago, the *Sunpapers* team was dismayed to realize that for the
first time in history the crowd was *dry*. Gone was the bubbling merriment that
Mencken had experienced in 1904, the popping of corks and the green fog of
hung-over mornings. "A strange quiet hangs over the whole scene," Mencken
reported, "and the crowds swarm in and out of the hotels in a stupid and listless
manner."

Not only was liquid stimulation lacking. The hall was an old armory that had
been used for prize fights, dog shows, and a third-rate circus, and according to
Mencken, it still smelled of pugs, kennels, and elephants. Over this inferno was
a glass roof that turned the place into a Turkish bath. "They say that the press
gallery at the Republican National Convention was the hottest place known,"
reported *Editor & Publisher*, with a snapshot of an unmistakably bedraggled
Mencken: "Judging from the gentleman hanging on the rail halfway down and
taking the count, we believe it." Pushing past perspiring cops in the cramped
aisles, Mencken sneaked out to refresh himself. He descended to a grimy cellar

for a meager and disgusting meal, observing later that "The dirtiest man that I have ever seen in my life was in charge of the sandwich counter at Chicago."

The Republicans believed they could win the election and end the Wilson era. Among the candidates was General Leonard Wood, a confidant of Theodore Roosevelt. Others included Herbert Hoover, the successful Wartime Food Administrator, Calvin Coolidge, the governor of Massachusetts, and Warren G. Harding, the senator from Ohio who was a popular self-made businessman from a pivotal state.

Cheers and hisses marked the sessions as the hot, exhausted delegates roared themselves hoarse. Deadlocked, no one was in a mood to go into a second week and remain in that sweltering hall. It was the heat, Mencken contended, "far more than the machinations of the masterminds on the scene, that gave Warren G. Harding the nomination." At 2 a.m., on June 12, 1920, Harding was chosen with "Silent Cal" as his running mate, and the convention's delegates eagerly adjourned. "It was a poor show," Mencken complained to his brother. "Harding is of the intellectual grade of an aging cockroach."[2]

After suffering through the miserable Republican Convention, Mencken faced the Democratic Convention in San Francisco with forebodings. His colleagues likewise wondered about the food and the booze awaiting them. With Prohibition, their only expectation in the way of a drink was a mix of rum, turpentine, and rye, with odd things floating in it. Instead, the show at San Francisco would turn out to be the most delightful Mencken had ever attended. From then on, Alfred Knopf observed, Mencken collected political conventions the way other men collect books and paintings.

In sharp contrast to the Chicago accommodations, the rooms at the newly built Civic Auditorium were luxurious, with a sandwich counter attended by lovely creatures in clean white uniforms. The walls of the hall were padded with tasteful canvas and the ceiling with a canopy, destroying the disturbing auditorium reverberations that always annoyed the acoustically sensitive Mencken. Harmony within the aisles was kept not by burly police but, as Mencken put it, by "a force of cuties," coeds from the local colleges, armed with little wands demanding order. Better still, San Francisco Mayor James Ralph supplied delegates and guests with the very refreshments Prohibition denied: a request for a bottle of whiskey was met within half an hour by a committee of pretty women, with no bill attached.

A sense of delicious freedom engulfed Mencken. Three thousand miles away from Baltimore, Mencken felt a subtle but unmistakable escape from the rest of the country. No wonder he long remembered the Democratic convention of 1920. The heady mixture of a glamorous city, politics, and women—and one woman in particular—made for a sweet and sentimental episode.

At the St. Francis Hotel, Mencken attended a dinner in his honor hosted by the poet George Sterling, where the endless wine, including *grappa*, "damn nigh killed me." By the time Mencken came to his senses, he found himself in a strange bed with an unknown delegate. Jane O'Roarke—a friend of Sterling and a leading actress in a San Francisco stock company—was the angel of mercy who offered to look after Mencken, patching him up with a warm bath and a strong pot of tea. "I am in love," Mencken announced. He spent the remaining two weeks hugely enjoying every minute of the show while remaining gentlemanly about Jane O'Roarke, refusing to point her out to his friends in the press section.[3]

When the name of New York governor Alfred E. Smith was placed in nomination, it triggered the most dramatic and heartiest uproar of the entire week. "I have never, in all my newspaper days, seen another scene to match that one," Mencken recalled. The band swung into "The Sidewalks of New York" and then into a whole series of the sentimental songs of long ago. Mencken, rapt to every nuance of music, especially in waltz time, was caught where he was most tender. For one solid hour he was under the romantic spell.

This was a golden opportunity for an eloquent appeal to the delegates to vote for a superior candidate. Unluckily for Al Smith, no such rhetoric came. What was offered by his nominator, Franklin D. Roosevelt—then President Wilson's assistant secretary of the Navy—"was a line of puerile and ineffective bosh about the great achievements of the navy," reported Mencken. As the delegates listened, all of their enthusiasms oozed out of them." Smith might have been chosen for the presidency, Mencken believed, if Roosevelt "had not been such an ass."

Instead, on the forty-fourth ballot, the governor of Ohio, James Cox, became the Democratic Party's choice for president, with Roosevelt as his running mate. It was the starting point for Roosevelt's triumphs, which would delight and exasperate Mencken for years to come.

Once back in Baltimore, Mencken dispatched a first edition of *In Defense of Women* to Jane O'Roarke in San Francisco. Viewed as condescending by many women, its contents filled her with indignation, though not enough, apparently, to quench her admiration for its author. In a panic, Mencken wrote to Sterling: "As you know, my relations with her are brotherly. I have two girls in New York, God help me." Mencken's dilemma provided enough grist to keep his friends busy. Six months later, Dreiser joked to Sterling: "Mencken still writes of San Francisco. A fine killing it made in his case."[4]

The conventions had made it impossible for Mencken to generate enthusiasm for either candidate in the fall campaign. The dismal prospect before the voters led him to ask: what merit leads a man into elective office in the first place? If the candidate was a man of self-respect, the test was cruelly hard. "In the face of this singular passion for conformity," Mencken wrote, "it is obvious that the man of vigorous mind and stout convictions is gradually shouldered out of public life. . . . This leaves the field to the intellectual jellyfish and inner tubes."

> The Presidency tends, year by year, to go to such men. As democracy is perfected, the office represents, more and more closely, the inner soul of the people. We move toward a lofty ideal. On some great and glorious day the plain folks of the land will reach their heart's desire at last, and the White House will be adorned by a downright moron.

No shit!

Mencken's hunch was subsequently borne out by the election of Warren G. Harding. At his inauguration, Mencken was appalled by the man's oratory. It was, he wrote, "the worst English I have ever encountered. It reminds me of a string of wet sponges; it reminds me of tattered washing on the line; it reminds me of stale bean soup, of college yells, of dogs barking idiotically through endless nights."

Why, Mencken asked, did the speech seem so stupidly at war with sense? The answer was simple. "When Dr. Harding prepares a speech he does not think it out in terms of an educated reader locked up in jail, but in terms of a great horde of stoneheads gathered around a stand . . . an audience of . . . morons scarcely able to understand a word of more than two syllables, and wholly unable to pursue a logical idea for more than two centimeters."

Mencken pulled a random sentence from the president's speech:

> I would like government to do all it can to mitigate, then, in understanding, in mutuality of interest, in concern for the common good, our tasks will be solved.

"I assume that you have read it," Mencken commented. "I also assume that you have set it down as idiotic—a series of words without sense. You are quite right; it is." The *New York Times* praised Harding's "misty language" as "Presidential." Mencken spent a week looking through foreign newspapers for their reaction. "I find in them no echo of the *Times'* delight in the 'misty language' of that historic harangue. On the contrary, all of them seem to regard it uneasily, and a bit askance. They seem to be unimpressed by the fact that it shows 'a style that looks Presidential'; what they apparently hoped for was a style that would let them know what to expect from the United States."5

AMID MENCKEN'S DEPRESSING DETOUR into political coverage, his reputation as a catalyst in American letters rose. In October of that election year, *Prejudices: Second Series* had been published. By far one of its most significant essays was a lengthy discussion of "The National Letters" and a much expanded version of his 1917 *Evening Mail* column, "The Sahara of the Bozart." The latter was an example not only of Mencken's preoccupation with the South that would continue throughout the decade, but also of his increasing sensitivity to blacks immediately following the war.

As Mencken's interest in the South increased, his articles in the *Evening Sun* and the *Smart Set* conveyed his conviction that the hope for Southern literature lay in "the new school of Aframerican novelists, now struggling heavily to emerge." By 1920, Mencken's name had become familiar to black intellectuals. James Weldon Johnson and W. E. B. Du Bois welcomed "The Sahara of the Bozart" as a clarion call, as did other writers in the pages of the *Crisis*, the *Messenger*, the *New York Age*, and elsewhere.

White Southerners reacted quickly. "*Herr Mencken*" was nothing but a "miserable, uninformed wretch," a "self-appointed emissary of the Wilhelmstrasse," stated the *Little Rock News.* Many demanded that the Arkansas members of Congress seek Mencken's deportation.

To Mencken's surprise, however, his attacks against the South attracted a following among the liberal white Southern minority. Among them was Thomas Wolfe, who was studying literature at Harvard; Paul Green, an aspiring playwright from North Carolina, who would win a Pulitzer Prize; Allen Tate, a poet from Vanderbilt University; Julia Peterkin, a South Carolinian Mencken had advised to write novels of Gullah Negro life; and Frances Newman, a librarian from Atlanta whom Mencken had inspired to write *The Hard Boiled Virgin.* Southern journalists who also saw in Mencken's method the most effective way to correct Southern ills included Emily Clark, the moving spirit behind the *Reviewer*, which printed the work of new Southern writers whom Mencken had praised. Although corresponding with the new talent "bores me horribly," Clark confessed to Joseph Hergesheimer, she continued to cultivate them to "have a good report for Mencken."[6]

Until this time, Mencken had not visited the South, and after the publication of *Prejudices: Second Series*, Emily Clark advised him not to "for the next two or three years." But he could not resist an invitation from the ever-amenable Joseph Hergesheimer, who, besides being always in the mood for festivities (it was said he invented the daiquiri cocktail), finally decided that if anyone was to escort Henry into Virginia, it would be him.

After making a quick inventory of his stock, Mencken duly arrived in Richmond, according to one observer, with a portable saloon.

"Here is Henry Mencken," Hergesheimer, in rich tones, introduced the critic one weekend. Appreciative guests were transfixed as the Baltimorean delivered a blistering denunciation of New York and continued to extol all that was Virginian. The impossible Mencken was also unpredictable—and cleverly political. Southern writer James Branch Cabell exulted: "Mencken's visit to me was a profound delight. I was astounded to discover the boyishness in him," concluding, "and it is a pleasure to add that my wife, who is distinctly suspicious of the literary, was delighted with him."[7]

DESPITE SUCH DENUNCIATIONS OF NEW YORK for Dixie ears, Mencken still spent a great deal of time in that city. Quite often he could be found in the home of Phil Goodman, gloating over a feast of roast goose, or in the company of Tommy Smith, the colorful editor of the *Century* magazine. Short, cherubic, and foppish, with a pink complexion and silvery hair, when not giving parties, he prowled the city, making the rounds of speak-easies and ending each evening by quietly drinking a quart of milk.

One night at Smith's apartment, Mencken and Nathan were introduced to Sinclair Lewis, who promptly flung his arm around Mencken's neck. Mencken remembered him "far gone in liquor, and when he fastened upon me with a drunkard's zeal, declaring that he had lately finished a novel of vast and singular merits full worthy of my most careful critical attention, I tried hard to shake him off." Shaking off Lewis was no easy task, however, and when Mencken finally was able to round up Nathan, he complained about the inebriated red-headed Midwesterner.

> "Can you imagine such a jackass," I said, "writing a book worth reading?"
> Nathan couldn't imagine it.
> "Never again!" he said. "If Tom Smith has taken to such nuisances, then I'll never go to his house again."
> The next day I returned to Baltimore, and before leaving the *Smart Set* office gathered up an armful of review books to examine on the train . . . I took up a sheaf as soon as the train plunged into the Pennsylvania tunnel. By the time it got to Newark I was interested, and by the time it got to Trenton I was fascinated. At Philadelphia I called a Western Union boy and sent a telegram to Nathan. I forget the exact text, but it read substantially: "That idiot has written a masterpiece." The book was *Main Street.*

Mencken's positive reception was a joy for the author and his wife, Grace Hegger, whose years of struggle finally seemed to be at an end. As Grace reported to her mother, "We tread air."

In Lewis, Mencken had found a writer who could combine a "Dreiserian ruthlessness of observation" with a Rabelaisian richness of humor. As the decade progressed, Lewis portrayed a panorama of 1920s society in a series of novels, in each of which he acknowledged his debt to Mencken. After *Main Street*, Mencken proposed that Lewis tackle the portrayal of another American type. The country's current preoccupation with business recalled to Mencken his early days in Baltimore, when he had feuded with the Merchants' and Manufacturers' Association in his " Free Lance" column. Why not portray the typical businessman of the typical Baltimore? Startled, Lewis confessed, "that was precisely what I *was* then planning." The result was *Babbitt.*[8]

By 1920 Mencken was recognized as a major critic by European observers. In Paris, F. Scott Fitzgerald declared that "everybody is reading Mencken." For those who did not read English, his books had been translated into Spanish and German.

Yet in Baltimore, despite this growing success, *Prejudices: Second Series* seemed not to have caused a ripple. "Most prominent Baltimoreans imagine they have disposed of this extraordinary person when they have said, 'Oh, it's only Mencken,' or 'It's just Mencken,' or more laconically, 'Mencken,'" reported the *Sun*. "They are totally unconscious of the fact that the author of *Prejudices* is the most truly prominent citizen this town possesses. When he dies, it will take 10 years to raise funds for a tombstone, and even then the memorial will be cheap and hideous—like Poe's."

"There may be good reasons why a prophet is without honour in his own country," observed the *Sydney (Australia) Triad*. "Prophets are uncomfortable

Even then we were the Blowhards of the Earth! [handwritten annotation]

people to live with. They shatter the complacencies. Mr. Mencken is a staunch American, but a staunch American with a difference. He loves America so well, is at heart so anxious about her future, that he has courage to tell her the truth about her goings-on. In an American, courage can run no higher than that."9

No sooner had *Prejudices: Second Series* been released than Knopf desperately wanted a revision of *The American Language*. The orders rolling in were driving him frantic. Royalties on the small first edition were more than any of Mencken's other books had ever earned, leading him to joke, "The moral is plain: fraud pays." While he remained initially sarcastic about the project, Mencken saw it was the first work of its kind that transcended traditional barriers between scholar and layman. What had begun as drudgery came to possess Mencken, making more and more demands of his time as he saw how each new edition entertained an old audience and captured a new one.

The prospect of revising, however, filled Mencken with dread. The corrections and suggestions that accumulated after the publication of the first edition, he recalled, "were of such bulk that they almost alarmed me into abandoning the work altogether." Moreover, he was sure he was going to "make a mess of it."

When it came to writing *The American Language*, Mencken concluded the only safe plan was to compare the varieties of American English with what was currently regarded as standard English. The task was enormous. Mencken's revision of the text, along with the addition of four new chapters, an appendix, and an extended bibliography, was demanding physically and hard work mentally. Three new sections in *The American Language* elaborated on the theme of American slang. The first, "Specimens of the American Vulgate," included a facetious translation of "The Declaration of Independence" into common speech. Two pieces by Ring Lardner that combined the common argot of professional baseball players and actors were included. A second addition, "Non-English Dialects in America," acknowledged the influence of Spanish and Yiddish. The third contained a section entitled "Proverb and Platitude," with examples of "the national talent for extravagant and pungent humor."

The American Language became a declaration of linguistic independence, the end of literary colonialism and a new stage in the development of American literature. "American writers were finally able to take flight from the old tree and to trust for the first time their own dialect," Edmund Wilson observed. "Mencken showed the positive value of our own vulgar heritage."

The generosity of subsequent reviews of *The American Language* staggered Mencken for the rest of his life. "If you took me aside and plied me with drink I could show you enough errors and imbecilities in it to justify the public hangman in burning it," he wrote much later to the linguist Raven McDavid Jr. But, he explained, "I had to give it a show. The one central objective of the whole infernal labor was to convince 100% Americans that language is really interesting, and not only interesting but important."

With his work on *The American Language* and routine editorial work for the *Evening Sun*, Mencken closed the year in a state of collapse. He swore to friends "No more philology!" Yet even before the plates were cast, Mencken found himself laboring in the early spring on still another revision. He groaned, "The book will kill me yet."[10]

As MENCKEN WAS BEING HAILED as a major influence on an entirely new generation of American writers, he continued to pay his respects to James Huneker in New York, only now the disciple had become more famous than his mentor. Huneker's books would soon be selling so poorly that Scribner's had difficulty keeping them in print.

Mencken had seen the older man infrequently during these last few years; on his last visit, Huneker looked thin and pasty. Tired, bored, life no longer remained an adventure. "The work of his life was behind him and he knew it," Mencken later recalled. "The old battles were over and half forgotten; of the old friends, more were dead than alive; all the ancient haunts were dark." Since Prohibition, Lüchow's, where Mencken used to sit with *Rinderbrüst mit Meerretig* and Huneker with his tenth seidel of pilsner, now had "its taps running Coca-Cola." Still suffering from spells of vertigo and nausea, Huneker brooded, "What is there to live for?"

Less than two weeks later, on February 9, 1921, James Huneker was dead. "So passed one of the most charming fellows ever heard of, and the best critic of the American first line," Mencken mourned. There would be a time when the very same tribute would be paid to him.

Mencken's impact on the young generation following World War I was summed up by Hamilton Owens: "They were floundering in their disillusionment," he wrote, "uncertain where to turn for guidance. Some fled to the Left Bank to fritter away their talents. Those who remained at home did better: they discovered Mencken. . . . They followed him in the thousands . . ."

It was a tribute Mencken claimed he did not want, and tried constantly to avoid. He used to say that if another came along who could put on a better show, his fans would abandon him overnight. Therefore, he put on the best show his talents could provide. One reporter, dispatched to the *Smart Set* for an interview, sat in the office in absolute wonder. Later he said he felt as a young Mencken had years before, after being in the presence of Huneker: "I left in a sort of fever . . ."

Yet despite Mencken's protests to the contrary, such declarations tickled him. He could recall those years with satisfaction: "It was at this time that I became known as 'That Man in Baltimore.'"[11]

22

THAT MAN IN BALTIMORE

B Y THE AUTUMN OF 1921, Mencken's workload had assumed such proportions that, reluctantly, he was forced to make the decision he had been postponing for years. And so, riding the Baltimore streetcar, he spotted a small black sign advertising secretarial services, got off, walked into the office of Margaret Redding, and handed her twenty pages of typing. "You meet but one Mencken in a lifetime," she later wrote in an unpublished memoir. "Meeting him, knowing him, is an experience never to be forgotten."

The secretary's recollections are valuable as an account of Mencken's idiosyncrasies; a rare look into the private life of a man within the walls of an exceedingly private home and family. Outside of Baltimore, Mencken created a public persona while taking care to conceal his real self. Many people, especially those who had shared a night with him drinking, imagined themselves to be Mencken's pals. James Cain recalled: "They'd say to be sure and tell Henry Mencken hello for them, and oh boy did we have a night that time. I said, I sure will, so when I'd see Mencken . . . I'd deliver the message and a blank look would cross his face. No recognition of any kind whatsoever."

Few ever gained admittance to 1524 Hollins Street, and those who did were a select circle of Baltimoreans. The Mencken house offered a rare glimpse of its inner workings to Margaret Redding. It did not make any effort to conceal its oddities because no member of that family ever thought them odd. The house was dominated by Mencken. Each family member saw that his work was not in the slightest way disturbed. As he gained in prominence, guests were quick to observe how deferential Anna Mencken was to her eldest son.[1]

For the next eight years, Margaret Redding regularly came to the house. Should New Year's Day fall on a workday, she was nevertheless instructed to appear. During that time she missed only one day because of illness. The experience was an exhilarating one for her: "Never in all the time I worked for Mencken did I fail to catch my breath and feel my heart beat faster as I stood on his front steps at 1524 Hollins Street, waiting for the door to open to me." And this despite the fact that her arrival was invariably greeted with virtual indifference.

Walking up the stairs to the third floor, she would come at last to Mencken. He would be sitting at a small table, where he had been since eight that morning, preparing for dictation. At his right was a revolving bookcase; on the walls was a miscellany of sketches, paintings, and cartoons, among them a cigar poster of Oriole pitcher Matt Kelley. (A medical portrait of a uterine carcinoma had been briefly considered until the family rebelled.) At Mencken's left a pile of books awaited review; before him, the manuscript of a book he was rewriting, and there in a corner was a basin where he occasionally washed paste and carbon from his hands.

Mencken observed that his mother and sister never spoke of his room save in terms of horror, but to him it was the most orderly place of the house. It was a separate and distinct world that physically never spilled out into the other rooms by as much as a postage stamp, yet it dominated just the same. The room was in fact so small that if Mencken pushed back, his chair would touch a chest of drawers against the wall; if Miss Redding pushed back hers, she would collide with the small sofa where Mencken took his three o'clock nap. Outside was a walled yard and beyond that the alley, where they could hear the shouts of the neighboring children at play.[2]

His secretary soon discovered that Mencken was not a man to let her screen his mail, though he admitted being deluged with letters from "nutty strangers." In the morning, rather than wait to have his mail delivered on the regular route, Mencken called for the incoming letters at the post office near his house. Whether they numbered ten or eighty, he read and answered them all. After dictation, Miss Redding neatly typed his replies and delivered them to him in the afternoon. He signed each with his spiky signature, then sealed, stamped, and mailed it himself on the day it was received. This was not only for reasons of practicality but with a sense of propriety that his father had instilled in him. "I answer letters promptly as a matter of self-defense." he explained. "My mail is so large that if I let it accumulate for even a few days, it would swamp me. I also believe it to be only decent politeness. If I write to a man on any proper business and he fails to answer me at once, I set him down as a boor and an ass. So far, I have never heard of any evidence tending to upset such a judgment."

Letter writing for Mencken also imposed its small ceremonies. Before mailing, he sometimes mischievously stuffed the envelope with wine labels or religious brochures announcing the second coming of the Messiah, with a penned inscription: "This is authentic. Get ready." He also sent printed hoaxes of his own devising: a flyer for the Tobacco-Chewer's Protective and Educational League of America, and cards advertising the Friends of the Saloon or Ming Aaron's Kosher Chinese Restaurant. On other occasions he might affix labels above his address: "Booklets on Sex Education," once even a picture of skull and crossbones, in bold red letters marked "POISON."

Then there were the letters to ill friends, stuffed with medical documents and Mencken's recommendation that they dispense their physician, drink three stiff glasses of *Gluhwein*, and sleep on a stolen Bible. Most recipients forgot the advice, until, two days later, a worn Bible would arrive by parcel post, its cover blazoned with gold: "PROPERTY OF THE HOTEL ASTOR," the flyleaf bearing the inscription: "With the Compliments of the Author." In a long list of Menckenisms, the Bible caper became legendary; Mencken guessed he had stolen at least 75. As one associate reflected, "His writings, his conversation, his letters are all of apiece—and it is a beautifully integrated pattern."[3]

IN THE 1920s, when the question "What do you think of Mencken?" was a recurring phrase, there were those who believed receiving a letter from Baltimore was an honor to be treasured. Sherwood Anderson wrote in his memoirs: "We got the letters and the letters made us proud. 'Well, I had a letter from Henry Mencken today.' You said it casually, but in your heart, you felt that it was like being knighted by a king." Other authors echoed the reaction of Ben Hecht, who used to save his letters and "show them around as if they were citations."

Mencken composed at least 100,000 letters during his lifetime, an average of 1,500 or more a year, on plain half-sheets of white paper, single-spaced, with neatly worded letterhead. Their recipients ranged from journalists and authors to a rich assortment of other celebrities, from Groucho Marx to J. Edgar Hoover. "When Mencken found the time to write remains one of the great unsolved mysteries," Knopf mused. "His letters, of course, were masterpieces of condensation . . . and I think the half-sheets of stationery helped in this respect." Long letters or those of special interest, such as those to Dreiser, Mencken usually typed himself, but these were few.

The letters were dictated in a lively voice in staccato bursts. Mencken could switch his tone from warm to cold. Formality lay behind polite words, stock phrases that conveyed when a new author had little chance of having his manuscript accepted. Yet even here the sting was softened with a helpful suggestion. When he wrote to those he liked, the detached manner vanished and he could be brisk and engaging, but he could also be courteously frigid. In answer to long, boring letters, Mencken invariably replied: "Your *note* received and I agree absolutely with all you say." Very few were ever routine. Some recipients were unable to tell when Mencken was spoofing; as a consequence they interpreted everything literally and thereby misunderstood him. An awed Margaret Redding could scarcely look up from her notebook, for "there was suspense and a wonder-what's-coming-next feeling about sitting opposite him with the pencil poised."

The routine was rigorous. Three times a week Margaret Redding would appear at ten o'clock sharp—not five minutes before or five minutes after. One morning she arrived ten minutes late. As she took her seat beside his small desk, eyes on pad, pencil ready, Mencken suddenly boomed: "I would like you to be here at ten." "The streetcars," she faltered. "Oh, yes, the streetcars," he clipped in his unique, coarse grain. Nothing more needed to be said: "I had not yet learned one does not make excuses for failures to Mencken."

Moments for small talk were few and far between. When they did occur, Mencken would become "boyish, delightful, almost gay," but, as Margaret Redding realized, these moments were not a priority when work needed to be done.

Finally, at precisely twelve noon, Mencken would lead the way down the marble steps scrubbed so hard they shone. Then the front door would close behind her. Afterward, riding the streetcar, an envelope tucked neatly under her arm, Margaret Redding would think of the man she had just left behind at Hollins Street. Ruminating on all that she had been privy to in the morning's dictation, Margaret concluded that "typing Mencken's stuff gave me a taste for the emphatic. Gradually I awakened to his body of thought; it was far from my own. He did not convert me, but he widened my horizon."[4]

Initially, Margaret wondered why the house seemed so silent. Later, she realized that Mencken's need for quiet and routine was paramount. Hollins Street was his one retreat for writing, which for Mencken was not always easy. He would wrestle with what he called "intolerable complexities . . . shadowy notions that refuse to reveal themselves clearly, doubts that torture, hesitations that damn." Sometimes, Margaret thought, "I feel he was sensitive to the point of agony." In such moments, every sound became enormously magnified. Each jangle of the telephone cut into him like a knife, and he would rage that "no man can hear his telephone ring without wishing heartily that Alexander Graham Bell had been run over by an ice wagon at the age of four."

Writer's block was worst of all. "The writer must plod his way through many days when writing is impossible altogether—days of doldrums, of dead centers, of utter mental collapse. These days have a happy habit of coming precisely when they are most inconvenient—when a book has been promised and the publisher is getting out of patience. They are days of utter horror. The writer labors like a galley-slave, and accomplishes absolutely nothing. A week of such effort and he is a wreck. It is in the last ghastly hours of such weeks that writers throw their children out of sixth-story windows and cut off the heads of their wives."

FAMILY OBLIGATIONS OFTEN INTERRUPTED Mencken's writing routine, putting him "in a stew" with his projects "gone to pot." Much of this was brought on by his self-appointed role as the dutiful and affectionate son. Mencken made certain that the wants of each family member were attended to, however trivial, whether it be assisting at weddings, meeting relatives at trains, seeing that the bin was full of coal, or mending a leak in the plumbing. Even Tessie, the beloved family dog, was carefully scrutinized for signs of the malignant tumor that had plagued her for years.

One such interruption came when his brother Charles, accompanied by his wife, Mary, and their daughter, Virginia, arrived early one morning at Hollins Street. Mary was to have a kidney operation—a procedure Mencken had arranged with his friends at Johns Hopkins and planned to witness in order to relay full medical details to worried members of the family. Grandma and Aunt Gertrude greeted the visitors at the door. Uncle Harry had to be awakened—a privilege duly accorded to baby Virginia, who had grown into a bundle of bounces and dimples. Happily she climbed up to the third floor bedroom, burrowed to the bottom of numerous layers of blankets, and gleefully shouted into the ears of her groggy uncle, now grunting and snorting, that the relatives had arrived.

The boundless energy of Uncle Harry's four-year-old niece could be tiring. "She seemed to have a thousand legs—and she used all of them." In addition, "I hear her babble all day long," he wrote, "—agreeable music, but not favorable to literary composition." When not playing in the garden and chatting like a parakeet, the little girl could be found writing on a sheet of copy-paper in Mencken's room and singing at the top of her voice. Privately, he confessed, "It will be a strenuous week."

Nevertheless, Mencken adored Virginia, a fact not lost on his friends. Every February 14, they obediently mailed Mencken's valentines from where they lived so that the little girl could receive anonymous greetings from all points of the country. Virginia reflected later, "As I look back, it never ceases to amaze me that a bachelor could know so instinctively just what to do and say in pleasing a child." One of the highlights of a trip to Baltimore was a visit to the toy store around the corner from the house. "Once we were inside I was given carte blanche and could choose any and everything that caught my fancy. Tucked away in a box I still have a glass eye that he bought for me. I can still hear him chuckling when we got home from our shopping expedition and I displayed my purchase. 'It was all she wanted,' he said, 'and I had to get it for her.' Later he sent me a monocle to go with it."

Mencken never seemed to tire of watching her antics. One afternoon, he reported to a friend, after the little child had been "raising hell" throughout the house, "a very flashy looking woman came in, trying to sell me some Mss. The kid wandered in, observed the visitor speechlessly, and has been imitating her flirtings of the skirt ever since. They begin early." When it came to having children, Mencken advised all expectant parents that they should give birth only to daughters. Nonetheless, it was not until the imp had finally scampered down the steps of 1524 Hollins Street and was on her way back home to Pittsburgh that Mencken could look forward to getting enough sleep.

Harmony was restored after a series of renovations to the Mencken house. New parquet floors were laid, a larger kitchen was added, appliances to lessen the burden of housekeeping were purchased. The old-fashioned hissing gas globes

"She seemed to have a thousand legs—and she used all of them." Mencken and his niece, Virginia.
H. L. Mencken Collection, Enoch Pratt Free Library.

were replaced by electric lights; the entrance was rebuilt with a wrought-iron handrail in the shape of a lyre on the front steps. Slowly, much of the monstrous and heavy Victorian furniture of his childhood was hauled away and replaced by more modern pieces. Along with the rest of the country, 1524 Hollins Street had become firmly launched into the new era. Still, a host of sentiments clung to every item; it was a cherished sanctuary that Mencken had no intention of leaving.[5]

The females of the clan: Anna, Virginia, Gertrude, and dog, Tessie. H. L. Mencken Collection, Enoch Pratt Free Library.

MUCH OF MENCKEN'S CORRESPONDENCE WAS the compensation of a lonely man. Mencken's private life was orderly and austere, admittedly one of isolation. It was broken on Saturday nights, when Mencken left the maternal comforts of Hollins Street to continue his habit of spending recreational time in masculine company.

The Saturday Night Club still remained an integral part and would continue for another half a century. A colleague recalled: "It symbolizes, in a way, what are probably the chief interests of Mencken's life—friends, music, good food and drink and, above all, conversation. The rest, however important to the world, remains secondary."

This was the Henry Mencken Baltimore knew, the private man screened from observation of press and public, through which ran a stream of sentiment and warm humanity. The club was well known, though little known about, in and outside of Baltimore. As he looked back to these years, Mencken remarked: "Next to journalists, doctors, liberals and waiters, I have probably spent more of my time since 1900 with musicians than with any other class of men."[6]

The club began in 1904. Over the years, several professional musicians joined the original founding members. German-born Theodor Hemberger, with the Peabody Conservatory of Music, made arrangements of compositions. Max Brödel, a gifted German medical artist at the Johns Hopkins Medical School, played first piano to Mencken's second. Gustav Strube, former conductor of the Baltimore Symphony Orchestra and later of the Baltimore Symphony, had become, as Mencken put it, "a deckhand" of the club, with fiddle and baton. Joining them was Adolph Torovsky, the Naval Academy Band leader. Raymond Pearl, professor of biology at Johns Hopkins, contributed his French horn; Heinrich Buchholz, a Baltimore publisher, ranked as secretary and librarian.

The only rules were that you had to play or like music, have something to say when the conversation got serious, and above all, be congenial. When a man died, his chair would be tilted up against the table for one evening and a song played in his honor. Not even funerals could break the routine; the club never missed a night unless Christmas Eve fell on a Saturday.

Mencken remained the undisputed leader of the group. It was *his* letters from abroad that club members read aloud on those rare occasions when he could not be present; his impromptu speeches, accompanied by some outlandish antic, which club members laughed over uproariously and mulled over years later. As scholar Charles Fecher has pointed out, when it came to the Saturday Night Club, Mencken was at all times its mind, its heart, and its inspiration.

On a warm spring evening, Louis Cheslock, a composer and violinist with the Baltimore Symphony and chairman of Theory at the Peabody Conservatory of Music in Baltimore, first met Mencken. He found the editor seated at the piano, coatless, shirt sleeves rolled up, necktie removed, wearing a pair of suspenders, as if he were going to do some honest work.

Then Mencken began to play.

From the notes it was obvious to Cheslock that Mencken knew his music. While Mencken could sight read (though he confessed, "I read scores by moving my lips like a moron"), and would sometimes remark that he was tone deaf, like his father, this was far from true. "He could recall tunes by singing them more accurately in tune than I have ever heard sung by trained musicians of repute,"

The Saturday Night Club, 1937. H. L. Mencken Collection, Enoch Pratt Free Library.

recalled Cheslock. "And as for his memory of musical motifs, like his memory in general, it was nothing short of staggering."

Moreover, Mencken had the deepest love of music. The same rogue who anonymously slipped a note to a classicist pianist requesting that he play "Yes, We Have No Bananas" could also discuss techniques of composition, harmony, counterpoint, orchestration, and contemporary trends. He took a keen interest in the progress of young musicians, suggested projects to professionals, even helped create Baltimore's Park Band. Each spring he made trips to Bethlehem, Pennsylvania, to hear the Bach festival at a time of year that, as he put it, "his music rises in me like sap."

"To hear Mencken sing, of course, is a distinction," one contemporary noted. After the removal of his tonsils, friends noted that the operation had changed his voice from a mellifluous baritone to a very squawkish tenor, "but he loves to show it off." As for Mencken's piano playing, all agreed it was the loudest in the world. It is fair to say that when it came to the Saturday Night Club, the music was enjoyed more by the players than by the audience. "It was more like rhythmic *noise*." Often members practiced for weeks on a particularly difficult composition, although Mencken later confessed that the only thing the club could really play well was, in fact, "The Beer Barrel Polka."

Members, including Mencken, contributed original pieces. But he remained convinced he would have never gotten anywhere as a composer, that "a happy music-lover would have been sacrificed to make a bad musician." There were fervent music-lovers who could neither compose nor play, but who were none-theless invited to the club to listen, and later, to hoist a seidel. Members of the club had their names embossed on pewter lids; those for guests were engraved

DEADHEAD—a term that applied to Alfred Knopf, James Cain, Edgar Lee Masters, and an assortment of eminent governors, judges, and doctors, all of whom were only too happy to gain admittance to the club and so claim the title.

During Prohibition, the club met at the homes of members who were expected to have on hand a generous supply of home brew. At Hollins Street, the dining room would be filled to the point of suffocation. Feasts of fried chicken, steamed crabs, corn pudding, and peach pie would be prepared; after that, women and children were expected to disappear. Few resented it (many were only too happy to relinquish their husbands to a hobby). But there was at least one wife who was not eager to have a group of bawdy, lusty men wandering through her house, shouting uproariously, and continuously trooping up and down the stairs in search of the bathroom.

One summer evening, between blasts of laughter and music, Raymond Pearl's wife heard the screen door to the kitchen sporadically swing open and shut with a loud bang. This went on for quite some time, until, horrified, she discovered the side of the back porch was being used as a substitute for the bathroom upstairs. "My mother always tried to keep this a secret from me, which I caught on to," remembered Pearl's daughter, who also distinctly recalled the indignant reprimand her father received the next morning: "*What will the neighbors think?*"

Eventually, the club made its final move to Schellhase's, a German restaurant known for its pilsner and cuisine. After playing, members arrived in a body, with Mencken leading the way, clumping past staring patrons, his eyes fixed straight ahead, in a single-file procession to the back room. Then it was time to eat, drink beer, and frequently argue. Their discussions had a recurrent theme—who do you consider the greatest composer and why; other times they would listen to Mencken's impromptu discourse on, say, the intricacies of tapeworms and ringworms. Whenever thirsty, members rapped the table or raised an empty seidel, which an attentive waitress would silently refill.

Winding up a convivial evening, Mencken would then stand up. Holding aloft a fork for a baton, his eyes agleam, he would lead the group in bawling out some American or German folk song—"O, Susanna" or "Du, Du Liegst Mir Im Herzen." Then it was on to more beer and a rendering of one of the club's own compositions—"I Am a One Hundred Percent American"—and then the chorus, with a heavy banging of seidels on the table:

> *I am a one hundred percent American,*
> *I am, God Damn! I am!*

"They would be a little tight when it was over," recalled an observer, as club members stumbled away, their ties off, and their coats slung over their arms, leaving behind them the lovely reek of alcohol, cigar smoke, and sauerbraten.[7]

FOR MENCKEN, MUSIC WAS more than a hobby. His library included the best scholarly books on music available, with titles ranging from Mozart's operas to African American spirituals, from the humor found in cowboy songs to the physiological mechanics of piano technique. His knowledge of contemporary scholarship, as well as his involvement with the Saturday Night Club, gave Mencken's music criticism a performer's insight. This was especially important when one considers that in Mencken's day, no mass market for musicology existed. The large orchestrations of the Romantics overshadowed the smaller, more restrictive forms of earlier composers such as Haydn. Mencken's music criticism became a useful corrective, precisely because he examined a musical composition the same way he judged a work of literature: on the basis of its design and shape. One of his articles on Haydn, written in 1916 for the *Baltimore Sun*, pointed to the virtues in that composer that remained generally unrecognized for another forty years. Mencken delighted in the waltzes of Strauss; Jerome Kern remained his favorite American composer; likewise, the works of Gilbert and Sullivan provided constant joy, as did the rhythms of the old Negro spirituals.

Mencken had his blind spots, as guests to the Saturday Night Club were quick to recognize. "At first, hearing him on Beethoven, noting his hospitality toward modern music, hearing him quote friends, such as Stokowski, you would assume his taste to be vast, in all ways cosmopolitan," James Cain wrote. "But then," continued Cain, Mencken "would let drop, in a grimace or glancing crack, an opinion that verged on boorish" showing "the obtuseness, the Philistine prejudice, and the crassness of a saloonkeeper." He would simply proclaim: "There is German music—and other music." As for jazz, Mencken could find nothing in it. George Gershwin was only "a competent Broadway composer"; when Aaron Copland showed Mencken the score of his piano concerto, it seemed to be "rather obvious stuff." That his gusty passion for music was rigidly old-fashioned, confined mainly to Bach, Beethoven, and Brahms, was confirmed by Alfred Knopf. "I remember his being with us once at a performance of a new piano concerto by the Spaniard De Falla," the publisher said. "His only comment at the end was, 'It would have been better without the flats.' "8

Music simply dominated Mencken's thinking. As he put it, whenever he had a beautiful idea, it always came to him in the form of music, not words. References to music terminology saturated the text of his books, articles, and criticism. It followed that the highest compliment he could pay an author was to compare his writing to music. Even so, Mencken admitted, "I'd rather have written any symphony of Brahms than any play of Ibsen's." But as a musician, he said, "I shall die an inarticulate man, for my best ideas have beset me in a language I know only vaguely and speak only as a child."

For all of Mencken's assertions that he had the taste and not the capacity, he nonetheless underestimated his own talent. Even then, during that warm spring evening, as Louis Cheslock watched Mencken's untutored fingers master the

"Music dominated his thinking." Photograph by Carl Van Vechten. Courtesy The Carl Van Vechten Trust and H. L. Mencken Collection, Enoch Pratt Free Library.

keys on the piano with such surprising facility, the young man realized that these were the very same stubby fingers that composed with such color and rhythm on a typewriter. Indeed, Mencken had made the same comparison years earlier. The process of writing on the typewriter, he observed, was the same as playing the piano: it was unconscious, leaving him free to proceed with fluency from mind to paper without the slightest interruption.

The image is a memorable one. It is this, what Edmund Wilson called "some strain of the musician," that made it possible for Mencken to turn his ideas into literature. And while the Saturday Night Club remained a private side to Harry Mencken, as integral a part of him as his skin, in a much more subtle and fundamental way, music is what helped the shape the artist otherwise known as "That Man in Baltimore."9

23

THE DUEL OF SEX

THERE WAS ANOTHER PRIVATE SIDE to Mencken, extending beyond his domesticity at home and his musical evenings with the Saturday Night Club. Mencken's social life had now entered a new phase. Though there would be brief reconciliations with Marion, their meetings often terminated in volcanic eruptions. "She accuses me of various atrocities, including a lewd affair with some imaginary cutie," Mencken complained to Estelle. "What could be more idiotic? I never look at cuties."

As Marion was well aware, in New York during the twenties the literary and theatrical worlds mingled, with plenty of actresses, chorus girls, and cuties joining in a tumultuous social whirl. It was a time famous for parties, as Carl Van Vechten reflected many years later, with "lots of talk and certainly a good deal of lewd behavior." As soon as Mencken arrived at the Algonquin, he would cross over to the Royalton, where Nathan greeted his guests with cocktail shaker in hand. Then the two would be off to attend gatherings with gin brought in gallon jugs and the revelry lasting until the small hours. Mencken admitted it was not uncommon for him to encounter acquaintances outside of the Algonquin at four o'clock in the morning, when he was, as he put it, in "a sad state of dilapidation."

Mencken noted that Nathan seemed to have many affairs: "His flat is full of hairpins, garters and stray drawers." He was, according to screenwriter Anita Loos, "a blatant Don Juan." His custom of dating younger women no taller than his eyebrows extended to merry little Ann Pennington, a beauty of the *Ziegfeld Follies*, who with her closest friend, the glamorous Kay Laurell (otherwise known

as "the Girl with the Most Wonderful Figure in the World"), playwright Zoë
Akins, and the maliciously witty Loos, formed the easy company that Mencken
now mingled with. "Our M., once the pride of our alley, seems satisfied grazing
among the Broadwayites," Marion Bloom bitterly complained to her sister. " '*Old*
Kay Laurell,' '*Old* Zoë Akins.' . . . Can you picture this Jenny Wren competing
with them paradise birds? Life would be one long ghastly sweat."

Such glitter, however, provided intellectual ammunition for a social critic
like Mencken, who seemed to be the only male in New York unaffected by Kay
Laurell's wide-set violet eyes. In her, Mencken recognized an extremely shrewd
judge of the male species, with "all the arts of the really first-rate harlot." She was,
in fact, "the most successful practitioner of her trade of her generation in New
York." Helen Hayes, an ingénue at the time, described Laurell as a thoroughly
practiced gold digger ("the skull and crossbones were right there on the label for
all to see"). Any woman could get money out of a man, Laurell explained. What
took real skill was getting the money and evading the sleeping. "Much of what I
got from her, in fact, went into *In Defense of Women*," Mencken admitted; already
he was determined to publish a revision.[1]

These women were part of a new generation. As Mencken had noted at the
Democratic Convention, never before had women taken such an important role.
With the passing of the Nineteenth Amendment, women had gained the vote,
but "they are duly making fools of themselves," he said. Every day, he noted, "it
appears that a woman politician is indistinguishable from the male politician—
they both have their eyes centered upon the swill in the trough, and are quite
willing to do anything, however idiotic, to get their share. What becomes of the
old theory that women in politics would refine the science? Nothing remains of it
save a faint whiff of staling perfume."

Only when, in a repudiation of the Victorian and Puritan past, the hated
corset went into the closet and long black cotton stockings gave way to silken
hose did Mencken sense that the sexual revolution had arrived. Before the war
Mencken had championed women's use of make-up (as he said, "who wants to
kiss pale lips?"); now cosmetics had grown from a minor business to one of $500
million a year. In every town women were cutting their locks in favor of the new
bob. Mildly shocked when Marion did the same, Mencken told her family that
the look "suggests a Greenwich Village hussy." One can only imagine his reaction at Hollins Street when he found Gertrude sporting an identical style.

Women had achieved a new freedom, but in doing so achieved a predicted
result: innocence had been killed and romance sadly wounded by "smutty
artillery." In *In Defense of Women*, Mencken observed: "There is still much debate
of the old and silly question: Are platonic relations possible between the sexes?
In other words, is friendship possible without sex? Many a woman of the new
order dismisses the problem with another question: why without sex?" Their
new frankness was all highly embarrassing to the more romantic sort of men,
among whom Mencken considered himself. "If women, continuing their present

"Much of what I got out of her . . . went into *In Defense of Women*." Kay Laurell of the *Ziegfeld Follies*. The Billy Rose Theatre Collection, The New York Public Library.

tendency to its logical goal, end by going stark naked, there will be no more poets and painters, but only dermatologists and photographers."[2]

With the success of *In Defense of Women* (it would have eleven printings by 1928), much attention had been focused on Mencken's celibacy. When one newspaper reporter chided that he did not seem to be "over-fond of the female sex," Mencken rushed in to deny the charge. "Oh, yes, I am," he replied emphatically. "I have fallen in love very often—but not for very long. I like 'em not too young—with dark eyes and a sense of humor." Only when he was slightly stewed, he vowed, did a woman genuinely amuse him; even then, he confessed that what interested him most "is the consciousness that my hat and walking stick are standing in the hall, and that I am quite free to grab them and run whenever the spirit moves me."

That Mencken could remain so popular with females baffled many of his friends. Certainly Mencken's flirtations provided plenty of food for gossip. When news of an impending marriage was circulated by various newspapers, Mencken wrote to Hergesheimer that the report "played hell with my chances with a certain fair creature. She won't listen to my denials." As for Jane O'Roarke, his cutie from San Francisco, she lost her appeal to Mencken by 1923, when the papers reported her arrest for credit fraud. "She calls up my office every now and then, but I have her on the 'out' list," Mencken wrote poet George Sterling. "She seems to be pursuing a lamentable career, and I fear for her soul."[3]

FOR EVERY JANE O'ROARKE AFFAIR, there was another tender one to add to his list of conquests. Of these, the only women Mencken was "not afraid of" and knew well, according to Carl Van Vechten, were "the Broadway kind and middle-aged intellectual ones." Mencken came into regular contact with chorus girls in New York. Recalled Anita Loos: "I knew any number of *Ziegfeld Follies* beauties who went about carrying copies of his *Prejudices* under their arms on a chance of running into its author in that circuit of the West Forties that included their theater and his hotel."

Joseph Hergesheimer recalled that at his celebrated weekend parties in Wilmington, Delaware, Mencken could be engagingly diffident when introduced to very attractive women; obsequious, entertaining, and good-mannered, the very essence of gallantry. Here he met charmers with whom he exchanged photographs. To the Chicago journalist Fanny Butcher, he professed his love: "Fanny, I wish you wasn't so far off. . . . Fanny, we might set around when the shades of evening come busting down." Bee Wilson, an attractive journalist, was another whom Mencken accused of being "grossly untrue to my devotion." The *Smart Set*, Nathan bragged, provided each editor with a steady stream of flirtatious female literati. For seven years, between 1920 and 1927, letters and meetings passed between Mencken and the poet Bernice Kenyon. Mencken teased another contributor named Dorothy Taylor, "You are neglecting my welfare shamelessly," and that her absence from his side "fills me with despair." Letters scrawled with his wish for "making elaborate love to you" would give way to the hint, a few weeks later, that another female already had laid plans for his marriage. "What shall I do?"

Most women knew Mencken was kidding. Even Margaret Redding suspected that he could "gently ridicule the more forward gals by suggesting: 'When we are married you must remember to call me *Herr Mencken*.'" But years later, after Anita Loos had looked through the sheaf of letters from Mencken, she observed: "I can accuse him of a subtle type of come-on that kept our romance very actively alive."

Anita Loos had been obsessed with Mencken's editorials in the *Smart Set* long before she met him. To be in New York meant to be "breathing the same air as Henry Mencken." Shyly, she spied him in the lobby of the Algonquin. "My first impression of Mencken was of his arresting masculinity," she recalled. "He was smoking a big cigar which he held, like Pop, at a jaunty angle; aside from that sign of maturity, Henry Mencken looked like a young farmhand who was dressed in his best, with too much starch in his shirt and too high a collar. His boyish appearance made him all the more fascinating, for it aroused a girl's motherly instincts." His hair was full of cowlicks, of which a tuft or two always stood on end, "but Mencken's pale blue eyes had the permanent expression of an impudent schoolboy, and one felt that he was in full control at all times." They were the kind of eyes, Carl Van Vechten noted, that a widow might feel free to confide in. For Loos, Mencken was "an idol to adore for a lifetime."

Blondes, especially silly ones, chased after him. "They were all alike, and he had one after another—they never lasted very long!" Anita Loos recalled. "I will say Mencken never went after the blondes, they went after him." But one evening, the fact that one of these same blondes had "bedazzled one of America's foremost intellects" had Anita seeing fire, for "I was in love with Henry Mencken." Taking up her pencil, she began to scribble on a pad; the result was *Gentlemen Prefer Blondes*. Although the name of Lorelei was invented, her birthplace was not; yet even here "Mencken had a hand in that, for I wanted Lorelei to be a symbol of our nation's lowest possible mentality and remembered Mencken's essay on American culture where he branded the state of Arkansas as 'The Sahara of the Bozarts.'" Thus one of the most well-known blondes in American literature came from Little Rock.[4]

Mencken's affairs reached such proportions that, as Ernest Boyd told him, "your lecheries are becoming fabulous." A succession of "amazing and charming" and "exotic" creatures would press Boyd with questions soon after Mencken escaped on the train bound for home. On his own turf, Mencken did not have to dine unaccompanied either. Caroline Williamson, another *Smart Set* contributor, regularly met the "sweet and adorable Menck" before going home to Washington on the train at night—alone. "Did you ever *hear* of such a thing?" exclaimed Emily Clark to Hergesheimer after digesting this scintillating piece of tattle. "She must be one of the blondes that you said would wait for him for hours."

If, upon meeting one of Mencken's girls, friends were astonished by their features ("she was so queer looking" was one observation), then they did not understand that feminine attraction for him was primarily aural, rather than visual. Referring to "my peculiar taste in women," he once added: "I seldom give much heed to the faces and forms of women, and I never notice their clothes. But when a woman has a low-pitched and soft voice, with a good clang-tint, she is free to consume my wealth and waste my time whenever the spirit moves her." As one gossip columnist put it, "he knows very well he will fall in love with the next gal with a smooth, drawling voice who is fetched up to be laid as a sacrifice at his feet."

That women played a role subordinate not only to his work but also to men was a key principle in Mencken's view of society. It was Nietzsche who called women the recreation of the warrior, Mencken reminded his readers. With their "infinite capacity for rewarding masculine industry and enterprise," females were "incomparable companions when the serious day of business is done." Women may emancipate themselves, Mencken asserted, may "borrow masculine tricks, cure themselves from the vegetable security of marriage, but they will never cease to be women, and so long as they are women they will remain provocative to men."5

When asked to give a description of his ideal woman, Mencken told reporters to read the last page of *In Defense of Women*. "Get it out and judge for yourself if she isn't almost perfect," he said.

> It is the close of a busy and vexatious day—say half past five or six o'clock of a winter afternoon. I have had a cocktail or two, and am stretched out on a divan in front of the fire, smoking. At the edge of the divan, close enough for me to reach her with my hands, sits a woman not too young, but still good-looking and well-dressed—above all, a woman with a soft, low-pitched, agreeable voice. As I snooze she talks—of anything, everything, all things that women talk of: books, music, the play, men, other women. No politics. No business. No religion. No metaphysics. Nothing challenging and vexatious—but remember, she is intelligent; what she says is clearly expressed. . . . I observe the fine sheen of her hair, the pretty cut of her frock, the glint of her white teeth, the arch of her eyebrow, the graceful curve of her arm. I listen to the exquisite murmur of her voice. Gradually I fall asleep—but only for an instant. . . . Then to sleep again—slowly and charmingly down that slippery hill of dreams. And then awake again, then asleep again, and so on.
> I ask you seriously: could anything be more unutterably beautiful?

Helen Jerome, later a successful British dramatist who had been seeing Mencken off and on, answered with a scathing parody of this "nonsense" in *The Secret of Woman*, dedicating her work to Mencken "with the faint hope of reforming him."

> His god-like form reclines majestically upon a divan in front of a fire. . . . "At the edge of the divan" sits the Incomparable She . . . She sits at a respectful distance —the "edge" of the divan. Not near enough to incommode him, just sufficiently near to feel the pat of the royal hand in any stray moment of condescension. She has not had the impertinence to be too young . . . she knows her place well enough to be good-looking (*still* good-looking, he puts it, somewhat ungallantly) . . . nor does she offend him with any sordid topics such as "business," "politics," or "metaphysics." Far from this tactful, agreeable creature to offend him in any

way! And "Remember," he puts up an admonishing finger, "she is *intelligent.*" "I listen to the exquisite murmur of her voice and then gradually fall asleep. . . . The situation," he says, "is enchanting! ennobling!" and then he drifts into unconsciousness! I wonder what reflections pass through the mind—that "intelligent mind" of his hostess as she presides over the sleeping Jehovah on the divan.

Probably she wonders why he does not try massage.

But if Helen Jerome ever hoped to reform Mencken, she failed miserably. "All it did," she reflected years later, "was to send Mencken's book back into another edition."[6]

Throughout all this, Marion Bloom remained Mencken's best girl. For the preceding two years Mencken had been telling Marion, "you are the only woman I give a damn about," but for nine years their relationship had been marred by a series of ruptures. It shook Mencken's inner integrity off its base, "beyond any intelligible thinking," although when explaining its uneven course, Mencken cheerfully said, "This is normalcy." This served in a way only to strengthen the bond between them. As Marion reported to Estelle, "He says we'll never really be separated. As he says, we've both been through the fires and came out caring for each other."

During this period of reconciliation with Marion, during the last few weeks before he was to set sail for Europe, marriage seemed to play most often in Mencken's thoughts. One day he came across an old wedding invitation. Looking at it closely, he saw it marked his twenty-first anniversary as best man and decided to make this a subject for a Monday column. "For Better, For Worse" Mencken argued that most marriages were happy, though he concluded, with profound disregard for his own situation, early marriages were best: only before the age of 25 could love affairs properly described as beautiful. "When a man is a bachelor after 35 it is not necessarily a proof that he is a fellow hard to snare. It is simply a proof that no presentable woman has ever made a serious effort to marry him."

Mencken's column on the subject caused him to be psychoanalyzed, criticized, and accused of a desire to be wed. Friends customarily asked Anna Mencken what she thought of an article her son had written. "I haven't read it," she replied. "I never read anything he writes. That's his business."[7]

Arriving in London in September 1922, Mencken was surprised to be beset by friendly reporters. Throughout the war he had been critical of the British and had made no attempt to conceal the fact, yet now they politely acclaimed him as a phenomenon. It was Mencken "and he alone, who has put America on the literary map."

In outlook and manner Mencken was so thoroughly American and yet so biting in critique that the British dubbed him "the Yankee George Bernard Shaw." Walking along the Strand, the brim of his fedora curled at a stylish angle, his cigar sputtering like a tugboat, a trail of newspapermen listened open-mouthed to his criticism of his own country. The entire nation, Mencken said, "is rotten with money" and Americans "drunk" with its power. The American businessman was a futile sort who came to work merely to get in touch with his bootlegger and make engagements to play golf.

Newspapers back home groused after reading the cables. Across London there was silent rejoicing: "A truthful American at last." But when later in the week Mencken suggested that London had become too Americanized and that the British, who were imitating American skyscrapers, should "hang all the architects," the average Englishman began to bristle: "Throw the blighter out."

On the whole, however, Mencken was impressed by what he considered the freedom of the British—"the only people I know who have any real liberty left." England was recovering from the war in a very wonderful way, Mencken told reporters. "But when you ask me who won the war, I am reminded of a remark of Irvin S. Cobb. 'Who do you think will win the war?' asked a woman of him in 1919. 'My dear friend,' he replied, 'may I ask you who won the San Francisco earthquake?' "[8]

When Mencken moved on to Germany, the war was still uppermost on his mind. He was eager to examine the effects of the Treaty of Versailles. The icy gloom of 1917 had been replaced with green trees and flowers. Not a trace of the war was visible although the mark had climbed to one million to the American dollar. The hyperinflation had produced a spirit of recklessness. Although most foreigners were taken in by the gay whirl and abandoned night life, Mencken found Berlin in a state of frenzy, with drinking and prostitution the order of the day. While locals starved on a diet of rats and birds, it was difficult for Mencken to spend more than fifty cents on a meal; his stay in one of the finest hotels cost only $1.50 a night.

The world war had marked a turning point for Berlin, engulfed in a wave of violence and decay. The day before Mencken's arrival, a Communist uprising killed one man.

Mencken came away from Munich convinced that the days of the Weimar Republic were numbered and that anti-Semitism was on the rise. A number of these revolutionary Communist leaders happened to be Jewish. As Mencken reflected, "Munich remembered them and was already ripe, in the autumn of 1922, for reaction against democracy in all its forms." He wrote to Paul Patterson in September: "Outwardly, everything looks serene, but every intelligent man looks for a catastrophe. If it comes, then there will be a colossal massacre of Jews."

Mencken finished his European sojourn on the windswept isle of Wieringen in Holland, where Crown Prince Wilhelm, former heir to the German throne, was in exile. Of all the Germans, military and civilian, he had been the most detested by the allies, an object of ridicule and contempt, the "Clown Prince."

The prince told Mencken he was surprised at how little concern the United States showed for the economic situation in Europe. The cause, he said, was the Versailles treaty, "made in anger and in total disregard of the most elementary economic laws and common sense. Today the fact that it is utterly unworkable is obvious to everyone . . . but the United States opposed the treaty before it was signed and has never ratified it since . . . I can see no way out save through a catastrophe. That catastrophe, remember, is not remote: it lies directly around the corner."

Inside Germany, Mencken's *Baltimore Sun* interview did not seem particularly new. "The Prince rehashed a good deal of what he has always said," Mencken's friend, the German author Hermann George Scheffauer, wrote him, and no German paper wanted a translation. But in the United States, the piece was well received by the *New York Times*, which stated that Mencken's interview "practically compels a revision of former judgments of the Prince and his conduct."9

Prince Wilhelm's forecast coupled with what Mencken had been observing for himself in Germany made a powerful impression on him. "The newly created states in central Europe, including Poland, are artificial," he told reporters in Berlin. "They are steering straight for bankruptcy and will collapse when their big backers withdraw." Mencken was astonished about how much ignorance prevailed in the United States about the burden of reparation payments. Privately, Mencken offered to assist the German Foreign Office in publicizing information regarding its dire economic condition. Once in the United States, he met with German officials and offered to distribute 500 copies of a pamphlet, *Germany's Economic and Financial Situation*, where they would have the most effect. That he might be accused of spreading propaganda was of no concern to him. He was convinced that the "imbecilities" of the Versailles Treaty could never be corrected by argument—only blood and iron could rectify them. Moreover, "the German people would see to the business in due time, and with a reasonable chance of success."

Finding himself back in Germany, especially in 1922, made Mencken feel an even closer personal tie to his roots. At the University of Leipzig he acquired copies of four Mencken family portraits in oil and a large number of engravings. He thrilled at walking along the Menckestrasse. At the Thomaskirche Mencken saw the memorial Mencke window: "It is directly under the choir," Mencken exulted in a letter to his little brother, "where Johann Sebastian Bach used to hold forth."

It was vital, not only as an author in his own right but as a *Mencken*, to have his work appear in Germany. To this end, his friend and translator Hermann George Scheffauer helped lead the way. Calling Mencken "one of the few really modern literary critics," Friedrich Schönemann of *Die Neue Zeit*, one of Germany's leading periodicals, observed: "In particular, German Americans should take note and evaluate him in his . . . tenacity. He did not let the one hundred percent American harass him . . . he has triumphed in his own field in his own way."

The German press was impressed by "that man in Baltimore," and Mencken left his new companions telling one another vivid accounts of his visit. "Those were hallucinative days and nights you brought us—I was immensely bucked up by you, and felt how much I needed someone of your dynamic presence," Scheffauer wrote. All fell victim to his charm, including Scheffauer's two-and-half-year-old daughter: "Fiona Francisca talks of Onkel Mencken almost every day, and habitually kisses his picture good night."[10]

AWAITING HIM at the Bristol Hotel in Berlin was a long essay from Marion, lecturing Mencken on the virtues of Christian Science, to which he responded: "What you say, Madame, has a very sweet reasonableness," but "good cooking is a damned sight more important in this carnal and loathsome life than accurate theology."

When Mencken's ship returned to New York, Marion experienced a repetition of the emotions that had scarred her so painfully during his previous return from Europe five years before. Their affair simply resumed as it always had, with Christian Science renewing Mencken's doubt that marriage to Marion could ever work. "Do you blame me," he asked her, "if I hesitate to take on a Civil War?" Marion complained to Estelle: "Once again he had changed bases and wanted to build on a tottering foundation. And so we ended. Ended! Ended puny physical meetings."

Expressing her anger to Mencken, who by this time had become less tolerant of Marion's metaphysical speculations than he had been in Berlin, did not exactly elicit the reply from him that she craved:

> You are very charming, but I also think you are somewhat unjust. You seem to be trying to conjure up a picture of a very selfish and thoughtless fellow, bent on securing his own convenience. This is certainly not true. What you have actually before you is a fellow who had his eyes on a certain person and then suddenly found before [him] quite another person. The shock dam near bowled him over.

Finally, Mencken in a frank statement revealed the real nature of their problem: that work, not marriage, was his firm goal in life, to which all else had to be subordinated.

Marion, in the meantime, as Mencken was fully aware, now had another suitor—a Jewish Roumanian named Lou Maritzer. Several months before, Mencken had already met "my hated rival and gave him my blessing."

Desperately uncertain which suitor she should ultimately choose, Marion's letter to Estelle revealed the extent of her anguish: "I never pretended to cease loving him. In spite of everything, I have never ceased adoring him. The most trivial thing was in terms of H sharing it. The approach of the train to Baltimore, after Lou had started me off, meant H . . . Oh, it is awful."

Then, when Mencken least expected it, Marion dropped the bombshell. The wedding date to Maritzer was set for July 28, 1923.

"Lou wants me to marry him at once," Marion wrote to her sister in midsummer. "Waves of sickness came over me—no more letters from H., with the half-defiant thought, 'What did they ever amount to but evasion, anyway?' " How could she love him, she asked: "Can one love and respect a man who has caused one humiliation and pain? It seems as if H cruelly punished me for loving him."

While the prospect of never seeing Mencken again haunted Marion, she fully recognized the real nature of their problematic relationship: that "inner urge for what he called freedom. I discerned that he saw in me (the woman I believe he loved) an enemy to that freedom." Even with this bitter realization, she sought to protect Mencken; her marriage to Lou Maritzer, Marion warned her sister, *must* be kept secret. Then, abruptly changing tactics, Marion asked her sister to do her one favor. "Gloom, will you please tell H? And be very gentle and sweet about it and tell him everything is utterly crazy and I am much better off and he is much better off free of me forever."

Thus it fell to the ever-patient Estelle the task of breaking the news to Mencken. He had written a book about the wiles of the female; now Marion had made a fool of him. It was a bad hour for her; he cursed Marion for being "a goddam gentleman" not to have grabbed him years before and instead granting him his freedom to work. But his fury could hardly cover the hurt he actually felt. In a letter to Estelle, Mencken reflected:

> Well, such is human destiny in a world run by a damned jackass. Little will that gal ever suspect how near she came to cooking, washing and ironing for the next President of the United States. But certainly you must know what happened: the Christian Science fever simply scared me to death. Worse, my general rampaging in late years scared *her* to death. The thing would have been hopeless.

"She lives in a world of dreams—many of them beautiful," he concluded. "I am 43, and all things begin to seem far off. But I shall not forget."

Mencken also mailed Marion what he thought would be his final letter.

> What am I to say? That I wish you the happiness that no one deserves so much as you do. That I have got out some old letters of yours, and re-read them and burned them, and now sit down and smoke my pipe, and wonder what in hell it is all about.

As he once said to Zoë Akins, "The heart forgets, but the shattered nerves remember."[11]

OTHER MATTERS WOULD DISTRACT Mencken the rest of 1923, though at the time he did not suspect how one of them would result in a major change in his own life. Some time before Marion's wedding, Mencken had accepted an invitation to lecture on writing at Goucher College and "about the one thing they are interested in. I tell them how to catch a man." Now, on this warm spring evening, the female students gathered to sit quite literally at his feet.

To the student Sara Mayfield, Mencken's "neat blue serge suit, stiff collar, and hightop shoes gave him the appearance of a professor from Johns Hopkins rather than a high-flying, hardhitting idol smasher." With his cowlicks carefully slicked down and a manner of rocking slightly back and forth on his heels and twisting a handkerchief as he spoke, his china-blue eyes brimmed with amusement as he surveyed his audience. Then his eyes rested on one young lady in particular.

Tall, slender, and willowy, Sara Haardt looked straight at him with large, soft, brown eyes. At 25, she was the youngest member of the faculty. Later that evening, Sara attended a dinner for Mencken with other members of the school. When, during the course of the dinner conversation, he heard that besides teaching she wrote short stories, he asked if he could see her work. Afterward, she would admit she had been sending manuscripts to the *Smart Set* ever since she had been "big enough to lift a stamp." It seemed clear to Sara Mayfield that Mr. Mencken, "with the grin of a small boy showing off before his girl," was trying to angle Sara "into casting a line his way." As for Sara Haardt, reported Mayfield, she listened to Mencken with wide, admiring eyes, as well as "with the rapt attention she reserved for those marked for conquest."

All too soon, the evening was over. Mencken lifted his fedora straight up from his head in the gesture of a Southern gentleman and bade the women goodnight with the promise, "We must do this again soon." H. L. Mencken, the women agreed, was one of the kindliest, most courteous of men.

Later, slipping into the room of her closest friend and confidante, professor Ola Elizabeth Winslow, Sara Haardt declared to her astonishment, "I'm going to marry that man!"

The older woman looked at Sara. "Well," she could only answer, "*That* will take some doing."[12]

The next morning, Sara Haardt turned up at Baltimore's Chelsea Pharmacy where Goucher College women habitually gathered. A copy of *In Defense of Women* was on the top of a pile of blue exam books. "Well, hussies, let me read you what our host of last evening has to say about us." Laughing, she began to leaf through the book, reading out loud Mencken's view of the female species.

As the weeks progressed into the summer of 1923, so did the meetings between Mencken and Sara. To anyone observing the two of them seated at lunch, the sight must have seemed incongruous: the stocky individual with the table manners of—as he himself put it—Cro-Magnon man, and the willowy, delicate creature eighteen years his junior, a Confederate from Montgomery, Alabama, from a region Mencken had labeled "The Sahara of the Bozart." Mencken ate with gusto, while Sara usually ate, according to Mencken, "like an Armenian refugee," picking on "fruit salads and other cobwebs."

A contemporary wrote that from across a crowded room Sara looked "alarmingly beautiful: oval face full of magnolia blossom texture, fine features framed in dark curls; luminous almond-shaped eyes, full sensuous mouth"; a graceful figure with a soft cheesecake-y form that James Cain admired, and "well dressed, in a quiet, tasteful way." As for her voice, it was low, like that of her childhood friend

Tallulah Bankhead, gently Southern, as another put it, "without a trace of *cawn pone*." Sometimes Sara's voice could verge on a growl when she said what she thought of people. Cain recalled that he never heard her cuss, "but profanity seemed to lurk just under the surface, in a most amusing way. She wasn't funny, and had none of Mencken's compulsion to clown, but she had plenty of wit, of a smoldering, ironical kind," accompanied by a throaty laugh.

To her Goucher students Sara seemed remote and mysterious, "a born writer who *looked* a born heroine." Many of them tried to imitate her slow, gracious movements, others, her large, legible handwriting. She had, as Mencken later said, "a full measure of that indefinable, pleasant thoughtfulness which passes commonly under the banal name of Southern charm." It was this charm of manner that, said R. P. Harriss, one of her later admirers, "in a less prosaic age inspired men to go out in the field of honor and shoot each other full of holes."

Nonetheless, as Mencken always maintained, "No unmarried woman can be polite to a bachelor without beginning to speculate how he would look in a wedding coat," adding, "this fact, which is too obvious to need proof, makes friendly dealings with them somewhat strained." In time, Sara discovered for herself how far Mencken would go to keep girlfriends at bay. Like Marion, Sara was not invited to the house, nor was she introduced to Anna Mencken. Her disappointment in this matter was only casually revealed during the course of conversation among her friends. Then, her eyes would darken, she would go into a sulk, and she would become dour, squint-eyed and introspective.

Yet when it came to marriage, Sara gave the impression of just as vigorously agreeing with Mencken. A modern woman, as she later wrote in a novelette, does not rush into matrimony: "I would advise any woman to wait. . . . There is so much in life—so much for a woman to see and do—it would be a pity for her to miss it. Of course, marriage is a career. But it isn't life, it isn't everything!"[13]

Over time, Mencken and Sara grew to respect each other's intelligence, humor and culture. In Sara, Mencken had found a soul mate.

Before going to lunch, Mencken and Sara often met at the Timanus Rock Mill, an old stone structure on the fringe of Druid Hill Park. The abandoned grain mill was in a state of ruin during the 1920s, but it was scenic and afforded a place to sit and watch the gurgling stream while being lost in the heart of the city. Here, during Prohibition, Mencken and Sara would brave the cold to share a sip of liquor.

SUCH ACTS WERE HEROIC FOR SARA. In January 1924, Mencken learned shocking news—she was seriously ill. Outside, the weather had taken a turn for the worse. Temperatures plunged to nine degrees Fahrenheit and were accompanied by high gusty winds. Even with a fever, Sara insisted on rising from her sickbed to meet with Mencken. When students came back to Goucher College from Christmas vacation, they found that their professor had suffered throughout the holidays with an acute bronchitis bordering on pneumonia.

"... a soulmate." Sara Powell Haardt. Photo by Eareckson. Courtesy Bettina Patterson.

Marjorie Hope Nicholson, an assistant professor of English, had always looked upon Sara as her little sister. Feeling responsible for her now, she turned to general practitioners who were all they could afford. There was a flu epidemic raging, and hospitals were so crowded it was impossible to get Sara a room. Protective as ever, Mencken stepped in, lining up an appointment with his friend, the radiologist Max Kahn. The prognosis was not good. Sara had a spot as big as an orange near the back of her left lung—the sure sign of tuberculosis. Upon hearing the news, Mencken immediately sought to comfort her. "A brave gal you are indeed! I hadn't suspected half your difficulties."

Sara's own reaction to the news was to spiral into depression. The only recourse open to those in her condition was isolation, but the prospect of languishing for years in a sanitarium seemed to her too dismal to contemplate. "I'm not going to live this way," she told Marjorie Nicholson. And then, on the eve of her eventual departure for the clinic, in a most dramatic gesture of all, Sara asked Marjorie to retrieve the pistol she had stored in a trunk downstairs from her hall bedroom. Marjorie obeyed, but took the precaution of first unloading the weapon.

"But you haven't put anything in it," Sara said.

"Oh," fibbed Marjorie, the bullets secretly hidden in her pocket. "I didn't know what to put in pistols."

Sara ordered her to look anew. "You go downstairs because I'm going to kill myself," she said. Marjorie delayed her supposed search until the doctors arrived to take Sara to Maple Heights, fifteen miles from Baltimore. The entire macabre episode was a secret Nicholson did not divulge to the public until half a century later. Only to Mencken did she apparently confide: "He was awfully good to people who needed comfort."[14]

MARCH 1924 WAS ICY AND WINDY, the coldest and wettest spring in Baltimore since 1917. Despite the snow, hail, and rain that plagued Baltimore from January to June, Mencken battled the elements and visited Sara at her hilltop sanitarium. "If you hear a sound like a washing-machine's at 2:30 tomorrow," he told her, "it is a sign that I am coming up the hill and making heavy weather of it." During this period of recuperation, Mencken helped Sara with her short stories. Mencken also loaned her books that he considered models of humor and realism: the latest published work of Ring Lardner, Edgar Lee Masters, and especially, Sinclair Lewis. During their visits, they would discuss literary gossip over sherry that he brought with him. Often, their conversation would go on for so long that Mencken had to race down the alpine hill to catch the train back to Baltimore.

Mencken's company afforded Sara an intellectual stimulus and raised her spirits at an especially difficult time. He continued to light up his letters with encouragement, refusing to let her admit defeat: "Courage, Camille!"

Without Mencken, there was an immense void. Advice on how to best deal with a famous bachelor came from the older and wise Marjorie Nicholson, who told her not to besiege a busy man with long letters: "All he wants is notes, and he'll pay attention to you. And *don't* keep writing." But for a man who was in constant receipt of mail from women all over the country, Sara's reticence was distressing: "Why don't you write? I never hear from you!"

Their relationship was hardly one-sided. During the eight months of Sara's convalescence, Mencken's affection flourished. She possessed a rare quality that Mencken had always admired in women: a talent for listening tempered with insight, understanding, and wit, not always devoid of a certain acidity. James Cain would later write that Sara "could see through most people." The writer James Tully, after meeting her, wrote admiringly: "It is amazing how many young women try to solve life with fluttery questions. You don't." By the end of a few visits Mencken was already writing, "I suspect that I am mashed on you."[15]

When Sara departed Baltimore to recuperate in Montgomery, their correspondence continued, but in the years ahead, even after her return, there would be other flirtations that questioned Mencken's ardor.

24

OLD DISCORD AND NEW ALLIANCES

W HAT A STORY the true history of the rise and fall of the Mencken-Nathan partnership will make someday," Alfred Knopf mused in his diary. There were ominous rumblings in the relationship as early as 1923 although the complete break would not come until 1932. In the interim, the two men outwardly maintained a superficial friendship and most people never knew the depth of their schism. To those observing them up close, however, the partnership was, as one contemporary noted, "like a bad marriage that should not have been made in the first place."

Their association had initially been fruitful, "unique in American literature," as Ernest Boyd put it, "for never were two men so dissimilar." Mencken charged the air with energy; according to some, Nathan looked "as if he were born tired." Of the two, Mencken remained popular within his own circle; others recalled that no one seemed to like Nathan. Edmund Wilson called Nathan "a pernickety and snubbing little man" whose "insolence has intimidated people, so that they have been afraid to point out how badly he writes and thinks a good deal of the time."

Even Philip Goodman found Nathan "a terrible poseur," whom he held in contempt for his foppish clothes that, by some mysterious law, never seemed to wrinkle. Surely it must have taken a considerable effort to maintain the image of the suave sophisticate, like the critic in Joseph Mankiewicz's screenplay *All About Eve*, for whom Nathan served as a model.

The partners were constantly accused of imitating each other, a notion Mencken found absurd. No two men could possibly have been more unlike in style and thought. "Nathan detests philosophical questions," Mencken said. "He

Played brilliantly by George Sanders!

sees life purely as an idiotic spectacle. I delight in such questions, though I reject all solutions. Nathan aims at a very complex style. I aim at the greatest possible lucidity."

But for all these differences, there remained an essential similarity between the two men. They shared the passion for introducing the work of fledgling American writers, the humor, and the relentless attacks upon sacred cows. While very different species, the two complemented each other.[1]

The truth is that neither could have produced the *Smart Set* alone. Mencken would not have left Baltimore for Manhattan, and, Ernest Boyd believed, Nathan could never have achieved that patience toward struggling authors on whom Mencken lavished so many hours of a busy life. The result of their collaboration was a magazine that Edmund Wilson felt was one of the great stimulants of the era, when the creative and liberating spirit of the magazine seemed "a dazzling phenomenon."

But much had changed in both men in the years following the war; Mencken wanted to publish the facts that no one else dared to print, to conduct a realistic investigation of the "whole, gaudy, gorgeous American scene." Nathan, on the contrary, said the great social and political questions of the time did not concern him in the slightest: "I care not who writes the laws of a country so long as I may listen to its songs."

Knopf once again raised the subject of launching a new review that would focus directly upon culture, society, and politics. It was an idea much embraced by Mencken, who had been planning such a magazine for more than a decade; he was sick of the *Smart Set*. Of the three, it was Nathan who balked. The *Smart Set* had served its purposes, he argued, and its essential features, if not its name, should be preserved.

Nathan's resistance disconcerted Knopf, who recognized, if Mencken initially did not, that the new monthly they envisioned would go far beyond Nathan's range of interest. Were it not for the fact that nine years before, under similar circumstances, Nathan had stuck by their partnership, Mencken no doubt would have been tempted to edit the new publication alone. Out of loyalty to his friend, he insisted that Nathan be retained as co-editor. Nathan agreed.

The death of President Harding on August 2, 1923, led to the departure of Mencken and Nathan from the *Smart Set* to the new venture. They had lampooned Harding in the magazine; now they saw no reason not to publish a mildly satiric parody on the funeral train and the saccharine efforts of the press to drum up national mourning for an amiable president whose journey home was being compared to the legendary cortege of Lincoln. When the copy reached the printer, a compositor called its conservative publisher, Eltinge Warner. Had he seen what his editors were saying about their president? Warner had not. The essay was read to him over the phone.

Warner exploded. "I don't give a damn what you thought of him," he stormed to Mencken and Nathan. "Harding was our president, after all." Besides,

Nathan contended, the issue was in print. "Write something else—run it blank—
I don't give a damn!" the publisher yelled. "But I won't have that kind of dis-
respect in *my* magazine. And I can tell you this much: you won't do it again. The
Smart Set's for sale!"

In the end, Nathan vetoed the piece himself, but the damage had been done.
Warner eventually found a new buyer, William Randolph Hearst, who acquired
the rights for $60,000, of which Mencken and Nathan reaped $15,000 each.
Under Hearst, a typical issue of the *Smart Set* featured an article by the Reverend
Billy Sunday, a poem by Edgar Guest, and articles such as "Is Marriage an Aid to
Success?" and "When a Man Laughs at Love." "I am glad that the change is so
violent," Mencken observed. "Now nobody will ever suspect that I still have a hand
in it." The "Magazine of Cleverness" had become a moneymaker, a confirmation
of Mencken's comment that "No one in the world has ever lost money by under-
estimating the intelligence of the great masses of the plain people."

For Mencken, the outcome was for the best. As he wrote in his final *Smart Set*
editorial, the objective of the magazine in 1908 had been accomplished: the
young American novelist, dramatist, or poet was now *free*. Back then, any protest
against him was damaging; "today it is only ridiculous." Mencken could now
devote his energy to planning a new review that would present a realistic survey
of what was going on in the country, with as much good humor as possible. The
magazine, however, was not dedicated to reforming the United States; if anything, Mencken believed reformers were frauds. But even reformers, Mencken
recognized, had human juices in them, so the new publication would spotlight
their fraudulence and other varieties of quackery, without indignation, "and
above all, without any howling for the police." "It is my hope . . . to stir up the
animals," Mencken enthused to his friend Max Brödel. "The prospect makes me
young again."[2]

In September, letters solicited advertisements and subscriptions for the new
magazine, which was to be called the *American Mercury*. Mencken, meanwhile,
sought articles on American themes from such authors as Upton Sinclair, James
Weldon Johnson, and Theodore Dreiser. From his friends in medicine and
chemistry, Mencken requested articles on osteopathy, patent medicines, and
death.

Obtaining contributors, however, was a frightful job. Mencken found writers
to be "a bit nervous, fearing that I shall advocate assassinating Coolidge in the
first issue. After two or three numbers it will be easier. I resign Coolidge to God."
Not everyone was enthusiastic about the new review. The fact that the editors
had embarked on a serious magazine sounded to some as though Mencken and
Nathan had completely lost their sense of humor.

As Thanksgiving drew near, the *American Mercury* organization was completed. The original print order was a modest 10,000 copies, with the date of the
first January 1924 issue set for sale on December 25, 1923. Contrary to Knopf's
recollection that the press was unfailingly cordial, there was little actual support
in the newspapers. F. Scott Fitzgerald announced that the appearance of the

"The young novelist was now free." *The Smart Set*, June 1922. H. L. Mencken Collection, Enoch Pratt Free Library.

American Mercury in 1924 promised to be "the real event of the year," but that was by no means the overwhelming opinion.

By the eve of publication, the editors were understandably tense. For a month the printers had delayed their work. At the eleventh hour when all arrangements were to have been made, Mencken was dramatically summoned to New York. There he found Knopf "with a pulse of 245 and his forehead cold and clammy."

The printers were objecting to what they called James Cain's scurrilous attack on unions in his article "The Labor Leader." Mencken's reaction was violent. Since when did a printer set himself up as a censor of the matter for which he assumed no responsibility whatsoever? But the Rumford Press stood firm. At the last minute, a new printer was procured.

Mencken and Nathan were under tremendous pressure. An interviewer found Mencken solemnly pacing the floor.

"We have wanted to do this for years," Nathan told him. "We don't want a rest; we want another round." Yet neither editor was willing to commit himself wholeheartedly to the *American Mercury*. Nathan would only go so far as to say "it will not be a bore." Mencken silently nodded. The interviewer, a fervent admirer of the *Smart Set*, deeply regretted its passing and wanted to give his readers the assurance that the new magazine was going to continue in the same vein. The editors assured him they would still be staging a circus—"with the horses running around," said Mencken; "and the band playing," added Nathan.[3]

THE FIRST ISSUES of the *American Mercury* quickly sold out. Its reception boggled the wildest expectations of the editors. In format and content, the periodical was hailed as the most significant event in literary circles in America for many years.

Knopf had taken pains to give the magazine a distinctive appearance. The *American Mercury* was handsome, with a Paris-green cover decorated with elegant marginal scrolls by Elmer Adler, a noted typographer of the day. The paper was imported Scotch featherweight; each issue's bindings were sewn in such a manner that it readily opened out flat like a book; there were no illustrations. It cost more than its competitors: 50 cents a copy, $5 a year.

The first issue set the pattern more or less consistently for the next years, reflecting Mencken's passions and prejudices. Inside were portraits of key figures: a debunking of "The Lincoln Legend," a study of Stephen Crane, and a collection of personal letters to friends by the late James Huneker. An article on "The Drool Method of History" criticized the tendency of historians to succumb to sectional, racial, and nationalistic bias. There were articles on politics and military matters, a poem by Dreiser, and three short stories, one contributed by Ruth Suckow.

By far the strongest section was on "Arts and Sciences," containing brief essays on medicine, architecture, and language—something quite new in quality journalism. In time nearly all of Mencken's interests were featured under this heading: science, the law, theology, pedagogy, music, as well as subjects with which he was not especially concerned, such as fine arts and radio. "The Theater," which dealt with the latest new plays and Broadway personalities, was written by Nathan. Though contemporary literature was treated in various articles, comment on the writing of the day was concentrated in Mencken's own book reviews.

Mencken's influence could be keenly felt in "Americana," a standard department originated in the *Smart Set*, which lampooned publications across the country. Not all were treated humorously. Dozens of contributions arrived at the office every day. The criterion for selection was his plea to stick to stuff that was utterly idiotic. Later, his assistant was told to remember that "The Americana must be *very* grotesque. Anything that may be defended logically is barred out." Foolish literary judgments, brutality in the South, religious oratory were all subjects for ridicule.

In Mencken's introduction to *Americana 1925*, a representative sampling of the clippings in book form, he said the items, as the rest of the *American Mercury*, offered documentary evidence and a revelatory insight into daily life and "what is going on in the minds of the masses—the great herd of undifferentiated, good-humored, goose-stepping, superstitious, sentimental, credulous, striving, romantic American people."

Mencken's aims in humorously setting forth the absurdities of American life were, however, the least of his concerns. One of the principal aims of the *American Mercury* was "to introduce one kind of American to another." Mencken was among the first to deal seriously with journalism and regularly commissioned such essays as "Schools of Journalism Today," "The Immigrant Press," "The Yiddish Press," and "Newspaper Girls." It was also the *Mercury* that brought the Paul Bunyan folklore to readers; before that, it was chiefly known only to folklore specialists. Other articles dealt with neglected authors of American literature, resurrecting Poe, Crane, Twain, and Whitman. Still others examined education, language, race, eugenics, medicine, business, religion, even America's past as reflected in Mencken's childhood. Regional differences were explored as well, through discussions on individual states as well as their local press and poets.

A much smaller part of the magazine was written by established creative writers—Ben Hecht, Dorothy Parker, Sherwood Anderson, F. Scott Fitzgerald, William Faulkner. Other *Mercury* contributors wrote profiles of one another—a feature later made famous in the *New Yorker*. Instead of assigning topics to professors thousands of miles from Washington, he had political pieces written by newspapermen who saw politicians week in and week out. Every hero (and rogue) of more than local interest was included. Mencken's discoveries included hobos, bricklayers, generals, Indians, doctors, lawyers, a bishop, and a U.S. senator. He even found contributors in prisons, with the unhappy result that "half the crooks in the United States seem to be going in for beautiful letters," Mencken commented. "I have to be polite to all of them, poor dogs!" At that, he published eighteen essays of the damned.

It didn't matter if some of the authors remained unknown. Mencken had scoured the country for interesting people to tell their own stories. "They have run the whole scale from visionaries to criminals, from heroes to poor fish," he argued. "But all of them, living out their own lives, have written with that earnest simplicity which is beyond all art, and some of their papers have been among the most moving and interesting things the magazine has printed." He was convinced that there were thousands of backwaters in America that remained to be explored.

At a time when black writers were not featured in white publications, when most Americans regularly tuned into *Amos n' Andy* on their radios, Mencken was the first white editor to dispense with stereotypes and try to depict the complexity of black life. He published 54 articles and devoted 15 editorials by and about blacks on a multitude of subjects—politics, religion, art, folklore, newspapers, music, and race. Writers such as Walter White, W. E. B. Du Bois, Langston Hughes, James Weldon Johnson, and Countee Cullen were regularly published; George S. Schuyler's article, "A Negro Looks Ahead," created a sensation not only in the South but also throughout the country.

"Appearing in the *American Mercury* was regarded as something, and if a Negro was good enough to appear in the *American Mercury*, then there must be other Negroes who could write well or better," recalled Schuyler. The *American Mercury* was an important factor in the development of African Americans as a writing group; *Harper's* and the *Atlantic* later followed suit.

"What Mencken actually accomplished was nothing less than a revolution in American journalism," reflected a colleague. Although Mencken denounced the *booboisie* month in and month out, he actually democratized quality journalism. "The intellectuals of the big cities were thrilled to read all about this America that only the newspapers had hitherto dealt with, and skimpily at that."

In less than a year, the magazine won credit for influencing widespread changes in the industry. Older and well-established magazines such as *Harper's* and the *Century* published articles that earlier would have been unheard of. "Americana" and the profiles were openly imitated in such established publications as the *Saturday Evening Post* and later the *New Yorker*. It was the first popular monthly to establish a music department, giving Mencken more influence on music criticism than any other editor. The *American Mercury* also got credit for stimulating the make-up of magazines. *American Printer* noted that other monthlies had brightened their covers and improved stodgy typography. The *American Review of Reviews* and the *Living Age* dropped their familiar old size and enlarged their pages; *Harper's, Forum, Dial, Scribner's, Century,* and *Current History* changed their typefaces.

While the buoyant and challenging tone was partially induced by the spirit of the twenties, many viewed the *American Mercury* as the primary influence in the revitalization. "But when all is said and done," the *New York Telegraph* noted, "it has been the literary personality of Mr. Mencken which has made the publication."

By December 1923 a second printing of the *American Mercury* had been prepared, then a third, with 22,000 copies quickly sold. Its popularity was all the more surprising because the magazine boasted of appealing only to "the civilized minority," leading one wag to comment: "Either many Americans are becoming civilized, which Mencken would never admit, or Mencken and his partner are becoming popular, which is an idea abhorrent to both of them."

The situation elicited Mencken's own rejoinder. "Whom gods would destroy," he commented wryly, "they first make popular. Let's not forget that the embalmer may be waiting just around the corner."4

MENCKEN'S LIFE NOW TOOK ON A ROUTINE similar to that of his days as editor of the *Smart Set*, although the magazine's new quarters in Knopf's suite in a conspicuous tower at 730 Fifth Avenue could not have differed more from the shabby office of Mencken and Nathan at their previous location. The entrance boasted a luxurious tiled floor and a reception room (referred to by the *Mercury* staff as "the Undertaking Parlor"). There was also a library, heavy Oriental rugs, and deeply shaded lights.

Once a month, Mencken would take the train from Baltimore and spend a week at these quarters. His morning entrance was heralded by a wide swinging of the outer door, a cheery "Good morning!" and the banging of the door of his private office. After a few moments came the heavy aroma of a cigar, then a succession of telephone calls with a resonant voice that could be easily heard throughout the offices. As the hours went by, the aroma of the cigar became stronger, the room enveloped in a thick blue haze. The editor was at work.

Mencken required that every man do his job and do it well. To achieve this, Mencken set an example of working at top speed, and it seemed to garner results. "When he sweeps through the office on his way to his inner rooms—the entire office force takes on new life as if a breath of fresh air has swept from the hills," one staffer wrote. "Not because they fear he will see that they are not working but because they can't help feeling his force and vigor. And it lasts all the time he is here. Everyone is conscious of the fact that 'H.L. is here.' The advertising men go out and sell twelve-page contracts and wonder how they did it. The stenographers speed up to 150 words a minute and wonder what someone put into the water cooler. The circulation department writes letters that bring in two subscriptions to a letter. The business manager balances the books two months ahead of time before he realizes it. One wonders why Mr. Knopf doesn't bribe Mr. Mencken to remain in New York all of the time."

Mencken would then dictate a series of letters. Copies were rarely kept, however. Twice a year the files were cleaned out, and manuscripts by writers such as Sinclair Lewis selected for distribution to libraries; the rest would be thrown out. In the period Mencken edited the *American Mercury*, only one file cabinet was kept for the entire office.

His efficiency set a standard in editing. James Branch Cabell lauded Mencken as "one who gives immediate attention to your manuscript, pays spot cash, encloses a return stamped envelope with the proofs and gives you second serial rights without asking. Authors began spreading the word: "If you write anything, send it to the *Mercury*."

When not dodging visitors and phone calls, Mencken spent his time plowing through the mountain of manuscripts on his desk—dog-eared pages written with worn-out ribbons, full of bad errors and untidy corrections. "It is to curse!" Mencken complained to Sara Haardt. For, as he later wrote, "despite the conviction of every Vassar girl that reading Mss. is as simple as mixing gin rickeys, it actually takes a great deal of skill and judgment . . . concealed among the rubbish is some stuff of great promise, and once in a great while the alert reader discovers the pearl of great price." So Mencken kept fishing, always hoping, even though he said the chances of bringing in a good haul ran at least 10,000 to 1.

At the end of the day there would be a last fleeting glimpse of a big black cigar and soft felt hat, then a hearty "*Good* night" and a slamming of the outer door.[5]

As KNOPF HAD UNEASILY ANTICIPATED, trouble between Mencken and Nathan finally erupted when, in the spring of 1924, the smooth system of cooperation between the two editors collapsed. Mencken wanted more social and political commentary in the magazine; Nathan insisted upon a counterbalance of literature. For the February issue Nathan wanted to include Eugene O'Neill's play *All God's Chillun Got Wings*; Mencken objected. Six months earlier, while at the *Smart Set*, he had already turned down one of O'Neill's plays for what he considered its weak realism. Finally, Knopf interceded, and the play was published, to enthusiastic response.

The argument, however, had taken its toll. After losing the battle over *All God's Chillun*, Mencken grew increasingly irritable with his co-editor, especially when Nathan, refusing to deal with subjects alien to his interests, left them entirely to Mencken. When it came to the *American Mercury*, Nathan confessed his interest had waned. As he put it: "The *Smart Set* was fun. The *Mercury* was a job."

Mencken had expected Nathan to take care of routine office business as he had during the days of the *Smart Set*, but Nathan was reluctant. By the summer, Mencken had decided that Nathan was "completely incompetent." Mencken's worries over the magazine, aggravated by the tension between the two, began taking a toll on his health. For weeks a pain in his left foot disabled him, reducing him to hopping down the office hall on one leg. Finally, in July 1924, when he covered the national conventions for the *Baltimore Evening Sun*, it became clear to him how far apart he and Nathan had become.

It is significant that when Mencken looked back on the first year of the *American Mercury*, he thought the best thing to appear in it was not Eugene O'Neill's classic play but a derogatory sketch of Coolidge's career by Frank Kent. To Mencken, the election of 1924 encapsulated all that had gone wrong with the American government. Mencken considered Coolidge "a stubborn little fellow with a tight, unimaginative mind." The fact that big business supported him was sufficient to make Mencken regard the candidate with suspicion, because, he wrote, "Big Business, in America, is almost wholly devoid of anything even poetically describable as public spirit."

Mencken distributed copies of Frank Kent's Coolidge article at the national conventions that year. The reprints not only reaped an enormous amount of advertising, but also gave the impression that the *Mercury* was vigorously against the Republican, which, as Mencken reasoned to Knopf, would do them good. "Try to imagine any Coolidge man reading the *Mercury*. Two numbers would get him to flight. We'll never get anywhere trying to woo the Babbitts."

The 1924 Republican convention in Cleveland confirmed Mencken's view about the candidate. Reporters cutting through the smoke at the Hollenden lobby eagerly accosted Mencken for his opinion. "Let us at once admit," Mencken said, his eyes sparkling and scorning at once, "that all such affairs as this are the most dreadful buffooneries conceivable." He added, "Coolidge can't arouse any more enthusiasm than a spittoon." In a well-oiled sequence of events, Coolidge was nominated on the first ballot; in two days it was over. The entire business, Mencken wrote, had been conducted "with the air of grocery clerks wrapping up packages of ginger snaps."[6]

In contrast to the harmony of the Republican convention, the Democratic National Convention in Madison Square Garden took place in a spirit of dissension. For sixteen days the Democrats battled over the Ku Klux Klan. Leading the anti-Klan forces was Alfred E. Smith, the popular governor of New York. New York, Mencken discovered, had made Smith its folk hero. Mencken could not come into the Algonquin without being stopped by the doorman and the elevator boy who would ask, Is all going well for Al? Will he be put over?

As the convention dragged on through a heat wave, reporters wearily feared they were doomed to remain at Madison Square Garden all summer. Mencken looked like a poached lobster, dripping from nose and eyes. "The convention had done one good thing if it hadn't accomplished anything else," reported one newspaper: "It has worn Henry Louis Mencken to a frazzle."

As lame as he was, Mencken still found the energy to promote his new magazine. While members of the Texas delegation were milling around their headquarters, he introduced himself. Late in the afternoon, two of the delegates were discovered carrying copies of the *American Mercury* under their arms, with puzzled expressions on their faces. They were looking for a dictionary.

It took thirteen days and 103 ballots for the deadlocked delegates to abandon their choice of Al Smith and nominate John W. David of West Virginia. "It seems to me the essence of comedy was here," Mencken noted, and a moral lesson: "that it is dangerous, in politics, to be too honest. The Hon. Mr. David won the nomination by dodging every issue that really stirred the convention." The collapse of Al Smith and the Democratic party, Mencken stated, was tragic. Hidden under the debris of hot dogs and wastepaper on the floor were "blasted hopes and broken hearts."[7]

WHILE THE DEMOCRATIC CONVENTION raged in New York, it was frustrating for Mencken to realize that Nathan did not even bother to feign interest in the battle for the presidency that was taking place under his very nose. To Mencken, this is what the *American Mercury* was all about; the political convention represented the frauds that the magazine was committed to debunking.

Mencken challenged Nathan's indifference to the state of the nation by listing his grievances in a memorandum to his colleague. The *American Mercury* needed to lead, "not a furious rabble, but the class that was serious at bottom." He proposed a change in the editorship. The magazine, he decided, must be a one-man show—and he would be the one man.

Nathan was also unhappy, but he sought reconciliation, putting his friend's discontent down to nervous strain. He beseeched Mencken not to act rashly; it would be sad to have their long association broken at the time of their greatest success. Mencken was still unsure whether the *American Mercury* was indeed a success. He was overburdened by routine chores, Mencken complained. He could work smoothly if he had a competent slave, but not if he had to be that slave himself.

Mencken was still wondering how to proceed with Nathan when he received a letter from a certain Charles Angoff that would make his decision much easier. The 1923 Harvard graduate had spent the summer applying for newspaper jobs. Might there be any position for him at the *Sun*?

The timing could not have been better. On November 8, Nathan reluctantly presented his resignation as co-editor of the *Mercury*, to become effective on February 1, 1925. The very next day, Mencken offered Angoff a position. The boy, Mencken recalled, was "speechless with astonishment and gratitude." On November 9, 1924, a jubilant Angoff telegrammed home: "Will become Managing Editor of the *Mercury*."

This was an exaggeration. Mencken had actually hired Angoff as assistant editor and office manager for a trial period of six months, to begin work in January. However, unknown to Angoff, Mencken made sure to have two other candidates on ice in case the Harvard graduate proved unsatisfactory. Not everyone was eager to work for the *Mercury*. Another man had earlier turned down the offer, sensing the editors "wanted to run the thing. Being *the* editors of the *American Mercury*, they just wanted slaves."

Christmas day found Mencken still unresolved and feeling guilty over his partner, with their last discussion on his mind. It was not enough that Nathan had resigned as co-editor of the magazine; Mencken was determined that eventually Nathan should depart completely.

But Nathan, who held a one-sixth interest in the firm, refused to be swayed. As Knopf later remarked, Nathan's strategy was always to sit and do nothing, hoping that the other side would eventually have to make a move.[8]

ON JANUARY 26, 1925, Angoff reported to 730 Fifth Avenue for his first day of work. The pile of unsolicited manuscripts awaiting him made the young man gasp. The *Mercury* received between 600 and 700 contributions a month. His duties included not only sorting the manuscripts and proofreading, but also assisting in the compilation of "Americana" and looking for new material. In the meantime, he was to help Mencken with a *Mercury* style sheet. "The slave looks very promising," Mencken reported to Sara Haardt. "He fell upon his work instantly, and was running without bumping in 24 hours. He goes along for hours without saying a word."

At the impressionable age of 22, Angoff noticed everything. These were not the memories he captured in *H. L. Mencken: A Portrait from Memory*. Published soon after Mencken's death in 1956, this book was an exercise in annihilation based on unsubstantiated and refuted anecdotes. "You cannot write out of hatred," Angoff later said to an interviewer, an ironic observation for a man whose biography of his former boss has been dismissed precisely because of this bias. On the other hand, Angoff's biographical novel, *The Bitter Spring*, written with a more balanced attitude, effectively captured his impressions when, as a young man, he arrived in New York and began working at the magazine. "Brandt, largely based on Mencken, is a much fuller portrait of Mencken than is my nonfiction book on him," Angoff acknowledged.

The novel portrays the heady glow Angoff felt at finding himself in New York during the 1920s, working with such important figures at the country's most popular magazine. He had entered a strange, exciting, and turbulent world. He was aware that the two men were celebrities of their age. On Fifth Avenue, when Angoff was in the company of either man, he noticed the reaction aroused in the passersby, as men and women, old and young, would turn around with admiration. Mencken's fame was more pronounced; from waitresses to secretaries to Alfred Knopf himself, everyone seemed to pay him smiling homage.

Angoff had mixed feelings about Mencken. He sensed in him a mixture of kindness and harshness, of sensitivity and cruelty that seemed indicative of an inner conflict. Like others who also knew Mencken, Angoff quite often saw that the editor's moods could alternate between loquaciousness and deep silences. At these moments, he sensed a deep well of sadness in the critic. Every now and then, the young man would look up from his pile of manuscripts and catch Mencken staring out of the window. "In those times there was something very appealing about him, something almost childlike about the eyes," Angoff would write of Brandt in *The Bitter Spring*, "something that bespoke tenderness and sympathy, even love and charity." This description belied the boyish braggadocio of the man, and Angoff later wrote of his wonder as to why anyone would fight so hard to keep this side hidden. As time went on, it was obvious that Mencken became more and more of a puzzle to him. He seemed the most complex and mysterious personality Angoff had ever encountered.

Mencken must have appeared just as enigmatic to the music and literary critic Isaac Goldberg, who in 1925 decided to expand a recent article into a book on Mencken. The prospect appealed to his subject, who thought it would be good for business. Mencken noted there had been too many hack jobs about "gaudy blobs," "the slobbery biography of the rich nobody," "vastly perfumed and white-washed." There was a need for a new sort of portrait, "with its brave realism and its freedom from professional pedantry." What he wanted instead was one enriched with illuminations into a man's character, giving it the intimacy and human interest that Huneker achieved in his criticism: "Not only a clear account of what the artist has done, but also a clear account of what he tried to do, and wherefore, and why."

To help Goldberg with this new task, that spring Mencken began unearthing childhood records, producing 200 pages of family history for the author's use. Before mailing a bundle of manuscript, Mencken warned his biographer that none of this should appear "as coming from me." He inundated Goldberg with so much material that the writer could not realize how much Mencken had actually omitted. Goldberg would have done well to take note of what Mencken had written two years earlier in a review for the *Smart Set*: "No man, of course, ever does an autobiography that is absolutely . . . honest." If, as Mencken admitted, preparing material for Goldberg had been a tremendous job, just as surely he had tried to ghost his own book.

Moreover, Mencken had certain reservations about the ability of Goldberg to do justice to his subject. He could never get over the concept that the young man was an academic who could not get himself decently stewed; to his dismay he discovered Goldberg only swallowed ginger ale. "I am full of doubts that he can get any sort of grip on me."9

WITH ANGOFF'S HELP, Mencken's need for Nathan diminished. Nonetheless, by April 1925 their parting had still not been resolved to Mencken's satisfaction. "But if I am to remain sane I must be completely free, and it will be worth a hundred rough fights to be so," Mencken told Sara Haardt.

Part of the difficulty was that Nathan was refusing to divorce himself completely from the *American Mercury*. Though he had resigned as co-editor, he continued to contribute to the magazine, was still a member of the board, and retained financial holdings. "The difficulty and anathema between H. L. Mencken and George Jean Nathan was that Nathan was still earning stock from the magazine when he was not involved with it at all," recalled William Koshland of Knopf, Inc. Mencken had written another formal memorandum outlining their separation. Nathan made a series of revisions, addressing such issues as his title, salary, duties, even details concerning stationery. An exasperated Mencken confided to Sara: "It may be necessary to murder the defendant. If it be God's will, then so be it."

Mencken finally proceeded in a manner most brutal. He had Nathan's name removed from the building's lobby directory and had his desk removed to an outer area among the stenographers. The space Nathan was given, writer Huntington Cairns noted, was "like a bull pen," so noisy he could hardly carry on a telephone conversation. In addition, he was told to expect a minimum of secretarial and phone service. Nathan wrote to Mencken that he resented "the unreasonable and often insulting attitude you have displayed towards me."

Astonishingly, however, the two men continued to inscribe their books to one another and on occasion went out socially. Nathan never publicly admitted there had been any sort of animosity between them. Why Nathan chose to remain at the *Mercury* was a mystery to Mencken's acquaintances. "George had enough reason to hold a grudge against Henry," Knopf said, "though he had only himself to blame for suffering the indignities to which he was subjected when the partnership broke up." By staying on, "Nathan had abandoned all pride and self-respect." Knopf reasoned that Nathan needed Mencken more than Mencken needed Nathan. "After all," Knopf wrote, "the theater and H.L.M. were, I think, the two great experiences of his life."

Eventually, the relationship between the two had deteriorated to such a degree that "besides the bitterness that Henry felt toward George, their quarrel had a trivial side as well," reflected Knopf. "Thus Nathan objected to our advertising the *Mercury* on the wrappers of his books. Mencken retaliated by objecting to our advertising George's books in the *Mercury*." Later Mencken removed all references to Nathan from his entry in *Who's Who*. "It's just another example of how the best friends when they once fall out become the bitterest enemies," Alfred Knopf jotted into his diary. "Outwardly all is calm and amiable: actually Henry will never rest 'till he ruins George. Poor game it seems to me for Henry—not worthy of his ammunition."

It took repeated meetings of the two partners, with the added intervention of Samuel, Alfred, and Blanche Knopf, before Nathan could be persuaded to sell back his stock in the *Mercury*. Eventually Knopf bought out Nathan for $25,000. Afterward, the stock market crash of 1929 made any stock held by Mencken and the Knopfs virtually worthless. In the end, Knopf admitted, "George was the only one . . . to get any cash out of the magazine."[10]

THE PUBLIC ANNOUNCEMENT of Nathan's resignation as co-editor caused rumors throughout New York. Gossipmongers gave as the main reason the need to cut down expenses. The *American Mercury* was changing its editorial policy, went the story; it was steadily losing vast sums of money because of its expensive composition. Mencken had begun sending letters to a select group, asking their opinions of the publication. This, plus the simultaneous announcement of Nathan's withdrawal, was met with sickly silence from the New York literati: the magazine, they said, was doomed.

No one was more surprised at these rumors than Mencken himself. Only a few advertisers had made suggestions, Mencken told a reporter from the *New York Telegraph*; many said they wanted no change at all. Another was afraid the *Mercury* would march to outside orders; his letter advised Mencken to stand by his principles. "If we can't depend on Mencken," the advertising agent told a reporter, almost in tears, "on whom can we depend?" Upon hearing this, Mencken gave a gargantuan laugh; nonetheless, he was greatly pleased.

Despite the *Mercury*'s success, the *Telegraph* sounded a warning. There had been other periodicals like the *Mercury* in America during the last half of the nineteenth century, but they had ossified. "The same fate may await the *Mercury*," the paper predicted. "In a generation or even a decade it may be lost in an avalanche of ignorance as was lost the intellectualism of a generation ago—lost so completely that even the intellectuals of today are hardly aware that it existed."[11]

Nathan was officially to depart the *Mercury* as co-editor on July 25, 1925, when his name would be removed from the masthead. Mencken's relief was palpable: "So all things pass!" No one, least of all Knopf, thought that Mencken would not continue his work with his customary zest, and indeed he was encouraged to do so by the success of the venture. In not aiming to make money, the *Mercury* was making it tenfold, printing 55,000 copies—remarkable for a periodical whose projectors had counted on a circulation of 20,000. By the end of 1925, it would reach 75,000. For a magazine that was scarcely a year old, copies of its first issue were already becoming collector's items, selling at $20 apiece.[12]

With the immediate problem of Nathan now resolved, Mencken could concentrate more freely on other issues—one in particular that was obsessing him and would take him, of all places, to Dayton, Tennessee, for one of the more colorful episodes of his journalistic career.

". . . for never were two men so dissimilar." Mencken and Nathan, *Theatre* Magazine. Courtesy Cornell University Library.

25

THE SCOPES TRIAL

I F THE SCOPES TRIAL HAD NOT EXISTED, one wag observed, H. L. Mencken would have had to invent it: "Nothing so perfectly illustrated his conception of the typical behavior of *Homo sapiens*."

Earlier, in the spring of 1925, it had come to Mencken's attention that an obscure member of the House of Representatives in Tennessee had drafted a bill that made it unlawful for a teacher in any school supported by state funds to teach the theory of evolution.

Shortly after the law was passed, leaders of the American Civil Liberties Union (ACLU) decided to make a test case of the dispute. George Rappelyea, a young mining engineer in Dayton, Tennessee, called on the town's popular athletic coach and 24-year-old substitute teacher, John Scopes, and pressed him to test the legality of the law. Scopes did so and, on May 7, 1925, he was arrested.

The battle gained national prominence when the Christian Fundamentalist Organization asked William Jennings Bryan to help with the prosecution of John Scopes. Bryan was 65 years old and at the twilight of his career, but even then the populist leader was an idol to many people for his anti-evolution crusades throughout the country. Now he jumped into the fray. "The Rock of Ages is more important than the Ages of Rocks," he asserted; scientists were "dishonest scoundrels." As for the ACLU, Bryan dismissed it as "a Communist organization," composed of a group of "unbelievers."

Clarence Darrow was famous for defending unpopular causes. He agreed to undertake the defense, asking lawyers Dudley Field Malone and Arthur Garfield Hays, the most influential member of the ACLU executive committee, to assist him. Hays's actions on behalf of free speech had made him a key figure at the ACLU. In 1925, the organization was only five years old and was seeking its first court victory. Hays called on Mencken to help prepare their strategy.

The aim of Darrow and his team was to have Scopes acquitted, but Mencken disagreed. The best way to handle the case, he argued, was to "convert it into a headlong assault on Bryan." It was he who was the international figure, "not that poor worm of a schoolmaster." Mencken proposed that the lawyers put Bryan on the stand if possible, "to make him state his barbaric credo in plain English, and to make a monkey of him before the world." The team agreed, although Hays still insisted Scopes could be acquitted.

As the skirmish began, newspapers promised that the trial would be a world sensation.[1]

Meanwhile in Chicago, Clarence Darrow sat at his desk, surrounded by heaps of mail that attested to the emotion the conflict had aroused in the nation. At stake was freedom of speech, freedom of religion, separation of church and state, public education, and modern concepts of individual liberty. "Scopes isn't on trial. Civilization is on trial," said Darrow. "I get no fee in this case. I enlisted like the boys who went to France, for liberty and humanity. We are not attacking the Bible. We are willing to let those who worship it, worship it, or anything else they want, but we insist they must let those who disagree have as much right."

The trial, Dudley Field Malone promised, "is going to be a good education for the people, *and* for the newspapers." Accompanying Mencken as part of the contingent for the *Evening Sun* were reporter Henry Hyde and cartoonist Edmund Duffy. "I hope to keep out of jail myself," Mencken pledged, "but resign myself to the will of God."[2]

DAYS BEFORE THE TRIAL, Dayton became a feverish home to the press. As hordes of newspapermen spilled from trains and buses, they were greeted by clanging hammers as carpenters applied the finishing touches to concession stands lining the sidewalks. A loft above the hardware store became a makeshift pressroom. Because Dayton was miles from a telegraph line, wires were now strung to accommodate the thirty operators sent by Western Union. The telephone company and post office hired additional staff, and a bank of phone booths for the reporters was installed outside the courtroom for the reporters. Even a field was cleared so that a plane transporting bundles of evening papers could put today's news in the hands of readers today.

Windows of the courtroom were washed, the floor scrubbed, the walls freshly painted. While workmen pounded the last nails into a platform for movie cameras, others set up microphones to feed the loudspeakers on the courtroom lawn. WGN, the radio voice of the *Chicago Tribune*, arranged for the first time to broadcast the entire trial live, through special telephone lines costing $1,000 a day. Some reporters considered it the most significant assignment of their careers. One newspaperman vowed, "I'm prepared to have my arm torn off."

It proved to be one of Mencken's most crucial stories. The trial was a culmination of the anti-evolution crusade that the fundamentalists had begun as a counteroffensive against modernist theology. Throughout the decade Mencken had taken it upon himself to champion the cause of the "beleaguered cities" against the "barbaric yokels" from the hinterland. One of the reasons for Mencken's hostility toward agrarian America was its ties to Protestant Fundamentalism, which he considered anathema to the nation's well-being. He went to Dayton as a combatant in what he sincerely took to be a struggle of civilization and science against bigotry and superstition. Long after the Scopes Trial was over, he was determined to write a record with Dudley Field Malone because "the real facts of history are always lost. Only balderdash survives." Although he never did so, the Scopes Trial remained first-rate drama he would never tire of recalling. Anecdotes from the trial filled his letters and books, including *A New Dictionary of Quotations*; enough material to last him the rest of his life.[3]

Meanwhile, hundreds of newspapermen, photographers, and newsreel crews from across America and Europe poured in, "fed upon a thousand different ideas of the south," scoffed the *Chattanooga News*, which noted that the majority of the American reporters hailed from the northeast. "If any cities of the south have any [Civil War] colonels there should be a rush order for them at once. They should be addicted to wide hats, long cigars, and have a mania for mint juleps and say 'Suh' on all occasions." New arrivals immediately sought out John Scopes, who had spent the last few days trying to elude them. The slight, freckled young man, who blushed easily whenever asked a question, finally took off his spectacles and tucked them inside his coat pocket—thereby succeeding in passing unrecognized by many of the reporters.

Bryan was the first of the star performers to arrive. Surveying the crowd before him, his pith helmet protecting his balding head from the glaring sunshine, he exclaimed with satisfaction: "This is the day I have been waiting for." In every possible action after he arrived in Dayton, Bryan believed he was making the greatest fight of his life. For several days before the trial, Bryan delivered thundering speeches that mesmerized crowds. Bryan may have been venerated as a Christian, Mencken observed, but it was not as a Christian that he had been called in, "but as one adept in attracting the newspaper boys—in brief, as a showman." As Will Rogers commented, "It's the most publicity any politician ever got in an off-year."

Clarence Darrow arrived a few days later. Although there was no torchlight parade to greet him, a considerable number of newsreel cameras were on hand to capture the scene of John Scopes embracing his lawyer—an image that was played over and over again in movie theaters across the nation.[4]   *1925*

Mencken arrived in Chattanooga on July 9, the day before the trial. Hiring a local driver, he and his *Sun* colleagues set off across forty miles of treacherous curves and hills for Dayton. The driver raced around each bend, plunging headlong across every unmarked crossing. Looking out the window, Mencken could see signs painted in red letters on the cliffs: "PREPARE TO MEET THY GOD." "SWEETHEARTS COME TO JESUS." "WHERE WILL YOU SPEND ETERNITY?" The frenzied drive through the mountains gave him one of the worst scares of his life. To his relief, the car eventually entered the shady streets of Dayton, a town one mile long and five blocks wide, cradled in the hills of eastern Tennessee, now the center of world news.

Strolling through the main street, Mencken reveled in the carnival atmosphere. Around him stretched newly constructed hot dog and lemonade stands, colorful banners, and posters depicting monkeys and coconuts. Little children raced through the throng, holding toy monkeys and giggling at the assorted apes, gorillas, baboons, and chimpanzees that the Ringling Brothers had sent into Dayton for the event. The latest jazz melody floated in the air.

Behind Mencken trailed several reporters, scribbling his observations in their notebooks. Each iron fence and neatly shingled home reminded the Baltimorean of country towns in Maryland—"a somewhat smallish but nevertheless attractive Westminster or Belair." Outside Robinson's Drug Store, under a banner that read "WHERE *IT* ALL STARTED," Frank Robinson rushed out and introduced himself. In a town where the local Reader's Club studied Edgar Guest, the Baltimorean was pleasantly surprised to discover many knew of him and of the *American Mercury*. Mencken, the *New York Evening World* reported, had to recover from "emotional convulsions" when Mrs. Robinson stated how pleased she was to meet the man who selected such lovely pictures for the American magazine.

When Mencken caught sight of William Jennings Bryan "parading in the street and basking in the veneration of the yokels," the two men greeted one another effusively and parted "in the manner of two Spanish ambassadors." But as Mencken later recalled, "that was the last touch of affability that I was destined to see in Bryan." By the end of the first week of the trial, Mencken noted, whenever Bryan caught Mencken's eye, "he would glare at me as if I were Beelzebub."

John Scopes said it was an embarrassment to the townspeople of Dayton that "every Bible-shouting, psalm-singing orator poured out of the hills," but for Mencken the spectacle was a source of sheer joy. He delighted in the presence of such characters as "John the Baptist the Third" and one who called himself "The Absolute Ruler of the Entire World, Without Military, Naval, or Other Physical Force."

Of particular delight to Mencken was the diminutive T. T. Martin, field secretary of the Anti-Evolution League of America, the only Christian in the entire town "who did not perspire hate." A picturesque character with a long-tailed coat and collar so large, said Mencken, "that he could pull his head into it like a turtle," Martin roved through Dayton, busily passing out leaflets that advertised "Mass Meetings for Infidels, Scoffers, Atheists, Communists, Evolutionists, and Others." He gave sermons discussing "Who made God? Did He make Himself?" and sold dog-eared volumes with such titles as *God or Gorilla* and *From Puddle to Heaven*.

"Mencken helped produce one of the screwballs," recalled Scopes. Mencken had 500 copies of his own circular readied for distribution. It suspiciously resembled those of T. T. Martin, except that this one advertised the work of the fictional fundamentalist Elmer Chubb, who promised to perform miracles on the public square. Dr. Chubb, it claimed, would allow himself to be bitten by any poisonous snake, scorpion, Gila monster, or other reptile, and would drink any poison brought him. There were testimonials, including one from Bryan ("With my own eyes I saw Dr. Chubb swallow cyanide of potassium") and Mencken himself ("Chubb is a fake. I can mix a cyanide cocktail that will make him turn up his toes in thirty seconds").

"Hundreds of copies of the circulars were flying about on the grass," recalled Mencken, "and dozens of yokels had them in their hands, but no one showed any interest in Dr. Elmer Chubb. A few discreet inquiries told us why. It was that the miracles he offered were old stuff in upland Tennessee."

As Dayton settled in for the night, boarding houses overflowed. Bryan stayed at the home of the town druggist; Darrow at the home of a local banker. More than one hundred reporters slept in the hardware store that doubled as a pressroom. Mencken's lodgings were the farthest away from the main street and the courthouse, in the comfortable home of a dentist.

At 6:30 on the morning of July 10, a loud cowbell rang from the Acqua Hotel, guaranteed to arouse those newspapermen who lodged there. Writing to Sara Haardt, Mencken rejoiced: "The show has just begun."[5]

CARS AND WAGONS STREAMED into Dayton before seven. For two hours farmers filed into the courthouse, their sober faces tight-lipped and expressionless. The Scopes Trial was causing nationwide interest; there was a demand for books by Charles Darwin in public libraries. In Dayton, locals announced that a fundamentalist college would be built on a hillside overlooking the valley and Blue Ridge Mountains and named the William Jennings Bryan College.

In the courtroom a hum filled the air as newspapermen squabbled over the seats at the rail surrounding the courtroom and photographers sought special vantage points. Above this sound could be heard the clatter of typewriters and the muffled click of telegraph instruments as some reporters began drafting articles for the afternoon papers.

The case promised to become more of a media event than a simple public trial, with some of America's best reporters present to tell the story: Joseph Wood Krutch, Frank Kent, Westbrook Pegler. But no one attracted more attention than the man whom the *Chattanooga News* described as "the foremost living iconoclast on the trial." As Hays put it, "in Dayton the yokels gaped at Bryan, defender of the Word, and Darrow, the devil's advocate. The press revered one god, Mencken."

Finally, in came Judge John T. Raulston, carrying a Bible, accompanied by a fundamentalist minister and his family. As the lawyers for the defense approached the courthouse, a large sign caught their attention: "READ YOUR BIBLE DAILY FOR ONE WEEK." As Arthur Garfield Hays later admitted, "I never passed that sign without mentally transposing the words, 'Read Your Bible Weakly for One Day.'" Of greatest amusement to Mencken was finding the command repeated on the wall to the outhouse—billboard space apparently even the fundamentalists couldn't resist. Darrow trailed behind, shedding his coat, his face, noted one, "softened by a quizzical twinkle of his deep-set eyes."

The lawyers for the prosecution were the last to arrive. A gentle handclapping greeted Bryan, who well understood the effect of a delayed entry. A full-throated roar erupted when the hero of the hour stepped into the railed-off enclosure in front of Judge Raulston. For fifteen minutes the photographers and movie men took pictures; then, realizing they had forgotten John Scopes who was trying to make himself as inconspicuous as possible by standing off to the side, they began the process all over again.[6]

Jury selection concluded after lunch, sooner than expected. Most of the candidates were middle-aged farmers from rural Rhea County, with little formal education, all of whom subscribed to fundamentalism. Evolution for them was not only foreign to their way of thinking but also a challenge to their beliefs. "Such a jury," Mencken wrote, "in a legal sense, may be fair, but it would certainly be spitting in the eye of reason to call it impartial." The *Pittsburgh Courier* expressed its reaction; such a jury, it said, is composed of the same type that black men and women must face in Southern courtrooms every day.

Inevitably, the jury presented to the rest of the nation the spectacle of illiterate farmers sitting in judgment in a trial that revolved around scientific theory. Since there was no disputing that John Scopes had taught evolution in the classroom in violation of Tennessee law, Darrow's tactic was to prove that the law itself was foolish and flawed. Reporter Watson Davis of *Science Service* had helped the defense enlist a dozen leading scientists from across America to testify and to test the validity of Darwin's theory. The prosecution, however, was determined to rest its case on the narrow point that Scopes, as an employee of the state, had violated its law. Bryan based his case on the fact that "A confessed minority in Tennessee is trying to set aside the wishes of a majority."

When the crowd left the courthouse on the first day, two small planes buzzed overhead, carrying newsreel footage of the trial, which would be shown in northern cinemas the next afternoon. As Dayton quieted down for the weekend, time hung heavily on the hands of the newspapermen. Those like Mencken, who suffered bellyaches from sampling local moonshine, discovered that the only place to obtain liquor was in Chattanooga. For the remainder of the week, taxis ferried reporters back and forth as they hauled bulging bags that clinked suspiciously.[7]

NELLIE KENYON, A YOUNG REPORTER with the *Chattanooga News*, found Mencken smoking a cigar at the Acqua Hotel, his mischievous blue eyes taking in the scene.

"Mr. Mencken! I would like to interview you! May I?"

Mencken half bowed. "I'm always charmed by an attractive little lady." Nellie Kenyon was barely five feet tall.

"What does one do for entertainment?" Mencken asked Kenyon. She was taken aback; anxious to interview the great H. L. Mencken, now it seemed as if he were interviewing her.

"There's a picture show across the street, the drugstore, a baboon in a cage down the street and a Holy Roller meeting from out of town."

"What's a Holy Roller meeting?"

"A meeting of religious people."

"Will you take me to one sometime?"

"Yes, sir, sometime," said Kenyon, anxious to get on with her interview.

Mencken's eyes twinkled. "How about tonight?"

Shortly before seven o'clock, Mencken and *Evening Sun* reporter Henry Hyde clambered with Nellie Kenyon into a Model T Ford and went chugging down a hilly road about two miles west of Dayton. After parking the car, they sneaked along the edge of a mountain cornfield. Dimly, they could hear shouts emanating from the woods. Far off in a glade, a flickering light was visible. Creeping closer, they could see fireflies twinkling around kerosene lamps hung from the branches of nearby trees. Quietly sliding into a long, unpainted bench in the last row, Mencken stared at the individuals who rose in the ghostly gloom. Decades later, Hyde would recall: "I'll never forget the night."

In the light of the lamps, Mencken and Hyde could see the preacher, a tall, thin mountaineer in dungarees, pacing back and forth. At each turn he thrust his arms into the air. "Glory to God! Hally-oo-ya!" Throwing back his tousled head, the preacher shouted toward the stars and the distant hills, in an archaic English that fascinated Mencken.

Suddenly there was a change of mood, and the little group of women and men began a monotonous, unintelligible chant. To Hyde, it had "the perfectly timed beat of a drum or tom-tom. Presently it began to have a hypnotic influence on those who listened. They rocked back and forth on their low benches, swayed from one side to the other." There were shouts of "Amen!" and "Hear ye! Yeah, yeah!" What followed, Mencken later recalled, "quickly reached such heights of barbaric grotesquerie that it was hard to believe it real." Women jumped in the aisles, swaying wildly, tossing their hair. Some lay moaning, tossing and grunting in the grass in great, convulsive gasps. Some simply fainted, exhausted.

The climax came when the preacher began to speak in tongues. Each second his voice rose to a higher register, and then, Mencken later wrote, it broke into "a shrill, inarticulate squeak, like that of a man throttled. He fell headlong across the pyramid of supplicants. A comic scene? Somehow, no. The poor half wits were too horribly in earnest. It was like peeping through a knothole at the writhings of a people in pain."

Years later, Nellie Kenyon remembered Mencken's reaction:

"Do you really think these people are serious?" he asked, breaking the long silence.

"Yes, sir, I do."

He sat there, shaking his head, his blue eyes getting bigger and bigger as he repeated the same question.

"They are not pulling our leg? They really believe all this?" Each time I would answer yes.

Finally, Mencken, the great iconoclast, the man reviled in the Bible Belt as an infidel . . . suggested we move closer to the front. We were alone on the beech bench. I said that mountain people do not take kindly to strangers. I remember earlier in the week trying to interview a mountain woman in Dayton as she stood eating an ice cream cone. She simply hitched her skirts and took off running.

Mencken and I remained on the last bench, out of the glow of the lights. As the meeting drew to a close we passed our way back to my car through the cornstalks, Mencken still wanting to know if the people were serious and where they came from.

When they returned to Dayton it was after eleven o'clock. The whole town was still gathered on the courthouse lawn, hanging on the words of the visiting evangelists. To Mencken, the revival he had just witnessed represented all of the falsehoods William Jennings Bryan and the lawyers for the prosecution represented. Yet at the same time he was so fascinated by the Holy Rollers that he visited their camp again and again, sitting on the ground, his hands on his knees, spellbound.

Mencken dispatched a long account of the Holy Roller performance to the *Evening Sun.* "Such is human existence among the fundamentalists, where children are brought up on Genesis and sin is unknown," he concluded. "I have done my best to show you what the great heritage of mankind comes to in regions where the Bible is the beginning and end of wisdom, and the mountebank Bryan, parading the streets in his seersucker coat, is pointed out to sucklings as the greatest man since Abraham."

Back in Baltimore, a small knot of reporters gathered to read Mencken's description that had been tacked up on the bulletin board with the comment: "That's reporting!" But at Dayton, the reaction was far different. As soon as the bundles of the "Airplane Edition" were distributed at Robinson's Drug Store, resentment toward newspapermen, and in particular to H. L. Mencken, began to form.

In an effort to prove to Mencken and the other journalists that their reporting was biased, that within those same hills there also existed educated circuit preachers, drugstore owner Fred Robinson made a special effort to introduce out-of-state reporters to a highly educated minister. The *New York Times* subsequently wrote in amazement of the Tennessee mountain man who had, along with his old clothes and unpolished boots, a scholar's knowledge of Greek and Hebrew as well as Darwin's *Origin of the Species.* But to Robinson's dismay, "Mencken kept with the hillbilly story of the Holy Rollers."[8]

"Dayton was now home for the press." John Scopes, right, reading the newspaper outside Robinson's Drug Store. W. C. Robinson Collection, Special Collections Library, University of Tennessee.

THE FOLLOWING MONDAY, local spectators and the press jammed the courtroom. Those lucky enough to perch near the windows had some chance for air. There were only three portable electric fans, and these were conveniently placed near Judge Raulston and the prosecution, and nowhere near the defense who occupied the sunniest part of the room.

Bryan's countenance struck everyone. Other reporters had described it as tired and dull; Mencken found "a vague, unpleasant manginess" about the "Commoner," with a bitterness that made his face hard: "By the end of the first week he was simply a walking malignancy." Sitting in the courtroom that day, Darrow admitted that "the merry twinkle had vanished" from his old friend's eyes. "Now he was like a wild animal at bay."

The defense spent the morning on a motion to dismiss the indictment of Scopes. Hays, who had occasionally attended the "weird ceremonies" of the Holy Rollers, later said he had perhaps not realized "that those in the Court were almost as weird." At one point, holding a lawbook in his hands, with his glasses at the end of his nose, General Ben McKenzie for the prosecution shook his finger, commenting on the inability of "New York lawyers" to understand the Tennessee anti-evolution law, "so simple a 10-year-old Rhea County boy could

"That damned infidel." Clarence Darrow addressing the court during the Scopes Trial, 1925.
W. C. Robinson Collection, Special Collections Library, University of Tennessee.

understand it." Dudley Field Malone sprang to his feet: "We are here not as
New Yorkers or Chicagoans, but as American citizens defending our liberties."
Judge Raulston interrupted; perhaps the "foreign" counsel did not understand
McKenzie as well as the natives did.

Pacing as he spoke, Darrow argued that the statute against the teaching
of evolution violated the principles of freedom guaranteed by the Tennessee
constitution. Only the clicking of telegraph keys disturbed the silence. Mencken
glanced at Bryan, whose mouth was tight-lipped as he tried to cool himself and
shoo flies with his palm-leaf fan. There was no reason Darrow's words should
shake him, Mencken noted: "He has those hillbillies locked up in his pen and he
knows it."

Darrow continued passionately, thrusting his thumbs under his blue suspenders, his collar limp. Facing the WGN microphone that conveyed his words
across a nation, he concluded:

> If today you can take a thing like evolution and make it a crime to teach it in the
> public schools, tomorrow you can make it a crime to teach it in the private
> schools, and the next year you can make it a crime to teach it in the hustings or in
> the churches. At the next session you may ban it in books and in newspapers.

Soon you may set Catholic against Protestant and Protestant against Protestant, and try to foist your own religion upon the minds of men. If you can do one you can do the other. Ignorance and fanaticism are ever busy and need feeding. Always they are feeding and gloating for more. Today it is the public school teachers, tomorrow the private. The next day the preachers and the lecturers, the magazines, the books, the newspapers. After a while, your Honor, it is the setting of man against man and creed against creed until with flying banners and beating drums we are marching backward to the glorious ages of the sixteenth century when bigots lighted fagots to burn the men who dared to bring any intelligence and enlightenment and culture to the human mind.

Telegraphs transmitted 200,000 words from Dayton, a record for a single event in the nation's history. Newspapers reprinted Darrow's speech at length. "You have but a dim notion of it who have only read it," Mencken wrote. "It was not designed for reading, but for hearing. The clanging of it was as important as the logic. It rose like a wind and ended like a flourish of bugles." The *Chicago Tribune* rated it as "one of the greatest speeches of his career."

Not all, however, were similarly impressed. When Darrow concluded, some spectators hissed; one remarked, "They ought to put him out!" Two women, leaving the courtroom, exclaimed in horror, "The damned infidel!" That night, a storm knocked out the electricity in Dayton. The next day some suggested that Darrow's heresy had incited the wrath of God. The *Memphis Commercial Appeal* captured local sentiment with a front-page editorial cartoon depiction of Darrow as the Anti-Christ. No matter that it later developed the power outage was due to a careless stroke by a ditchdigger who had driven his pick through the main electricity supply. To Mencken, Darrow's eloquent appeal of that morning had been wasted on a public that had ears only for Bryan. The net effect "seems to be precisely the same as if he had bawled it up a rainspout in the interior of Afghanistan."9

Nonetheless, the sensational case had now become the focus of the world. It was difficult for other nations to comprehend how anyone could dream of attacking the basic principles of nature within a courtroom. To them, the Scopes Trial was simply a vaudeville show. In Germany, there was a curious disdain; in France, any mention of Dayton caused laughter. "Let America look to it, and let the newspapers and pulpits of Tennessee rally to their duty, lest their state become a mere reservation of morons and moral cowards," wrote George Bernard Shaw. "They can put a stop to this monstrous nonsense in a single Sunday if they have the courage of their profession, and no Sunday in America can ever be better spent!"

"I have met no educated man who is not ashamed of the ridicule that has fallen upon the State," Mencken reflected. The civilized minority had known for years what was going on in the hills, wrote Mencken: "They knew what the country preachers [had] rammed and hammered into yokel skulls." Now Tennessee was paying the price.

In spite of the trial's lack of dignity, the columnist asked that his readers "not make the colossal mistake" of viewing it "as a trivial farce." But the next American who finds himself with an idle million on his hands, Mencken proposed, should dedicate it to civilizing Tennessee, "a sort of Holy Land for imbeciles." He concluded that one of the best ways to test the enlightenment of a state was to look at its newspapers. If the readers of the newspapers were "well informed and sensible, if they see what is in front of them clearly and discuss it honestly and courageously, then you will find a general interest in ideas and a disposition to hear new ones. But if they are ignorant and bellicose, if they seek to put down discontent and heresy with the weapons of the professional patriot and evangelist, then you will find only idiocy."

The reply was not long in coming. Tennessee's Governor Austin Peay dismissed Mencken as "an intellectual skunk." He added: "I don't think anybody pays any attention to him. What surprises me is that the newspapers print his stuff."[10]

Mencken soon noted that a sort of permanent town meeting was taking place daily at Robinson's Drug Store. Sobered by the lack of eminent society figures descending on the town, a dismayed Dayton discovered that its visitors were mostly reporters, photographers, telegraphers and radio operators, few of whom spent any money. As a consequence, prices for meals and rooms were reluctantly lowered by the local tradesmen. Those who had expected the two main thoroughfares to be heavily packed with limousines from Fifth Avenue found instead that their town attracted only a few curious farmers from East Tennessee, who came in dusty wagons driven by tired mules, and a scattering of rival evangelists, who set up their tents from which came the shrill echoes of gospel hymns.

No one seemed to be reading the brochure the town leaders had printed that described the many assets of the area and the factories and businesses that could be located there. Everyone was devouring the headlines. One businessman concluded that "it was the worst publicity we could get." "Two months ago the town was obscure and happy," noted Mencken. "Today it is a universal joke."

"Everyone's nerves are racked to shreds," observed *Editor & Publisher*. "The trial drags along slowly, tiresomely, bitterly. At the other end of the wire it no doubt reads like good copy, but to the sweltering, agonized, exhausted group of men and women on the job . . . it has already gone on long enough." *Editor & Publisher* reported at least a dozen reporters were sending 3,000 words each night.

Howard R. Hale, a Western Union telegrapher assigned to handle the copy of the most famous reporter at the trial, recalled that "Mencken strutted around like a big gobbler turkey, and demanded that his stories be given first priority." Hale was sometimes awakened at two or three o'clock in the morning when Mencken had a sudden idea. But despite his exhaustion, Hale found Mencken the most effective of all the reporters: "He knew how to scoop everyone else, including the Associated Press."

Reporters found the Scopes trial their most difficult assignment in years. Lawyers tripped over spittoons. Dogs roamed between spectators' legs and barked under the courtroom seats until they were forcibly ejected, only to return. Babies wailed. The space allotted to the press was so overcrowded that reporters were forced to stand. Through the windows came the smell of barbecued meat sizzling over a trench of coals directly below on the courthouse lawn. One astonished reporter wrote to his wife, "The courtroom is a madhouse."

When not sitting on the window next to Quinn Ryan of WGN Radio or sharing a desk with Watson Davis of *Science Service*, Mencken chose to plant his feet on top of a table located at the extreme left-hand corner of the courtroom. Though it faced advocates and audience, it provided the best view; at that height, said one onlooker, Mencken had "the look of a bloodhound on his eager face as he sniffs the air, mops the perspiration from his brow, and clasps his big hands behind his back in a stoic gesture. He is alive, truculent and omniscient—the highest figure in the room—the most respected, hated, reviled, feared, and loved person in the City of Light today."

Whenever a member of the prosecution spoke, spectators glanced in Mencken's direction; one recalled his expression of "delighted incredulity." When, at one point, the table he was standing on came down with a startling crash, the *New York Herald Tribune* recorded one of the "sisters" in the audience

"The most respected and reviled person" in Tennessee: Mencken standing on a table at the Dayton courtroom during the Scopes Trial, 1925. H. L. Mencken Collection, Enoch Pratt Free Library.

as saying: " 'It's a jedgement. The walls are falling in and Mr. Mencken is the first to go—and he won't go to glory, either.' "[11]

PROCEEDINGS RESUMED. The case that had begun as a fight for freedom of speech was sidelined into a discussion of when humans first walked the earth, a point to be decided by a jury of six Baptists, one Methodist, one Disciple-of-Christ, and one nonchurchgoer. As the afternoon drew to a close, Dr. Maynard M. Metcalf, an evolution expert from Johns Hopkins University, was called to the stand. Immediately there was a flurry of protest on the admissibility of his evidence. The judge asked the jurors to leave the room; they would remain out for the rest of that week.

"Then began one of the clearest, most succinct and withal most eloquent presentations of the case for the evolutionists that I have ever heard," Mencken wrote of Metcalf's testimony. "Is the earth more than 6,000 years old?" Darrow finally asked Metcalf. The scientist scratched a rather thin thatch of hair. "Well, 600,000,000 years would be a moderate estimate, I think," he replied. Judge Raulston gasped and called for a glass of water; Bryan flushed. To Mencken's disgust, court was adjourned before Metcalf was able to get to the Bible.[12]

Throughout the week not much had been heard from Bryan beyond a cough, as he fanned himself furiously. It had previously been agreed that he would give only a rousing summation at the end of the trial, an arrangement that would allow free rein to his oratorical style. Word that Bryan was finally to speak drew large crowds on the appointed afternoon. When he rose, the New York Times reported, "Bryan, with the sweat streaming from his face and his great arms going like flails, was not to be denied this chance that he had so long waited for."

To Mencken, it quickly ceased to be an argument addressed to the court and instead became a sermon at a camp meeting. "This old buzzard, having failed to raise the mob against its rulers, now prepares to raise it against its teachers. He can never be the peasants' President, but there is still a chance to be the peasants' Pope." Only days before, many Southern congregations had compared Darrow to Satan, and Bryan to Jesus.

Bryan's strength in making long and inspiring speeches to neutral or friendly audiences had made him an effective politician and public crusader for many reforms. "It wasn't so much what he had to say, it was how he said it," recalled Scopes of that day. "By the time he was finished, I was mesmerized." Years later, Scopes mused that Bryan's day had come too early. With unlimited access to television so that he could have gone into every American home, Scopes reasoned, Bryan could have defeated his Republican opponents in every national election. "I've seen no one else like Bryan. Franklin D. Roosevelt could not approach him as a public speaker."

But the speech Bryan gave in the Dayton courtroom in 1925 was far from his best. He trembled at times and his face was flushed; sometimes he switched his thoughts in midsentence. Mencken characterized it as "meandering, feeble and

"... broken [and] furious." William Jennings Bryan, 1925. Reproduced from the Collections of the Library of Congress.

downright idiotic. Presumably, he was speaking to a point of law, but it was quickly apparent that he knew no more law than the bailiff at the door. He dragged in snatches of ancient chautauqua addresses; he wandered up hill and down dale."

The climax came when Bryan launched into what Mencken called a "furious denunciation of the doctrine that man is a mammal. It seemed a sheer impossibility that any literate man should stand up in public and discharge any such nonsense. Yet the poor old fellow did it. Darrow stared incredulous. Malone sat with his mouth wide open. Hays indulged himself one of his sardonic chuckles." Mencken wrote Sara Haardt: "I almost swooned." In fact, he found the whole performance depressing. "One somehow pities [Bryan], despite his so palpable imbecilities. It is a tragedy, indeed, to begin life as a hero and to end it as a buffoon."

God save us all from this!

Nevertheless, the crowd sided with Bryan. During his oration he became so intent talking to the people that he faced the courtroom and kept his back to the bench. "The one beauty about the Word of God is, it does not take an expert to understand it," Bryan concluded. "The facts are simple, the case is plain, and if those gentlemen want to enter upon a larger field of educational work on the subject of evolution, let us get through with this case and then convene a mock court, for it will deserve the title of mock court if its purpose is to banish from the hearts of the people the Word of God as revealed."

There was applause, Mencken noted, but the old magic had failed to work; there were no exultant shouts. "Worse, I believe that he somehow sensed the fact," Mencken mused later. "I saw how it fell flat and how Bryan himself was conscious of the fact. . . . He sank into his seat a wreck." Mencken could see Mrs. Bryan hunched in her chair. "I think that some appalling prescience was upon her, and that she saw in Bryan's eyes a hint of the collapse that was so near."

"Papa is looking like an old war-horse," Mrs. Bryan wrote home to her children, with "a tired look, however, which does not please me." She confessed "I never saw him quite so agitated. He trembled when he stood up, and it has alarmed me very much." Miles away in Washington, Bryan's family physician had been examining the newspaper pictures; he, too, was apprehensive. Bryan had a haggard, gaunt look about him.[13]

The audience did not expect Malone to rise in answer to Bryan, but he spoke for half an hour. There was no loudspeaker in the courtroom, but he did not need it. Mencken observed that even "trains thundering by on the nearby railroad sounded faint and far away."

"Keep your Bible," Malone roared. "Keep it as a consolation, keep it as your guide, but . . . keep your Bible in the world of theology where it belongs." Then, pointing his finger at Bryan, Malone shouted:

There is never a duel with the truth. The truth always wins and we are not afraid of it. The truth is no coward. The truth does not need the law. The truth does not need the forces of government. The truth does not need Mr. Bryan. The truth is imperishable, eternal and immortal, and needs no human agency to support it. We are ready to tell the truth as we understand it, and we do not fear all the truth that they present as facts. We are ready.

"Women shrieked their approval, men could not restrain their cheers," observed a reporter. A policeman pounded on the table so hard with his nightstick that the surface split; when another officer rushed forward to assist him in quieting the crowd, the first shouted back, "I'm not trying to restore order. Hell, I'm cheering." To J. W. Butler, an anti-evolution lawmaker seated in the audience, it was "the finest speech of the century."

Years later, Scopes recalled, "Malone's words, read today, seem dry and uninspiring; delivered in full heat of battle . . . they were electric." Decades later, that trial day remained for Scopes "the most dramatic event I have attended in my life." The press broke its silence and gave a standing ovation. "Dudley," said Mencken, clapping Malone on the back, "that was the loudest speech I ever heard." The cheer that went up was four times as hearty as the one the crowd had given Bryan; endlessly it went on.

Mencken wrote that Bryan "sat through it in his usual posture, with his palm-leaf fan flapping energetically and his hard, cruel mouth shut." But when it was over, Bryan offered his congratulations. "That was a great speech, Malone," he said, coming over to the lawyer's chair. "It was one of the greatest I ever listened to. I have forgotten the others."[14]

MALONE'S ELOQUENT ORATORY DISCONCERTED members of the Bryan family, who loyally felt it "really had no bearing upon the question involved." As for the prosecution, Mrs. Bryan confided, Darrow suffered from a "lack of faith" and Hays was "as forward and self-asserting as the New York Jew can be."

The Bryan family, like many others in Dayton, had already concluded Clarence Darrow was in the "employ" of "the hostile Eastern press," who they felt had been Bryan's "enemies all his public life." If the press promoted the trial strongly enough, it would mean "money in their pockets from the tremendous sale of newspapers," thereby putting "an end to Father's career." In reality, *Editor & Publisher* found there had been no appreciable jump in circulation, even though the story was front page news.

Mencken's syndicated columns for the *Evening Sun* made him the target of resentment in Dayton. Even before the trial began, the primary mood and theme of the rest of the press was one of ridicule. "For the newspapermen it was a lark on a monstrous scale," remembered Nunally Johnson, the noted Hollywood screenwriter, then covering the trial for the *Brooklyn Eagle*. "Being admirably constituted fellows, they were of course all evolutionists and looked down on the local fundamentalists."[15]

What disturbed the local townspeople of Dayton most was to be portrayed as religious fanatics. While many of the population admitted to being conservative Christians, the residents disliked being described as mountaineers. Two who fell into this category were college graduates from northern Pennsylvania. Others gave interviews, only to find their speech had been liberally sprinkled in print with words like "*hain't*" and "*sech*."

"Some of the newspaper correspondents attending the trial have apparently lost no opportunity for exaggeration if not downright misrepresentation," complained the *Chattanooga Times*. It was noted that in their thirst for local color, "they have seized upon the most narrow, ignorant, backward aspects of the community and harped upon them as though they were representative. . . . Such writing is obviously unfair and unjust and beneath the ethics of anybody who adheres to an enlightened code of intellectual honesty."

Locally, much of the unfairness was blamed on Mencken. To this day, Mencken's name is mentioned in Dayton with contempt; in 1925 he was anointed "the stinker." ("Mr. Mencken did not degenerate from an ape," one local said, "but from an ass.") It was not, as Mencken supposed, his description of the Holy Roller meeting that caused the most fury, but his caricatures of the "Babbitts" and "backward" locals, "hillbillies," "yaps," "yokels," "peasants," and mountaineers from the hills of East Tennessee that infuriated citizens who prided themselves on their intelligence.

Eloise Reed, a girl of twelve at the time of the trial, much later recalled the rancor toward Mencken in her Dayton home: "Father would read the stories and get madder each day." About the nicest thing Mencken was able to say of the community was that "The Klan never got a foothold here, though it rages everywhere else in Tennessee." While Mencken admitted Daytonians were outwardly polite, even he began to comprehend, as the week wore on, that "I ranked with atheists and German spies in their menagerie of monsters."[16]

"In a way it was Mencken's show," John Scopes recalled in 1967. "In the public mind today, a mention of the Dayton trial more likely evokes Mencken than it does me. His biting commentary on the Bible Belt and the trial itself was one of the highlights of the entire event." Yet even Scopes disagreed with Mencken's portrayal of the Dayton townsfolk as "morons"; many were his friends. Looking back at the trial years later, Scopes dismissed Mencken as "a sensationalist."

During the trial, Paul Patterson had given George Fort Milton, publisher of the *Chattanooga News*, the rights to reprint Mencken's reports. "In a little while my dispatches became so offensive to the local Christians that printing them became dangerous to Milton," Mencken wrote. Mencken's columns were prefaced with a carefully worded caveat:

> These dispatches are in no way a reflection of the belief of The News as to the issues involved. They are merely printed to afford our readers a better insight into the attitude taken toward Dayton, Tenn., and the south by other sections of America. The words of Mr. Mencken, brilliant, bitter, provocative, are typical of one viewpoint.

As the days passed, this polite introduction gave way to printing Mencken's articles with so many typographical errors that they were unintelligible. Headlines were changed so that one article criticizing Rhea County went under the incongruous title, "Mencken Pays His Respects to Chattanooga's Police." Soon whole paragraphs were omitted; filling the extra space were refutations by the local clergy.

Yet enough of Mencken's articles leaked through. When it came to the Baltimorean, one reader wrote to the *Chattanooga Times*, "his one ambition seems to be to ridicule the south, slur its people, and deride its customs and conventions. Certainly, the south is horribly behind—but we do have trains and even though Mr. Mencken may not believe it—they will take him back to the country he idolizes—the wonderful east."[17]

Excited whispers that Mencken would be run out of Dayton escalated. Rumor had it that anonymous letters were being sent to Mencken that he either leave peaceably or be escorted on a rail in tar and feathers—the latter, joked Richard Beamish of the *Philadelphia Inquirer*, being the choice most favored by Bryan.

Dayton was not alone in this view of Mencken. The *Daily Oklahoman* on its front page asserted that Mencken's attacks "went beyond the limits of reasonable and tolerant criticism." Other papers followed. In churches throughout the South, Christians were lectured by ministers about "the nerve of Mr. Mencken," a notorious "radical Red":

> Mencken is just a dirty buzzard and the folks that follow him are no more than damn scoundrels. . . . Well, I'm here to tell you that the biggest set of fools that walk on earth today walk on Broadway. Why, there are more ignorant, pot-headed fools to the square inch in New York than in any part of America.

"But don't get alarmed, folks," called out one minister from his pulpit. "All the spilling of all the buzzards like Mencken can't change the great, intellectual state of Tennessee."[18]

COURT RESUMED Friday morning, July 17, with a prayer that included blessings "upon those who are members of the press as they send out the messages to the waiting millions of the world." "H. L. Mencken was still present," wryly noted the *Boston Transcript*—"not yet having been ridden out of town on a rail."

Of main import to Mencken that day was the expert testimony he felt would demolish the fundamentalist case that imperiled freedom of education and scientific inquiry. Throughout that week he had spent much of his free time in the company of scientists, waiting in the wings while the court decided whether the jury should hear them. On July 17, Judge Raulston announced his decision regarding expert testimony: the answer was no.

When court adjourned for the day, a disgusted Mencken decided to leave Dayton. Other reporters left with him. The Scopes trial, Mencken concluded, was a "damnable obscenity." Nearly everyone believed that Bryan had won, and the streets of Dayton suddenly became deserted. Even those who favored Scopes assumed there was little that Darrow could do. "The trial has blown up," Mencken wrote to Sara Haardt. Nothing remained except "the formal business of bumping off the defendant." It proved to be a gross miscalculation of journalistic judgment.

In his memoirs Mencken said his motivation for leaving town was his loyalty to the *American Mercury*; two weeks' absence was the maximum time he felt he could leave the magazine. From the moment of his arrival in Dayton, he had said he was "merely here to write articles" and not news accounts, and that as little as a week's stay would be "long enough for my purpose." By leaving Dayton when he did, Mencken missed the climax of the trial—"a deprivation," Mencken later admitted, "that I have always regretted heartily."

As for the people of Dayton, one newspaper headline announced they were "Glad to See H. L. Mencken Leave." Thirty townspeople gathered around the foot of the flagpole in the center of Main and Market streets, blocking traffic. When it came to Mencken, one local citizen angrily told a reporter, "We still believe in our God, our country, our flag and prayer."

The rumor that Mencken had been forced out of town spread across the South. Mencken wrote: "I have reason to believe that many of the yahoos themselves now accept it as true, and that there are heroes among them who claim to have been members of the posse, and to have taken pot shots at me as I ran screaming down the road." In Dayton the myth continues to be believed by some to this day.[19]

On his return to New York, Mencken found his desk piled high with abusive letters. His departure from Dayton, he reported to Sara, "had the usual accursed effect: it brought in a ton of mail, mainly from idiots, Christian and infidel." He advised George Milton of the *Chattanooga News*: "I think that printing the letters against my stuff is a very wise strategy. The best way to handle such idiots is to give them perfectly free rein. They inevitably reduce their case to an absurdity."

Meanwhile, Darrow quietly began preparing a plan that would become legend in American folklore. Not until late Sunday did the few remaining members of the press sense that the defense was preparing "a coup d'etat," as the *Nashville Banner* predicted. "Tomorrow comes the crisis!" T. T. Martin addressed his congregation from the pulpit of the Dayton Baptist Church. "Whatever mean things Darrow and Mencken may say or do I beg you not to lose your tempers." But by that time, Mencken was already gone.[20]

DARROW'S SECRET STRATEGY soon became evident. If the court would not let him call in expert witnesses to test the validity of evolution, Darrow and the defense would call in an expert witness—Bryan himself—to test the historical authenticity of the Bible. When Bryan was summoned, there was a gasp from the crowd, but he welcomed the opportunity Darrow had given him. The case had been going well for him; furthermore, he believed that eventually he would get his chance to interrogate Darrow. The great agnostic was now about to question the great defender of the faith.

High on the platform above the audience, standing three inches away from Bryan's face and snapping his suspenders, Darrow asked him to explain some of the stories from the Bible. Where did Cain get his wife? Do you believe the first woman was Eve? Do you believe she was literally made out of Adam's rib? Did a whale swallow Jonah? Such questions, Darrow later wrote, compelled Bryan "to choose between his crude beliefs and the common intelligence of modern times," or to admit ignorance.

Reading the reports later, Mencken was compelled by the drama. On the courthouse lawn, where the trial had been moved, many found Darrow insulting, even abusive, as he peppered Bryan, giving him little time for explanation.

Darrow's manner, recalled one listener, "made us all uncomfortable and squirmy." As the questioning progressed, one spectator seated immediately behind Bryan could see his neck getting redder and redder, his hands trembling, and his lips quivering. Intensity ran so high that, during the heat of debate, one mountaineer had his hand on his gun and said afterward that if Darrow had taken hold of Bryan, Darrow would never have left the platform alive.

Darrow was relentless. He asked Bryan about the record of the flood and the age of the earth. As the lawyer pushed his questioning, all the while snapping his suspenders, Bryan was forced to admit that he did not know the answers. This lack of scientific knowledge undercut his credibility. Darrow asked Bryan if God made the world in six days.

DARROW: Does the statement, "The morning and the evening were the first day," and "The morning and the evening were the second day," mean anything to you?

BRYAN: I do not think it necessarily means a twenty-four-hour day.

DARROW: . . . Now, if you call those periods, they may have been a very long time.

BRYAN: They might have been.

DARROW: The creation might have been going on for a very long time?

BRYAN: It might have continued for millions of years.

The crowd was stunned. By admitting to "millions of years," Darrow had just succeeded in getting Bryan to admit to the basic tenet of Darwinism. In one afternoon, Darrow had turned the case in his favor. Darrow later wrote to Mencken: "I made up my mind to show the country what an ignoramus he was and I succeeded."

It was an ordeal for Bryan. "In all my days of public life, I have never been so abused by anyone as by the evolutionary crowd—not even by the Republicans," he later told a United Press reporter. "They misrepresent me and they vilify me. The defense in this case cannot open their mouths without hurtling insults at me." As soon as court was adjourned, Bryan began gathering ammunition for his own cross-examination.

But the trial concluded the next day. Scopes never took the stand. Bryan's testimony was expunged from the record by the judge, and the simple question presented to the jury was whether Scopes had violated the state law. By waiving his right to a closing argument, Darrow thus deprived Bryan of his chance to end the trial with a stirring oration. Shortly before noon, the jury huddled together briefly, returning nine minutes later with their verdict: Guilty. A minimum $100 fine was imposed, which the *Baltimore Evening Sun* offered to pay. It was an anti-climax to what Mencken had hoped to be a great test case of the Constitution.[21]

THE SCOPES TRIAL DID NOT END the anti-evolution crusade. As Mencken confided to a friend about his trip to Dayton, "I set out laughing and returned shivering. The Fundamentalists are on us! They will sweep the south and middle west,

Bryan or no Bryan." After the trial's conclusion, Bryan took the offense, revising his closing argument and later delivering it to the newspapers, putting the best political spin on the event. He talked of an expanded crusade against the teaching of evolution. At an open-air meeting in a town not far from Dayton, with Mencken undoubtedly in mind, he expressed indignation at "the way the correspondents have maligned and slandered" the men and women of Tennessee by calling them "yokels." "But in the end," Bryan angrily told his audience, "every critic you have will be rotted and forgotten." As the *Chicago Tribune* observed, "It is only Henry L. Mencken who has used, extensively at least, the nouns and adjectives to which Mr. Bryan objected."

Fundamentalists and evolutionists continued to clash over the question of the public educational system. Baptists in Kentucky voted to contribute no money to schools where evolution was taught; the Florida legislature proposed a law not to employ teachers who taught Darwinism; in Texas, the board of regents ruled "no infidel, atheist, or agnostic" be employed at the university. In the nation's capital, a group of fundamentalists proposed that Congress refuse salaries to those who taught "disrespect for the Bible." "Heave an egg out of a Pullman window," Mencken observed, "and you will hit a Fundamentalist almost anywhere in the United States today."

Only five days after the Scopes trial, the incredible news flashed across the nation that William Jennings Bryan was dead. In Baltimore, Mencken joked, "No doubt Heaven is in turmoil today, with Bryan just arrived," adding, "God aimed at Darrow, missed, and hit Bryan instead." To Joseph Krutch, he gloated: "We killed the son-of-a-bitch!"[22]

Bryan's private physician said the immediate cause of his death was "the heat and his extraordinary exertions due to the Scopes trial," but diabetes and Bryan's heart condition were later determined to be responsible. At Dayton, men and women from all across Rhea County came to pay tribute. "It was like somebody in the family had died," Eloise Reed recalled. "Soon afterward," John Scopes observed, "there was a rumor about town that the old Devil Darrow had killed Bryan with his inquisition." If so, Mencken said, that was "a job of public sanitation" that Darrow "never regretted."

From Dayton, the Bryan funeral train headed north toward Arlington Cemetery. Along the route church bells tolled; on houses, black crepe was draped; at each stop, parents lifted their children to gaze at Bryan's casket. In Ohio, Ku Klux Klan Klansmen ignited tall crosses in the night sky: "IN MEMORY OF WILLIAM JENNINGS BRYAN, THE GREATEST KLANSMAN OF OUR TIME, THIS CROSS IS BURNED: HE STOOD AT ARMAGEDDON AND BATTLED FOR THE LORD."

For days the news of Bryan's death dominated the nation's front pages. Where once reporters had derided the Commoner, now they obliterated all references that ridiculed him: *Life* destroyed 20,000 copies; the *New Yorker* pulled articles and cartoons that lampooned him; *Judge* apologized to readers for being unable to stop its publication while the staff hastily wrote an editorial in tribute for the next issue. Meanwhile, a popular country music ballad, recorded only a week after the event, began to feed a legend:

> *He fought the evolutionists and infidel men, fools*
> *Who are trying to ruin the minds of children in our schools.*

Determined not to permit the country to descend to "its national custom to sentimentalize the dead" or to forget the overriding issues from the Scopes trial, Mencken launched his strongest assault in a withering obituary, simply entitled "Bryan." Critic Alfred Kazin noted, "It was significant that one of the cruelest things he ever wrote, his essay on Bryan, was probably the most brilliant."

It was plain to everyone, when Bryan came to Dayton, that his great days were behind him—that he was definitely an old man, and headed at last for silence. . . . Hour after hour he grew more bitter. What the Christian Scientists call malicious animal magnetism seemed to radiate from him like heat from a stove. From my place in the courtroom, standing upon a table, I looked directly down upon him, sweating horribly and pumping his palm-leaf fan. His eyes fascinated me; I watched them all day long. They were blazing points of hatred. They glittered like occult and sinister gems. Now and then they wandered to me, and I got my share. It was like coming under fire.

What was behind that consuming hatred? At first I thought it was mere evangelical passion. . . . One day it dawned on me that Bryan, after all, was an evangelical Christian only by a sort of afterthought—that his career in this world, and the glories thereof, had actually come to an end before he ever began whooping for Genesis. So I came to this conclusion: that what really moved him was a lust for revenge. The men of the cities had destroyed him and made a mock of him; now he would lead the yokels against them. . . . The hatred in the old man's burning eyes was not for the enemies of God; it was for the enemies of Bryan. . . .

The Bryan I shall remember is the Bryan of his last weeks on this earth—broken, furious, and infinitely pathetic. It was impossible to meet his hatred with hatred to match it. He was winning a battle that would make him forever infamous, wherever enlightened men remembered it and him. . . .

It was hard to believe, watching him at Dayton, that he had traveled, that he had been received in civilized societies, that he had been a high officer of State. He seemed only a poor clod . . . full of an almost pathological hatred of all learning, all human dignity, all beauty, all fine and noble things. He was a peasant come home to the dung-pile. Imagine a gentleman, and you have imagined everything that he was not.

The job before democracy is to get rid of such canaille. If it fails, they will devour it.[23]

Reaction was not long in coming. At the Baltimore *Sunpapers*, the phones rang incessantly as angry readers canceled their subscriptions and advertisers pulled notices. It was early afternoon and the first edition had just hit the street when Mencken came charging through the revolving doors.

He seized an extra copy of the *Evening Sun* and, taking out a pencil from his coat pocket, began marking up his own column with quick jabs. "Here," he said

cf Dickens Scrooge – Child personification of want and
Ignorance – Must fear ignorance the most!!

to Walter Sondheim, who was manning the downstairs desk, and thrust the paper into the boy's hands, "Send this up to the editorial office." Then, his face mottled, Mencken pushed through the doors, leaving them spinning.

Looking at the copy that had just been handed him, the young boy began to read. In one second he recognized before him the obituary that had been the topic of all the irate phone calls. In place of "*fool*" Mencken had substituted "*figure*"; "*mountebank*" became "*leader*"; whole paragraphs and sentences had been excised. Deleted were other phrases "—a political charlatan of the worst type, without principle and without honor," and the one describing Bryan as "a peasant come home to the dung-pile. Imagine a gentleman, and you have imagined everything he was not."

The pressure on the *Sunpapers* had been too much. Later a rewrite man recounted the sequence of events. Edwin Murphy, the managing editor, had caught a glimpse of Mencken's article and hit the ceiling. "STOP IT!" Murphy yelled to his assistant. "They usually only stop the presses in the movies," the rewrite man later recalled, "but Murphy actually did stop the presses that day to take the vitriol and sting out of Mencken's article." A call was placed to Hollins Street. It was the apparent reason for the afternoon visit and for the changes. Editors at the *Evening Sun* called upon editorial writer Gerald Johnson to write a sober account of Bryan's life, if only to lend balance to Mencken's column. Downstairs, at the front desk, young Sondheim sent the reworked obituary upstairs to the pressroom through the vacuum tube. "They're censoring *Mencken*," the boy thought, aghast.

In his memoirs, Mencken repeatedly insisted that he did not mind being edited; nowhere did he ever mention his obituary of Bryan. During the heat of controversy, however, Mencken confided to Fielding Garrison that the *Evening Sun* had its doubts about the obit even before it was printed: "Sentimentality dies very hard. For two weeks I denounced him as a mountebank daily; now he must be praised. But not by me, by damn!"

Years later, long after "the trial of the century" was over and Mencken was in a mellower mood, he admitted that dismissing Bryan "as a quack pure and unadulterated" was perhaps not "really just." But his rejection of the principles that Bryan defended at the trial continued unabated. In hundreds of communities around the United States, freedom still rested on a shaky foundation, dependent on local beliefs and biases.

Moreover, Mencken could not stop thinking it a pity that only two reporters had remained in Dayton when Bryan died, and that he was not one of them. "They were quite unequal to the story, which was badly manhandled. If the old boy had died while the trial was going on he'd have been turned off much more competently, for many virtuosi were then on hand." The whole episode served as a lesson, Mencken observed. He and Darrow were both in superb condition; meanwhile, Bryan was in hell. "Trust the Devil!" he said to a friend. "He takes care of his own!"[24]

26

IN THE CRUCIBLE

I T IS GIVEN TO VERY FEW WRITERS to have books written about them while they are living," noted the *New York Telegraph* shortly after the Scopes Trial and upon the publication of Isaac Goldberg's *The Man Mencken* and Ernest Boyd's *H. L. Mencken.* "But H. L. Mencken, with his God-given gift for getting publicity without asking for it, is doing very well."

Mencken's work had been made easier by the manner in which Anna Mencken provided a comfortable, orderly home for her family. The Mencken kitchen was famous for its old-world charm, for knockwurst and *Apfleschnitten*, for *Baumküchen* at Christmas, and for cookies that looked like Valentines. They were all thoroughly enjoyed by Anna's eldest son, who did not have to give any thought to the running of a house that hummed along in an organized routine which betrayed no sign of the hard work that went on to make it that way. Anna, like other German women, Mencken wrote, still labored under "the pitifully antique delusion that it is fine and honorable and glorious to be an industrious housewife and a good mother—that the life is not wasted which transforms a house into a home—that the woman is deserving of lasting honor who seeks no public notice, but sends a healthy, clean-minded son into the world to serve his fellow men."

At sixty-seven, Anna Mencken was still a handsome woman. Her hair was iron gray, a bit fluffy, and becomingly dressed; her complexion pale and clear, almost translucent; her figure shapely. She, more than any of the others in the family, caught the eye of visitors and held their attention. During the years following his father's death, Mencken had grown closer to Anna. "Despite the uneasiness that some of my ventures aroused in her," she had always stood loyally by him. Though it was quietly understood that together Henry and Anna would shoulder the responsibility of his younger siblings, the emphasis was primarily on Henry having the freedom to focus on his own activities. "I have been able to express my views because I have always been free from any financial pressure. If I had to worry about buying the baby's shoes from the weekly pay envelope, my attitude might have been different."

Mencken recognized with increasing gratitude this special relationship with his mother. Remembering the transgressions of his father, he made sure to call his mother whenever he was going to be late for meals or when another engagement prevented him from coming home. Yet when Mother's Day was established in America, he was its biggest critic. Mencken thought that the man who had to inform strangers that he loved his mother "is a cad." Instead of honoring a mother one day a year, he wrote, "he serves her by doing his work in the world, whatever it may be, in a way that does her credit, and remembering his debt to her every day of his life."[1]

ONE AFTERNOON IN MID-DECEMBER 1925, as Mencken passed by his mother's sitting room, he found her at her table, "sitting idly (an unheard of thing for her) and obviously ill. I took her temperature and found it was 103." When her condition worsened, Mencken rushed her to Union Memorial Hospital. She went bravely, even gaily. "It amused her to think she was having her first surgical operation at 67," Mencken recalled, for acute tonsillitis and a streptococcus infection. "All the rest of us, including the house dog, had been on that [surgeon's] table, but she had always escaped." Her cheerfulness buoyed Mencken, leading him to declare up to the last moment that he believed she would get well.

Mencken sat upstairs in his third floor office, typing a few sentences of *Notes on Democracy*, but the thought of his mother ailing in the room directly below tormented him. "The sight and thought of her made work almost impossible," he recalled. "My mind was filled with horrible imaginings, and I resented bitterly the fact that medicine could do so little for her." Nervously, he repeatedly walked down to her room to check on her. He even asked the convent on the corner of Hollins Street to stop ringing their bell so that its heavy clanging would not disturb her early morning rest.[2]

"To add to my distress," Mencken later recalled, "my uncle, Henry Mencken, now sole proprietor of my father's old firm of August Mencken & Bro., had seized the time of my mother's last illness to go bankrupt." On December 11, 1925, while Anna clung to life, Mencken had been summoned hurriedly to his uncle's office and told the firm was insolvent.

Mencken went to great pains to prevent his mother from hearing about this misfortune, not because she had any concern for her brother-in-law (she had always regarded him as lazy and incompetent) but because she had pride in the good name of the firm. Now Mencken devoted himself to settling its affairs without public scandal.

One day, Theodore Dreiser showed up on Mencken's doorstep. Since 1919, their friendship had stood on shaky ground. At this point, Dreiser was on his way to Florida, concerned, Mencken said later, only about a bottle of Scotch to take with him. When Mencken informed Dreiser of his mother's condition, his old friend seemed uninterested and offered no word of hope that she would recover. Politely, Mencken bade Dreiser sit by the fire, but after they had been conversing for several minutes, Dreiser told him he had left his girlfriend, Helen Richardson, seated in the car in the cold outside. Indignant, Mencken invited her in, but the couple did not stay long. Dreiser left, still saying nothing about Anna Mencken. "The episode caused me to set him down as an incurable lout," Mencken wrote. Of all the other evidences of behavior during their friendship, none seemed "so gross and disgusting."

Helen remembered Dreiser's words as they left Hollins Street that afternoon. Mencken's resentment was painfully clear to Dreiser, who commented to Helen: "It doesn't matter what he ever says about me or does to me, he is a great guy and a great friend and I'll always love him."

Anna Abhau Mencken died the very next day, on December 13. The end had been painless. "She simply went to sleep and passed quietly out of life," her eldest son noted. "Her last words to me were that she felt much better."

Alone in his room, Mencken penned two brief lines to Sara. "It is the end of many things for me." A month later, a letter from Dreiser straggled in from Florida, asking about Mencken's mother, but it was too little and too late. There were other matters that would strain their friendship. For the next nine years, the two men maintained a guarded silence.[3]

MENCKEN REGARDED ANNA'S DEATH as nothing less than "pure disaster." Her loss filled him "with a sense of futility and desolation." Among the first telegrams of condolence was one from Sara Haardt, a comforting caress from Montgomery for which Mencken was thankful. "It reached me when I needed it."

Each time he passed his mother's sitting room he could not help but see her there. "The house seems dreadfully empty. My mother and I had lived here together for 42 years," he later reflected. "What a woman she was!" he wrote. "And how I'll miss her!" Anna had been only 22 years his senior; now, with her death, Mencken admitted to feeling very old. The loss of both his parents made him sense that "we are all on our way. Nothing stands ahead of us. Somehow it makes me shiver."

In the days ahead he had to deal with the terms of his mother's will. All of the property had been left in trust to him with the provision for Gertrude to occupy the house until her marriage or her death, with an annuity of $900 a year from bonds worth a total of $30,000. As executor and head of the family, Mencken was required to deal with any monetary disbursements.

Mencken felt a particular concern for the welfare of his younger sister. He fretted how he was to find company for Gertrude when travel to New York took him away from Hollins Street. "My sister, all her life, has been used to having my mother about," he worried. "Of late they slept in the same room. Now she will be immensely lonely."[4]

Christmas was only nine days away when the family buried Anna in the Loudon Park cemetery. Baltimore was decked in its routine holiday bustle and cheer. Bells pealed throughout the city; up and down the streets mailmen delivered packages to families. Missing from inside 1524 Hollins Street was the merriment their mother had infused on previous holiday seasons: the cozy smell of baking, the sharp tang of pine needles draped over the mantel, the Christmas tree in the corner of the living room. Instead, that afternoon when the family returned from the burial, a bow of black crepe greeted them at the front door. Inside, to Mencken, it seemed "as empty as a cave."

"Christmas here would have been awful," Mencken wrote to Sara that evening. Gertrude planned to travel to Charlie's house in Pittsburgh; August and Mencken would join them Christmas Eve. While the dreadful day of the funeral had mercifully ended, it had left Mencken in considerable confusion. So many things had come to a close that year—his partnership with Nathan, his friendship with Dreiser, his father's old factory, and now the family home, the property that he once thought would keep him when he was old, essentially belonged to Gertrude. Above all, it seemed inconceivable to Mencken that his mother was gone forever, that he could not at that moment go down the stairs to find her calmly reading in her sitting room below.

"Somehow," he mourned, "I always thought of her death as something far off."[5]

The day after the funeral, Margaret Redding arrived at Mencken's office for the usual dictation of the morning mail. Mencken, unlike himself, did not rise when she entered. Instead, he remained sitting with his hands on his desk, eyes downcast, not even looking at the pile of letters stacked in front of him.

> I walked around his chair and before I sat down I said: "Mr. Mencken, I am so sorry to hear of your mother's death."
> He answered at once as a cued actor says his line . . . "She was very ill for a long time," he said. "It was expected."
> I sat down, feeling chilled. Even to himself, his voice must have sounded cold. He added less mechanically: "We had a mask taken as soon as she died."
> His face was impassive, his body very still, like a drawing: the small room where we sat seemed airless, motionless, without sound waves or stirrings.

Then, the secretary lifted her pen and Mencken began dictation, his voice maintaining the same pitch throughout the session. "It is noteworthy that he kept to his routine," Margaret observed.

"That routine," Mencken reflected years later, "happily, was so heavy that it rescued me from myself."[6]

WITH GERTRUDE SAFELY in Pittsburgh, Mencken resolutely resumed his tasks at the *American Mercury* office in New York, where observers noted he was in a much better mental state than anyone had anticipated. Such outward composure could only be maintained through hard work. After putting in a day at the *Mercury*, he sought the company of James Cain and Lilly and Ruth Goodman, who accompanied him to the Hofbrauhaus at Union Hill, across the Hudson River in New Jersey. "Mencken cried in his beer, while Ruth and I took ourselves out of the way, and had one or two dances," James Cain recalled. "He seemed utterly inconsolable, as though his world had fallen in."

The stupendous debt that Mencken said he owed to Anna, and which he promised to express at a later date, was neither written in 1925 nor in the many years that followed. What was the most painful to Mencken, and therefore the most private, was often passed over in silence. In truth, the gratitude this son felt for his mother had already been expressed a quarter of a century earlier, in the pages of an unfinished manuscript, written during the years of his troubled adolescence: "Often I do remember her sitting, at twilight, at the large window of her room which opened toward the town, with an old leather volume lying in her lap."

Sometimes I bounded into the room to pour into her ear the story of my boyish troubles, she would bid me sit at her feet, and as I rested my head beside the book, she would read to me some story. . . . The tale and her manner of telling it were oftentime so romantic that I would sit spellbound until rudely awakened by the loud Sunday supper bell. . . .

I have more than once thought of those glorious evenings. . . . and whatever I may have done in this life that deserved to be called good or noble, whether it were a great action or small, found its inspiration, I know, in my mother's angelic example and influence. That I have not been a greater credit is my fault, and mine alone.[7]

". . . how I'll miss her!" Anna Abhau Mencken. Courtesy Admiral William Abhau.

27

BANNED IN BOSTON

IN 1926 MENCKEN WAS FORCED to turn his attention to what he called the "snouting and preposterous Puritan" who now dominated the landscape, "wearing out his eyes in the quest for smut." Borrowing an Australian term, Mencken concluded that "We are run by wowsers." A *wowser* bears a divine commission to relegate and improve. "So long as you and I are sinful, he can't sleep," Mencken said. "So long as we are happy, he is after us."

From the time Mencken read Dreiser's first novel, he knew he had found the writer whose work he could use in his battle against Puritanism. He rallied the literary community to keep the censors from suppressing Dreiser's *The Genius*. He continued the fight against all censorship in his columns for the *Evening Sun*, his essays in the *Smart Set* and the *American Mercury*, and his books. The culmination of all these battles took place in 1926, when Mencken precipitated a confrontation by selling a copy of the censored April issue of the *American Mercury* to the Reverend Franklin Chase in Boston Common. The very next day the local judge dismissed the complaint on grounds that no offense to public morals had been committed. By midafternoon, Mencken found himself a hero, surrounded by eager Harvard students cheering his name, as flashbulbs popped and hands reached across to shake his.

The day Mencken broke the law for the sake of freedom of speech would long be remembered. Many more marveled that such an hour had not arrived sooner. James Cain wrote to Mencken: "How you keep out of jail is a mystery to me."[1]

Inside Boston's Copley Plaza Hotel, Mencken's room bounced with reporters, assistants, women, and bellboys; above the din came the sound of a jangling telephone. First came a call from Arthur Garfield Hays; then one from the Harvard Liberal Club with an invitation; another, from the Harvard Union offering a monster dinner and testimonial in Mencken's honor. When the phone rang again, it was a representative from the student newspaper at Boston University. "And always the bell, bell, bell, until it seemed to fill the room," noted Isaac Goldberg, also present. "It looked for all the world like the headquarters of a political campaign."

Moving about in his vest and shirt-sleeves, red-faced and radiant, puffing a cigar that would not stay lighted, Mencken boomed, "The boys and girls came across splendidly." With the afternoon sun shining just behind Mencken, it seemed to Goldberg that the editor "looked like a college man himself, on the eve of an inter-collegiate debate." He was having, in fact, the time of his life. "He looked, and felt, fit for the deviltry he is always talking about, yet beneath his joviality was a genuine seriousness. Mencken laughs, rasps, jests, but he means business and is a cruel, dangerous opponent."

A bellhop arrived with a letter. "Ah, my famous four-bit piece," Mencken exclaimed. Apparently, one reporter noted, Mencken's wit was more effective than his molars; no marks of his teeth could be found upon the enclosed coin that he had accepted when Chase had bought the banned magazine. "I had my attorney demand its return. This I shall cherish for some time. It is what you might call my blood money."[2]

Although Mencken had been absent from Baltimore for only three days, he was not one to permit his correspondence to lag. The trial had already brought in fathoms of mail. Before returning home, he dispatched a telegram to his secretary: "Can we have a session at eight this evening?"

A debonair Mencken, wearing a tuxedo and freshly shaved, greeted Margaret Redding at the front door. Mencken was all business while dictating, but when he finished he entertained Margaret with stories about "those imbeciles." As long as Margaret had worked for Mencken he had maintained an almost impenetrable façade. The memory of his vibrant presence on this particular evening, of hearing him speak with such clipped elation, stayed with her for years.

At last Mencken escorted Margaret down the stairs. "I am heading for Paul Patterson's house. We are going to have a session." Years later, Margaret recalled, "Coming from Mencken the word *session* sounded like a call to arms. Whoever shared his life shared a battle-ground."

At the foot of the stairs, Mencken suddenly wheeled around and hurriedly bounded up the steps. Returning, he handed his secretary a copy of the "Hatrack" issue of his magazine. "I almost forgot," he said, triumphantly: "The *American Mercury*, April, 1926!" Ever on cue, he opened the front door with a flourish.[3]

Meanwhile, the Reverend Chase had been arranging a surprise reprisal of his own. From across the country, the attorney general had received letters of complaint about the *American Mercury*. Taking advantage of the situation, Reverend Chase quietly persuaded authorities in Washington to suppress the distribution of the April issue through the mails. It did not seem to matter that Mencken had already been acquitted in Boston. Instead, bowing to the Watch & Ward Society, the full force of the United States government came down upon Mencken. The *American Mercury* was federally banned across the country.

Elated, Reverend Chase gloated to reporters, "I knew I was right."

Losing no time, Mencken joined Arthur Garfield Hays in Washington for a meeting with Horace J. Donnelly, the postmaster general. "I am glad you are going after all those fellows," Clarence Darrow encouraged Mencken. "We have got to fight and you are the best fighter I know."

The hearing lasted more than three hours. The postmaster general sat behind a wide desk, piled high with periodicals and books, including a copy of Ernest Hermingway's *In Our Times*. Donnelly spoke seldom, and then in a dry, clipped voice from the corner of his mouth; the perfect model, Mencken later wrote, of a third-rate bureaucrat: "vain, cocksure, and unintelligent."

Hays stepped in, arguing energetically that a great principle was at stake; the entire procedure was contrary to the fundamentals of American law, in taking action against a client without a hearing.

Donnelly remained unmoved. "Why so much rumpus about that case?" the irritated Donnelly later grumbled to reporters. "It's just one in a hundred. Dubious books and magazines pour in here, 10 to 20 a day. Hardly a night I don't sit up until midnight reading."

Did he think he should be the sole judge of the nation's literature?

"Well, someone has to do it," the postmaster general replied. "The works of Boccaccio and Rabelais have been banned at various times. But I've found that somehow the word 'literature' is used to cover up filth."[4]

This calculated unfairness seemed to Mencken to threaten the very existence of the publication. The *American Mercury*, at that time, was little more than two years old. "I'll be damned if I want to be plastered in the newspapers as the publisher of a smutty magazine," Mencken contended. Yet this was exactly what was happening. Police throughout the country were now treating the magazine as it if it were just another piece of erotica.

A new class of bootleggers sold copies of the April issue for as much as sixty dollars; others made money by selling the article itself. Too late, horrified librarians discovered the offending story about the prostitute Hatrack had been ripped from their only copies; they began locking the magazine away. Newsdealers' stocks quickly depleted, though not an hour seemed to pass without their being asked for it. One man chained his only edition to his stand, charging customers ten cents a read; he made more than fifty dollars.

Entire communities seemed to agree with the *Christian Index* that either parents must provide something wholesome for their reading tables or be faced with the alternative of allowing "Mencken to provide our children with the poison which will eat out their hearts and drag their souls down to hell."

Mencken had long been accustomed to public abuse, but now he felt embittered by the hostile reaction from his colleagues in the press. He had expected some negative comment from the Boston papers and also from the South, where he was excessively unpopular, mainly because of "The Sahara of the Bozart" and his reports from the Scopes Trial.

He had felt sure, however, that his fight against censorship would draw sympathy from the big-city dailies, especially in the northeast. "The fact that I was fighting a battle in which the whole press of the country had a stake was seldom mentioned," he observed. Yet, the majority was united in its condemnation. He was accused not only of having bad taste, but also of being cheap, tawdry, and vulgar. Perhaps one of the most venomous reactions came from the *New York Herald Tribune*. Mencken's loyalty to Germany during the war was cited, with the dismissal: "He is completely alien to America."

There was another issue to consider—the danger to Mencken's own fortunes. "I had accumulated, through my writings during the war and afterward, a large crop of bitter enemies, and some of them were extremely enterprising," Mencken recalled. "They now had, thanks to the two wowsers, a good stick to beat me with, and they employed it with much industry. . . . It seemed intolerable that all my efforts should now be set at naught by such frauds as Donnelly and Chase."

Herbert Asbury, the author of "Hatrack," fared little better. When pressed by reporters, the mayor of his hometown said Asbury "must have gotten a little out of balance since he left Farmington," the unfortunate victim of Mencken's baleful influence.

That nothing had been done in this same moral town regarding Hatrack's unfortunate plight seemed to have been forgotten. "Those worthy citizens of Farmington simply prove Mr. Asbury's case," Mencken told the United Press. "My suggestion is that they hang all the town evangelists and begin to read the Sermon on the Mount."[5]

Mencken's euphoria from the initial days in Boston had now largely evaporated to be replaced by a fierce determination. He refused to admit exhaustion or defeat. To quell the criticism that he had risked imprisonment as a mere publicity stunt, he wrote a circular entitled "To the Friends of the *Mercury*" that mollified his critics and reduced the astounding number of individual letters Mencken had to write subscribers and friends. He told Alfred Knopf that he had been dictating an average of 125 a day for ten days.

He found solace in the words of Victor L. Berger of Wisconsin, the only member of the House of Representatives who showed any interest in the case. Marching to the podium in the House, Berger attacked all unlimited censorship over free speech and a free press:

> Mr. Speaker, have the American people lost their faith in democratic insti-
> tutions? There seems to be less concern here about the loss of civil liberty than
> in any Western European country. There is surely less resistance against
> Federal, State and local tyranny. We have truly become a docile people.

Afterward, Mencken wrote a full account of the "Hatrack" case, hoping it
might some day interest a historian of American culture in the early twentieth
century.[6]

A FEW WEEKS AFTER THE HEARING in Washington, a New York judge, Julian Mack,
granted an injunction against the U.S. postmaster. After reading the article in the
American Mercury, he said: "No one but a moron could be affected by it."
  Sensing defeat, the government shifted its attack from "Hatrack" to an
obscure advertisement in the magazine. Clearly, the Puritans had lost and they
knew it. Mencken failed to collect damages, but he handed the Watch & Ward
Society a major setback. Many Bostonians were indignant over the bad publicity
the case had given the town; many withdrew their support from the society. One
year after the *American Mercury* case, the Society concluded in its annual report
that the publicity had given "advertisement to the very thing it is seeking to
suppress. . . ."
  "While I personally would not consider the attack of Mencken scarcely
worth a thought," the president of the World's Purity Federation wrote to the
Watch & Ward Society, he was nonetheless concerned over the resignation of
many members of the board.
  "Wowsers always desert one another in times of stress," Mencken wryly
noted, "and when they begin to quarrel their fighting technique is extraordinarily
foul." Now that the U.S. Post Office had been defeated, the influence that the
secretary of the Watch & Ward Society had so long wielded was collapsing.
Discredited and shunned, J. Franklin Chase quit his post.
  The episode had taken its toll. Eight months later, the reverend died.
Compassion was notably absent when Mencken heard the news. "I am told," he
wrote with glee, "that worry over the case, especially over the reprisals we held
over him, helped to kill him. I hope so."
  "He belonged to the type of cleric that is extraordinarily obnoxious to me,"
Mencken observed. Beneath all of Chase's burly geniality and strict morality,
Mencken remarked, "Boston was full of reports that . . . he was extremely fond of
the dirty literature he professed to hold in such holy horror, and he was in the
habit of exhibiting it clandestinely to his friends." A criminal record on file in
Boston showed that over the years, he had been accused of adultery, forgery,
assault and battery. As Mencken said, "Now he was dead at last in defeat and dis-
may, and we were rid of him."[7]
  The war against censorship, Mencken admitted, had been "a hard sweat."
Tired yet exhilarated, he was gratified to see that the story was reported around

the world. Sinclair Lewis called it glorious; at Kansas City a dozen preachers were "tickled to death that you had put it all over Chase, and all of them referred to you as 'Menck' with an affection which I think would really astonish you."

Other battles followed, but Mencken's fight against censorship in April 1926 made his name forever identified with freedom of speech. "Mr. Mencken nearly always makes me angry when I read him, which I am sure is the only effect he would wish to have on me," a reporter from the *London Sunday Express* pointed out, "but I always have to admit to myself that here is a man who deserves well of his age, because he is against humbug when humbug is terribly successful on two sides of the Atlantic."

Even the least sympathetic of Mencken's readers, the *Express* acknowledged, had to allow that "Mencken is really a brave man, and further, that he is a devoted and uncompromising American patriot." If "the coming generations of Americans will, I believe, witness an increasing honesty of intellectual and moral life . . . the credit will be due to the men of Mr. Mencken's courage."[8]

28

THE GREAT GOD MENCKEN

H<small>E IS THE MOST POWERFUL PERSONAL INFLUENCE</small> on this whole generation of educated people," Walter Lippmann said of Mencken after his victory in Boston. Like a mere handful of other literary critics in American history, Mencken had become a celebrity, that exalted individual whom Mencken once defined as "One who is known to many persons he is glad he doesn't know."

Hundreds of newspapers printed stories about his influence or his personal life, the way he parted his hair, his fondness for cigars (it was proposed one should be named after him). In New York, a doctor used extracts of *Prejudices* to test his patients' vision. At Carnegie Hall, an orchestra played a song with words taken from Mencken's *Ventures Into Verse*. When Mencken listed suggestions for the improvement of rail travel, "The Most Quoted Man in America" discovered his tips soberly considered by officials of *Railway Age*. When he praised Henry Ford, the distributors for the car lifted the quotation for full page advertisements of the Model A, then about to make its debut.

Meanwhile, Isaac Goldberg's biography of Mencken had become a best seller, and there was a clamor for his autobiography. In library catalogues, cards for his books were blackened from being fingered by so many readers. Rare book dealers noted that the first editions most in demand were those written by H. L. Mencken, surpassing even Mark Twain's. Mencken's plays, *The Artist* and *Death: A Discussion*, were shown in theaters in Baltimore, Los Angeles, Chicago, and London.

"No other contemporary critic is so well known in the colleges," attested Carl Van Doren. At Harvard, students were asked to "explain the reference

"*Mother, Junior's being Mencken again.*"

Cartoon by Rea Gardner in *The New Yorker*, May 11, 1929. © TheCartoonBank.com; Rea Gardner 2005.

of Mr. Mencken to the Bible Belt." All this was a remarkable change from a few years before, when an undergraduate at the University of Michigan was attacked by fellow students for criticizing the school in the *Smart Set*. Now, at Northwestern University, a special edition of the campus magazine imitated the *American Mercury*, and the editors, who were threatened with expulsion, were being hailed as heroes by the rest of the student body. "So many young men," mused Jake Barnes in Ernest Hemingway's *The Sun Also Rises*, "get their likes and dislikes from Mencken."[1]

As usual with this controversial figure, praise was offset by fierce opposition. Across the country, Rotary Clubs packed houses with such talks as "The Fallacies of H. L. Mencken." If some Moslems called him a seer, there were clergy who were giving sermons on such topics as "God Is Still God, In spite of H. L. Mencken." The Reverend John Roach Stratton, one of the era's best-known fundamentalists, said he had prayed for Mencken for years. He now invited the editor to a revival service (Mencken declined). At Harvard, laughter echoed when Stratton addressed students on the Bible. After this fiasco, it was suggested that forty priests be sent to universities across the United States to preach to youngsters "who should be saved from H. L. Mencken and his ghoulish crowd."

At some faculty luncheons, heads of English departments offered variations of the sentiment that "Mencken is the worst menace to the glorious Republic." As for his critical ability, it was dismissed as "zero." When the president of Rutgers

University blamed a wave of college suicides on "too much Mencken," Mencken's subsequent proposal that there be a wave of suicide among college presidents was greeted with a roar of student approval.[2]

"It is hard to describe the way we felt, I mean our generation on the campuses, about Mencken," reminisced Philip Wagner, later an editor on the *Baltimore Evening Sun*. "For one thing, he gave us an attitude. . . . He shook the dust from early literature. He persuaded us that good writing didn't have to follow old models, although it might take the best of them. He knocked down a whole shooting gallery of sacred literary sheep and cows. But he didn't stop at that: he talked about new men and pulled us to them."

Not until 1926 were both editor and publisher reasonably sure that the *American Mercury* was not, as they first worried, only a short-term success. That year, the circulation rose to 70,000 a month; at its peak, two years later, it reached 84,000 copies—a solid achievement for a magazine without any illustrations that cost fifty cents. Whenever a new bundle of *Mercurys* was delivered to the shops, young men eagerly tore open the package. The publication was passed from hand to hand until it became tattered.

A generation of novices began copying Mencken. His style was "immediately imitated to nausea," observed Edmund Wilson, and was borrowed, said F. Scott Fitzgerald, by "four-fifths of the younger critics." Emily Clark, the editor of the *Reviewer*, was inundated by "an unprecedented number of cheap and obnoxious imitations." James Branch Cabell referred to "Menckenoids," others to "Menckenettes." Mencken admitted he was to blame for his imitators; it put him in an icy mood. "They are stealing my stuff," he told a reporter; the college boys constituted "a public nuisance."

The younger generation was not done in by this worship; established writers sometimes yielded as well. "Henry Mencken was our great hero," Sherwood Anderson wrote of his circle in Chicago, among them Ben Hecht and Carl Sandburg. "The younger generation of newspapermen was captivated by Mencken's iconoclastic and vernacular style," recalled Southern author Virginius Dabney. The list of his admirers was remarkable: Sinclair Lewis, William L. Shirer, Margaret Mead, Arthur M. Schlesinger Jr., William Styron, John Huston—all attesting to the powerful influence Mencken exerted.[3]

In 1926, he was named in the *Nation's* Honor Roll for "adding with his books and the *American Mercury* to the gaiety and sanity of the nation." ("God save us!" was Mencken's reaction.) The Mencken cult was especially apparent among the young in Baltimore. "There was a sense of excitement to be living in the same city as H. L. Mencken," one youth recalled. Some took to driving their cars by Hollins Street to peek at his house. Others rang the front doorbell, forcing an annoyed August Mencken to poke his head from an upper-story window to yell that his brother was not at home.

A letter came to the *Sun*: "Why not put Baltimore on the map by boosting a movement to change the name of our city to 'Menckenapolis'?" The gawking his

"... he gave us an attitude." H. L. Mencken Collection, Enoch Pratt Free Library.

appearance caused became so frequent that Mencken was forced to slip through the alley and enter his own home through the back entrance.[4]

In Memphis, a lonely African American teenager named Richard Wright borrowed a friend's library card and forged a note: "Dear Madam: Will you please let this nigger boy have some books by H. L. Mencken?" A block away from the library, he opened one of the books and read the title: *Prejudices*. "I knew what that word meant," he later recalled. "I had heard it all my life."

That night as the boy read, he was shocked. "This man was fighting, fighting with words," he wrote. "He was using words as a weapon, using them as one would use a club." The boy read on. "What amazed me was not what he said, but how on earth anybody had the courage to say it."

Long before *Native Son* established Richard Wright as a Pulitzer Prize–winning author, he had discovered what members of the Harlem Renaissance, already in full swing by 1926, had recognized for themselves: that H. L. Mencken was a force in their own literary movement. That year, Carl Van Vechten's best-selling *Nigger Heaven* paid Mencken homage by identifying him as the editor responsible for the success of black literature.

Mencken's reputation for encouraging the works of James Weldon Johnson, George Schuyler, and Langston Hughes also gave courage to Reginald Clyne, a redcap at Penn Station in New York, who purposely waited on him so he could speak to him about his manuscript. "He surprised me by suggesting that I mail it to him," Clyne recalled. "This I did. And after a couple of weeks, he complimented me on my style." Mencken went even further, sending the manuscript to Knopf.

It was a scene that would play itself out over and over again, leading Countee Cullen to praise Mencken for "performing a great service for us in banishing bigotry, prejudice and ignorance so effectively." Not only was Mencken "judiciously fair" in his attitude toward African Americans, according to W. E. B. Du Bois; black leaders such as Adam Clayton Powell declared him to be "the most distinguished, learned iconoclast on the American continent."[5]

OVERSEAS, "MENCKENISM" HAD ALSO REACHED new heights. Europeans had been the first group to recognize his merits; now, the growth of his reputation abroad was one of the literary phenomena of the time. In London, a club met every month when a new issue of the *American Mercury* appeared: meetings were called to order, whiskeys were mixed with soda, and the secretary, in a grave voice, read from the latest collection of "Americana." Each time a new volume of *Prejudices* was published, British reviewers complained that the author was too vulgar for refined consumption; nonetheless, the acclaim for the Baltimorean continued. Elsewhere on the Continent, Italians liked the fact that the "*iconoclista*" was so "*allegro*"; in Paris, the French affectionately labeled him "*l'enfant terrible de la critique americaine.*"

By far Mencken's most eager disciples could be found in Germany, where he was praised for his European outlook and as the only modern critic who possessed a deep insight into American character. This was especially gratifying to Mencken, who had made special efforts to have all of his books translated in his "mother" country. *Notes on Democracy* made a great impression on the kaiser, who read it in English and later sent Mencken two large autographed pictures of himself.

Mencken's popularity also extended to Poland, Norway, South Africa, Venezuela, even to Japan, where his work was used to teach pupils English. Letters addressed to H. L. Mencken without any street, number, or city found their way to him. Mencken, Carl Van Doren asserted, was "one of the most American things we have." The recent discovery of articles in the tomb of King Tut inspired the *London Outlook* to propose that a book of essays by Mencken, along with a Model T Ford, be likewise buried, so that posterity would have an idea of life as lived in the twentieth century in America. By 1926, Mencken was no longer merely a literary personality; he had become an institution.[6]

Mencken, like Babe Ruth, did not need a press agent. Every time he finished a book, Mencken visited Knopf in New York to "scheme some publicity for it—an enterprise which really revolts me," he joked to Hamilton Owens, "and for which, as you know, I have no hand." As Owens well knew, Mencken had an expert hand; Owens had been on the receiving end of some of those schemes, such as instructions to send his Monday column to clergymen in the South "to stir things up."

Knopf Inc. sent thousands of circulars on what the foreign critics were saying to college teachers, public libraries, press associations, and individuals—all compiled from lists Mencken had prepared. Billboards promoted his work. Up and down New York's theater district, brightly colored couriers paraded placards displaying the latest book titles, with Mencken's opinions on each and his name as large and as prominent as the title of the book.

Mencken suggested that strong sales of his books be emphasized in any advertising. "It seems to me to be a far better selling point than good reviews," he advised. "Americans always want to do what everyone else is doing. If we could spread the impression that the book is a success, it might really become one."

During 1926, more than 500 editorials on the sayings and doings of H. L. Mencken were printed in the United States, many of them unfavorable. Even these were fodder for publicity. As Mencken once advised Dreiser when he complained of an unflattering press: "Don't bother about it. *Any* mention of your name is good." Sara, back in Baltimore, helped Mencken gather the clippings and group the insults into categories—the zoological, the genealogical, the Freudian. *Menckeniana: A Schimpflexicon* was the result and sold well.

Even the admittedly flawed *Notes on Democracy* did not completely discourage his fans, for all of New York seemed to be reading the little volume. In the course of only a few hours, one reporter found seven individuals reading the book on the subway; in Central Park, a flapper with bobbed hair was seen reading it aloud to her boyfriend.[7]

DURING THE HEIGHT OF THIS CELEBRITY, Joseph Hergesheimer invited him to a party, "with a pleasing variety of gals and refreshment." Mencken headed north to Wilmington, his suitcases loaded with Maryland terrapin. Waiting at the station with Dorothy Hergesheimer was a small, sparkling, animated woman— Aileen Pringle, a movie star from California, one of the "wenches" Joe promised to help entertain his friend. As Mencken's train pulled into the station, Aileen said, "I clapped my eye on the handsomest man this side of Hell." It was, she later confessed to Mencken, "the first really beautiful moment in my life. You were so 'bubbly' . . . so gorgeously full of yourself—and why not."

As the group made its way toward the Hergesheimers' home, Dorothy Hergesheimer chatted gaily in the car. Aileen Pringle hardly said a word, but, she told Mencken later, "I knew somehow that you were mine." Aileen got a speck of dust in her eye and Mencken, looking into those pools of unearthly turquoise, showed her the method of rolling the lid over a pencil. That did it. By the time they reached the house, she later confessed, "I knew I loved you." Mencken was totally smitten.

"I shall never forget how perfectly roguish you were—about four years old— when you took me to the library," she recalled. Mencken had made a pretense of showing Aileen an autograph in a book he had given to Joe. Most of the guests had drifted elsewhere, leaving the two of them alone. "You always remind me of just having discovered and robbed the jam jar," she said. "Three-quarters of an hour later I was in your arms. Even Valentino would have congratulated you—no sheik could do better."

Thirty years later, Aileen Pringle could still recall the exact minute of their very first encounter on June 19, 1926, "a day I shall long remember."[8]

She was born Aileen Bisbee in San Francisco on July 23, 1895. Her mother was of French Basque lineage; her father was president of the Pioneer Fruit Company. When Aileen was living in New York, her father had to go to Jamaica on business and asked her to go with him. "I was frankly bored with Manhattan at the time," remembered Aileen. "Since arriving, I had had, believe it or not, seven proposals of marriage." In Jamaica she was told she must meet Charlie Pringle, a confirmed bachelor whose father was the governor of Jamaica and the largest landowner. "Give me 25 minutes alone with him, I said, and I'll bet he proposes." He did and she accepted. Once ensconced on his Jamaican plantation, however, it did not take long for Aileen to realize she had made a tremendous mistake. Returning alone to California, with her husband hundreds of miles away and no doubt wondering how she could possibly want anything besides seventeen servants and two homes, in 1919 Aileen launched her movie career.

Because of her regal appearance and aristocratic upbringing, directors who wanted their films to reflect correct social etiquette took her opinion as definitive. Word went around the movie lot: "Ask Pringie; she knows." That Aileen's family background was brilliant was almost a curse: every motion picture magazine had spasms of delight over her family tree. "You had shop girls like Joan Crawford trying to impersonate society people, and you had real society people like myself doing little more than elaborate walk-ons," she said. "And so I have probably appeared in the worst roles that any woman was ever cursed with. If I have any admirers I am certainly surprised. How anyone could like me in the stupid roles I have played is always a source of the greatest amazement to me!"

Her big break came in 1923, when the British writer Elinor Glynn demanded Aileen be cast as Queen of Sardinia in the scandalous novel of its day, *Three Weeks*.

"The darling of the intellectuals." Aileen Pringle in 1926. The Billy Rose Theatre Collection, The New York Public Library.

Glynn's only singular contribution to literature and the motion picture industry, observed Aileen, was the word "It," but the studios hung on her every word. Glynn searched the country for a woman beautiful and refined enough to be her heroine. When Glynn declared Aileen had "It," she was cast in the role. *Three Weeks* led to other films, with Aileen carving a niche for herself as a modern vamp. When, in *His Hour*, a tipsy John Gilbert spat out some champagne on her bare shoulder, "I called him an s.o.b., but it was deserved. Neither of us knew it was the 'take' that would finally make it to the big screen."

Hergesheimer had met Aileen the year before, on a visit to Hollywood as the guest of Samuel Goldwyn, who hoped to entice an original film story from him. Aileen became the novelist's favorite partner at dinner parties. Hergesheimer wrote to his wife, Dorothy, that he found the actress "very charming and naturally well bred." That she was also pleasingly curvaceous, flirtatious, with a low melodious voice (attributes that made her, according to *Photoplay*, "a lady surrounded by men"), Hergesheimer failed to mention. Aileen's arrival at Hollywood parties was always an event.

Aileen Pringle's beauty was not the only draw that had men flocking to her home. She also had been tagged throughout the Hollywood community as "First Wit." Her *bons mots* passed from mouth to mouth until they were passed off by others as originals. With far more frequency Aileen was labeled "the darling of the intellectuals," a phrase that infuriated the actress but nonetheless stuck. The studio chiefs, not knowing what to do with her, loaned her out to other studios. Finally they decided to make her an unofficial greeter of arriving New York writers. "I knew that Mr. Mayer's people were buying properties from the best sellers listed in the *New York Times*," she said years later, "and I also knew they hadn't bothered to read any of them."

Ignoring the advice of her friend Greta Garbo, who thought she should refrain from being a greeter and demand to be regarded as a serious actress, Aileen decided that being with authors was not such a bad way to spend one's day. A captivated Carl Van Vechten found "an ironic tinge to her most serious comment and a touch of sentiment in her most jocular remark, qualities which give her a very real fascination for me." He immortalized her as Auburn Six in his novel *Spider Boy*. "But what struck me, even more than her physical grace, was the vigor of her personality," Hergesheimer wrote in 1926. "There was no hesitation in her attitude, no doubt in her speech."

In 1926, Aileen Pringle was still waiting for her "big picture" when she met H. L. Mencken. She "took one look at those china blue eyes and we fell into each other's arms."9

DATING A FAMOUS HOLLYWOOD ACTRESS forced Mencken to pay closer attention to his own appearance. Nathan had often teased him about his clothes. Now, he obediently began following Aileen's suggestions: old-fashioned buttoned shoes instead of laced ones; lower collars; fashionable suspenders rather than a belt. He even went so far as to have four small moles removed from his left cheek. Valentino, Mencken jested, "will be jealous of me now."

Occasionally, when Aileen chanced to be in New York, they would be joined by Mencken's partner Nathan and Lillian Gish. Nathan had become obsessed with the diminutive former D. W. Griffith star, to the point that the walls of his apartment were covered with her photographs. Aileen recalled: "When the four of us went out together it was more of a man's evening. They paid more attention to each other talking than they did to us . . . and the talk often centered on literature and the new books and plays." Sometimes they would be joined by Anita Loos, and "Lillian took in everything—short of taking notes like you do at school. A book or play could be a future film for her. She was very smart that way. She scouted her material by attaching herself to the greatest sources possible, after she had left D. W. Griffith. Who better than Mencken or Nathan?"

In August, Mencken and Aileen were again guests of the Hergesheimers in Wilmington, with an impromptu movie filmed on the lawn. Mencken reported that the film was very thrilling and mildly salacious, and Aileen "very amusing." Jim Tully wrote a profile of the weekend, but as he told Nathan: "I dealt very kindly with the Great Lover—for when a man is goofy about Pringie he has enough to bear." During their time together Mencken dined with Rudolph Valentino in New York, with Aileen as hostess. Valentino had sought out Mencken for his advice, irritated by an unfriendly press that accused him of being responsible for the effeminization of the American male.

Valentino's predicament touched Mencken deeply: "Here was a young man who was living the daily dream of millions of other young men. Here was one who was catnip to women. Here was one who had wealth and fame, both made honorably and by his own effort. And here was one who was very unhappy." Mencken summarized Valentino's problem as "the agony of a man of civilized feelings thrown into a situation of intolerable vulgarity, destructive alike to his peace and his dignity."

The observation could well have been applied to Mencken himself. Earlier that year, his free speech efforts in Boston had been misunderstood as mere publicity. What was being remembered was the public character, the national wag. The public personality that Mencken had wholeheartedly lent himself to, and that was being exploited in the press, had ended up producing a persona that seemed forced and overdone.

When, soon after, Valentino took ill and died, Mencken wrote in his obituary that one of the biggest jokes of the gods was "that man must remain alone and lonely in this world, even with crowds surging about him."

Ironically, during the peak of Mencken's popularity, a deep well of loneliness gripped him. When Aileen headed back west from Wilmington, Mencken stuffed a note in her bag, telling her, "I have left the whole of me at Wilmington." Aileen replied: "I shan't be normal again until you come to Hollywood. In spite of the mosquitoes, wilting collars, drooping underwear and the preventions for pregnancy I think we did awfully well—at least it recommends our dispositions and if we ever meet on a cool day we would probably become so perfectly angelic that we would be obliged to continue our affair in Heaven." She concluded "I love you too my dearest one and somehow I feel I will always continue to do so."

In Hollins Street that summer, Mencken took a page of *Sun* copypaper, put it in his typewriter, and began to write about "the sweet and dreadful passion of love. It is as tenderly personal and private as a gallstone." Then he crossed it out.[10]

29

A SENTIMENTAL JOURNEY

D ESPITE THE EXCITEMENT of a new love affair and the professional heights
Mencken had achieved, the strain of the preceding six months of 1926
had left his spirit depleted. Overwork was understandably a factor. He
had been kept jumping with *Notes on Democracy*, and *Prejudices: Fifth Series*, by
continued litigation over the "Hatrack" case, and by the bankruptcy of August
Mencken & Bro. In addition, the family had been going through the sorrowful
process of reorganizing the household following Anna's death. Her memory still
haunted her son. "A hundred times a day I find myself planning to tell her something, or ask her for this or that," he wrote Dreiser. "It is a curious thing: the
human incapacity to imagine finality."

All the links with his past seemed broken, not only in his personal life but in
the country around him. His contributions to the editorial page of the *Baltimore
Evening Sun* were mainly devoted to denouncing two things: the interference
with free speech and civil rights, and, as he put it, "the growing complacency and
imbecility of the country under the so-called Coolidge Prosperity." To Mencken,
the United States had become a nation where wealth exceeded any other value.
Each time he visited New York he noted that in every block new office buildings
were going up; one right next door to the Algonquin. Each morning explosions
jolted Mencken awake; at night, coming home, he often stepped into potholes.
Getting from his office at Fifty-seventh Street to the Algonquin on Forty-fourth
took twenty minutes by bus or taxi. New York was inconceivably rich; nothing
seemed out of reach. Mencken oscillated between liking and loathing the town,

yet each time he boarded the train headed back to Baltimore, he confessed to feeling "an absurd kind of thrill."

But there was little to recall the Baltimore of forty years before. A few blocks from Mencken's home were at least a dozen stores with radios going full blast. "They are maintained by poor fish who yearn to be noticed," he wrote, "and have no other means of accomplishing it. [The] very essence of their pleasure is that what they do is unpleasant. If silence were a nuisance they would like it, and be silent." Steuart's Hill, the canyon where Mencken used to play as a boy, was half ditch and half sewer. Neat rows of red brick houses with white trim were increasingly giving way to architectural horrors. "The only substantial liberty left to Americans is the liberty to be offensive to their neighbors," he observed. The old-time Babbitts, whatever their faults, were at least Baltimoreans. Their successors were strangers who aspired "to put Baltimore on the level of Chicago."

As the great boom of the 1920s moved into its sixth consecutive year, Mencken lamented a wiping out of all the old traditions. A relentless and all-pervading standardization and a continuing desire for consumption had taken over. A sense of remoteness gripped him. In his most despondent moments Mencken spoke of the "grandiose futility" of life. "What could be more preposterous than keeping alive?" he asked. "The end is always a vanity, and usually a sordid one, without any noble touch of the pathetic." The secret of contentment, said Mencken, was "the capacity to postpone suicide at least another day."

It was not the first time that Mencken had expressed such negative thoughts. As an adolescent, while at the cigar factory, he had toyed with the notion of ending his life. At the *Herald*, he had been depressed over his inability to measure up to his ideals in poetry and fiction; later, he suffered frustration over his lack of musical training. In 1919, a year of disillusionment with his country and his first break with Marion Bloom, he had spoken of "the terrible years between twenty-five and forty," a time when he felt so world-weary, he wrote to Gamaliel Bradford, that he felt "at least 98."

Anyone acquainted with Mencken knew his spirits were always low during the midst of hay fever season. Nor was it uncommon for friends to receive dejected letters from him during the suffocating gloom of December through March. His moodiness turned to philosophical pessimism. "My belief is necessarily transient," he would say. "The natural state of a reflective man is one of depression. The world is a botch."

Anna's death had clearly marked a turning point in Mencken's life. During the summer of 1926, at the very height of his fame, even the act of writing became difficult and exhausting; during this period Mencken confessed, "I got to sitting in front of a typewriter and staring into space."[1]

In an effort to distract himself, Mencken abandoned his first idea of visiting Europe and canceled any plans of seeing either Dorothy Taylor or Marion Bloom in Paris. Instead, he invited Paul Patterson to accompany him on a tour of the American South. The announced goal was to drum up publicity for the *Sunpapers* and for Patterson to make contact with newspaper editors in the region. But its real purpose was as the first real vacation Mencken had had since his launch of the *American Mercury* in 1924.

The trip also marked Mencken's increasing attraction to Aileen. "I may also drop off in Los Angeles, to see the movie gals. As I descend into senility I become very susceptible," Mencken coyly wrote to Marion, who, upon hearing the news, was predictably angry. On the basis of his hints, she had canceled her own plans to take a trip to Egypt. In her fury, she sent "a dirty cable" to "a dirty fellow," although it achieved none of the effect Marion intended for it. Mencken took it in his stride; he was used to her indignation.

In October 1926, Mencken and Patterson left Baltimore. At each city Mencken was interviewed several times a day. In Raleigh, the *News & Observer* reported: "Apparently people expect to meet a volcano when they meet Mencken. They stand around very much as they do in Yellowstone National Park." Excited reports set forth at length the staggering discovery that Mencken was *human*. In Atlanta, a female admirer timidly asked him to autograph a copy of the *Mercury* for her. He obliged by drawing a one-gallon jug. At Vanderbilt University in Nashville, Rupert Vance remarked, "I thought he ate children for breakfast—until I saw him." These were all loyal Confederates who had valiantly defended the South from Mencken's attacks. Now, reported the *New York World*, "the Sahara of the Bozart blossomed with bouquets."

From New Orleans, Mencken made preparations for Hollywood. "What are you going to do in California?" a reporter asked.

Mencken's large blue eyes twinkled. "I'm going to join the movies," he said.

"Scenarios?"

"No. I'm going to take Valentino's place."[2]

MENCKEN ARRIVED IN LOS ANGELES tired, hungry, worried about his baggage, late for a dinner engagement, and impatient over the tardiness of his reception committee of one. The weariness and concern vanished from his face, however, when Aileen Pringle's shining automobile loomed into view. It did not take Mencken long to discover that Hollywood was a relatively peaceful, pastoral town, perfumed by orange blossoms and surrounded by eucalyptus trees and lemon groves. Anyone who could prefer Florida to California, he thought, must be suffering from senile dementia.

With Hergesheimer's arrival the next day, Mencken's weeks of pure holiday began. "Most of that trip was about playing tricks on Hergesheimer," Anita Loos recalled. "He was not only naive, but tremendously impressed by anyone with social importance." A welcome party of four—Mencken, Anita Loos, Aileen Pringle, and *Photoplay* editor James Quirk—met the novelist at the station wearing paper hats, blowing horns, and waving small flags. A floral horseshoe was placed on Hergesheimer's neck; everyone gave him kisses on both cheeks.

While Hergesheimer seemed to be quite taken with Los Angeles, Mencken was not. "This place is a genuine horror," he wrote Sara. "If I described it literally I'd be set down as the damndest liar ever heard of." As Carl Van Vechten had noted, America's famous film paradise had more of everything—more money, jewels, Rolls Royces, fur coats, luck, heartbreak, and dissatisfaction—than anyplace else in the world. Mencken found movie queens living "in superb Venetian palaces, with $3,000 radio sets."

As for the architecture, Mencken told Sara that it would "make you yell. The noblesse of Spotted Cow, Idaho, come here, erect gaudy Spanish palaces, then fill them with Grand Rapids furniture. The effect is really *kolossal*." The implausibility of the town surprised Mencken wherever he went. One morning, motoring, he and Hergesheimer ran into what seemed to be the whole German army. "It was a herd of 1,000 movie actors, making a war film," Mencken explained. "I *hoched* for the Kaiser, and felt at home."

Surrounded by a local population that seemed devoid of any intellectual pretensions, he found southern California to be "solid moron," inhabited by higher forms of ape who were building a civilization resembling that of man. There was nothing more corrupting to the human psyche, Mencken asserted, than the mean admiration of mean things, the continuing desire for material goods which became the primary means of defining one's class and personality. "The movie-parlors, I suspect, are turning out such victims by the million," he wrote, so debauching the American proletariat that eventually it would place movie stars on a level above George Washington.

A notable difference in the status of writers versus movie idols became palpably clear to Mencken when he attended the premiere of Lawrence Stallings's *What Price Glory?* with Aileen. He recalled, "The proletariat on the sidelines gave us a rousing cheer. But though they knew her, of course, they didn't know who I was, and so they began to speculate. . . . A private agent later informed me that they had come to the conclusion that I was [movie cowboy] Tom Mix," he joked. "This somehow flattered me."

By 1926 there were more than 20,000 movie theaters across the country, offering celluloid refuge and glamour for a mere 35 cents. But the films of the silent era, with their postures and grimaces and nineteenth-century ideas of love and adventure, did nothing to convince Mencken of their merit (though he did suggest they be shown on long journeys aboard trains). He tried watching Lillian Gish in *Broken Blossoms* but had to walk out after only fifteen minutes. Charlie Chaplin amused him, but again he quit watching one film long before it was over. The new medium made the former drama critic, accustomed to the theater, believe that movies were ruining the ancient and noble art. Talent was wasted: one could only see an actor "as one sees a row of telegraph poles, riding in a train." The entire procedure, Mencken asserted, "would have made the late Richard Mansfield yell."

Nonetheless, after spending three weeks in Los Angeles, Mencken could not continue to ignore the industry. He heard movies talked about day and night, and by people who knew a great deal about them. Movie makers, Mencken concluded, were on the horns of a sad dilemma. "In order to meet the immense cost of making a gaudy modern film they have to make it appeal to a gigantic audience," he later told a reporter for *Photoplay*. "Soon or late," he predicted prophetically, "the movies will have to be split into two halves. There will be movies for the mob, and there will be movies for the relatively civilized minority. The former will continue idiotic; the latter, if competent men to make them are unearthed, will show sense and beauty."[3]

For all his criticism of the movies, Mencken appeared in a film himself, but it was never commercially released. When the caricaturist Ralph Barton informed Mencken that he was filming a production of *Camille: The Fate of a Coquette* with Anita Loos in the title role, he beseeched Mencken to be in it.

The film had a cast of characters unlike any assembled before or since, with Mencken portraying the founder of Prohibition, Andrew Volstead, and Kaiser Wilhelm. Hergesheimer played the ghost of Valentino. Charlie Chaplin later told Mencken he had a great deal of acting talent. Mencken joked to Nathan: "If you meet Louis B. Mayer, tell him to bear me in mind. . . . Chaplin will coach me in the necessary grimaces." Apparently Mencken did not need any coaching at all.[4]

The California press hyped his celebrity visit to the tabernacle of Aimee Semple McPherson. Revival fan as he was, Mencken found nothing to make his eyes pop. On a sunny Sunday afternoon, he found himself gaping at the reverend sister "with the oldest, safest tricks out of the pack of Billy Sunday." Her sex appeal was enormous, Mencken told friends, perfect for Los Angeles, which seemed to be full of fundamentalists. "It is a literal fact that Dayton seems almost like Paris beside it."

Mencken attended various parties, in sunlit gardens full of palm trees. The director James Cruze entertained Mencken at his home. In a moment Mencken was surrounded by a variety of shimmering beauties, among them actress Betty Compton. Thinking of his home city, Mencken told her: "When I was a young-ster the girls in the sporting houses called me professor." Betty Compton looked coyly at him. "I thought your face was familiar," she said.

However, night after night of lavish parties could be exhausting. As Hergesheimer recalled, it had all been "a thin if dazzling interlude." Both men were overwhelmed by the social whirl. "Finally, we were happier, in a bungalow at the Hotel Ambassador grounds, over bottles of scotch planning our return east. After all, one lovely or loved girl was a lot of girl."[5]

OF FAR MORE INTEREST to Mencken was his visit to San Francisco, where five years earlier he had attended the Democratic National Convention. With the poet George Sterling once again playing host, he expected a lively time. Mencken was surprised to find how much Sterling had changed. While he had always been given to spells of melancholia, these seemed to pass away and he would become the life of every gathering. Now, however, his drinking had a new ferocity to it.

"Weeks of pure holiday." Walter Wanger, Mencken, and John Hemphill examine Joseph Hergesheimer's brains. John Emerson and Helen are to the left, with Aileen Pringle, May Alison, and James Quirk to the right. The baby in the bassinet is Anita Loos. The Harry Ransom Research Center, The University of Texas at Austin.

Earlier attempts at suicide had been prevented by friends. The poet had taken to carrying a tiny bottle of cyanide in his pocket or keeping it handy in his dresser drawer, always with an idea of taking it if he should ever feel himself slipping. "I really fear for his life," Mencken told friends. He visited Sterling at the Bohemian Club and tried to divert the poet's thoughts from his own mortality by discussing his literary plans. Sterling only rambled aimlessly, apologizing for his condition. Mencken left and paid a return visit; again he knocked on Sterling's door. Assuming he was still asleep, Mencken scribbled a note and slipped it across the threshold, but the poet was dead and had been for more than twelve hours. His body was found twisted in agony; an empty bottle of cyanide was near his bed.

"Good God," Mencken exclaimed, upon hearing the news. "This is terrible. I came up here especially to see him." Greatly affected, Mencken babbled on. "We were going to have all sorts of good times." A few seconds later, a shaken Mencken composed himself. "He was one of our greatest poets. He was a Bohemian but avoided Bohemian writing. I had a tremendous respect for his work and admiration for his style."

On the back of a menu found in his room, Sterling had written "My Swan Song":

Has the man the right . . .
To sever without fear
The irksome bonds of life,
When he is tired of strife?

Penciled on the page was a message: "Send a copy to Mencken!"

Numbly, Mencken told reporters: "If I have any sorrow for George it is for the agony of body and mind to which he was forced to surrender. But I am sorry only for myself. For I have lost a splendid friend—the kind one needs."

In his eulogy in the *San Francisco Chronicle*, Mencken expanded on this theme. His lament over Sterling's death could also be seen as a commentary on the heat and fury of the Jazz Age, "the massive triumph of regimentation" that he saw across the country and that he had found so distasteful in Los Angeles. As for Sterling, he had remained a free spirit, faithful to the classical tradition. "Such charming fellows make life more bearable among us. They stand against the idiotic strivings of a vain and preposterous age. The things they admire, in the arts as in life itself, are genuinely admirable. They know the high value of simplicity. They are without guile. The world would be happier if there were more of them."

Badly shaken, Mencken quickly cut short his visit and returned to Los Angeles. San Francisco could never be the same for him; he vowed never to go back again.[6]

Mencken that summer had spoken of "the grandiose futility of life"; when confronted with the suicide of Sterling he was forced to face the problem again. He later stated frankly to a reporter:

What keeps a reflective and skeptical man alive? Mainly it is this sense of humor. But in addition there is curiosity. Human existence is always irrational and often painful, but in the last analysis it remains interesting. One wants to know what is going to happen tomorrow. . . . The uncertainty is the thing. If the future were known, every intelligent man would kill himself at once, and the Republic would be peopled wholly by morons. Perhaps we are really moving toward the con-summation now.

IN MID-NOVEMBER, Mencken started east on the 63-hour Los Angeles to New York train. Before Mencken's departure, Aileen secretly tucked little notes into his bags, expressing jealously of the contents within: "Happy little shirts! I wish I could pop out at you from your collar box, snuggle down beside you—never to leave your side again." She confessed each "wretched day" that took Mencken farther from Los Angeles only made her feel more confused. "My darling: Why are you going away from me when I have only learned just how much I love you? Why must we part when we have only just met and there is much I want to say to you? If the answer is that when we next meet there will be no good-byes, only then will I believe that you love me." Finding Aileen's letters tucked into his clothing, Mencken told her: "Your notes saved me from imitating George."

Upon his return to Baltimore, Mencken bought a porcelain figure and sent it to Aileen. "I hope it will be in *our* home one day," she replied, wondering why so many miles should stand between herself and Mencken. "Aren't you ever to do anything about it?"[7]

Meanwhile, Sara decided to spend Christmas in Baltimore, but if she thought she was going to see Mencken, she was sadly mistaken; he was going to Pittsburgh, to spend the holiday with his niece. Especially now, during this season, 1524 Hollins Street reminded Mencken anew of his mother's absence; Christmas had become for him the worst of possible holidays. He wrote to Sara: "I wish I could get drunk this damned season, and wake up in the middle of May." As for Marion, it seemed 100 years since he had last seen her, although the homesickness he had felt for her now was completely overshadowed by his experiences in Hollywood; he had not even sent her a Christmas card. "He is a hog," Marion complained from Paris to her sister Estelle. "Last year when his mother died I was very sad for him; now I am over here alone and he doesn't even type me a card. Such things depress me. I wish Henry would die or I would. He makes me sick."

Mencken said no more about the gloom of earlier that summer. Now, as 1926 drew to a close, he had to admit that his luck had been "magnificent" during the year. He sent a Christmas telegram to Aileen in Santa Monica: "My devotion to your charming mother. Tell her I begin to suspect that you have enslaved my love forever."

Slyly, Mencken began dropping her name to friends. At the home of Phil Goodman, family members nudged one another. An ever-curious Blanche Knopf asked the actress to visit: "I have been hearing simply superb things about you from Mencken." Before long, the Hollywood gossip columnists were gleefully reporting that the bad boy of journalism had fallen for one of their own. "It is useless to conceal the damning fact any longer," Mencken wrote in a telegram to Aileen. "I begin to suspect that I am mashed on you. What is to be done about it? I hope you are not insulted by this humble devotion." In another he sent the simple statement: "I'LL ALWAYS LOVE YOU."

Across the country, newspapers whispered that the two were engaged, overlooking the fact that Aileen was still married to Lord Pringle of Jamaica. Aileen's photograph was plastered all over the press, though the one printed made Mencken want to tar and feather the photographer. "Can it be that I have got mashed on the Hoor of Babylon?" Mencken commented. "A more lascivious smile I never saw." If anyone asks for the wedding date, Aileen joked to Mencken, "I shall tell them that it will be June 19th, 1927."

The reports of an engagement were of special interest in Baltimore, where gossip about Mencken's love life had been the subject of curiosity ever since his "Free Lance" column days in 1913. From the Guilford neighborhood to Highlandtown, the question was: "Have you heard about Henry?"

Intrigued beyond endurance, one newspaper reporter called Mencken's home. Were the reports true? A member of the family answered pleasantly that the engagement between Mencken and Aileen was old news—and a joke. When asked if the joke was on Henry or Aileen, the telephone receiver at the Mencken home was promptly placed on its hook.[8]

30

THE GERMAN VALENTINO

THE WOMEN A MAN SLEEPS WITH make charming episodes in his life, but it is seldom that they influence the main course of it," Mencken wrote in his diary. "Yet no novelist would ever think of telling about his hero without telling about his women," he once told Edmund Wilson. In his memoirs, he deliberately concealed the fact that throughout his adulthood he maintained a stable of devoted girlfriends.

Never would his juggling act and his strict notions of privacy be put to a more severe test than in 1927 and 1928. Even as the public was wondering about his supposed engagement to Aileen Pringle, he confessed to Nathan he had turned up a new girl in Washington who "looks very promising."

She was Gretchen Hood, a free-spirited woman who had had a short career as an opera singer. It all started when she suggested to the *New York World* that Mencken run for president. They began a frequent exchange of playful banter that would go on for four years. The attraction seemed mutual. Gretchen's familiarity with the journalistic and political life of the nation's capital (her father had been the Washington head of the Associated Press bureau), her musical background, her good looks and witty repartee were obviously alluring to Mencken. As for Gretchen, by their second meeting she had decided she wanted to spend the rest of her life with him. Suitors such as Congressman (later Mayor of New York) Fiorello La Guardia soon gave up the idea of seriously courting her, saying she was already "too far gone on Mencken." Like Marion and Aileen before her, Gretchen was curious about the other women in his life. Mencken brushed her inquiries aside, stimulating her curiosity all the more.

Such conduct was a consistent pattern in Mencken's behavior. His suggestions of commitment were contradicted by his actions, with the unhappy consequence that many women who became seriously involved with him believed mistakenly that they could hope for a serious outcome. He was gallant, generous, and sympathetic; he encouraged their careers and tried to help them achieve their professional goals. Many of his letters to women were full of compliments, signed "Love forever" or "Yours devotedly," accompanied by kisses and assurances that he was their "devoted" or "elderly" slave. He showered many with thoughtful and generous gifts. He even broached the subject of marriage on more than one occasion, and not always in jest.

Part of the process of seduction was his ability to paint pictures of life with the person involved. He often said, "Any plausible gal who really made up her mind to it could probably fetch me." In confusion, girlfriends consequently read too much into his letters and promises, even going so far as to analyze his signature. Aileen even scrutinized the romantic homespun illustrations he chose for his Valentines, although she admitted that his behavior was disturbing: "Let me always believe, in any case, that your intentions are honorable. I never want to be told, in the coming years, that you were toying with me."

If and when a woman was lulled into the belief that she was the exclusive object of Mencken's fancy, he soon disabused her of the notion by extricating himself. Long before, Marion Bloom had painfully discovered that Mencken could be, as she put it, "as slick as a ribbon." Yet, excuses he might give for his repeated absences seemed logical. Surely anyone could understand the professional demands that would justify his disappearances: the work, the appointments, a schedule that kept him hopping between cities—these activities were not a major mystery, they were public news. That in addition Mencken was elusive and charming seemed to make him all the more desirable. For those who had become addicted to his promises and emotionally dependent on him, however, the relationship was sheer torment.[1]

THE COURSE OF MENCKEN's seven-year courtship of Sara Haardt had unfolded unevenly. Early on she had realized she was only one of many and had tried to be casual about their relationship. In January 1927, she announced brusquely, "He's a closed chapter in my book."

According to one of her friends, Mencken seemed to be more upset by their falling out than Sara. She was acutely aware that at least some of what was being written about Mencken's relationships was true. In addition to rumors linking him with Aileen Pringle and Gretchen Hood, there had been suggestions of other matrimonial aspirants. Adherents of eugenics, according to the *Los Angeles Herald*, had already selected Ellen Glasgow, considered one of the best of modern novelists, as perhaps the most suitable wife for Mencken.

Even if Sara knew the notion of Ellen Glasgow was not true, she was not quite sure when Mencken was linked with the author Frances Newman. "Where such

"The German Valentino." Mencken in 1926. Photo by Alfred A. Knopf. H. L. Mencken Collection, Enoch Pratt Free Library.

charming tales originate I don't know," Mencken confessed to another of his female admirers, Dorothy Taylor, but the frequency of the reports began to annoy him. Perhaps he sensed how much they irritated some of the women in his life, particularly Sara. "Twice they have picked out ladies with husbands," he complained to his friend Betty Hanes. "I used to send out polite denials, but I found that the Hearst vermin simply used them as excuses to print more and worse stuff. Such is journalism in the United States."

The rumor linking Mencken and Frances Newman persisted, though untrue. "It would be quite an achievement marrying Mencken," Newman confessed to reporters, "Nobody has ever done it, thus far." Nonetheless, it led Marion Bloom to call Nathan to inquire of its veracity. As she later told Mencken, "George agreed that a man of your years and dignity had bigger work to do than to spend his time disentangling the ambiguities of a neurotic woman." Shortly

This plot has universal application?

thereafter, Sara met Frances Newman at a party hosted by Joseph Hergesheimer. As Sara Mayfield recalled that meeting:

> Seeing that Miss Newman was eyeing Sara Haardt, who was bantering with Mencken and Nancy Hoyt, with a nod at Sara, Mr. [Ernest] Boyd asked Miss Newman, "How do you like the future Mrs. Mencken?"
> "The future Miss Sara Haardt," she retorted acidly and emphatically.
> A few minutes later, when Mencken brought Sara over to introduce her to Frances, Miss Newman appraised her at close range. "Miss Haardt?" The serpentine curve of Miss Newman's mouth slithered into an ophidian smile. "From all I've heard of you, I should not have thought you were so good-looking," she said in a tone that implied that she was disappointed not to find that Sara wore flat-heeled shoes and horn-rimmed glasses.
> "And from all that I've heard of you, Miss Newman, I should have thought that you were," Sara replied suavely.
> To her indignation, Mencken later reported to Cabell and Sinclair Lewis that she had "floored Frances with a dreadful clout." Lewis, who had just read Miss Newman's *The Hardboiled Virgin*, groaned, "Jesus, such a woman! By God, if I spent a year on a desert island with Frances Newman, at the end of it she wouldn't be so hardboiled but she'd still be a virgin."

Yet, despite the gossip, Sara could not remain distant toward Mencken for long, and by the summer of 1927 their feelings were rekindled. Mencken told Hergesheimer he was seeing Sara "very often; she is better looking than ever." There were those who suspected the possibility of a match. Among Sara's friends, this belief was widespread: "Although you never spoke of him, I knew the feelings you had for him," one of them later said to her. In August, Sara accompanied Mencken to Dower House. Dorothy Hergesheimer, who had become very fond of Sara, afterward broached the possibility of marriage to a radiant Mencken, who responded with characteristic banter: "The idea is charming! Ah, that it could be executed! But I already have one foot in the cemetery, and spies hint that she is mashed on a rich Babbitt in Birmingham, Alabama."[2]

Although Mencken continued to be attracted to Sara, he was still very much taken with Aileen Pringle, to whom he would write ardent letters, sometimes twice a day, a gesture she confessed "chains me to you for life." At one point he sent her six separate envelopes with "I Love You" written in each. The blossoming romance was well known to all their friends, especially to Blanche Knopf and to F. Scott and Zelda Fitzgerald, then visiting Hollywood. But as time went on, her response to a query by Arthur Krock gave some indication as to where the relationship was headed:

> I have been harboring an illusion that I was a clever woman but you have shattered these notions by discovering I'm mashed on Henry. . . . The really sad part of this tale comes last. Henry remains unstirred. The dragon's blood has made his heart and hide impenetrable. If, by chance, you know where the lime leaf fell—tell me at once. The suffering I can endure no longer.[3]

In his friendship with Sara, Mencken played the part of mentor, helping her in her ambition as a writer. Sara's finances had never been good, and early in the fall of 1927, Mencken seemed to have arrived at a solution for her problem. Little did he suspect that in helping Sara regain financial independence, he would be setting off a chain of events that would eventually unmask the depth of his feelings for her.

In the fall of 1927, Sara's writing had attracted the notice of Famous Players-Lasky Studio, which would later become Paramount Pictures. In the 1920s, the studio was contracting writers for five- to six-week stints, then retaining their services if they provided usable material. The suggestion that Sara be invited to join was a tribute to her work and to Mencken's influence. She had already drawn attention with her short stories, and under Mencken's direction they had improved to the point that in 1924 they were included in the "Roll of Honor of American Short Stories" and in "The Best Short Stories" for that year. In the spring, Mencken introduced her to Herman Mankiewicz, then an executive of Famous Players. Mankiewicz recognized fresh material when he saw it and gave her a job as a screen writer at a salary of $250 a week, with travel expenses paid both ways and a bonus of $3,750 if a story of hers was produced.

While Mencken believed Los Angeles swarmed with literary aspirants of little worth ("The town really enjoys a vague eminence: it houses more bad authors than New York"), he recognized that Sara's stint would bring in enough money to enable her to write her novel. For the last few years Mencken had been paying Sara $100 a month to conduct research and copyedit his books. He also supplemented her income by having her write reviews for the *American Mercury*'s "Check List of New Books." While her stories were being published by various magazines, through the intervention of Mencken several of her ironic pieces about Southern club women also ran in the *Evening Sun*. As editor Hamilton Owens recalled, "They created many disputes between Henry and me as to her skill as a writer. Henry undoubtedly thought she was more skillful than I thought she was."

Friends questioned the reasoning behind Mencken's packing Sara off to Hollywood. "To get rid of her? In fear that she was becoming a bigger part of his life than he wanted her to be?" There were those, including Philip Goodman, who thought this might be so. When it came time for Sara to leave, however, Mencken was reluctant to let her go. "If I seemed idiotic yesterday," he wrote in apology, "blame it upon the fact that it had suddenly dawned on me that I'd not see you for weeks."

Sara's experience in Hollywood was quite different from that of Mencken, who had arrived there as a celebrity. She was also less enraptured by the glamour than Mencken had been on his visit with Hergesheimer the year before. Every day, she returned from the studio to her room at the Mark Twain Hotel off Hollywood Boulevard, on a busy, dusty thoroughfare. It was quite different from the Ambassador Hotel where Mencken had stayed, where Hollywood and New

York society mixed freely, where Pola Negri dined alone in her bungalow, complete with candelabras and butler. The clientele at the Mark Twain Hotel consisted of would-bes and has-beens, and poor relations of the VIPs of the film industry—screen writers, cameramen, and bit players. "I never saw her speak to anyone," recalled Marcella Pierce, whose husband managed the hotel. Sara was "pleasant but aloof," although "obviously 'A Lady.' She picked up her mail, messages, and keys at the front desk and proceeded right up the wide staircase from the lobby to her hotel suite." Pierce concluded that Sara "must have been very lonely."

Forty-eight hours after Sara arrived in Hollywood she met the writer Jim Tully, who took a genuine liking to her, reporting to Mencken: "She is too genuine to be impressed by the infamies out here. There is no need to worry about her." What amused Sara most, it turned out, was what she called "the high-brow complex running through the movies," especially "the synthetic ladies boasting of their conquests among the literati" and the actresses who struggled to "not only appear a lady, but an intellectual!" Quite possibly Sara's comment to Mencken was a pointed barb against Aileen Pringle. But even if she was not mentioned by name, Sara nonetheless made sure to let Mencken know how "cheap and pretentious" she found the whole Hollywood community to be.

What Sara detested most in Hollywood, more than its vulgarity, was its hypocrisy. "Her adventures there," Mencken reflected, "were typically grotesque." She wrote for months on end, never knowing if her work was being read, struggling feverishly night after night until the small hours of the morning. Eventually she was able to sell the idea of her movie, *Way Down South*, to James Cruze, then the highest paid director in Hollywood. Sara recognized that if she had accomplished anything, in large part it had been due to Mencken's encouragement. "You are so thoughtful and so reassuring," she wrote to him. "And I love you for it."4

DURING SARA'S HOLLYWOOD EXILE, Mencken had not been socially idle. He had attended a round of dinners in New York, as he said, "with a great deal of gadding about and too much gin," and the annual stag party at Maryland's Eastern Shore. In Washington, he enjoyed the company of Gretchen Hood, who, in turn, introduced him to Speaker of the House Nicholas Longworth. Not wishing to jeopardize his friendship with Gretchen, some time later he assured her that his "engagement to A. P." was off, even though he had arranged to meet Aileen a week later in New York.

At the station, Mencken found Aileen half frantic with joy at escaping from Hollywood, even if it was only for a few days. Their stay with the Hergesheimers at Dower House was cut short when Dorothy suffered an attack of appendicitis. Perhaps Mencken and Aileen might have moved closer to marriage had the visit not been interrupted. He got in a panic seeing her off. The feelings Aileen aroused in him during their reunion surprised Mencken. He tucked notes into her bag, admitting his love for her. Along her route home she was handed telegrams from Mencken that told her she was "infinitely, completely and perfectly dear." Two days later he wrote her, "You are grand, lovely, gorgeous, incomparable, peerless, perfect." Without her he was "unutterably low" and "completely desolate." He confessed to Hergesheimer that he mourned for Aileen "like a cow robbed of its calf," and to Blanche Knopf he uttered the simple statement that he was "dizzy" with "love."

Yet, at the same time Mencken was also meeting with Sara Mayfield, Mary Parmenter, and other friends just so he could talk about Sara. She had once been a fixture in Baltimore; now that she was away, Mencken's beloved hometown seemed empty.

Finally, in December, Sara's contract with Famous Players-Lasky expired and she headed east with more money than she had ever had. The three months Sara had been away felt to Mencken like five years. "The days seem endless." Along her route to Baltimore, he showered her with telegrams and letters, and while they were less passionate in tone than those he had sent to Aileen, they still demonstrated his fondness. "It is charming to think you are a thousand miles nearer," he told her. He promised to meet her train, whatever the hour, warning her: "You are apt to be hugged in public, with all of the redcaps gaping."

It is probable that by this time Mencken was already beginning to regret a casual promise he had made to Aileen to visit her the following January. Whatever the reason, he grew moody that December, a month that always recalled for him the anniversary of his mother's death. Downcast letters went to a series of women. Aileen responded: "You just think you are a moody person" but "that may be because you need me." When Mencken hinted again to Aileen his hesitation about his visiting her in January, she reacted indignantly: "Goddammit, I won't have you writing me such vomit as 'then maybe I'll see you, if you still want to see me.' " Aware that perhaps she had been putting too much pressure on him, she began to suspect that perhaps "I have been the cause of your depression."

Back in Baltimore, Sara regaled Mencken with marvelous tales about Hollywood. Seeing that city anew through Sara's eyes seemed to confirm some of Mencken's own views. At the same time, he was being bombarded by letters from Aileen, who had decided to see a lawyer and get a divorce immediately from Charlie Pringle. But she irritated him with constant references to her salary ($30,000 in 1926 alone, though he had made equal to that). It did not threaten him as much as it confirmed his view, as he wrote in *Photoplay*, that "the objection to swollen salaries should come from the stars themselves—that is, assuming them to be artists. The system diverts them from their proper business of trying to produce charming and amusing movies, and converts them into bogus society folk."[5]

If Aileen sensed a degree of annoyance on Mencken's part, she hastened to assure him she loathed shopping, was not interested in fashion, that her needs were small, and that he needed never to worry about not having enough money to meet her requirements: "Eating beans with you is better than eating caviar with

Condé Nast. Sleeping with you should have advantages over sleeping with [John] Gilbert. In other words I think you are perfect and I'll stay yours for richer for poorer, for better for worse for all time."

But that was as far as it went. With each new advance from Aileen, Mencken retreated ever further. Mencken sensed that he was falling in love with Sara. In a column, he wrote a lengthy passage in which he seemed to be trying to convince himself:

> I see no reason why a man sliding into his forties should not marry satisfactorily, and make a good husband. His illusions may be gone, but if the lady he claps his eye on is really charming there may be a great many soothing realities. The plain fact of it is that many females of the species are lovely, and that their loveliness survives even the harshest of spotlights. They make pretty pictures, especially when completely made up. They have nimble wits, and are amusing. They are tolerantly cynical, and do not expect too much, either of God or of men.

As Aileen's feelings of desolation and uncertainty over Mencken intensified, she wrote him an agitated, scarcely decipherable letter, giving full release to her torment.

> Tell me honestly—would you prefer not to marry, always to live with your sister at 1524 and have me whenever you want me. I have never particularly thought of myself in that relation . . . but primarily I want you content, footloose and fancy free. If marrying means giving up any of those attributes I am the last to contribute to its cause. You are the important factor—I am your slave. Do quite what you like with me regardless of what I might normally accept.

But, she added, her scrawl becoming even more desperate:

> I couldn't ever do it openly—even if my mother were not living. I haven't been brought up a slut—as you know. I simply couldn't bear being pointed out as Mencken's girl. . . . If, professionally, you would be an idiot to marry me—for God's sake, don't. You said if you ever married you would do it suddenly—as a man shoots himself.—How can I make you out a liar? Darling, I love you.[6]

IN JANUARY, MENCKEN ESCAPED temporarily from Aileen's pursuit when he headed for Havana to cover the Sixth Pan American Conference. The entire conference was a charade, slavishly deferential to the United States. Being in Cuba convinced him that the American administration "now takes its place definitely among the maniacal imperialisms of all times." As Mencken noted in the *Evening Sun*, "Nations get on with one another, not by telling the truth, but by lying gracefully."

Lying was nevertheless Mencken's method of dealing with his various women friends, especially with Aileen. Depressed that a bundle of fifteen letters to Havana had been returned unread, she nonetheless rallied when she received a telegram from a "Menchen" in Cuba, stating "YO TE AMO." It inspired her, as his "devoted slave," to do all in her power to make him "content and happy." When she heard that his beloved Corona, dating from 1916, which had traveled with him nearly 100,000 miles and recorded at least 10,000,000 words, had finally given out, she wrote to the factory and, after much painstaking research, had them ship a 1920 model to his house in Baltimore. She could have hardly guessed at his reaction.

While she was at the movie set, her mother read his telegram to her over the phone. Aileen was not to send him the Corona; to do so would make him extremely annoyed. When it arrived, Aileen insisted he keep it (even if he relegated it to the cellar), but he wrapped up the machine and sent it back. From then on, letters to her were few and far between. Eventually Aileen realized that Mencken was determined that no one was to run his life. She apologized for being bossy, but the damage was done.

From mutual friends in New York, Aileen began hearing the names of other women in Mencken's life. She was aware of the flappers who chased Mencken and Nathan ("Both men could find those types, and did, all the time") and knew Carl Van Vechten's assertion that many women followed Mencken around "who would marry him." By now, author and screenwriter Lawrence Stallings had told Aileen of the depth of Mencken's relationship with Sara, and she made sure that he knew that there were others in Hollywood who "didn't think much of your girl." But in time Aileen cooled off and told Mencken "I, too, am sorry I didn't meet Sara. If she comes out here again be sure to let me know. I'm sure from all I have heard—including Stallings' reports—I would have liked her."

Just as had been the case with Marion Bloom, the more Aileen Pringle's obsession intensified, the more Mencken distanced himself. "I'm always blabbing about you," she confessed; others noticed as Hollywood gossips commented: "It's Henry this and Henry that." At one point, while entertaining Van Vechten, Aileen unconsciously called him "Henry." For his part, Van Vechten said he had not felt so flattered in years. If the postman did not arrive with letters from Baltimore, she was furious. "I'm afraid you spoiled me so much in the beginning that a day with no letters from you is a horror," said Aileen. She began marking anniversaries. Every June 19, the date of their first meeting, that rolled by made her think of him.

At age 32, she confessed that she had given up the idea that anyone else could meet her specifications. Now that she had met Mencken, "Every man, in comparison, seems like a heavy, dull, thoughtless, stupid creature." Nonetheless, she knew that things were not the same between them. Aileen's frenzy had reached such a state that her mother became preoccupied with her daughter's emotional health.

Finally, in desperation, Aileen tried the direct approach since Mencken's own letters seemed so indirect. "You told me you were born practical and couldn't help thinking of certain implications," she wrote to him. "You said we discussed them gingerly—some more obvious—others more subtly and they should be gone into frankly. Then you said someday soon you would tell me what you were up to and how you would accomplish it. . . . Tell me my darling—really be quite frank with me. . . . Tell me—what are your plans and how do I appear as a pattern in them?"

By the spring, Mencken tried once and for all to extricate himself graciously from his involvement with her. His reply was a masterpiece of evasion, remarkably similar to the one he had written to Marion Bloom five years earlier.

> My dear:
>   Your lovely letter hangs me on the hooks of a dilemma. Need I tell you that I want to take you at your word, and give three rousing cheers? I am too immensely fond of you to even think of hail and farewell. But there always remains the uneasy feeling that you have deceived yourself—that the whole thing is simply an illusion, beautiful but yet an illusion. After all, every shred of common sense is against it. You are still young, and beautiful, and still eager for life, and the best of it is ahead of you. But I am beginning to crack, and in a few years I'll probably regret it. What is ahead for me? I see a few more books (if, in fact, I can actually pump up the energy to write them), and then a long dullness. . . . What I fear is that you have never actually visualized it. You know me only on holiday. I wish to God that you were near enough for a palaver. In two days we'd really know each other. More, I think we'd agree. You have invented a fellow that doesn't exist. But it is lovely of you to imagine him. . . .

If Mencken had hoped that Aileen would make the decision to end their romance, thereby shifting responsibility away from him, she did not fall for his ploy, but continued writing desperately of her own undying love. Almost in response, Mencken gave a new round of interviews to the press, in each renewing his vow to remain a confirmed bachelor, which she resented. "Seriously," she warned him, if she ever fell into a low frame of mind—"then you will have a broken heart to mend!"[7]

One entanglement, however, did not deter Mencken from becoming involved in another. Disillusioned with Aileen, he now turned not to Sara but back to Marion Bloom. "I feel without brazenness that I am sticking pretty firmly in Menck's old heart," Marion confessed to Estelle with some confidence. It was now fourteen years since those bygone days when a younger Mencken, flush with his success with the *Smart Set* and the "Free Lance," had first courted the "bold, bad, haughty, violent gal." She knew him better than most, discerning the vulnerability of the man beneath a protective, defensive shell that made his actions toward women difficult to fathom. "He was completely masculine with the most divine streaks of tender sentiment, though he loved being thought tough," Marion once said in a generous assessment, considering all of the heartache he had caused her.

With her divorce from Lou Maritzer now complete, that spring Marion returned from Paris to care for her ailing mother. The thought of reuniting with Mencken was not far from her mind ("it's been creeping around like a snake"). But deliberately, in her instinct to protect herself from the anguish she had experienced years before, she tried to isolate herself from him. She told Estelle, "I wish to God I'd hear he was married or dead."

While Estelle had no illusions about Mencken's failings, she recognized how deeply Marion was committed to him.

I won't make any brilliant caustic remark about people who are no more facile than to love one unworthy man for so long. But it has crippled you and colored your feeling for every other man you've met. I've often wondered how much feeling you'd have for him if he were not America's leading bastard critic. I don't mean you love him for that, but it dazzles you, doesn't let you see things clearly. At bottom, without the searchlight of fame, Henry is a very selfish, dictatorial man. He is no longer young. He likes to carouse on lots of parties, stag or mixed, on which he wouldn't want the same woman every time. You'd be pushed into the background. While Henry was in New York every two weeks, little Marianne would be back in Baltimore keeping the home fires burning. And then there would be another howl.

Mencken invited Marion to have lunch with him in Baltimore and discovered that his desire had not abated in the years they had spent apart. "Now," he demanded peremptorily, "What has happened to you, and what about Maritzer?" Marion answered, "I can't discuss him without his being present. It wouldn't be fair." Mencken croaked out, "Always the gentleman, eh? The goddamned little gentleman." It was a veiled reference to what Estelle once termed as Marion's being "too chivalrous to grab Mencken," of keeping up the fable that she did not want marriage because, deep down, she was terrified that it would ruin his writing career. Five years had passed since Mencken shed tears over Marion's marriage and cursed her for being a gentleman in granting him that freedom. His hurt over her decision had not abated, even now.

Again Mencken invited her to have lunch with him, this time in New York in his suite at the Algonquin, with Estelle as chaperone. "Everything seemed lovely," recalled Marion. The hotel had whipped up the usual delicacy; the white wine was chilled on ice. Then, when Estelle momentarily disappeared, Mencken grabbed Marion, kissing her with such force, she later said, that "he almost broke me. He said, 'There's nobody in the world like you.' Then threw me from his arms." Mencken was staggered when he later learned that his action might have offended her. "What else was there to do?" he confessed. "I was delighted to see you again, and the last thing on my mind was to do or say anything that would wound you." Sensing they might be drifting back to their old pattern of behavior, he commented: "Certainly we ought to meet without holding a watch on each other, and figuring out the meaning of this or that."

Meanwhile, back in California, Aileen's letters to Mencken became even more wistful as she sensed a definite change in his attitude. His letters had become short, the tone cool and distant; they were "curt little notes with all the warmth of a coroner's notice" that were "eating away at my vitals." He was evasive about visiting her for their summer meeting. When he wrote that he would not, after all, come to California after the Democratic convention in Houston, she responded: "The news . . . finishes me."

By this time, she realized that her chances of marriage to Mencken had finally dissolved. It had been a long time since Mencken had told her he loved her. "My heart aches sometimes, honestly it aches," Aileen responded to a query from *Picture* magazine, "Are Actors Unlucky in Love?" "Women are primitive creatures," she explained. "They wouldn't believe they had been in love if they did not allow it to hurt." A newspaper reporter spent one long afternoon in the company of Aileen at her home in Santa Monica. Spread on the table were clippings Mencken had sent from the campaign trail with Al Smith.

Certainly, Aileen told the reporter, she had fancied herself in love before. There had been a time, she confessed, when her spectacular courtship and marriage with confirmed bachelor Charlie Pringle had made her think highly of herself: "No man could resist me, I decided."

Unspoken, but perhaps not far from her thoughts, was the resistance of one confirmed bachelor who remained 3,000 miles away in Baltimore. "I think sometimes of the years ahead, when I am older," said Aileen. "People ask if I will be lonely—but we're all lonely really."[8]

IN BALTIMORE, SARA HAARDT was hardly faring any better, as friends began to ply her with questions about the status of her romance. "Do let me know what progress H. L. has achieved in 'making haste slowly,'" wrote Sara Mayfield. Others played matchmaker with other men. Her friends William and Margaret Cobb invited Sara for a weekend at the beach: "They have invited, very specially, a man, highly eligible and a knock-out—for me and my entertainment," Sara wrote to Mary Parmenter. "Well, we shall see, we shall see. . . ." Anne Duffy, wife of the cartoonist Edmund Duffy, took Sara to dinner to meet John Owens, editor of the *Baltimore Sun*. "He is a widower with two children and said to be very eligible," Sara wrote to Mayfield, not very enthusiastic about the evening that stretched before her. "He will probably have a gold tooth."

Robin Harriss, a young man from the staff of the *Evening Sun*, one of Sara's latest admirers, began sending her long-stemmed roses and invited her to go dancing at the roof garden of the Southern Hotel, where there was a good band and a breeze from the harbor. "Don't think he didn't fall like a log," Sara wrote to Sara Mayfield. "The way he hangs upon my words is something completely refreshing, and it really is."

Harriss was aware that his attentions seemed to bother Mencken. There was a touch of jealousy in the older man's manner, as in the instances when Mencken extravagantly called him "a dashing young blade." Harriss would escort Sara to parties, and observers commented at how he would stay "blissfully at her side 'till late in the evening—then H. L. Mencken arrived and it was instantly obvious that a bond existed between those two. He didn't monopolize her, but from the moment he arrived, she had eyes only for Henry." That Mencken and Sara were an item soon became obvious to other suitors as well. James Cain stopped seeing her, he later wrote, only when he learned that she was Mencken's "special weakness."

"How is the German Valentino?" Jim Tully joked to Nathan. Even Mencken admitted that his balancing act had reached an exhausting intensity. He complained to Lillian Gish of "my unfortunate love affairs. I am, as they say, damn nigh all in." Growing more despondent, he wrote to Van Vechten: "I am full of troubles. A mere recital of them, in a low monotonous voice, would bust your heart." As was often the case with Mencken during periods of high emotional intensity, he had been plagued by a recurrent series of illnesses and subjected to various minor operations, feeling rocky the entire year.

In August, he wisely slipped down to North Carolina for a much-needed respite, to cool off in the Blue Ridge Mountains at the home of his friend Doctor Fred Hanes, of Duke University Hospital. A fog surrounded the valley, and a quiet hour spent fishing took him back to innocent days when he was a boy. Best of all, he was far away from the demands of work and girlfriends, and this "feeling of isolation . . . was very pleasant."9

Revived, Mencken turned his attention now to the approaching presidential election. With the nation enjoying unparalleled prosperity, the odds against a Democratic upset seemed long from the start. New York governor Alfred E. Smith felt sure he could win against the Republican contender, Herbert Hoover. Religion quickly became a major issue in the campaign: "A Vote for Al Smith Is a Vote for the Pope," shouted Klansmen.

Although Mencken considered Al Smith the better man, he predicted few votes would come of it. "The American people prefer safer men. That is to say, they prefer vacuums." Prosperity advantaged Hoover, who promised his audiences "a chicken in every pot and two cars in every garage." Hoover, Mencken concluded, "is no more than a fat Coolidge."10

FOR MONTHS SARA HAD BEEN AILING, then suddenly underwent surgery. To her shock, she learned that the doctors had removed one ovary and debilitated the other, so that any possibility of her ever having children was gone. Friends found Sara propped in bed at her room at Union Memorial Hospital, surrounded by bouquets of chrysanthemums. "She was a badly broken blossom," Mary Parmenter reported to Sara Mayfield, "nothing but big black eyes." Mencken arrived from the campaign trail with a suitcase full of beverages and a pack of Methodist and Baptist newspapers. "His idea of an uproarious afternoon," observed Mary, "was apparently to read what the hardshells were saying about Al Smith."

Sara's health had never been the best, and after her return from the hospital friends noticed that she had still not fully recovered from her ordeal. Nonetheless, after Hoover's election, a pale but determined Sara joined Mencken for a luncheon party with the Hergesheimers. Sara afterward glowed to friends, "Henry is his usual thoughtful self."

Yet on the very day Sara was praising Mencken, he was joining Marion for lunch at the Belvedere Hotel. Sara's illness had thrown him into a tumult of conflicting emotions. Torn between his affection for her and guilt over his continued attraction to Marion, his ambivalence betrayed itself that Sunday. As Marion recalled, it was during this meal that they had their "sad parting." He denounced her for being "hopeless" in her devotion to Christian Science, telling her brutally she was "no longer in his intellectual class and a disgrace to mankind." It was, she said, "one of a dozen renunciations." When it came time to escort Marion back to the train station, instead of hailing a taxi Mencken helped her onto a bus. It seemed odd to Marion that they should be riding this mode of public transportation when they had never done so before. Sometime later she asked him, "Why did you make me ride on a bus that day?" Mencken simply answered, "Because I knew if I kissed you, I'd never let you go."

As with all of Mencken's outbursts, his angry conduct predictably vanished the next day. Marion was used to his mercurial changes of moods; Mencken "was as full of whim as a gal." He now wrote her:

> I have a notion that we called the coroner's inquest before the patient was actually dead. He is up today, walking around the room, smoking a cigar and singing like a bird. I report the fact, and leave you to determine why medical science failed. The truth is that such things are ordered by incomprehensible and humorous gods. We theorize and plan—and then the band begins to play, and it is all off. I hesitate to puff you up with flattery, but God roast me in hell if you ain't getting better looking all the time. Probably it is an optical delusion—but a man has only his own eyes.

Marion had realized, all along, that Mencken's aspirations for her, although cruelly expressed, were what she needed to gain on her own: self-respect and self-possession. "I suppose he wanted a writer—nothing was too great or too much for a pot-bellied, slope-shouldered clown," she had written to Estelle. "He had me climbing unreachable stars, lashing and cursing my dumb self because I lacked. Well, that's over. These days I might ask him what he could have accomplished working with my inadequacies. No; if I ever stand self-respecting again I may be amused to look over the man who colored my life so much, but not these times, when I lack the least self-possession. I have no wish to go about apologizing for a living."

But by this time, late fall of 1928, Marion had had enough. For years her most profound yearnings had been to share her life with Mencken. Now she was determined not to fall victim to Mencken's charm or his "slobber-gobble," not to ever again have her happiness "dependent on him or his moods." After that upsetting lunch at which she had listened to his bitter renunciations, "I built my own farewell renunciation soon after and asked him not to write again. After five years in Paris I was again in the mess." [11]

CHRISTMAS ARRIVED at Hollins Street, and for the first time in the three years since Anna's death, there were decorations and a tree. From afar, Aileen expressed her wish that Mencken visit her. He had promised to come in the fall; now that autumn had passed, "Couldn't you break the rule and send me a wire, saying you were coming next week?" Apparently, he could not. "I wish I could go to the coast with you, but it is a sheer impossibility," he told Joseph Hergesheimer, who was about to depart for Los Angeles. "If you encounter Aileen, kiss her hand for me."

In perhaps the most truthful assessment of his actions that season, Mencken told Betty Hanes: "I shall spend Christmas in the Christian manner. That is to say, I shall ingest ethyl alcohol until my higher faculties are suspended." On Christmas Eve, he sent a flurry of telegrams and letters to girlfriends from the safe haven of Hollins Street. "But it will never be a good Christmas so long as you are so far away," he wrote to Aileen Pringle, unaware of the irony of his message. Another went to Gretchen Hood in Washington, who resided much closer than California, yet comfortably far enough to prevent Mencken from making the trip. He sent Gretchen his wish: "I would like to be close to you and toast you with a loud voice, 'A Merry Xmas and Happy New Year.'" He also sent a card to Sara Haardt in Baltimore, with what had become his customary holiday greeting: "A less miserable Christmas than usual!"

One evening Mencken came by to call on Sara. He turned to her not only because she filled a void left by his mother, but also because she was a comfortable presence who exacted less pressure on him than any of the other women in his life. She was also a woman who, despite her physical ailments, refused to cast herself in the role of victim or martyr. Increasingly, Mencken's respect for Sara had developed into more closeness and equality between them. He trusted her maturity and felt confident that she could understand his moods without recourse to the quarrels he had experienced with others. It seemed a great relief for this intensely private man to be able to abandon in her company the jaunty facade that he felt he must always demonstrate to the outside world.

"He was very low, having returned from the cemetery only the Sunday before from placing wreaths on his mother's tombstone," Sara reported to Mayfield. "God knows I have had a cheerful lot of admirers in my day."[12]

31

THE SEA OF MATRIMONY

THROUGHOUT 1928 MENCKEN FOCUSED on Sara, constantly asking her to be at his side when he had to play host. She helped him give dinner parties at the Rennert Hotel, and he took her to the Hergesheimers for the occasional weekend. Later, in New York, she accompanied him at Emily Clark's salon (or "saloon," as Sara called it) and also met the Goodmans. In Baltimore, they continued their ritual of lunch at Marconi's and Schellhase's for beer. "We like to do the same things," Mencken later said of Sara. "One of these is to sit around at night and just gabble after the day's work is done. We have spent many delightful evenings doing just that."

But there were more substantial bonds of commonality. Both were agnostics; both shared a sense of discipline and common sense (she was noted for her "cool, sane judgments"); both looked on life as a human comedy (although Sara's outlook was, Mencken reflected, more "charmingly pessimistic" than his). Despite her independence and feminist point of view, Sara with her traditional Southern upbringing was appealingly soft in her ways, a fine example of those Southern women Mencken maintained knew "how to handle a man."

No man looks for a woman, Nathan liked to say, who "has a repertoire of ever-changing moods that make an evening spent with her the equivalent of suffering an emotional vaudeville show acted on a rapidly revolving turntable." Mencken had already experienced—and contributed to—this kind of roller coaster with Marion Bloom. Every argument with her left their relationship on such shaky ground that any minor disagreement felt like a major earthquake. Aileen Pringle's intensity and need to control his life remained equally upsetting. "You may resent it when she tries to run you, as she undoubtedly will," he wrote to James Cain years later upon Cain's impending marriage to the actress, "for there's a regular army general hidden in her soft and disarming exterior." Both Mencken and Nathan preferred women whose fellowship was, in short, something "like a good piano minus the loud pedal . . . music that is well composed, soft and lovely."

Moreover, Mencken always had the sneaking suspicion that what most women wanted from him was an extraordinary man but a very conventional one. Sara remained one of his few female companions who had seen him not only "illuminated and refined by wine" but also hard at work. More than any other, she understood the demands it entailed. Likewise, her devotion to her own work, and responsiveness to his suggestions, was dramatized for him by her success in Hollywood in 1927. Despite the fact that *Way Down South* was never produced (that year, talking pictures revolutionized the industry), she had demonstrated a steadfastness that he found admirable.

This had not been the case with Marion or Aileen. Mencken had tried to direct Aileen's talent toward writing articles about servants or her experiences with Hollywood. Surely her continuous rounds of tennis, dominoes, and suppers with the likes of Greta Garbo, Marion Davies, and Gloria Swanson could yield something. "I never hear from Aileen save that she is playing tennis with mimes all day and going to movie parties at night," Mencken complained to Carl Van Vechten. "It is a life wholly devoid of spiritual elements. I hope Aimee [McPherson] works on her." Aileen's efforts at writing produced nothing, however. "I become self-conscious and sound like a schoolteacher trying to be funny," she confessed. As for the article on servants, she got only so far as the title, "Home of the Free and Home of the Slave," which she thought of "while I was curling my hair and as usual thinking of you." When it came to sitting at a typewriter, the ordeal of punching the keys made her nervous, though to prove herself to Mencken she did send him six pages filled with carefully typewritten rows of the alphabet. What Mencken made of this substitute one can only guess.[1]

Sara shared Mencken's love for Baltimore; Marion Bloom and Gretchen Hood preferred Washington. Aileen, despite her protests to the contrary, was so embedded in the social life of Hollywood that there did not seem any chance that she would ever be happy moving to Maryland. Sara's years at Goucher College had stimulated her curiosity and broadened her intellectual horizons. Returning to Montgomery was always difficult for her; staying home ("stuck," she called it) was part of what Mencken called her "revolt against the threadbare Confederate metaphysic." The social life of the well-to-do was focused on the women's clubs, the ladies' literary clubs, the country club. To Sara, it was "like being buried alive. The same old bores mouthing the same old platitudes. Nobody with any sense to talk to, much less to have a date with . . . at least I don't pretend to be a lot of things I'm not."

In trying to analyze the spell Sara cast over Mencken, friends observed that while Sara's upbringing was Southern, by blood she was German. It thrilled

Mencken to know that their points of contact extended to the fact that they both had German ancestors who were scholars—and in one case, actual colleagues. One of the Haardts in the late seventeenth century had been a professor, an associate of Otto and Johann Burkhard Mencken at the University of Leipzig. In Mencken, there was a love for all things Teutonic, and it was the reason, James Cain believed, that his mother and Sara "enchanted him so, for both by blood were German, and to this they owned everything—their looks, their charm, their love. I doubt if they would have possessed him so if they had not been the beautiful personification of Germanism."

To crown Sara's other virtues, as Mencken pointed out, there was "a great deal of the traditional charm of the South" in her, the kind of elegance and self-confidence from Southerners of high breeding that Mencken had felt lacking in Marion Bloom and even Aileen Pringle—despite her pedigree. During his stay in Hollywood, when Aileen played the "Blue Danube Waltz" on the piano, and "I did the bump-bump-bump-bump with my bottom," she recalled, Mencken had been horrified. "He turned white and I laughed clear out to the patio." It took her almost half an hour of pleading to make him snap out of his rage, but to Mencken, such vulgarity toward Strauss was repellent. It certainly was not what he encountered with Sara. There was a reason that Sara had been nicknamed "Soulful Highbrow" at Goucher College. "Sara was always the lady—always proper, always reserved," recalled a classmate.

Of all Mencken's friends, Joseph Hergesheimer summed up Mencken's attraction to Sara best: "She was endlessly companionable, a bounty dearer to monological men than any precarious digression. Henry and I lingered evening after evening in her apartment on Read Street, steeped in her attentive tact. Drinking the traditional Maryland rye, we watched Sara's slow consumption of gin, Coca-Cola, and lime juice incredulously. While Henry applied the salt of a verbal pretzel-bender to the Bible Belt, her latent composure was swiftly animated by the amusement that never quite reached her grave eyes. At middle age Henry and I ignored the swiftness of time; we were happy, obviously, in Sara's house; at our best, complacent."

Even as he broached the subject of marriage during the first half of 1929, Mencken hesitated to set a definite date. A letter from Mary Parmenter to Sara Mayfield gave some indication of the relationship: "She and her boyfriend have been very realistic of late. At least she has been to him. Then she gets sorry she was mean, and him with bad sinus trouble." Unlike previous girlfriends, Sara seems to have been more adept at setting limits, at clarifying to her partner what she wanted and what she would no longer tolerate. While many of the wives of Mencken's friends were sure that eventually Henry would succumb, none of the men believed it.

One afternoon, while Hamilton Owens was lunching with Emily Clark and her stepmother, he was asked: "When is Henry going to marry Sara?" Owens brushed off the query. "Don't be silly. Henry isn't going to marry anybody. He's a confirmed bachelor." The women simply laughed at the man's naiveté, and looked at each other: "That's what you think." Their conviction made Owens stop and wonder. But as the weeks went on, without any announcement forthcoming, he, like so many other of Mencken's male companions, simply dismissed the feminine intuition as idle gossip.[2]

THE SUMMER OF 1929 had caused a drought in the Midwest, and in Baltimore the humidity rose to record heights. Sara had been planning to escape the heat and go to Europe, until she became violently ill with a kidney infection that put her in Union Memorial Hospital. The treatment was rigorous but only produced transient relief. "Now and then she feels better, but always, in a few days, she is worse again," Mencken worriedly wrote to Mayfield. "She is bearing the thing very bravely, but it is beginning to wear her out."

As he had before, Mencken took control, consulting with Sara's doctors to make sure she received the best possible care. "I can't bear to see you in pain," he told Sara. "It must be stopped." He dashed letters to friends out of town, and Sara began receiving cheerful notes that bolstered her spirits. In one, Paul De Kruif advised her: "Don't listen too much to Henry, who is so damned fond of hospitals that he'll try to keep you there indefinitely just to be able to talk to you about your experiences in them." Illness did seem a link that bound Mencken and Sara closer together. Mencken was fascinated by the frailties of the human body—his own and everybody else's. But far more than that, he was deeply impressed by the courageous way Sara faced suffering.

Throughout Sara's illness, Mencken tried to hide the reason for his concern, and he strictly advised all of her friends to do so as well, so that Sara could make a complete recovery. Although Sara believed she had a small local infection, her illness had been diagnosed as a secondary bladder infection, and possibly a recurrence of tuberculosis. The date of Sara's operation was suddenly advanced from July 15 to July 6.

In early July, as Sara faced surgery, she repeated to Sara Mayfield her instructions for administration of last rites. Mencken hastily turned his head to the window. Two nurses eased Sara's stretcher out into the hall. When Mencken and Mayfield were waiting for the surgery to be finished, he told her that he and Sara had been planning to get married that fall. According to doctors, although the operation was successful, Sara's kidney was tubercular and she had, at most, only three years to live. "If she pulls through," Mencken told Mayfield, "I've promised myself that I'll make them the happiest years of her life."[3]

"Poor Sal," Margaret Cobb wrote to Mayfield. "The way hard luck has been pursuing her is almost incredible, were we not seeing it with our own eyes." Privately, everyone praised Mencken's solicitude, but Sara's history of ill health gave few of her friends hope for a recovery. Anne Duffy, recently back from Europe, inadvertently broke the shocking news to Sara. "Please do not be uneasy," Mencken tried to comfort her; he assured her that doctors were natural pessimists. "You will get well and completely."

Later Mencken wrote Raymond Pearl, "What will follow, God alone knows."[4]

SARA WROTE TO A FRIEND: "I've had a pretty awful time of it, but it looks as if my time still isn't yet, God knows why." After two months at the hospital she was back at her apartment, but so weak doctors forbade her to travel. Sara's tenuous future was a drastic reality that finally forced Mencken to come to terms with the status of their relationship. After years of postponing the decision to marry any of the eligible women with whom he had been involved, if anything, this current turn of events made him rise to the occasion. If he did not seem as passionate about Sara during the initial months of their engagement as he had been openly passionate with Marion and Aileen, years of marriage to her would change all of that; in time, she replaced all others in his heart.

Mencken continued to show Sara off to his brother and sister while keeping careful tabs on his family's reactions. Afterward, Mencken praised Sara: "You were lovely as always, and won the family all over again. What a gal!" For the next six months, they had resolved to keep their engagement secret. With Sara's return to health, Mencken devoted his energy to finishing *Treatise on the Gods*. The task before him was daunting, but at least it served as an excuse to keep Aileen at bay. When he wrote telling her he could not see her until 1930, she retorted violently: "I'll be damned if I go to a psychoanalyst or fall in love with an actor to please you. Forever thine—and to hell with you."

His labors continued through Thanksgiving. After a celebratory drink, Mencken sent Sara a jubilant telegram: "THE BOOK WAS FINISHED AT NINE FIFTEEN TONIGHT GLORY HALLELUJAH." Deciding that he had earned a vacation, and on Sara's insistence, Mencken embarked for Europe. Leaving Sara behind in Baltimore, however, was more difficult than he had anticipated. He was tempted to tear up his ticket. Before he set sail, he called Sara from the dock in New York and sounded, she told her friends, "quite doleful. I'll miss him terribly." With thousands of miles of ocean between them, he wrote to Sara: "You will never know how much I think of you, and depend on you, and love you." He repeated his vow to love her "forever." From London, he assured Sara, "I think of you every minute."

This, however, was not quite the case, even if he did think of Sara quite often. The very same day, he also wrote a flirtatious letter to Aileen, telling her that a fortuneteller had informed him that a beautiful lady, well known to him, would soon be in New York. "What do you have to say to that?" At the American Express office he checked for Sara's letters but also looked for mail from Aileen. It was a splendid deception that Mencken continued to maintain even when engaged. Still, he must have known that sooner or later he would have to give it up.[5]

IN APRIL, despite his own qualms, Mencken finally decided to tell his family of their engagement. Gertrude was genuinely delighted; August gave Sara one of his highest compliments: "For a woman she had a good sense of humor." Little Virginia remained the most astonished, especially after all that she had heard her uncle say against marriage. But she told him: "I know that I will like my new aunt and I hope that she will like me." Such positive family reaction, Mencken confessed, made him feel "immensely relieved. So we seem to have got around the first corner without breaking a leg."

Sara traveled to Montgomery to break the news to her family. Mencken had arranged and paid for the trip, even supplying her with a jug of cocktails to share with her family. Nothing could compare with the jubilation Sara felt during the spring of 1930. To begin with, she received the news that Doubleday was going to publish her novel, *The Making of a Lady*. In the span of one year she had been launched as an author and had become engaged to "America's Foremost Bachelor," her mentor through all of her literary endeavors. Now, she was back in the familiar landscape of the deep South. Around her, gardens of jasmine and Mexican primroses blossomed; the perfume of kiss-me-at-the-gate wafted into the warm sunshine: "I am so happy I am dizzy."

A few of Mencken's close associates were informed of the tremendous secret. "The poor gal is Sara Haardt. Resort to the jug at once," Mencken wrote Nathan. "When you recover send me your blessing." As for his marrying a Confederate, he joked to Blanche Knopf, "I only hope it gets us some subscriptions to the *Mercury* in the South." He told his *Mercury* secretary, Edith Lustgarten, he was counting on his upcoming marriage to promote the sales of *Treatise on the Gods*. Mencken asked for the prayers of all his friends, begging them, in jest, "to please say nothing about my heavy drinking or about the trouble with that girl in Red Lion, Pa., in 1917." Most friends reacted as had Fielding Garrison—rubbing their eyes in disbelief and asking others whether the news was authentic. One member of that masculine bastion, the Saturday Night Club, wondered "what will Sara do to the club!" But many more responded with pleasure. Hergesheimer wired: "You are doing exactly the right thing at the right time and with the right person."

In order to spare Aileen the shock of reading about his decision in the newspapers, Mencken sent a letter telling her himself. By coincidence, it arrived on June 19, a date she held most dear, for it was the fourth anniversary of their first meeting. Immediately she fired off a telegram:

> WIRE ME AT ONCE AND TELL ME EVERY WORD IN YOUR LETTER IS NONSENSE   AND
> DID YOU TIME ITS ARRIVAL FOR THE NINETEENTH   I THOUGHT SOMEHOW THAT YOU
> WOULD ALWAYS BE THERE THE LAST TO LEAVE THE SHIP   IM HAVING A RATHER
> ROTTEN TIME OF IT   WONT YOU BEAR WITH ME = AILEEN.

The upcoming marriage was hailed as the most sensational since that of Anne Morrow to Charles Lindbergh a little more than a year before. Internationally, newspaper editors mourned the loss of the sole survivor of "The Last Man Club." Mencken had been the patron saint of single men. Now, with the prospect of his wedding, one reporter noted that "bachelors of the nation are aghast and sore afraid, like sheep without a leader."

"The Sea of Matrimony." Cartoon by Richard Q. Yardley, 1930. H. L. Mencken Collection, Enoch Pratt Free Library.

Naturally, everyone was clamoring to know who the young lady was who had subdued America's best known bachelor. The *Mobile (Alabama) News* had an answer of sorts: "H. L. Mencken, who has been regarded as almost a professional bachelor, has at last succumbed to the charms of an Alabama girl, which only goes to show that if he had been in contact with some Alabama girls earlier he would have never been known as a bachelor, or even as an iconoclast."

The press concluded that the author of *In Defense of Women* was probably in the most embarrassing position of any fiancé in recent years. Reporters were bent on trotting out the old quotes. Long before, he had defined love as "the delusion that one woman differs from another," maintaining "bachelors know more about women than married men. If they didn't, they'd be married, too." How, reporters insisted with glee, will he explain it to his fiancée? To these queries Mencken replied, with mock seriousness: "I formerly was not as wise as I am now . . . the wise man frequently revises his opinions. The fool, never."

The one who professed to be least puzzled by Mencken's marriage was George Jean Nathan. He alone had been privy to most of Mencken's love affairs throughout the years, and Mencken valued Nathan's role as confidante. "Henry always was like a married man," he loyally told reporters. "He really is just a home man, and he hollers if he doesn't get his noodle soup at six o'clock." Mencken brightly told a member of the press: "I have never said that I would not marry. I have been very careful not to say anything like that. Very careful." He turned frankly to his interviewer. "I have often imagined that I would be as perfect a husband as a woman could find," he continued. In fact, he had vowed to draw up a contract with his wife that would consist of just two sentences: " 'I hereby promise to do my damndest. You are hereby notified that I expect you to be polite.' "

For all the excitement, many still scowled at the news. "This was the worst shock I ever had—never heard him mention to me Sara Haardt's name," recalled a wounded Gretchen Hood. She later bitterly confessed, "I never got over it."

"Gentlemen might prefer blondes," quipped Anita Loos, "but they marry brunettes." In time, Loos confessed, "I came to realize that my poor mother's clichés were uncommonly sound; a man worth marrying chooses a wife he can visualize as his mother."

Marion Bloom tried to remain philosophical, arguing that Sara was Southern and "Southern women are famous for grabbing their men." Yet for all her resolve that she would not spend the rest of her life writing her memoirs about him, Marion and Estelle made sure to keep a detailed record of the tempestuous love affair, perhaps so that posterity could come to its own conclusion as to whom Mencken loved best.[6]

It HAD BEEN DECIDED THAT, in accordance with Anna Mencken's will, Gertrude would remain at Hollins Street, and that Mencken and Sara would move into a new home of their own. The apartment house at 704 Cathedral Street was within easy proximity to beer *stubes* such as Schellhase's and to the Enoch Pratt Free Library. For the next few weeks Sara spent her time dealing with plumbers, carpenters, carpet layers and floor waxers. Various bottles of bootleg liquor were toted from the Hollins Street cellar, a job that took four days, with Sara keeping careful watch all the while. After all of this hard work, Mencken could only hope that the janitor would not raid his wine while he and Sara were freezing in Canada on their honeymoon.

It did not take Mencken long before he concluded that getting married was a more tedious business than he had expected, especially having to deal with so many tradesmen. "Outfitting a swell apartment turns out to be very expensive," he said to his secretary at the *American Mercury*, advising her to tear up Sara's card in the index: "If she works for the magazine it will have to be for nothing!" The comments were made in jest, probably to cover up whatever awkwardness he may have felt in preparing to take so big a step. More than ever, he missed his mother's sound counsel. Turning to Goodman, he asked in all seriousness if his wife should handle all the money: "This may seem a small matter, but it has given me some concern."

As the date drew ever closer, increasingly Mencken jested that he had begun to tremble and wobble; with alarming frequency he referred to the officiating reverend as "the hangman." To his old friend A. H. McDannald, he wrote: "The hour approaches. I can almost hear the sheriff's stealthy step." Even so, he managed to pull himself together and obtain his marriage license, where, the clerk noted, Mencken mumbled and blushed like any young fellow.

Somehow in the midst of interviews and preparations, and an appalling amount of mail, Mencken found time to meet with his friends. Raymond Pearl offered to instruct him in "The Facts of Life"; the Saturday Night Club gave him a dimestore wedding shower, complete with a medal and a diamond-studded belt buckle. The night before his wedding, Mencken hosted a party in a private room at the Rennert Hotel. A few members of the Saturday Night Club were invited, those whom Mencken considered his closest friends in Baltimore: Raymond Pearl and his wife, the Willie Woolcotts, Mr. and Mrs. Heinrich Buchholz, and, from the *Evening Sun*, the editor Hamilton Owens and his wife, Olga. Mencken had gone through a great deal of trouble to obtain the right cocktails and wines, and plenty of champagne. As the evening progressed, the hilarity and singing grew louder and louder. "As a result of all these wonderful drinks," Owens agreed, "we were all feeling quite gay and happy and jolly."

Olga Owens vividly remembered how very woebegone Sara Haardt looked throughout the festivities: "She wasn't enjoying it at all." Part of the reason may have been because Sara hardly knew anyone at the party: "She was somewhat overwhelmed by these intimate friends of Henry's who had known him so many years," so consequently, "she was very quiet" but also "very sad. She did not enter into anything."

Raymond Pearl got up and made a toast. So did the others. In the midst of the gaiety, Buchholz's wife, whom no one had met before, leaped on one of the tables and began, with her stout body, to dance the shimmy. Her performance "seemed particularly awful," recalled Olga. "Nobody could stop her. She got noisier and noisier." Mencken was obviously appalled. "Henry, you know, was a great stickler for being correct. He didn't like raucous behavior [before women]. He was a

Victorian." The party broke up quickly after that, but probably not without Sara's private but firm resolve that, when it came time to have Henry's friends over to 704 Cathedral Street, there was at least one who would not be invited to gather around her antique mahogany table in the new dining room. Ashamed, Mencken sent notes of apology to all of his guests.

In a successful coup to avoid the press, Mencken and Sara had secretly advanced their wedding date by a week, from September 3 to August 27. Mencken devoted the day to answering his correspondence and submitting to an interview with the United Press.

There remained one unfinished piece of business before the church ceremony.

The prospective groom wrapped all of Aileen's letters to him with pages of a German newspaper, made three packets of them in thick brown paper, then tied each one securely with string. Ceremoniously, he sealed the packets with blobs of red and green wax and, as was his custom—even on his very wedding day—took them to the post office himself and mailed them first class.

One can only imagine Aileen's reaction when the bundles arrived and she saw the familiar handwriting, or for that matter, the wedding announcement that came shortly thereafter, addressed to her in the hand of her rival. It took Aileen four months before she was able to comply with Mencken's request to return most of his letters to her. For this she received his thanks: "As always you are a grand gal!"

Contrary to his wishes, however, instead of burning her half of the evidence of their relationship, Aileen kept the brown parcels Mencken had sent. Years went by before she could bring herself to open them. Until her death, they were kept behind her living room sofa in the small apartment in New York to which she later moved—a constant reminder of their love affair and of Mencken's broken promise. Long before, she had made a prophecy to him, which her collection of letters now fulfilled: "My devotion shall haunt you beyond the grave."[7]

THE AFTERNOON OF THE WEDDING was humid and cloudy, with a dull overcast. Shortly after 4 p.m. a long black limousine that looked like a funeral hearse pulled up to St. Stephen the Martyr. Sara emerged with a worried expression, wearing a beige crepe ensemble with fluffy sleeves and a fluffy neckline. Hamilton Owens was standing at the church steps. Apprehensively, Sara asked Owens if the groom had arrived. "Well," he joked, "There's been rumors—" "No rumors!" Sara snapped. "Has Henry arrived?" Even then, it seemed to Owens, she was unsure whether "America's Best Known Bachelor" would wobble in his intentions.

The vestibule was practically empty, with only ten guests, but this was exactly as they had planned it. As Mencken had once written, "Being married with all your friends around you is as private and as discriminating as eating in the window of a restaurant." Paul Patterson had arranged for only one *Sun* photographer and had promised the press associations copies of all pictures taken. Within moments, Sara saw Mencken waiting for her at the altar. If, as friends said, on ceremonial occasions Mencken dressed "like a plumber got up for church," at least it can be noted that the suit he wore on his wedding day was not wrinkled.

Soon it was over and rice was scattered about the head of the man who had written of weddings as "barbaric rites." Only when their train was speeding toward Canada were bride and groom able to relax. Sensing Mencken's nervousness, Sara changed from her wedding clothes into a simple gingham dress, putting him at ease. At each stop, Mencken bought a pile of papers. To his horror, the wedding photographs published on the front pages were extraordinarily bad.

Somehow, Mencken managed to conceal them for a time from his bride, but at the next train stop Sara discovered for herself the most appalling one of all. Staring at her from a newsstand, on the front page of one newspaper, she saw a picture of herself looking dour and forbidding, her left eye freakishly reduced to less than half its size; her other eyeball was a large, blurry black smudge. "No Hearst photographer, trained upon divorcees and murderesses, could have done worse," Mencken reflected. It took some time before Mencken was able to quiet her lamentations: "It was a dreadful blow."

In New York, they sent a telegram to Nathan:

PASSING THROUGH YOUR GREAT CITY WE SEND YOU THE BLESSING OF OLD MARRIED FOLKS   ON OUR RETURN IN TWO WEEKS WE SHALL CONSIDER YOUR SITUATION SERIOUSLY   YOU GET THE TWO KISSES AND AN EXTRA ONE FROM THE OLD MAN   LOVE TO LILLIAN SARA AND HEN

Once in Halifax, they were greeted by the splendor of blue skies and cool ocean breezes. While Sara shopped among the antique stores, Mencken spent the afternoon writing an article for the *Evening Sun* on the malt liquor situation in Quebec. Mencken's devotion to work even on his honeymoon did not seem to bother Sara, who was blissfully happy. From their hotel room window, they watched the tugboats lazily go back and forth across the water, and planned the dinner parties they would have in their new home. The emerging Depression and its hardships seemed far, far away.

"It is a grand experience to be able to look a hotel detective in the eye," Mencken confided to Nathan. "I begin to feel like an old married man already," he wrote to another old pal of the Saturday Night Club. As soon as his friends could manage it, they must meet his bride. "She is a grand girl, but somewhat optimistic. Coming from the South, she is not used to real beer kings, so I have promised her to drink no more than 20 seidel on Saturday nights." In a postcard to a friend, Sara wrote glowingly: "You were right: I have the one perfect husband."[8]

32

VARIATIONS ON A FAMILIAR THEME

THERE HAD BEEN A CERTAIN IRONY in Sara's health crisis of 1929, occurring just as Mencken was deeply immersed in writing *Treatise on the Gods*. Although he was hardly a religious man and often given to ridiculing the clergy and its domain, he did at times admit to friends, half in jest, that he did a lot of soul searching. He was the first to admit that when "I am in low spirits and full of misery, I never feel any impulse to seek help, or even mere consolation, from supernatural powers." To do so would be "as foreign to my nature as the impulse to run for Congress." When facing the loss of his mother or physical pain, it never occurred to him to send for a clergyman. When he was in trouble he sent for a doctor, lawyer, or a policeman. Faith for him was in conflict with the scientific point of view, which remained his complete answer for as long as he could remember. "It leaves a good many dark spots in the universe, to be sure, but not a hundred times as many as theology."

Yet Mencken was not an atheist. As he said, to deny all gods is "simply folly." Something made the stars spin, he said, because some will ordained it. While he did not believe in souls or the afterlife, he was once willing to concede that perhaps after death a person's spirit was transformed into electrical energy. He hadn't the slightest objection to churchgoing in others (provided, he added, "they are not hypocrites, which they usually are"), and, as could be seen in his interest in Billy Sunday, Aimee Semple McPherson, and the Holy Rollers, he continued to be fascinated by religious ceremonies. On those occasions when he listened to solemn liturgy, he enjoyed it, if only because of the sensuous delight in its beauty —"a delight exactly like that which comes over me when I hear, say, Brahms' first symphony." Among his acquaintances were clergymen of every denomination. In Baltimore he could be found sharing a beer at Schellhase's and discussing theology with pastors, rabbis, and priests.

Mencken was aware of the principal arguments in favor of some of the dogmas. He described himself as "an amiable skeptic," whose true religion was a devotion to truth: "Any man who was born with that impulse leads a fundamentally happy life, though his quest may never bring him anything, either in worldly rewards or in truth itself." In pursuit of truth, Mencken admitted to being a lifelong "student of the sacred sciences." The Reverend Francis C. Kelley, bishop of Oklahoma, declared that Mencken knew more about the canons of the Church than most of the members of the American Catholic hierachy. *Commonweal* hailed Mencken, half ironically, half affectionately, as Defender of the Faith. A number of theological works were reviewed over the years in the *Smart Set* and the *American Mercury*, which, despite their bantering tone, were commended for their fairness and studied by editors of the *Christian Union Quarterly*. Nonetheless, there were those who were firmly convinced that Mencken was headed for hell—"and what is more, that I deserved it." They may have thought twice if they had known that Mencken confessed to having deep within him an incurable nostalgia for the nether region.

Books on hell, however, were not the only theological studies that graced Mencken's bedside table. As early as 1921, he had been thumbing through his 1904 Bible until it was finally worn to tatters, all with the aim of writing a book on religion. "I find myself in considerable difficulties," he wrote to Fielding Garrison. "The material in front of me is colossal, and I must boil it down to a small compass. I am sure to be accused of overlooking important facts. But I see no way to do the book save to confine myself to facts that seem important to *me*, letting the anthropologists, theologians and other such criminals be damned." Later, he seems to have recanted that view, since one of the principal objects of the book was to show how religious beliefs and practices had entered human culture from its origins. Sara helped him in his research on primitive man and savage tribes, going through volumes of the *Journal of the Royal Anthropological Institute*.[1]

Treatise on the Gods was the culmination of his thinking on the subject. It dealt with the nature and origin of religion, its evolution, its varieties, its Christian form, and its state in modernity. It was his first book since 1927, and, unlike the cut and paste jobs in *Prejudices*, nothing in it had been printed before, either in the *American Mercury* or elsewhere. Originally, the book was conceived as the second volume of a trilogy of statements on democracy, religion, and ethics. Claiming *Notes on Democracy* was "the worst of all my books," he resolved to do a better job with *Treatise on the Gods*.

Treatise on the Gods would remain by far Mencken's favorite book. "It is smooth, good-tempered, and adroitly written," he wrote. The draft as a whole remains an impressive demonstration of his ability to turn out clean copy on the first attempt. Mencken praised it as "a model of condensation; I can think of no other American book in which such a large body of material is brought into such small compass without any sacrifice of form or style. Most current critics put *The American Language* series in first place, but that is only because they are relieved when I avoid dangerous subjects."

In *Treatise on the Gods*, Mencken did not duck controversy. The book began with the assumption that the origin of religion was primitive man's fear of the unknown. Although Mencken touched on the Eastern religions, a large part of the book was devoted to the origin and development of Christianity, emphasizing what was distinctive and original with the Jews and harmonizing that with the Gospels. He believed in the historic existence of Jesus and praised the Bible as "a mine of lordly and incomparable poetry, at once the most stirring and the most touching ever heard of." Here, he said, nearly all of its beauty "comes from the Jews, and their making of it constitutes one of the most astounding phenomena of human history." He went on in a diatribe on the Jews that, more than previous remarks, generated the allegations of anti-Semitism that would haunt him:

> For there is little in their character, as the modern world knows them, to suggest a talent for noble thinking. Even Renan, who was very friendly to them, once sneered at the *esprit semitique* as *sans entendue, sans diversité,* and *sans philosophie.* One might still go further. The Jews could be put down as the most unpleasant race ever heard of. As commonly encountered, they lack many of the qualities that mark the civilized man: courage, dignity, incorruptibility, ease, confidence. They have vanity without pride, voluptuousness without taste, and learning without wisdom. Their fortitude, such as it is, is wasted upon puerile objects, and their charity is mainly only a form of display. Yet these Jews, from time immemorial, have been the chief dreamers of the human race, and beyond all comparison its greatest poets. . . . All of this, of course, may prove either one of two things: that the Jews, in their heyday, were actually superior to all the great peoples who disdained them, or that poetry is only a minor art. My private inclination is to embrace the latter hypothesis, but I do not pause to argue the point.[2]

When *Treatise on the Gods* was released in the spring of 1930, the reaction to that one paragraph was swift in coming. During the 1920s Mencken was accustomed to being accused of many things, but anti-Semitism had seldom been among them. There were a few moderating voices: in the *Jewish Chronicle Supplement* Jacob de Haas downplayed Mencken's importance, scolding other Jews for paying any attention to "the perfect fault finder." Dr. Edward Israel, rabbi of the Bolton Street Temple in Baltimore, dismissed *Treatise on the Gods* as "pseudo academic," pretending to a scholarship that it did not possess. As for the insulting paragraph, its author was "intoxicated with the exuberance of his own verbosity."

But there were Jewish and gentile critics who came to Mencken's aid. Meyer Weisgal wrote a defense in the *Brooklyn Daily Eagle*, although its three-decker headline alone told the story:

Benjamin de Casseres summed up the matter as he saw it in *New Masses*: "Mencken criticizes in Jews the thing any intelligent Jew deplores. Because he is a non-Jew and says them does not mean he is an anti-Jew."

Samuel Knopf was upset by the hostility, but his son Alfred remained philosophical. By April 1930, the book was already in its fifth printing, with sales exceeding 13,000. It would go into three reprints in three years. Mencken's name was on the best-seller list on the East coast and in the Midwest. Even in the Bible Belt, where his name was anathema, the book was widely read. Alfred Knopf was convinced, as he told Mencken, that a large proportion of the book's sales went "to the very Jews who are objecting to that paragraph." Many rabbis demanded that Mencken change it or omit it altogether. "In as much as these demands were invariably accompanied by loud threats I refused to heed them," Mencken reflected. Fifteen years later, he rewrote the passage. In 1930, however, he remained determined not to yield under fire. Those who denounced him most, Mencken told Isaac Goldberg, were "professionals of the familiar type." He maintained that the "professional Jew," through something close to paranoia, was as much to blame for anti-Semitism as the gentiles.[3]

The only interview Mencken granted at this time was to Joseph Brainin for the Seven Arts Feature Syndicate. The two sat in the comfortable lounge of the *American Mercury* office. After 75 minutes of what the reporter admitted to be a "strange" interview, full of contradictions, Brainin still did not know what Mencken thought of Jews. "I gained the impression that Mencken has done very little thinking about Jews," Brainin reflected later. "He is too close to them. He always has been, since his early childhood. I am sure he almost feels like one of them. That is why his approach to things Jewish is straightforward, betraying no conception of the problem involved."

Despite a slight cold, Mencken seemed to be in the best of form. Asked, "Are you an anti-Semite?" his smile broadened into a grin; then he laughed. "I never answer critics," he said. "I will make no exception in the case of my Jewish critics. They can go to hell. Jews don't know when they're well off. In the three hundred pages of my book I have devoted just one paragraph to them. If the Jews don't like what I say about them, what should the Catholics and Protestants say? As a matter of fact they do say it. The Catholics, I mean. The Protestants are so used to being dragged about and trampled upon they haven't the guts to protest. I used my best abusive vocabulary on them. I called the Jews unpleasant. I don't apologize. What are you going to do about it?"

"The trouble with you Jews," Mencken continued,

is that you have professional Jews. They have a special knack for making themselves unpleasant. They shout and protest when they should smile. They smile and look the other way when they should protest. . . . They train their heavy artillery on a sentence that might well have been overlooked if they had not projected a spotlight upon it. . . . Don't forget that my book is about religion, not about individuals. I don't like religious Jews. I don't like religious Catholics and Protestants. So everything should be in order. And it would be in order without your professional Jews. . . .

Jews should learn from what happened to the German Americans. They were a decent lot, just like the Jews. But for every two thousand Germans one could find about five professional German Americans. That proved their doom. They became chesty and super-sensitive. American politicians exploited them for their own political ends. These politicians were always on hand, at all German functions, and never failed to praise old Bismarck. They were always ready to drink *Bruderschaft* with the German American voters. But when the United States entered the war and overdid itself in Germanphobia these *Bruderschaft*-drinkers were in the front ranks of the hysterical anti-Germans. Bismarck suddenly became a Hun.

Mencken paused to light his cigar. The interviewer asked: "But why are we such a disagreeable race, Mr. Mencken?" Mencken corrected him. "I used the word 'unpleasant,' and advisedly. It's a nice word," he chuckled, "that's exactly what you are." He went on,

The Jews go about like sandwich-men carrying big signs: "I am a Jew." They parade it in front of you. They shout it in your face not as an answer to a question, but aggressively, without solicitation. Now I am a German, but I don't recite aloud from morn to midnight: "Every day in every way I am becoming a better and bigger German." But these professional Jews insist on yelling: "I am a Jew. Make no mistake about it—don't think I am one of you fellows. I am a Jew." . . . It's just like these Catholics clamoring that they are the only people who will go to heaven. . . . All that makes them downright unpleasant. . . . Well—isn't unpleasant the right word?

Mencken smiled, grinned, and then burst out laughing, but, Joseph Brainin noted, his Teutonic blue eyes looked genuinely annoyed. Just then, Knopf crossed the room; Mencken followed the reporter's glance. "Here I have a Jewish publisher, a Jewish assistant, a Jewish proof-reader, a Jewish secretary," he said. "They all read my last book. Not one of them felt offended. They are not professional Jews."

Clearly bothered, Mencken could not let go of the topic. "Sure there's a difference between Jews and Gentiles. It is the Jews, however, who erect the Chinese walls, who emphasize the lines of demarcation. In literature and science there is no anti-Semitism, unless you put it there. Who cares that the heads of the Rockefeller Institute are three Jews? Or even in the professions."

Mencken praised intermarriage and called on Jews to further assimilate into the country, noting that Zionism was an inhibiting factor toward that goal. This echoed the thesis put forth by Maurice Fishberg in his book *The Jews: A Study of Race and Environment*, which Mencken had read in 1911. "If you want to live differently and have your own two-by-four country just like all those Wilsonian creations in the Balkans," he said, "go right ahead."

> It's not going to last anyhow. Nationalism is now on its highest crest. It will break its back before long. But then you have to accept the cry: "Go to Jerusalem," as the Americans used to tell the Germans to "Go back to Berlin." I am sick and tired of this nationalism, anyhow. That goes for racialism. There is no pure race, the anthropologists tell us. So why not mix? Why not get our bloods intermingled? Something interesting might result. I want to travel without visas, on one passport, without crossing any frontiers. I am sick and tired of calling a man a Catholic or a Jew.

"And when you write your interview don't put on the soft pedal," Mencken concluded. "I don't apologize. I am entitled to my prejudices. If you want to call me an anti-Semite, you're welcome to it. There is one thing I want you to remember, however. I am not half as anti-Semitic as some of your own Jews. And that goes for the best of them."[4]

Two of Mencken's closest Jewish friends dealt with their heritage in strikingly different ways. George Jean Nathan all but disavowed it; Philip Goodman, as a German Jew, briefly joined Mencken in making fun of the recent arrivals of Eastern European Jewish immigrants.[5]

Mencken could hardly have suspected in 1930 that during the next few years a series of events would occur that would magnify his every subsequent comment regarding Jews. Nor would he have ever suspected that before the decade was over, he would lose some of his closest friends.

Part Four
1930–1935

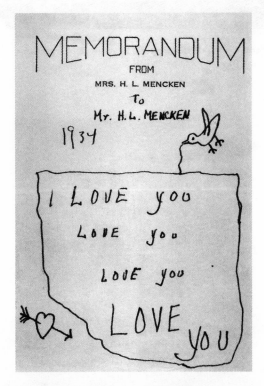

Note written by Sara to Mencken. H. L. Mencken Collection, Enoch Pratt Free Library.

Mencken and Sara, "at all times in divine humor." Photograph by Carl Van Vechten. Courtesy the Carl Van Vechten Trust.

33

THE TAMED OGRE OF
CATHEDRAL STREET

THE HOME OF MR. AND MRS. H. L. MENCKEN, arch agnostics, was on Cathedral Street, almost entirely surrounded by churches, including a Christian Science parish house right next door. The irony did not escape Henry Mencken, who often heard the cheerful songs of its congregation, each singer shrilling along in a different key.

Located in what had once been the brownstone mansion of a Baltimore banker, the Menckens' apartment was on the third floor right. There was no elevator and many wondered, in light of Sara's poor health, how the couple dealt with this situation. The stairs were numerous and steep. Mencken felt called on repeatedly to apologize for them to visitors (who, if need be, he noted, could be hoisted by rope). He promised that those who successfully survived the climb would be rewarded with comfortable chairs and a good bar.

Once on the third floor, visitors were led into a succession of spacious rooms with tall ceilings. The apartment's east windows faced Mount Vernon Place, in the middle of which, Mencken liked to point out, was "the greatest damned monument ever erected to the memory of America's first and only gentleman— George Washington." The decor of the living room was decidedly feminine—so much so, in fact, that members of the Saturday Night Club felt distinctly ill at ease in it, and younger visitors were so in awe that they hardly dared look around. As Mencken's nephew, William C. Abhau, later said, it "seemed a bit elegant for our family."

With the aid of her friend Anne Duffy, Sara had decorated the drawing room with green chenille and mulberry silk—so delicate that, as Mencken recalled, it

"The Victorian Palace." Interior view of 704 Cathedral Street." H. L. Mencken Collection, Enoch Pratt Free Library.

cost him plenty to have everything cleaned. Elsewhere hung gilt mirrors, fancy fans, lace valentines, and glass bells. A cast-iron plug hat served as a cuspidor. "I spit in it only once," Mencken confessed to Hergesheimer. "The ensuing uproar dissuaded me thereafter."

"I often wondered, walking into that room, how a boisterous and rambunctious fellow like Henry could manage to be comfortable in it," Hamilton Owens marveled. Instead, Mencken mostly sat in the dining room, where a lithograph of the Pabst Brewery plant operating at full steam was hung, a monument to the days before Prohibition. Whenever he showed the lithograph to guests, a fleeting look would come over his ordinarily cheerful countenance. He would drop his hands resignedly toward the print and, without another word, sit down at the table with his back to it. In addition to the picture, decorating the room were his 267 beer steins, a collection of ivories ("made out of the skulls of bishops," Mencken assured guests), and an autographed portrait of Kaiser Wilhelm II. All the other furnishings in the apartment, Mencken told visitors, had been chosen by his wife. When it came to the "Victorian Palace," many friends privately felt that the lithograph of the Pabst Brewery plant was Mencken's one salvation.[1]

A corridor ran from the dining room, spanning the length of the apartment. On one side was a shelf where Sara kept her collection of 300 Victorian pin boxes, many of them acquired in secondhand shops on countless visits. "My brother didn't approve too highly of the collecting," August recalled, "and every time

"The poster was his one salvation." Here, with lawyer Clarence Darrow. H. L. Mencken Collection, Enoch Pratt Free Library.

she'd start unpacking, he'd say, 'Aw, for Christ's sake!' But she thought it was all right, so that's all there was to it."

Sara's explanation of what she called this "curious perversity of mine" was a revealing confession of her concept of femininity. "I like to remember a time when ladies in their hearts were sorely tired and troubled," she wrote, "they could fashion such charming trivia as lavender baskets and wax flowers. . . . Far from a silly picture as it is, it has, for me, a quiet heroism. If, as I have so often heard, knitting is soothing for the nerves, then surely making a nosegay of wax flowers must have concealed many a heartache. Whenever such a specimen of a lady's gallantry comes to my notice, I can almost never resist adding it to my collection." To all of these examples, Mencken added his own collectable: a sign on the wall pointing— THIS WAY TO THE AIRPORT—that led to the bathroom.

Completing this magnificence were Sara's books, a large number of which reflected Victorian manners and household economies. All had been rescued from various junk shops; yet, taken together they provided a portrait of the American lady in the mid-nineteenth century, with the feminine virtues necessary to produce an ideal spouse—the ideal, Sara once told Mencken in mock seriousness, by which she lived. Among the qualities were good humor and moderation.

In an interview, Sara agreed with her husband that politeness was the chief requisite of the perfect marriage. Mencken defined it in terms of understood liberty, as "the absence of the reformer complex: of any desire to improve other people." As he now put it: "Leave them alone. They're doing the best they can, poor fishes, wishing they were in heaven and afraid to try and get there. But then of course, it's easy for her," Mencken added, beaming at Sara's tall graceful figure. His eyes snapped with amusement. "She's married to the perfect man."

"Henry is Victorian, though he won't admit it," Sara drawled quietly. "So am I."

If, later on, Mencken looked unhappy whenever he was not in the usual seersucker suit that looked as if it had been slept in for a week, and was seen instead in an expensive dinner coat, "it was all Sara Haardt's notions of being High-Toned," one critic scoffed. Much of Mencken's discomfort may have been due not so much to the formality as to the fact that he was simply bursting at the seams. Marriage had inflated him to 192 pounds—twenty pounds above his normal weight, thereby prompting Sara to put him on a diet. From then on, any candy sent to 704 Cathedral Street was nibbled by Mencken in stealth.[2]

His own study was on a lower level, overlooking a small green courtyard. It was here, on certain rare occasions, he entertained the Saturday Night Club, where the men could indulge in talk of Beethoven while munching on the crab salad Sara had arranged for. Many of Mencken's papers were still stored at Hollins Street, to which he returned weekly to file. Next to Mencken's office was his private cellar; beyond were their bedrooms.

While everything at Hollins Street had been quite proper, family members quickly noticed that in Cathedral Street all was on a superlative level: the very best wine was served in crystal, the very best terrapin on Dresden china. Linen and silver, doilies and finger bowls accompanied every meal. "Dinner at their home was an experience," Mencken's niece, Virginia, recalled. A succession of maids had come and gone until finally it was determined that Hester Denby was the only perfect cook, and Bessie Lee the only one suitable to serve—which she did, dressed in a black uniform and a crisp white apron.

Visitors included old friends Clarence and Ruby Darrow, Joseph and Dorothy Hergesheimer, Ola Elizabeth Winslow, Harry and Constance Black. The fundamentalist Howard Kelly, delighted with his dinner, requested that Sara write her recipe for *brockwurst* in his prayer notebook. Once Sinclair Lewis arrived late with a bloody nose and insisted upon seeing Sara, who was in bed. "There he sat for twenty minutes or so," Mencken recalled, "gabbing at his usual dizzy pace and dripping gore on her coverlet." F. Scott Fitzgerald, who had moved to Baltimore for Zelda's psychiatric treatment at the Sheppard-Pratt Hospital, was another frequent caller. Sara, a little older than Zelda, had known her in Montgomery, but Zelda had little to say. ". . . every few minutes she would drop her knife and fork and grab and squeeze the arms of her chair," Mencken observed. "Obviously, she was trying to desperately hold herself together, and equally obviously she was finding it difficult."

Mencken deeply sympathized with Fitzgerald over the constant and costly care Zelda demanded of him; he had his own problems with Sara's illness.

Fitzgerald's worries, however, were compounded. They drained his energy during the day and denied him sleep at night. His exhaustion showed in his face. By this time he was drinking on a grand scale, leading Mencken to tell Dr. Benjamin Baker, "This Fitzgerald is nearly driving me crazy," begging him to "please do something to stop this."

At Johns Hopkins Hospital, tests revealed that Fitzgerald was suffering from cirrhosis. For his next four years in Baltimore, he kept promising to stay on the wagon but failed to do so, calling doctors in the middle of the night for help but asking them to bring him a bottle of gin. During sober intervals, Fitzgerald would sometimes come to visit "The Venus of Cathedral Street." Once, driving around the Washington Monument in an obvious state of inebriation, he went over the curb. Many times, Mencken would watch an intoxicated Scott and Zelda drive off in their car and say, "That's the last time we'll see them alive."

Other visitors, however, flocked to what Goucher friend Marjorie Nicholson called "a kind of social place." Mencken told Phil Goodman: "They come in clumps, and ought to be studied mathematically. The sweetest announce their arrival in town from Los Angeles, New Orleans or Stuttgart at 11:50 a.m. and expect to be entertained royally at lunch, with the wine at just the right temperature." The table was always set for four.

Such engagements initially disrupted Mencken's writing schedule. The freedom to write was precisely the reason he had given Marion Bloom and Aileen Pringle for remaining single. Normally, he was able to deliver a manuscript in less than twelve months; during his marriage to Sara, it took him four years to write *Treatise on the Right and Wrong*. While embarking on any new book was difficult ("It tires the soul" was his expression), social engagements delayed the project further. "Such work cannot be done at odd moments," he declared. "It is necessary to pull oneself together before launching into it."

Yet, Mencken insisted that married life in itself ultimately did not invade his freedom; it had actually given him more. A worse intrusion was the telephone, "the greatest boon to bores ever invented." Mencken was convinced the contraption set the "ancient art" of bores "upon a new level of efficiency," enabling them to "penetrate the last strongholds of privacy." Some even called every day for a week. "Boring is an art like any other," Mencken said. "A born bore gives it his passionate devotion."

Sara greatly assisted in diverting unwanted intruders. She was now, Mencken said, in charge of the pests who continued "to call me up, urging me to read their vile poetry, endorse their application for public jobs, or makes speeches for their dismal clubs. She is an immensely polite woman, and gets rid of them in a very suave and humane manner. Many call up again the next day, to thank me for having so courteous a secretary."

In the same vein, Mencken wrote that his wife "had all the Southern taste and talent (for it is a talent like any other) for an easy and gracious hospitality, and all the Southern skill at making people (and especially black people) want to do things for her, and a full measure of that indefinable and pleasant thoughtfulness which passes commonly under the banal name of Southern charm. Of this Southern charm she was very critical, and once she wrote a short story to expose and ridicule it, but she could no more shed it than she could shed the accent that left all her r's as soft and thin as gossamer."

Visitors who came to 704 would find a loving couple who held hands and called each other "darling" and "dear." The first time Virginia heard her uncle use this form of address it came as something of a shock. "It sounded so natural that I knew he meant it," she reflected. Until then, she had never realized how well Uncle Harry had become accustomed to married life. Others noticed the same. He seemed healthier, more buoyant than ever. "In all the years I have known you," Alfred Knopf wrote Mencken, "I have never seen you looking so thoroughly and completely happy and at home."

A reporter observed: "One reason for the Menckens' happy marriage, obviously, is that they never breakfast together." Sara explained: "No one has anything to say at that time of day. I want my papers and Henry wants his!" They worked out a routine that followed closely Mencken's own at Hollins Street. From nine to twelve, he wrote in his office or dictated letters to Rosalind Lohrfinck, his new secretary, while Sara wrote or attended to managing the household affairs. At noon they met in the dining room ("I never leave Henry to lunch alone," Sara told Knopf), and from 2:30 to 5:30 they went back to work again, he to his study and typewriter, she to hers to write in longhand and pencil.

Unless they dined out, which was seldom, after an early dinner they would work again from 7 until 10. Then it was drinks in the drawing room of which she was so proud. There, Mencken with beer at hand, Sara with the inevitable Coca-Cola, they would discuss the projects on which they were working or he would play the piano. On Sunday nights, when the servants were off, Sara often made supper in the kitchen, and the two would eat together there, and, according to Mencken, "just gabble."

"Marriage is largely talk, and I still recall clearly the long palavers that we used to have," Mencken wrote later. "I don't think we ever bored each other. I know that, for my part, the last days of that gabbling were as stimulating as the first. I never heard her say a downright foolish thing. She had violent prejudices, but so did I have them, and we seldom disagreed. It seemed to me that she always maintained hers with great plausibility. I have never known a more rational woman, nor another half so charming." And he declared early on: "I am still convinced that the American wife is normally far more intelligent than her husband. I have been married less than a month but I can recall at least 40 massive proofs of it at my own hearth."

"Life runs along pleasantly and smoothly and not too fast," Sara once observed. "Both Henry and I enjoy a routine that gives us time for work, time for play, and time for seeing friends we like to have drop in. I don't think either of us would ever be happy where the tempo of life is faster. This suits us just perfectly."

If marriage was "a beautiful adventure" for Mencken, he also recognized that it was a safe harbor for Sara, giving her the kind of security she had not known in years. Free of the financial difficulties she had suffered since college, she could indulge in dinner parties with a circle that included some of America's most notable personalities. Women's magazines rushed to print stories and articles written by Mrs. H. L. Mencken, and organizations such as the National Council of Women invited her to speak.

Visiting Mencken at home, a reporter from NBC Radio observed that six months of married life had created no lines of care or worry on Mencken's face. "That's because Southern women do not harass their husbands," Mencken said. Sara countered that "it stands to reason that a bachelor would make a good husband. A bachelor is likely to be much more interesting, because he has had a more varied life. Then, he is set in his ways. I think it is pleasant to live with someone who knows what he wants."3

Nevertheless, opinions about their life together did vary. Sara's sister Ida commented that "he was so considerate of Sara—so gentle and *darling*," but others disagreed. In the opinion of Dr. Benjamin Baker, the family doctor who lived two doors down on Cathedral Street, "he could be difficult. I don't think Henry was a very thoughtful husband." Mencken put in fourteen hours a day in his office, and even though Sara never played the role of a neglected wife, in her diary there might appear the forlorn entry, "Alone." Mencken later admitted in his own diary, "on many a day I did not see her until lunchtime, and then left her all afternoon, and worked all evening. She was busy herself, and knew the burdens of writing. When she was ill in bed in the house, and I could spare all too little time to entertain her, she often suggested that I go out when my day's work was done, saying I needed change and the talk of men."

The idea of having children was never far from Sara's heart, though illness had ultimately forced her to put the thought out of her mind. Her stories were full of profiles of small children, and one could detect the note of longing in a letter to Mrs. Edgar Lee Masters, from whom she had received a photograph of her infant son. The image had caused Sara to think of the boy for the remainder of the day. Without their own children, the couple's energies were focused on Mencken's niece, Virginia, and nephew, William, who attended the Naval Academy at Annapolis. He often stopped by the apartment, as did the adolescent Virginia. As she grew older, Mencken gave her a violin and encouraged her to take lessons. He sent her a desk, typewriter, and a dictionary, and reviewed her school essays. When it came time for her to attend college, Mencken paid her tuition to Sweet Briar, and Sara sent her pretty things for formal dances.

"If they ever had a serious quarrel, I never heard of it," Sara Mayfield recalled. "Between Henry's insistence on amiability and politeness in marriage and Sara's on conjugal courtesy, I doubt that they ever exchanged a cross word with each other. This is not to say that they didn't have their ups and downs—they did, before and after their marriage—but the end product of their disagreements was not a quarrel but an interlude of silence, occasionally so glacial on both sides that I shivered between them and dared not say a word to either."

"Sara seemed to be very docile but I have an idea that she ruled with the 'iron hand in the velvet glove,' " observed Virginia. "I don't mean to imply that she browbeat him or nagged. But Uncle Henry was so entranced with her that any-thing she suggested was fine with him. I often heard Sara say, 'Henry, I think we should thus and so,' and they did it, even if it was the farthest thing from his mind." This behavior, in part, was in keeping with Mencken's view of how to get along with a spouse. "Marriage is largely a matter of give and take," he advised Phil Goodman's daughter, Ruth, when she became engaged. "Each must respect the individuality of the other."

IT WAS NOT ONLY VIRGINIA who suspected that in many ways Sara took charge of Mencken's life. For all of Mencken's protests against reform, many of his old friends resented the manner in which they thought Sara was trying to change her husband. In some ways her influence was for the good. She helped him see the merit in Thomas Wolfe's *Look Homeward, Angel* and caused him to view the work of other Southern authors. She may have prodded him to publish several stories by William Faulkner in the *American Mercury*. Her friendship with Ellen Glasgow altered his opinion of *Barren Ground*. This novel, which he had described in 1925 as "being somehow weak in its legs," he now placed among her best books.

On the other hand, James Cain believed that it may have been due to Sara that her husband broke off with some of his closest friends. His version was some-what at variance with the view of Sara as soft and feminine. "She had a catty gift, she could see through people magnificently," he recalled. "Sara must always be regarded as the real whisperer into his ear. Of course, she really didn't whisper, she was very slam bang in her estimates of people, very given to salty expressions which must have caught his ear, as a lot of them began creeping into his own copy. And of course there was just enough truth in her cracks and enough indication of reality with enough proof to warrant the attention he paid them. She wasn't unkind, but perhaps she was malicious." Ruth Goodman also recognized that "beneath her soft manner there lay some malice, much intelligence, and a certain ferocity."[4]

Sara could not abide particular members of the Saturday Night Club. "It is easy to understand how so completely feminine, not to say delicate, a person like Sara would find it difficult to adjust herself to great hulking males like Raymond Pearl, or that deliberate vulgarian Heine Buchholz," observed Hamilton Owens, in whom Sara confided after her marriage. She felt Hamilton understood her better than most of the hearty, rather rough acquaintances who surrounded her husband. Owens recalled that on one occasion he met her for lunch and she bluntly announced, "I want to get rid of some of Henry's friends." He asked her which one in particular. She was boiling. She said, "Raymond Pearl, in particular. He is, to me, an insufferable human being."

When it came to separating Mencken from Pearl, James Cain noted, "Sara began having an ascendance over him that seems most remarkable considering how headstrong he was." Except for Paul Patterson, Raymond Pearl was the most intimate of Mencken's Baltimore associates. Six foot three with a shock of black hair, Pearl cut an imposing and charismatic figure. Wherever he went, he infected his associates with his own indomitable zeal.

Raymond Pearl was chief statistician at the Johns Hopkins School of Hygiene and Public Health, and professor of biology at the Johns Hopkins University School of Medicine. Characterizing himself as "a hard-boiled realist," Pearl pioneered studies in longevity, changes in world population, and genetics. His research, often controversial, concluded that heredity predominated over environment in shaping one's destiny. Of Pearl, Mencken wrote: "We had a common bond in music, but were both also interested in many other things, ranging from good eating to the congenital infirmities of the human race." Mencken was especially interested in how Pearl related biology to the social sciences.

Pearl's daughter described her father's friendship with Mencken as sensitive and sentimental. Pearl's wife, Ruth, who was somewhat reclusive, was jealous of the time the two men shared, but it was Sara who publicly complained of it. The unhappy result was that Mencken saw somewhat less of Pearl than he had before his marriage. "It's because of *her* that Henry can't see us," the Pearl children would hear their father growl. "A good time by all" was *not* the phrase Pearl used in his diary in describing an evening of the Saturday Night Club held at 704 Cathedral Street. "Everybody blamed Sara when the old friendships didn't continue," Olga Owens recalled.[5]

Nonetheless, opinions about Sara differed radically. "She was far too reserved to be described as the popular favorite," Mencken acknowledged, but his unwavering devotion caused him to remain blind to any undercurrent of resentment anyone may have felt toward his wife. He was convinced that "she always made a good impression on people of sense, and it delighted me to see how all my old friends liked her." In fact, some found Sara "self-consciously intellectual and pompous." Other women, recalled Elliot Wheeler of the Enoch Pratt Free Library, "loved to make little cracks about Sara. She was a great topic of conversation among Henry's friends."

In much the same manner that Sara had her dislikes among Mencken's friends, Mencken tired of the officious and domineering Anne Duffy. Anne lived only two blocks away. As Olga Owens recalled, "Whenever things weren't just the way Sara felt they ought to be or if Henry was having friends in, she would just go to the Duffys for the evening." This irritated Mencken to the extent that on one occasion he approached Hamilton Owens at his office.

> I said, "What's the matter?" He said, "It's those damn Duffys. I never go home but Anne Duffy is there and often Duff too. She's trying to run Sara. She's got Sara under her control."

Sara gave Anne the keys to the Menckens' apartment, and the two were insepar-
able. It seemed to Olga Owens that Anne had "the perfect subject to work on with
Sara, because Sara depended on her." Anne "was convinced that Sara was being
crushed by Henry" and was the instigator of Sara's attacks on many of Mencken's
friends. "When Anne disliked anyone, she was very articulate. Her dislike of
Raymond [Pearl] and Willie Woolcott and others was just poisonous," Olga
Owens recalled. "Anyway, she was trying to break off Sara from a good part of
Henry's life."[6]

THE MONOGAMOUS EXISTENCE apparently proved too much of a burden for
Mencken. Perhaps as an escape, he retreated to past associations with female
admirers. He wrote to a mutual friend: "Dorothy Taylor has apparently put me
on her blacklist. I haven't heard from her for months and months." Mencken's
overtures of this kind were met with resentment. Dorothy cynically commented:
"He's getting that second wind—after matrimony!" Aileen Pringle simply returned
one of his initial overtures unanswered. When he sent her another letter, encouraging her writing and exchanging bits of gossip, he warned that if she returned it,
"I shall get out some sort of writ against you." As for Gretchen Hood, she simply
refused to answer. Only Marion Bloom seemed to have escaped such attention;
surprisingly, Sara dined with Estelle Bloom, whom she liked a great deal.

If Sara ever gave any hint of insecurity, it came in one of her short stories.
In "Solitaire," a young woman marries a man who, once jilted, "distrusted all
women." Then, one night, he proposes. "She was so flattered that she didn't
realize he hadn't said he loved her." As time passes, the wife worries that her
husband is still in love with the former girlfriend. The thought of her rival, Sara
wrote, "grew on her until her whole body throbbed with sickened fear." To out-
siders "she seemed as happy as ever," yet not even her closest friend suspects her
"painful uncertainty. . . . She tried to tell herself that those long silences between
them, when Tom sat staring at the walls, didn't mean anything, that he was merely
tired, but then she found the box . . . containing all of Leila's letters to him . . ."

Yet, Sara's trust in her own husband was not misplaced. Sending the
occasional polite letter to former girlfriends was as far as Mencken would go. He
confessed: "I had a prejudice against adultery, if only because it involved a breach
of faith." He repeatedly insisted to friends (and himself) that he felt "completely
happy" in his marriage to Sara, nor could he recall a single moment during their
years together when "I ever had the slightest doubt of our marriage, or wished
that it had never been." Whenever confronted with a reminder of a former affair,
Mencken felt pangs of guilt. Once, at the Bach Festival in Pennsylvania, he came
across a good-looking friend of Aileen. That very evening he wrote a letter to
Sara, expressing his love and vowing: "No more of these solo flights! I miss you
too much."

Doubtless, Mencken had ample opportunities to stray, especially when
forced to keep "a bachelor's hall" during Sara's numerous stays at the hospital. He

found himself wandering through their apartment like a stray dog. After only a few months, he confessed to Dorothy Hergesheimer: "I am lonely here without the Wife. I have come to this."[7]

Sara's illnesses were very costly, as Mencken's canceled checks attested. In light of her history, she took every health precaution, often visiting the hospital for treatments and having a private nurse at home three times a week. "She loves to be coddled by doctors and nurses periodically but there seems to be nothing seriously wrong with her," Raymond Pearl groused to a mutual acquaintance. Mencken's sister, Gertrude, agreed. Her own sturdy constitution caused her to think that Sara overacted the role of a spoiled Southern belle. "That silly wife of his," Gertrude called her.

But in all matters of health, Sara had Mencken's full support, as repeatedly he opened his green checkbook, scrawled his spidery signature, and the checks went out—to doctors, to nurses, to McGarvey's Pharmacy located around the corner. In one month, he paid Union Memorial Hospital $300, at a time during the Depression when five dollars could buy a week's groceries. It was an expense, Mencken confided to Goodman. "But I was always taught that a good wife is worth anything she costs."

After Sara suffered a bout of influenza, Mencken took her to enjoy the sun and sea spray of Atlantic City. (Sara commented, "It is a cheap Coney Island but I have low tastes and enjoy such things.") Later jaunts included a visit to the beaches off the coast of Georgia and, during the bleak cold of winter, cruises to the Caribbean and the Mediterranean. During the oppressive heat of summer, Mencken made sure Sara had an escape to the cool forests of the upper New England states. Even though she had put on so many pounds she thought she was beginning to resemble a German soprano, he was encouraging. "I tell her that obesity is far preferable to pleurisy."

As time wore on, Sara became paler and paler, with only a slight flush to her cheeks. "It is a literal fact that despite all of her illness she was invariably patient and in good humor," Mencken told one of Sara's colleagues at Goucher College. "She was the perfect patient, and cheered her doctors when there was little that they could do to cheer her." Through it all, illness never seemed to come between husband and wife.

Within a year of their wedding, Sara told Mrs. Louis Philip that she had never thought life could be as easy with anyone as it had been with Henry. Henry's account corroborates Sara's. He wrote Phil Goodman:

Frankly, I expected to make rather heavy weather of the first year. I feared I'd be homesick for Hollins Street, and that it would be more difficult to work in new surroundings, eating purely Southern cooking—hams and greens, corn-pone, hot biscuits, etc. Nothing of the sort ensued. I am far more comfortable than I was in Hollins Street. Sara takes all telephone calls. The bills leave me $1.50 a week for Uncle Willies. Such is life with a really Good Woman.

Joseph Hergesheimer told reporters their calling Mencken "the ogre of Cathedral Street" was misplaced. All the virtues his friend had kept hidden for so long had "now burst into bloom like spring flowers. He is at all times in divine humor." With marriage, the gossip columnists observed, Mencken had become among the most polite and cheerful of men in America.[8]

Really!

34

HARD TIMES

THAT MENCKEN WAS, as Joseph Hergesheimer claimed, "the ideal husband of the Western hemisphere" seemed to annoy some of his most loyal fans. They resented the taming of "the Bad Boy of Baltimore." A reader of a local paper complained: "No wonder the *American Mercury* shows signs of decay." Mencken's essays were no longer "the diatribic effusions of a virile and volatile bachelor, but the pale and gloomy ramblings of a domesticated, yes, 'ideal husband.' And you editors call it romance. I call it tragedy."

It was only natural that Mencken in his marriage should devote himself to domestic life. Yet, even he was aware that the *American Mercury* was in need of attention, that it lacked the fire of its heyday. In part this undoubtedly was due to the economic downturn and the stock market crash of 1929. The magazine had always attracted a wealthier reader; newsstand purchasers had now become less willing to spend fifty cents for it. If its printer abandoned him, Mencken joked that he could always turn to the mimeograph.[1]

While Mencken put up a brave front before his friends, he was worried by the downturn. Advertising income for 1931 had dropped from an all-time high of $120,000 to less than half that amount, and profits had fallen from $15,000 only two years before to less than $4,000. Elaborate graphs and charts comparing the fortunes of the magazine with those of *Atlantic, Harper's, Scribner's* and the *Forum* were not encouraging.

One day, Mencken vowed he would tell the "true story" about the demise of the *American Mercury*; its woes would "fill a book." The manuscript's title was *My Life as Author and Editor*, but the chronicle remained unfinished and the history of his resignation from the magazine untold. The easy and early success of the *Mercury* had misled the Knopfs about its future. The basic scheme for the magazine was that it would earn money by circulation alone. But Samuel Knopf, encouraged by the magazine's prosperity, became, in his son's words, "more ambitious to sell advertising space than was good for us." In addition, stock in the *American Mercury* was acquired from individuals who held it in exchange for stock in Alfred A. Knopf, Inc. "It turned out to be a very bad move," Alfred Knopf realized. As the magazine began losing money, the *American Mercury* became a considerable liability for the publishing firm.

In an effort to coax more advertising and attract potential contributors, Knopf and Mencken went on a recruiting campaign in Boston. Alfred Knopf regarded most professors, especially history professors, as his betters and had published many books by them. At Harvard, Arthur M. Schlesinger Sr. recommended professors who would be willing to collaborate as writers.

More characteristic of Mencken were his methods of securing readers in spectacular undertakings, such as his three-part series in 1931 in quest of the "Worst American State." A hundred and four tables of statistics from a variety of sources, including the NAACP, revealed the relative standing of the states in wealth, literacy, crime, public health, numbers of newspapers, libraries, hospitals, even cases of lynching. Massachusetts was rated the best; Mencken's own beloved Maryland ranked twenty-seventh, and Mississippi finished last. Indeed, Mencken concluded, the entire Cotton Belt was the least advanced section of the country.

The hotly disputed findings drew the shrillest protest from Arkansas. "My only defense is that I didn't make Arkansas the butt of ridicule," Mencken replied. "God did." This provoked another uproar; one state representative suggested that "we have a few minutes of prayer for him." Mencken had been the recipient of both curses and blessings from Arkansas years before; now, he told a reporter, it interfered with his work. "I felt a great uplift, shooting sensations in my nerves and a throbbing in my head and the sound of many things in my ears," he said. "And then I knew that the House of Representatives of Arkansas was praying for me again."[2]

Despite all the publicity, by the autumn of 1931 the situation at the *American Mercury* had not improved. Knopf invited a businessman named Henry Sell and Mencken to dinner at his home to discuss how to reverse the magazine's fortunes. After two hours' discussion in which Sell kept hammering home how they could go about "making the old girl work," Mencken was convinced that if Sell had his way, the *American Mercury* would become as radically transformed as the *Smart Set* had been after it was sold to Hearst. He resolved to take the most radical approach possible. The next day he announced his resignation from the publication.

Mencken contended that he couldn't edit a magazine such as Sell outlined, and he would not want to write for one edited by someone else. Knopf later recalled of the meeting, "So in the end at my suggestion we agreed to give him

[Mencken] full sway—to let him forget advertisers and circulation alike and give a good show." Even so, Mencken's authority had been dealt a severe blow.

Mencken outlined his grievances in a fourteen-page memo that was a passionate defense of his role as editor. The essential difficulty, he argued, was the wide disparity between the editorial plan and the business office point of view. Samuel Knopf, who handled the finances for the firm, had been insisting that the difficulties facing the magazine stemmed from the editorial side. Mencken countered that he was being forced to "do two disparate and irreconcilable things—to produce a magazine of strong and unusual character, and to produce one that could be sold to the general run of advertising men." It was a faulty strategy to tackle the wrong advertisers and try to convert the wrong people into readers: "Little if any stress was laid upon the *quality* of our circulation."

Mencken balked at Samuel Knopf's rejection of many editorial ideas. To Mencken's disgust, he found out that "the job before me was not to find and print the best stuff obtainable; it was to find and print stuff that would not upset an elaborate business office campaign for advertising and circulation." Mencken suggested that the magazine change its appearance with a new cover and lower subscription rate. Both ideas were dismissed. Samuel Knopf was convinced that striking, sensational articles on finance would build circulation.

Trying to reason with the elder Knopf was notoriously difficult, for Samuel would roar and pound the table at meetings and want everything done his way. "There was no way of disagreeing without a row and probably being thrown out," Blanche Knopf recalled. When it came to improving the *American Mercury*, Samuel simply could not comprehend Mencken's unwillingness to expand the magazine along his lines, and Mencken concluded that the problem was "the extravagant and indeed almost insane management of Knopf's father. . . . We had a great many palavers on the subject, and there were promises of reforms and reorganization, but I came to the conclusion that the elder Knopf was hopeless."

Even so, Mencken held fast to his conviction that hard times would pass and the magazine would prosper again, and he so reassured Alfred Knopf. "But," he warned him, magazines "are sold, both to advertisers and subscribers, not by graphs and tables of statistics, but by their contents. Those contents are not improved by compromise and irresolution."

From then on, Mencken and Alfred Knopf discussed editorial matters on a weekly basis. A new cover appeared on the January 1932 issue that sought to attract more attention with better headlines. Yet no sooner had Mencken made his case when a headline on which he had laboriously worked was killed by Samuel Knopf.

One scheme on which Mencken did yield was to place his editorials at the beginning of the magazine, under the general heading "What Is Going On in the World." But once he agreed, he became uncomfortable with the arrangement. "I find myself hanging upon a precarious branch trying to unhappily figure out what is going to happen next," he complained of the economic situation. "I am driven nearly frantic trying to find subjects that will not be out of date by the time we come out." A tired air crept into much of the magazine, Mencken confessed, because he was having difficulty coming up with ideas for editorials. There were times when none were printed at all.

"We can do better with what we have, I'm sure, and he will make a better magazine," Knopf mused. He began meeting with other colleagues on how the *American Mercury* could be improved. Only Henry Luce, editor and founder of *Time*, seemed to agree with what Mencken had outlined in his original memo. He advised selling the *American Mercury* to advertisers as a unique medium, the circulation of which was relatively unimportant.

"Easy to say and see," Knopf despaired in his diary. "But how to do?"³

AT THIS JUNCTURE, Nathan decided to show Knopf his memoirs. *Friends of Mine* was a collection of portraits of literary personalities that included Sinclair Lewis, Eugene O'Neill, Theodore Dreiser, Joseph Hergesheimer, Ernest Boyd, and Mencken. He had high hopes that it would entertain; after ten months of hard work, it seemed to him the product was one of the best books he had ever written. When Nathan brought the manuscript to Knopf, he assured his publisher, "We are going to *sell* this one."

When Knopf read *Friends of Mine* that evening, he became outraged. "It's absurd to think for a moment that we could publish it," he wrote in his diary. Not only were chapters on mutual friends "grossly offensive" and "malicious"—the one on Mencken was in "execrable taste." "None of the book, save the chapter on Eugene O'Neill," Knopf wrote, "has any dignity and the book if published will show George as one of the worst bounders of his day. Is he stupid and naif or really an unfriendly fellow acting subtly, as Henry always believed. In the *mss.* of course he protests endlessly that these men and especially HLM are his friends."

Nathan had sent a copy of the proofs to Mencken, who spent the morning reading and becoming more incensed by the minute. The manuscript, he said, was simply "impossible" as it stood. The chapter on himself, Mencken argued, was "full of malice," however much Nathan insisted that the stories he told were "charming." Mencken could not get rid of the feeling that the book had, in places, the flavor of a mere gossip column in the manner of Walter Winchell.

What appeared to anger Mencken most was not Nathan's implication that Mencken was not the man he once was (for instance, listening idiotically to radio tripe), but his pointed criticism of his old partner's taking to Holy Church instead of marrying Sara in a simple civil ceremony. Mencken, in a letter, assured Nathan that he had no other choice; Baltimore did not have civil ceremonies. Moreover, he had *not* kneeled at his wedding service with Sara. "There is a hell of a difference between mere comic exaggeration and actual misstatements of fact," he wrote Nathan.

There were disparaging anecdotes about Mencken's mother and a visit to an honored shrine. "If there is anything sacred to Mencken there are three things:

his mother, Beethoven, and his wife," commented Margaret Redding, who had been shown the manuscript by her sister, Rosalind Lohrfinck, who had replaced her as Mencken's secretary. Margaret believed that Nathan was satisfying a private spite, and that "the *American Mercury* complex has got Nathan by the ears." She went on: "If Nathan purports to be writing really his impressions of Mencken, why does he drag in everything 'small' that he knows, or thinks he knows about his 'friend'?" Mencken felt exactly the same, and wrote Nathan to that effect.

Nathan asked Mencken to consider the treatment of the other authors in the book: "Is it not precisely in the same vein? You know damned well—or, if you are not an idiot—should know my feeling toward you. Maybe I am simply a clumsy writer. But don't lose your humor, for the love of God!" He went on:

> Loyalty is a quality you deride, but it is one of the few good ones I've got. And stop my "Mercury complex" talk. I didn't fit in with the magazine, I admit it freely; and it would have been tragedy for me—and certainly for you—had we tried to operate it together. You have done a much better job on the magazine than I could have done, or that you could have done if I, with my editorial views and prejudices, had been in the way. . . . Again, I am disappointed in your verdict. I should have liked to please you.

Sinclair Lewis also saw validity to Nathan's criticism. But after reading the chapter on Mencken, Lewis advised a measure of diffidence. "No matter how much you have to lie, I think I would end the account of Menck a little more affectionately and favorably. I would try to get in some 'nevertheless' paragraph which would keep the chapter from indicating so decisively that he is no longer Menck." While the book was "shocking" and "not altogether factual," Lewis nonetheless felt strongly that it should be published. "If Alfred doesn't want to publish it, I'll damned well see to it that somebody else does." Lewis added his hope that Nathan would not be "idiot enough to let Alfred influence you" against the book.

While Mencken's feelings of betrayal by his friends intensified, he limited himself to typing a list of corrections. When Nathan responded that "it is too bad, after more than twenty years, that we should find friendship threatened," Mencken replied: ". . . if you ever want to print the book, changed or unchanged, go ahead. As far as the chapter on me is concerned, far worse stuff about me is printed every day, and I certainly never object to it. The question is simply whether the general attitude of the chapter would seem to anyone to be that of a friend, or could be so considered on any rational theory. On that point, unfortunately, I still have some doubts."

Ultimately, Nathan relented. Over lunch at the Plaza Hotel, it took only ten minutes for Blanche and Alfred Knopf to convince him that the book simply could not be published. At first Nathan told Knopf he didn't have the heart to destroy *Friends of Mine*, but then he recanted. He promised to eliminate all the parts that were offensive. Privately, Knopf vowed that the final manuscript would have to be considerably revised before he would consent to its ever reaching the public.

A contrite Nathan apologized to Mencken, asking his advice. But all he earned for his gesture was Mencken's further repugnance. "Imagine falling into my arms after all the rancor of that chapter!" Mencken commented to Knopf. "I shall steer clear of the gentleman hereafter."

Friends of Mine was eventually published in 1932 under its revised title, *The Intimate Notebooks of George Jean Nathan.* There is nothing in the final version that gives any indication of the original offense it caused. In his chapter on Mencken, Nathan modified his tone, limiting himself to the oblique comment that "the four-handed scherzo that we used to play vivacissimo together on the barroom piano of life has become for him—as, I suspect, for me as well—rather more suggestive of a Ländler waltz."

Other incidents related to Nathan caused Mencken to bristle in the months ahead, but it was primarily because of his manuscript that any friendship remaining between the two men seemed irrevocably terminated. "So far as I am concerned, Nathan can do his worst and be damned," was Mencken's final condemnation. "If he doesn't do it openly he will do it behind the door. I am through with him."[4]

IN RETROSPECT, THE IMPENDING DOOM of the *American Mercury* and the end of the friendship between Mencken and Nathan were commentaries on a larger change taking place. Many still held Mencken to be the principal catalyst for bringing American literature the vigor of a true and native realism. The very fact that Sinclair Lewis had won the Nobel Prize in 1930 was a testament to Mencken's influence. An end had nevertheless come to a particular phase of twentieth-century American literature.

Literary criticism in America had taken on a self-consciously serious tone, and with it came the burial of what the *Bookman* called "the dear dead days of 1915–1925," the days of Mencken and the *Smart Set*. Contributing to the new critical tone was the *American Spectator*, a monthly publication set up by his old friends George Jean Nathan, Ernest Boyd, Theodore Dreiser, James Branch Cabell, and Eugene O'Neill. Although these were all men whom at one time Mencken had defended, their magazine ran articles that disparaged him. Other former allies of Mencken, including many liberals, also rejected him. "Today his articles in the *American Mercury* arouse about as much controversy as the daily reports of the weather man," wrote Mortimer Smith.

This changed mood could be noted in a new generation of college undergraduates. At Harvard, the very campus where Mencken had been idolized during the "Hatrack" episode of 1926, one student primly summed up the difference in attitude: "Dreiser, Mencken and Sinclair Lewis we have put aside as too destructive. We want to be built up."

The revisionism was ruthless. As Budd Schulberg remembered, "my generation thought of F. Scott Fitzgerald as an age rather than a writer, and when the economic stroke of 1929 began to change the sheiks and flappers into unemployed

"Something is stifling me—I think it's Mencken."

Krakusin for *The New Yorker*, March 22, 1930. © TheCartoonBank.com; Krakusin 2005.

boys or underpaid girls, we consciously, a little belligerently, turned our backs on Fitzgerald. We turned our backs on many things." Even Mencken struck a valedictory tone in one of his essays. "Any man engaged habitually in controversy as I have been for twenty years," he declared in the *American Mercury*, "must enter upon his declining days with a melancholy sense of its hollowness and futility."

Two years after the Wall Street crash, in what Fitzgerald called "the dark autumn" of 1931, he wrote an obituary to "the most expensive orgy in history" in *Scribner's* magazine. The Jazz Age, Fitzgerald wrote, seemed far away. "It all seems rosy and romantic to us who were young then," he wrote sadly, because "we will never feel quite so intensely about our surroundings anymore."

As the year 1931 drew to a close, Mencken met for lunch with Alfred Knopf. Much of their discussion inevitably centered on the fate of the *American Mercury*, and Knopf put it clearly to his friend that he must make a success of it. The outcome of such talk made Mencken sink even lower. Knopf wrote in his diary: "He talks about getting old—that perhaps he is not the right editor, that we ought to be looking around for someone else, etc. I told him that we must reformulate his purpose in producing the magazine and we should see the magazine as best we could, on that basis."

In typical fashion whenever he was in a blue mood, Mencken told his publisher he saw little hope for the human race. Even Knopf had to agree.[5]

Many Americans during this period would have said they shared Mencken's gloomy prognosis. All over the country, men and women had been in a state of shock as the reality of the Depression set in. Only twelve months prior, several prominent individuals, among them Mencken, had been asked by the Associated Press to say what they hoped to see in the new year; by December 1931, it was clear none of their hopes had been realized. The stock market had not rallied but retreated; unemployment had not vanished but grown larger; prosperity had not returned. When it came to solving this "hell of a mess," Mencken threw up his hands. However, although he saw little future for the human race, he told Knopf, he hoped that the American people would demand once more "the strict observance of the Bill of Rights."[6]

This would continue to be Mencken's clarion call for the decade to come, but whether it would be made from the pages of the *American Mercury* remained to be seen.

35

"HAPPY DAYS ARE HERE AGAIN"

TIRED, ILL, AND DEPRESSED, on January 9, 1932, Mencken boarded SS *Columbus* of the North German Lloyd line for a trip to the Caribbean, fully suspecting the cruise was going to be a frightful bore. A knot of reporters, concerned by Mencken's wilted appearance, noted that he hardly displayed his usual robust and hearty manner. What did he think of the Prohibition amendment? one newsman called out. "It will not be repealed in our time, nor in our children's time," Mencken grumpily predicted. "Americans prefer to ignore amendments rather than repeal them." After this, there seemed to be nothing more to do but head for the smoking room.

Once Mencken was at sea, however, the sun baked all vexations from him. Lulled by the rhythmic slap of water along the ship's side and fortified with massive doses of German *Müncher*, Mencken soon returned to his old self. The voyage, indeed, surpassed his expectations. His and Sara's cabin was so grand that he was almost ashamed to hang his old shirts on the hooks; he locked his corncob pipe in the hold. Never one to be absolutely still, he left Sara to lounge on a deck chair while he sat in his room typing his column for the *Baltimore Evening Sun* on his decrepit Corona. At odd moments he amused himself by writing articles for the ship's newspaper, the *Caribbean Caravel*, where he offered an outlandish fictitious history of the North German Lloyd.

The ship made eight stops—each of which gave Sara the chance to go ashore and buy antiques. Mencken's first glimpse of the islands, as seen through the porthole of his cabin, brought him rows of pink and yellow houses amidst green palms; it made a pretty picture. A leisurely excursion through Jamaica's mountains, their peaks lost amid the clouds, enabled him to share with his wife a tropical view that had impressed him as a young man in 1902. Other stops offered less sentiment and more useful material. Such was his mood that he remained unfazed by Sara's shopping; instead, after she returned to the ship laden with perfume, he used her example to describe the free port of Curaçao. "Scents that sell for $25 a bottle in Baltimore may be had there for $24.65," he wryly noted for the *Evening Sun.* "It is a saving."

At last the cruise was almost over. As their ship slipped past Nassau, bottles of alcoholic beverages awaited in the dining room; even Mencken found it impossible to get through more than one-third of them. By the time they finally disembarked in New York, the couple felt fully recovered. The trip had been perfect from end to end. "Mr. Mencken was not only sober during the entire cruise," Sara told the assembled newsmen, "but he was also in good humor." A sunburned Mencken flushed with pleasure, mumbling his gratitude. He had restored his health, he said, on a diet of beer.[1]

ONCE HOME, Mencken turned his attention to politics, his principal theme for the remainder of the year. "The two national conventions of 1932 were the most fateful in American history," Mencken later reflected, "but no one knew it at the time." The New Deal was unheard of, but there was a widespread belief among Mencken and his colleagues that once Hoover was defeated there would be a rapid improvement in the nation's economy. In the March 1932 issue of the *American Mercury*, Mencken preached an optimism based, he insisted, "not upon fantasies, but upon realities." The Depression, he contended, had taught Americans the difference between speculative and real values, and had hastened the death of sick industries, thereby proving the vigor of sound ones.

> Best of all, it has taught millions that there is really no earthly reason why there should be two cars in every garage, and a chicken in the pot every day. . . . Life in America had become an almost unanimous effort to keep up with the Joneses, and what the Joneses had to offer by way of example was chiefly no more than puerile ostentation. So many luxuries became necessities that the line separating the one from the other almost vanished. People forgot altogether how to live well, and devoted themselves frantically to living gaudily. It seems to me that the depression will be well worth its cost if it brings Americans back to their senses.

As for the effects of the Depression, that spring Mencken told the United Press they were "greatly exaggerated." He was old enough to remember the panic of 1893: "There was a Depression with real teeth in it." Although it was true that on a per capita basis the unemployment figures during the winter of 1893–1894 were likely the greatest in the nation's history and that hard times haunted Americans for five years after 1893, the crisis after 1929 deepened for five years and persisted for twelve.

In addition, Mencken was living in an exclusive neighborhood, far from the poverty of the rest of the city. Moreover, Baltimore congratulated itself on being better off than other cities. The large proportion of mortgage-free homes meant fewer evictions and foreclosures. Fewer of the big banks failed. Even during the infamous bank holiday, Mencken and many of his friends were unaffected, and Baltimore was the only city in the country that invited the Metropolitan Opera to perform that year. Statements of public officials offered no reliable clues to the gravity of events; the society page continued to report a whirl of parties and teas. Indeed, it was not until 1934 that Baltimore eventually arrived at the same low point as the rest of the country.

Throughout his life Mencken had viewed the world through the prism of his city. So it was little wonder that during the spring of 1932 he continued blithely to advise women to stop riding the wave of postwar easy money. Mencken recalled how his own mother ran a household: with thrift, hard work, and simple living—ideals, he said, that had made the country great. Mencken did not see why other women could not stop "acting like a lot of idiots" and do the same.

The seriousness of the economic situation seems to have been finally brought home to Mencken during June 1932 in Chicago, where both national conventions were held. Below his window outside the Blackstone Hotel, on the grass of Lincoln Park, he could see hundreds of homeless men sleeping every night; in the morning he would see them washing at the park fountains. Cardboard shacks sprouted along South Michigan Avenue. "The Depression," he recalled, "was making itself felt at last."[2]

When Mencken's assistant, Charles Angoff, later took him by Times Square in New York to see the long lines of homeless men waiting for their bowls of soup, Mencken turned his face to a wall and could not speak. "A few days later, after he had returned to Baltimore, Angoff was called to his desk by a stenographer to greet a man who had come to see 'the editor of the *American Mercury*,'" William Manchester recalled. "In the hall he found a frail and miserable tramp, wearing an overcoat that somehow looked familiar. The vagrant had come to thank the man who had talked to him encouragingly in Times Square and had ended by stripping off his overcoat and giving it to him. It was Mencken's overcoat."

The Mencken family considered whether it could afford to send Virginia to Sweet Briar. Surely, Mencken reassured his niece, he would find a way to pay for the education of the family's "fairest flower." But he privately told her father the Depression put the matter in doubt, and he joked maybe she would be better off going to Hollywood instead. Nonetheless, he acknowledged "we are more fortunate than most. Two-thirds of the people I know are completely broke, and it would be no more possible for them to send their children to college than it would be for them to buy yachts."

As the Depression deepened, any thought Mencken had of taking another cruise with Sara or making a visit to Germany was postponed; he fully believed the years ahead would be economically even worse than 1932.

By this time, Mencken wrote, Hoover had become "the pebble in every American's shoe." If the president had any friends left, "they must all be deaf and

"... this hell of a mess." Apple selling in the shadow of the U.S. Capitol. Reproduced from the Collections of the Library of Congress.

dumb, for nothing is ever heard of them." The legislation that had promised to assist the top of the economic ladder, in the trust that sooner or later it would somehow trickle down and improve the lot stuck at the bottom, had backfired with a public that was growing more disenchanted by the day.

Thus, the Democrats were confident of victory when they met on June 27. Franklin D. Roosevelt, two-term governor of New York, became the front runner. The 1932 convention not only ushered in the long reign of Roosevelt, but with it came a blow to Prohibition. Delegates showed far more concern over this than over unemployment; they had been torn apart by the liquor issue during the 1920s and were determined it would not happen again. Most newspapermen of the time, including Mencken, believed the chief significance of the conventions rested upon this probable outcome.

How the resolutions committee threw out a wishy-washy plank against Prohibition and substituted one flatly for repeal, Mencken later said, deserved to be ranked as one of the great dramas of American politics. It was not until one o'clock in the morning that, for all practical purposes, Prohibition died. After this, the nomination for president began. "All the brethren in the press stand, like the delegates on the floor, were dripping with perspiration," Mencken wrote. "As for me, my seersucker suit came to resemble a bathing suit, and my necktie took on the appearance of having been fried."

At three o'clock in the morning a violent thunderstorm broke, and a cool breeze swept through the hall as the last of the nominating speeches finally ended. The remaining delegates were ready to go home, but Roosevelt's managers, anxious to begin the balloting, launched the process at 4:27 a.m. Mencken enjoyed every minute of it, chewing a burnt-out cigar at the press table, pounding out copy with his glasses halfway down his nose. At seven o'clock he went out for breakfast, and as he ate hamburgers in the company of Walter Lippmann, they wondered when the whole thing would be over. The delegates, however, did not adjourn until 9:15 that morning, as politicians worked frantically to line up additional votes to put their candidate over the top.

Roosevelt rushed to Chicago by air to accept the nomination—the first nominee in American history to do so on the spot. The moment when, in his mellifluous tenor, he bellowed the magic word "beer," the whole convention hall rose and cheered. And Mencken? "I laughed for hours on end."[3]

By the time Mencken returned to New York, Knopf had convinced him to reprint his convention articles as a book, to be called *Making a President*. Knopf believed it would show Mencken's reporting at its best, exhibiting a vigorous style and shrewd intelligence that needed to be preserved beyond the pages of a newspaper. The book was originally intended as first in a series that would come out at four-year intervals, covering each of the national conventions. Upon his publisher's insistence, he performed a cut-and-paste job in record time, finishing the project within thirty-six hours.

As soon as the book was released, Mencken recognized its defects. *Making a President* proved to be a dismal failure (fewer than 2,000 copies sold), convincing Mencken he should never do anything like it again. As for the subject in question, Roosevelt wrote Knopf he was delighted with the little book, "as I happen to know Mr. Mencken very well." When Knopf proudly displayed his letter, Mencken was unimpressed. Instead, he wondered at his publisher's naiveté. As early as 1920, Mencken had called Roosevelt an ass and accused him of losing the Democratic nomination for Al Smith; as a reporter who had covered many contenders, Mencken well knew a politician would say just about anything to get elected.[4]

Nonetheless, by Election Day, Mencken joined millions of others in casting his vote for the Democrat. When the results swept Roosevelt to stunning victory, the outcome made Mencken feel "almost ashamed." After years of Mencken's voting for the underdog, Roosevelt was "the first candidate of my choice ever to win," capturing every state south and west of Pennsylvania. By contrast, Hoover held only six states. Save for 1912, no Republican candidate had ever been defeated so badly.

Part of Hoover's defeat, Mencken observed at the time, was not only "his long and preposterous efforts to deny that there was any Depression," but "his almost incredibly incompetent dealing with Prohibition. He was too stupid to see that the vast majority of people were sick of it."[5]

Prohibition of hard liquor actually came to an end much later. Before that could happen, Roosevelt knew the repeal amendment would take months for its final passage in Congress. On the other hand, the president knew all that was needed to bring back beer was one simple revision: to legalize the sale of beverages containing no more than 3.2 percent of alcohol and make the shift from "near beer" to the real thing. In keeping with his promise to move the nation forward, Roosevelt made an impression Hoover had never been able to create: of a man who knew how to lead. In one simple act, the official return to sanity was set for April 7, 1933.

As the date approached, it seemed as if the entire eastern seaboard wanted Mencken's opinion regarding the return of legal beer. Mencken insisted the real hero of the hour was the nation's press, who alone among public agencies refused to accept the law. Many more, however, recognized that when it came to beating an incessant drum against corruption, whether it had been in the pages of the *Smart Set*, the *American Mercury*, or the *Evening Sun*, no reporter had worked harder than Mencken to bring about Prohibition's end.

In a train stop between Baltimore and New York, a reporter for the *Philadelphia Record* nabbed Mencken for an interview. Beer signified the return of joy, the editor of the *American Mercury* announced, it inspired song as well as story. He hailed the new administration's accomplishment. "Under the leadership of a personable, attractive and forceful man," Mencken said, "we have cast off the cursed yoke imposed by a parcel of umbrella-brandishing halitotic harridans who forced the standards of Goosetown and Waterville, Ohio upon New York, Chicago, Philadelphia and Union Hill, New Jersey."

Boarding the train, Mencken cocked his cigar at a defiant angle, jammed his derby over his ears, and winked a blue eye. "If you can't stand up to the bar," he demanded, "how the hell are you to toss the bartender for the drinks?"[6]

ONE MONTH LATER, at midnight on April 7, 1933, the Anheuser-Busch clock in Times Square in Manhattan chimed "Happy Days Are Here Again." In Washington, a big truck, gay with festoons, rumbled to the service entrance of the White House, bearing two cases: a brewer's gift to the president.

Throughout the United States rang the discordant din of cheers and singing, as parched throats drank an estimated 1,500,000 barrels of beer within 24 hours.

> *Take me down, down down*
> *Where the brown lager flows;*
> *It goes down, down, down, but*
> *nobody knows!*

Mencken had arrived in a gala mood at Baltimore's Rennert Hotel on the invitation of its manager, who wanted to have the honor of serving the very first draught to the Baltimore journalist whose untiring attacks on Prohibition were legendary. For his part, Mencken promised to down it to the glory of God.

At 11:59 p.m., as the fated hour grew near, the bartender began manipulating the newly fitted ebony spigots at the old mahogany counter. As soon as the liquid foamed forth from the knobs, the crowd gave a whoop. Outside the window auto horns blared. Hundreds jostled close as the first glass drawn was ceremoniously handed over to Mencken. Many of those assembled shared the

"Not bad at all. Fill it again." The legalization of beer, April 1933. H. L. Mencken Collection, Enoch Pratt Free Library.

Such fuss over 3.2 ?

sentiment of one young Johns Hopkins student, who later said he had gone to the Rennert bar just to see history being made.

"Here it goes!" announced Mencken, his eyes dancing to the battery of flashbulbs as photographers captured the moment. "*Prosit!*" "*Skol!*" "Down the hatch!" echoed the throng. There was a moment of apprehensive silence as Mencken bent his elbow, tilted his head back, and drained the contents in practically one gulp. Then came a collective sigh as Mencken grinned. "Pretty good, not bad at all," he pronounced. "Fill it again."

Privately, Mencken admitted the Rennert brew had actually been "a sad hogwash." To get rid of the taste, he later washed down several Piel's *Dunklas*, a magnificent dark beer that happily restored him to a state of optimism. But he agreed with the universal declaration that no New Year's Eve celebration ever equaled that glorious night. Not one arrest for drunkenness was made for the first time in years. It was, Mencken asserted, "an epochal event in the onward march of humanity. It is perhaps the first time in history that any of the essential liberties of man has been gained without the wholesale emission of blood."[7]

36

MARYLAND, MY MARYLAND

THE END OF PROHIBITION, Mencken asserted, may have brought with it the renewal of civil liberty, but many individuals' rights still were being trampled. The difficulties of the Depression and the rise of fascism in Europe had encouraged white supremacists in the United States. Throughout the 1930s, the Klan regrouped and public lynching increased as these atrocities continued to go unpunished.

The lynching of Matthew Williams in Salisbury, Maryland, spurred Mencken's continuing battle for civil rights through a responsible press. For the next four years, Mencken aggressively assisted the NAACP in forging a growing movement of opposition to lynching.

IN DECEMBER 1931, Williams, a 35-year-old African American, had shot and killed his employer in his factory office in Salisbury. Williams fled, but not before the employer's son shot him in the head. That evening, a bulletin was posted on the front of the *Salisbury Times*.

> The nigger who murdered Mr. Elliott, a prominent citizen, has been reported as being dead.

"Ain't that a damn shame that nigger died so soon," one bystander remarked. "There was going to be some fun here tonight." No sooner was it said when another notice was posted, announcing that Matthew Williams was not dead, but in fact recovering in a local hospital. Cries of "Lynch Williams!" erupted, as white men entered the hospital in search of the suspect. "If you must take him," said the superintendent nurse, "do it quietly."

Williams was pulled from his cot, pushed out the first-floor window and dragged, blindfolded, several blocks to Courthouse Square. A schoolboy climbed a tree and dropped a rope over a limb. A noose was tied around Williams's neck and he was hoisted fifteen feet into the air. Three times the body was dropped to the ground; three times it was jerked back. "Pull him up, boys!" cried one man to the cheers of two thousand onlookers, including women and children. After the corpse had dangled in the air for twenty minutes, the mob hauled Williams's body to a vacant lot at the edge of town. There it was tied to a telephone pole, doused with gasoline, and ignited. The stench of burning flesh drove some of the onlookers away, but not all. One member of the mob cut off several of Williams's toes and carried them off as souvenirs.

It was the first lynching the state had witnessed in twenty years. The local townspeople celebrated the occasion by draping the tree with an American flag.[1]

Mencken's reaction was immediate. It revolted him that no one had done anything to stop Williams's murder. Equally disturbing was what Mencken perceived as the cowardice of some of the local press. The managing editor of the *Salisbury Times*, to cool off the explosive atmosphere, decided to play down details of the murder. Repetition of the "demonstration" would be "superfluous," the newspaper stated. The slaying of Mr. Elliott was "deplorable, as was also the mob scene," but readers were warned to "pay little heed to the overdrawn pictures that will be painted by the metropolitan newspapers whose only purpose is . . . to increase their own circulation."

Half a century later, managing editor Charles Truitt still thought his decision the right one. "Unless you've been through a thing like that, you can't comprehend what it's like," he said shortly before his death in 1982. "When you see people ready to do anything, follow any suggestion that's made to them, you know you'd better be careful or you'll upset the whole community."

The decision produced a storm of criticism of which Mencken's was the fiercest. In his column, "The Eastern Shore Kultur," he singled out the *Salisbury Times* and the *Cambridge Daily Banner* as prime examples of a "degenerating process" that had been undermining the region for years. The *Banner* had criticized the lynching "formally, but only formally," Mencken scoffed.

The Eastern Shore, Mencken went on, was being run by "its poor white trash" who still accepted the "brutish imbecilities" of the Ku Klux Klan. Mentally and morally, "it has been sliding out of Maryland and into the orbit of Arkansas and Tennessee, Mississippi and the more flea-bitten half of Virginia." And he thundered: "Certainly it would be irrational to ask for enlightenment in communities whose ideas are supplied by such pathetic sheets as the *Cambridge Daily Banner* and the *Salisbury Times*."

Sunpapers cartoonist Edmund Duffy drew an image of the lynching to accompany Mencken's article on the *Evening Sun*'s editorial page, ironically

"Maryland, My Maryland." Pulitzer-winning cartoon by Edmund Duffy. Courtesy Sara Anne Duffy Chermayeff and the H. L. Mencken Collection, Enoch Pratt Free Library.

captioning his cartoon with words of the state anthem, "Maryland, My Maryland." Duffy's cartoon incited vicious attacks on Mencken and himself by the *Worcester Democrat* of Pocomoke City, Maryland, accusing them of being "jealous" because they had not gotten to "enjoy" the lynching. Mencken reprinted extracts in his subsequent column. "They serve very well," he said, "to show what effect the lynching spirit, if it is allowed to go unchecked, has upon the minds of simple people—even among the more literate minority thereof." He wrote:

> The question before the house is thus quite simple. It is whether the Salisbury lynchers will be permitted to escape punishment for their crime, and so inspire a long series of like atrocities among similar town boomers, or whether the decent people of the lower Shore will band themselves together effectively and see that the guilty are brought to heel. Every schoolboy in Salisbury knows who was in the mob. The names of those who dragged the victim from the hospital, blind and helpless, are known, and so is the name of the hero who made off with the souvenir toes. The leaders are on public display at this moment, bathed in moron admiration. . . . The sole question to be determined is whether the civilized people of Maryland will permit such crimes to be perpetrated with impunity.[2]

Within 48 hours, orders from the city's retailers worth over $148,000 were cancelled by Salisbury businesses. Other cities on the Eastern Shore followed suit. As the 1931 Christmas season approached, many Eastern Shore residents began shopping in Wilmington, Delaware, instead of Baltimore. The *Sunpapers* were burned or thrown in the streets before they could be placed on sale. Trucks carried placards proclaiming,

I Am An

EASTERN SHOREMAN

And Proud of It

Alarmed, the executive committee of the Baltimore Association of Commerce spoke glowingly of the ties between Baltimore and the Eastern Shore. A number of businesses joined in the appeal, including the Western Newspaper Union: "Please do not judge the people of Baltimore by what appears in the *Baltimore Sun*. The *Sun* is being condemned on all sides by the people of this city, who feel that Mencken's article was a most disgraceful attack on one of the finest sections of the State."

The boycott went on for weeks. The editor of the *Easton Journal* advised Mencken not to set foot in the Eastern Shore "for the next 20 years. In Salisbury, at least, they'd rather lynch you," warning that *his* toes, and perhaps *his* ears, might be taken as souvenirs. The *Sunpapers'* office was besieged with complaints. One reader took the *Sun* to task for printing a paper that was not even fit for his outhouse, adding: "neither of you know anything about the shore and still less of the lynching of the nigger." The letter was just one example of the bundles received, which Mencken preserved "as illustrative of the state of civilization on the Eastern Shore of Maryland in 1931."

If Mencken had lost his following among many white voters at this time, he had, by his stand on racial issues, strengthened his hold with his black audience. George Schuyler of the *Pittsburgh Courier* said Mencken and the *Sun* "had guts." Clarence Mitchell of the NAACP in Washington repeatedly told his sons that

"Mencken is on the side of the black man." In 1931, the *Nation* magazine gave Mencken an award for distinguished journalism in the face of personal danger. When it came to the race question, Mencken declared to an African American audience, "If everybody could see the Southern Cracker as he really is, they could understand lynching. He is the lowest type of humanity in America."[3]

BY 1933, ROOSEVELT'S REFUSAL to speak out on the most recent atrocity on Maryland's Eastern Shore was a matter of discussion throughout the country. In Baltimore, African Americans began to look to Mencken to help them. It was clear to Mencken that the federal government had to adopt an official stance against these crimes and inflict heavy penalties that would make it "crystal clear" that lynching "is murder plain and unadulterated." Determined that this outrage not be dismissed, Mencken joined forces with Clarence Mitchell to promote the Costigan-Wagner Anti-Lynching Bill that would make lynchings and attempted lynchings federal offenses. The bill was endorsed by a long list of mayors, governors, clergy, writers, artists, and college presidents, as well as other organizations.

While Mencken had serious doubts about the efficacy of the bill, he nonetheless wanted to see it passed—if only, as he confided to Henry Hyde of the *Sun* Washington Bureau, because "it would put good Franklin [Roosevelt] on the spot." But as time passed, Mencken's confidence in the bill's passage waned. He felt that congressional hearings would be "a vain battle of mere opinion" by a series of "bogus experts," including himself. Moreover, there was little that Mencken could do to make sure that the bill would not die. With his flair for drama, Mencken proposed an idea that would ensure publicity and jolt the president into action. It was to put on what surgeons at Johns Hopkins Medical School called a clinic. "The best way to show the need of this bill will be to show how all State agencies failed in the case of the two lynchings in Maryland." When this was rejected, Mencken counseled the NAACP how to achieve the maximum impact for the cause in the nation's newspapers, writing letters to white and black journalists himself.

NAACP leader Walter White believed the bill would pass if the president supported it. Predictably, Roosevelt refused to challenge the Southern leadership of his party. "If I come out for the anti-lynching bill now, they will block every bill [needed] to keep America from collapsing," he said. Congress adjourned without considering the bill, and despite the repeated pleas from the NAACP, the president did nothing to advance it.

Mencken outlined his own views in the *Crisis* magazine. The fight for constitutional rights must continue, he said; the Negro could not afford to submit. Although Mencken doubted that Negro civil rights would be achieved in any near tomorrow, he expressed "my private hope is that he will get them soon or late, for the only future I can endure to think of is one which no man will lack what he reasonably wants, and can show that he deserves."[4]

A new hearing on the Costigan-Wagner Bill finally took place before a Senate Judiciary Subcommittee on February 14, 1935. Mencken was the only writer to testify (others supported the bill by the usual telegrams). The fact that he was doing so under trying personal circumstances, while Sara was ill, was a testament to how passionately he felt about the issue. In a caucus room filled with spectators of all races and colors, Mencken urged the government to take action and "make every possible effort" to stop lynchings. "The chief virtue of the bill, as I see it, is that it does not try to set up lynching as a new crime and provide new penalties for it," Mencken told the committee. "It presumes lynching is murder, which is precisely what it is, and it punishes it as such."

Mencken's words seemed to have galvanized the subcommittee. After Mencken's appearance, subcommittee chairman Frederick Van Nuys of Indiana predicted that the bill would pass, but his testimony also prompted a new wave of hate mail. "If you think a Negro's life is equivalent to yours, most of us *white* people do not," one man wrote to Mencken. "Most of us wish you would sail for Africa or Germany or some other place, where you may find more congenial companionship and environment."

Organizations whose total membership numbered more than fifty million people sent telegrams to the White House. But Southern senators continued to argue that lynching was a historically sanctioned tradition, protected by state's rights. President Roosevelt, ever sensitive to his Southern state supporters, remained silent. The Costigan-Wagner Anti-Lynching Bill died as the Senate voted to adjourn.

The end to lynching, Mencken believed, lay in new leaders, black and white—"leaders who want nothing, and have nothing to sell. I believe that wherever and whenever such a leader bobs up in rural America, whether North or South, East or West, he will meet with a very hearty response, and have a lot of fun. And if he is lucky he may also achieve some good."

When it came to better relations between the races, Mencken insisted that "it is impossible to separate one group from the other." Failing that, however, Mencken could see only trouble ahead.[5]

37

THE TUNE CHANGES

OF ALL MENCKEN'S CONTROVERSIAL VIEWS, what most alienated liberals closest to him, and especially Jewish Americans, was his seeming blindness to the rise of Adolf Hitler, the Nazi party, and anti-Semitism in his beloved Germany.

In 1933, when Hitler became chancellor of Germany, he was largely dismissed as not representing a peril to anyone. The *London Daily Herald* described him as "a stubby little Austrian with a flabby handshake, shifty brown eyes, and a Charlie Chaplin moustache." Mencken, likewise at first, thought Hitler little more than "a clown," and he commented with the same flippancy that he had displayed toward other "fools" not to be taken seriously: "Certainly a man who wears a Charlie Chaplin moustache can't be altogether bad."

Journalist William Shirer proclaimed after the 1934 Nuremberg rally that the West in general and "our newspapers above all had underestimated Adolf Hitler." Of the stories on the German situation that were written at that time, only a few focused on the persecution of the Jews. The majority of American newspapers concentrated on the violence perpetuated by Storm Troopers against socialists and communists. Many papers and magazines, among them the *Chicago Tribune*, the *Baltimore Sunpapers*, and the *Los Angeles Times*, labeled early reports of persecution wild rumors, convinced that the "amazing tales of oppression" were either exaggerated or incorrect.

Such was the atmosphere of disbelief when in early 1933 Blanche Knopf approached Mencken about a book proposal that had been submitted to her on the history of Jewish persecution "from B.C. to the present performance."

Mencken replied that such a topic would "fill volumes and require a lifetime of investigation . . . incidentally, I note by the *Sun* of this morning that the slaughter of Jews in Germany is imaginary. In fact, the leading Jewish organizations of the country say so."

Mencken remained convinced that a leading cause of anti-Semitism had been the "shrill" complaints of it by the Jews themselves. As already noted, Mencken applied the same line of reasoning to his German American friends, telling them that the best way to stir up anti-German feeling in the United States was for them to raise their voices. Rather unfairly, Mencken refused to recognize that Rabbi Stephen Wise's role as chairman of the American Jewish Congress obliged him to sound the alarm about Germany's persecution of the Jews. In this, however, Mencken again was not alone. From the press to President Roosevelt in the White House, many Americans continued to have doubts about the rabbi's claims.

Moreover, Mencken's own experience in Berlin during 1917 convinced him that American reporters, with minor exceptions, were little more than mouthpieces for the London War Office; he felt justified in dismissing the American correspondents in Germany as biased and fraudulent. He gave more credence to reports from Stephen Miles Bouton, the Berlin correspondent for the *New York World* and the *New York Times*, whose article, "False News from Germany," had been published in the September 1932 issue of the *American Mercury*.

The general disbelief in the persecution of Jews in Germany rested also on the laudatory reports of some American tourists. Impressed by the cleanliness and low unemployment in Germany, and by the seeming politeness of Nazis they met, they denied that anything unusual was happening. The *Nation* complained that it was "difficult to restrain the silly people who after a week or two in Germany, during which they have seen no Jews beaten up in the streets, go back to their own countries and declare that the stories told in Germany are all untrue." Mencken, too, was receiving positive accounts from friends in Baltimore.

Other visitors to Germany, however, had a very different view of the Nazi regime. Philip Goodman had moved to Europe for an extended stay after he lost a considerable fortune in 1929 producing the musical *Rainbow*, a dreadful failure. Now he was barely surviving, living in inexpensive *pensiones* and, according to his daughter Ruth, feeling at sea.

Mencken felt sure Hitler would be "bumped off very quickly. The fellow is plainly pathological," but he qualified his criticism with a virtual apology for the Nazi leader's program: "Hitler seems to me to be a shabby ass, but I can well understand why so many Germans are supporting him in the present situation. He is at least against the idiotic internationalism that has kept Germany impotent since the war, and equally against the corruption that the post-war movement toward the Left introduced into German internal policies." When Goodman disagreed, Mencken wrote: "Your mercurial disposition leaves me gaping: three months ago you were filling the mails with arguments to the effect that Germany was the only civilized country in the world, and urging me to abandon my American citizenship and settle down at Wurzburg. Then a few Jews had their *doki* [behinds] bumped, and now you are arguing that Germany is unfit to live in, that the Germans are all maniacs, and that their country is about to be partitioned by the Poles. Rabbi Stephen Wise himself has gone no further."

Goodman finally became so fed up with Mencken's defense of Hitler's Germany that he wrote him point by point replies. Goodman's daughter Ruth recalled: "He showed them to me before mailing them, and I saw Henry's answers when they came. He defended himself savagely against my father's assaults, saying as best I can remember it that '*rentiers*' who live in Europe without any '*rent*' were hardly in a position to judge how honest taxpayers felt about the excesses of the Roosevelt administration and his speeches against Hitler. That letter did it. After twenty-five years of almost daily exchange the friendship was over." Goodman told Ruth: "Henry's just a clown."

Upon Goodman's return to the United States in the autumn of 1933, he met with Mencken for the last time at a New York sidewalk café on lower Fifth Avenue. Again he tried to convince his friend of what he had witnessed but found an unsympathetic ear. August Mencken later recalled that "my brother told me that listening to Goodman's opinions about Hitler and his doings for a whole evening was more than he could stand." A considerably offended Goodman repeatedly complained to his family about "that crazy son-of-a-bitch Mencken."

Mencken admitted that "the termination of my pleasant relations with Goodman must be laid to Hitler. When the first laws against the Jews were promulgated in Germany he was staggered, for, as I have said, he had always been in love with all things German. So far I could hardly blame him, but when he started bombarding me with letters denouncing the Germans as fiends in human form, going back into history for evidence of it, I began to suspect that the troubles of the time had somewhat addled his wits, and when he announced that he had become a Communist I was sure of it. After that our correspondence naturally languished, and in the end I suggested to him that we had better suspend it." Mencken said Goodman "began ranting like any other hysterical Jew, so I stopped seeing him."

It was not a step he took lightly. During the period Goodman was abroad, Mencken had written to him, "It is a literal fact that New York seems desolate without you." No one else was fit to drink with; their favorite watering holes in Hoboken and Union Hill, New Jersey, were Goodman's discoveries. Nor could Mencken forget that Goodman, whose chief interest besides theater was philology, had spent a month annotating the first edition of *The American Language*, saving Mencken from blunders.

The break affected Mencken more deeply than he let on. August Mencken confirmed how "greatly hurt" his brother had been when "Goodman started denouncing him as a Nazi." Mencken, who in the 1920s joked with Goodman about recently arrived Eastern European Jewish immigrants, now suddenly felt betrayed. Most of Mencken's Jewish friends had been German Jews—Goodman, Knopf, Untermeyer, Nathan—a fact that colored his attitude. Gertrude, whose own correspondence showed streaks of anti-Semitism, said that although Mencken disliked Jews as a race, he still liked certain Jewish individuals. For that matter, the same could be said about Mencken's attitude toward the British and many other nationalities. But of all ethnic or religious groups, Mencken seemed to be most fascinated by Jews.

Goodman was more vocal in his feelings about the termination of the friendship. According to Ruth Goodman, the entire family "would discuss Mencken's anti-Semitism around the dinner table, *ad nauseum*." How could a man who expressed an admiration for Jewish culture, language, politics, and cuisine, who had praised Jews to be vastly more civilized and more honest, who asserted that "some of the most intelligent people in America are Jewish, and not only some of the most intelligent, but also some of the most charming," at the same time speak so disparagingly of them? Ruth admitted that "no one could figure him out."[1]

Mencken's readers were equally distressed. Many Baltimoreans wrote the *Sunpapers* asking why he did not speak out against Hitler. "A man with a gifted pen," one man charged, "and does not use it to fight the powers of darkness and savage barbarism is not a friend of humanity." Mencken retorted: "What makes you believe that I am 'a friend of humanity'? As a matter of fact, I believe that humanity well deserves to be blown to hell." If letter writers to the *Sun* had let him alone, he later admitted, "I might have said in print . . . what I had already said [in private], but in the face of their attempt to browbeat me I could only refuse to write a line." Mencken did insist, however, that the *Sunpapers* publish the letters that denounced him as a Nazi and anti-Semite.

Mencken did on occasion express rejection of Adolf Hitler and the Nazis. One of the first pro-Nazi societies in the United States was called Friends of Germany. When its leader, Col. Edwin Emerson, awarded Mencken honorary membership, he rejected the offer outright. "By talking and acting in a completely lunatic manner," Mencken wrote Emerson, "Hitler and his associates have thrown away the German case and given the enemies of their country enough ammunition to last for ten years." Any defense of Germany was impossible "so long as the chief officer of the German state continues to make speeches worthy of an Imperial Wizard of the Ku Klux Klan, and his followers imitate, plainly with his connivance, the monkey-shines of the American Legion at its worst."

At the same time, Mencken was preoccupied with the treatment of Germans in the United States, as he complained to Dr. Walther Fischer in Germany:

> I have been greatly distressed by the reappearance of violent anti-Semitic feeling in the United States. The idiotic speeches made by some of the German politicians have been a God-send to the surviving anti-Germans of the war days, and they have made adept use of them.

Mencken's silence was entirely consistent with his demeanor during the years of the First World War. Few Americans not of German heritage would have understood or remembered the trauma German Americans had undergone during that period, the inner martyrdom described in memoirs and interviews published long after the war. Since that time the quiet submersion of German America had proceeded virtually unchecked.[2]

THE ISSUE OF NAZISM would dog Mencken as long as the German chancellor remained in power. When he did write about the subject, it led to such heated arguments with Alfred Knopf that he eventually decided he would not write about Germany or Hitler again. Mencken was in Baltimore when Knopf began looking over the proofs of the final issue of the *American Mercury*. In the "Library" column, Mencken had reviewed five of what promised to be a long procession of Hitler books. The translated and abridged edition of *Mein Kampf*, entitled *My Battle* and published by Houghton-Mifflin—and at the time the only translation available in the United States—had sanitized its more vitriolic references to the Jews. This was unfortunate. According to William Shirer and journalist (and later senator) Alan Cranston, Hitler set down the anti-Semitic blueprint of the Third Reich in the original edition in appalling crudity and detail.

By relying on the material from the abridged edition, Mencken's review from the start was destined to be distorted. He recognized that much of Hitler's success was due to his extraordinary talent as a mob orator, and that what he said was "often absurd." This was, however, as far as Mencken would go in criticism of the man. As for Hitler's anti-Semitism, Mencken like so many others at the time failed to recognize that it was a fundamental element of Nazism. Instead, he said that the Nazi view of Jews was hardly a surprise, for such hatred was latent all over Western Europe.

In his review of *Mein Kampf*, Mencken criticized the harassment, intimidation and murder of "perfectly innocent and helpless people, some of them Jews," though he added probably more of them had been Christians. While these actions were "certainly not creditable to the German people, nor indeed to the human race in general," the main question was "how long the orgy will last, and whether it will wear itself out or have to be put out by external force." Boycotts were not the answer, Mencken believed, for such action would only serve to strengthen Hitler, not weaken him, in his own country.

Mencken felt it was inevitable there would be another world war, though he clung to faith in the ultimate intelligence of the German people that Hitler would go the way of so many other former leaders in other countries, such as William Jennings Bryan, whose "following had shrunk to a feeble rabble of half-wits," and Lloyd George, who today "bosses only himself."

That was the extent of Mencken's denunciation of Hitlerism. His opinion was typical of the division in the press between reporters stationed inside

Germany, who tended to be severe in their evaluation of the Nazis, and and commentators studying the German situation from afar, who were generally lenient in their judgments.

Alfred Knopf was especially sensitive to reports from abroad. He had visited Munich himself and subsequent conversations with friends returning from Europe intensified his concern. Protesting to Mencken that his review of *Mein Kampf* was "just not worthy of you," Knopf argued: "You simply can't make such a statement as you do about its being unimportant if the American edition suppresses the worst of Hitler's notions, without a great deal of elaborate support."

Mencken heatedly defended his review: "If any customer takes it for a defense of Hitler, then I can only say that I must give up trying to write plain English. It is actually an attempt to disentangle the facts from the blah of both sides, and present them as objectively as possible." It was the last dispute Mencken and Knopf would have about editorial matters in the magazine.

Unlike Philip Goodman, however, never once did Knopf view any of Mencken's comments as indications of anti-Semitism, nor that Mencken had sympathy for the German Nazis. Knopf denied that he and Mencken had ever argued about the subject; instead, he would continue to view Mencken as "a dearly beloved friend." Yet, the accusation of anti-Semitism seemed to make Mencken uncharacteristically tense. For all his professed refusal to be intimidated, he made sure to change the wording in certain columns and even in casual conversation to avoid offending Jewish critics.

As Hamilton Owens recalled,

> I remember that one day he came into the office and quite seriously asked, "Hamilton, you don't believe that I am a Nazi or anti-Semitic, do you?" Reassured, he made one of the frankest concessions of his faith I ever heard from him. "I believe," he said in effect, "in only one thing and that is human liberty. If ever a man is to achieve anything like dignity, it can happen only if superior men are given absolute freedom to think what they want to think and say what they want to say. I am against any man and any organization which seeks to limit or deny that freedom." I made the obvious comment, that he seemed to limit freedom to superior men. His reply was simple, to the effect that the superior man can be sure of freedom only if it is given to all men. So far as my observation goes, that little exchange gets close to the core of the Mencken philosophy.[3]

38

THE LATE MR. MENCKEN

M R. CROWNINSHIELD SAYS Mencken has ceased to interest anybody," managing editor Clare Boothe Luce jotted in her notepad after a 1933 editorial meeting at *Vanity Fair*. More historians began referring to Mencken in the past tense, as "The Late Mr. Mencken."[1]

With the lessening of Mencken's influence came the further decline of the *American Mercury*, as evident in February that year, when Knopf shared with Mencken the figures for the previous year. Circulation had hit a new low. So had the income from advertising. Unfortunately, this was at a time when Knopf's other revenues were enormously diminished. Then there was the matter of editorial costs; after developing authors at great pains, Mencken had lost them to *Harper's* and *Scribner's*, which paid more than the *Mercury* budget allowed. Meanwhile, for a second time during the Depression, office salaries were slashed, while Mencken's own expenses went unabated.

Looking back at this period, Alfred Knopf reflected:

A really shrewd publisher and editor would have said, "This is the end of the chapter, let's call it a day and quit." The times began to be clearly out of joint for the kind of thing Mencken was interested in doing. Basically I have always felt that his battles had been won. Censorship had been laid pretty low; writing talents had been developed and found plenty of elbow room; it was pretty hard to imagine any American writer going through what Theodore Dreiser had gone through earlier. The political scene, though, was quite different. There wasn't the same kind of younger generation at all, eager to read the sort of thing Mencken was feeding.

"This is like that awful afternoon we telephoned Mencken."

Cartoon by James Thurber in *The New Yorker*, May 5, 1934. Copyright © 1943 James Thurber. Copyright © 1971 Rosemary A. Thurber. From *Men, Women and Dogs*, published by Harcourt Brace. Used with special permission of the James Thurber Literary Estate.

But despite this, Mencken was devoting more time and energy to the magazine than ever. By his own account, he never gave less than five hours a day to it and sometimes as much as twelve, seven days a week, all year round. Mencken's efforts to vary the general contents of the *American Mercury* led Blanche Knopf to comment, "I don't see how anyone can seriously maintain that the magazine isn't as good as it ever was." There had been several articles discussing the economy and unemployment, including one that discussed the death rate during the Depression. There were essays on George Bernard Shaw in Moscow, the troubles of a radical editor, and men at the bargain counter. Replacing Nathan's theater reviews was a music department. The *Mercury* continued to be popular among musicians with its analysis of new compositions, the radio, and the phonograph. Such improvements, however, as Mencken well knew, were too small to offset the larger weakness. What was needed was a general overhaul.

Sensing that her husband was working too hard with little gain, Sara once again encouraged Mencken to leave the *Mercury*. There were many reasons for him to find the idea attractive. Even with Samuel Knopf's unexpected death in 1932, Mencken continued to be at constant loggerheads with Alfred Knopf over the editorial content of the magazine. Knopf had always professed admiration for *Harper's*; now his praise went to *Fortune*, a periodical Mencken found "preposterous." Such differences naturally strained the relations between the two men. Their association had been pleasant, Mencken admitted, "until we began to hold our continuous coroner's inquest."

Eventually, after long discussion, Knopf reluctantly accepted Mencken's view that the venture had been mismanaged by his father. Samuel Knopf's fight for a large circulation and heavy general advertising had forced negative policy changes on Mencken. "I told Alfred that I thought it should be far more literary than it has been, and far less political," Mencken wrote in his diary after their meeting in 1933.

This last remark had a certain irony to it, since Mencken, against the wishes of both Knopf and Nathan, from the very first issue of the *Mercury* had made it a vehicle for political and social commentary more than literature and the other arts. Such a course proved fatal, according to Theodore Dreiser, who had warned Mencken in 1926 that Nathan's lighter touch was important to the success of the magazine. "He disagreed with me," Dreiser now reflected to Nathan, "and, of course, since he pursued his intellectual course so ponderously, the *Mercury* failed and, to a certain extent, I think, rightly."

But this was not the only reason for Mencken to resign. For the first time in his life he had begun to give serious thought to money. His income for 1932 was less than that of 1931, and in 1933 he knew that there would be an even further drop. His book royalties for one year actually declined 80 percent. Not long before, he had received generous invitations to contribute to other magazines. In all cases, because he was editor of the *American Mercury*, he was forced to say no. But "the demands for money are incessant," he told a friend. There were not only the expenses of Sara's illnesses but also college tuition for Virginia, and the $2,400 a year Mencken paid from his own pocket to run his magazine. "Mencken was a very sound businessman," affirmed William Koshland of Knopf, Inc. "After all, he was a stockholder himself and he did not want to keep losing money. He got out while the going was good."[2]

Ultimately, Henry Hazlitt was chosen by Mencken as his successor. He had been literary editor of the *Nation* but had spent most of his professional life as a financial writer. Mencken classified Hazlitt as one of the few economists who could write. Moreover, Mencken thought Hazlitt could broaden the scope of the *American Mercury*.

This early in 1933, to the public and staff alike Mencken kept up the pretense of staying on, though he had already made up his mind to quit. To encourage advertisers, Knopf had used several of the closing pages of the January 1933 number to emphasize the solvency of the periodical. Thus it was a surprise when, in June of that year, the estate of Samuel Knopf was made public. A startled industry learned that the stock in the *American Mercury* had been eliminated from the balance sheet since the shares were worth nothing. In an affidavit, Joseph C. Lesser, comptroller for the Knopf company, argued that the Depression had hit the magazine particularly hard because it was a one-man publication dependent entirely upon the popularity of its editor, and that popularity was largely reflected by what Mencken had written years before. The magazine, Lesser told the press, did not have the "ordinary chance of being revamped."

This "imbecilic statement," Mencken fumed, had been made without Knopf's knowledge while he was in Europe. It took some considerable convincing on Mencken's part to persuade Hazlitt that the *Mercury* was not going to be abandoned. Lawrence Spivak, a small, owlish, Harvard man who knew the workings of every aspect of magazine operations, was persuaded to come on board as the magazine's new business manager.

There still remained, however, the search for capital. The task of convincing investors to sink money in the financially shaky iconoclastic review was left to Mencken himself. Assuring Edwin R. Embree of the Rockefeller Foundation that there had been a profit in May and that new advertising was coming in, Mencken downplayed the magazine's losses: "Such magazines have their ups and downs, but new blood usually revives them."

Having apparently convinced Embree, Mencken left their meeting and walked out into a terrific storm. As thunder roared overhead, a bolt of lightning suddenly struck very near him. It was a cataclysmic moment, "but a fellow as pious as I am is never in any real danger," he later joked. By his own admission, Mencken had always been extraordinarily lucky. During the summer of 1933, he had every reason to feel so. With each day his spirits began to lift as his new freedom approached.[3]

AT THE *AMERICAN MERCURY*, editorial assistant Charles Angoff—shaken by pay cuts, nervous over reports of job layoffs, passionate about social issues and about what it meant to be a Jew in America—was enraged by what he saw as Mencken's contempt for the great issues of the day. The bank failures and misery had only been incidentally discussed in the *American Mercury*. There seemed, on the other hand, little purpose to articles on the monastic life, on the lowly farmer, on the passing of the locomotive, all of which made the magazine seem removed from contemporary reality.

On the cultural front, the contrast between the *Mercury* and one of the best of the literary monthlies, *Scribner's*, was strikingly obvious. Mencken failed to review books by such writers as William Faulkner, Thomas Wolfe, and John Steinbeck, authors who were then transforming the nation's literature. Indeed, Mencken was of the opinion, he told the Associated Press, that American writers continued to "labor in the literary doldrums." In the field of poetry, Mencken was likewise convinced that in its new form, "not one percent of it has any merit whatsoever," even though e. e. cummings and others had steadily gained popularity. Angoff noticed that fewer newspapers were printing comments on Mencken's editorials. Gradually he concluded that he was working for a has-been. "What does he know?" Angoff griped to members of the staff. "Mencken doesn't know anything."

Since joining the magazine, Angoff admitted to having "many and sometimes torturing doubts" about Mencken—"about his knowledge, about his professional integrity, about his whole attitude toward people." There had been a time when Angoff had been overwhelmed by Mencken's reputation and his sheer editorial skill, and grateful for having been given the chance to witness him in one of the most colorful eras in American publishing history. No one could comprehend Angoff's private grievance. "He may be the kind of person who always turns on a benefactor," August Mencken concluded.

One of Mencken's friends found Angoff "a somewhat humorless Russian who didn't know when he was being kidded." His excessive seriousness, Ruth Goodman said, combined with a loping walk, frizzy, pale-orange hair, rabbitty eyes, and a soft voice that still echoed the accents of Eastern Europe "made him the perfect goat," the kind of person whom James Cain described as "a target for some of the heavy hoaxing that both Mencken and [Philip] Goodman indulged in." Years afterward, Knopf reflected: "Henry's great mistake, of course, was exposing himself to such a fellow while at the same time regarding him essentially as his slave. Slaves have a way of turning ultimately on their masters."

Edith Lustgarten, Mencken's secretary at the *Mercury*, was aware that despite Angoff's growing antagonism, Mencken continued to be very thoughtful to his young assistant. He encouraged Angoff's proposed history of American literature and promoted the project to Knopf, though he found Angoff's writing "hopeless" and his ideas "uncatholic and dull." Nevertheless, Mencken saw to it that eleven articles by Angoff were printed in the *American Mercury* while he was editor.

Mencken recognized and appreciated Angoff as a diligent managing editor, and he so informed Alfred Knopf and others. "He was very sure he had chosen a good man," commented one acquaintance. Mencken often spoke kindly of "my boy, Angoff" and worried that the young man was driving himself too hard. "Don't you want a holiday?" he would ask his assistant.

If Angoff's account is to be believed, Mencken was genuinely embarrassed by the pay cuts that Knopf had forced on the staff, seeing them as a shabby penalty afflicted on workers who deserved better. That March, Mencken had drawn up a contract that would make Angoff a co-editor of *A New Dictionary of Quotations* with a share in its profits. Edith Lustgarten, who would watch the editor and his assistant going off for lunch together, later commented: "My feeling always was that Angoff should have been *grateful* working for this man."[4]

Whatever Angoff's former attachment to Mencken, by the mid-1930s it was no more. Years later, Angoff blamed the anti-Semitic ideas Mencken harbored "without fully knowing he did so" and credited his later hatred of Mencken to his calm indifference to Nazism in Germany.

Angoff's self-analysis told only half the story. In his autobiographical novel *Summer Storm*, he expressed his anger at "having wasted" so many years of his life. Until September 1933, Angoff was not sure if the rumors of Mencken's resignation were true. But if they were, Angoff was certain that Knopf (with whom he felt allied by ties of religion) had some plan for his future once Mencken departed. When this was not the case, it came as a severe blow to his pride. In his vanity, Angoff had not foreseen that Mencken and Knopf viewed him as a useful subordinate only, and nothing more. Lawrence Spivak remembered that "when Mencken got Henry Hazlitt to be editor of the *American Mercury*, it *infuriated* Angoff," who had expected to be given the post.

Mencken, in fact, had saved Angoff's job by interceding with Knopf, and spoke of him unreservedly to his successor, Hazlitt, as a hard worker and "completely loyal." Mencken wrote thanking Angoff for his years of excellent performance. Angoff sent a simple note to Baltimore that only further deluded Mencken into believing the young man's devotion. "It is difficult for me to write to you everything that I want to write," Angoff said. "All I can say at present is that I reciprocate your feelings twice over. I shall never forget our nine years together on the magazine."

Friends suggested to Angoff that he "cut loose" and "write something against Mencken." While Angoff remained resentful at his situation, for the time being he remained silent, brooding darkly about the one man to whom he acknowledged he owed so much.[5]

In December 1933, in this atmosphere of unease in his personal relations, Mencken's twenty years in the field of magazines came to an end. It would not be easy to think of the *American Mercury* without him. Many in the literary world felt they were witnessing a historic parting.

Nathan's *American Spectator* sounded a different albeit more popular note. In what seemed a veiled reference to Mencken's book review of *Mein Kampf*, the magazine stated: "It was most fitting that his last pieces were contributed to an ideologically bankrupt American Mercury and that intellectual hari-kari found him there." Yet, as the weeks wound down, Knopf assured Mencken that his old *Mercury* customers "are going to miss you more than you think." In its notice, *Time* predicted the same reaction: the *American Mercury* without Mencken was like imagining a highball without whiskey.

Knopf harbored some doubt as to whether the new editor could carry on the magazine. Where Mencken was clownish and blatant, Hazlitt was grave and austere. Hazlitt assured his readers that in its new incarnation, attuned to the more somber times of the 1930s, the *American Mercury* "will not be devoted merely to the entertainment of its readers; it cannot pretend to be aloof and complacent when 10,000,000 Americans are unable to find work." At the same time, in a direct departure from Mencken's brash irreverence, the young editor said he did not believe that the major social, political, and economic evils of the day were inherently incurable.

Hazlitt, however, was unable to rekindle the Mencken spark. Few readers decided to stay with the periodical, and after only four months Hazlitt was replaced. It remained Knopf's firm belief that "once Hazlitt gave up the active editorship, "we should have closed it down."

The night before Mencken's official resignation, he received reporters at the *American Mercury*. He announced a series of literary projects. He spoke with anticipatory zest, chuckling often and contagiously, treating his retirement like a long-awaited adventure for which vast stores of energy had been hoarded through the years. "All my books," he said, "with the exception of one or two, have been made up of mere magazine material. This has been a job, a daily job, here at this office." Now, he said, "I'm going to have a chance to be *mobile*."

Last, there was *The American Language*. "I have enough material to fill that couch," he said, pointing to a large divan in the library. He had been amazed by the response that greeted the previous edition; "That work I'm keenly interested in—tremendously interested in."

There was also his column in the *Evening Sun*. "There are lots of things happening all the time," he said with eagerness, "that I like to write about when they're happening. For a magazine, you know, what you really do is write a book hurriedly, trying at the same time to foresee what will have happened by the time the issue gets out. It's ghastly. As a matter of fact, I'll probably do more news-paper writing than I've done in some years."

Sara awaited him in her Victorian parlor of gold brocade in Baltimore, which replaced 730 Fifth Avenue in New York as Mencken's new headquarters. "There is no twilight of the gods in Cathedral Street," commented one newspaperman. It may have been the end of an era, but no one expected "The Ogre of Cathedral Street" to remain silent for very long.[6]

39

A TIME TO BE WARY

ENCKEN INAUGURATED HIS FREEDOM from the *American Mercury* with a
Mediterranean cruise with Sara. Concerned about Sara's condition,
he had booked passage to another sunny destination in the hope that
shipboard life would once again restore her health.

The trip also marked the beginning of a newfound mobility after years of
being chained to a desk. When he was not busy playing shuffleboard, he could be
found mixing beer and theology with Bishop Francis C. Kelley of Oklahoma
City, an old *Mercury* subscriber and one of the many pilgrims en route to the Holy
Land. Together they debated whether Mencken would qualify for absolution if
he were to heave a YMCA delegate overboard—a discussion that persuaded the
bishop that while Mencken was "intellectually very close to the Church, spiritu-
ally, he is about one million miles away."

Sara did not fare as well as her husband. Part of the trouble was the heavy
itinerary of 14 countries with 38 stops. The trip was, indeed, what Sara called "a
blur of ports," with sailors heaving anchor into exotic waterfronts whirling with
honking buses and goats leaping out of the way. Mencken made the usual tourist
rounds, riding jitneys with guides howling out the names of the villages, all of
which sounded to him like the names of Oriental rugs. Halts in sightseeing
allowed time to buy a plentiful supply of crucifixes and yarmulkes for members of
the Saturday Night Club. At the River Jordan he collected a small container of
water and mailed it to Birmingham, Alabama, where Sara's niece was soon to be
baptized. Sara remained in her cabin, away from the *souks* and boys in long gowns
demanding *baksheesh*. As a result, Mencken was usually late returning to port,
rendering Sara terrified that the ship would leave without him.[1]

What enchanted Mencken most during the trip was Palestine and the Jewish colonists. In Jerusalem, he discovered the Hebrew University had the best general library in the Near East (its catalogue even listed a copy of *In Defense of Women!*). While Sara remained on board ship, Mencken went by car with a member of the Jewish Agency over bare mountains and blistering desert, visiting Jewish colonies in the north. The contrast in the manner that Arabs and Jews cultivated arable land astonished him. The Arabs, Mencken noted, raised the same crop year after year and never bothered to fertilize the soil. "Their draft animals look as starved and flea-bitten as they do themselves. Thus it takes the largest tract to support a meager Arab village, and famine is always around the corner." The Jewish colonists' land, on the contrary, was intelligently planted, with fat cows grazing in the meadows and every barnyard swarming with Leghorn chickens.

Despite the impression of harmony, Mencken felt an air of foreboding. As he watched the men plowing their fields, each with a rifle strapped to his back, he realized that beyond the healthy orchards was a vast reservoir of Arabs, "all hungry, all full of enlightened self interest." He feared for the future of the region, characterizing the Arabs as the "dirtiest, orneriest and most shiftless people who regularly make the first pages of the world's press."

So enchanted was Mencken with the diligence of the Jewish colonists that he joked to Knopf that he hoped to convert him to Zionism. When he returned to Baltimore, he spoke of little else. He wrote two articles on the subject for the *Evening Sun,* and later a privately printed little book entitled *Eretz Israel.* He would again refer to this leg of his trip in the third volume of his autobiographical trilogy, *Heathen Days.* Journalist Philip Rubin later noted in *Congress Weekly* that at least Mencken was "honest enough to give [Jews] credit when he thought they deserved it."

As for his relationship with Sara, Mencken looked back on the Mediterranean cruise as "perhaps our happiest time together," despite the shadow that hung over them through the journey. Sara had left New York feeling ill and the trip seemed only to make her worse. She had borne the fatigues of travel very badly; in Cairo, she developed a slight temperature and had to be put to bed by the ship's surgeon. "The cruise was only fairly pleasant, and far too strenuous," Sara confessed. Later she developed a high fever, which the doctors failed to diagnose, concluding vaguely that perhaps she may have picked up some sort of malaria.[2]

IN SEPTEMBER, Sara became well enough to leave her bed for a trip to Montgomery. She had traveled the road from Baltimore many times before, but never as sadly as this time. Her mother was dying. "I was going home to say goodbye," Sara later wrote, not suspecting that it also would be her own farewell to the South.

Mencken counted the days until he would meet Sara's return train. "You don't need it, but I append a certificate that I love you, and to excess!" he wrote. "These four years, in fact, have made me your slave, and by the time we have gone ten I'll be in a completely lost and abject state."

When Sara arrived, Mencken could see at once how ill she was. "Her face was pale and in the bright morning sunlight she looked almost transparent," he recalled. The gossipmongers did not make the situation easier to bear. For weeks Mencken had to wave off rumors in Walter Winchell's column that his wife was expecting; salesmen descended on him, selling rattles and cribs. (He instructed that the bills should be sent to Winchell.)

So preoccupied was Mencken over Sara's health that what little work he accomplished was due to her encouragement. Save for the incipient *American Language* revision, nearly all of Mencken's writing at this time was a polemic against the New Deal.[3]

AS EARLY AS PRESIDENT ROOSEVELT's first inaugural speech, Mencken cautioned Americans that it was "a time to be wary." Mencken had always been a supporter of a balanced budget and a federal government of limited powers, an exponent of the Jeffersonian belief that the best government is one that governs least.

Like his father before him, who had always been suspicious of governmental authority and power, Mencken watched with uneasiness as Washington accumulated "a horde of bogus 'experts' " renewing themselves "like the lost claws of the Chesapeake crab." FDR's Brain Trust, he said, was composed of "sorry wizards" who would bring the country to the verge of bankruptcy. New Deal programs bloated the federal budget. Wherever Mencken looked, he saw an alphabet soup of government agencies spring into being—the WPA, the CCC, the National Recovery Act. Overnight, the NRA symbol of a blue eagle appeared everywhere, proclaiming "WE DO OUR PART." Mencken hung up the banner, wore the button, and used the rubber stamp—ironically—pounding the image on his letterhead repeatedly in quick succession. If the NRA did nothing else, Mencken pointed out, it gave people hope again. Nevertheless, it had acquired a formidable chorus of critics, and Mencken called it a flop.

Long before the WPA was liquidated across the country, Mencken was holding forth vociferously on New Deal waste. Once, in Florida, he told a team of reporters, gathered like a flock of seagulls: "I was down at your WPA project. There were about a dozen men working on a roof. Not more than two or three would touch that roof at a time. A private contractor would go broke on that kind of labor. The people of your city will pay for that job," Mencken observed, his eyes glinting brightly. "They're not getting it for nothing."

By the end of 1934, the government had spent more than two billion dollars on relief and even Roosevelt felt he had little to show for it; some twenty million Americans were receiving public assistance. Mencken resented having to pay more taxes; the concept of the New Deal under Roosevelt had "only one new and genuinely novel idea: whatever A earns really belongs to B. A is any honest and industrious man or woman; B is any drone or jackass."

Mencken was of the generation that remembered the response to the Depression of the 1890s. Neither in the literature of that time nor in the debates of Congress was the idea ever broached that the problem of unemployment and relief were the concern of the national government. More often than not, some individuals during the 1890s were expected to be self-reliant, avoiding direct handouts.

By the mid-1930s, thanks to the New Deal, all that self-reliance had changed, prompting Mencken to declare: "There is no genuine justice in any scheme of feeding and coddling the loafer whose only ponderable energies are devoted wholly to reproduction. Nine-tenths of the rights he bellows for are really privileges and he does nothing whatsoever to deserve them." Despite the billions spent on such an individual, "he can be lifted up transiently but he always slips back again." Thus, the New Deal had been "the most stupendous digenetic enterprise ever undertaken by man. . . . We have not only acquired a vast new population of morons, we have inculcated all morons, old or young, with the doctrine that the decent and industrious people of the country are bound to support them for all time. The effects of that doctrine are bound to be disastrous soon or late."

When someone asked, "And what, Mr. Mencken, would you do about the unemployed?" He looked up with a bland expression. "We could start by taking away their vote," he said, deadpan. Mencken was not surprised when the majority disagreed. "There can be nothing even remotely approaching a rational solution of the fundamental national problems until we face them in a realistic spirit," he later reflected, and that was impossible so long as educated Americans remained responsive "to the Roosevelt buncombe."[4]

When Congress ceded more unprecedented powers to the president, Mencken was not the only conservative democrat raising the fear that constitutional checks and balances were being eroded. It was in time of crisis that presidents needed the most scrutiny, Mencken declared. Citing the nation's two previous encounters with "dictatorship"—the administrations of Lincoln and Wilson—he sounded his alarm: "At the end of each, the courts were intimidated and palsied, the books bristled with oppressive and idiotic laws, thousands of men were in jail for their opinions, and great hordes of impudent scoundrels were rolling in money." Whenever government was overturned in a free country, vigilance was required. This was, however, as far as Mencken went. On the whole, during the 1930s he directed his attacks at the "quacks" of the Brain Trust rather than at Roosevelt himself. He treated the president with relative restraint until, finally, an event at the end of 1934 confirmed Mencken's hunch—that Roosevelt was "the most adept politico who has ever sat in the White House, save only Abraham Lincoln."[5]

THE GRIDIRON CLUB was a male bastion of the Washington press corps that met once a year for dinner, with political lampoons the main entertainment. Its main speaker was usually a leader from the opposition party who delivered an essentially humorous attack on the chief executive, his administration, and programs. The president was then given the opportunity to respond in kind. In 1934, the

Gridiron Club bypassed asking a Republican leader to give the main address and approached H. L. Mencken to do the honors.

The prospect, however, plainly made him anxious. Ever since he had been chosen valedictorian long ago at the Baltimore Polytechnic, he disliked giving speeches. Now he practiced before Sara, stumbling over his lines until she advised him not to memorize but to read instead. He went over the text with great care, crossing out and substituting words up to the last minute. Mencken wanted his speech before the Gridiron to be as good-humored as possible. Toward that end, he shared drafts with his colleagues. "Do you think it is in the proper tone?" he asked Fred Essary of the *Sun*'s Washington bureau. Essary confidently predicted: "It will be a joy for us to show the politicians what a writing man can do."

At the White House, Press Secretary Stephen Early had been poring over Mencken's volumes. Suddenly, he had an inspiration. After sharing his thoughts with Roosevelt, an obviously elated press secretary wrote in his diary that his ideas had "made a great hit with the President."

On the night of the dinner, Mencken rose from his chair, bursting from his formal suit. Governor Albert Ritchie of Maryland, who sat next to him, expected Mencken to be extremely nervous, but when the time came, he found him collected and at ease. "Mr. President, Mr. Wright, and fellow subjects of the Reich," he began, launching into an attack on the New Deal. "For if the current flow of ideas is somewhat confusing, it must still be admitted that the show that goes with it is a very good one. Here we come upon one of the really sound and salient merits of the great American republic. It is the most amusing country ever heard of in history. It tackles all of its most horrible problems in the manner of a young fellow necking a new girl. . . ."

Mencken then speculated how long it would take for the New Deal to bring the country to ruin. In its early days, he confessed, "I used to do a great deal of worrying about the Constitution, and even allude to it once or twice in print." But he did so no longer. The Constitution was really very well taken care of; it was in a museum.

New York Times political commentator Arthur Krock felt that Mencken's speech was so mild that "Roosevelt didn't know what to do with it." He found the president's expression "absolutely marvelous" in its bafflement. Cabinet members also seemed to be taken aback at the absence of savagery in Mencken's speech. Secretary of the Interior Harold Ickes thought Mencken "cleverly cynical, as usual, but he wasn't particularly ill-humored." Everyone in the audience seemed to enjoy Mencken's jabs; the applause was hearty and the laughter loud.[6]

At eleven fifteen it was the president's turn. Flashing his famous smile, he made a few humorous introductory remarks. He welcomed the entertainment presented at dinner, yet he wondered at the choice of Mencken as speaker, traditionally reserved for critics of the opposition party. How was Mr. Mencken to be classified? "I never regarded him as either a Democrat or a Republican," Roosevelt stated. "After following his writings I'd rather listed him as a follower of that famous old Irishman who landed on our shores some years ago and announced, as he got off the boat, 'I don't know what sort of government you've got over here, but whatever it is I'm agin' it.'"

It soon became apparent that while Mencken's speech consisted of harmless spoofing, Roosevelt, thinking that Mencken's treatment of him was going to be rough, had come armed with a violent reply. "When his time came," as Mencken put it, "he launched into me with a savage attack." After the initial pleasantries, Roosevelt began reading: "The majority of [newspapermen] in almost every American city are still ignoramuses, and proud of it."

He added, grinning at Mencken:

I know of no American who starts from a higher level of aspiration than the journalist . . . He plans to be both an artist and a moralist—a master of lovely words and merchant of sound ideas. He ends, commonly, as the most depressing jackass of his community—that is, if his career goes on to what is called a success.

It was "one of the most fiendish jokes ever perpetrated on an adversary," recalled James Cain. As "the chill got colder and colder," it turned out this was not Roosevelt's indictment. It was from Mencken's *Prejudices: Sixth Series*. The effect, according to Ickes, was "devastating. I looked over at Mencken two or three times while the President was speaking and it was clear to see that he didn't like it at all. He seemed to me to be distinctly put out." As Arthur Krock recalled, "The more the President alluded to their friendship and kept calling him 'Henry,'" the redder and redder Mencken's face became. "I'll get the son of a bitch," Mencken whispered to Governor Ritchie at his side. "I'll dig the skeletons out of his closet." As the president spoke, Mencken began busily jotting down notes, readying himself for a reply—if the chance ever came.

Finally Roosevelt reached the end of his response. Grinning triumphantly, he informed the crowd that the quotations he had used were from the words of "my old friend, Henry Mencken." A roar went up. The president had "simply smeared him all over," Ickes concluded. A victorious Roosevelt then changed tone as he concluded with a homily from the Bible, pleading for a new "Era of Good Feeling."

After Roosevelt sat down, the president of the Gridiron Club asked him privately why he had replied so ill-humoredly to Mencken's good-humored speech. Roosevelt replied that he couldn't help it; the text was before him and he couldn't think of anything else to say.

Mencken was given no chance for a rebuttal. As he prepared to leave the ball-room, Roosevelt wheeled past Mencken's chair. "It was fair shooting," Mencken said graciously to the president, putting out his hand. The president seemed somewhat taken aback, apparently expecting to find Mencken angry. Guests standing nearby spontaneously applauded.

"I knew that there was a good deal of feeling under the smiling exterior from which that speech issued," columnist Arthur Brisbane said, congratulating the president. "I wonder that you keep your temper as you do." FDR, evidently pleased by the reaction, later wrote to Brisbane: "I did not really intend to be quite so rough on Henry Mencken, but the old quotations which I dug up were too good to be true, and I felt that in view of all the amusing but cynically rough things which Henry has said in print for twenty years, he was entitled to ten minutes of comeback!"

Not all members of the press corps were amused. Arthur Sulzberger of the *New York Times* told Mencken he thought the president's speech had been in grossly bad taste, out of harmony with the usual Gridiron Club spirit. "I heard the same from various other people," Mencken later wrote, "but they were probably simply trying to be nice. As a matter of fact, his reading extracts from my writing was a fair device, and he carried it off very well. Despite his wide smile and his insistence that I was a friend, it was plain enough that he had a grudge and was trying to get revenge. He has had plenty of ground for wanting to do so, and he will have more ground hereafter."

For all of Mencken's efforts to gloss lightly over the event, those who knew him well understood how deeply he had been humiliated. The president had made a fool of him. John Owens of the *Sun* recalled Mencken's remark the day after the event. "Well, we'll even this off," he had said. Owens realized that as much as Mencken might try, it was not a possibility; if Roosevelt "hit below the belt," as Owens believed, any president always had the upper hand. Fighting Roosevelt, James Cain admitted, "was like stabbing a rapier into the Mississippi River." "It was a malicious thing on Roosevelt's part," said Owens. "Mencken would have never done that had the situation been reversed." Friends felt that Mencken had made a mistake in speaking at the Gridiron. One said: "He sort of exposed himself."

"There was not room enough on the planet for Franklin Delano Roosevelt and H. L. Mencken," William Manchester later concluded. Mencken sensed in years to come that much would be made of the event. "In a little while, I daresay, rumors will begin to circulate that Roosevelt attacked me with his fists. Even people who were present begin to remember things that never happened. But this, of course, is the fortune of war. Get into the paper at all and you are bound to become a character in highly fantastic tales."

Some may have had the impression that Mencken's subsequent criticism of FDR stemmed from his treatment at the Gridiron. In fact, Mencken's motivation went far beyond a single simple slight at a dinner. He was angry not only against New Deal policies and what he saw as the abolishment of traditional Constitutional guarantees, but later by what he considered the duplicitous way the president led America into war. Moreover, to Mencken, the defender of liberty, FDR's manipulation of the press and later his censorship policies were far more significant. He would speak of the president with such rancor that his companions would be amazed. It would come to a halt when Sara, interrupting

Mencken midstream, would lightly pat her husband's hand. "Now, Henry, let's not talk about that," she would say softly; only then would he calm down.

Indeed, Sara always seemed to be the tonic that soothed, though she herself was ailing. It was an old superstition of Mencken's that December was his unluckiest month. In Montgomery, Sara's mother died on Christmas Eve, and was buried on Christmas day. Sara, too ill to attend the funeral, lay in bed, bearing up bravely while grieving. With Sara bedridden, Mencken suffering from a sinus infection, and the anniversaries of their parents' deaths at hand, Christmas ran its usual infernal course. "Let us give the Holy Ghost credit," Mencken wrote to Edgar Lee Masters. "He has got off some masterpieces in 1934."

Despite his problems, Mencken told Knopf he had already started work on his revision of *The American Language*. If all went well, he planned to take Sara to Germany before the end of next summer to visit his Tante Anna in Oldenburg. During the weeks ahead Mencken would have further reason to hope, when Sara was finally able to sit up and leave what he called "her bed of pain." Perhaps good fortune *was* around the corner. As the New Year approached, Mencken issued his customary greeting to friends: "Here's hoping that we are all lucky in 1935."[7]

Worse was yet to come.

40

A WINTER OF HORROR

S ARA CONTINUES IN PRIME CONDITION," Mencken wrote with relief to his
family. In March 1935 she had returned to Johns Hopkins, but in better
health than in past years. "I am very hopeful that her rest cure will rid her of
her troubles permanently."

The snow had cleared and the weather was warming; soon, Mencken noted
happily, it would be spring—though he could not contemplate the season without being reminded that in Hollins Street the crocuses were already in bloom.
Sara's impending release from the hospital meant she soon would be able to
resume work on her new book. "Having to stop it is what chiefly upset her, next
to the pain," Mencken confessed to Ellen Glasgow.

But with the arrival of spring, Sara's health was not better. Each day
Mencken was sure she would return home, only to be told otherwise. She continued to run a temperature that made her recovery depressingly slow. The
doctors seemed baffled by her case. "All the wizards come in and look at her, but
the best they can offer is surmises," Mencken worried. He told Blanche Knopf:
"The poor girl has had a horrible year. She has borne it bravely, but if the quacks
don't turn her loose pretty soon I think she'll begin to shoot."

Somehow, in the midst of all this, he managed to get a few more pages written for *The American Language*. But as the days passed he became more distressed
at Sara's condition. He developed bronchitis that completely incapacitated him,
renewing his doubts about completing the manuscript before his self-imposed
deadline of July 4. Within the same period several of his friends died, among them
the medical historian Fielding Garrison. "Again I was a pallbearer," he unhappily

reflected, "and again I had to hear a Protestant Episcopal ecclesiastic give assurance over the body of an agnostic that an immortal soul had just taken flight from it." Simultaneously, his sister-in-law became ill, and August Mencken developed a sinus infection that required surgery.

None of these concerns was revealed to Sara when Mencken was at her bedside. "I enjoyed Henry so much, and so did the whole hospital," Sara wrote from Johns Hopkins. On one such visit he came to her room toting a portable record player. She was particularly fond of a German song by Werner R. Heymann, playing it so often the grooves in the disc became worn. Years later, Mencken would write there had been something prophetic about the words of the refrain:

> *It exists only once,*
> *It doesn't come again;*
> *It is too beautiful to be true . . .*
> *Perhaps it will be gone tomorrow.*[1]

APRIL ARRIVED, COLD, DARK, AND WET, day in and day out, for three weeks running. "If only the sun would shine," Mencken despaired. He was convinced that after a couple days of sunlight on the porch Sara would be ready to sign off from the hospital. But despite his wishes, her temperature remained the same, with little sign of lowering.

April always reminded Sara of springtime in Alabama. For her, this meant the "blue sky and a dazzling green and yellow flame of jonquils blowing everywhere," of the garden at her home in Montgomery, with its scents of lavender, narcissus, and iris. Scrunched under the heavy blankets of her hospital bed, in her mind's eye Sara floated over the border of boxwood that formed the northern garden wall, past the trailing rose bushes, toward the golden glimmer of open fields, breathing in "the sweet wild smell" that hovered over the plum thickets.

Sara had experienced such fevers before, in similar hospital beds with nurses fussing over her. In an essay entitled "Dear Life," she vividly described the torment of being a convalescent. She wrote that "death, and a full tropical death at the moment of greater promise, was a peculiar heritage of the South, and all Southerners. I was merely coming into my own." All she had to do was close her eyes and the mists rolled over, as they had rolled over the river down in Alabama.

Outside her hospital room window, the rain continued to fall. It also fell on Cathedral Street, making the pavement slick and a shiny gray. It fell in streaks against the window of Mencken's office as he worked. "The house is horribly lonely and gloomy," he wrote to her. He was counting the days until she came home: "I love you."

Eventually the skies cleared and the air grew warm again. Sitting outside on the hospital porch, Sara felt her spirits begin to revive. To the relief of both Mencken and Sara, Dr. Baker still found no sign of tuberculosis in her x-rays. Nonetheless he advised her to go to the mountains for a complete rest and not undertake housekeeping anywhere—"and that makes me feel all the worse," Sara groaned; "I am heartbroken, for it was the one thing I was looking forward to." Together, she and Mencken made plans to rent a summer home in the Adirondacks beginning June 1, believing that a few months in the mountains would restore her completely.

Before heading there, Sara continued writing notes for her new novel on Southern life to be called *The Plantation*. She asked a friend in Montgomery for a list of the flowers that grew in the garden. She remembered the young intern from Duke who had taken care of her at Johns Hopkins and tried to obtain a permanent position for her. "My house—my life in it among my own used things— had never seemed so precious," she had written in "Dear Life." Now she was back in her retreat, ready to resume her routine. The telephone rang all day and friends dropped in to see her. "I greatly fear that she'll overdo it," Mencken clucked anxiously.

In spite of his misgivings, Mencken remained fundamentally confident that the danger had passed. While declining an invitation to visit friends in Massachusetts, he reassured them that they would see the Menckens again soon, for "we all have hundreds of years of life ahead of us."[2]

Then, in the middle of May, Sara took a sudden turn for the worse, with raging headache following raging headache. "She is bearing up with incredible patience," Mencken reported to Alfred Knopf on May 25, "but I greatly fear if the thing goes on much longer she'll begin to crack." Despite Sara's pain, she continued to write. When Mencken heard her start to type at her desk, stop, then resume, only to stop entirely, he realized Sara might have to be hospitalized again. Indeed, back she returned to Johns Hopkins, to the miserable routine of stethoscopes and rubber tubes. She scrawled a note, describing herself as "quite weary with my miseries and all."

The next day Sara became even more desperately ill. When the full nature of her illness was revealed, and denial was no longer possible, Mencken steeled himself for the inevitable. "I greatly fear that she can't recover," he wrote to the members of her family. He had known before they married that her chances were not too strong, he told Raymond Pearl. "Four or five times since then I have been in terror." Now he was confronted with the brutal reality. To his friend Max Brödel he wrote:

Sara has meningitis, with t.b. bacilli in the spinal fluid. It is, of course, completely hopeless. She seems comfortable—at least far more comfortable than she was a few days ago. The horrible headache has passed off, and she sleeps peacefully all day long. She may be aroused for half a minute, but hardly for more. This is the climax of her long series of illnesses. It would be silly to say that I have not anticipated it; in fact, I have dreaded it constantly. But it is appalling to face.

All visitors except her husband were barred from her room. Mencken saw her for the last time on Wednesday, May 29. So much morphine was being used, it was difficult to arouse her, yet briefly she regained consciousness and inquired in good humor about the sheep on Gertrude's farm. At the end of five minutes she fell back into unconsciousness. It was plain for Mencken to see that she was dying. "I fear I'll never hear her speak again," he mourned. "It is dreadful to see her slipping away."

Keeping him company that evening were his siblings August and Gertrude, his friends Raymond Pearl and Hamilton Owens. In the morning came the news that Sara continued to hold her own. He endlessly praised her brave spirit—"*My poor girl . . . ," "My dear girl . . . ,*"—as she remained "fighting magnificently in the shadows, with a strong heart and a steady pulse." His hours were filled with such confusion, he later confessed, that he hardly knew what was going on around him. Theodore Dreiser's letter offered Mencken a solution for his sorrow: "As I see it, life furnishes just one panacea, if so much, for all the ills and accidents of life: it is work—and more work." It was exactly the way that Mencken usually sought to conquer grief, but this time he was so heartbroken, he could not. He tried composing his column for the *Evening Sun* but was unable to do so. Frantically he wrote notes to family and friends, feeling the need to unburden himself. "Poor Sara, I fear, is now beyond all help. It seems a dreadful end to her long and gallant struggle."

When the doorbell rang on May 31, Dr. Baker brought the news that Sara had died at 6:40 that evening. She was 37 years old. At the end, Mencken summed it up poignantly. "When I married Sara," he said, "the doctors said she could not live more than three years. Actually she lived five, so that I had two more years of happiness than I had any right to expect."³

LETTERS STREAMED IN from friends and strangers alike, including from several people from his past with whom he had lost contact: Phil Goodman, George Jean Nathan, Willard Huntington Wright, Wells and Arthur Hawks, the families of his former mentors on the *Herald*—Lynn Meekins and Max Ways—even from former girlfriends. "I am beginning to suspect that life is not a party," mourned Anita Loos. The telephone rang with calls from the proprietors and waitresses of restaurants Mencken and Sara had frequented together, from Schellhase's and Moneta's, from the manager of the Hotel Stafford across the street. Of some consolation was the letter from Marjorie Nicholson, Sara's confidante from Goucher College, who had comforted her during the first siege of tuberculosis years before.

Sara's years with Mencken had been a time of greatest happiness, Marjorie told him. "She could not have appreciated more all that you did for her in every way; and her one regret was that her health was such a constant drag; her only worry was that she was not doing her part. I knew she was and used to tell her so; and she really knew it—but she used to feel that it was hard for you to have to come home again and again to a sick wife. She wanted your happiness more than her own. . . ."

Among the hundreds of letters, many came from people who did not even know Sara. One of the bores who had called Cathedral Street praised Sara's thoughtfulness for giving him pointers in his writing. Others felt compelled to reach Mencken because they had been so moved by Sara's short stories and her essay "Dear Life." Running through the letters were the same expressions of shock and distress. "I so resent the loss of great beauty or a fine gift," summed up one, "and with Sara's passing we have lost both."

Dazed, Mencken set about the sad task of answering them all. To Aileen Pringle, whom he had jilted to marry Sara, he expressed his regret that the two women had never met: "You would have liked her." Eventually, every condolence letter was methodically filed and put away.[4]

August and Anne Duffy took care of the funeral arrangements. Though Sara was an agnostic, to Mencken it seemed "intolerable to part from her without a word," so an Episcopal minister was asked to conduct the service. She had requested that her body be cremated and the funeral be held with no flowers or pallbearers. The ceremony was held on a beautiful spring day. For Philippa, Ida, John, and Mary Kelley, there was an acute pain in losing their elder sister so soon after the death of their mother. Present were the Hergesheimers, the Knopfs, and Governor Ritchie of Maryland. Mencken was hardly aware of their presence. His marriage to Sara had been "a beautiful adventure while it lasted," but "all beautiful things must end." Somehow, he could never think of her as gone forever. Now it was over. "What a cruel and idiotic world we live in!"

The week of anxiety, of hoping against hope, had left Mencken in a state near collapse. Returning to his empty apartment, Mencken confided to Sara Mayfield, ". . . I hate to think of the months ahead." It had been determined that Mencken and August would take a trip to England "if only to get away, for a little while, from the endless reminders of Sara in Cathedral Street." Henry hoped the sea air would revive his spirits and blow the fog from his head. On board ship, a photographer captured his agony as he stared into the ocean, the thumping of the engines an accompaniment to the whisper of the waves.[5]

IN LONDON, NEWSPAPER HEADLINES heralded his arrival: "The Frankest Man on Earth Is Here!" He could be easily identified walking through the city wearing a boater with a bit chipped off the side. Nothing seemed to persuade him to wear any other hat, although the press commented he was the only man in London to wear a boater apart from the fish salesmen at West End.

Throughout his meetings with the press, Mencken resorted to discussions of his work to avoid mention of his wife's death, the subject uppermost in everyone's mind. He spoke of Roosevelt, saying that the American president would make a good king. Reporters duly filled their notebooks. "In spite of his caustic raillery and flippant observations, there is a look of sadness in the eyes," wrote one reporter. Then, just as suddenly, Mencken would stop, apologize for a dull interview, rub his hand over his tired eyes, and promise to have some more prejudices for them to quote on another day.

"What a cruel and idiotic world we live in!" En route to London, 1935. H. L. Mencken Collection, Enoch Pratt Free Library.

Paul Patterson had advised the London office of the *Sunpapers* to be especially attentive to Mencken during his stay. Newton Aiken secured tickets for a session at the House of Commons, where Mencken sat entranced during a speech by Anthony Eden. "I am convinced that the death of his wife had been a blow to Mencken," Newton Aiken later recalled. Away from the scrutiny of the press and his pals, where he possibly felt the need to put on his public persona, Mencken had spoken a great deal to Margaret Aiken about Sara's things and how to dispose of them. Throughout his life, women had provided him with an emotional outlet for his private feelings. "But otherwise," Aiken reflected, "he gave no great indication of his grief."[6]

After two weeks spent in England, Mencken on his return said he now felt "more or less rational again." Nonetheless, the apartment at Cathedral Street was full of ghosts. To his immense gratitude, August had agreed to keep him company until November.

During this period Mencken carefully arranged Sara's mementos from the Margaret Booth School, her Goucher College notebooks, and other papers, and had them bound in blue morocco leather. In the flyleaf to one notebook he typed the hopeful comment, "It may be that in the future some historian of Southern letters will want to go through her work with some care." He was astonished at how much she had written and published. Responding to those Southerners who had asked that an edited volume of Sara's short stories be collected, Mencken selected what he felt to be her best creations and put them together in one volume entitled *Southern Album*. He wrote a long preface to the collection, the hardest thing, he later confessed, he had ever tried to write.

The rest of Sara's possessions remained in the apartment exactly as she had left them. Mencken refused to touch anything, so much so, Anne Duffy told friends, "it verged on the gruesome." One night, she picked up a rag doll and told Mencken she was taking it to her daughter, "and he blinked, but he didn't say anything." It broke the spell, she said, and after that Mencken proceeded to clean things up. A barrel of Dresden china was sent to Sara's family; an inkwell that he had once given his wife was mailed to a Goucher pal. All the pin boxes were given away, as was her clothing.

His only distraction during this period was the infant Bridget Duffy, whom Anne, at Mencken's request, had decided to rename Sara in honor of her best friend. Mencken had never been a fan of Anne Duffy. He had, in fact, thrown her out of the apartment the night of Sara's death when he found her rummaging through his wife's things, collecting armfuls of lace doilies. But the two of them had become reconciled through this baby, of whom Sara had been immensely fond and whom Mencken now recognized as a link to his wife. When, that summer, Anne brought the six-month-old child to Mencken, and the little girl sat up boldly and looked at him straight in the eye, he was enraptured.

Eagerly, Mencken began collecting trinkets to put in shiny brown and yellow cigar boxes filled with the kind of things a child would love: marbles, old stamps, candy, small toys. "I used to delight in such things myself in my early days," Mencken explained to her mother, "and I assume that the taste of the young has not changed much." To these he added an elfin pearl necklace, a tiny silver knife and fork, a miniature sideboard with Lilliputian china plates and a collection of "gaudy" paper dolls. Where Sara Anne Duffy was involved, "my interest in that lady grows every time I see her."

But even the captivating spectacle of little Sara Duffy failed to assuage Mencken's grief. He continued to long for *his* Sara, whose presence was everywhere.

He discovered the hundreds of letters the two of them had exchanged over the years; intermingled among his books were many of hers; on the shelves he came across volumes of old Southern magazines. For weeks on end he was deluged with mail addressed to his wife, despite his sending letters to Baltimore shops that she was no longer present to read their circulars. One polite notice arrived from Sara's favorite antique store at Hanover Street, asking what should be done with the items she had purchased only a few short weeks before her death.

"She had gone on living as if no menace hung over her," Mencken reflected. "Unto her last days she kept on adding to her vast and disorderly collection of Victorian glass and china, and piling up the preposterous Victorian books that were her delight. I find it hard, even so soon after her death, to recall her as ill. It is much easier to remember her on those days when things were going well with her, and she was full of projects, and busy with her friends and the house, and merry with her easy laughter."

On the morning of their wedding anniversary, Mencken visited Sara's grave with Sara Mayfield, and found it looking green and peaceful. The sight of him looking out the window of the taxi, his cigar clenched between his teeth, his face set stoically, was one his companion would not forget. For a while they stood there together at Loudon Cemetery, in silence. Thinking of his beloved wife, Mencken later confessed: "I can well understand the human yearning that makes for a belief in immortality." "Finally, with the effort of a man attempting to throw off a burden too heavy for his shoulders," Mayfield recorded, "Mencken tried to shake off the weight of his grief. 'Come on,' he said huskily. 'Let's go. I think a libation is in order.' "

Mencken got so lonely he even considered letting Reverend Henri Wiesel of Georgetown Prep teach him golf: "I realize that as a patriotic American I must learn it sooner or later." But if the days were intolerable, the evenings were even worse. To fill the hours he invited many of his friends to the apartment for dinner. On September 12, Mencken fled to New York—mainly to get away from the house—to celebrate his fifty-fifth birthday soberly in the company of Alfred Knopf, who shared the same birth date. "I was fifty-five years old before I envied anyone," he privately recorded, "and then it was not so much for what others had as for what I had lost."[7]

THAT SEPTEMBER MENCKEN WAS GIVEN a foretaste of the honors posterity would award him, when the Enoch Pratt Free Library presented a window display of Menckeniana. Arranged around an enormous photograph of a contemporary Mencken was another of him at age six months, still another in the backyard of his home at Hollins Street, and others showing him being arrested in Boston in 1926. Bound copies of the *Smart Set* and *Menckeniana: A Schimpflexicon*, which Sara had helped Mencken assemble, were also on display. At the back of the window was a copy of *Ventures Into Verse*, far from the reach of any roving bibliophile who might be tempted to steal the precious volume.

Mencken had passed the same window many times, each instance hesitating to stop for fear of being recognized. But one evening, under the cover of darkness, he stood before the window, quietly gazing at the material dedicated to him. Indeed, as Anne Duffy observed, the exhibit seemed to revive his spirits; Mencken after his birthday seemed to be getting on with his life. He had resumed his "slavery" on *The American Language*, a task that he had been eager to do ever since publishing the revised edition in 1923. But no matter how hard he labored, behind every batch of notes another began to bloom. New material accumulated almost faster than he could work it into the manuscript. He actually had thirty pounds of newspaper clippings alone. Weaving it into a coherent pattern was a formidable job. He noted there were at least 150 footnotes in the chapter on the grammar of the vulgate.

"Why I undertook this job God alone knows," he joked to his Uncle Charles Abhau. "Conscientiousness . . . is one of the curses of this family." There were moments when grinding away horribly for thirteen-hour days seemed to drag him down.

In October, Mencken donated Sara's scrapbooks and four hundred volumes from her library to Goucher College. Included in the collection of Victorian tomes were autographed copies of the books of Sinclair Lewis, Ellen Glasgow, and Robert Frost, not to mention an almost complete set of her husband's work. Accompanying him was his old friend Hergesheimer, "to sustain me," Mencken wrote Dorothy Hergesheimer, "while I hand over Sara's books. How she would have larfed to see us!"

The proofs of *Southern Album* having already arrived from Doubleday, Mencken now turned his attention to making lists of the libraries and friends to send copies to. Determined that Sara's work not be consigned to oblivion, he gave her papers to Goucher College and sent a packet to the Alabama Archives. Upon publication of Sara's collection, he observed that "she could evoke simple feeling without any elaborate machinery, and knew how to be pathetic without becoming maudlin." He admitted *The Making of a Lady* had been apprentice work, but he had held high hopes for *The Plantation*. "It seems to be idiotically irrational that a person of her potentialities should die so soon. She had been finding herself professionally during the past few years, and her writing was improving very rapidly. My belief is that the novel she had in mind would have been a really first-rate job. I always told her that no one had ever done a first-rate work of fiction before the age of forty."

He dedicated *Southern Album* to Sara Anne Duffy. "What she will think of it when she grows up I often wonder." Reviewers were on the whole very friendly, although Mencken found most of the critics ignorant. "What ghastly imbeciles review books in this great country!" he later cursed. "I begin to blush for having been one of the gang myself." Yet, the *New Republic* commented that, had Sara lived, "it is tantalizing to speculate on what might have been."

It had taken him six months to finish sorting through all of Sara's papers, and now that he had completed the task he admitted to feeling at a loss. With the exception of his preface in *Southern Album* and to the first volume of his auto-biography, *Happy Days*, Mencken did not publicly allude to Sara in his writings again except in the limited privacy of his diary and memoirs. He beseeched his friends not to forget her. "She is still tremendously real to me," he said. "I simply can't think of her as vanished."[8]

LATE IN THE FALL, August returned to Hollins Street. As the days grew shorter, Mencken spent them shivering in his "gloomy cell," finishing the indexes to *The American Language*. Working with the temperature hovering between 47 and 52 degrees was not easy; it left him "longing for sunlight and cursing God." Nonetheless, on many days he was at his desk from 9 in the morning to 10 at night, with only brief intervals for meals and a cat-nap in the late afternoon. "But the late evenings are ghastly," he told Betty Hanes, for then the servants would go home and the apartment was empty. He wrote of feeling "dreadfully lonely. In all my life I have never lived alone. Before my marriage I was always at home."

Just as stubbornly, Mencken refused to make any concession, perhaps deciding that in keeping the apartment he could retain another bond of union to Sara. "I suppose I'll have to learn to endure the fact that my wife is no longer in it." Then, in desperation, he would plow through the snow to Schellhase's to meet with his brother August and his old friend Heinrich Buchholz, "a godsend to me in those dismal days." He knew, however, that this routine could not go on forever.

The sheer labor and nervous strain had, Mencken admitted, left him drained. In December James Cain saw him wandering through the Victorian rooms, mechanically talking nonstop. He was almost afraid that Mencken had lost his reason. "It must have been a winter of horror—living in that place alone," August later reflected. "I don't see how he stood it."

As Christmas approached, Mencken braced himself for the onslaught. "The holiday will be a really dreadful one and I want to forget it as much as possible," he wrote his niece, Virginia. The easiest way to escape its worst horrors was to spend all of December 25 toiling on the indexes to *The American Language*. He also completed several short pieces for the *Evening Sun*, though fully aware that the material he struggled to get on paper was certainly not the best. "It was the worst Christmas I have ever had and I am delighted that it is over."

It was agreed that part of the holiday would be spent with his family. Recognizing, perhaps more acutely than most, that their older brother could not remain living in such solitary confines surrounded by painful memories, Gertrude beseeched him to leave that apartment: Why not return next spring and set up housekeeping with August back at 1524 Hollins Street? As for Gertrude, she was spending more time at her farm and far less in Baltimore.[9]

The effect of Gertrude's speech was almost as if it were the invitation he had been desperately awaiting. Only then did Mencken finally allow himself to return to his beloved Hollins Street. But only then.

Part Five
1936–1940

Inside of Mencken's desk drawer. Photograph by A. Aubrey Bodine, The Maryland Historical Society, Baltimore, Maryland.

"Like an anxious parent . . . concerned for the health of his petunias." Mencken in his beloved garden at Hollins Street. H. L. Mencken Collection, Enoch Pratt Free Library.

41

BALTIMORE'S FRIENDLY DRAGON

AUGUST'S FIVE-YEAR STEWARDSHIP of the garden at 1524 Hollins Street had left it in a sorry state. In no time Mencken changed all that, sowing seeds, transplanting hundreds of violets, and trimming the ivy. Of the two grapevines, one seemed to be dead, but the other was putting forth shoots; Mencken fertilized it with yeast from a brewery. He mailed a handful of soil to the University of Maryland for analysis; like an anxious parent, Mencken was concerned for the health of his petunias. Soon the little garden was bursting with life. At one corner a patch of mint flourished, with leaves enough to make a host of juleps.

A bigger challenge awaited inside. Tables and chairs from 704 Cathedral and at least twice as much furniture as Mencken could find space for were piled to the ceiling. He fell over furnishings every time he entered a room in the dark. In the meantime, he despaired over what to do with the barrels of china and glassware that Sara had accumulated and now crowded the parlor. Eventually the items were dispatched but the process took weeks.

Finally, in early summer, Mencken was able to settle back in his new office, roll a sheet of stationery into his typewriter, slash a line through "704 Cathedral Street," replace it with "1524 Hollins Street," and breathe, "It is good to be home again." Best of all, Mencken confided to Hergesheimer, his move back to Hollins Street meant that after the loneliness following the loss of Sara, "there will be a meal on the table, with a drink beside it and some one to talk to whenever I get home." August provided the company he was lacking. "They had an almost perfect relationship," the writer George Schuyler observed. "They could anticipate what each other was thinking."

"It is a pleasant life for two elderly Christians, with the icebox handy nearby," Mencken remarked happily. "No one expects a widower to be clean," he added. "That assumption has added a great deal to my comfort." As August noted, theirs had become a life conducive to work, and on Mencken's return to Hollins Street he was again at his most productive. That spring, thirteen years after the appearance of the third edition of *The American Language*, Alfred Knopf published the fourth edition.[1]

Thanks to Mencken, a tremendous growth had taken place in American linguistics since his first edition in 1919. Various tomes on language had been published, including the ongoing *Dictionary of American English* and a linguistic atlas of the United States and Canada. The Linguistic Society of America was founded, and a group of scholars, encouraged by Mencken, launched the *Journal of American Speech*. In addition, Mencken's generosity in acknowledging even the most trivial contribution from the rankest amateur had served to make him a catalyst to many budding linguists, giving them an appreciative audience when such audiences were not common.

Mencken's fourth edition differed from its three predecessors, although the fact that the revision was rather more scientific made it rather less amusing for him. In 1919 Mencken had observed how American English diverged from the British; now he argued that the American language would displace its model, and with the addition of new waves of immigrants, the foreign influence would contribute new words to colloquial speech, making English a dialect of American. However much Englishmen might be opposed to American idiom on principle, they were unconsciously using thirty or forty Americanisms a day.

Mencken made no effort to present a comprehensive lexicon of Americanisms (a task he left for the *Dictionary of American English*, then under way at the University of Chicago). Instead, he chose a few examples to show the general principles underlying their formation and how they had infiltrated the language. It was a colossal achievement. By the time his manuscript arrived at his publisher's desk, it weighed fifteen pounds.

The work had not only sustained him following Sara's death; its reception marked, in scholar Charles Fecher's phrase, "the beginning of his critical rehabilitation." It was reprinted fourteen times, was issued in Braille and in a British edition, and was a Book-of-the-Month Club selection that sold more than 90,000 copies. At the Knopf office, orders arrived from as far away as Moscow. *The American Language* would eventually fulfill Mencken's prediction that it would "outlast anything I have ever written."[2]

Now that Mencken was back at Hollins Street, with its garden and familiar alleys, he resumed work on several light essays about his early boyhood. Editors at the *New Yorker*, among them St. Clair McKelway, thought they could use more. With some trepidation, McKelway approached the legendary Harold Ross, who instantly said: "I'm against most reminiscences because most writers

"The Mencken family." Here, with children from the alley behind Hollins Street. Courtesy Sara Anne Duffy Chermayeff.

remember the wrong things, but Mencken's safe. Jesus, Mencken can even write about politics."

Delighted, McKelway introduced the two men over lunch.

I remember Ross saying, "Say, Mencken, that was a good trick of yours that time in Boston when you bit the quarter, but what the hell do I do with a fifteen-cent magazine?" "Raise the price ten cents," said Mencken. At some point, they talked about boobs. "Boobs love me," Mencken said. "They are always coming up to me and slobbering over me. Of course that's because they don't know I'm a fellow boob. I'm the boob that asks the waiter what is especially good on the menu." "I'm the boob who says 'Fine,' when the barber holds the mirror so I can look at the back of my neck," said Ross. The talk went all over the place, all over the world, with never a mention of Mencken's reminiscent pieces or the fact that we wanted him to do more of them.

So began a lifelong friendship, blossoming later into a trilogy that came to be seen as the most memorable of Mencken's writing, forever fixing the way later generations would remember him, marking the triumphant comeback of an author that the emancipated writers of the current age—whose freedom he had secured—had claimed they no longer needed.[3]

SINCE MENCKEN'S RESIGNATION from the *American Mercury*, magazines had interested him only as a lucrative forum. His relationship with the *Sun*, which had been an integral part of his life for thirty years, was another matter. He was immensely interested in the endless problems that confronted the paper. To his duties as board member, reporter, and columnist were now added the functions of consulting editor in the news and editorial departments.

Mencken felt that the 1936 elections offered an ideal opportunity for revitalizing the newspaper. The New Deal had become too powerful with little opposition. It was generally believed that Roosevelt would be reelected in November, but Mencken, unconvinced, was sure the New Deal had lost its strength. He recalled that after the midterm elections of 1934 there had been a drop in the president's popularity, and early in 1936, a Gallup poll showed that his support had sunk to a fraction above 50 percent. Mencken was sure the president could be defeated.

What is more, he sensed a certain insecurity on Roosevelt's part, in FDR's cynical attempt to attract votes by directing public money where it would be most effective on Election Day. "If he became convinced tomorrow that coming out for cannibalism would get him the votes he needs so sorely," Mencken wrote in the March issue of the *American Mercury*, "he would begin fattening a missionary in the White House yard come Wednesday." The people were catching on, Mencken wrote. If they can beat Roosevelt at all, he said, "they can beat him with a Chinaman or even with a Republican."[4]

Although Mencken considered his article, "Three Years of Dr. Roosevelt," a mild attack, it was seen by the public as one of the most scathing assaults yet published on the administration. There had been other articles but, as the *Mercury's* Lawrence Spivak reflected, "No one went at it in Mencken's language." Calling Roosevelt "the boldest and most preposterous practitioner of political quackery in modern times," Mencken claimed that the president "has carried on his job with an ingratiating grin upon his face like that of a snake-oil vendor at a village carnival, and he has exhibited exactly the same kind of responsibility." Even the *London Times*, Spivak recalled, was amazed by the severity of Mencken's language. It compared its tone to that of "a Tammany thug."

The article created a great deal of excitement in the offices of Knopf, Inc. "I have never heard as much talk about a single article anywhere," Blanche Knopf wrote to Mencken, "and people are now clamoring to subscribe to your *Baltimore Sun* pieces." When asked at a White House press conference what he thought of Mencken's article, Roosevelt replied disdainfully that he had not read it; Mencken suspected it was a diplomatic lie.

Mencken, however, was correct in surmising that Roosevelt still had a challenge ahead of him. One of the first speeches he delivered in the campaign took place in Baltimore, where the president did not initially enjoy much popularity. At the Fifth Regiment Armory, the president offered a new policy to be called Social Security. The crowd's negative reaction was personified by Mencken, who sat impassively chewing his cigar throughout. He summed up the proposals as "demagogic." Here was a capital chance for the *Sunpapers* to write one of its strongest editorials, for Roosevelt's speech had received a rather indifferent reception from the crowd. Instead, Mencken thought, the *Sun* treated it mildly.

The opportunity for Mencken to air his grievances over how the press was handling such a powerful leader came at the annual luncheon of the Associated Press. Before 500 editors at the Waldorf-Astoria, Mencken studiously avoided politics, concentrating his ire on the newspaper business and referring to the editorial pages as "our grandest and gaudiest failure." Newspapers had become too refined, he argued; its writers seemed to have a constitutional apathy to offending anyone. "The newspaper is not only a newsmonger; it is also a critic," he declared. "Printing the bare news is only half the job. The rest is interpreting it, showing what it signifies, getting some sense and coherence into it."

> This leaves the field open to the newspapers of the country. They constitute its only effective opposition, and one of their clearest duties is to keep a wary eye on the gentlemen who operate this great nation, and only too often slip into the assumption that they own it.[5]

In EARLY JUNE 1936, Mencken went to the Republican convention in Cleveland where Governor Alfred M. Landon of Kansas was nominated. Mencken brought several Maryland madstones—basically, an ordinary rock that Mencken had attached to a card that listed the stone's powers, promising a remedy for various ills. He now began distributing the madstones among his friends; the Republican party was going to need all the luck it could get. Up to that time he had been hopeful that the Republicans might find someone capable of defeating Roosevelt. But he realized that unseating him was going to be a challenge.

In contrast to Franklin Roosevelt, who made each of his deliveries a clarion call to the country, Mencken said Landon might have been "reciting the multiplication table" for all the effect his speeches produced. Mencken traveled with Landon on three of his four campaign trips, and each state event had "no more thrills in it than a game of checkers." Most of the speeches were not spoken at all: they were simply recited badly. "If it was possible, by any device, however tortured, to stress the wrong word in a sentence, he invariably stressed it. If the text called for a howl of indignation, he always dropped his voice, and if a sepulchral whisper was in order he raised it." The effect of the governor's voice was that of "a muted xylophone."

Landon was smart enough to realize that his chief asset in the campaign was his character. If his speeches were not those of a rabble-rouser but simply plain talk of a plain man, it was in that character that Landon hoped to reach voters. He concentrated on what he considered the waste and extravagance of the current administration, a theme he was sure would please Republicans and conservative Democrats alike.

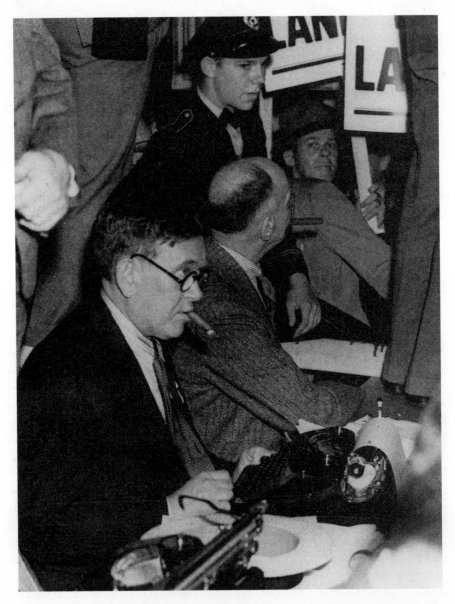

"Landon would need all the luck he could get." Covering the 1936 Republican convention.
H. L. Mencken Collection, Enoch Pratt Free Library.

While Mencken considered the Landon campaign futile, he personally
enjoyed the governor's company. The Kansas governor epitomized to Mencken
a typical, frugal, hard-working American, and for the first time, he endorsed
a candidate for the presidency. The support of Landon by Mencken seemed
incongruous to the liberal press, which felt betrayed by its favorite son, the self-
admitted lifelong Democrat who had grown up to be a querulous Tory. Seeing

Mencken under a Landon banner with a sunflower on his lapel, the columnist Westbrook Pegler observed, was one of the hilarities of the campaign. There were those who accused Mencken of being too much of the governor's confidant (a "lapdog," according to the liberal papers).

There were so many denunciations of Mencken that he found he had enough material on hand for ten *Schimplexicons*. "In quiet moments of soul searching," he confided, "I suspect that my patriotism has often fallen below the ideal vehicle." That same month, the *American Spectator* published an "obituary" for Mencken, stating that future generations would remember him as "one of the hollow men," with "the bite gone from his invective; the savor from his yawp."[6]

Nonetheless, Mencken's criticism of FDR transformed him into the darling of the conservatives, just as he had been the darling of the liberals less than a decade before. The *Sunpapers* received many requests for copies of Mencken's reports as they appeared. Conservative publishers such as William Randolph Hearst read Mencken's columns aloud to their friends. After reading Mencken's accounts of the convention, journalist and historian Mark Sullivan urged the *Sun* to submit them for the Pulitzer Prize. Mencken discouraged the *Sun*; he felt the prize ought to be given whenever possible to relatively younger recipients.

Nor did Mencken's conservatism dampen the admiration of a new generation of newspapermen, who found the older man to be a hard-working reporter who chased down every source of every major event. He would walk enormous distances or hitch a ride on bus, a streetcar, or a taxi just to get the missing fact to complete his report. At West Middlesex, Pennsylvania, site of Landon's boyhood home, Mencken arrived at the Sunday services ahead of the other reporters, generously furnishing them with data regarding the candidate and the city. Later he could be seen in the fifth pew, hymn book in hand, glasses halfway down his nose, singing lustily "Onward, Christian Soldiers," as if he had attended services all his life. When it was over, Mencken rushed down the church aisle to the pulpit, grabbing the notes of the minister. He reported his sermon in full for the *Sun*, later sending him a personal invitation to visit Baltimore.

When the indefatigable Mencken was not writing his own dispatches, he often acted as legman for his colleagues. He plied local reporters with questions about every town through which they had passed. This method enabled him to acquire knowledge of the countryside that was a veritable compendium of American folklore.

Being a good newspaperman did not lack its tribulations. "The reporter often has to do his work under great difficulties and to his own extreme discomfort," Mencken noted. At one point, the record-breaking heat in Pennsylvania made it too uncomfortable to work, and he took refuge in an air-conditioned train to write his stories. Two days later, in Buffalo, the temperature dropped forty degrees overnight and he was half frozen to death in the press stand. Mencken spent his birthday in Portland, Maine, listening to Landon make a dull speech in an open field full of mud puddles, with a cold fog blowing in from the sea.

"An indefatigable and hard working reporter." H. L. Mencken Collection, Enoch Pratt Free Library.

Liquor was a powerful antidote for such brutalities (after Portland, Mencken was convinced that a massive dose of Scotch had helped him overcome pneumonia). With the support of alcohol, he would regale the younger men until the small hours with tales of his early life and his reminiscences of the great and near-great. However, obtaining liquor was not always easy when traveling with a presidential candidate who was a Kansas progressive with one leg in the Anti-Saloon League. One evening on the train, passengers overheard Mencken call repeatedly for bourbon, then for some Scotch, then for some wine, and finally for beer. Upon being refused each time, Mencken complained to the waiter, "What in the hell is wrong with this goddamned train?" The waiter replied: "We is in Kansas." Kansas, the state of Alfred E. Landon, was a "dry state," and its constitution forbade the sale of any alcoholic beverages. "So that's it!," replied Mencken. "I might have known it!" He was certain that the full tale of his sufferings for God and country would break the hearts of his friends.

Even so, Mencken persisted following Landon from state to state, in what he termed "my devotion to the cause of Sound and Sane Government," although he could not shake the feeling that his candidate was doomed to defeat. By October, Mencken was one of the few journalists left aboard what he now called "the Landon funeral train." If the campaign trail had nearly worked Mencken to death, so, too, had it dealt a similar blow to Landon. At one point doctors compelled him to rest in bed, a fact that only further highlighted the contrast between the two candidates. Even under the strain, Mencken noted, the handicapped president was bearing up beautifully. "The Roosevelt family is completely superhuman," he wryly noted. "No member of it ever becomes tired."[7]

WHAT ENGAGED MENCKEN far more than the race between Roosevelt and Landon were the antics of the candidates of the third-party movements. Millions of dissidents opposed the New Deal, and in 1936 the new Union Party nominated William Lemke, a Republican congressman from North Dakota. He was supported by

Some suggested his columns on the 1936 Convention be nominated for a Pulitzer. H. L. Mencken Collection, Enoch Pratt Free Library.

Father Charles E. Coughlin, Michigan's "radio priest," and the Reverend Gerald K. Smith from Louisiana, who passionately believed FDR's policies were communistic (a "Brain Trust cake baked in Moscow," according to Smith).

When Smith stripped off his coat, gulped ice water from a pitcher, held aloft a Bible, and launched into a speech, even the reporters in the press stand at the convention stood up to cheer. At one point, Smith leaned over toward Mencken and gave him a wink, asking: "How'm I doin', Henry?" Smith nevertheless attacked attacked the columnist, calling him the "menial hireling of the prostituted *Baltimore Sun* papers."

Father Coughlin gave a show that fell short "no more than a yard or two" of that of Gerald K. Smith. In a fit of rhetorical passion, Coughlin ripped off his clerical collar and called the president "Franklin Double-Crossing Roosevelt" a "liar." The word "liar," Mencken reported, "came out like a discharge of artillery."

Mencken had taken an instant dislike to Coughlin, "a fraud of the first caliber," but his harangues were worthy of Billy Sunday at his best. One newspaperman, peering into Mencken's hotel window, recalled watching him at work alone, pounding out the copy on a typewriter on a desk. He would type a few sentences, read them, slap his thigh, toss his head back, and roar with laughter. Then he would type some more lines, guffaw, and so on until the end of the article. As Mencken told Edgar Lee Masters, "I was worn out by laughter far more than the weather." He had been at it from 9 a.m. until 3 a.m. the next day; but, said Mencken, "it is the best show since the Scopes trial."[8]

In late October, a poll published in the *Literary Digest* predicted a Landon victory. Great, traditionally Democratic newspapers also endorsed Landon, including the liberal *Evening Sun*. In Maryland, the *Sunpapers'* shedding of their long Democratic allegiance was seen as a betrayal of trust. When publisher Paul Patterson announced the decision at a luncheon for the *Evening Sun* staff, he cleared his throat and said he hoped there would be general acceptance. Patterson "was so nervous that his hands were shaking," writer R. P. Harriss recalled. "He probably felt someone might jump up and object in strenuous terms, or even resign."

First, there was a silence. Then Gerald Johnson quietly rose. Although the decision was obviously a *fait accompli*, he gave a careful, reasoned argument against it. No one said a word in rebuttal; the rest of the reporters remained silent, looking sheepish.

Mencken stepped in. "Johnson is violently opposed to this move, and I maintain that he ought to have his say," he announced. "I'll give him my space in the *Evening Sun* next Monday and take his on Thursday." It was a remarkable action by Mencken, considering his own opinion of Roosevelt. But he was determined that the paper must be fair in the opinion column, and that there should always be a free discussion on public issues.

Roosevelt's main fear about the election of 1936 may have been an antagonistic press, but the voters were strongly with him. The campaign, despite the press's opposition, was a long victory parade, with cheering crowds shouting their appreciation of the president.9

ELECTION DAY FINALLY DAWNED with Mencken firmly committed to the Landon ticket. In Baltimore, great crowds watched the returns flashing on a screen in Sun Square, their yells of approval growing louder as each tally came in. When a map depicting the Roosevelt sweep was displayed on the screen, there was an uproar. It was a victory without precedent.

Liberals now began roasting Mencken for previously stating that Roosevelt could have been "beaten by a Chinaman." Mencken wrote his niece that there was no reason for dejection. "Four years more of Roosevelt will make plenty of material for me." Besides, he told friends, the mob always rises up against its Messiah and crucifies him in the end. Mencken had already begun the countdown.10

If Mencken thought the Era of Good Feeling toward FDR would only last a few months, he soon discovered he was hopelessly mistaken. On this point, Mencken became convinced, lay the greatest challenge for the nation's press.

42

MENCKEN AS BOSS

F RANKLIN D. ROOSEVELT, IT WAS SAID, had three things going for him: a
great name, a great voice, and a great smile. With these gifts, he made
masterful use of the media changes then sweeping the country. If he had
followed the precedent set by Herbert Hoover and Calvin Coolidge, he would
have avoided the newspapermen. Instead, four days after his first inauguration, he
began a procedure that he soon elevated to an art form—the press conference.

The president would grin broadly, lean back in his armchair, take a cigarette
from his case, light it, puff leisurely, and greet reporters with a "Well, boys, and
how are you today?" One British newspaperman described the atmosphere "like
that of a gathering of friends for a friendly chat." Nicknames and first names were
used and exchanges were sprightly and humorous, leaving some of the reporters,
already sympathetic to New Deal policies, in an absolute glow.

But Mencken was preoccupied not just by Roosevelt's management of the
media, or even the fact that correspondents—after being invited to the White
House for clambakes, baseball games, and picnic lunches—were forging personal
relationships with the president. In his estimation the practice ruined reportorial
objectivity. As the *Wall Street Journal* put it: "A man would be less than human
[after all this] if he did not feel kindly disposed toward the Master of the New
Deal."

The New Deal publicity system particularly irked Mencken. Under
Roosevelt, Washington became the world's most important news center. Before
he occupied the White House, there was a tendency to cut down the size of
administration staffs dealing with the major newspapers and press associations.

But the New Deal, with its surfeit of information, changed all that. The National Recovery Act, for instance, manufactured news at a rate almost too fast for daily newspapers and wire services to handle. Established government departments such as Interior, Treasury, and Justice had become hot sources of news. The government's new press agents stepped in, many of them former journalists who were adept at writing copy. They shoveled out mimeographed handouts that were converted into stories in newspapers under Washington datelines that often won public support for New Deal programs.

Newspapermen were relying more and more on the handouts, which, as Arthur Krock of the *New York Times* pointed out, though useful did not tell the whole story. Despite the best efforts of some correspondents to look beyond the official versions, a study showed that Roosevelt's attempts to set the agenda worked extremely well. The administration's publicists also strove to close off hitherto open news sources. Roosevelt had become, as some called him, "the Master Manipulator."

The situation that confronted newspapers of the country was daunting. Mencken wrote a memo to publisher Paul Patterson: "The primary aim of the *Sunpapers*, both in their news columns and on their editorial pages, must be simply and solely to tell the truth . . . for we confront a high development of government propaganda. . . . Every public official with large powers in his hands should be held in suspicion until he proves his case, and we should keep him at all times in a glare of light." This had been the general policy of the *Sunpapers* ever since Mencken had written the White Paper in 1920. When it came to free speech, Mencken confessed to a friend, "I believe in it now more than I did in my early days."[1]

Mencken had long urged Patterson to remedy a palpable lack of ideas that was damaging the *Sunpapers* and making its editorial page so banal. As a result, Mencken was persuaded to drop his column and take over the editorial page for three months.

Before taking the helm, Mencken wrote a letter to each member of the staff, stating how much he was counting on him for scintillating ideas, assuring that "it will be pleasant to return, if only temporarily, to the editorial page where I first disported in 1910." Thus, even before he began, editorial writer R. P. Harriss commented, Mencken "started off making you feel that you were close to him." This was a boon to the demoralized group, already nervously speculating as to the real reasons for the reorganization. Even so, it was an unhappy period for the writers on both papers who felt that Mencken's Toryism would probably be hard to bear.

IT TOOK MENCKEN only a few days to assess the staff. To his disappointment, he discovered he did not have the men to revive the kind of editorial page he had in mind. As amiable as Mencken found them to be, he thought their individual talents third-rate for the requirements of the editorial page, with writing that was unimaginative and useless. Mencken later thus summarized his findings: an editorial writer, he wrote, was: "*(a)* a man who could write with some eloquence, *(b)* one who has sound information, and is always hunting for more, and *(c)* one who is not ashamed to be indignant." If an editorial could not arouse a reaction in the reader, it was "worthless."

Determined to make the editorial page less somber so that it was not only read but talked about, Mencken made a series of changes. Within 24 hours, R. P. Harriss jotted in his diary, Mencken "began making the place spin round and round." One of his first acts was to redesign the book page. It was given a check-list of new books, as it had been during his days at the *American Mercury*. Mencken also changed the overall typesetting, abolished the rule that there had to be a set number of editorials each day, and made use of large and bold illustrations, some of them maps, line drawings, even an eight-column cartoon. A quotation was printed under the masthead each day, out of the immense stock Mencken had been accumulating for his *New Dictionary of Quotations*, under such rubrics as Democracy, Government, Free Speech, and Free Press, all of them subjects on which Mencken held strong personal views. Soon the whole office was agog.

By far the most revolutionary change was Mencken's new schedule. "Under Hamilton Owens the work put into the editorial page had been reduced to a luxurious minimum," Mencken later explained. There had been a daily editorial conference at 9 a.m., followed by a series of brief editorials written in a matter of minutes and submitted to the composing room by 10:30. After the first edition appeared, the copyboy brought in a tray of coffee and buns, and the writers relaxed and read their pieces.

"I had this beautiful scheme of editing without pain wrecked in two days," Mencken recalled. He abolished the daily editorial conference and saw all the editorial writers individually before they set to work. If he did not like their idea, he tried to substitute another. When an idea *was* approved, Mencken saw to it that it was given careful and thorough treatment, and not merely dashed off. "This, of course," reflected Mencken, "usually made it impossible to finish the job by 10:30, and so the gentlemen of the staff began to suffer the novelty of working in the afternoons, and what is more, working hard."[2]

Mencken began his tenure as editor full of bounce. At ten o'clock Mencken would proudly don his beer jacket and, staff in tow, descend to the composing room to make up the editorial page. Most of the printers, awed by his presence, accorded him great deference, except for old Nick, who had known Henry since his youth and who treated him familiarly as if he were a bright but wayward schoolboy. Yet, it seems that none of them, not even Nick, was prepared for what came next.

To bring home to the ordinary man the enormity of the New Deal largesse and the scope of the federal dole, Mencken had hit upon the idea of presenting his message in the form of a graphic illustration, under the title of "OBJECT LESSON." Six of the seven columns were filled with black dots, over a million in all, representing "the Federal Government's immense corps of job-holders."

The screen used was so fine that to some subscribers it simply looked like a large gray area, and they besieged the paper with complaints that day and the following. To Mencken's delight, "Object Lesson" attracted national attention and was quoted across the country in magazines ranging from *Time* to *Printer's Ink*. "Many of these Federal job-holders, we fear," one paper editorialized, "do as little work as Mr. Mencken's corps of editorial writers did on that particular day."

The ensuing publicity inevitably focused attention on the *Evening Sun*'s editorial page. As the weeks passed, its innovations were universally praised; Mencken, stated the *Kansas City Journal-Post*, has "violated the basic journalistic law that editorial pages should be profound, self-consciously serious—and extraordinarily dull."

Mencken's next stunt was to print the longest editorial in journalistic history. By his personal order, the entire page was to be devoted to a single subject: "Five Years of the New Deal." It was to begin in the upper left-hand corner of the page and not end until it reached the lower right-hand corner. The task fell to Philip Wagner and Gerald Johnson, who did a conscientious job of reviewing critically, but fairly, the negative side of the Roosevelt administration. To their dismay, Mencken rewrote much of the piece, concluding that there was only one idea running through "the sorry farce from the rise of the curtain in 1933 to the present depressing scene." The New Deal, Mencken concluded, "teaches that whoever is getting on in the world is a suspicious character, and whoever is left behind is a hero and a martyr."

The general effect of the comments, R. P. Harriss grumbled in his diary, was to produce an editorial that was "grossly unfair and full of Tory venom. . . . Wagner, who had worked very hard to produce a sound review of the administration, was depressed over the way Mencken handled it." Wagner classified the editorial as "awful," adding, "Fortunately, [Mencken] has sprinkled characteristic adjectives and a fine spray of abuse all over the part I wrote, so that my share of the undertaking is perfectly concealed."

It did not take long for members of the staff to note that their editorial page had become largely a one-man show. Some thought that articles by Gerald Johnson, who did not conceal his admiration for Roosevelt, were often kept out of the paper because of that, though he was permitted to write his own rebuttal to "Five Years of the New Deal" under a four-column head: "On the Profit Side: A Reply to the Huge Editorial." The rebuttal evoked more interest and was reprinted in more papers than the original article, though Mencken thought it feeble stuff. After a while, Mencken gave Johnson no more assignments. "Instead, I let him write whatever he pleased, and then picked out the little that was printable."

Apparently sensing revolt among a staff of fervent New Dealers, Mencken called a general meeting. He reiterated his plans. These, Harriss privately reflected, seemed oriented to one sole aim: "to fill the *Evening Sun* editorial columns with long-winded venomous attacks on Mr. Roosevelt." The more the editorial writers listened to Mencken, the more alarmed they got. From then on,

Mencken told them, few if any editorials were to be written in the morning. He opposed the Hamilton Owens system of many short, pertinent comments on "spot news." This made for snap judgments and errors, he argued. Instead, Mencken wanted carefully written pieces on a few topics only, preferably written the night before—much in the same way he had handled his own Monday column or "The Free Lance" decades ago.[3]

Frequently, the assignments Mencken gave could not be done overnight—indeed, as Hamilton Owens subsequently commented, Mencken's standards of thoroughness and precision were so great that they might take a week, "so that when the morning came and the paper had to be made up, the material to fill the page simply wasn't there." As Wagner remembered, "when it came to contributions from the rest of us, here came his total intolerance of any writing not first class. Nearly everything we did went into the wastebasket, with the result that his anxiety about a daily crisis was justified, daily. We solved this by sneaking things into type ahead of time. When makeup time came, he had no choice but to use them." They were not precisely the kind of editorials that Mencken would have liked, Owens admitted, but "the fact is that they *were* printable, publishable editorials, and the page did come out."

This method proved frustrating both for Mencken and the staff. "We wore ourselves out trying not to be traditional," Harriss remembered. His diary recorded their dilemma. One entry read: "Wagner has been much annoyed because of the difficulty of finding editorial topics which Mencken will approve. About the only subject Mencken will accept is the New Deal—Its Iniquities." Harriss was sure that Mencken was "not always careful about the facts, nor [did] he hesitate to juggle them to suit his argument." Moreover, he suspected him of interlarding editorials written by staff with expressions of his own, "which changed the general tone and tended to give the writer a Tory complexion." Yet, Mencken insisted that he did not want any member of his staff to feel forced to write against the grain.

The page itself varied wildly from day to day, remembered Harriss, "reflecting both Toryism and radical change, pedestrian pomposity and high-jinks." Indeed, "if you take the three months and look them over, they were not necessarily the brightest three months in the history of the editorial page of the *Evening Sun*." Day after day, local issues were bypassed in favor of editorials that censured Roosevelt. In one of these, Mencken excoriated the TVA—which may have accomplished more for recovery than many of the other New Deal programs—as the only place where the president had a following, "among the anthropoids of the Tennessee Valley, where $200,000,000 of the taxpayers' money has been laid out to buy their votes." In another, Mencken simply displayed across the top of the page a huge eight-column, Edmund Duffy cartoon showing shabby men shambling in a bread line, titled "The Abundant Life—1938." Under a thin guise of an editorial celebrating the two-hundred-and-sixth anniversary of the birth of George Washington, entitled "Man of an Extinct Species," Mencken attacked "the character of high American officials" who were unlike Washington, who "kept promises," "never sought popularity by the arts of a demagogue," and "had a modest view of his own capacities and did not pretend to be wider or better than other men."[4]

None of this differed substantially from the stances Mencken had taken in the past. His denunciation of Franklin Roosevelt and the New Deal reminded readers of the *American Mercury* of the treatment he had given Coolidge and Hoover. His insertion of his own expressions into the text was a carryover from his days as editor of the magazine. What was different was the passion behind his purpose: to fight, as he told Patterson, for the chief liberal goals: the limitation of governmental powers, economy in all public services, the greatest tolerable degree of free speech, and a press secure against official pressure.

When Mencken was not denouncing Roosevelt, he went after Communists, whom he dismissed as jackasses and dishonest to boot. Mencken's view of radicalism, Harriss noted in his diary, "almost amounts to a phobia. Wagner and I call him, privately, the Red Hunter," constantly on the alert to pick up statements in such publications as *New Masses* and the *Daily Worker* to discredit suspected communists. Mencken also wrote against socialized medicine, a topic on which he would expand in his own column much later. One day, when Harriss showed him a mild phrase in a review that A. D. Emmart had written for the books page, Mencken said: "He's no good, he's a pink. A goddamned pink. I don't like a man around me that I can't trust."

In all fairness, other topics were covered during Mencken's tenure as editor. He focused on minorities; he spoke for the advancement of women; and he raised the issue of anti-lynching legislation. He also voiced support of Robert L. Vann, the black editor and publisher of the *Pittsburgh Courier*, as a candidate for the Supreme Court. When Vann was bypassed in favor of Hugo Black, Mencken insinuated that FDR's racial prejudice blocked Vann's nomination. Mencken also wrote a moving piece on the death of Clarence Darrow, reminding the public of the fury and righteousness he had shown during the Scopes Trial.

On the international front, Mencken wrote on Mexico, but paid very little attention to the rise of Hitler in Germany. His tenure as editor of the *Evening Sun* editorial page coincided with Hitler's invasion of Austria. During the weeks that followed, German actions were front-page news in the vast majority of American papers; according to the *Press Information Bulletin*, more than 1,400 editorials on the subject were printed, half of them devoted to the plights of the Jews. But Mencken devoted only one editorial to the Anschluss, explaining that at least Austrians had been taken over by one of their own. There was not a single mention of the plight of Jewish refugees.

The fact that Mencken had not devoted any space to the fate of the Jews did not pass unnoticed, and letters to that effect came into the office. Mencken took over the letters column himself, cutting the space in half. He lifted the "Points from Letters" feature from the *London Times*, editing down yard-long letters to one inch. Mencken dismissed these correspondents: "Most of them were Jews of low mental visibility, and in the early part of 1938 virtually all of their letters were devoted to denouncing Hitler. This rubbish," Mencken argued, "had driven all intelligent correspondents out of the paper."[5]

Throughout this period, Mencken was frustrated that although plenty of "graceful nothings" had been produced, he felt there was not one good editorial writer among the present staff. For all of his coaching, the future of the *Evening Sun* editorial page seemed just as unpromising as when he had taken the helm. Now and then, his patience wore thin. "Wagner and I have had several loud but good-natured arguments with Mencken over matters of make-up," Harriss recorded in his diary one day in March. "One of them became violent, with Mencken bellowing 'No, No, No,' and waving his arms, yelling, 'You and Harriss are ganging up on me and by God I won't *let* you two put that Katzenjammer over me!' A photographer who overheard the row looked in and was amazed. He thought I was going to hit Mencken with the bungstarter—which I keep on my desk against nuts who come in with grievances and threaten to wreck the place." The photographer fled to the city room, telling his colleagues that murder was being committed in "Brain Alley."

"The Mencken instinct for order in all things was equally manifest," Wagner remembered. It was not only in the manner he insisted the editorial page be composed, but even in his care in choosing a stenographer. Elsinor Roman was the stenographer in question, and she soon learned that no matter how quickly she took notes, Mencken was always one sentence ahead of her. "It was exhausting," she admitted. "I remember thinking, when I left his desk that first day, 'It's *inhuman* to dictate that fast.' But someone told me he just couldn't think slowly."

At first, Mencken found his new duties enjoyable. He wrote a correspondent: "The truth is that a newspaperman is never happier than when he is worked fifteen hours a day." This was of some comfort to the rest of the beleaguered staff, who had only to glance up from their typewriters to see that Mencken was completely absorbed in his own work; he did not even get up for a glass of water. He paid no heed to a sculptor working in the corner of the room, busily molding a likeness of the famous editor. For Mencken, that clay bust was "just a big mud pie." He kept going until after four in the afternoon, when he would glance at his watch and head for Hollins Street for an early dinner and his own private mail. Such a schedule did not leave much time for leisure; weekends were filled with the work he was unable to do at the office.

According to Harriss, "despite the fact that we worked like dogs" and disagreed with Mencken's views, relations between the editor and his staff were positive. "He was a taskmaster, he was a slave driver, but you did it because it was fun to do it," Harriss said. "And he did some nice things." Wagner noted that Mencken's "distress over the incompetence of his subordinates—and I may say that each of us displayed incompetence of a different sort—had the effect of increasing his personal kindness and courtesy to the very people who were driving

"One of the highlights . . . was to pour a glass of water over his head." Mencken at the *Sunpapers*, 1938, oblivious to the bust being made of him. H. L. Mencken Collection, Enoch Pratt Free Library.

him wild. . . . I have never known anyone more *considerate*, if I may, by the use of that mawkish word, expose him to posthumous embarrassment."

"To us smaller fry in the organization he was consistently genial and consistently helpful, although he could be sardonic," Gerald Johnson later wrote. "To me one day he observed, blandly, 'He is a great cartoonist, but in politics, of course, [Edmund] Duffy is an idiot.' Since Duffy's politics and mine were identical I got it, all right."

And yet, Johnson went on, "It would be difficult, indeed, to identify a man who didn't hate H. L. Mencken," the public figure of the signed articles. But the private figure was another story. "He was too expansive, too free of envy, too obviously void of any disposition to grasp at personal advantage. Even those most captious of critics, writers who knew that he could out-write them, once they came within the magnetic field of his personality lost the capacity to hate. They could be exasperated by him, they could denounce him with fire and fury; but they had trouble doing it with a straight face."[6]

WHILE MENCKEN WAS LAMBASTING FDR and his administration on the *Evening Sun* editorial page, uppermost in his mind was the situation in Germany. With the Anschluss had come the persecution of the Jewish population in Austria, which shocked the American press in a way that prior events in Germany had not. The news that Nazi authorities in Vienna had treated abusively Sigmund Freud

"... a zest for life ..." Mencken and the American scene. H. L. Mencken Collection, Enoch Pratt Free Library.

and Albert Einstein was the topic of many editorials that presented their situation as typifying the woes of the Jewish refugee.

Mencken did not share the sense of outrage of the rest of the nation. "My belief when history is written at last the one indubitable white mark to the credit of the Nazis will be the fact that they threw Freud out of Vienna," he said. "They will also get a gray mark, in my opinion, for chasing out Einstein." And while he

Cheeeriost!!

"Difficult to hate him." At a *Sunpapers* picnic. H. L. Mencken Collection, Enoch Pratt Free Library.

claimed that his natural inclination was against Hitler, he wrote to a nun that he was "still willing to be convinced." As American outrage intensified, Mencken persuaded himself that the dispatches reaching America were exaggerated. As he wrote to friends in Germany, "Three times out of ten they are obviously nonsensical."

It may have been this added to the pace of his editorial job that kept Mencken's nerves on edge and his chest pains acute. All his life Mencken had combatted pain by lying down for an hour or more, or taking two or three days of rest from his work. But now there was too much work to allow him such routines. He settled for gulping glasses of water mixed with a half teaspoon of bicarbonate of soda.

After weeks of discomfort, Mencken visited Dr. Baker, arriving, his doctor recalled, "in characteristic fashion—in a great rush and a minute ahead of a fit, saying he had a peculiar sensation about his heart." A cardiogram indicated arteriosclerosis. Over the course of Mencken's tenure as editor, spells of dizziness had plagued him. Every time he took a prescribed dosage of belladonna he had a troublesome reaction as he sat at his desk trying to write. At night, his sleep was frequently broken. Mencken soon realized that the anxiety of managing a staff and being responsible for the editorial page of the *Evening Sun* was taking its toll. In letters to friends, Mencken began to see his post as a purgatory he was more than eager to escape.

If Mencken felt limp, so did the staff. Frantically, Elsinor Roman asked a doctor to prescribe something to help her keep up with Mencken's pace; he advised her to give up her job. One of her duties was to wet the clay of the Mencken bust that had yet to be completed. One of the highlights of her day, before staggering home, she recalled, was to "pour a glass of water over Mencken's head."

Hamilton Owens wryly observed: "I wouldn't say the place was a shambles by the time Mencken's three months were over, but I would say that everybody concerned was happy, and Mencken was the happiest of them all."

Shortly thereafter, Mencken suggested to management that Philip Wagner become editor of the *Evening Sun*. As for himself, he again checked into Johns Hopkins Hospital where again he was diagnosed with arteriosclerotic heart disease. He confidently told doctors that a trip abroad would cure him of troubles. He had not been to Germany in ten years, he confessed, "and I am eager to find out what is really going on."

As Mencken's departure for Germany approached, he would have done well to recall a letter from his old friend, Philip Goodman, from whom he had been estranged since their argument over Hitler four years before. Noting that Mencken was about to visit "the land of the Barbarians," Goodman gave him several suggestions. At the bottom of the page, he made another. "Only, henceforth," he pleaded with Henry, "try and remove your heart from your head."[7]

43

BERLIN, 1938

Whas Mencken arrived in Berlin, orchids were in bloom in the public gardens and the red flags of the Nazi party, displayed from various buildings, flapped in the unusually warm summer breeze. The momentum of the successful 1936 Olympics continued unabated. Under the Nazis, the *Reichscapital* was the new focal point for Germany. Throughout the weeks of Mencken's stay, it seemed that in almost every other street some new building was being erected in Nazi neoclassical style. For the majority of Berliners, the mid-1930s had brought an unprecedented prosperity. For those who were favored in the new racially pure Reich, the times were productive and positive, making it all the easier to turn away from disturbing scenes in the streets, to accept quietly the increasingly repressive measures taken against Jews and other "enemies of the state."

The victims of the regime were more dehumanized and isolated as 1938 progressed. The fate of the Jews was discussed in hundreds of papers across the United States, with editorials devoted to their plight. In Berlin, however, Mencken took a limited view of the damage he learned about firsthand. During his stay, a group of vigilantes chalked the front windows of the small Jewish shops in the western neighborhood off of Kurfurstendamm, but by morning the police had removed all traces of the paint. Mencken dismissed all this. "Save for one or two smashed windows, I could see no evidence of violence," he wrote, although he admitted to his sister, "In that neighborhood every Jewish place now shows the real name of the proprietor. Thus, under the sign of a dress-shop called Imogene's or Mlle. Fifi's one reads: Inhaber: Max Cohn. But they are all open. In other parts of the city I find no Inhaber [proprietor] signs at all."

The fact that Jewish businesses remained open initially misled Mencken into thinking that the situation was not serious. He still held stubbornly to the view that there had been "some plain exaggeration" in newspaper reports. "The situation of the Jews is dreadful," he wrote to a correspondent, "but perhaps not as dreadful as the American papers make it out. I begin to realize more and more that journalism is not an exact science." In his quest for gifts for family and friends, he patronized Jewish-owned shops, each time reporting in letters to the United States that these were still doing a fair amount of trade. He repeatedly underscored that the *Inhaber* signs were not many, that "only a few" shops were marked *arierische Geschäft* (Aryan business).

Alarming as these actions were, they did not seem to dampen Mencken's enthusiasm for the country he loved, and he continued to look at everything through a soft haze. His romantic view of Germany was stimulated by good food, good beer, and music; by spending evenings sitting in a courtyard picturesquely lit by a row of flambeaux, listening to the Berlin Philharmonic Orchestra playing concerts under the open sky; by the knowledge that the Mencken clan had originated in this very land and rose to become dominant figures in the seventeenth century as world renowned scholars at the University of Leipzig. The contemporary German Jews, though harried, still seemed to be surviving. In fairness, as historians have pointed out, no bureaucrat in 1933 could have predicted what measures would be taken in 1938; nor was it possible to foretell what would happen during the 1940s. The steps toward total destruction of the Jews were introduced sequentially: first, the concept of the Jew is defined; then the expropriation operations are inaugurated; third, Jews are concentrated in ghettos; and finally, the decision is made to annihilate European Jewry.[1]

Mencken nevertheless still exhibited a stupefying naiveté about Hitler and his ultimate aims. Even at this stage, after five and a half years of Nazi rule, many other Americans did not understand that anti-Semitism was one of the keystones of Nazism. So while Mencken in letters termed Hitler an "idiot," "lunatic," "maniac," a "preposterous mountebank" whose "whole scheme seems to be insane," to some degree he continued to see him basically as a "buffoon" and essentially harmless.

He sent his friends postcards portraying Hitler smiling in the company of small children. It was certainly a far different Hitler from the raving madman customarily shown in American newspaper photographs and newsreels. "Does this look like a tyrant?" Mencken scribbled on the back of one postcard that showed Hitler beaming at a blond, pig-tailed little girl busily devouring a bowl of cherries. "You have been deceived by Heywood Broun and the Elders of Zion." Another postcard depicting Hitler and the Goebbels family enjoying themselves at Obersalzburg led him to comment: "More proof—as if more were needed.

"mistaking . . . a macabre sense of humor." A postcard from Nazi Germany, 1938. Courtesy Sara Anne Duffy Chermayeff.

This is an actual photograph. No fake." Another: "How could one who loves children be wicked? You have been grossly misinformed by Bolshevik propaganda." And still one more, as Hitler stooped to chat to a toddler: "Find me if you can, a similar picture of Stalin. You have been misinformed about Hitler." When Anne Duffy replied to these, Mencken continued with the banter: "I am delighted to hear that you have changed your attitude toward Hitler. He is really a genuine

How could the arch-critic, debunker of all— see a postcard us exculpatory "evidence"! ?

genteel fellow and a great lover of humanity. If he had his way war would be abolished altogether and every sincere patriot would be presented with forty acres of land and two mules."

Conceivably, this was typical Mencken spoofing, as Alfred Knopf once noted, a sense of humor that misled only those readers who did not know him well. They "would make the mistake of taking literally whatever he wrote in a letter—and he sometimes wrote shocking and startling things—when he was merely giving rein to his lusty and sometimes macabre sense of humor," Knopf said. The best way to vanquish enemies, he believed, was to laugh at them.

After Mencken's death, Gertrude made sure to tell her brother August to dispose of anything that might be misunderstood by posterity. "During Hitler's early days we [she and Henry] wrote of him in a friendly way. I think Henry destroyed such letters but maybe you had better go through the file to make sure."[2]

Mencken's incredible lack of suspicion toward Hitler during 1938 was in keeping with what many German citizens in that country felt at the time, and what many German Americans felt at home. "Hitler, whatever his outrages, had found a way to restore hope and self-respect to the country, and what is more, confidence," Mencken argued in his memoirs in 1942. The defeatism he had observed in 1922 had given way to assurance. In a little while, Hitler would have the military strength to enforce his demands. Mencken could identify emotionally with the proud new Germany Hitler had created out of the debris of war, reparations, and depression. Everywhere Mencken went, the weather was glorious, the fields bountiful, the economy thriving, with "Help Wanted" ads scattered throughout the press. Gradually, he no longer saw Hitler as a joke but as a master economist and powerful leader. "The Hitler New Deal," Mencken remarked, "seems to be working better than Franklin's. There is actually a shortage of labor."

In reality, the Berlin of the 1930s was a schizophrenic mixture of material success and terror, but Mencken complained that only one side of the picture was being reported by the British and American press. For instance, much as he thought that "Hitler's attitude toward learning is ignorant and preposterous," he insisted that in the field of science Germany remained the world leader.

While Mencken was in Berlin during the summer of 1938, he read in a newspaper that a bacteriologist attached to the veterinary institute there had discovered a vaccine against foot and mouth disease. "Upon my return to the United States I inquired if anything had been heard of it here," Mencken recalled. "I found that the American newspapers had not reported it. The correspondents in Berlin were all too stupid to see its possibilities. They devoted all of their dispatches to political speculations, most of them inflammatory and unwarranted by the facts."

Mencken's lack of confidence in the American foreign press stemmed in part from his experience in Berlin during 1917 and the traumatic aftermath of the mass hysteria against all things German during and after World War I. In that period, he had come face to face with the deliberate falsification of news reports, many of which originated in London. During the winter of 1917, as in the summer of 1938, German papers protested against what they saw as an anti-German campaign propagated mainly by the British press. "New instigation with old lies," as one newspaper headline had it. Mencken remained mired in the mindset of two decades earlier, choosing to remain loyal to the German point of view.

Mencken in 1938 purposely stayed at the Bristol Hotel, several blocks away from the Adlon where most American journalists resided. "They are, as I knew, mainly duds." His experience during World War I convinced him that the best and most accurate information about what was going on in Germany came from well-placed German friends.

One of these was the widow of Henry Wood, a professor of German at Johns Hopkins University, who had obtained for him an introduction to Kaiser Wilhelm in 1922. Mencken heard stories from her of the brutality by the Poles against some of her friends. Otto J. Merkel, an aircraft manufacturer with access to the highest army circles, was another witness. His information on military matters was of immense interest to Mencken; Merkel submitted himself to frank questioning about the Czech and Polish armies, then being subsidized on a large scale by both England and France. Mencken was surprised when Merkel told him the chiefs of the new German army did not fear old enemies: "He said that they counted on capturing most of the *materiel* of both, and using it against France."

Mencken shared more in common with Georg Kartzke, a lifelong liberal with strong ties to the United States and especially to Yale University, where he had once taught. On Unter den Linden, Kartzke's fierce denunciation of the Hitler regime was so loud that, even though he was speaking in English, Mencken felt called on to warn his friend to be careful. But while Kartzke confessed to being terribly upset by the harsh manner in which Jews were being treated, in the same breath he said, "he had come to the conclusion that their own gigantic folly was to blame for it."[3]

ALTHOUGH MENCKEN WOULD NOT ADMIT IT, the longer he remained in Germany during the summer of 1938, the harder it would have been for him to dismiss as exaggerated all American and British newspaper reports about the Jewish plight. Even with the contention that there were no active signs of persecution, Mencken had only to read the German papers to feel a frightening sense that massive prejudice did exist, with promises of more to come. Mencken was in Berlin during its midsummer festivities, when there were parades and bands playing throughout the city, and when Goebbels made a speech in the Olympic stadium. Although there is no record of Mencken's attendance, even with his faulty German he surely could not have overlooked the headlines and nationalistic cover stories in the German newspapers and Goebbels's vehement denunciation of enemies of the new Germany. Newspaper accounts described how the masses had supported anti-Semitic declarations with enthusiastic cheers. When Goebbels cried: "Is it not disgusting and doesn't one turn red with anger, if one remembers that during the last months not less than 3,000 Jews migrated to Berlin?" indignant shouts roared through the stadium. "What do they want here?" asked Goebbels. Agitated cries of "OUT!" shook the air.

Whether or not Mencken read these reports, he admitted that the situation of the Jews was "very bad." He wrote to Max Brödel: "They have been driven out of many small towns, and are concentrated in the cities. The Public Health Service doctor at the American consulate told me that many of the richer ones are trying to get visas for the United States. Only those who have well-to-do friends or relatives in America are passed."

Day after day that summer, new legal measures added to the pressure. Beginning in July, the ministerial bureaucracy obliterated any remaining Jewish businesses. Jewish property was confiscated, an action ostensibly justified by claims that half the property in Berlin was owned by Jews and either dependent on their capital or administered by them. Germans argued that all Jewish capital in Germany really belonged to them because the Jews could not have acquired it honestly. That July, a decree by the Interior and Justice Ministries required all Jews of German nationality to apply for identification cards; still another prohibited Jews from practicing certain professions; throughout, newspapers emphasized the need for blood purity among Germans. Mencken's only comment was that "outwardly, everything looks placid. The crops are enormous, and the country is lovely. But the state of the poor Jews is very depressing."4

Prior to Mencken's stay in Germany, Patterson had asked him to send home dispatches for the *Sun.* The paper was relying on a team of reporters sent by the Associated Press to cover a conference of the Intergovernmental Committee, at Évian-les-Bains on Lake Geneva, called by Roosevelt to find ways of helping Jewish refugees. During the conference, it became painfully clear that few nations, including especially the three great powers—the United States, Great Britain, and France—wanted to open their doors to Jewish immigrants. Mencken's reports would have been valuable not only to the *Sun* but to the public back home. But he was vehemently opposed to the idea and could not be persuaded to touch the subject in his new Sunday column.

During 1938, many in the United States, like Mencken, deeply respected and admired German culture, and were distressed by the conformity and behavior of the Germans. Unlike Mencken, they went public with their criticism. How, one reporter asked in the *New Republic,* "can the German nation, this mighty and splendid nation, have sunk so low as to build a whole system on prejudice, construct a philosophy out of inhumanity? How can the ordinary, friendly, good-natured people one sees in the streets and the beer gardens and shops, the clear-eyed German people, accept such twisted and darkened and hideous nonsense as being a rule of life?"

If Mencken felt any torment over the behavior of his ancestral homeland, he chose to turn away from the whole business. However, by refusing to write a single newspaper article or column during the summer of 1938, he opened himself to criticism from his own profession that he had failed miserably as a newspaperman. "How could anyone," Lawrence Spivak mused years later, "least of all a journalist, go to Germany and *not* write about his impressions?"

William Manchester recounted that an entranced Mencken, before leaving Munich in 1912, "had so pledged his soul to his dream of Bavarian culture that no war, not even a Hitler, could ever shake him awake." That loyalty was evident in Mencken's trepidation, in advance of his trip, over what he would find in Germany once he got there. He said at the time: "My suspicion is that the situation there is really very bad and I hesitate to be the one to have to report it." When it came to matters about Germany, Mencken was a romantic first, a newspaperman second, despite the sound advice that Philip Goodman had given him. Mencken insisted upon viewing Germany not with his head, but with his heart.5

In any event, it was the Germany of his ancestors, not Hitler's Berlin, that Mencken had gone to see. Rather than dwelling on the reality before his eyes, he retreated to a Germany that no longer existed. He was impatient to get out of the city and head for the remote villages to see "all of the backwoods that I have never visited." After seeing Leipzig, the home of Otto Johann Burkhard and Friedrich Mencken, he drove to the birthplace of his grandfather Burkhardt Ludwig Mencken, a tiny village called Laas. Another day, peering through the dim light of the old cathedral at Marienwerder, Mencken found the tablet of his ancestor Eilhard Mencken, dated 1641, fifteen feet above the stone floor, on one of the gaunt, interior walls.

Then it was on to East Prussia, through long stretches of dense primeval forest and small lakes to the region he had last seen in 1917, when it had been buried under many feet of snow. Now the sun shone brightly on the trees and water. Mencken celebrated the Fourth of July roving over the battlefield of Tannenberg, the location of Germany's biggest victory during World War I, and gazed at Hindenburg's tomb. Along the route, Mencken carefully picked some flowers, making sure not to crush the petals of a *Kaiserblum*, so he could send one to his sister as a souvenir.

Onward Mencken traveled, first to Halle and then to Wittenberg, where the Menckens had been professors and practioners of law during the eighteenth century. As his train ran along the foothills of the Hartz Mountains, Mencken was enraptured with the scenery: "Never in this world have I seen more smiling fields or more charming villages." His last trip took him south and west of Berlin to the Schwarzwald, then on the Rhine by steamer to Koblenz, up to Cologne, finally terminating in Oldenburg, in the flat, marshy country where the Mencken clan may have originated, and where Helmrich Mencke, the earliest Mencken patriarch, died in 1570.

By the end of his stay, Mencken had traveled three thousand miles by train and car. As much as he enjoyed these adventures, in all of them a sense of loneliness accompanied him, with only a chauffeur to keep him company or local townspeople with whom to practice his halting German. In many of the church-yards, it was difficult to decipher the inscriptions on the ancient graves.

But if Mencken thought he could escape the tensions of Berlin by retreating into the past, he was mistaken. Germany was on the brink of war. Everywhere Mencken went he could see soldiers marching along the rolling country roads; airplanes roared overhead. Trains in the Polish Corridor were packed, ostensibly with émigrés. The only mention Mencken made of all this in his memoirs was that he had to stand throughout most of his journey. His ship was not to sail for another week, but he cut short his stay.

Mencken started for home feeling that a chapter had ended and that he would probably never visit Germany again. He was 58 years old, and his health was showing the effects of a lifetime of hard work. He was conscious that one day his name, too, would be a line on a crumbling stone. Moreover, another great European war was certain. He was convinced that the Germans were not eager for it, not because they wanted to avoid war but because they were as yet unprepared. But, as Mencken put it, they were making fast progress to "face the music with confidence."

When the *Europa* finally sailed into New York harbor, reporters were waiting on the dock to interview the more notable passengers as they disembarked. Notepads in hand, they surrounded Mencken. What did he think of the situation in Germany? The country, Mencken replied in denial of what he had just seen, "looked like a church to me, it was so quiet." Mencken on his return made history, noted one columnist, "by being the only arriving celebrity in three years who did not venture on the prospects of a European war."

Mencken's reticence extended to friends of the Saturday Night Club, awaiting his homecoming that following weekend. Mencken, Louis Cheslock recorded in his diary, "has been inordinantly uncommunicative about the scene under Hitler." Instead, he preferred rather to speak "of the 'Christmas-card' prettiness of the Black Forest [and] the church where one of his ancestors was dignified with a [memorial] some centuries ago."[6]

44

POLEMICS AND PREJUDICES

ALTHOUGH MENCKEN SAID NOTHING on his return from Europe about the
Jews in Germany, it is clear from his private writings that he had the
matter on his mind. It was not until *Kristallnacht*, on November 9, 1938,
that he publicly spoke out against the physical persecution.

In the weeks that followed, a thousand or more editorials were published
on the subject, the overwhelming majority expressing American contempt for
German behavior while nevertheless remaining opposed to any changes in
refugee legislation. The anti-Semitic mood of the country was reflected in
answers to a question posed by a Roper poll in 1938: What kinds of people do
you object to? More than half of Americans believed that Jews were different
from everyone else and that these differences should lead to restrictions in business and social life.

In spite of prevailing opinion, Mencken adopted a contrary stance. On
November 27, 1938, his column "Help for the Jews" directly proposed that the
United States open its doors to them. Arguing that the American plan for helping
the refugees was limited to "weasel words and flattery," yet "so curiously stingy
with actual aid," he attacked the British alternative of resettling the Jews in
remote colonial areas. Mencken's principal criticism, however, was reserved for
Roosevelt. Politically vulnerable during the latter part of 1938, FDR was, as
Mencken put it, "sorry for the Jews, but unwilling to do anything about it that
might cause him political inconvenience at home."

The decision that America not serve as a home to Jewish refugees was not
only welcomed by citizens of the United States, but as Mencken observed, "the

American newspapers with their usual credulity, applauded it gravely." This was not the case of the black press, Mencken pointed out, referring to a sympathetic article by George S. Schuyler in the *Pittsburgh Courier*. Walter Lippmann in *Time* magazine, however, said nothing could be done for the persecuted Jews except to find refuge in Africa.

While Mencken's column clearly demonstrated his defense of civil rights and liberties for all men and women regardless of country or race, it also revealed a certain prejudice; when it came to a discussion as to where refugees should be allowed to settle, he specified the United States only for German Jews who "constitute an undoubtedly superior group." He downgraded the Eastern Jews, saying they should be sent to Russia, where their opportunities would be "immensely better," a position in accord with the prevailing view of mainstream America.

Mencken still did not agree, however, with the alternative proposal of the Zionists for establishment of a Jewish state in part of Palestine. Having visited there himself only five years earlier, he sensed prophetically that the establishment of a Jewish homeland in Palestine would result in increasing tensions. He felt certain that the Jews had been naive in accepting the British government's Balfour Declaration in 1917, which favored the establishment of a Jewish homeland. He wrote:

> There was nothing in the document, in fact, justifying their common assumption that the whole of Palestine was to be turned over to them. The most they were *true* promised was the right to live there—but only under such circumstances that the rights of other inhabitants of the country would not be invaded. They always forget this provision.

Mencken remained convinced that renewed pleas for Palestine by Zionists would inevitably further stir up anti-Semitic feeling in the United States. He wrote a Baltimore cleric that Jews' constantly propagating the notion they are a separate people with distinct interests "is the sort of thing that gives anti-Semitic demagogues their chance." More than once he resolved to "write nothing more about the Jews, no matter how poignant their sufferings. It is impossible to discuss their troubles with any show of sense without bringing down a storm of hysterical objurgation."

Behind the scenes, however, Mencken did what many others declined to do: he helped Jewish refugees emigrate to the United States. He submitted affidavits and petitions to the U.S. Consul on behalf of family members of his friends, including Oscar Levy, the Nietzsche scholar, and Leon Kellner, an early contributor to the *American Mercury*. Moreover, his assistance continued once the refugees had arrived in the United States. He agreed to sponsor others, promising authorities at the State Department he would "take care of them in case they get into difficulties." For all of Mencken's private charges of "hysterical Jews," he nonetheless became, as Leon Kellner's daughter wrote him, the "embodiment of hope" for the "Disinherited and Exiled."[1]

Thus, it was a shock to Mencken when he read an essay in the *North American Review* by his former assistant Charles Angoff, accusing him of being lukewarm toward Nazism. "Isn't Hitlerism, which deprives millions of people of their civil rights and persecutes helpless minorities, also worth a few resounding attacks?" Angoff argued. "Does Mencken's interest in honor and decency stop at the Rhine?" Angoff, in a thinly disguised reference to the break in friendship with Philip Goodman, observed that many of Mencken's old associates "have reasoned with him in vain so often" about Hitler and Germany "that they have been inclined to give him up."

Mencken had never suspected how deeply his former assistant resented him. He dismissed Angoff as "a poor fish consumed by gigantic ambitions." Angoff's bitterness was confirmed years later by his daughter, Nancy Gallin. She had learned not to discuss Mencken, because whenever the name was mentioned, "Father cursed him, and always in connection with an epithet."

Yet, Mencken was far more troubled by the article than he was willing to let on. Angoff's pointed inference about the loss of his friendship with Goodman reopened old wounds. He found himself feeling "in the dumps," unable to do any sustained work. His irritability was evident to his friends. "One had the impression," Edmund Wilson wrote, "that Mencken was more disagreeable and bitter, becoming rather nasty in his arguments in a way that had not been characteristic of his hard-hitting but good-humored ridicule." Wilson ascribed Mencken's demeanor to the fact that his "ideal of Germany was contradicted by the behavior of Hitler and the Nazis, of whom Mencken had never approved. . . ." In the *American Mercury*, Mencken had compared Hitler to a harmless buffoon, a demagogue worthy of William Jennings Bryan. As far back as 1912, he had declared with some pride that "mountebanks" such as these would be unimaginable in Germany.

Too proud to admit error, he now wrote of his concerns. As Mencken put it in 1939, "I am a great deal less interested in what Hitler does to the Czechs, Jews and Rumanians and so on than I am in what he does to the Germans. My fear is that after ten or fifteen years of his rule, free speech will be dead in Germany and almost beyond hope of resurrection. Inasmuch as I believe that it is one of the greatest values cherished by modern man, I can only conclude that its destruction will be costly to German civilization."[2]

DETERMINED TO SET HIS OWN THOUGHTS down on paper, Mencken renewed his labor on "Advice to Young Men." The book, as he planned it, was to open with a discussion of values. "The test of every individual is really the values he cherishes," he typed in a note to himself. "The chief mark of the inferior man is that he immensely admires mean things. His values are all false ones—patriotism, conformity, respectability."

Mencken had visited these themes before, in *Notes on Democracy*. Mencken's musings in "Advice to Young Men" constituted a penetrating examination of his ideals and his thoughts on the United States as events escalated toward World War II. The real question, Mencken jotted in his notes, was not whether the country was right or wrong, but whether it was gallant or not. "I can support it against odds, but not when it tackles a puny antagonist or is not hard beset by other enemies. Here we can open another of the differences between honor and morals."

In this book, Mencken played with the notion of writing a treatise on the human species, following the line of Thomas Henry Huxley. His interest in medicine and biology accepted the Darwinian hypothesis of natural evolution. But Mencken's view that the biological process proved "superiority is deserved and what is more, real" remained the most conflictive of positions. These were no different from those views he had outlined in 1910 when he had written *Men Versus the Man*.

What is especially disturbing about all these entries is what one writer from the *Baltimore Jewish Times* later called their "grim seriousness. The customary Mencken wit is largely absent, leaving only the opinions themselves."

Mencken's stubbornness in relinquishing nineteenth-century views inevitably made his opinions racist. The idea of biological superiority had obsessed many American thinkers in the latter half of the nineteenth century. The noted anthropologist Franz Boas led a generation away from this theory, challenging biological heredity and replacing it with the notion that environmental influences were determinative. Although this was a significant conclusion in racial studies and substantiated by later investigations, Mencken as late as the 1940s was writing that it was "absurd." Boas had "yielded to his native Jewishness in his old age," Mencken wrote; any doctrine that stated racial differences were entirely imaginary was simply "drivel."

As a reaction against the "Aryan imbecilities of Hitler," Mencken believed Boas had gone to "extravagant lengths." Moreover, when it came to the relationship between Jews and other minority groups, blacks especially, Mencken argued that despite "Jewish propaganda for tolerance," there was little sign of them welcoming "Negroes into their homes, offices, clubs, synagogues, and stores." The department stores in downtown Baltimore, he observed, "nearly all of them owned and operated by Jews, discourage colored trade."

He found it "curious that no one has ever attempted a really scientific investigation of anti-Semitism." The truth, Mencken believed, "lies, as usual, in the middle ground, and it ought to be unearthed. But the moment any attempt is ever made to unearth it the inquirer will face the rage of all Jewry, and in a little while he will be defending himself against the charge that he is propagating a new and most horrible variety of anti-Semitism, and it will be impossible for him to go on to any profit."

Missing, too, in "Advice to Young Men" are Mencken's frequent assertions of admiration for African Americans; like his entries on Jews, there remains little but denigration. In one such entry, he writes: "I should start out by saying frankly that I don't admire the darker races." Four months later he writes: "I believe that white people of America will always run the country and that they will forever object to intermarriage and equality. Nevertheless, the Negro still has certain clear rights, and some of them at least are realizable . . . the educated and intelligent Negro should be permitted to vote precisely as an educated white man should be permitted."

Such conflicting views throughout the manuscript represented a devilish conundrum. As Alistair Cooke pointed out, "in the first quarter of the century Mencken's assumption that everybody he dealt with—of whatever race or persuasion—was to be equal, was rare." Mencken's actions on behalf of African Americans, when juxtaposed against entries in "Advice to Young Men," serve as just one more example of the contradictions in Mencken's personality that made him so controversial.

The lynching episode of 1932 was one instance; publishing and promoting the work of black authors when no other white editor was doing so was another. He repeatedly urged Paul Patterson to devote space to features on African American issues in the *Sunpapers*, arguing they should not just write news stories when blacks were in the hands of the police. This was the same man who cried out for common decency against race discrimination when Donald G. Murray, a black graduate of Amherst College, was refused admission to the Law School of the University of Maryland; when Countee Cullen was denied entrance into the Maryland Club of Baltimore; and when another African American was denied a seat in the reserved white section of a cafeteria in New York. These were the kinds of things that happened in Mississippi, Mencken argued.

Here was a man who, during the height of racial tension in Baltimore (and at the urging of his mother), also worried about decreasing property values and hired "a Jew lawyer" to induce others in Hollins Street to segregate "the coons who menace" his neighborhood. Taken alone, the sentiment is outrageous. But as Mencken wrote in his newspaper column, the "low riffraff" migrating from other cities were "driving out the more respectable people of their own race." Rents were being forced too high, Mencken argued, displacing "colored gentry" with "crapshooters," a process helped by the same "scoundrels who exploit the black tenant—almost always white men. . . . If all colored folk of Baltimore were housed as the better sort now try to house themselves this would be a far healthier and happier town than it is."

At the same time, here was a man who delighted in poking fun at the racial comments of his friends, and, in doing so, displayed racial tendencies himself. "But when it was a question of individuals," recalled Hamilton Owens, he "judged them on an individual basis, and, in my observation, no consideration other than individual worth entered into the equation. In his house I have dined with Negroes and Jews as well as with Scots, Englishmen and Heaven knows what other races. He was a compassionate man and was determined that none of these social taboos which operate in all communities against certain groups would cloud his judgment of any human being."

George Schuyler agreed: "There was very little gabble about civil rights in those days." Mencken had "none of the mawkishness that comes from a lot of professional liberals, which is rather nauseating. And so he could chuckle over many things that other people wouldn't deign to mention. Because he had no illusions about the Negro or about whites, for that matter—it was all about the individual."

"Advice to Young Men" was never completed, even though Mencken later confessed to having accumulated "40 or 50 tons of notes" for it. It was not until 1945 that Mencken began putting his notes into better shape, some of which he mined for *Minority Report*. He gave the material another combing in 1955, expurgating some of the racial opinions contained therein. In the end, the passage of time that Mencken had spoken of, with all of its horrors of the Holocaust, of mounting racial tension in Baltimore and elsewhere in the country, may have been responsible for causing Mencken to reject these entries. In the end, he decided to reserve his pen exclusively "for braggarts and mountebanks, quacks and swindlers, fools and knaves."[3]

DURING THIS TIME, Blanche Knopf had been urging Mencken ("perhaps nagging would be not too strong a way to put it," Alfred observed) to get on with his autobiography, excerpts of which had appeared in the *New Yorker*. "I am thinking of calling it 'Happy Days,'" Mencken wrote to Blanche. The writing turned out to be a genuine pleasure, enabling him to retreat from the distress of the approaching war and slip back to the Golden Age between 1880 and 1892. Here were the light-hearted accounts of Mencken's introduction to music and his genesis as a bookworm, character sketches of his family and the men who lived in the alley behind Hollins Street, the routine of Americans from an earlier time, a record of a whole era, as Mencken put it, "now fast fading into the shadows of forgotten history." If, as Mencken had confessed, he had been "in the dumps," with the writing of *Happy Days* "I begin to feel alive again." Cautiously, he showed an advance copy to his brother Charlie, who immediately recognized the neighborhood characters populating the memoir.

The book was written in a lively style that had not been seen since Mencken's early days on the *American Mercury*; every page demonstrated the ease of a highly skillful writer. Unlike the diary entries of "Advice to Young Men," the tone of *Happy Days* was placid and benign, detecting the ridiculous side of man without judging him harshly. Helen Essary, who had grown up with Mencken in the Hollins Street neighborhood, had little trouble seeing through her friend's many contradictions. "Underneath the hard-boiled armor you wear for your debunking crusades," she wrote, "you are just a first-class sentimentalist."

Despite Mencken's enchantment with *Happy Days*, he was discomforted by chest pains brought on by his arteriosclerosis and the seriousness of world events. On July 21, 1939, while walking, he was struck by "a far-away feeling" and numbness behind his left ear. Then, in varying intensity, the whole side of his left face

"I am my own party." At home in his office at Hollins Street. Photo by Alfred A. Knopf. Harry Ransom Humanities Research Center, The University of Texas at Austin.

became numb, then his left hand and arm, accompanied by a pain behind his forehead. The event, Mencken said later, was "a sudden blow that served warning that, with sixty approaching, I was no longer the resilient and indomitable youngster that I had once been." He was admitted to the hospital, where doctors verified that he had just had a heart attack. Only too well Mencken realized that "I was growing old at last, and that the end of my sojourn in this vale was looming into view."

On September 1, 1939, Hitler invaded Poland; two days later England, fulfilling its treaty obligation, declared war on Germany. It seemed inevitable to Mencken that the United States would be involved sooner or later. With each passing day, he renewed his resolve to quit writing for the newspaper. "Not only is Congress going along with Roosevelt, but the newspapers with very few exceptions have abdicated their right to criticism," he complained to friends in Berlin. "We are going through the bogus neutrality of Wilson all over again."

With his usual bravado, Mencken claimed he had never paid serious attention to contemporary opinion and suspected that most other writers did the same. "Certainly there is no sign that Shakespeare did," Mencken wrote. ". . . he steered down his own course regardless of what the morons who supported him believed or not believed." Writing in his study, Mencken felt "quite distinct and separate from the masses of men. It is very comforting on blue days. I belong to no party. I am my own party."

At the same time, Mencken was plagued with self-doubt. He had written a few columns protesting the course of events, but realized "they are too feeble to accomplish anything." He might well have wondered, as Fred Hobson wrote in his biography, "if Angoff might have written, with only slight exaggeration, what many others were thinking—that [Mencken] was, indeed, finished." Toward the end of the year Mencken reflected to his brother Charles: "I begin to suspect that my best days of labor are now over."

He spent Christmas Eve with the Duffys. Earlier that year, little Sara Anne had burst her appendix and slipped into a coma, terrifying family members who thought the child would die. For weeks Mencken had been tenderly solicitous of his late wife's namesake as if she were his own daughter. Now that the patient was fully recovered, he presented her with a miniature doctor's kit. Clambering up on Mencken's knee, the little girl placed the toy stethoscope to his heart. After a moment, she looked up at him, worried. "I don't hear anything!" she said.

"Just what I thought," commented Mencken. "I've been dead for years."[4]

45

TRIUMPH OF DEMOCRACY

I N THE SPRING OF 1939, as the world hurtled toward war, Franklin Roosevelt's repeated promises of American neutrality had been dismissed outright by Mencken, who thought them just as bogus in 1939 as such promises had been in 1917. "Whenever two gangs of thieves come into conflict anywhere in the world, it quickly appears that vital American interests are involved," he argued, "and that unless one or the other gang is put down at once not a sharecropper's wife in Arkansas will be safe from licentious generals." He was convinced that American security in the world would depend, like Switzerland's, on abstention from European conflict.

Warfare was not made by the common folk, "scratching for livings in the heat of the day," he wrote. It was made by "demagogues infesting palaces." The overwhelming majority of Americans did not want war again and hoped that it would not come, as did the majority of Europeans. He went on:

> But the main reason why it is easy to sell war to peaceful people is that the demagogues who act as salesmen quickly acquire a monopoly of both public information and public instruction. They pass laws penalizing anyone who ventures to call them to book, and in a little while no one does it anymore. . . . On the day war is declared the Espionage Act will come into effect, and all free discussion will cease. No one will have access to the radio who is not approved by the White House, and no newspaper will be able to dissent without grave risk of denunciation and ruin. Any argument against the war itself, and any criticism of the persons appointed to carry it on, will become aid and comfort to the enemy. The war will not only become moral over all, it will become the touchstone and standard of morality.

Newspapermen who tried to resist, Mencken continued, would be threatened "both socially and psychologically. The dissenter is not only suspected by his neighbors; he also begins to suspect himself."

> Thus the job of demagogy is completed, and a brave and united nation confronts a craven and ignominious foe. It is not long afterward that anyone ventures to inquire into the matter more particularly, and it is then too late to do anything about it. The dead are still dead, the fellows who lost legs still lack them, war widows go on suffering the orneriness of their second husbands, and taxpayers continue to pay, pay, pay. In the schools children are taught that the war was fought for freedom, the home and God.

Mencken was disturbed most of all that the outbreak of war would pose a threat to freedom of the press. He sounded a warning at the annual convention of the American Society of Newspaper Editors (ASNE). William Allen White, editor of the *Emporia Gazette* and a supporter of Roosevelt, had opened the ASNE convention by advising fellow editors not to get "hot and bothered" when the press of the country was under attack. But Mencken rejected such complacency, bluntly warning his colleagues that in a little while the problem of freedom of the press would indeed become critical. Once more, Mencken hammered away at the theme that was so central to his life.

"There are some of you, I suppose, who are old enough to recall what went on the last time democracy was saved," he began, referring to the censorship of 1917. "It will be undoubtedly worse the next time," he warned, as President Roosevelt prepared to run for reelection. "He will carry into his campaign an animosity against daily newspapers that began to reveal itself during his first term, and began increasing in intensity."

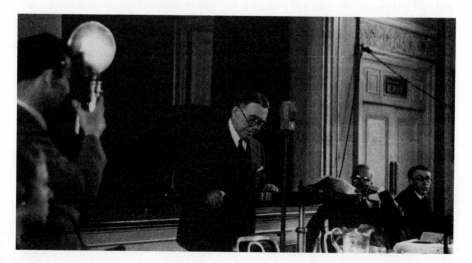

"the only effective opposition . . . against the gentlemen who run this great nation." Mencken stressing the importance of a free press. H. L. Mencken Collection, Enoch Pratt Free Library.

The administration's reaction was predictable. Insisting that censorship plans had neither been formulated nor anticipated, Stephen J. Early, press secretary to the president, called all such ideas "spinach!" But the most vituperative reply appeared the week following Mencken's speech: Harold Ickes asserted that columnists—"that curious, eccentric malady" which had "infected the American press"—were "journalism's Public Enemy No. 1." After mentioning every major columnist in the country, Ickes added rhetorically, "By the way, whatever became of Henry L. Mencken, the crusty old Baron of Baltimore?"[1]

Meanwhile, disagreements between the crusty old Baron of Baltimore and Paul Patterson over the editorial positions of the *Sunpapers* had become a daily trial that escalated into angry arguments, unprecedented in decades of friendly discussion. With the onset of war, Patterson and other members of management were willing to shelve their prejudice against Roosevelt. Even though numerous letters came to the *Sun* frantically calling for strict neutrality, Patterson wanted the paper to back Roosevelt and England; Mencken insisted upon a newspaper's responsibility to remain independent. At a staff meeting, strong hints were given to the editorial writers not to "go off the deep end on any matter of foreign policy." An exception was made for Mencken, since the public drew a distinction between his views and those of the *Sunpapers*.

Members of the *Sun* staff were aware of Mencken's unhappiness, but they did question his position; as one of them commented, "Strange how his Germanomania persists."[2]

ALL THROUGH EARLY 1940, as speculation grew about Roosevelt's serving an unprecedented third term, Mencken expressed his alarm. The Republicans had enjoyed some success in the midterm elections of 1938. The nation was in a deep and sudden recession that had a chastening effect on the New Deal and encouraged a flurry of presidential contenders. The surprise Republican nominee was Wendell L. Willkie, a Wall Street lawyer without political experience but with an appealing homespun quality. Willkie's victory at the Republican convention, however, could not compare with the show that was about to unfold before Mencken at the Democratic convention in July at Chicago Stadium.

A battery of spotlights had been installed for the accommodation of newsreel photographers, and in the glare the red chairs of the hall looked, according to Mencken, "downright incandescent. Some of the delegates sat down in them as gingerly as a condemned fellow takes position in an electric chair." Gazing through a green eye-shade, Mencken saw for himself how radio had come into its own: special quarters had been erected for its reporters. In the next few days, Franklin Roosevelt, who was skilled at employing radio, would again dramatically demonstrate his mastery of the medium.

Although most of the delegates supported Roosevelt, many wanted a change and a rest from New Deal reforms. It fell to the president's advance men—particularly his deputy Harry Hopkins—to see that FDR was again the

Democratic candidate. The nomination and the manner in which it was made turned out to be particularly significant to Mencken, who had been eager to see how successfully the president managed to squelch the opposition.

By the time the convention was called to order, most of the delegates were pledged to the president, but as the evening went on he refused to declare himself a candidate. No one knew whether Roosevelt's name would be placed in nomination, and if so, by whom. Insistent he not be seen as actively seeking a third term, Roosevelt issued a statement that he had no wish to be on the ticket again and that all the delegates to the convention were free to vote for any candidate. There was dead silence, which Mencken saw as a transparent "pretense of indifference." He looked around the hall to see the effect it was having: "The delegates sat as if flabbergasted." He sent a postcard to August in Baltimore. "The whole show is full of unreality," he wrote. "It seems like an idiotic stage play."

Then, from a loudspeaker, came a single shout: "*We Want Roosevelt!*" From the press stand, Mencken saw delegates gaping while small groups paraded the aisles. Once again the voice boomed: "*The world wants Roosevelt! Everybody wants Roosevelt!*" The unseen voice was eventually traced to a small basement beneath the stadium. There, huddled before a microphone, Chicago's superintendent of sewers, Thomas D. McGarry, acting on instructions to use his lungs to full effect, did so repeatedly in a roar: "*Roosevelt! . . . Roosevelt! . . . Roosevelt!*"

In the early morning, when what came to be known as the Voice of the Sewer finally subsided, Mencken wrote that "the two-term tradition, held almost sacred in American politics for nearly a century and a half, went out of the window." Only a single ballot was required for Roosevelt's renomination—"just as scheduled." Mencken returned to the *Sun*'s headquarters in the Blackstone Hotel, and there, with Paul Patterson and Dorothy Gish, drank beer until 4 a.m. "I needed it, God knows."

Many delegates bitterly resented what Mencken called Roosevelt's "hypocritical maneuvering for a third term." He became even more inflamed during the president's "imperious insistence" on choosing his secretary of Agriculture, Henry A. Wallace, as his vice president. There were at least ten more popular vice presidential possibilities, but as Mencken noted, all orders were being dictated from the White House, and from nowhere else. When the name of Henry Wallace was presented to the convention, jeers and catcalls from the delegates shook the rafters.

To quell the mood, Eleanor Roosevelt flew to Chicago, where she had the uncomfortable task of sitting on the podium next to Mrs. Wallace as the storm of boos rolled over them. When it came time for Eleanor Roosevelt to rise from her chair and speak on behalf of Wallace, however, even Mencken, who was no great fan of Eleanor, saw how the delegates listened in respectful silence. It was now eleven o'clock, and the heat in the hall was becoming oppressive, but in a few hours Wallace received the necessary votes.

A beam of light shone on a huge drawing of the president's face on the wall, as Roosevelt's voice, telephoned from Washington, finally closed the show. The delegates listened with grave politeness, Mencken reported, "but the eminent speaker's violent denunciations of dictatorship must have struck many of them as almost ironical, for they had just experienced the passage of his own steamroller over them, and were still feeling flat and used up." It was, in form and substance, "precisely like the Reichstag sessions that Hitler calls at long intervals," Mencken said. There was only one choice before the delegates: "They could vote *Ja* or they could be damned."

By the small hours of the morning it was over. Softly the lights began to wink out in the radio cages, and the mop-up squads moved in with brooms. Bright red blotches representing empty seats could be seen in the galleries. Mencken slammed on his stiff straw hat, savagely bit his cigar, gave his last piece of newspaper copy to a messenger boy, and stalked down the aisle. He paused to shake the hand of a colleague. "Goodbye, old chap. No, we won't see another in 1944. This is the last political convention that will ever be held in this country."

Mencken wondered about the possible outcome, in the long run, "of this stupendous fraud." He recognized that it was hardly fair to lay all the blame on Roosevelt, though he saw him as the chief instrument of a revolution that had been in the making since the age of Jackson. In that remote age, he wrote, "judicious men saw what was coming."

> They realized the essential weakness of democracy, and predicted some of its worst excesses—now unhappy and inescapable realities. They warned that giving the vote to incompetent, despairing and envious people would breed demagogues to rouse and rally them, and that the whole democratic process would thus be converted into organized pillage and rapine.

In spite of his reservations, Mencken joined the Willkie campaign as its train dragged its glittering length through the great open spaces of the American west.[3]

WHILE WILLKIE'S CHANCES WERE SLIM, Mencken initially found himself admiring "the wonder man." In Willkie he found a plentiful stock of hard common sense, a sense of the ludicrous (even in himself), and a kind of sloppiness that was somehow attractive; "His hair is tousled, he perspires freely, his pants hang loosely, and he enters upon no conspiracy with his tailor to conceal his paunch." In the course of Willkie's whirlwind campaign, the candidate worked so hard that he actually lost his voice at times, to the extent that it was no more than a croak.

Yet, no matter how energetically Willkie traveled across the country, the reality of the Nazi victories in Europe worked against him. Americans began to realize that the events then taking place across the Atlantic were more precarious than they had ever thought. Mencken gauged the reaction of the crowds. "Hey, who are you for?" he shouted out the window of a bus to some startled schoolchildren who lined the streets. "Roosevelt," the first replied. "Roosevelt," said the second. "Willkie," said the third. For Mencken, that informal poll simply confirmed the challenge that faced the Republican candidate. In the face of a war scare and a war boom, it was almost impossible to beat a sitting president, especially one who had succeeded in pushing through $17 billion in appropriations and contract authorizations on national defense. "No politician is ever benefitted by saving money," Mencken noted. "It is spending it that makes him."

Mencken was convinced that Willkie's principal weakness lay in the shakiness of his position on the war. On the one hand, he spoke against Europe's dictators, and on the other, he promised that no American boys would be sent to fight Europe's war. Physically exhausted and severely disillusioned, Mencken felt that what Willkie represented was "only sound and *pfui*, signifying nothing. The more he hollers, the plainer it will become that he is really saying nothing. He will be lucky if his laryngitis returns, and his friendly doctors lock him up for the duration." On November 3, as the returns came in, it was as Mencken predicted: the country resoundingly reelected Roosevelt.

"It is my serious belief that the American Republic as we once knew it blew up last night," Mencken observed the next day. "We are probably in for some sort of totalitarianism, though it will undoubtedly wear some other name." He assured friends in Germany it would be nothing like Hitler's. The forms of democracy would still be maintained, "but the thing itself is dead." To distract himself, Mencken made arrangements to visit Aileen Pringle in New York. "You will see a greatly changed man," he promised. "The political horrors I have witnessed have pretty well wrecked me."[4]

DESPITE THE SUCCESS of Mencken's *Happy Days*, he closed 1940 in an unhappy frame of mind. In addition to his forebodings over the constitutionality of the third-term election and the likely return of press censorship, a series of personal losses made the season especially dismal, leading him to wish he were in some faraway place. In Pittsburgh, Charlie's wife, Mary, died of a heart attack; next he learned of the death of his old friend Philip Goodman; then came the passing of F. Scott Fitzgerald. On November 20, one of his closest friends, Raymond Pearl, suddenly died of a coronary thrombosis. With Pearl's passing, he said, "there ends a pleasant and unforgettable chapter in more than one other life."

On top of so many losses came another: Mencken's association with the editorial page of the *Sunpapers*. Paul Patterson could no longer tolerate Mencken's views on Hitler and Roosevelt. But having to tell this to Mencken, he later confessed, was the most embarrassing moment of his life. Mencken's actual resignation came on January 16, 1941. Patterson half-heartedly attempted to talk Mencken out of it, but Mencken stuck stubbornly to his resolve. At Hollins Street, Patterson sat listening without interruption for a full hour as Mencken expressed his anger and disappointment. He claimed that the *Sun* had failed to be the really great newspaper that it might have been; it had lost its independent character that the two men had dreamed of during the 1920s. Patterson protested but made little attempt to dissuade him. The fact that Mencken had quit his column came as a relief. It was only after some effort that he let himself be persuaded to

"God help the United States!" Franklin D. Roosevelt's third inaugural, January 20, 1941. OWI Collection, Franklin D. Roosevelt Library at Hyde Park.

stay on the board of the *Sunpapers*, and he insisted on a reduction in pay. After another drink, the two called it a day.

Thus ended a partnership of thirty years. Although Mencken and Patterson were seen together thereafter, they were no longer as close as in the past.[5]

Four days later, Franklin D. Roosevelt was inaugurated for an unprecedented third term. "There are men who believe . . . that freedom is an ebbing tide," the president said, as he stood before a cheering crowd that stretched across the front of the Capitol. "But we Americans know that is not true."

Mencken's only comment was, "God help the United States!"[6]

Part Six
1941–1948

Union Square in front of Hollins Street. Photograph by A. Aubrey Bodine. Copyright © Jennifer B. Bodine.

The First Casualty

Cartoon by MalOvery, June 15, 1941.

46

THE WEAPON OF SILENCE

THE COMMON NOTION THAT FREE SPEECH prevails in the United States
always makes me laugh," Mencken wrote in his diary. "Twice in one
lifetime I have been forced to shut down altogether, first in 1916 and
then in 1941.... The American people, I am convinced, really detest free speech.
At the slightest alarm they are ready and eager to put it down.... War, in this
country, wipes out all the rules of fair play."

While Mencken had been critical of Roosevelt's social programs during the
1930s and continued to rebel against the United States entering the war, at the
core he was focused on issues of liberty and censorship. His increasing bitterness
toward FDR during the 1940s had more to do with government efforts to throttle
the press than with any personal slight at the Gridiron dinner. He carefully filed
memos to the *Sun* on censorship issues and kept copies of important documents,
including the *Code of Wartime Practices for the American Press*, a pamphlet issued by
the Office of Censorship in 1942 that used George Creel's World War I chart as
a guide. Mencken poured his daily rage into his diary. These entries were not
included in its posthumous publication, but in light of Mencken's passion for free
speech and a free press, his observations of contemporary events on these matters
do much to explain his violent reaction against the popular president. Mencken
also began writing a quieter, more even-handed discussion of his disappointment
with his newspaper, colleagues, and profession in his memoir, *Thirty-Five Years of
Newspaper Work*. In his *Diary* was the hopeful comment that his papers would
offer useful material for a history of American journalism in his time—"that is, if
anyone ever thinks to write it, or wants to learn the truth."[1]

Back in his 1939 speech to the ASNE convention and in subsequent columns, Mencken had predicted the truth regarding censorship that he now saw unfolding before him. The events of December 7, 1941, soon confirmed this reality. With the bombing of Pearl Harbor, the fundamental dispute between the military and the American press came to a head. One of Roosevelt's first actions was to order FBI director J. Edgar Hoover to supervise censorship. As the war proceeded, Hoover's influence grew. Labor unions, radical political groups, civil rights organizations—all were wiretapped. Reports on individuals or newspaper stories critical of Roosevelt were forwarded to the White House. An entire file was labeled "AP Stories Showing Distinct Bias Against the President and Administration."

Under the authority of the War Powers Act, Roosevelt soon established an Office of Censorship and made Byron Price, formerly the executive news editor of the Associated Press, its director. The president promised he would avoid the post office censorship excesses of World War I in which thousands were arrested. Instead, Roosevelt said, censorship would be administered only in harmony with other free institutions. After all, as he had once stated, democracy would be compromised if freedom of the press were hindered.

The administration's censorship codes, released in 1942, called for voluntary compliance. During the first months of the codes, nearly 2,000 stories were submitted to the Office of Censorship prior to publication, and in every case, its advice was followed. Mencken, who remembered that there had been much more opposition to the Wilson version of censorship during the first weeks of World War I, found it "astonishing" at how "docilely" the American newspapers had submitted to this new form.

But Mencken failed to take into account how Pearl Harbor had changed the relationship of the press and the military. Unlike during World War I, hardly any anti-war dissent surfaced in the United States during the years 1941 through 1945. In the days following Pearl Harbor, columnist Arthur Krock of the *New York Times* wrote that you could almost hear the unity of Americans click into place.

Ever the social critic, Mencken suspected that the very idea of censorship "had been promoted by the growth of the New Deal mania, with its wholehearted confidence in governmental regulation." Millions of letters in the international mails were combed for dangerous information, and from time to time Mencken's own letters from overseas contained gaps where the censor had cut out words or names, even though they were, in all probability, quite harmless.

In addition, there were nearly a thousand people who waged the war with typewriters in wartime Washington agencies that made George Creel's 1917 Committee on Public Information seem a huge publicity mill. The chief propaganda agencies were responsible for the statements regarding the defense program —all of which cost the government $10 million in one year even before the nation entered the war. The propaganda machine raised a multitude of questions, not the least of which, for Mencken, was the disgraceful state to which journalism had succumbed, making it a profession of "public office seekers, title hunters, social pushers, dollar diddlers, mountebanks and cads." He had always been against newspapermen who became press agents, but by 1940 he was even firmer in his view that any journalist who took a political job and later tried to come back to the profession should be locked up in the office doghouse.

As had been the case during World War I, Mencken concluded that the journalist in wartime was constrained by many factors besides military censorship; that strong political, social, and professional pressures skewed the reporting in favor of the home team. While many newspapermen thought Mencken's casual remarks were unfair and reckless, others agreed. A. J. Liebling, a war correspondent who would later risk his life in Normandy and North Africa, derided the misuse of military censorship to support political positions and public relations. On the matter of censorship, however, the president was firm. On occasion, he called a *New York Times* editor to the White House to chastise him for the way that the paper was handling news of the war.

Many wondered what had become of Mencken's celebrated column in the *Sun*; Walter Winchell asked in his own column if the Baltimorean had been censored, but he had not. Measures were taken, nevertheless, to rein in reporters. The FBI went after columnists Drew Pearson and Robert Allen for what J. Edgar Hoover saw as their unpatriotic statements in their column, "Washington Merry Go Round." Press secretary Stephen Early threatened to bar their column and stop their access to government sources, and he told reporters there was a need for wiretapping and such investigations: "The President's feeling is that handcuffs ought to be taken off the FBI and put somewhere else." In his effort to curb Westbrook Pegler, censor chief Byron Price put pressure on King Features syndicate, which distributed Pegler's column.[2]

Any kind of censorship infuriated Mencken. A record snowstorm throughout the East Coast on Palm Sunday, 1942, finally brought the issue of restrictions on weather reports to a ludicrous point. A dazzling whiteness covered Washington. New York had almost the same amount of snow, but the *New York Times* did not comment on the fact, explaining that censorship restrictions allowed mention of storms in only one area of the country in any one issue of the paper. Baltimore had the largest snowfall, but the *Sun* not only ignored the Washington storm, it neglected to report the 22-inch depth in Baltimore, explaining it had prepared its weather story after consultation with Army officials and the Weather Bureau.

Mencken looked out of his third floor study and watched the snow pile in drifts across the street at Union Square. From his sunporch, he took photographs of the powdery flakes that had blanketed his backyard. Then he read his copy of the *Sun* with disgust. After the holiday was over, he stormed into the office, complaining to Paul Patterson that it was an absurd compliance with the wartime order against giving weather information.[3]

Omitting weather reports was only one instance of voluntary press censorship. The biggest change would concern the president's whereabouts. In

September 1942, FDR wanted a complete blackout of an impending military inspection trip, and he was determined to take no reporters with him.

The situation angered Mencken, who wrote in his diary, "Roosevelt is on a two-week tour of the country, but not a line of it is being printed in the papers, though thousands of people are seeing him every day." When a labor union weekly, *Aero Mechanic*, broke the story about the president's visit to an airplane plant in Seattle, the FBI moved in rapidly, destroying copies of the paper and asking union workers who had received copies to turn them in for suppression. Throughout the president's trip, editors had been receiving angry letters from men and women who, once having discovered that the president was visiting their community, attacked their local papers. "You hate the president so much," a typical letter read, "that you even refuse to report it when he comes to our town!"

"The Washington correspondents are naturally greatly upset," Mencken observed. But nothing could be done; even a report on the controversy was a violation of the censorship code. Thirty-three Washington newspaper correspondents wrote a letter to Byron Price, remonstrating against the secrecy that surrounded the presidential tour. Price tried to soothe them by complimenting them on their patriotism, but behind the scenes a flurry of memos inundated the White House.

Protesting newspapermen carried their appeal directly to the president at his press conference on October 1, 1942. Over half a century later, the palpable tension in the room on this critical day leaps off the transcript page. Every time Roosevelt congratulated the reporters for their voluntary censorship, a reporter asked what the president had against the press. Roosevelt gave a sweeping denunciation of forces at work in the capital to weaken security, including congressmen, lobbyists and, especially, the owners of the press.

Yet, even as loyal a staffer as Byron Price, in later years, admitted that Roosevelt not only "overestimated the government's power over the press in wartime, but he took unexpected advantage of the immunities afforded him by the Code." The president used censorship policies to shield his frequent visits to his girlfriend, Lucy Mercer. "In my book," Mencken later commented, FDR "was an S.O.B. in his public life and an S.O.B. in his private life."

After the president's trip, Mencken met with his colleagues in New York to discuss the implications of the censorship and recorded their reaction in his diary. "Soon or late," Arthur Sulzberger of the *New York Times* said to the group, "we may have to throw off the chains with which we have shackled ourselves, and begin to tell the truth." As Mencken told his colleagues, their trouble was that "you discovered that Roosevelt is a dictator too late. You should have gone to him in 1932."[4]

ROOSEVELT'S USE OF INTIMIDATION by other agencies to stop information prompted Mencken to later label the president "an unmitigated S.O.B." When the Justice Department complained that the Associated Press was operating in violation of the Sherman Anti-Trust Act, Mencken saw an ulterior motive. He was convinced that the real purpose was blackmail to force the AP into giving membership and access to their wire service to the *Chicago Sun*, as a way of punishing the rival *Chicago Tribune* for its anti–New Deal bias. *Tribune* publisher Robert R. McCormick insisted on his rights to pursue an editorial line of his choice.

While Mencken had been an admirer of the *Tribune*, he recognized what "a quarrelsome fellow" McCormick personally could be. In this case, however, Mencken thought that the conduct and character of the publisher were irrelevant, and that all newspapermen should stand behind him. In a memo to Paul Patterson, Mencken outlined a strategy to win the case.

"Is [McCormick] to be permitted to run his paper as he thinks it ought to be run, taking all legal responsibility for what he prints in it, or is it to be run as the White House thinks it ought to be run?" Mencken asked Patterson.

> Not once, but several times dishonest and nefarious efforts have been made to suppress him directly. Now that they have all failed, it is proposed to get at him indirectly by damaging his property . . . I can think of nothing more indecent than this attempt to use a general law to attain private end. Nor anything that deserves better the whole-hearted and unanimous condemnation of American newspapers. In this case, and for all the purposes of this case, McCormick is every American publisher, regardless of how sharply any or all of them may dissent from his practices.

Mencken's newspaper colleagues agreed with him that the suit against the Associated Press must have been ordered by the president himself and that the Justice Department lawyers had functioned "merely as yes-men." Only a few weeks before, Attorney General Francis Biddle had met with the president and later, in a private memo, reminded him that bringing the Associated Press case to court would look like "persecution" against a newspaper. Sincere in his defense of civil rights, Biddle was often forced to compromise under pressure. "The last time I backed the press," Biddle wrote in his diary, "the president had slapped me down pretty hard. . . ." Unhappy though he might be, after several pointed remarks made by the president, even Biddle recognized that there was nothing more he could do.

The antitrust case was argued in 1945 before the Supreme Court, which found for the government by a vote of 5–3. Justice Frank Murphy wrote in his dissent: "Today is the first time that the Sherman Act has been used as a vehicle for affirmative action by the Government in the realm of dissemination of information. . . . We stand at the threshold of a previously unopened door. We should pause long before opening it, lest the path be made clear for dangerous governmental interference in the future."

Mencken deplored the lack of "some really violent writing" against the decision, but he had retired as a *Sun* columnist. As for the rest of the press, he always believed that Washington correspondents were "too stupid to penetrate the fraudulencies by which they are surrounded." To Mencken's disappointment but hardly to his surprise, the Associated Press case spurred little reaction or sympathy among the public. "In Peter Zenger's day, the people might feel that the defense of his rights was the defense of theirs," commented the *Atlantic Monthly*. "Now they [are] jaded and silent. . . . perhaps . . . they had begun to regard the newspapers no longer as trustees of constitutional liberty."[5]

FRANKLIN ROOSEVELT DID NOT LIVE LONG ENOUGH to see the AP suit brought to a close. On Thursday, April 12, 1945, at 4:35 p.m., Eastern War Time, he died at Warm Springs, Georgia. The funeral was held on Saturday at the East Room of the White House. Wire service teletypes halted, then printed, slowly, seven letters: S I L E N C E.

At home in Baltimore, Mencken examined the newspapers to see how they had handled the news of the president's death. None, he concluded, could compare to the column by George Schuyler in the *Pittsburgh Courier*, whose calm appraisal of Roosevelt's record, especially as it related to the mistreatment of blacks and Japanese Americans, elicited Mencken's praise. "The pale face journalists unanimously resorted to crooning and blah," he wrote Schuyler. "You alone tried to tell the whole bitter truth."

Months later, as Early cleared out his desk at the White House, he wrote a letter to Price, congratulating him on a job well done. Early felt certain President Harry Truman would continue with the censorship practices Price had put into place as director of the Office of Censorship. Indeed, the repercussions of such actions lingered long after World War II. As historian Betty Winfield pointed out, "There was and still is a danger of a possible media tyranny by an adroit president and his advisers over a mediocre press." Fears over executive cover-ups and lack of openness in government have continued. Mencken did not misjudge Roosevelt's legacy over the control of governmental information in a democracy.

A young reporter once asked Mencken about the future of journalism. Mencken was deeply pessimistic. One day in the future, he surmised, the United States would develop "super-Roosevelts who will make Franklin himself seem cautious, and even more or less honest. Let us not forget that he opened the path for these heirs and assigns by abolishing the only stop that stood in his way, to wit, the Constitution of the United States. It is now extinct, and it will not be revived. Its three basic guarantees—free speech, equality before the law, and the limitation of government—have all gone with the wind."

As was his habit, he turned to Thomas Jefferson: "Our liberty depends on the freedom of the press, and that cannot be limited without being lost."[6]

47

ON THE HOME FRONT

MENCKEN WAS THE FIRST TO ADMIT that World War II hardly affected him personally. He pointed out to a friend in London, who had lost his house in an air raid, that for most of his countrymen the war was a remote series of events whose dangers and hazards failed to strike home. Few had ever seen an enemy airplane in flight or heard a bomb explode, and Mencken doubted they ever would.

The idea of giving the population gas masks Mencken dismissed outright: the joke was that the air pollution was so bad, no conceivable war gas could make it worse. With more than 14,000 wardens at their posts, Baltimore staged a series of air-raid alerts, plunging the city into blackouts. Such public alarm resulted that August began to talk about building a bomb-proof shelter at Hollins Street, but Mencken refused to take any such notion seriously. For one thing, it seemed to him highly improbable that any bomb could ever reach Baltimore; for another, he had been given access to the caves of a brewery not far from his house, which promised to be not only quite safe but also extremely comfortable. He did wonder, though, how long the two thousand barrels of prime malt liquor stored there would last.[1]

Unlike the First World War, when Mencken was briefly in Berlin and found himself thrown into the main current of contemporary history, in World War II he was safe at home. His family and friends were not in any danger of being drafted as they had been during the previous war.

Mencken believed that the United States had been duped into declaring war by the British. "I am no isolationist," he argued, "but I can see no reason why

American blood and American money should always be devoted to fattening the share of the English." World War I had produced only "a debt and a headache." If the United States had stayed out of it, "the Russian menace to Western civilization would have been disposed of for two or three generations, the European powers would have been forced into something approaching a workable arrangement, and England would have been prevented from setting up artificial bases for the next struggle—for example, Poland and Czechoslovakia." This and nothing else, he argued, had produced Hitler, who would not have been taken seriously if the defeated Germans had been dealt with in a decent manner. "But the threat to their trade, their food lines and their very lives from both east and west naturally alarmed them, and after trying various tame and puerile saviors they followed democratic procedures by calling on the loudest and worst."

Mencken believed that while many Americans solidly opposed entering the war in 1939, Roosevelt had been preparing the country for a showdown, and that the English would have never engaged in World War II if they had not been sure of Roosevelt's help. Mencken said Roosevelt had so cleverly brainwashed the American public that only one incident was needed to force the country into a declaration of war. "He goaded the Japs into making war on us," Mencken argued. "If the true story of Pearl Harbor is ever honestly told, it will be the most disgraceful story you have ever heard."

Mencken's antiwar position this time elicited little outrage against him. No one molested him or called him a German spy, as in the First World War, although individuals from Baltimore and within the White House sent complaints and queries to the Department of Justice, which continued to add material to his file. Mencken's books still received good notices. *Happy Days* became a GI favorite, issued in pocket size for the armed forces overseas, and uniformed readers in all parts of the world wrote to Hollins Street saying how much they enjoyed the book. "That is the difference between a soldier and a civilian," Mencken commented wryly. "The letters you get from civilians are from those who don't like your books."

What did affect Mencken was the manner in which the war began to interfere with the routine of American life. Shortages and restrictions were now normal. America was warned to tighten its belt as the federal government rationed essential goods, such as canned food, gasoline, and fuel oil. The lack of gasoline presented no problem for Mencken, who walked everywhere, but it did present a dilemma for his siblings. If an emergency were to arise for Gertrude who lived in the country, her small reserves would have made it hard for her to undertake the drive to Hollins Street. "You would hardly recognize the streets of Baltimore," Mencken wrote to his niece, Virginia. "They are almost bare of automobiles."

If the war had altered lives in countless ways, for Mencken most noticeable of all were the transformations being wrought in his city, particularly in his neighborhood. It was slowly going downhill; he predicted it eventually would become a slum. "The face of Baltimore had changed between 1924 and 1942," reminisced

"Fifteen million . . . to work at war plants and shipyards." The first Liberty ship, the *Patrick Henry*, is launched from the Bethlehem-Fairfield shipyards, 1941. Copyright © 1941, The Baltimore Sun. Used by Permission.

H. K. Fleming, the managing editor of the *Baltimore Sun*. "All night long the hammers were pounding in the Bethlehem shipyards and from North Carolina, Kentucky and Tennessee a flood of mountain people had poured into the city." These were the "Oakies, lintheads [and] hillbillies" that Mencken described in his diary, poor Southern whites from Appalachia and elsewhere who migrated to Baltimore in search of jobs. Baltimore suffered a severe housing shortage; within a mile and a half of City Hall, the Health Department noted, a three-story house was occupied by as many as ten defense workers per room.

Sidewalks were crowded with servicemen passing through town, seamen on liberty, and war industry workers on late night shifts. Wastepaper swirled along Charles and Baltimore Streets in such a maelstrom of rubbish that motor traffic had to creep along to avert accidents. Baltimoreans discovered that life was also becoming more dangerous with a sudden surge of street violence. Mencken was sure after reading the *Afro-American* that serious race riots were not far off. The solution, he believed, was to limit the excessive wartime immigration, especially from the South, that was directly responsible for crime and disorder in the ghettos.[2]

To investigate the changes in Baltimore, the managing editor of the *Sun* assigned his entire reporting staff to survey one city neighborhood. A block was a city in miniature, H. K. Fleming asserted, and the 1500 block of Hollins Street— Mencken's block—was more representative than most, since some of the old families of Baltimore lived there but others had suddenly invaded it as a result of the war.

An influx of poor white immigrants swarmed into Hollins Street, as Mencken put it, "reeking with hookworms and idealism." Within a few days another family would move in; two weeks later, relatives of both families would join. With the flood of new residents, lawns were trampled and many of the shrubs torn up. In the evenings the newcomers launched themselves on endless drunks at Union Square, waking the neighbors with their caterwauling. "Their behavior inspired a saying in Baltimore: 'There are only 45 states in the union. West Virginia and South Carolina have moved to Maryland, and Maryland has gone to Hell.'"

Four doors from 1524 Hollins Street lived one Southern family who had never before seen, let alone used, a gas stove. Another tenant had never seen an electric light. "The night she got here she turned the light on and off, just amused that it really worked," Leon Asner, the landlord, noted with disdain. Still another pried a wooden mantle from the wall and burned it, along with tables and chairs, as firewood. In the old days, Hollins Street had been the most peaceful and sedate block in Baltimore. Now, August Mencken told a *Sun* reporter, "It's a madhouse."

From downstairs, the reporter could hear the clatter of typing from the floor above. As a form of escapism, Mencken had begun writing a series of random reminiscences covering the years of his childhood up to 1936. After grappling with ideas for a title, he decided to call these memoirs *Heathen Days*. It was the last volume to the trilogy that had begun with *Happy Days*. The second, *Newspaper Days*, which recalled the atmosphere and spirit of Mencken's salad days as a journalist, had been published in 1941 to great acclaim. The autobiographical stories in *Heathen Days*, with their exuberance and high spirits, contained what one critic called the most accomplished prose since Mark Twain. There were a series of tributes to the public mountebanks Mencken had ridiculed years before and other recollections, ranging from the equine lessons taught by Frank (perhaps the most hilarious Shetland pony in literature) to the deviltries of the Saturday Night Club.

But if Mencken was the chief human character in *Heathen Days*, many came to recognize that the real hero of the book was the city of Baltimore, and Mencken, its most famous and loyal son. The *Days* trilogy was a valentine to a day long past, appealing to those who yearned for relief from the tribulations of the current age. As Mencken told Edgar Lee Masters, "We were passing through Utopia, and didn't know it."[3]

IF THIS WAS NOT ENOUGH to occupy him, Mencken embarked on a new project. Since 1918 he had been collecting a card index of sayings that struck his interest but were not included in the existing quotation books. The final manuscript made a package fourteen inches high that weighed more than 35 pounds. Mencken personally toted his latest newborn from 1524 Hollins Street to Knopf's office in New York—and picked one of the warmest days of early summer for the journey. He warned Knopf to be careful when he read it: "If it slips from your grasp it may break your leg." In 1942 Knopf declared the result, *A New Dictionary of Quotations*, one of his most distinguished publications of the year.

The book was aimed at readers whose general taste and ideas approximated Mencken's own. "There is no reason why a book of quotations should be dull," he argued. *A New Dictionary of Quotations* differed from other collections in that it was historically precise, with quotations, dated whenever possible, from Aristotle to Franklin D. Roosevelt to the Head Keeper of the National Zoo. Special attention was devoted to the Bible, the Koran, Oriental scriptures, the decisions of the higher courts (both English and American), the speeches of statesmen, and the papal encyclicals, and "the proverbs of all peoples, for in them some of the soundest thinking of the human race is embodied, and also some of the most pungent wit." It was the least banal or solemn dictionary of quotations yet published; as Mencken put it, "the Congressman hunting for platitudes to embellish his eulogy upon a fallen colleague will find relatively little to his purpose."[4]

The *Days* trilogy, like *A New Dictionary of Quotations* and his massive study on the American language, had revived Mencken's reputation. Readers once repulsed by the scorn Mencken had heaped on Roosevelt now felt free to open the doors of their homes to him. With so much praise, Mencken took stock of his trade. He noted that its cash rewards were seldom lucrative, except by accident, nor was there much satisfaction in reading reviews—"for the bad ones, only too often, are written by those one knows to be scoundrels, and the good ones by persons one suspects of being idiots."

Meanwhile, the fourth edition of *The American Language* was showing signs of age. As in the last war, Mencken realized that prevailing censorship made this subject the safest and perhaps the only one he could tackle. Almost two decades since the "Hatrack" case in Boston, censorship of books, magazines, and newspapers had increased at a steady rate. Under provisions of the 1917 Espionage Act, hundreds of publications were suppressed during World War II. While Roosevelt had stated that some degree of censorship was essential in wartime, many of the barred books had nothing to do with the country being at war. Boston banned an issue of *Life* because it reprinted six nude pictures on display in a Dallas art museum. Governor Herman Talmadge of Georgia urged that books dealing with better race relations be burned.

In addition, a number of publications had been deprived of their second-class mailing privileges for various alleged violations of regulations, over which the Post Office had been both the prosecutor and judge in every case. The only notable protest against this form of censorship came from the American Civil Liberties Union, which saw a grave danger to press freedom in the apparently unlimited power vested in the postmaster general.

One of the biggest cases centered on *Esquire* magazine, directed at the male population, without which no dentist's office or barber shop was decently furnished. Because it offended the Post Office's sense of morality, it lost its mailing privileges. The Post Office attorneys sought to show that the magazine was not only obscene but lewd. For Mencken, the case was yet another example of the erosion of freedom he had spent a lifetime trying to combat. He told a correspondent he could imagine nothing more dreadful than an attempt to police the American language: "It is no more susceptible to regulation than a litter of kittens."

Esquire marshaled a long list of witnesses of whom its most forceful was undoubtedly Mencken. He dominated the subsequent hearing, clearly demonstrating the utter confusion and lack of intelligible standards the Post Office had applied to the case. Against a backdrop of the American flag, three government attorneys rustled through some 2,000 pages of testimony.

The Post Office censors read aloud the items they said proved the magazine's guilt.

POST OFFICE: Now, what about the words, "sunny south"?
MENCKEN: It is not alleged that "sunny south" is obscene, is it?
POST OFFICE: I believe it is.
MENCKEN: I can't answer such a question. It is too absurd. "Sunny south" is obviously an attempt at humor. I myself in such a situation use the word "caboose," but then everybody has his favorites. You have to sometime in this life, living in a biological life of mammals, refer to backsides, and in humorous writing, which this is, there is an effort to invent charming, and, if possible, enough backsides. There may not be enough euphemisms and this man is inventing "sunny south." I never heard it before. The idea that it was

> obscene shocks me. I didn't know anybody was absolutely so indecent that he should consider it that way.
>
> POST OFFICE: It seems to me to be a term of limited situation and only applied when a woman is facing north.
>
> MENCKEN: Apparently so, only what he would call it if she was facing south, I don't know.

What, then, did Mencken think of the word "fanny"? Again, Mencken countered, "fanny" was completely harmless: "Little children five years of age use it." After a few minutes of this even the Post Office seemed to grow aware of the ludicrousness of their position:

> POST OFFICE: What can you say about the use of the word "behind"?
>
> MENCKEN: Is "behind" the word complained of?
>
> POST OFFICE: I am afraid so.
>
> MENCKEN: Gracious. I knew no other word for the rear part until I was probably four years of age, . . . and became sophisticated.

"Before it was over," Mencken recalled, "I had them laughing."

In the cross-examination, when the Post Office attempted to impeach Mencken's testimony by dragging in the story of "Hatrack," the government dramatically illustrated the mistake they had made in bringing the censorship case against *Esquire* in the first place. In doing so, they handed Mencken a chance to tell the Post Office that, in its pursuit of its "filthy course of trying to persecute me" over twenty years ago, it had failed miserably. For the first time that afternoon, Mencken became heated. "I went to court on that," he answered, "and I had injunctions against the Post Office by two federal judges, both of whom denounced the Post Office as obscene, indecent, unfair and ignominious. I agree with the verdict thoroughly and I believe it was just to this minute."

When his testimony was over, Mencken admitted that defending *Esquire* had given him genuine pleasure. "It at least gave me a chance to state under oath my opinion of the Post Office wowsers." The hearings would drag on for another two years, until the Supreme Court ruled unanimously in favor of *Esquire*. Justice William Douglas declared the existing law gave the postmaster general "the power of censorship . . . abhorrent to our traditions."

The case proved to be a personal triumph for Mencken; his prestige as the expert on the American language remained undisputed. Lawyers, in arguing the case, stated "No one today would question either Mr. Mencken's eminence or his complete respectability"—an opinion that in itself, Mencken joked, was something of a marvel.[5]

48

MENCKEN AND THE GUILD

ALTHOUGH HE WAS NO LONGER writing for the *Sun*, Mencken remained a dominant presence as one of its foremost directors. Employees could hear him thumping briskly up the hall, aware of his arrival at the office even before he walked through the door. "Everyone bowed and scraped when he came in," recalled copyeditor Grace Darin. Through the thick boardroom doors came a muffled uproar, often of laughter, or when Mencken boomed his displeasure at poor content, typographical errors, and bad grammar.

More often than not, Mencken's anger was provoked by the American Newspaper Guild, which had won representation at the *Sun* in 1938 but did not achieve a contract with the paper until 1949. The Guild had been arguing that irregular hours and lack of compensation for unusual assignments was making life burdensome for workers. This was anathema to Mencken. "Most of the youngsters I run into devote two-thirds of their time complaining about work," he reflected. "The old-timers who welcomed it and delighted in it seem to have vanished, along with the buffalo." He looked forward to the impending battle.

Mencken's relationship with the Guild bared the contradiction in his role as a free speech advocate. He insisted that the Guild was setting up "a very cockeyed kind of free speech" by saying that employees could demand certain benefits and management had no right to oppose the union. Mencken refused to recognize the difference between an employee with no economic power advocating membership and management officials, like himself, pressuring employees against their right to join.

In 1934, Mencken received an invitation to attend the first annual convention of the American Newspaper Guild; members thought his very presence would aid their success. But Mencken was convinced that the Guild, "in seeking to prove that all newspaper proprietors are rogues," had only succeeded "in proving that a large number of newspaper men are idiots. It has rounded up all the misfits in the business and all the envious and baffled men . . . no newspaperman of genuine skill and dignity has anything to do with the management of the Guild." Mencken considered syndicated columnist Heywood Broun, a socialist who had organized the American Newspaper Guild and was its first president, "a second-rater" who had always quarreled with his employers.

Broun's death on December 18, 1939, precipitated a battle for control of the national organization. Mencken was convinced that the Guild's subsequent seizure by "a group of New York Jews" was converting the organization "into an outhouse of the Communist party." Only a few years before, the Guild had affiliated itself with the CIO and extended its membership to elevator operators, copyboys, rackmen, as well as editorial employees. "I believe good reporters should get more money than they do," Mencken told a reporter for the *Nation*, "but I don't see why they should fuss over the wages of understrappers." In this Mencken and the top executives at the *Sunpapers* fully agreed. So strong was their distaste for the Guild and Broun that the day after the columnist's death editorial writer R. P. Harriss recorded in his diary:

> Shortly before the Evening Sun went to press this morning an order came from P. P. [Paul Patterson] that we were to print no editorial on Heywood Broun— so we killed the one we had in type. [Philip] Wagner was sore, but not half so sore as I was. I asked him if H. L. M. had been chiefly responsible.—Yes. And so, simply because Mencken hated Broun, and because Broun was president of the Newspaper Guild, we must pretend he never existed, never wrote, never died. [There was] an editorial in virtually every paper in the country—except the Sunpapers. What a long way we have come during the last 10 years! Mencken's arteries harden; his adrenalin dries up; his prejudices grow like cancer,—but his grip on the Sunpapers grows stronger every day.[1]

During the spring of 1941, a new and intensive campaign to negotiate with the *Sun* to improve salaries, minimum wage standards, hours, working conditions, and job security was launched by the local branch of the Newspaper Guild in Baltimore. In prior years, the combination of Mencken's stonewalling and the Guild's internal politics, especially its lack of major support, had been responsible for that organization's failure to negotiate a contract.

The Guild, however, was determined to gain a foothold at the *Sunpapers*, the second wealthiest publishing property in the United States, leading the country in advertising linage. The *Sunpapers* prestige was based on a tradition of excellence (it had averaged a Pulitzer Prize every other year), a reputation for comprehensive coverage by a staff that included bureaus overseas and a dozen top Washington correspondents. That prestige, however, was countered by its reputation for penuriousness. The joke went around the newsroom that the paper's motto, "Light for All," applied to the company's pay envelopes. "Among faithful old *Sun* hands," staffer and later columnist Russell Baker wrote, "poverty was something to be accepted gracefully, for not everyone was privileged to work for the *Sun*." Some executives also justified the low salaries with the claim that the cost of living was less in Baltimore than in other cities in the East. "This was true to a degree," recalled Miles Wolff, one of the editors, "but not to the degree cited by the management."

Notwithstanding the poor pay, there was never any difficulty in attracting competent newsmen, a few of whom did rather well in perks and status. But as one *Sunpapers* employee remembered, "the majority, often just as worthy, grubbed along, forever hoping to join the Chosen Few." According to Mencken, Patterson usually resolved the question of pay increases by giving them to "those who showed a reasonable spirit and were good at their jobs, and excluding the incurable malcontents and incompetents." Mencken sided with him, declaring that "I don't believe in giving gratuities to men who cause trouble and annoy their betters." Whether or not they were members of the Guild played no role in such decisions.

What made the pay situation hardest for the staff was the erratic and capricious system of raises. One competent, loyal employee had been hired at a certain figure "to start." Four years later he commented, "I must still be 'starting.' " It was quite a blow to the copyeditors when a new man arrived at a higher salary than any of those then on the desk, including the man on whose recommendation he had been hired. To ask for a raise was a precarious venture. As late as 1946, copyboys were earning only 40 cents an hour. "It was a sweatshop operation," remembered Stanley Harrison, a former employee. "Copyboys turned over like leaves in winter time."

Although the paper was famous for its wretched rates of pay, the American Newspaper Guild's efforts to unionize the *Sun* newsroom alarmed the more timid among the staff, who were aware that revealing union sympathies was likely to irritate management and perhaps ruin their careers. As financially desperate as many reporters were, no one wanted to be branded the office Bolshevik. Employees were forbidden to discuss Guild matters in the *Sunpapers* building or at lunch. Even Mencken, who defended the right of free speech so vociferously, declared that "nobody has the right to use the cafeteria as a circus lot or Union Square."[2]

Mencken handled the *Sun*'s negotiations with the Guild in conjunction with Neil H. Swanson, the executive editor, universally detested by the employees. A cigarette dangling from his mouth like a character from *The Front Page*, Swanson was not shy in sharing his own grandiose conceptions of the paper or of himself. Russell Baker recalled that "Swanson's imperial military manner and boyish pleasure in pushing people around to show who was boss contributed to making him villain-in-chief of the *Sun*." His periodic outbursts made negotiation virtually impossible. Guild organizers who met with him would emerge after long sessions with nothing to show for their efforts.

The other formidable personal hurdle for Guild negotiators was Emmett P. Kavanaugh, the business manager. Saying the wishes of the employees were of "no concern," he complained that the Guild had given him more trouble than all other unions put together in the years he was the *Sunpapers'* labor representative. One Guild chairman recalled that when other newspaper editorial pay scales were shown to Kavanaugh, he responded that he would give "only what you're strong enough to take." It was a lesson never to be forgotten. Another equally difficult opponent was William F. Schmick, the executive vice president, who, with his business department background, did not always appreciate how reporters functioned.[3]

Given these choices, Mencken's assignment to serve as the chief negotiator was a shrewd move on Patterson's part. As a former reporter who had risen through the ranks, Mencken was best suited to provide the necessary sympathy for the ink-stained wretches of the company. The Newspaper Guild remembered Mencken's youthful struggle at the Baltimore *Morning Herald*, when he wondered how he could stretch his paltry salary to last him an entire week. In those days he was enough of a realist to recognize that "a reporter's code of ethics are all right so long as they do not menace newspaper profits; the moment they do so the business manager, now quiescent, will begin to growl again."

But that was then. Now, as a pillar of management, Mencken was a member of the posh and exclusive Maryland Club in Baltimore, a holder of *Sunpapers* stock. At the height of the Depression, when reporters were making $30 a week, he earned more than $17,000 a year from the *Sunpapers* alone. By 1943, his net worth was $185,000. As a negotiator, Mencken admitted, "I was now representing the papers, not myself, and had to make the best bargain I could."

Guild negotiators initially appreciated that Mencken was inclined to be less arbitrary than the other executives. He was prone to intercede calmly whenever arguments became too heated. He reassured the Guild that he was glad to hear whatever complaint they might have and to use his good offices to get their requests considered by the proper people. Everyone knew that when Mencken intervened with Paul Patterson things would happen. No one dared to defy Patterson, and more often than not, Patterson chose not to defy Mencken, who became indignant when he considered that management behaved unfairly.

Moreover, Mencken was generally well liked by the Guild negotiators. Some believed the rumors that he had left the *Sun*'s editorial pages because he had been silenced from above, although Mencken told them this was nonsense. He endeared himself to them by adding, although "I did not question the good faith of my late associates . . . their ideas seemed to me to be haywire." This, as it turned out, was the Guild's own view, "which indicates," Mencken later joked, "that I must have been closer to the Party Line than I ever suspected."

Guild members thumbed through Mencken's history *The Sunpapers of Baltimore* and found information they tried to use in their negotiation for a pay increase. Although following the Mencken angle was, Guild members discovered, their best chance for success, it took only a few weeks for them to realize that Patterson had been guilty of a wonderful charade in putting Mencken in charge of labor relations. There was a broad streak of mischief in Mencken, which he now brought to the bargaining table. At his first negotiating meeting, he drew up a tentative contract and read it aloud. As Philip Wagner recalled:

> It was larded with references to "the gentlemen of the press," "the aforesaid gentlemen," "the gentlemen known as the parties of the first part," and so forth. When he had finished reading this tentative contract, one of the Guild negotiators cleared his throat and said:
> "Mr. Mencken, ah, what is the reason for the repeated use of the word 'gentlemen'?"
> Mencken was quick on the reply. "I used the word," he said, "in order to have something to concede when the bargaining gets tough."

While equally at ease with all, Mencken nonetheless exuded such authority that few dared to contradict him. Fluent in debate, Mencken was so precise with facts and so devastating in logic that his arguments seemed impossible to overcome. He brandished Latin legal terms in the course of his speeches that cowed his opponents. Moreover, he was clearly willing to stay and argue a point, as he put it, "until the cows come home." At times he spoke so fast that members of the Guild complained that they could not get a word in. For this reason Patterson had given Mencken the role of labor negotiator: when it came to the Guild, as Mencken himself recognized, the publisher "believed that in the long run, I could always talk them down and get rid of them." As the meetings progressed into 1942, the local Guild in desperation appealed for help to national headquarters. With Mencken at the helm, they complained, "we got nowhere fast."[4]

THROUGHOUT THE 1940s Mencken sat in on meetings, a third of a cigar hanging limp from the center of his mouth, his nose red, his cheeks ruddy, his necktie clumsily twisted in a rumpled collar. But the alert blue eyes roamed the room like twin cameras—not the slightest detail escaped—and the famous Baltimore rasp was as vibrant as ever. Clearly dominating the room, Mencken took up the issues of vacation, pay increases, even whether or not copyboys could smoke.

For his part, Mencken could not care less what the "labor bravoes" thought of him. While he claimed that "I enjoyed my sessions with the Guild brethren" he admitted that "I had no respect for most of them." Unions may have improved the lot of the individual, "but they have killed his desire for opportunity and responsibility." Very few had "amounted to a hill of beans as a newspaper man." And he added crushingly, "I did the best I could for the *Sunpapers* against the Guild, and with an easy conscience, for it was dominated by highly dubious persons athirst for power, and its concern for the welfare of working newspaper men and women was always less than its yearning to afflict publishers."

Mencken resented those who did not have real grievances but simply "went to the wailing wall." As long as a person did his work, Mencken said, he would see his lot improve. As a young reporter, he had supplemented his income and risen through the ranks through his own industry and skill; there was no reason others could not do the same.

For all his harsh words against strikers and labor leaders—recalling the words of his own father against the cigarmaker's union over half a century before —Mencken insisted that he remained on the side of the individual. As long as the Guild promoted tenure and actually increased salaries he supported it, as he had long advocated these aims in the *Sun* office. "The tendency there, as in every other newspaper office, was to overpay the men at the top and underpay those at the bottom. Against this I began to protest as early as 1920, and I never let up. . . . I insisted that it was disgraceful for a corporation as rich as the A. S. Abell Company to pay such starvation wages, and proposed a resolution of the board setting a minimum wage for all *Sun* employees, and instructing the administration to clear out all sweatshops at once." He also advocated longer vacations and full salaries in sickness.

Recognizing that the Guild undoubtedly had some influence in the elimination of hidden sweatshops, Mencken applauded its efforts, later confiding that if he were a young reporter he would probably be a Guild member himself, if only to get better pay. In this, as in other matters, Mencken was contradictory; he had all along fought against the Guild's organizing the paper's staff. The New Deal had provided workers an opportunity to organize the workforce; Mencken must have known that most of these workers had been sympathetic to Roosevelt. When the Guild finally did come to Baltimore at the invitation of a group of *Evening Sun* employees in September 1946, Mencken was no longer the chief negotiator for management, and the policies and actions of the paper continued to be hostile to the Guild. Kavanaugh's advice to the dissatisfied was that "anybody who thinks he can make more money elsewhere is a sucker to stay on the *Sun.*" Eventually some did leave, but many stayed.[5]

A Guild contract was finally negotiated in 1949, but by then morale was at its lowest. The minimum for reporters was set at $100 a week, twice what had been offered by Mencken a dozen years earlier. It would be decades more before the Guild was able, as Russell Baker put it, "to lure the *Sun* into the twentieth century on things like money, sick pay, and retirement."

Two reasons the *Sunpapers* could get away with such miserliness were that radio and television posed no major threat at the time and there was little serious competition from other papers. But another reason was Mencken's celebrity. "They could hire people who were talented and available to work for peanuts because they thought it was an honor to work for the papers H. L. Mencken had once worked for," recalled former *Sun* reporter John Goodspeed, who joined the paper in 1949. "So—miserly pay notwithstanding and thanks mostly to Mencken's reputation—the *Sunpapers* attracted some very talented people."

As for a retirement plan and life insurance, there was a rumor that such things existed, but the details were available only to a select few. It would have surprised many staffers to know that those who did receive help could thank Mencken, who convinced Patterson of the need, especially during World War II, to give help whenever needed to the families of deceased employees. Despite his acerbic criticism of "Roosevelt's war," Mencken felt that he could not overlook the fate of employees fighting abroad and the families they left behind.

During the war, the *Sunpapers* hosted a Christmas party for the children of employees at the front. They were picked up by a uniformed chauffeur driving a limousine and then deposited in the board room, which had been decked out with fancy linens and butlers in white coats who served petits fours and ices in the shapes of strawberries. This was an honor, but the youngsters who had been formally ushered into the imposing paneled room, dressed in their Sunday best, seemed baffled. Who were the men in suits, and why were they droning on? "It was an awful party," recalled Mary Ann McCardell Daily, the daughter of reporter Lee McCardell, then stationed in Europe. "We were bored to death and very uncomfortable with all the elegance."

> I remember the ices in particular, for I had never seen such beautiful things, and my younger sister, who was three, could not be convinced that they they were to be eaten as ice cream. There was a fully dressed Santa Claus who distributed very expensive presents, the kind of gifts my parents never could have afforded, and some makeshift entertainment which consisted of a young man playing the accordion, and a quartet of men who looked very uncomfortable in suits and ties, who sang Christmas music. While this quartet was performing, Mr. Mencken came in, looked around and promptly saw that the guests of honor were having an AWFUL time. He left for a few minutes, and then returned with a Santa Claus mask on his face, and joined the singers. It didn't help. We didn't know who he was, and we continued to have an awful time. But he had made an effort no one else had thought to make.[6]

It was a glimpse of why so many reporters still liked Mencken. Such kindly gestures, however, could not compensate for Mencken's energetic actions against the Guild's collective strivings for better conditions. He clung to the belief that a man's individual labors must speak for him. Above all, he admired competence, "for it is very rare in this world, and especially in this great Republic," he insisted. "Those who have it in some measure, in any art or craft from adultery to zoology, are the only human beings I can think of who will be worth the oil it will take to fry them in Hell."[7]

49

FRIENDS AND RELATIVES

I SEEM TO LIVE in the midst of death and disaster," said Mencken. So certain was he that his turn might be next, he turned over the matters of his estate to the Mercantile Bank to make sure his siblings would be left well provided for. The truth was, as he confessed to James Branch Cabell in 1944, "you and I seem to be among the few old timers who are still on their legs. Edgar Lee Masters is hardly able to walk; Dreiser is a wreck . . . and Joe Hergesheimer is sick and quite unable to work."

Edgar Lee Masters was one of the few friends Mencken visited during his infrequent trips to New York. To one neighbor at the Hotel Chelsea, the poet seemed "the saddest, loneliest and most bitter man I have ever known." It had been years since he had published a book; he was alienated from his former wife and most of all from his friends. With the exception of Theodore Dreiser and a young woman named Alice Davis, Mencken was one of few who continued to associate with him.

As Alice Davis recalled, Mencken "used to say of dear Edgar that he had *deteriorated*, a word which stabbed and hurt me." Together the three would dine at Lüchow's, where a beaming circle of waiters would be properly respectful and Masters would shed his crabbiness and perceived injustices and become jovial. Alice remembered that the restaurant seemed to restore Masters to his natural element. Lüchow's had the same effect on Mencken. It was the only place in New York, he declared, that had not changed since he had first patronized it in 1901— good food and beer and wonderful music. "The musicians always play the Brahms waltz in A flat when I come in," Mencken observed. "Somebody told them that it was my favorite. It isn't, but it is still very lovely."

Eventually Masters checked into a nursing home in the Bronx, where Mencken encountered a listless old man. "He did smile when Mencken pulled his usual good-humored jokes, but on the whole he seemed depressed," according to Alice. Mencken was left shaken by the encounter. Hilary Masters later wrote, "like every husband since Ulysses who has strayed, my father quickly reclaimed the shore of domesticity." When Masters did leave to reunite with his estranged wife and moved to Charlotte, North Carolina, Mencken said that he could not imagine how a civilized man could remain content in such a town. He eventually accepted the fact that he would never see his friend again.

Mencken found compensation in his renewed friendship with Theodore Dreiser. World War II brought the two men back together after their estrangement from 1926 to 1934. Like Mencken, Dreiser had maintained his hatred of the English, criticizing Roosevelt for his pro-British sympathies. Dreiser was well aware how much Mencken's support of his work had meant for his career.

Dreiser's death in 1945 dealt Mencken a terrible blow. "It recalls to me the long-ago days when hope hopped high in both of us, and we had a grand time," Mencken mourned. "I can hardly imagine grand times hereafter." The fact remained, he wrote to Dreiser's wife, Helen, "that he was a great artist, and that no other American of his generation left so wide and handsome a mark upon national letters. American writing before and after his time differed almost as much as biology before and after Darwin. He was a man of large originality, of profound feeling, and of unshakeable courage. All of us who write are better off because he lived, worked and hoped."

Of Mencken's friends now remaining, none seemed to show decay more than Joseph Hergesheimer. At one time he had been acclaimed everywhere as America's novelist. "Hardly any one disputed his preeminence," recalled Carl Van Vechten. But in so many ways, Hergesheimer was the product of a bygone age, his writing replete with descriptions of a romantic past. All too clearly, Hergesheimer himself was aware that his books had been cast to a "dark, questionable fate."

Hergesheimer's sudden abandonment of writing after an extraordinarily busy career—he had published 22 books in 20 years, besides many short stories and magazine articles—caused widespread astonishment. Mencken attributed it largely to ill health. But as Knopf well knew, the reason for his sudden silence mainly stemmed from an overwrought writing style that was no longer popular. In the 1940s he hesitated to make an offer to publish any of his works sight unseen. To Mencken's despair, Hergesheimer was reduced to living on his somewhat limited savings. Suicidal moods often besieged him.

Among other ailing friends Mencken visited was Ezra Pound, who was confined to St. Elizabeth's Hospital in Washington, charged with treason and ultimately declared insane. If the illness of such acquaintances disturbed Mencken, the death of several more plunged him into the deepest gloom. One by one, members of the Saturday Night Club disappeared. The week following the deaths of two brought the demise of three others: Jim Tully, Fred Hanes, and Ernest Boyd.

Of those left during these years, Mencken met regularly with Alfred Knopf, attending concerts and the annual Bach Festival in Bethlehem, Pennsylvania, with him. Many of the publisher's friends attributed Knopf's increasingly conservative attitude to Mencken, who could never forget that Knopf was once a New Dealer who had voted for Roosevelt in 1936 and 1940. "Alfred has no political sense. He is a very emotional fellow, too irascible, gets himself up to look like Abercrombie & Fitch, is a fresh-air maniac," Mencken said, referring to Knopf's mania about skiing and golf. Moreover, Mencken continued, "He's not a merry man; he's a sad man. Not the kind of fellow who ever kicks off."

It was true that Knopf, Mencken's junior by twelve years, affected the manner of a considerably older man. Mencken's visits to Knopf's Tudor country house in Purchase, New York, where he often stayed overnight, were relatively somber affairs. The two men discussed music and books or the intricacies of Knopf, Inc. And while Knopf's view toward alcohol was respectful (reverently bringing out rare vintage wines from his cellar), it was also temperate. His only frivolity seemed his addiction to purple shirts and loud neckties, so multicolored that it led Mencken to tell Nathan that "Alfred must think he is an Easter egg."

". . . the manner of a considerably older man." Alfred Knopf at his home in Purchase, New York. The Harry Ransom Humanities Research Center, The University of Texas at Austin.

With Alfred's wife, Blanche, Mencken could be more carefree. Her world was almost the exact opposite of her husband's; bilingual and bicoastal, she cared little for quiet evenings in the country, preferring the worlds of New York and Paris. Although Blanche's intensity toward her work and her friendships could be tiring for Mencken, he could share subjects with her he probably would have never felt free to discuss with Alfred—news about "a new gal" or, formerly, his feelings for Aileen.

Besides their love of quality and books, Alfred and Blanche shared their appreciation of Mencken as adviser and confidant. "He had more influence on me than any single person whom I have ever come into contact," Alfred confessed. From the very beginning of their firm, Mencken took an active part in reading manuscripts and recommending projects and ideas. With his magazines, Mencken introduced Knopf to such authors as James Cain and Ruth Suckow. He first urged the Knopfs to import *The Magic Mountain* by Thomas Mann and laid out in detail the blueprint for Logan Clendening's huge best seller, *The Human Body*. Even after his retirement from the *American Mercury*, Mencken continued to have an impact on American literature, when, as a board member of Knopf, Inc., he promoted the work of new writers for publication.

When Blanche tried to have a baby, she sought Mencken's medical counsel. When her eyesight began to fail, Mencken escorted her to Johns Hopkins. He advised both parents about their son, Pat. Mencken consistently paid tribute to a couple whom he felt had brought integrity to the book industry. The friendship among the three was affectionate and respectful, the kind of sentimental relationship between author and publisher that Knopf later admitted had become far less common.[1]

YEARS HAD PASSED since Mencken had read George Jean Nathan's *Friends of Mine* and vowed to Knopf that he never wanted to speak to Nathan again. However, the two resumed their friendship over lunch one spring day during the late 1930s; from there began a renewed exchange of letters that, like the inscriptions in their books, gave the impression that they had been corresponding daily without a break. By the 1940s the two were meeting regularly, lunching at the Colony or dining at Lüchow's before heading for drinks at 21 or the Stork Club, squiring old pals Zoë Akins and Anita Loos.

Nathan, whose own *American Spectator* magazine had collapsed in 1937, was clearly delighted at the reconciliation. Since he had never admitted publicly that he and Mencken were alienated, it was not difficult to pick up the threads of their friendship. Their reunion caused much wonder. Blanche Knopf found it "most strange to sit at dinner with you and G.J.N. again." Others understood better; Mencken may have acted like a hurt little boy years before, observed one, but deep down there had always been great affection for Nathan. In February 1947, the two posed for Irving Penn for a full-page portrait in *Vogue*, prompting Mencken to comment to Nathan that it made them look like a pair of 92-year-old roués.

While Mencken seemed glad of the opportunity to recapture the carefree days of his youth, there was another bonus to his renewed association with Nathan. At odd moments he was still at work on *My Life as Author and Editor*, and Nathan, whose memory was said to be like a safe-deposit vault, was able to fill in some of the missing details of the days when they co-edited the *Smart Set* and *Black Mask*—though he joked to Mencken that he would charge $87.25 for mental strain. On those rare occasions when he failed to remember missing names and dates, Mencken would say that Nathan's magnificent memory had finally yielded to senility and that he should be locked up at Johns Hopkins for a week's examination.

After so many years apart, Mencken found Nathan very fit, though somewhat graying. His figure was still trim. He still held his cigarette holder jauntily aslant, and his dark eyes still sparkled. Nathan's reputation had not been doomed to the fate of Mencken's other companions. He remained a Broadway institution, the man George Bernard Shaw ranked as "Intelligent Playgoer No. 1." Although the day had passed when he could kill a play with a mere quip, he was an acute and acidulous observer of the theater as drama columnist for Hearst's King Features Syndicate and the *New York Journal-American*, who disdained the movies ("at their best," Nathan sniffed, "they are tenth-rate theater").

Moreover, Nathan had kept busy writing, publishing articles for as many as thirty magazines, though executives at Knopf, Inc. were quick to point out that his books had never made any money and that Knopf himself viewed Nathan as one his more "difficult" and "fussy" authors. Nonetheless, he was still considered, then as now, the dean of drama critics, the champion of Ireland's Abbey Theatre players, instrumental in seeing that Sean O'Casey and other Irish playwrights found an audience on Broadway—a force not only in raising the level of the American stage but in developing a public.

During the 1940s, Nathan could be found at 21, where he ruled at his corner table as the most gracious of hosts. Nothing seemed to have changed in Nathan's routine from decades before. On cold nights he still insisted on wearing his ancient fur coat to the theater; his apartment at the Royalton was more cluttered than ever, only now books piled high on chairs almost reached to the ceiling. The most unreconstructed of hypochondriacs, Nathan had currently adopted the habit of carrying two thermometers in his pocket—to test one against the other, he maintained. "I spend an hour a day groaning," he told reporters, "but Mencken says he groans a quarter of an hour more than I do now."

Meanwhile, although his heyday as a Lothario was in the past, attractive women continued to parade softly through his years. The first of these was Lillian Gish, then came the soft-spoken, halo-headed actress Julie Haydon. Intermittently there were Chinese beauties, including a Miss Noel Toy, whom columnist Elsa Maxwell described as "a girl finely drawn as a curlicue of incense smoke, and who, on the side, could strip like a banana." Nathan insisted on referring ladies as possible companions to Mencken, but cautioned his former partner to "avoid

Toy. At your age, such women are fatiguing." According to Nathan, she was a passionate creature habitually falling for men who wore bowler hats; he advised Mencken to get out his fedora and be on the safe side.[2]

If Mencken had any reservations about getting together with his former partner, they were quickly dismissed. Nathan offered a comforting link with the past while demonstrating a heartening vitality in the present. Female company offered a similar refuge. Although Mencken tried to give the impression that he led a monastic life in Baltimore, Nathan knew better. For had he not spent hours listening to women confide to him the enduring attractions about his partner? During the 1940s, he was again assigned this role. One evening, before Aileen Pringle married the writer James Cain, Nathan patiently listened to her speak of Mencken at length. On another occasion, Zoë Akins admitted to Nathan that, having recently seeing Mencken, she had realized after all these years she was still in love with him. For his part, Mencken suggested to Nathan that they dine quietly alone and avoid the company of ladies. He had already received a box of candy in the mail from one female admirer—it was crushed, but a fragment bearing the word *kiss* survived.[3]

But women continued to pursue Mencken. A slim pantherlike creature named Virginia Alvarez began sending him passionate letters from Venezuela, confessing that since her first meeting with him in March 1919, "you have never been out of my mind. When you married . . . my soul cried silently while I wished you all the happiness you deserved." Now that Mencken was free again, she tried to convince him what a good companion she could be: "I love home life, like you; I am a very good cook . . . ," and while she sensed his desolation without Sara, she was certain that Mencken would find her own charms irresistible: "My hair is still very black; my teeth are mine and very even; plump now but not much . . . my body is firm."

Two years later, Alvarez moved to Philadelphia, determined to visit Mencken in Baltimore, despite her own impending marriage. She was adamant that "I am going to see you this time, if it is the last thing I do in this world." She compared him to mature wine, "full of flavour and taste." In an effort to dissuade her, Mencken responded: "What you say is far too flattering. You have in fact, always overestimated me, both as a writer and as a man."

Such polite demurrals did not dampen Alvarez's ardor; if anything, they only seemed to make her more enthusiastic. There was only one recourse left to Mencken: he fled.

The company of young Clare Leighton was considerably more welcome. A single Englishwoman in her late thirties, she had come to Baltimore supplied with several letters of introduction from mutual friends who thought it would be great fun if the two met. Clare tried her best not to feel shy about approaching this famous man, but her letters of introduction must have spoken well of her, because the very next day Mencken called and suggested they meet for lunch at the Belvedere Hotel.

As Clare came into the lounge, she saw a ruddy-faced man reading. Her first impression was that he was so "unexpectedly tough looking" that he reminded her of "an English pork butcher." But while Mencken may have looked tough, Clare Leighton quickly discovered he was "one of the most sentimental of creatures." Their twelve-thirty luncheon date lasted until four o'clock in the afternoon. It was the first of many encounters.

Friends began to suspect that perhaps there was more to these visits than met the eye. Members of the Saturday Night Club teased Mencken about seeing him with "a ravishing blonde at the Belvedere." It did not take long before Mencken told his new luncheon companion that he thought meeting her at the hotel was "a bit formidable" and began squiring her to Marconi's or Haussner's instead. Soon others began to question her as to the nature of her friendship with Mencken. When it came to her suitors, Clare Leighton assured her inquisitors that "our Henry is not one of them. We are great friends but it is in a roguish sort of way, with both of us squeezing what we can out of this strange mess called life." When she left Baltimore to move to Chapel Hill, she was aware that her departure made Mencken "resentful and sad. We had grown accustomed to our 'sessions.' "

That was the last time she saw him. Their friendship was somewhat circumscribed. Not once was she invited to his home, not once did she meet his brother August, or hear from his lips any mention of Sara, his deceased wife. "I realized the limits of our friendship and never thought to intrude beyond its ordained confines," she admitted. "There was about him a tragic, lonely dignity. The cynicism always veiled his true sentimentality."

Other women of that period came to a similar conclusion. Among them was Marcella DuPont, a close friend of the Hergesheimers, who made Mencken's acquaintance in 1934 when he and Sara were on their Mediterranean cruise. The two exchanged many letters, including some that were allegedly burned at Mencken's request. Mencken, while fond of the "very talkative and energetic" Marcella, often tired of her company, dismissing her as "a considerable gossip" and "far from reliable." At the end of his life, his wording was somewhat less diplomatic, referring to her striving for social status as an excuse for avoiding her friendship. Nonetheless, Mencken always treated his women friends courteously, demanding that everybody else do the same—"even some people that I thought were quite villainous," recalled August, "he said, 'Here, you gotta be polite to be them.' "

Those who met Mencken for the occasional lunch at Marconi's included Sara's companion, Ola Winslow, and Ellen Hawks, the wife of his boyhood friend Arthur. "I was sassy with him, too young to know any better," Ellen Hawks remembered of their banter. Mencken liked her voice, the way she pronounced certain words; Ellen was from the deep South. She recognized that in this way, perhaps, she reminded him of Sara.

"I think maybe that was what Henry was looking for—some way of having a clever, jolly person to spend an hour or two with," observed Olga Owens. Among those with whom Mencken enjoyed a mild flirtation were the newspaperwoman Doris Fleeson and Ruth Alexander, a lecturer from Chicago, who found him "too utterly fascinating to live so far away." Those who met Ruth recognized she had quite a wit. "I used to hear Henry mention [that her husband] was dull but that she was fun," recalled Olga Owens.

Yet, all of these faded into insignificance beside Sara. She "still remains living to me, and seldom a waking hour passes that I do not think of her . . . with tenderness and a kind of longing." These moments could come swiftly and involuntarily, giving strangers a glimpse into the most private recesses of his heart. The poet Julian Lee Rayford recalled meeting Mencken for lunch during this period. Afterward, "all of a sudden, as we were crossing street—right in the midst of traffic, with cars bearing down on us in both directions, he stopped. With his hands over his face, his face turned to the ground, he said, 'My poor wife! She has been dead eight years.' "

For those previous eight years, Mencken had tried to be loyal to Sara's memory, but whatever pangs of guilt he may have felt did not prevent him from enjoying the company of others. All of his life he had admired women. After Sara's death, he did not hesitate to arrange something beyond the casual flirtation; according to his own confession, there were two women in New York who were willing partners. But he could also declare, quite truthfully, about the gap his wife's passing had left in his life. As he said to one of his doctors, "After Sara, there was no other."[4]

all these circumlocutions – I suppose they did fuck

AS FOR HIS IMMEDIATE FAMILY, with the exception of August, Mencken saw less of his other siblings during this time. As a child, Mencken had been competitive with his brother Charlie; now that they were grown, their divergent interests became a gulf between them. Charlie readily acknowledged he had never cared for books; his favorite evening pastime was listening to *Amos 'n Andy* on the radio (a medium, according to his elder brother, meant only for "idiots"). The most serious difference between the two, however, remained unspoken: Charlie drank but, unlike Mencken, could not hold his liquor, and sometimes became surly. Such conduct, in Mencken's world, was an offense against order and discipline. With Charlie's wife, Mary, now dead, and Charlie roving from job to job, Mencken nonetheless worried from afar and often tried contacting his brother, to no avail. "We rarely saw him," August confirmed.

Mencken was particularly devoted and protective of his unmarried sister, Gertie—affectionately nicknamed "Sweet Teeth." In exchange for his sole use of the house on Hollins Street, he paid her rent for a furnished apartment during the winter when she was not at her farm, Choice Parcel. He would often visit there, clearing land, planting trees, and tending to her cows. But as with Charlie, there were glaring differences between the two.

Unlike her brothers, Gertrude was devout. But the main problem that kept Mencken at a distance was, as August put it, "her unending gabble." She had a

"He enjoyed tending to her cows." Mencken at Choice Parcel. H. L. Mencken Collection, Enoch Pratt Free Library.

habit of monopolizing the conversation and interrupting anyone who broke in. About half an hour was all that Mencken could stand and then he wanted to be rescued. Friends recalled of her visits to Hollins Street, "the moment she entered the house she would start talking and bossing August around." At lunch the two brothers would be held prisoner as Gertrude blithely leapt from subject to subject like a grasshopper across her fields, punctuating her monologue with instructions of what they should or should *not* do. August and Henry would exchange looks and stare at each other across the table; as soon as Gertrude left, Mencken would quickly shut the door: "*Jesus Christ!*" And then, almost as if to make up for such intolerance, he would dash off a brotherly note to his sister, offering to lend a hand to whatever needed to be done at Choice Parcel.

Mencken always spoke of his little brother affectionately. "Henry always said that his best ideas came from August," Hamilton Owens remembered, "and from what I know of August's mind, I think there was more than a trace of truth in that statement." In school August had been known as the odd genius. Mechanically inclined, as was Charlie, August had also had a successful career as an engineer, but his interests extended to science, archeology, and travel, with an emphasis on the bizarre. Notably, he was the only sibling, other than Mencken, of literary bent. An avid reader, he possessed an amazingly retentive memory. By avocation he was an author. In his lifetime August wrote four books, all of which required an enormous amount of research: *First Class Passenger*, on ocean travel; *By the Neck*, a history of hanging; *The Railroad Passenger Car*; and *Designing and Building the Great Pyramid*.

August was a caricature of Mencken in appearance and voice. Although taller, he had the same blue eyes and family trait of squinting when he became interested in what another was saying. Even when dressed, he looked disheveled. By nature he did not share the exuberance of his elder brother. "If you said hello, he would mumble and keep on going," a neighbor recalled. It was the complete opposite of Henry Mencken, who would stop and chat and inquire about the neighbor's family, or kneel to play marbles with the children of the block. Painfully shy, August remained a character unto himself. In his youth, he had fallen in love with a German American neighbor, but he never married, and as he grew older he had no ambition to do so. The first impression he gave women was of "an unsmiling rather good-looking man, a very pink forehead, a dignified almost cold manner." He detested going out to dinners and cocktail parties if he could avoid it, for the reason, he explained, that "it was just a hunting ground for that type of woman"—women "who give dinners and try to get people there that they hardly know."

Instead, August liked to surround himself with a small coterie of men who were not intellectual but who appreciated his dry sense of humor. In him, they found a genial pipe smoker and a good companion, very patient and not easily disturbed. As he grew older, August felt happiest in the company of his brother Harry, and it was during these years that the two became the best of friends. "They loved each other with a singular devotion," former secretary Margaret Redding recalled, "though Harry's love was the less possessive of the two." So loyal was August toward his brother than anyone slightly critical of Mencken promptly felt his anger.[5]

Although Mencken was content with his sibling's company, Hollins Street seemed an empty place, its silence relieved to an extent by the procession of small children, sons and daughters of his friends, who seemed to be as fond of Mencken as he was of them. Tokens of their admiration would arrive at Hollins Street, letters and drawings in childish scrawl: "I Love You, Be My Valentine," said one; another simply asked: "Dear Uncle Henry, Can I see you soon?" After returning from a weekend with Julian Boyd in Princeton, who was collecting a massive amount of Mencken's letters for publication, Mencken discovered he had so impressed Boyd's small son Kenneth that the boy had promptly christened one of his toy animals "Mr. Mencken."

Mencken made frequent trips to the toy store for one child or another. Over the years, Sara Anne Duffy received more than two hundred Valentines, including a plush satin heart upon which Mencken had stamped FOR DEPOSIT ONLY. She became a regular visitor to Hollins Street, where Mencken would be chivalrously waiting at the curb; if it was raining, he would be holding an umbrella. During lunch, he would play butler, opening the lid to a silver platter with a flourish to reveal a row of hot dogs, all in their buns. Of course, this was only after he had been patiently instructed by the child's mother as to the kind of food children *liked* to eat, and that it did *not* include sauerkraut. He took his role as godfather seriously. When Sara Anne was ten years old, he presented her with a large chest of silver. When she was in boarding school, he sent her a typewriter and a complete set of the works of George Bernard Shaw, along with postcards of Baltimore landmarks upon which he had jotted how far they were from the nearest department store.

When he was not entertaining Sara Anne Duffy, Mencken combed the beaches for seashells and driftwood that he would put in a cigar box and mail to Davy, the adored son of his niece, Virginia. To all of his bulletins to Virginia, Mencken bestowed advice on the care of the little barbarian: "You are beginning to discover that the logic of children is sharp and merciless. It is very hard to fool them and they are seldom deceived by facile and specious explanations. When they grow older, of course, they improve in stupidity and by the time they are ready to vote they are down to the common American level."[6]

As Mencken confessed to Benjamin de Casseres, "I should have had, not six children, but eight or ten. I am a natural born Polonius, and an audience that couldn't escape me would have been a considerable consolation in my old age." It was an admission of a growing feeling of loneliness as age crept up on him. With so many reminders of mortality, the urgency to get his own affairs in order spurred him on. He therefore proceeded with the job of arranging family albums, the typescripts of his books, the hundred or so volumes of clippings, an eight-volume set devoted to the "Hatrack" case, and his bound copies of the *American Mercury* and *Smart Set*.

At regular intervals these would be loaded on a truck sent over to the Enoch Pratt Free Library where they were placed into a locked enclosure at the third stack level. Already 2,000 volumes of manuscripts and first editions were piled there, with volumes doubled on some shelves. Employees were startled when, passing by "The Mencken Cage," in the dim light of the stacks they sometimes saw the subject himself, seated on a stool, his back propped against a steel upright, his glasses halfway down his nose, peacefully chewing a cigar and checking the pages of a volume of clippings. All offers of a more comfortable work space would be brushed aside. "I'm fine," Mencken would murmur, "be out of here in a minute."

He had no doubt about the importance of the papers he had donated. He realized that his memoirs—namely, *Thirty-Five Years of Newspaper Work* and *My Life as Author and Editor*, his "Additions" to his *Days* books, and other confidential manuscripts—included "some swell scandals," and he hoped that "they'll provide entertainment for dozens of nascent Ph.D.'s in the years to come." He made plans for three libraries to have copies of this material: in addition to the Enoch Pratt Free Library, the New York Public Library and the library at Dartmouth College. Over lunch with Alfred Knopf, Mencken spoke in detail about his plans. "Characteristically," Knopf noted, "he said that if it weren't for the war he'd leave something to the University of Leipzig!"

Meanwhile, he kept an envelope marked "Library" near his desk. Whenever he came across menus, butcher lists, clothing catalogues, war or presidential campaign material, and other such souvenirs of social history, he mailed them off to the Enoch Pratt Free Library to enlarge the Maryland collection, where it was filed for the thankful use by researchers not yet born. Sheets of music and magazines were also sent to expand the library's archives; and ideas were liberally supplied and editions loaned to boost the library's window displays. "My debt to the Enoch Pratt Free Library is immense," he wrote its director. "I only hope that the people of Baltimore come to understand its incalculable value to the town."[7]

AT LAST, THE FOURTH EDITION of *The American Language: Supplement I* was completed and Mencken closeted himself in his room to proofread the galleys. When the long, solitary labor was over, he wrote down his initials and dated it, neatly tying the long sheets together with string. Then he tried to reach a few of his closest friends to celebrate, but not one of them was in Baltimore at the time. "He told me that in a state of desolation he walked into a strange bar and sat at the counter for a drink," Marcella DuPont recalled.

> A sailor and his girl were there, too, and were the only other customers. They were racking their brains to find the answer to some historical question that had come up between them. Henry said that he leaned over and gave them the answer. Instantly the sailor flew into a fury and railed at Henry for interrupting his tête-à-tête with his girl. Henry confided to me that he left the bar at lowest ebb. I could measure the extent of his loneliness by this extreme sensitivity. Normally, he would have found the sailor grotesquely funny or just abysmally stupid.

If, as the saying goes, the surest sign of age is loneliness, it was a considerably older and sadder Mencken who walked home alone through the streets of Baltimore that evening.[8]

50

THE MAN WHO HATES EVERYTHING

WITH THE ARRIVAL OF 1945, Mencken was experiencing more and more the effects of his age. At dawn the pear tree at 1524 Hollins Street rustled with birds, filling the yard with such a chorus of song they habitually woke him up. He no longer felt refreshed or invigorated in the morning; each vertebra cracked as he rolled out of bed; his knees felt so stiff they would not bend at all; he wheezed as he climbed over the edge of the bathtub.

During the day, he often felt suddenly weak and at times seemed to be on the verge of fainting. Lying down failed to give him relief. He also noted an alarming loss of memory; on one occasion he could not even remember what year it was. Night after night he had trouble sleeping. Once, he recorded, "I awoke from a disturbed and idiotic dream with a sense of smothering, and lay awake the better part of an hour." He felt his pulse and found it normal, and his heart still beat strongly, but the next day he wrote in his diary that he had felt considerable discomfort with a sense of impending collapse.

All of this should have normally turned his mind to thoughts of mortality, but Mencken professed to remain sanguine on this score. "It interests me to note how little the fear of death is present at such times," he reflected. "It ought to be there, but it simply isn't." Instead, his thoughts were of his business affairs. On a trip to New York, he shared with Alfred Knopf ideas for several more books: a rewrite of *In Defense of Women*, *Selected Prejudices*, an omnibus of his own writings, an anthology of writings by others, and *Supplement II* to *The American Language*. As Knopf sat listening to Mencken, he observed his friend closely. "I don't like the way he looks," he later recorded in his diary. "Something not quite right about his complexion."[1]

Throughout their conversation, Mencken chatted genially about a range of topics unrelated to his health. On some level, though, he harbored the regret that his demise would make it impossible to finish some of the projects he had long had in mind. But his conscience was clear: "Looking back over a life of hard work, I find that my only regret is that I didn't work even harder. But this is somewhat absurd: I have actually worked hard enough."

While Mencken took comfort in the fact that his own affairs were generally in good order, he was keenly aware that the rest of the world was in chaos. Thousands of tons of bombs had been dropped on Germany. Dresden, once called the "Florence of Germany," was completely destroyed; Nuremberg, Hamburg, and Berlin had also been hard hit. Most troubling to Mencken was the attack on Leipzig, though later he was relieved to know that in the university the portraits of his ancestors were unscathed.

In the spring of 1945, the *Sun* denounced the Germans as responsible for horrible crimes. As far back as 1922 Mencken had predicted that anti-Semitism in Germany was so great that one day there would be "a colossal massacre of Jews." But when the world discovered that the Holocaust was a reality, Mencken remained noticeably silent. Always loyal to Germany, he was not one to criticize it now, especially when so much of it lay in rubble. If Mencken seemed unable to face the atrocity of German concentration camps, he was not alone in initially refusing to believe the evidence.

It is difficult for those living in the twenty-first century to comprehend the skepticism that greeted preliminary reports about the destruction of the Jews. Many Americans, newspapermen included, assumed that accounts about the Holocaust were merely exaggerations, similar to the anti-German propaganda circulated during the First World War. All through the Second World War the Allies said little about atrocities. Without eyewitnesses and with doubts about the reports from the Russians who liberated the camps, the stories seemed unbelievable.

This changed dramatically once Western newsmen actually visited the concentration camps and photographers documented the brutal scenes of the dead and the dying. In a front-page story, Lee McCardell, the *Sunpapers* war correspondent, voiced his own shock after touring one of the camps, of seeing in a wooden shed, piled up like so much cordwood, the naked bodies of more dead men than he dared to count.

In Baltimore the Century Theater ran a ten-minute documentary made by the Army Signal Corps about the German prison camps and the Buchenwald atrocities. "It was sickening," R. P. Harriss of the *Sunpapers* wrote in his diary. "In the First World War, atrocity tales were not documented and were probably mostly lies. There is no doubting *this* evidence." In the *Sunday Sun*, the magazine published large photos of the horrors found in Bergen-Belsen.

Friends had learned not to mention the war in Mencken's presence. During those evenings at the Saturday Night Club, Louis Cheslock noted, "No one discusses the war—this we agreed on shortly after it began." Knopf reflected: "I still have not heard him say a word against Germany. He is personally about the kindest and most sentimentally generous man I've ever known but these large areas of discussion must simply be avoided." Mencken's refusal to admit the existence of concentration camps apparently was the main reason John Owens had drawn apart from him: "When Buchenwald was going on, Mr. Mencken still held fast to Germany."

Alistair Cooke recalled: "I have to say that I don't remember Mencken ever admitted that the gas chambers and the concentration camps existed." That he half believed they did seemed evident from "the uneasiness with which he brushed aside any mention of Nazi brutality and in a weary grumble equated such rumors with the First World War" reports. Mencken's characteristic reaction to subjects he found too disturbing even to contemplate was a stony-faced silence. Though he could not bring himself to admit aloud what was going on, he found himself unable to sleep at night and increasingly disturbed by nightmares.

Ultimately, in his correspondence Mencken stopped scolding those "hysterical" voices of American Jewish "propagandists" whom he had once termed "professional Jews" leading the charge against Germany. Later in 1945, as he prepared a revised edition of *Treatise on the Gods*, he took care to eliminate his 1930 statement that "the Jews could be put down very plausibly as the most unpleasant race ever heard of." Eventually, even Mencken came to recognize, as he said, that "better than the rest of us, they sensed what was ahead for their people."[2]

Mencken remained convinced that if other countries had behaved badly during the Second World War, the United States also had its share of the blame. "I am quite unable to agree that all the force of right, decency and justice were on the American side in the late war," he angrily commented to a correspondent. "Apparently, you have overlooked many things, including the intolerably barbaric use of the atom bomb and the wholesale looting that is now going on both in Germany and Japan."

The situation confronting postwar Germany disturbed Mencken acutely. The Second World War ended in Europe in May 1945 but, as Mencken was fully aware, the misery continued, with widespread hunger and turmoil everywhere. Berlin, as the symbol of Nazism, became a pawn in a battle of wills with the Soviet Union for postwar Europe.

As the United States celebrated victory and confetti billowed forth from the upper floors of downtown buildings in Baltimore, Mencken could not help but reflect on the fate of his fatherland, of friends and distant relatives still there. Eleven family members had died in Germany, including one during the bombardment of Berlin; another, a young German soldier who bore the name of his own grandfather Burkhardt Mencken, had been taken prisoner. Civilians in Germany scrambled for food, shelter, and protection as systematic pillage, looting, and rape took place under a Red Army seen as conquerors not as liberators.

News of conditions in Germany came in letters from correspondents in Berlin. Georg Kartzke, head of the Amerika Institut, wrote Mencken that his office at the university was now buried under a pile of debris from an attack by American and British planes—an irony, he commented sadly, considering so many notables from the United States and England had gathered there before the war.

Mencken felt powerless. He had no political influence, and he realized that his ideas about the war were such that his intervention would probably do more harm than good. "In the United States, as in all modern countries, the highest virtue of a citizen seems to be mere conformity," he wrote. "Unless he agrees with everything that the politicians preach, he is dismissed as a kind of criminal."

Hungry for more detailed information, Mencken pleaded with friends to send him copies of the German newspapers. The American correspondents in Berlin, he complained, "seem to be the most incompetent on record." Families, sorting through the debris of damaged buildings, were struggling to survive on less than 400 calories a day. Mencken sent packages of oatmeal, oil, rice, powdered milk, chocolate, and tea, and tins of meat, fish, and brown bread. These were genuine pleasures, unknown for years, their recipients assured him. "My heart was ready to burst," his friend Julie Merkel wrote. Mencken asked for the names and addresses of others who might be in need. He even managed to send gifts to the Russian zones, and, against the odds, some of his packages made it to their destination. In one were several pairs of shoes; in another, the necessary ingredients for a cake, along with a tin of coffee. In towns and cities across Germany, families sang Mencken's praise as they unwrapped delicacies otherwise unavailable except on the black market. Mencken had become "Santa Claus."[3]

A far more difficult challenge confronted Mencken when he tried to mail copies of the *Congressional Record* and *The American Language* to Georg Kartzke and to Heinrich Spies, an authority on English in Germany. They were promptly returned. "Certainly it is an absurdity to deprive a professor of American affairs and English *The Congressional Record* and books on language," Mencken wrote to the commanding general in charge of military government in Germany. For six months he continued this battle but received no answer. "The bureaucrat is a natural imbecile," Mencken wrote to Kartzke. "When he is put in a position to afflict and annoy his betters he leaps to it like a trout swimming upstream." And he added to another German friend: "The same frauds who still afflict the United States have opened an export branch."

Palestine, which had just been partitioned into Arab and Jewish states, also drew Mencken's special attention. He scoured the *Palestine Post* for news of the termination of the British mandate. Even the advertisements in the *Post* fascinated him, and when his edition did not arrive in the mail, he complained to journalist Paula Arnold, a Jewish émigré, who confessed she was surprised to hear from him. No other newspaperman, she wrote him, seemed to recall her name. He used his influence to try and place her news stories in the United States.

Mencken, meanwhile, was increasingly distressed by the conditions in the United States. Eight hundred thousand steel workers and others were on strike. Tests of atomic bombs continued, and shortages of meat and other goods persisted. He did not expect the year ahead to be any better. "Whenever I contemplate the state of the Republic," Mencken commented, "I think of Jefferson's saying, 'I tremble for my country when I reflect that God is just.'"

On New Year's Eve at the Pattersons' house, Mencken leaned against the mantel, surrounded by a group of admirers listening to his lively talk. Out the blue, one of the women, her head crowned with a pert little hat, asked him: "Mr. Mencken, have you had a happy Christmas?" To everyone's alarm, Mencken flew into a rage. "You know how perfectly awful Christmas is!" he boomed, eyes bristling. In one swift instant, geniality had been transformed into vehemence. The holiday only reminded him of loss; it was a day to pull the blinds, bring out the booze, and fervently wish it would just go away.

Too late, the questioner realized her mistake; she visibly wilted under Mencken's assault, as the rest of the crowd drifted away, embarrassed.[4]

MENCKEN'S MOOD LINGERED until he opened his paper a few months later, on March 14, 1947, and read Truman's address about aiding Europe. He was jubilant to note that the government of the United States had finally decided that the greatest threat to peace was no longer Germany but the Soviet Union. It was a considerable change from the official and popular viewpoint that had prevailed since the end of the war.

A corner had been turned. Gratified, Mencken argued in favor of the immediate economic rehabilitation of Germany and was convinced that the process of change would be far more rapid than it had been after World War I. "Altogether," he observed, " I find myself rather optimistic for the first time in years," for, as he told Heinrich Spies, "until the end of 1947, the Germans were still the enemies of mankind but now they are found to be very amiable people with high spirits and capacities. The current villains, of course, are the Russians. Everyone seems to be convinced that the war with them is inevitable soon or late."

Still, Mencken's overall assessment of the postwar outlook was reserved. Beyond "the few more conspicuous fruits of the second great crusade to save humanity," Mencken argued, World War II had left the world with a host of other problems. He listed some of them: "millions of young Americans, robbed of the most precious years of their lives, are dismally trying to start anew; the prices are rising, inflation impends, no American investment is safe, and another huge collapse seems to be certain."

Mencken's criticism prompted a reporter from *Life* magazine to ask him, "which would you rather be called—'The Sage of Baltimore' or 'The Man Who Hates Everything'?" He replied aggressively,

I don't care a damn what you or anyone else calls me, just as long as you don't call me an old dodo sneaked out of the dissecting room. I'm 66 years old, I work hard all the time, and while it is perfectly true that I may be snatched into heaven tomorrow I am still going strong today. I have written five books since I was 60, and all of them sold better than any of my previous books. In the present case, it is a little inaccurate to say that I hate everything. I am strongly in favor of common sense, common honesty and common decency. This makes me forever ineligible to any public office of trust or profit in the Republic. But I do not repine, for I am a subject of it only by force of arms. By birth and of free choice I am a citizen of the Maryland Free State.

Of the hundreds of letters that arrived at *Life* magazine, half praised Mencken for, as one put it, "the courage to say what many of us hardly dare feel," while the other half castigated him as "un-American." By the end of the decade, nevertheless, Mencken again found himself something of a celebrity. A new generation of authors knocked at his door, eager to write a biography of the great iconoclast.[5]

The first of these was Edgar Kemler, who had taken a year's leave of absence from teaching political science at Harvard University. Mencken had written so much about his own life in the *New Yorker* and in his *Days* trilogy that Kemler found it a challenge to obtain new information, especially on Mencken's private life. Not many of Mencken's contemporaries were willing to breach a confidence, especially when the subject was still living. But Kemler discovered a cooperative Mencken, inviting him to ask questions, reading chapters as they were completed. Mencken arranged for Joseph Hergesheimer to join them and reminisce over lunch.

If Kemler thought he was going to gain any insight into Mencken's private life, however, he was mistaken. From the distance, Hergesheimer could see Kemler ardently addressing Mencken, who, according to Hergesheimer, was leaning against the wall, clearly ill at ease, gazing "around him with his striking blue eyes and the faintly troubled frown that seldom lifted." At Schellhase's, Kemler lay a thick portfolio beside his plate and in short order produced an account of the week in 1926, when Mencken and Hergesheimer were in Hollywood. Mencken froze, his eyes going blank, staring straight ahead at the wall beyond the young man's head.

Kemler's well-intentioned interrogation continued through lunch. At one point, he reminded them of Mencken's meeting with Aileen Pringle at Hergesheimer's house. At the mention of the name, Mencken suddenly consulted his watch and reminded Hergesheimer it was time to catch his train. As Hergesheimer knew well from experience, Mencken was expert at detaching himself, and he left the young biographer with a host of questions that seemed doomed to remain unanswered.

On his train ride back to Philadelphia, Hergesheimer concluded that Kemler, while amiable, might not be best suited to write the story of Mencken's life. Mencken agreed. Hergesheimer thought Kemler too young to ever "plumb the springs of Henry's diversity"; Mencken dismissed the lad as "a New Dealer" who was "obviously not the man to write a really intelligent book on me." Hergesheimer subsequently wrote Kemler and advised him that in questioning Mencken, it was best not to pry *too* closely into his personal affairs.

The case of William Manchester was different. While in college Manchester had first become interested in Mencken, arguing the merits of the Baltimore columnist with faculty members. Afterward, using material from the public library and under the direction of Frank Luther Mott at the University of Missouri, Manchester had written a dissertation on H. L. Mencken and the *Smart Set* magazine.

With Mencken's encouragement, Manchester moved to Baltimore in 1947 and, with his help, got a job with the *Sunpapers* while writing the biography. Mencken was a generous mentor. Together at the Enoch Pratt Free Library, the older man and young disciple leafed through clippings and an incredible number of first editions. Once, as they emerged onto Cathedral Street, Mencken stepped in front of a taxicab. "I grabbed him by the arm and whisked him away just in time," Manchester remembered. "He spoke on the transience of life—and then proceeded to lead me right through the heavy traffic, against the light, again! He had no respect for lights or cars, it seems, though he was genuinely scared by that cab."

Manchester often saw Mencken and jotted his impressions after frequent walks together through downtown Baltimore. Strolling on Charles Street, Manchester recalled, "we encountered two sedate women from the *Sun's* library coming the other way, and [Mencken] cried out heartily, 'Hello, girls! How's the profession?' Later one of them said to me, 'Of course, he didn't mean it the way it sounded.' I knew that was exactly how he had meant it." In the *Sunpapers'* morgue Mencken advised a man updating his obituary to "Leave it as it is. Just add one line: 'As he grew older, he grew worse.'"

Unlike his experience with Kemler, Mencken felt completely at ease with Manchester. And while Mencken often told him that all authors were insufferable, he appreciated especially the fact that Manchester was not planning to remain a reporter all his life, but planned to become a writer of books, much as he had done. Their conversations would continue late into the night before a roaring fireplace at Hollins Street, a home that had become a kind of shrine for the younger man. It was not long before Mencken began calling Manchester "my last protégé."

Manchester, however, initially encountered the same obstacles as had Kemler: "Mencken repeats himself about city editors and reporters, and tells stories from his reminiscences, apparently unaware that he has published them." As Manchester's research continued, he realized that Mencken was the most complex subject he had ever tried to master.

For the next two years Manchester labored on his Mencken biography and continued to work at the *Sun*. Bit by bit, the young man accumulated such an overwhelming amount of data that he and his family were forced to find a larger apartment: "It rules my very life."

Years later, Manchester achieved further fame, writing several more biographies, books of fiction and history, including a hugely successful account of the assassination of President John F. Kennedy and a celebrated portrait of Winston Churchill. But the kindness Mencken had shown toward a struggling author most impressed Manchester in a long career of writing and affected him personally. "Our friendship was strong and my love for him genuine," he recounted. Many years later, when he was old and incapacitated by a stroke, he repeated his devotion: "Mencken is so close to me. He is always with me."[6]

YOUNG BIOGRAPHERS such as Kemler and Manchester, eagerly listening to Mencken recounting his days on the *Herald*, might have been further reminders to the older man of his luck in having been born when he was. A louder, more chaotic, less palatable world now confronted Mencken each day he left his house on Hollins Street.

One morning, on his way to the Pratt Library, Mencken encountered a crowd of young protestors, shouting and waving signs about the dawn of the atomic age. Nudging his way through the mob, Mencken reminded himself that he was all for free speech, but he later wrote to a library board member: "My heart bled for the honest folk who had to shoulder their way through Hyde Park in order to get at the card catalogue."

Mencken blamed the state of the country on "world savers"—especially Franklin D. Roosevelt and the New Dealers. As for his own city, "now completely bankrupt, completely filthy, and completely godless," he marveled "that our Heavenly father has not knocked it off with a blast of mustard gas." Home was Mencken's sanctuary, yet even here he was hardly free to enjoy a cigar without being harassed by the Human Engineering Foundation, which sent moralistic letters chiding him for continuing to smoke and demanding that he be an advocate of a better way of life for boys and girls in "this high speed, starving world."

It seemed to Mencken that America had lost its way. "As the shadows close in we can at least recall that there was a time when people could spend weeks, months and even years without being badgered, bilked or alarmed," he lamented. "The human race had not yet succumbed to the political and other scoundrels who have undertaken of late to save it, to its infinite cost and degradation. It had a better time in the days when I was a boy, and also in the days when I was a young newspaper reporter." It was, Mencken wrote, a time of joy in "this once great and happy Republic," now only "a dismal burlesque of its former self."

Again, Mencken found refuge in the past, this time to his days as a young newspaperman, in his book *Christmas Story*. Published in 1946, it was a harmless but ironic account of a holiday feast among the homeless. Mencken had a difficult time persuading Knopf to print it; his Canadian publisher withdrew the book because it was considered sacrilegious.

Playing music with members of the Saturday Night Club provided Mencken with another refuge. Yet, many of his colleagues had grown grumpy; not all showed up; others had long since died. At times the music played was mediocre and the conversation dull. More often than not, Mencken tired easily and seemed unwell. He began leaving at 11:30, "which is considerably sooner than in the old days, when 1 o'clock was more common," Louis Cheslock noted in his diary. "Sad days these."

Nor did it help matters that the brown and white mongrel belonging to the Fortenbaugh family next door barked day and night. The noise made it impossible to conduct conversation; it actually reduced Gertrude to complete silence when she came in for lunch. In his office Mencken could only sort out papers, but soon he had to abandon the job and flee to his office at the *Sunpapers*. When he returned home, "that damn dog" was still at it.

Though his typewriter had always been weapon enough against the assorted banes of mankind, eventually Mencken sought the help of the courts, seeking damages for "deprivation of normal peace, comfort and rest." The newspaper wire services picked up the story and flashed it across the country. Within 24 hours after Mencken filed his lawsuit, the dog disappeared, eventually becoming very useful as a rat exterminator at the Baltimore Humane Society, and so contented, the press reported, that he did not utter a sound of any kind.

Somehow, in the face of poor health and barking dogs, Mencken finished the first draft of the "accursed" *The American Language: Supplement II* by May of 1947; by June he was bashing out the preface on his typewriter. "At my age a man encounters frequent reminders, some of them—" he crossed out *unpleasantly surprising* and inserted *disconcerting*, typing an entire row of x's before continuing: "—that his body is no more than . . . unstable congeries of the compounds of carbon."

Mencken expressed his indebtedness to his secretary, "whose heroic struggles with an extraordinarily difficult manuscript—" Again he stopped; again the angry slash with dark pencil. With furious emphasis, applying more pressure to paper than before, he replaced *difficult* with a more suitable word. It was nothing less than a *maddening* manuscript. He later confessed to a correspondent that he had grown so intensely hostile to the American language, he could hardly imagine writing about it again.[7]

TWO MONTHS LATER, on July 30, 1947, Mencken awoke in a considerable state of confusion. Dr. Baker, on examining him, found that Mencken had suffered a stroke, caused by an embolism close to the speech center of the brain, that had produced temporary aphasia. "I look normal to the superficial eye but I find it impossible to write," Mencken told one of his doctors. "When I tackled the typewriter the letters jumped and when I used the pen I could not form them."

As usual, he put on a brave front, though he knew enough medicine to be aware of what was going on. "Such are the sorrows that have come to a man who

"An extraordinarily *maddening* manuscript." HLM at work on *The American Language*.
H. L. Mencken Collection, Enoch Pratt Free Library.

has led a clean life for nearly a century," Mencken told friends. "I begin to believe that virtue doesn't pay." In his diary he harbored a darker thought: "I fear I am in for it."

In the face of his declining health, Mencken nonetheless managed to finish the index for *Supplement II*, a task, he admitted, that reduced him to a pulp. To recuperate, he and August went to St. Petersburg, Florida. The trip rallied Mencken's spirits, but his health did not improve. At nights he would wake with a start, feeling discomfort around his heart. On such occasions, when he had trouble sleeping, he would turn his mind's eye to those scenes of his youth that he had recounted with such nostalgia in *Happy Days* and reflect on those long lost days of childhood.

There, unfolding before him, was Oriole Park. Beyond, he could see "the green sward, and the packed grandstand, and the long shafts of the setting sun as clearly as if I were back in 1892."[8]

51

THE GREAT UPSET OF 1948

Late in 1947 Paul Patterson and his son Maclean tried to persuade Mencken to cover the 1948 political conventions for the *Sun*. Their overtures were violently rejected. Mencken felt that the paper had greatly deteriorated; moreover, against his objections it had set up a television station. "I quit writing for the *Sun* in January, 1941, and it is highly improbable that I'll resume for the two conventions. Thus you had better chalk me off," he wrote to Maclean, adding sarcastically, "I am beginning to yearn for television. In a little while you'll hear and see me crooning."

Despite his resistance, Mencken missed the convention press stalls. "Shortly after [Senator Robert A.] Taft announced his candidacy," William Manchester recalled, "he showed up in the office wearing an enormous button bearing the legend 'Taft for President,' which, under close inspection, turned out to be a souvenir of the convention of 1908." Father and son again expressed the hope that Mencken would join them, for the spectacle if nothing else. To tempt him even further, Maclean sent him clippings of the campaign of the new Progressive Party under Henry A. Wallace. He broadly hinted that the present one promised to be as wild as the old Progressive party of Gerald K. Smith and Charles E. Coughlin that Mencken had enjoyed not so long before. Still Mencken remained coy. He was within two years of his seventieth birthday which, as a life-long hypochondriac full of very real arterial disturbances, he dreaded more than the average individual. One all-night session, he told Maclean, was sure to deliver him to the Pathology Department of Johns Hopkins: "Better not count on me."

Later, when Mencken was in New York promoting *Supplement II* of *The American Language*, liberally dropping random quotes and cigar ash in the Knopf board room, a reporter again brought up the subject of the conventions. "I'll probably end up by going and blowing up and coming home on a shutter," Mencken remarked. "Oh, well. It's a heroic death." Clearly, his defenses were weakening. "God knows I itch to see all three conventions but I seriously doubt that I'll be physically able to cover them," he told Maclean.

However critical Mencken had been of the *Sunpapers*, he was sentimental about his friendships and his allegiance to the paper. When Maclean kept up the pressure and wrote Mencken that "we are still holding a seat and a bed at the conventions," Mencken was genuinely touched. Convinced that by 1952 he would be too old for the job, Mencken now eagerly looked forward to the summer of 1948's orgies, declaring to Hergesheimer that "either they'll restore me, or they will kill me."[1]

The conventions and campaigns of 1948 constituted the beginning of a new era. It would be the last of the predominantly whistle-stop campaigns by train; it was the first time the conventions were televised. From his seat in the press stand, Mencken saw how television crews now hogged the glass-enclosed perch high on the wall behind the platform, squeezing out "the newsreel boys" and "radio crooners" who wanted nothing to do with the new medium. Edward R. Murrow and Eric Sevareid at CBS were among the big names who had been convinced by their employers, albeit with great difficulty, that they should take part, at least occasionally. What they provided was carried by 4 networks to 18 stations in 9 cities. But for many who attended in the hall, the television coverage would be the best-remembered part of the 1948 convention. On the floor was a mass of amplifiers, wires, and cables, one of which Mencken readily tripped over.

Mencken was stridently opposed to television, calling it "madness" and "a curse to newspapers." He wrote a friend: "I am thoroughly convinced in conscience that television is the most ghastly gadget yet invented by maniacs. I can see nothing in it whatsoever." Why public taste had reached such abysmal depths, Mencken could not fathom. "The old-time leadership of journalism has pretty well vanished," he concluded. "It is now simply a pander to imbecility."

Throughout 1947 and 1948 he had heatedly debated the advisability of the *Sunpapers'* involvement in television, which for him, was simply "a boobs and tubes business. It's Hollywood." WMAR-TV shared the *Sun* building; sometimes the anchormen would come downstairs to the city room in their make-up and costume and look around. "We thought they were comedians," laughed William Manchester.[2]

By 1948, there were enough people who thought differently. In the United States, the number of television sets had climbed past one million; in Baltimore alone, the number had grown from 1,600 the year before to more than 22,000. As television's popularity grew, recruiting to its ranks "more and more press agents and other such intellectuals," Mencken conceded that video verbiage had begun creeping into the American language. He wrote an article to that effect for the *New Yorker*, telling *Sunpapers'* colleagues that "I hate to see a good newspaperman wasted on its puerilities." Human nature being what it was, Mencken observed, "as soon as a television or any kind of radio enterprise gets into a newspaper an enormous number of men including some of the best become radio crooners, not newspapermen. . . . They get stage-struck, in brief. It shows in the newspaper instantly. The way for newspapers to meet the competition of radio and television is simply to get out better newspapers." He soberly concluded that "television, if it actually becomes profitable, will be a rival to newspapers rather than an auxiliary."

Within the convention hall in Philadelphia, Mencken could witness for himself the first signs of the medium's deleterious effect. The new light bulbs that made the newsreel lights of long ago seem insignificant in comparison exuded so much heat they made the place a steam bath. Although the auditorium had been refurbished, it was not air conditioned and the temperature at the rostrum was 93 degrees. Reporters wore dark glasses in order to work in the fierce glare; Mencken sported a green eyeshade. He doubted that any politician, however leathery his hide, could survive the heat or the lights without fainting or catching fire, or at the very least suffering a considerable singeing. From the press stand, Mencken observed that "the few hard-boiled fellows who faced it out on the platform began by looking almost transparent, and then showed a phosphorescent glow. The hardiest stood it only a few minutes."

Mencken soon wilted under the television superglare, though characteristically he refused to give up his post, writing at least one running story from the stand during an almost twenty-four-hour watch. He said he had "come back from the grave after eight years" to cover the conventions; then, smiling with cheery optimism, declared "I figure this will be my last one." The *London Spectator* reported that the air-conditioned pressroom was mobbed with reporters drinking beer and watching the show in comfort, rather than venturing into the blast furnace below. "Television may kill the old-fashioned reporter of the Casablanca type," the newspaper predicted. "Even the sight of H. L. Mencken seated on the burning deck whence nearly all but he had fled did not shame any of his colleagues to returning to the field of action where the temperatures, hot air, television and miscellaneous noise made reporting harder."

The escape from the heat of the convention hall to the luxurious air-conditioned bedroom in the *Sunpaper's* suite at the Ritz proved to be too great a temptation for Mencken. To the horror of everyone on the staff, he requested that the vents to his room be taped. Even so, he caught a bad cold, complaining that it was not the strain but "an attack of my old enemy, tracheitis" that forced him to leave the Republican convention and return to Baltimore before the presidential nomination of Thomas E. Dewey.[3]

Two weeks later, Mencken was back in Philadelphia to attend the Democratic convention, characterized as the most dispirited in American political annals.

"Television may kill the old-fashioned reporter." Surviving the heat at the 1948 Democratic convention. H. L. Mencken Collection, Enoch Pratt Free Library.

Previously, Mencken had predicted President Truman's victory—he "still has that war scare in his pocket, and war scares are always potent with American numskulls." But after witnessing the grim convention, Mencken was certain that he had misjudged the situation. It was only too evident that Truman seemed nervous about the outcome of the election, Mencken later said. He had sat less than twenty feet from him when he made his speech of acceptance in Philadelphia—viewed as the most militant presidential speech of either party since that of William Jennings Bryan. "It was the snarling and defiant harangue of a badly scared man," summarized Mencken. "The more he whooped and hollered the more manifest it was that he was fighting with his back to the wall."

Alistair Cooke of the *Manchester Guardian*, who sat next to Mencken, watched the older man work night and day. "He typed out his stuff in triple space, on a ribbon that might well have been installed at the 1904 convention," Cooke recalled. "But however faint and gray was the typescript, the sharp prose was no one's but his." Chewing on a cigar, Mencken "would glare in a steady trance at the keyboard while the loudspeakers rattled with the sobs and bawlings of the party chieftains, and would then slap out a woeful salute to '*the traditional weather of a national convention . . . a rising temperature, very high humidity, and lazy puffs of gummy wind from the mangrove swamps surrounding the city.*'" This was quoted, with great guffaws, as a typical Menckenism. After an eight-year absence, all agreed that he was one of the most welcome figures in what constituted a sort of old home week.

A small crowd of reporters would gather around to watch him work, their eyes glued not to what was happening on stage but to Mencken himself. The star of this show pretended not to notice, though every now and then he shot them a glance out of the corner of his eye. "See that man over there?" One newspaperman pointed out to another. "To us, Mencken was a god," Anthony Lewis, much later a *New York Times* columnist, remembered. So welcome was his reappearance at the Democratic convention that somebody actually yelled, "H. L. Mencken for President!" to which Mencken responded by standing up on his desk, bowing gracefully, and announcing: "I accept." Mencken at the same time was willing to remain as anonymous as any other reporter. When a photographer innocently asked for his name and occupation, Mencken solemnly wrote: "Retired six-day bicycle rider."

Much had been made of Mencken's return to page one of the *Sun*. The promotion staff of the *Sunpapers* had prepared oversize ads in advance. Paul Patterson made sure that a special typesetting format was given to Mencken's articles, with more white space between each line so that the words jumped off the page. Patterson had assigned a typographer in Baltimore exclusively to Mencken, whose articles alone were bylined. The result, commented Bradford Jacobs, one of the younger political reporters for the *Sun*, initially made "the rest of us feel faintly intimidated," but "everybody wanted to be Mencken." The conventions, copyeditors observed, had given the old man a new lease on life: "It was the old Mencken reporting."

Manchester, who could be seen walking behind Mencken and toting his typewriter for him, assessed the old man's reporting from the 1948 convention "as among the best he has ever done." As they had years before, editors in Baltimore delighted in reading Mencken's dispatches as they came over the wire

"Everybody wanted to be Mencken." Showing he was a working newspaperman to the end.
H. L. Mencken Collection, Enoch Pratt Free Library.

during the small hours of the morning. "It was the most rocking thing you could read," recalled former copyreader Stanley Harrison, "especially the material that came in from the Wallace Progressive Party convention." Who could forget Mencken's description of Wallace as having acquired such a "semi-celestial character" that "if when he is nominated today he suddenly sprouts wings and begins flapping about the hall no one will be surprised." Or his withering dismissal of Glen Taylor, Wallace's running mate, as "a third-rate mountebank from the great open spaces. . . . Soak a radio clown for ten days and nights in the rectified juices of all the cow-state Messiahs ever heard of and you have him to the life." "He was in rare form, and he knew it," according to Alistair Cooke, "determined to show that he was a working newspaperman to the end."

No one, including Mencken, knew how near that end was. The conventions turned out to be his last reporting stint. For those who shared the press stand with him in Philadelphia, poignant memories would remain of what Cooke called the last happy days of H. L. Mencken. Those who were there said Mencken was in a carnival mood. While the Progressives had produced "a surprisingly good crop," Mencken remarked to Cooke, they were "nothing so bizarre" as the eccentrics he swore he had seen at the Bull Moose Convention of 1912. Mencken and a young reporter, Murray Kempton, stood together looking out over the hall. "Well, the Communists here seem very smart," Mencken said, turning to the young man; "they didn't show up." Kempton later confessed: "I didn't have the heart to tell Mencken that around the hall were my Communist friends."

After 49 years of Mencken's attendance at national conventions, it seemed incredible to the younger set that his energy had not waned. He arrived early, as was his custom, interviewing doormen, policemen, and the band conductor. In the early hours of the morning, other newsmen began to decamp, but not Mencken. "It was very late, and I assumed that Mencken, after so much recent moaning about his approach to the grave, would beg off on account of his sinuses and go to bed," Cooke remembered. "But again he appeared to want to show that he was as casually professional as any other reporter, who on such assignments behaves like an oblivious infantryman, snatching sleep and food only when the firing lets up or the liquor has all gone." He knew a place to get German beer, and he and Cooke downed several schooners. When they got back to the Progressive Party's hotel headquarters, Cooke said, Mencken mingled with the crowd, listening to small groups of young people plucking on guitars. He gave little bows to the women, hailed the men as "Comrade," until finally he went across the street and into the Ritz. "Nobody had the slightest idea who he was."[4]

The next day, the official proceedings got off to a blundering start with Wallace, according to Mencken, "making a thumping ass of himself in his preliminary press conference." The candidate began by attacking the press. Many suspected that the real reason for his diatribe was to forestall harassment about letters that, Westbrook Pegler asserted, Wallace had written to the leader of a religious cult. Wallace was asked if he had indeed written the letters. His face a frozen mask, Wallace replied disdainfully, "I never discuss Westbrook Pegler." Two or three other reporters rephrased the question, to which Wallace gave the same inflexible answer. Pegler, who had been sitting near the back of the room, stood up.

"Did you or did you not write them?" he asked. Wallace coldly retorted: "I never engage in any discussions with Westbrook Pegler." By now Wallace was sweating profusely.

Suddenly Mencken was on his feet. Young newsmen, who had heard about Mencken but had never seen him before, climbed onto their chairs to watch the spectacle. Smiling, Mencken asked Wallace, "Would you consider *me* a Pegler stooge?" The entire room, Wallace included, broke into laughter. "No, Mr. Mencken," he said. "I would never consider you anybody's stooge."

"Well, then," gently continued Mencken, "it's a simple question. We've all written love letters in our youth that would bring a blush later on. There's no shame in it. This is a question that all of us here would like to have answered, so we can move on to weightier things."

Wallace answered that he would "handle it in my own way in my own time." "But why?" Mencken persisted. "These things have no importance," Wallace countered. "Let's get on to something important."

"Why not now?" suggested Mencken. "We are all here."

Pegler watched Mencken with a mixture of admiration and astonishment. His wheedling insistence, the columnist noted, "turned up an unsuspected streak of rug-salesman" that he had not expected to witness in the stately Mencken.

Nonetheless, Wallace's defiant refusal to explain himself had succeeded in making a mountain out of a molehill. A reporter later asked Mencken what he thought of the proceedings. "Everybody named Henry should be put to death," growled Mencken. "If somebody will do it for Henry Wallace, I promise to commit suicide."[5]

As MATTERS TURNED OUT, Wallace was not the only center of controversy. Another was Mencken himself. That evening, the keynote speech was given by the lawyer Charles P. Howard of Iowa, who was an African American. At issue was a historic plank regarding civil rights. Mencken, whose ears were always finely attuned to a melodious voice, praised the speaker's soaring baritone—but typically, went on to describe him as "a tall, full-bodied barrister of the color of a good ten-cent cigar" with "an African roll in his voice that is far from unpleasant." The next morning delegates of the Maryland Progressive party muttered against "that son-of-a-bitch Mencken." One of them presented Bradford Jacobs of the *Sunpapers* with a petition charging that Mencken "makes Hitlerite references to the people of this convention. Mr. Mencken Red-baits, Jew-baits and Negro-baits." It also charged that he was a racist and demanded that he be censured by the convention.

In addition to describing Howard as being "the color of a good ten-cent cigar," Mencken had referred to the speech as being "mainly devoted to excoriating Hitler, the du Ponts, the Rockefellers, Truman and other such malefactors," and slyly surmised the cost of the shining diamond ring Howard sported on his finger. He had also written that "if the night's proceedings were actually maneuvered by goons of the Kremlin, there was certainly no overt sign of it." Nor, Mencken wrote, were there many "dark faces spotted in the hall," that "distinctly Jewish faces were decidedly scarce," and "I saw no Indians, Chinese, Malays, Eskimos or Arabs."

Infuriated, the Maryland Progressives proposed a resolution censoring Mencken "and his contemptible rantings which pass for newspaper reporting" for demonstrating "that the fighting spirit of equality and brotherhood is entirely lost to him . . . he has resorted to un-American slander against the people of this convention, and . . . his obscenities against the American people mark him as unfit to report the proceedings of a people's convention."

Jacobs showed their resolution to Mencken, warning him it was going to be read and perhaps might even be passed. Mencken actually cared about his reputation more than he was willing to admit. In an unguarded moment, according to Jacobs, he was "visibly and badly shaken, really deflated. 'They don't understand,'" he kept repeating. "'They don't *know* me.'" Jacobs went back to the delegates. This was Mencken's manner, the way he used language, the young man pleaded, the sort of talk that was as natural to him as breathing. Then he defended Mencken with an account of what he had done for the civil rights of African Americans, as well as for other minorities.

Yet, the resolution was finally read aloud from the platform. Alistair Cooke, seated next to Mencken, recalled that he "goggled with unaccustomed pride. It was the first time in all his reporting years that a national convention had officially deigned to regret his existence, although the Arkansas state legislature had once petitioned for his deportation. He took a small bow to acknowledge the passing tribute of a boo but the resolution got no further. The chairman threw it out as a dangerous precedent inviting an endless litany of curses against other blasphemers, of whom there were plenty."

After the furor was over, Mencken quipped, "I'm only sorry the resolution was not passed." That night, over beef and beer, he complained about "the growing sensitiveness of politicians. Nobody denounced me as a white-baiter," he said, "when I wrote that Herbert Hoover had a complexion like unrisen dough." Then, as Cooke recalled, Mencken "took a swig and broke down into his schoolboy-crafty grin." With tenderness, Mencken began to recall San Francisco and the Democratic Convention of 1920.

"He realizes his era has passed," one columnist commented of Mencken during the 1948 conventions; nevertheless, "he is still one of the best reporters in the country."[6]

WHILE TRAVELING ON THE CAMPAIGN TRAIL no longer held its appeal for Mencken, whenever a candidate was in Baltimore, he was certain to be on hand to cover the speech. A few months later, as he went down in the elevator of the *Sun* building, someone tapped him on the shoulder. "Gonna tear them to pieces tonight, Henry?" Mencken smiled, threw a little salute to the elevator operator, walked out across the lobby, and went out the swinging doors; he had decided to celebrate his birthday by going to a Henry Wallace meeting. "They are still the same old frauds that we followed years ago," Mencken commented to his retired colleague Henry Hyde. While the candidates left him uninspired, Mencken thought

South Carolina Governor J. Strom Thurmond, defender of States' Rights, the best of all, though handicapped, like Wallace, by his followers. "Wallace has the Communists around his neck and Thurmond has the Ku Kluxers. Both are stupid, vicious and nefarious. Between the two, in truth, I think I'd rather take my chances with the Communists."

Mencken, like the great majority of reporters, was convinced that it was a no-contest between the two top contenders, Thomas Dewey and Harry Truman, who relied on a whistle-stop tour of the country to salvage his campaign. "Poor Harry is on the skids," as he put it. The final polls showed Dewey with an overwhelming lead.

On election night, Mencken sat among his *Sunpapers* colleagues as the returns flowed in. Executive editor Neil Swanson looked at the projections. "I think Dewey is in trouble," he remarked to the staff. "Truman is running better than expected in Baltimore." As it developed, Truman carried 28 states to Dewey's 16 —winning 303 electoral votes to Dewey's 189 with Truman carrying the popular election by just over 2,100,000 votes, one of the most startling upsets in the history of American presidential politics. As the news of Dewey's defeat went out over the wires, a stunned Mencken stood up, cigar in mouth, and announced: "This is it. This is the end of everything," stomped out of the room and went home.

"How could so many wizards be so thumpingly wrong?" Mencken asked in his subsequent column. The outcome "shook the bones of all . . . [the] smarties," of which he confessed to having been one. He heartily agreed with James Reston's column in the *New York Times* that claimed the press had lost its direction by being far too impressed by the tidy statistics of the polls instead of talking to the people or giving weight to the political direction of the time. Mencken concluded: "We should all go into sackcloth and ashes."

Yet the question remained: why such an astounding upset? The answer was the contrast in how the two contestants presented themselves to the voters. "Neither candidate made a speech on the stump that will survive in the schoolbooks, but those of Truman at least had warmth in them," Mencken wrote. In contrast to Dewey, who addressed "great multitudes as if they were gangs of drowsing judges," Truman made no such mistake. "He assumed as a matter of course that the American people were just folks like himself. He thus wasted no high falutin' rhetoric upon them, but appealed directly to their self interest."7

That week Mencken returned to Philadelphia to address the American Philosophical Society on how presidents were elected. The atmosphere was solemn. Mencken reminded his listeners of what they had witnessed in the last few weeks. "I think the answer is to be sought in the very nature of the democratic form of society," he suggested, quoting Thomas Jefferson that "whenever a man has cast a longing eye on office, a rottenness begins in his conduct." Afterward, Mencken heard that some members of the audience were shocked: "They thought I was too cynical," he commented. "It was plain that the assembled scientificos expected something far more optimistic and reassuring."

The next morning, once again Mencken discussed the matter of his health with the Knopfs. He had previously promised his publisher that he would speak before the Grolier Club in New York in January, "if I am still alive," and predicted "that on the night of the Grolier dinner I'll be laid up at the Johns Hopkins." Throughout that autumn, Mencken had again experienced pain around his heart, shortness of breath, and an occasional loss of memory. These symptoms had become more frequent in November. At one point, he was not even able to play the piano. There were times, he confessed to his brother Charlie, that "I could smell the angels."

Now, over breakfast, he turned to Knopf, who later recalled that Mencken "spoke for the upteenth time of his old uncle who had been bedridden and useless for years." For his friends, such gloomy forebodings were the usual conversation in a hypochondriac as superstitious as Mencken. After seeing Henry in Philadelphia, Blanche Knopf wrote to George Jean Nathan, "he seemed in fine form."[8]

THE CONVENTIONS HAD LEFT MENCKEN feeling somewhat depleted, with little time for rest. The mail was heavy; a stack of letters from all over the world awaited his signature, which had become more wobbly than usual. Every month he perused at least forty magazines, among them the *Supreme Court Reporter* and the *Congressional Record*; for fun he was reading *The Letters and Private Papers of William Makepeace Thackeray; Postscript to Yesterday: America, The Last Fifty Years; A Hog on Ice and Other Curious Expressions; The Dictionary of Clichés*, and *An Introduction to Linguistic Science*. Notes were still piling up on the American language, which he worked into articles for *American Speech* and the *New Yorker*. Meanwhile, he was also helping the Knopf publishing house with its publicity for *A Mencken Chrestomathy* for release in 1949. It promised to be a winner.

The year 1948 had once again seen a resurgence of interest in Mencken, with a cover profile in *Newsweek* ("Pamphleteer to Pundit"); he was the object of admiration in dozens of newspapers. "Something great went out of American life when the *Smart Set* and the *American Mercury* of the old days passed," one critic recalled. New books analyzing the dominant literary personalities of the 1920s concentrated on figures such as Sinclair Lewis, F. Scott Fitzgerald, and H. L. Mencken. "There is something in the air of this second postwar period—a growth of skepticism and pessimism—which has renewed the appeal of the Sage of Baltimore," the Scripps-Howard newspapers noted. Bookshops reported a revival of interest in his works, with a special demand for *Prejudices*.

While preparing *A Mencken Chrestomathy*, the Knopf office asked its clipping service to report all current mention of Mencken in magazines and newspapers. Within a few days the publisher was astounded. Of the scores of clippings that came in, only a few were concerned with *The American Language: Supplement II*, even though from coast to coast it was being rated as a must-have for Christmas.

At the request of the Library of Congress, Mencken was persuaded by *Sun* reporter Donald Kirkley to go to Washington for an interview. With courtly politeness, Mencken also ushered reporters into Baltimore's Maryland Club to give them a close-up. In the gray *Sunpapers* building, a new generation of admirers interviewed him, among them a young student from the University of Maryland who years later confessed, "If a Beatles fan were to spend an afternoon with Ringo, he might have some idea of the state of my nerves." Mencken was shorter than the young boy expected, he walked slowly and breathed with some difficulty. A longish cigar was held tightly in his teeth, and each drag brought about a mild cough. But his eyes were bright and his smile cherubic.

With a gravelly punch Mencken spoke on theology, journalism, and politics. What depressed him most about America? "The gullibility of its people, the ease with which they are rooked," he slowly answered. So what pleased him the most? "Besides being the most comfortable country, the United States is also the most comic. You can laugh yourself to death here everyday." The eyes lit up with the glee of a child caught pulling a cat's tail. Didn't Mencken have any hopes for the human race? "Yes! In course of time it will make some progress. The human race is still very new," he explained, only thousands of years old: "So the capacity to think is a recent acquisition. Only a few men have acquired it."

Everyone seemed to want Mencken's opinion on the trends and events then sweeping the country. A professor named Alfred Kinsey from the University of Indiana had published in 1948 *Sexual Behavior in the Human Male*, and for a while America was startled by the report. "If I had had to review that Kinsey book," Mencken commented, "I think I'd have called it *Pedagogues in Wonderland*."

Stranger still was America's being caught in the grip of a Communist spy mania, fueled by the House Un-American Activities Committee and by Senator Joseph McCarthy. Mencken suggested that the *Sun* report on the committee proceedings in the grand manner. When it came to the "Red hunt," Mencken thought the committee, "though burdened with manifest idiots, have done, on the whole, a good job" in "smoking out these rascals" left over, he said, from Roosevelt's New Deal.

As relations with Russia worsened, Mencken gave his own prophetic view of Communism. "It will probably disappear altogether when the Russian experiment comes to a climax, and Bolshevism either converts itself into a sickly imitation of capitalism or blows up with a bang." He was sure that sooner or later the United States would engage in a war with the Soviet Union, an observation he shared with Ilya Ehrenburg of *Pravda* and which the Soviets took quite seriously.

When it came to civil rights, the *Afro-American* acknowledged that Mencken's fight for equality was evident in every column he wrote. At issue was segregation on public playgrounds. "Is such a prohibition, even supposing that it is lawful, supported by anything to be found in common sense and common decency?" Mencken asked. "Why should a man of one race . . . be permitted to exclude men of another race?"

As the clippings poured into his office in New York, Knopf could have breathed only a sigh of satisfaction. So what of this talk of being disabled, of being laid up at the Johns Hopkins, of bedridden uncles? Mencken, Knopf was happy to say, was still a force in the Great Republic.⁹

ON THE EVENING OF Wednesday, November 23, Mencken left the Maryland Club to go to Rosalind Lohrfinck's apartment. He had recently finished writing another manuscript and was anxious for the typewritten copy. It was 7:30. Almost instantly, his typist noticed Mencken in a strange state: sitting, standing, looking distractedly at himself in the mirror, and speaking in an incoherent manner. Lohrfinck immediately telephoned Dr. Baker, who on arrival could tell at once that Mencken had suffered a massive cerebral hemorrhage. He drove at once to Johns Hopkins Hospital.

August Mencken had been uneasy for quite some time about leaving his brother on his own. He had been looking less well than usual. But Henry had urged him to go out and be sociable, and so, taking his older brother's advice, August had gone out that evening for Thanksgiving dinner at the home of a friend. "Nobody knew where I was," he recalled. "As soon as I got home, which was about 11:00 o'clock, my sister called up. She had been calling up every ten minutes." In a few moments, he, too, was hurriedly heading for Johns Hopkins, only to be told by an intern that there was nothing he could do to help.

He was leaving when he ran into Doctor Baker. "He started past without speaking, and after he'd gone a step or two he turned around and said, 'Here, I guess I've got to talk to you. Come with me.'" The two men went back inside the hospital. "'Your brother has got a massive hemorrhage,'" Baker told August. "'He can't conceivably live until morning. He was practically dead on arrival. That's the way he would have wanted it to be. Good night.' And with that he went on off." August returned home, lying awake all night, expecting any moment the call that would tell him that his brother was dead. But the call did not come.

Still, the word of Mencken's stroke spread rapidly among his friends, though it would not be known to the public until much later. Telephone calls came to Johns Hopkins and Hollins Street from all over the country. Press bureaus began harassing Benjamin Baker's office for bulletins. By December 1, late news bulletins announced "H. L. MENCKEN, FAMED WRITER, IN HOSPITAL."

"I know you are deeply concerned as all of us who are close to Henry are," Dr. Baker wrote to Hergesheimer a few days later. "It is a great tragedy, too great, in fact, to be measured. He is alive and promises to continue to be but just how much return to his former self there will be is a completely uncertain matter at present." From New York, Alfred Knopf wrote August. Just that very day he had been preparing to mail his friend the first proofs of *A Mencken Chrestomathy*. Thinking of the many things he wanted to share with him, and wondering if Henry would ever be himself again, he, too, called Johns Hopkins Hospital. Years later, he remembered the reply as clearly as if it had been yesterday.

"I called Baker. I have never forgotten his words: 'Mr. Mencken has suffered a stroke and I am *sorry* to say he is getting over it.' A wise man."¹⁰

Part Seven
1949–1956

Beethoven's death mask and the first bars to the Fifth Symphony outside in Mencken's garden. The
Harry Ransom Humanities Research Center, The University of Texas at Austin.

"Mencken, Back from the Dead." Returning to 1524 Hollins Street and being greeted by August. H. L. Mencken Collection, Enoch Pratt Free Library.

52

THE LAST DAYS

THE STORY OF his brother's final illness, August Mencken later said, was "a bitter one," partly because of dissatisfaction with the medical treatment he received. The medical profession, especially "the boys" at Johns Hopkins, "was a sort of sacred cow" to his brother, August said. "His attitude toward doctors and medicine would be roughly parallel to a Catholic's attitude toward priests. . . . He thought they could do miracles," but, he added darkly, "as a matter of fact, sometimes they do, but not as often as he thought."

When August approached the staffers to ask how his brother was, they simply shook their heads. He "jabbers and babbles" one told him. "Nobody can make out what he's talking about." Mencken's confusion was evident as soon as August entered his hospital room. "Why are you making this long trip? It's a terrible trip," Mencken asked. Perplexed, August replied, "It's not so far. I don't mind it." This went on for several days. Not until Mencken was wheeled out onto the porch did he recognize where he was. "I'm in the Hopkins! I'm in the Hopkins!" In the confusion of his illness Mencken had thought he was back at the 1948 convention and that August was traveling to Philadelphia every day. Relieved, he turned to his brother: "These boys will take care of me. They're all my friends."

Immediately after his stroke, Mencken did make some improvement. Since he had suffered no paralysis, he was able to get up and tend to his needs with little assistance. So well did he feel that Hamilton Owens reported to Paul Patterson that "he was sufficiently annoyed by the situation to complain that his night nurse was paid for doing nothing." But as for his speech, the doctors continued to claim impatiently, "You can't make sense of it."

It then occurred to August to ask Dr. Arnold Rich, a member of the Saturday Night Club and head of the pathology department, to examine his brother. Rich found Mencken sitting up in bed and laughing at a Christmas stocking sent to him by Anita Loos. In the toe was a copy of the New Testament. "He told Rich all about her, and then he showed him all these damned things she'd sent him, and Rich just sort of sat there looking at him," recalled August. After twenty minutes Rich left, saying repeatedly, "Marvelous. Marvelous." "From that time on," commented August wryly, "I didn't hear so much about this gibberish business."

According to August, one person was still unconvinced of Mencken's improved condition. Dr. Benjamin Baker called August into his office. "I understand you're thinking of taking your brother home," he said. "Your brother is insane. He's not only insane, but he's violently insane. . . . He might even kill you." Baker explained that he had already made arrangements with a sanitarium.

August left the hospital in a state of shock. "I didn't know what in the hell to do. Here I was, a layman, with no knowledge of medicine, and I am told by . . . one of the big figures of Johns Hopkins Hospital that the man is insane." After giving the matter serious thought, August decided to keep his brother at home. Reluctantly, Baker discharged his patient with a nurse to accompany him back to Hollins Street. "No instructions," the nurse allegedly shrugged to August. "It's just a mental case." August got rid of the nurse, retired from his job as an engineer, and became the full-time caregiver for his brother. "To lock that poor man up in that nursing home," August concluded, "he would have gone crazy without question."

During the first few months, only August could make out clearly what Mencken was saying. Acting as interpreter and trying to keep up with "the quiz program" proved exhausting for him. When Mencken wanted a certain object, he would have to describe its use, as in "the thing to cut with" for scissors. The Mencken siblings had left most of the caretaking to August. When he was alone, August would cry out desperately, "I have got to get some relief." His devotion was unflagging; there were times when he was afraid to leave even for an hour and Mencken was apparently afraid for him to do so.

On the suggestion of Dr. Rich, August put his older brother under the care of a specialist to help him with his reading and speech. Three times a week Mencken sat in the office of Dr. William Hardy of the Johns Hopkins Hospital, slowly reading aloud from a list of words: *blue, violin, Beethoven.* The ability to recognize words and numbers initially had a positive mental effect on Mencken. One day, August found him kneeling on the floor of his office, sorting out clippings into neat piles for Rosalind Lohrfinck to paste into scrapbooks.

Initially the family concluded that their brother might even be able to read within six months; even the patient believed that it was only a matter of time before he was restored "to something resembling normalcy." Mencken dictated a letter to Knopf, saying it might be a good idea to send him the proofs of the *Chrestomathy.*

When the galleys arrived, it was clear that although these were his words, try as he might he could not understand them; they were simply marks on a page. Neighbors accustomed to hearing Mencken typing late into the night now passed by the house and saw him gazing blankly out of the front parlor window. That was how bookshop owner Siegfried Weisberger found him by that same window, "depressed and blue . . . with a noticeable veil over his eyes." Mencken told Weisberger: "Had I lost both of my legs I would have been happy to be in a wheelchair. I could write and have a lot of fun. Now I am through and I don't give a damn."[1]

Mencken's frustration reached such levels that he said if it wasn't for his brother, he would commit suicide. Doctors would seek to encourage him by telling him he needed to practice drills for ten to fifteen minutes to synchronize writing, reading, and speaking. Rosalind Lohrfinck was called to Hollins Street where she would sit in Mencken's office just as she and her sister Margaret before her had done during the old days: notepad in hand, pencil poised.

Mencken would make an initial effort: "Despite my troubles of language I am still able to understand the letters sent to him. Whatever is printed in the newspapers I pass it quite easily, but it is still impossible for me to state—," he stopped, breaking off abruptly in confusion: "Why go on; it's damn foolishness." On another occasion, he turned to Lorhfinck and explained, "My intellectual has gone completely, and it is a terrible thing, but maybe they'll be able to . . . ," he trailed off. Disgusted, he observed, "They have made no mark at all in four months."

Sometimes, however, Mencken did make sense. He would speak about his ancestors, of the mess Truman had made of the presidency, of how the gang in Washington was ruining the country. All of this would be duly recorded by Rosalind Lohrfinck, although she noted, "I can't let him know I am taking notes of his conversation, for then he would blow up completely and would be unable to collect his thoughts." To her, it was "amazing how far HLM has improved on some days." Inspired by his own progress, Mencken would bravely launch into another drill:

It may seem incredible, but it is fact that I can spend more than half an hour without thinking at all. I don't seem to borrow much when I am sitting reading—that is to say, I don't care ordinarily what the result of my decision is.

Then he stopped. "The doctors should have let me die in November," Mencken concluded. "I'd have been much better off."

Often Lohrfinck felt like bursting into tears. "Great God he will never get well," she wrote in her diary. "Some days I feel as if I'll have to quit, the pain of seeing him is so great and so hopeless." Each evening as she prepared to go home, Mencken looked so dejected that there were times she spent most of the night crying. "I'd give my life to cure him."

The general public seemed initially to have little comprehension of how ill Mencken really was. Letters poured in that Lorhfinck was obliged to read aloud. " 'Dear Mr. Mencken,' " she might begin: " 'I hope that you will continue to progress and that *The American Language* will keep growing—' " Mencken would tell Lohrfinck to stop, advising she take a long vacation and not answer the mail. On his desk were circulars of various kinds, requests for articles, including one asking him for a book review; they only served to remind him of his own inability to read. His mail had once been a happy task; now it had been reduced to "God damn stuff all over the place."

Nonetheless, a lifetime of politely answering each and every letter as soon as it was received forced him to reply, even if it meant irritation. Somehow she was able to get the gist of what he was trying to say and would type a reply, handing the response to Mencken to sign a wobbly H.L.M. "It's a hell of a state of things when the only thing a man can read or write is his name," he would say. Then Lohrfinck would send the letters off, "hoping and trusting to God that they are right."

Mencken's doctors believed that if he had more visitors, his confidence would increase. But when it came to receiving guests, August confided, "he has days when he wants to see people and days when he don't, and it is not easy to tell in advance which will be which." There were few whose presence he welcomed. Women he had known well—Aileen Pringle, Lillian Gish, Marcella DuPont, Betty Hanes—sought to drop by, but all were gently discouraged. "They don't want to see a sick man, see what a wreck I am," he would say. "I can see *that* very well."

Those few who were allowed to visit noticed he did not talk as much, that his attention flagged on several occasions. "He did not like to give up," the writer James Farrell said. Yet he still wanted to know about old friends. Although Mencken was aware of the person whom he would be speaking about, he couldn't always remember the name.

"The novelist out there . . ." he would point with his right hand, lifted above his head. "He married a rich woman. He's not writing anymore."

"Cabell," said Farrell.

"Yes, Cabell. And Joe. He can't write a book anymore."

"Hergesheimer."

"The poet, his wife got him in the end."

"Masters."

On another occasion Mencken said: "George was here. George, George . . . ," he faltered and looked for help to August, hovering nearby, who then supplied the missing name: Nathan. Finally, as Farrell was leaving, Mencken asked that he be remembered to those mutual acquaintances whom he might encounter: "Tell my friends I'm in a hell of a mess."[2]

WHILE MENCKEN WAS REALISTIC over his condition, his ability to read and write did actually improve. One spring morning Lohrfinck came to Hollins Street to find, scrawled on a piece of notepaper:

It was the first legible memorandum Mencken had written since his stroke. The fact that he had become impatient to see a copy of the newly published *Chrestomathy* was interpreted by the entire household as an encouraging sign. Already the book was climbing the best-seller charts, an echo of some of the storms that Mencken's writings had stirred up decades before.

When the copies of the book arrived, Mencken thumbed through them, greatly pleased. For the first time he was able to add the correct date to his signature. "You are the artist of the book; you've done the main work," he generously praised Lohrfinck. "It is a monument to you, not to me." He handed it over to his secretary, who noted cheerfully: "He is returning to normalcy with the old blarney in full blast." But then came another entry in her diary:

> Today was the worst day I have spent since HLM's illness. He was in a truly terrible condition, for signing four copies of the *Chrestomathy* for various friends almost drove him crazy. He made mistakes signing them, which naturally irritated him, and he God damned everything and everybody. The strain of working for him at this time is pretty severe, but so far I have been able to keep my temper. . . . We went to the post office to mail the books later, and he fretted and stormed all the way about having to sign the books and bothering with the mailing of them. I suggested that I bring them home and mail them myself, which I have done heretofore, but he blew up and said emphatically that he would take them to the post office right that moment and mail them, so that was that.

Having accomplished this task, Mencken relaxed, insisting he treat August and Lohrfinck for dinner at their favorite restaurant, overriding August's protests by insisting that wine be ordered. But Mencken, "despite all his difficulties . . . remains kind and considerate," Lohrfinck wrote in her diary, "and this fact only adds to my own despair."[3]

ON OCTOBER 12, 1950, Mencken suffered a severe heart attack. The world had seen Mencken bounce back from many illnesses, but this time his doctors definitely did not expect him to recover. Over the next few weeks, August faithfully made his way to the hospital and tapped on Mencken's door. From within came a croak, "Come in!" There was his brother, up to his neck in sheets. He had lost a great deal of weight; one of his eyelids drooped. As the weeks went on, August began to prepare for the inevitable. Members of the Saturday Night Club agreed to disband permanently. All over the country newspaper editors prepared obituaries.

In the midst of all this, Mencken eventually rallied.

By December, a recuperated Mencken was insisting to his nurse that a barber be regularly brought in to shave him. He asked August about his mail. Was everyone getting along at home? How was their housekeeper Emma? Was 1524 Hollins Street functioning properly? Was Union Square being kept up? On some occasions Mencken would say, "Well, how about a little —" and finish his sentence by moving his hands as if he were tilting a glass; whereupon August would produce a bottle. Doctors had decided that their famous charge should not be denied any of his former luxuries. In Mencken's room, the scent of beer mingled with the smell of medicine; soon the patient was loudly demanding tobacco.

Editors tossed away their Mencken obits. Instead headlines read: "Mencken Laughs at Death Again." When Mencken complained that the hospital cooking was inedible, August brought dishes from home. After digging into Emma's lamb stew, Mencken would smack his lips and call for more. Soon it was not uncommon for August to find his brother listening to the radio while munching on Emma's chocolate cake. Before leaving, there came a new request—for peanut brittle. "August never misses a night," Mencken happily told his doctors. "He always comes in."

August's medical diary told the story:

> Nov. 6, 1950: H. L. M. was in a very depressed state today. . . . I found in the past that such depressed periods usually preceded an improvement and I hope that it will be the case this time.
>
> Dec. 4, 1950: I went to the hospital at usual time and took HLM a box of Uncle Willie cigars. I found HLM raising a racket and demanding that he be taken out of the hospital at once. He said the young doctors there are all bums and the hospital a dump and he didn't intend to stay.
>
> Dec. 25, 1950: Got to the hospital at 2. p.m. just in time to get "Hansel and Gretel" for HLM on his television. He enjoyed it immensely. He was propped up in bed and in the middle of it a nurse brought him a glass of eggnog which he got down quickly, saying it was fine, then lit a cigar. While the witch was being murdered he used the bed urinal and told me that he doubted that anyone had ever heard the opera in greater comfort.

Mencken's improvement was marked by a renewed sociability. He insisted on being wheeled into the hall to listen to the sounds of the ward and mingle with the other patients. His spirits lifted even further when a young and very pretty new nurse was assigned to him. Now he no longer talked about going home.

By January, Mencken was amazed at how much better he felt. He joked with his nurse: "How about a cigar, darling?" Then, puffing a Corona, he would watch a program on television, which he inevitably pronounced "horrible, perfectly terrible, unbelievably bad." Eventually, he began receiving visitors, including a Catholic priest who read aloud from William Manchester's newly published Mencken biography; Manchester had no way of knowing that his subject would be alive when the book came out.

By this time, Mencken was under the compassionate care of Dr. Philip Wagley, who had taken great interest in the case. He made a point of visiting Mencken's room before he made his rounds; even when he complained, the old man cheered him up for the rest of the day.

By March, Mencken was ready to be discharged. As he was wheeled out of the Johns Hopkins Hospital, he promised, "I'll be back." At the main entrance he stepped out of the wheelchair and walked unassisted to the car with Wagley, who, along with a nurse, was there to help ease his reintroduction to the world outside. As they pulled past the old YMCA building on Franklin Street, he gravely tipped

On the road to recovery: Nurse Lois Gentry, Dr. Philip Wagley, H. L. Mencken, and William Manchester return to Hollins Street. H. L. Mencken Collection, Enoch Pratt Free Library.

his hat. From the car window he spotted the No. 2 branch of the Enoch Pratt Free Library at Hollins and Calhoun. "My school," he said.

August greeted him at the stoop of 1524, where a crowd of neighbors was waiting. Mencken had been in the hospital for five months.[4]

RETURNING HOME REPRESENTED a victory of sorts, but every room that Mencken wandered through reminded him of a previous joy now out of reach. He stared at his bookshelves and the rows of volumes written by authors he had once launched to the forefront of American literature. "Oh, if I could read, I would be a happy man," was his constant refrain, spoken with infinite sadness.

A solution required sensitive treatment, for August said his brother detested people reading to him. Nobody could read a book as fast as he could scan it. Eventually, Mencken consented to have William Manchester come in four mornings a week to read aloud from those favorites he had especially once enjoyed—*The Adventures of Huckleberry Finn*, or *Youth*, by Joseph Conrad. The latter reminded him of himself half a century before, at the time of the great fire of 1904, when, as he once put it, "the hot ichor of youth" still roared in his veins. The two men sat under the grape arbor as Manchester began to read:

> As the years passed, I would remember my youth and the feeling that will never come back anymore—the feeling that I could outlast forever, outlast the sea, the earth, and all men. . . . Youth! All youth! The silly, charming, beautiful youth!

Mencken's eyes misted over. "Isn't that magnificent," he muttered, shaking his head. "What a genius he was." The book was closed; the young man was told to return home and read to him another day.[5]

As the years of illness wore on, there was something in the air on Hollins Street that was different: Mencken was not in absolute command. In the basement, the copypaper he once used for all his books lay in dusty stacks, piled high in a dark corner. There was a time when he would run his hands over his desk, enjoying the feel of the grain of the wood. Now that was all the desk was good for.

The shadow of this betrayal—whether by medical science or some higher force—hung heavily over Mencken. Prayer was not for him. "I envy you your religion," he confided to Bill Abell of the *Sunpapers* one day, "because as a Catholic you would be getting a great deal of consolation in your faith." The closest he could come was gazing from his study window and watching the nuns pacing through the sunlit gardens at the convent next door. One day he asked Rosalind to take a letter to George Jean Nathan.

"What shall I tell him?" she asked.

"Tell him," Mencken replied, "that I am in despair."[6]

He worried about the state of his affairs. One-fourth of his $300,000 estate was to go to Johns Hopkins Hospital, the rest to the Enoch Pratt Free Library because, as he put it, the library had been of more benefit during his lifetime than any other public institution of Baltimore. He called in his lawyer to review his will, dividing a sum of money among his cook, his secretary, and his relatives. Eager to get rid of his volumes on the American language, considered one of the best linguistics libraries in the United States, he scattered books in labeled piles on the living room floor. After they were hauled away, with some relief he noted that he did not have a single book on that subject in the house.

Only one item remained unassigned: the house itself.

In the family no one cared more for 1524 Hollins Street or had a greater attachment to it than Mencken. Its disposition caused a major squabble within the family. But in the end, all agreed with Mencken's decision that August should remain sole owner and later dispose of it in some proper way.

As August well realized, their brother had a special horror of the thought that when he died the house "would be wrecked." During the 1950s, Philip Wagner noted, Hollins Street had deteriorated. In daylight, Union Square looked shabby. But the trees were still in full leaf, and the light of a street lamp put the old bandstand into silhouette.

The view was as comforting and familiar to Mencken as it was haunting. There was no denying the old Baltimore was gone. On Sun Square, the broad intersection of Baltimore and Charles Streets, where Mencken and his newspaper came of age, the city now had a television tower; elsewhere were superhighways. One day the jackhammers of a construction crew came across a block of solid brick buried twenty feet beneath Fayette and St. Paul Streets: it was the foundation of the old *Baltimore Morning Herald*.

Gone were many of the remaining gadflies of the twenties and thirties; only George Jean Nathan was hanging on. Over the telephone he and Mencken deplored what they considered the present state of magazines and the pathetic condition of their health. Nathan was convinced he would not live through the year; as this seemed to be his normal outlook, Mencken did not worry. The deaths of Joseph Hergesheimer and then Paul Patterson, however, plunged him into grief.

One day, Siegfried Weisberger wrote that Estelle Bloom had died in Westminster, and that he had discovered boxes of material and "a batch of very touchy letters Marion has written to Estelle about you, and Henry is very much in the discussion." Mencken's past, which he had sought to bury so very long ago, vividly came rushing back. Eagerly he asked Weisberger to tell him more, carefully adding Marion's papers to the pile destined for the New York Public Library.[7]

MENCKEN'S MOOD DEPENDED LARGELY on the weather. Warm, sunny days were best, when he could work in his beloved garden, puttering among petunias and morning glories. As he could not sit idly, August gave him diversions, such as breaking branches into eight-inch lengths and binding them together with cord as fagots for the fireplace. Only the hottest weather would force Mencken to stop.

"Here now, I'd better quit this or I'll fall to pieces. This is knocking me out." But in a few moments his hands were busy again.

Together the brothers would roam the alley foraging for firewood. The booty might be a table leg, broomstick, or fence post. "Wow! Look at that, will you! Look what he's got!" Mencken would exclaim. "August, you've got some rich stuff there." Then the two brothers, in mock seriousness, examined their prize with great satisfaction. The more nefarious the item, the better it was.

Then there were the suits to clean. "Not that they need it," August explained, "but we do it as a matter of form." During those years a new home dry-cleaning product called Renuzit had come out, and for a while the brothers took to cleaning their own suits with Renuzit in a big washtub out in the backyard, then hosing them down on the line. Mencken liked to watch the dirt wash out until finally the water ran clear. This activity would continue well into autumn. On cold days the clothes would become frozen stiff. After they thawed, the brothers would haul them to the tailor to be pressed. "Once they even insisted on cleaning a pink jacket of mine," nurse Lois Gentry recalled. "It survived."

Occasionally, a little boy nicknamed Butch from next door would peer over the wall and pipe, "*Mencken! Mencken!*" whereupon the author of *The American Language* would trot over, chuckling, to pop his head up. "Butch had no idea what a "mencken" might be," an observer recounted, "but he knew that the word would almost always fetch that head, and it was a friendly head that sometimes supplied candy and toys." Another favorite was Alvin, a quiet African American boy with a shy grin, smiling and barefoot. "Well, come on in, boys. How are you today?" Mencken would say, before handing over a candy or a nickel. Another frequent visitor was little Martin Asner, who, like so many others, never knew he was talking to a famous man; to him he was just an old geezer with tired eyes, sitting out in the sun.

One lazy afternoon, while Mencken was sitting in the garden, half asleep, a squirrel came over the wall, climbed up his leg, and perched on his shoulder. "He grew fond of the animal and could summon him by whistling and he had August go out and buy a large bag of peanuts with the shells on," the journalist H. Allen Smith recounted. The squirrel became a steady visitor, coming from the park across the street to sit on Mencken's shoulder.

> A week or two went by with no sign of him and then Henry insisted that they cross the park and search for him. "He may be sick," said the man who was the scourge of the '20s. They went over and found the tree where the squirrel lived, and they scattered peanuts around. Now the squirrel started crossing the street to visit his friend again. There came an afternoon when Henry and August were sitting out front; they saw the squirrel come out of park and start loping across Hollins Street. Suddenly an automobile swished by, killed the squirrel, and went on without slackening speed. Henry was livid with rage. He cried out against the driver of the car, insisting that the man hit the squirrel deliberately, calling him a murderer and worse, howling that the gallows would be too good for such a villain. "He got madder at that man," said August, "than he ever got at the Anti-Saloon League."[8]

When inclement weather forced Mencken to remain indoors, word went out to family members that "Harry is in the dumps." "These were bad days," recalled Robert Durr, a young Johns Hopkins student who read to him, when Mencken was so blue that he could not speak.

Television, with its variety shows and endless commercials, was not an option. More entertainment was to be found on the radio, with its daily broadcasts of classical music and Saturday's Metropolitan Opera. It was a bad day when, during football season, the broadcast of games replaced music, and he would come downstairs from his room looking glum.

On such days, he would be taken to the movies at a neighborhood theater. Prior to his illness, Mencken had never seen more than a half dozen. Now he had to admit they were "a damn sight better" since the days of silent film. Sometimes he would see three in one day. The more preposterous the plot, the better he liked it. "I remember he used to make great fun of the Tarzan movies, with their mechanical crocodiles, but he loved them because they amused him," said his nurse. He got a great kick out of Betty Grable in *The Beautiful Blonde from Bashful Bend*. Rosalind Lohrfinck recalled him roaring "about the imbecilities of the thing." Spectacular musicals in Technicolor were his preference. One of his favorite actors was Fred Astaire; as for the actresses, as long as they were pretty he enjoyed them all, particularly Myrna Loy, Rita Hayworth, and Elizabeth Taylor.

On Saturday nights, the brothers would go to the home of Louis Cheslock. August would pull up in his decrepit 1937 Ford coupe. "How the two would emerge with bows and doffing of their hats!" Cheslock recalled. Mencken would empty a handful of Havana cigars into Cheslock's palm; August would follow immediately behind with a bottle of fine German wine. Once inside, Mencken could not pass by the piano without wistfully playing a few chords.

Food continued to be his passion, though at one point he had lost so much weight, the back of his pants was held together by a large safety pin. "When are you going to have those red things?" Mencken asked Elise Cheslock. Before him she would place a feast of steamed crabs, which would prompt Mencken to thump his hand on the table in approval. Usually, he would be the first to break into song. Together, the group would harmonize "*Du, Du, Liegst Mir Im Hertzen*" before swinging into a drinking rhythm, with chug-a-lugs added. Then: "Where the hell is August? August, come on!" and it was time to go home, with the brothers still singing as they clambered into their ancient car.

In truth, however, even these visits, with their good food and music, were not enough to satisfy him. "The trouble is," Mencken said, giving an impatient gesture with his cigar, "I didn't live long enough to write all I wanted."

There still remained, however, his files of papers. He refused to spend his twilight days in idleness. "If I did, it would kill me," he snorted. Lohrfinck had kept hundreds of notebooks from letters Mencken had dictated—there were said to be more than 100,000. After breakfast, she would sit with him in his small second floor office, where, surrounded by bound volumes of the *American Mercury*, she would read Mencken's replies to his correspondents, one by one, from her shorthand, and the two would decide which ones to keep and which to discard. Those that related to American literature were destined for the New York Public Library; the others for the Pratt.[9]

Mencken would suddenly turn around and say, "Oh, my eyes, I can't see! I can't see!" Mencken kept taking off his glasses, then putting them on again, smudging them with thumb prints that August patiently cleaned. New lighting fixtures were installed in an effort to help improve his sight, but to no avail: he suffered from hemianopsia, blindness over half the field of vision. August had amber yellow lenses ground for his brother, the type that pilots used during the war. As soon as Mencken put them on he cried, "Oh my God, this is marvelous! This is wonderful!"

Back went Mencken to the ophthalmologist for more testing. August discovered that the eye doctors, misunderstanding Mencken's speech, had made the proper lens for one eye but not for the other. When it was fixed, his brother was able to read every single letter on the eye chart perfectly. "Just that difference," August later mourned, "would have made those years bearable."

But time had run out. August was convinced "without the slightest doubt" that had his brother received the proper medical care from the very beginning, eventually "he would have learned to read again. Not like he used to, but enough to entertain himself." One of his speech therapists agreed. There is some medical question as to whether this might be so; the strokes had caused too much damage. But nothing could dissuade August from believing that his brother's vision problem was caused by "neglect."

When Dr. Wagley left Baltimore for military duty, the Menckens decided to abandon Johns Hopkins in favor of Bon Secours Hospital, within walking distance of Hollins Street. Here, the man who had denounced religion was given tender care by nuns.[10]

AFTER SEVEN LONG YEARS, Mencken, reconciled to the stroke that had whitened his hair and lined his face, refused to celebrate his seventy-fifth birthday because, he said, he had never celebrated any of them. It promised to be like any other day: after breakfast, he proposed to listen to the news read to him from the *Sun*; in the late morning he would work sorting the letters in his files, and after the noon meal he planned to rest and listen to the radio.

But to his great surprise, his birthday became a cause for national celebration. More than a thousand letters, telegrams, and clippings arrived at Hollins Street, as August was kept jumping answering the telephone. Boxes upon boxes of cigars arrived, along with candy and flowers. An entirely new collection of his essays, assembled by Alistair Cooke, *The Vintage Mencken*, appeared—evidence, Cooke and Alfred Knopf believed, that Mencken remained one of the master craftsman of daily journalism in the twentieth century.

The first printing sold out in two days.

Mencken was astounded. He was acclaimed America's Samuel Johnson, as celebrated as George Bernard Shaw, a native product unlike any other, a humorist on a par with Mark Twain. That year, *Inherit the Wind*, a play based on the Scopes Trial, had been performed to much praise, provoking an avalanche of recollections of Mencken's role during that hot summer in 1925. Mencken's books were touted (though, to his disappointment, no one mentioned *Treatise on the Gods*, which he still considered his best). His place in American literature seemed firmly established. So great was his popularity that in the personal ads for that year, one young woman described herself as "Menckenesque." He had become a part of the American language itself.

In prior years August had refused to let anyone arrive at Hollins Street unannounced. Now a new round of guests were welcomed as they paid homage to "The Sage of Baltimore." To each, Mencken gave the grand tour. With a gesture of his cigar, he pointed to paintings of his German ancestors. "Isn't that one a horror?" he remarked, then led them past book shelves covered with lint, to the quiet back garden where he gesticulated to the brick wall: "That wall of mine will be standing when the rest of Baltimore is dust." One visitor called off the names of politicians in the hope of carrying away a terse quote. He was not disappointed. Eisenhower? "Well, for a soldier, he's better than Grant." How about General Douglas MacArthur? "A dreadful old fraud who appears to be fading satisfactorily."

The Mencken revival took place against a background of a slow, creeping rot then taking place in the country's intellectual life. "Never had American youth been so withdrawn, cautious, unimaginative, indifferent, unadventurous—and silent," Manchester recalled.

Few audible white voices protested the racism and segregation that was a blight across the land. In a nationwide campaign to screen un-American material, textbooks in high schools and colleges were censored; in libraries, books were banned. Just days before Mencken's birthday, the mayor of Baltimore called a meeting of newsstand operators and presented them with an unofficial list of objectionable magazines.

There were no cries of indignation.

Fueled by affluence and confidence, across the country many middle-class American families were complacently watching TV between four or five hours a day.

"What tends to be forgotten was his courage," Alfred Knopf told listeners in a 1955 radio interview, "and the one [virtue] Mencken admired most in human beings." And that was what the country needed Mencken most; for, as Cooke said, "timid, suspicious conformity tends to come up during times of prosperity."[10]

One day in November 1955, Rosalind Lohrfinck came across a manuscript that had been stuffed into a folder, buried in the basement under a huge pile of

"An American Institution." H. L. Mencken at seventy-five, at home in his backyard. Photograph by A. Aubrey Bodine; Copyright © Jennifer B. Bodine.

correspondence headed for the Enoch Pratt Free Library. On the top was a type-written note: "A good title for my projected book of notes would be *Minority Report*." Inside were hundreds of such notes, some only a few lines in length, some running to several pages, on a wide variety of topics—government, organized religion, professional philosophers, pedagogues—collected by Mencken before his stroke, forgotten by author and publisher alike. "What delighted him most of all," Lohrfinck recalled, "was that he had already written the preface," which explained the reason for this proposed new publication:

> Ever since my earliest attempts as an author I have followed the somewhat banal practice of setting down notions as they come to me, sometimes in the form of hasty scrawls, unintelligible to anyone else, and then throwing these notes into a bin. Out of that bin have come a couple dozen books and pamphlets and an almost innumerable swarm of magazine and newspaper articles, but still the raw materials kept mounting faster than I could work them up, so I am printing herewith some select samples of them, partly for the purpose of getting them off my hands and my conscience, and partly in the hope that some of them, at least, may enkindle an occasional reader to more orderly and profitable lucubrations.

In New York, publishing staff member William Koshland arrived at the office and found Alfred Knopf seated at his desk, manuscript in hand, smiling. "Look!" he shouted. "Henry left us something we can publish!" The whole office, Koshland recalled, was more excited than it had been in long while.

There still remained, as Knopf put it, the task of balancing the text, which required the excising of entire passages that were criticisms of Franklin D. Roosevelt and observations on race, some of which had been lifted from random notes that Mencken had written under the title "Advice to Young Men" in 1939. Knopf explained to Mencken that these were deleted because he could not reply to criticism. While Mencken agreed with the editing, he knew that there remained enough contentious remarks to make the book controversial.

To advance publicity for the book, an Associated Press reporter was invited to 1524 Hollins Street to write a feature that would be distributed nationally. The two men sat by the fire. Mencken settled himself comfortably into his easy chair, encircled by cigar smoke. Flecking a speck of ash from his shirt, he announced with a grin, "It will be nice being denounced again."[11]

THE FOLLOWING SATURDAY, on January 28, 1956, Mencken listened to a radio broadcast of *Die Meistersinger* before taking a nap. As he ate a light supper, August read him the headlines of the *Evening Sun*. That day few stories interested him. "There were no robberies, or murders, or women shooting their husbands, or anything like that," August remembered. Then he played some more classical music.

That evening, Louis Cheslock called at Hollins Street, but Mencken was not waiting for him at his usual seat. "Harry doesn't feel well," August explained. A few moments later, Mencken came downstairs. To Cheslock's surprise, he walked straight up to him and put out his hand. He had never done this before. "Louis, this is the last you'll see me," he said. At these words, Cheslock later said, "a chill ran down my back."

Once they were in the parlor, Mencken went immediately over to the sofa and sat down, saying, "I don't think I feel well." After this, however, he felt remarkably revived. The evening progressed as if nothing untoward had happened. The men spoke about music, television announcers, and the forthcoming *Minority Report*. To the delight of all three, a crank had already written to denounce it before its publication. At one point, Mencken complained about a pain in his chest, and August handed him a pink pill. At nine he went upstairs. Before doing so, he briefly shook Cheslock's hand, and repeated, "Louis, this is the last you'll see me." Cheslock left shortly after. Outside the weather was raw, with rain eventually turning to sleet. When he reached his house, Cheslock told his wife that he had an ominous feeling about Mencken. "Don't say that," Elise reassured him. "You'll be there next week."

The Mencken household retired at 9:15. On Mencken's bedside table was a glass of water and his night pills. To his right, within easy reach, was his radio. The strains of music could be heard. It was Mozart. Long ago, on hearing the music of this composer, Mencken had mused that the only permanent values in the world were truth and beauty. This and only this, he believed, was the heritage of man. They were the things he had fought for all his life.

The symphony played until ten that evening. Silence descended on the house and the city. And then, sometime later, long after the last chord of music had registered itself upon H. L. Mencken, a gray light shone upon the icy rooftops, as the sun rose over Baltimore.[12]

Epilogue

THE PASSING OF AN ERA

I N THE OFFICES of the *Sunpapers*, staffers were busier than usual, arranging the layout of the final edition. Three major stories competed for their attention: on January 29, 1956, a fire had engulfed a crowd at an oyster supper, resulting in death and injury; a strike by the Baltimore Transit company had begun, with thousands of workers threatening to dig in for a long siege. In the middle of the page, above the fold, an editor carefully adjusted a headline to the third item:

H. L. MENCKEN, AUTHOR, DIES AT 75

It was difficult trying to fit together these stories in such little space. One copy editor, giving her colleague a nudge, asked: "Why couldn't he have died on a day when we didn't have *any* news?"

Hours earlier, a *Sun* librarian had struggled to unlock a metal box firmly screwed onto a shelf in the library. Inside, he found a piece of paper. On it Mencken had written: "TO WHOEVER COVERS MY DEATH." Inside was Mencken's earnest request that there be only a very brief announcement, with no attempt at a biographical sketch, no portrait, and no editorial.

Mencken might have known that such instructions would not be heeded. All that day and the next, August tried to cope with calls and the hundreds of letters that poured into Hollins Street. "I believe he was glad to go," August told a friend, "My only comfort was that the end was as he would have wanted it."

Always an agnostic, Mencken insisted he felt no animosity toward persons who were religious. He provided for the possibility, however, that he could be wrong

"Wink your eye at some homely girl." How to please Mencken's ghost. H. L. Mencken Collection, Enoch Pratt Free Library.

about the immortality of the soul. If, he said, he arrived at heaven and was confronted by the Twelve Apostles, he would simply say "Gentlemen, I was wrong."

Nonetheless, he insisted that no Christian religious service be performed, warning his brother to "be sure to not let Gertrude change the terms of my funeral as stated in my will." The body was sent to the pathology department at Johns Hopkins Hospital in compliance with Mencken's wishes that "the boys" look at his brain and "find out what went on in it." The autopsy provided a complete microscopic diagnosis of a man who prized science above all disciplines because of its cold reliance on facts. Duty accomplished, August faithfully adhered to his brother's final request: to have a few old friends around to speed him on his way.

They gathered on January 31 at the funeral home just around the corner from 1524 Hollins Street. Many more would have attended, but August discouraged them. Oh no, he said, why travel such a long distance for something that might last only a few seconds? Standing shoulder to shoulder were W. Edwin Moffet, the oldest surviving member of the Saturday Night Club, along with Louis Cheslock; Dr. Arnold Rich, professor of pathology at Johns Hopkins Medical School; and Siegfried Weisberger of the Peabody Book Store. Among those from the *Sunpapers* were William Abell and Hamilton Owens. Charles Mencken was there with his second wife, Ruth, and his daughter, Virginia. James Cain had driven from Maryland; Alfred Knopf had flown in from New York. Standing next to Knopf was Elise Cheslock. At one point, he turned to her: "Henry said you're the best cook in the world," he managed. Elise understood some of what Knopf must have been feeling. As she put it, "It was all that he could say."

Hamilton Owens was spokesman for the group. "August wanted me to tell you what most of you already know," he began. "Henry didn't want funeral services of any kind. All he wanted was a few friends to see him off on his last journey." Almost breaking down, Owens struggled to keep going: "And that is what we are doing here today." There was an awkward silence. Then, with a nod from August, the casket was closed and removed from the small room.

The entire procedure lasted less than five minutes. For many, the service, such as it was, had been unsatisfying. Hamilton Owens thought it cold and Knopf dreary. James Cain felt that August could have remembered, that "though Mencken disbelieved he was entering the next world, he was at least taking leave of this one, and permitted some sort of rites that would have served as a memorial to what he did, which was considerable. Somehow," Cain later recounted to reporter Arthur Krock, "we were made to subserve a gag, and the effect wasn't so much bleak as blank. The minute of silence didn't quite say it."

As the gathering prepared to leave, Siegfried Weisberger struggled with an overcoat obviously many sizes too large for him. He looked up, bewildered, into the smiling face of Hamilton Owens. "Siegfried, I think you have my coat," Owens said gently, and the smaller man quickly recovered, gallantly helping the towering Owens into his own coat. This seemed to break the ice, and there were some smiles as the friends filed out the door. Only August and Charles accompanied the casket to the cemetery. Newsreel photographers stood nearby; August threatened them with legal action if any pictures were taken. The hearse slowly rolled away from the curb, gleaming brightly in the afternoon sunlight, then headed for Louden Park.

It was Gertrude whom many remembered from that day. She disapproved of the lack of a service so intensely that, instead of shepherding the group back to 1524 Hollins Street afterward as planned, she stalked out of the funeral parlor, abruptly got into her car, and drove straight back to her apartment. Only a few feet away, housekeeper Emma Ball had prepared a luncheon, but none of the friends felt comfortable going into the house without any of its hosts. The group silently dispersed into the cold afternoon, some heading to Marconi's, others to their own homes.

Only Rosalind Lohrfinck joined the family at Hollins Street. No sooner had Mencken's body been taken to the grave than the household disintegrated into a minor sulk. Eventually Gertrude joined them. Cornering Lohrfinck, she unloaded a torrent of complaints. For seven long years while her brother was ill, Gertrude confided, she had suffered because of August's "insufferable conduct." Without meaning to, his protective intentions toward Harry had antagonized every member of the family. She recalled the many instances that August had kept her out of the house, when he had told her just what time to come in and when to leave.

As for "Auggie," Lohrfinck wrote in her diary, the most misunderstood member of the Mencken clan "sat at the head of the table slicing the Smithfield ham like a German *Fuhrer.*"

So the day ended at 1524 Hollins Street, with none of the graceful civility that Mencken had tried to impart when he had inhabited it.[1]

ALFRED KNOPF RETURNED to New York later that afternoon. His thoughts were fixed on that day, so long ago in 1913, when he had first met Mencken. His reverie took him forward to when he had shyly introduced his new bride to the young critic. "I'd warned her what a gruff boisterous fire eater she was to meet," Knopf recalled telling Blanche; instead, Mencken had gallantly presented her with a gift. Then came the publication of *A Book of Prefaces*, "and the beginning of a relationship that had only ended the past Saturday." It would be difficult, Knopf mused, especially in these times, for another generation to understand Mencken's importance, how much he had been bound up in both American and European fiction and changed its course. Now his friend was gone. The finality was almost too painful to bear. "Probably no one has had as much influence over us for as many years," Knopf wrote. "Thus ended a very, very important chapter in my life."[2]

THE SOBRIETY OF THE FUNERAL ARRANGEMENTS was countered by the public acclaim. Tributes filled the newspapers. One *Sun* subscriber summed up what everyone felt—"proud that I am from the same town in which Henry L. Mencken did his best work." The Baltimore Association of Commerce, which had scorned Mencken in the past, now acknowledged that city representatives, when seeking business, achieved success in some distant towns because they came from the place "where Henry Mencken lived." In death, H. L. Mencken had joined Fort McHenry, Edgar Allan Poe, and the Johns Hopkins Hospital as Baltimore's chief attractions.

Yet, there were those in Baltimore who, as Gerald Johnson put it, "were not much interested in what the world had lost—the incomparable reporter, the critic, the philologist, the social historian, H. L. Mencken. They were too much occupied in lamenting their own loss—Henry Mencken, the unique," the private citizen of Baltimore, "sitting at ease after the day's work was over, with a cigar in mouth, a seidel in hand," the man who "touched the dull fabric of our days and gave it a silken sheen."

As word spread, friends and strangers alike tried to come to terms with the news. George Jean Nathan was inconsolable. In Santa Monica, Aileen Pringle heard the news on the radio. It left her so stunned she found it almost impossible to write a coherent letter of condolence. Like Marion Bloom and Gretchen Hood, Aileen continued as the years passed to care for Mencken, critical of his behavior yet still in love with him.

In Washington, D.C., at the headquarters of the FBI, an agent added Mencken's obituary to an already thick dossier, while several blocks away, a young United Press reporter, Neil McNeil, crestfallen, derived some comfort by literally following Mencken's postmortem instructions as they had appeared in the *Chrestomathy*:

> If, after I depart this vale, you ever remember me and have thought to please my ghost, forgive some sinner and wink your eye at some homely girl.[3]

To Rosalind Lohrfinck remained the sad task of pasting into the scrapbooks thousands of clippings from all over the world. She spent her last years at the Enoch Pratt Free Library, assisting librarian Betty Adler in loyally cataloging material in preparation of the Mencken Room that would be, in Alistair Cooke's phrase, for "the comfort of sinners and the astonishment of the virtuous."

August Mencken continued to live at 1524 Hollins Street. The sudden death of his brother Charlie, within two months after Henry's, came as a profound shock. The blows eventually took their toll. August died in 1967. Gertrude, when she was not busy in works of piety or attending the Episcopal Church, remained at Choice Parcel, spry and alert, until her death in 1980. Two months later, Virginia Mencken was killed in an automobile accident and, shortly thereafter, her son, Davy, in an airplane crash.

In time, Siegfried Weisberger's hopes for a Mencken Society became a reality when scholar Carl Bode founded the organization and became its first president, to be succeeded by Arthur Gutman, who nurtured a membership that continues to this day. Repeatedly, Mencken's beloved 1524 Hollins Street was rescued from oblivion by a determined band of citizens; their passionate attempts go on.[4]

INSTINCTIVELY, MENCKEN KNEW he would continue to disturb the peace long after his death. He had left enough material, including his diary, to make that outcome inevitable. When it came to criticism, of charges of racism brought against him by Angoff, he told William Manchester, "It doesn't matter what they think of me. My work will depend, not on what those people think of me, but on what I've *done*." Certainly Mencken could be unfair; he could arouse feelings of betrayal and disappointment in those who had blindly set him up as an idol. That he was a man of maddening contradictions is without question. And yet, in many of his actions, especially toward minorities, Mencken demonstrated a greater appreciation than anyone might have thought. His fame, as Alistair Cooke noted, was "rightly grounded on the vigor and noble indignation he brought to unpopular causes."

He was, however, anything but a moralist—an attitude, he realized, that made him incomprehensible to most Americans. "The first passion of a good Americano is to make his fellow primates do something that they don't want to do," observed Mencken. "His second is to convince them that doing it will improve the world and please God." Here, Mencken recognized, "I lie outside the stream, at ease along the bank."

At the height of his powers, Mencken had proven "that iconoclasm, whatever its perils, is at least one of the most gallant and stimulating sports." He held to these guidelines: sound information, common sense, good taste, lively wit, and ready humor. In Mencken's hands, they were the best way to combat cowardice, censorship, the suppression of individual rights, and the hypocrisy of frauds (or, as he pronounced it, "frodds") that have existed since time immemorial. Beyond his brilliant writing style, Mencken's great contribution was his courage to write what he thought.

The man who found it "simply impossible to follow American patterns of thinking" was, as his European followers always recognized, most American: in language, in humor, in what Mencken observed in Mark Twain—his "curious mixture of sentimentality and cynicism," the "mingling of romanticist and iconoclast."

Such authors, Mencken recognized, are invariably denounced. The "national guardians" sound the alarms, the lavish praise is alternately given and withdrawn, the artist is "labeled, then relabeled."

What remains is "a destructive satirist of the utmost pungency and relentlessness, and the most bitter critic of American platitude and delusion." When Mencken remarked that "Mark Twain, dead, promises to stir up the animals even more joyously than Mark Twain, living," he could have said the same of himself.

As if on cue, the first of many posthumous storms occurred a few short weeks after Mencken's death. Under the vaulted dome of the Maryland State Capitol in Annapolis came the sound of shouts and jeers. At issue was a joint resolution "expressing the sorrow of the General Assembly of Maryland over the passing of Henry Louis Mencken." Such resolutions are customarily passed without a dissenting vote, but in the midst of the roll call, one senator from the Eastern Shore leaped to his feet, bitterly insisting that he be recorded against it. Mencken, he complained, had once described the Shore's residents as "barbarians," "an Alsatia of morons" with "ignorant and ignoble minds."

Nobody mentioned that Mencken had written these phrases in 1932, protesting the lynching of an African American in one of the most vicious murders Maryland had ever seen. Before the roll call could continue, another infuriated senator from the Eastern Shore rose to the floor. He, too, disapproved of the motion to honor Mencken, primly insisting that he simply "couldn't vote for a man who didn't believe in heaven or hell."

Their protests were resoundingly defeated as supporters of the bill erupted in a tremendous "AYE!"

The entire procedure left some convinced that Mencken, who always took delight in stirring up the animals, wouldn't have wanted the vote to be unanimous anyway.

As Mencken wrote in his own obituary for the Associated Press, "I have believed all my life in free thought and free speech." That made James Cain, on the eve of Mencken's death, find the prospect of life without his friend nothing less than "frightening. For we live in troubled times, with the censor, the bigot, and the patrioteer in full cry once more. And one wonders who the big bull elephant will be, to smash at them hard again, and whether there ever will be another one quite as big, quite as brave, quite as mad as Mencken."5

ACKNOWLEDGMENTS

In 1981, two weeks before my graduation from Goucher College, while I was researching the papers of alumna Sara Haardt, I literally tripped over a box of love letters between her and H. L. Mencken. Taped to the top of the collection was a stern command, written by Mencken, that it was not to be opened until that very year. To say that my life changed course at that moment would be an understatement. Suddenly, a door was swung open into Mencken's life through the tender route of romantic correspondence. During two decades, Mencken has pulled me through many happy adventures, both personal and professional, that included my editing two books of his work and culminated in my writing this volume.

I wish to acknowledge at the outset the extraordinary support given by the Enoch Pratt Free Library in Baltimore, Maryland, particularly by Averil Kadis, who manages the estate of H. L. Mencken, and Carla Hayden, director of the library. Access to H. L. Mencken's papers was just a part of why those years were so rewarding; even more welcome were the countless examples of help and encouragement from the entire staff, and the thoughtful manner in which so much was done to make my task easier. For expert assistance in dealing with all my inquiries I am grateful to the late Neil Jordahl, former curator of the Mencken Room, and Vince Fitzpatrick, its current curator, for constructive suggestions on important points in the manuscript. Staff members John Sondheim, Ralph Clayton, Jeff Korman, Judy Cooper, Ophelia Racelis, Mark Sober, Wesley Wilson, William S. Forshaw, Wilbur McGill, Faye Houston, Thomas Himmel, and Charlotte Gettes also provided valuable assistance and friendship.

This project could not have been undertaken without the financial assistance of institutions that gave not once but on several occasions: the National Endowment for the Humanities; the Goldsmith Research Award from the Joan Shorenstein Barone Center for Press, Politics and Public Policy at Harvard University; the Fleur Cowles Fellowship from the Harry Ransom Humanities Research Center at the University of Texas at Austin that enabled me to spend a fulfilling month researching its many treasures, including Alfred A. Knopf's personal papers; and the McCloy Fellowship from the American Council on Germany that provided the opportunity to retrace Mencken's footsteps and visit archives in Germany. Additional generous aid for research was provided by the Freedom Forum Media Studies Center at Columbia University in New York City, under the expert guidance of Everette A. Dennis, where I was able to profit from interchanges with scholars and journalists on widely varying projects. My thanks also go to Charles Overby and Peter Prichard of the Freedom Forum. Among those who believed in this project from its inception, I am grateful to the late historian and former librarian of Congress Daniel J. Boorstin, and his wife, Ruth; newspaper editor John S. Carroll; and biographers Richard Lingeman, Kenneth Lynn, Robert K. Massie, Edmund and Sylvia Morris; and my former graduate adviser from Emory University, the late Floyd A. Watkins.

The majority of this biography is based on primary sources, from personal interviews and manuscripts housed in private family collections as well as in libraries in the United States and Germany. Those who knew H. L. Mencken made the past come alive through vivid anecdotes, tempered by perception and wit. All are listed in the bibliography, but I would like to especially single out Ruth Goodman Goetz, Robin P. Harriss and his wife, Margery Harriss—who later not only had the diaries of her husband transcribed but also gave me complete access, without any restrictions, to them—Olga Owens, Elise Cheslock, and Betti Anne Patterson. All became dear friends while I lived in Baltimore and New York, and for me, neither city is quite the same without them; they are missed to this day. I am also beholden to the sons and daughters of Mencken's contemporaries, who provided candid insights and patiently searched their attics for material and entrusted me with these valuable treasures for as long as I needed. I should like to single out Sara Anne Duffy Chermayeff, Barry Cheslock, the entire Hawks family, Clarinda Harriss, and especially Gwinn Owens and Bettina Patterson, whose boxes of family papers are of the greatest possible value on which more Mencken studies can be based.

I would have liked to present a copy of this publication to the late Harold A. Williams, who selflessly lent me a trove of material from his archive and arranged for me to interview those who had worked with Mencken on the Sunpapers. It was under Hal's watch on the newspaper that vivid recollections of Baltimore were gathered in the feature called "I Remember When," on topics ranging from the Baltimore fire of 1904 to H. L. Mencken's Saturday Night Club. Historians are much in his debt.

Tribute must also be paid to Arthur Gutman, president emeritus of the Mencken Society, cherished surrogate uncle, who shared his own extensive private collection of Menckeniana with me and prodded fellow collectors to do the same. Among them are Richard Schrader, George H. Thompson, Steven Lauria, the late Charles Wallen Jr., William H. C. Wilson, R. B. Lasco, and Edward DeRussy—my warmest thanks to all of them. A steady stream of valuable items came to me from Jack Sanders, whose thoughtfulness and generosity over these many years goes beyond words. Likewise, my gratitude to author Roy Hoopes who, by providing a wealth of extensive interviews with James Cain as well as copies of Cain's unpublished memoirs and memoranda dealing with Mencken (many of which Hoopes had not used in his biography of Cain), offered otherwise unavailable insights. The late Helmut Winter also selflessly took time from his own series of German editions of H. L. Mencken's work to aid me.

The work of Mencken scholars has added much to the canon. There are four in particular who have had the most profound influence on my work, and I express my gratitude to them. When it comes to a critical analysis of Mencken's philosophy, Charles A. Fecher's *H. L. Mencken: A Study of His Thought*, as Alfred A. Knopf rightly put it in 1978, excels as "to leave the competition nowhere." Charles Fecher gave me unflagging support, reading an early draft and offering astute suggestions, and has been a gracious friend throughout. The late William Manchester, whose own masterful biography of Mencken continues to be read, was a generous mentor throughout his last ten years, cheering me on with letters and phone calls and providing personal material to help me write this book. Another critical influence was the late Alistair Cooke. Our first meeting was over lunch at the Carlyle in New York. There, at my place setting, balanced on top of an elegant china plate, was a mysterious packet containing more than twenty letters, many of them handwritten, from H. L. Mencken to one of his girlfriends, Dorothy Taylor. They had been sent anonymously to Cooke after the publication of *The Vintage Mencken* in 1955. "You're the best person to have these," he said magnanimously—one of several gifts, the most valuable of which were his articulate insights. Finally, the late Carl Bode, whose own work and interviews with Mencken's contemporaries, many of them long deceased, have provided a valuable inner glimpse of one of the most private of authors. The kindness of these four men, literary lions all, moved me; my admiration for their achievements goes hand in hand with gratitude from one who has long relied on their scholarship and enjoyed reading their prose.

Elsewhere the staffs of sixty libraries in the United States and Germany diligently aided me in tracking down elusive documents. While I cannot name them all individually, I trust these expert guardians of history realize the extent of my gratitude. For additional help, I must particularly thank Dirk Standen for his extraordinary industry during the nine months of my fellowship at the Freedom Forum's Media Studies Center in New York. In Germany, I am especially indebted to Hauke Hartmann and to Sonja Lueke. My thanks also for the assistance of Marianela Soto, Spencer Abruzzese, Karimah El-Bahtimy, Megan Balzer, Robert W. Barnes, Tina Braxton, Elizabeth Hubble, Ruth Kupperschlag, Philip Laredo, Abby Markwyn, Henry C. Peden Jr., and Andy Virkus.

Other scholars and individuals who provided information and hospitality include: Katharina Albrecht, Patricia Angelin, Susan Barron, Paul Bauer, Joe Beck, George Bell, Amy Bernstein, Paul Boytinck, Judi Buckalew, Thomas Butterbaugh, Bill Clarke, George Clarke, Zechariah Chafee III, John Clyne, Pablo Conrad, Roy H. Copperud, Richard Cornelius, Mary Ann McCardell Daily, Brother Patrick Ellis, Claudia Fielding, Laura Fortenbaugh, David Foster, Rod and Lee Frazer, Donald T. Fritz, Mary Anita Fulton, Martin Gilbert, Victoria Hawkins, Barbara Hellman, Sandra Hicks, Stephanie Jordan, Valerie Keane, Harry G. Kelly, Bruce Kellner, Betty Kondayan, Thomas Kunkel, John Larivee, Michael Lienesch, Nancy Magnuson, William K. Marimow, Howard Markel, Edward A. Martin, Hilary Masters, Victor Navasky, David R. Owen, Eddie Pattillo, Marcella Peirce, John Pentz, Gayle Peters, Alice Piper, Peter Prescott, Keith Richwine, Donald A. Ritchie, Carlin Romano, Stephan Russ-Mohl, Judy Sanger, Dodgie Schaffer, Kathryn Scott, Sam Sokolow, Dieter Spielberg, Barbara Strickland, Seth Tallert, Robert Taylor, Randy Tietjen, Doug Trussel, Barbara Vandergrift, and Barbie Zelizer.

The past, as biographer Richard Holmes observes, retains a physical presence in the form of words and images and in landscapes and buildings. It was a privilege to live in the city that Mencken cherished while I worked on this book. I am especially grateful to those dedicated citizens who battle to save Baltimore's heritage, including Mencken's house at 1524 Hollins Street.

My parents, Maria Arce Fernandez and William Livingston Rodgers, whose love sustains me, my siblings Linda and Bill Rodgers, who read several chapters of this book, and other members of my family have contributed much more than they realize. My hope is that one day Matthew, Alysia, and Anna will gain inspiration from Mencken's prose and his courage. When it came to navigating the world of computers, Paul, Amy, and Julie Witcover, Steven Sandford, and Nasser Rawashdeh were very patient with someone more at home in the early years of the last century than in this one.

Finally, there are those whose debt is of a very special order and who have done the most to help bring this work to fruition. My thanks to Sallye Leventhal and Arabella Meyer, who first brought the attention of this biography to the legendary Sheldon Meyer of Oxford University Press, rightly called "Editor Nonpareil" by historian William E. Leuchtenburg. Sheldon's patience and faith in this project have earned my deepest gratitude, as has the entire team at Oxford University Press, especially Joellyn Ausanka, Senior Production Editor, whose eagle eye and expert, gracious guidance has kept this manuscript on track.

My uncle, Leon Livingstone, professor emeritus of the State University of New York at Buffalo, now residing in London, reviewed each chapter. Across the miles, his steady hand helped me over many a rough passage; my love and thanks to him.

And, my husband, author and journalist Jules Witcover who, when we first met at a tribute to the *Baltimore Evening Sun*, hardly suspected that one day H. L. Mencken would invade his own home. There are no words of adequate appreciation for providing me with the atmosphere in which to write. Jules is, by nature, and has been through the course of our years together, a pillar of strength, and it is for these reasons among many that the lines of "Song of Love," by Chilean poet Pablo Neruda, resonate so deeply in my soul.

Marion Elizabeth Rodgers
Washington, D.C.

NOTES

These notes are for those who, in the words of H. L. Mencken, enjoy "running down the by-ways of the subject." Sources are listed along with guideposts for further study. Although principal secondary works are cited, in most cases a multitude of primary sources have been used. These include personal interviews and oral histories, contemporary newspaper and magazine accounts, office files, memos, pamphlets, and manuscripts located at libraries across the United States and in Germany, as well as diaries, memoirs, and letters held in archives and in private collections here and abroad.

Original manuscripts to H. L. Mencken's autobiographical writing are cited, not the edited versions published later. This includes his *Diary*, *My Life as Author and Editor*, and *Thirty-Five Years of Newspaper Work*, located at the Enoch Pratt Free Library in Baltimore, Maryland. Mencken purged his letter files before bequeathing them to the New York Public Library and elsewhere. Missing letters, especially those bearing on personal affairs, are to be found within the individual collections of contemporaries scattered in archives throughout the United States.

To avoid a large number of endnotes, all the references necessary to a particular passage are combined in a single note. The names of H. L. Mencken, George Jean Nathan, and Alfred A. Knopf are abbreviated as HLM, GJN, and AAK. The *Baltimore Sun*, the *Baltimore Evening Sun*, and the *New York Times* are *BS*, *BES*, and *NYT*. Abbreviations used in these endnotes for library and manuscript collections are in the Bibliography.

Prologue: Boston, 1926

1. "Mencken Creates Furor," *North Adams (Mass.) Transcript*, April 10, 1926; "Famous Editor Defies . . . ," *New Britain (Conn.) Editor*, April 5, 1926; "Mencken Ready For . . . ," *Boston Evening Globe*, April 5, 1926; "Mencken Sues After Arrest," *Boston Post*, April 6, 1926.

2. HLM, "Autobiographical Notes, 1925," p. 165, EPFL; "Judge Reads Piece in Mencken's Case," *NYT*, April 7, 1926; A. L. S. Wood, "Keeping the Puritans Pure," *American Mercury*, Sept. 1925, pp. 74–78; William T. Matchett, "Boston Is Afraid of Books," *Saturday Review of Books*, July 14, 1944, pp. 6, 7, 21; HLM to Sara Haardt, April 2, 1926, GOU.

3. "Mr. Mencken Craves Arrest," *Boston Herald*, April 5, 1926.

4. Edwin A. Alderman to John Barton Cross, President of the University of Virginia, Feb. 4, 1925, UVA; Farrar, "College Reading," *Bookman*, April 1926, p. 131; Singleton, *H. L. Mencken and the American Mercury Adventure*, p. 158.

5. "Crowd Assembled To Witness Mencken's Arrest," *Chicago (Ill.) Post*, April 6, 1926; HLM, "The 'Hatrack' Case 1926–1927, The American Mercury vs. The New England Watch & Ward Society, The Postmaster General of the United States, et al., With Newspaper Reports and Other Documents, 1937," Appendix LV, p. 49, EPFL; "Mencken Defies Watch & Ward and Is Arrested," *Boston Transcript*, April 5, 1926; Richard Massock, "About New York," *New York Leader Republican*, Sept. 30, 1930; author interview with William Manchester, May 23, 1995; author interview with Harvard graduate Wallace Cohen, Aug. 29, 1993.

6. Author interview with Wallace Cohen, Aug. 29, 1993 (the Baltimore native reported on the event for the *Harvard Crimson* in 1926); "Mencken Freed on Own Bond After Defiance of Boston Law," *BS*, April 6, 1926; "Watch & Ward Leader Denounced," *New Bedford (Mass.) Times*, July 11, 1916; Herbert Asbury, "The Day Mencken Broke the Law," *American Mercury*, Oct. 1951, pp. 62–63; "Editor Defies Watch & Ward," *Boston Globe*, April 6, 1926; author interview with William Koshland, March 15, 1995.

7. Author interview with William Koshland, March 15, 1995; "Editor Defies. . . . ," *Boston Globe*, April 6, 1926; Herbert Asbury, "The Day . . . ," *American Mercury*, Oct. 1951, p. 63; "Editor Arrested," *New Haven (Conn.) Register*, April 8, 1926; HLM, "The 'Hatrack' Case . . . ," Appendix LV, p. 51, EPFL; "Mencken's Simplicity Surprised Court Gazers," *Springfield (Mass.) Union*, April 11, 1926.

8. "Mencken Freed . . . ," *BS*, April 6, 1926; "Mencken Arrested," *Cumberland (Md.) News*, April 10, 1926; "Both Heard in Mencken Case," *Boston Herald*, April 7, 1926; "Mencken Arraigned; Sues Watch & Ward Society," *Boston Traveler*, April 6, 1926; "Mencken Decision to Be Announced Tomorrow Morning," *Boston Transcript*, April 6, 1926; Herbert Asbury, "The Day . . . ," *American Mercury*, Oct. 1951, p. 64.

9. "Clear Mencken and Mercury," *Boston Herald*, April 8, 1926; *The Editor, the Bluenose, and the Prostitute*, ed. Carl Bode, p. 71; "Mencken Finds Boston Isn't So Bad After All," *Boston Globe*, April 11, 1926; "Mr. Mencken Exonerated After Boston Judge Reads Article Appearing in the Mercury," *Chambersburg (Pa.) Repository*, April 10, 1926.

10. "Mencken Honored at Harvard Following Victory in Court," *BS*, April 8, 1926; "Mencken Raps Watch & Ward at Union," *Harvard Crimson*, April 8, 1926; author interview with Wallace Cohen, Aug. 29, 1993.

11. "Mencken Honored . . . ," *BS*, April 8, 1926; "Big Ovation to Mencken at Harvard," *Boston Post*, April 8, 1926; Felix Frankfurter to HLM, April 15, 1926, in HLM, "The 'Hatrack' Case . . . ," EPFL; Andrew J. R. Helmus to Harvard President Lawrence Lowell, April 18, 1926, HAR/arc; Harvard President Lawrence Lowell to Andrew J. R. Helmus, April 20, 1926, HAR/arc.

12. "Mencken Raps . . . ," *Harvard Crimson*, April 8, 1926.

Chapter 1: The Citizen of Baltimore

1. James Cain, "Memo to Dr. Bode re: Mencken," courtesy Roy Hoopes and Alice Piper; Gerald Johnson, "Henry L. Mencken [1880–1956]," *Saturday Review of Literature*, Feb. 11, 1956, p. 12.

2. HLM, *Happy Days*, p. 4; HLM, "The Free Lance," *BES*, July 9, 1912; HLM, "Old Soldiers Meet" in HLM, "Early News Stories Baltimore Morning Herald 1899–1901," p. 69, EPFL.

3. HLM, *Happy Days*, pp. 3–4; "A Brilliant Harbor Scene, A Fine Street Procession," *BS*, Sept. 14, 1883; "Pageant Night, Gorgeous Spectacle," *BS*, Sept. 15, 1883; Carol Dulaney, "Ignatius Donelly," *Baltimore American*, Oct. 14, 1934; Richardson Wright, "Tough Boyhood of the Pride of Baltimore," *New York Herald Tribune Books*, Jan. 21, 1940.

4. HLM, "Miscellaneous Typescripts, Carbons and Clippings 1946–1948," pp. 64–65, EPFL; HLM, *"Happy Days*: Additions . . . ," p. 157, EPFL; HLM, *Happy Days*, p. 71; Janvier, *Baltimore in the Eighties and Nineties*, p. 31; Janvier, *Baltimore Yesterdays*, p. 1. For information on how Baltimoreans lived during the turn of the last century, Mencken suggested readers refer to these delightful volumes. HLM, "School Drawing Books F. Knapp Institute Baltimore 1881–1882," EPFL. The musical notes appear in the entry for Oct. 4, 1888.

5. HLM, "Autobiographical Notes, 1941," EPFL; HLM, "The Schooling of a Theologian," *New Yorker*, July 8, 1939, p. 32.

6. HLM, "The Passing of 'The Hill.' A Chronicle of Boyhood Days in the Perilous Wilds of the Southwest Baltimore Steppes," *BS*, March 15, 1905; HLM, *Happy Days*, p. vii.

7. Henry C. Rauch, "107 Year Story of Union Square: Cool Greenness and Relaxing Quiet Mark This Little West Baltimore Oasis," *BS*, Oct. 31, 1954; "Hollins Street: Literature, Invention, Church and Social Life Give Far-Reaching Distinction to Thoroughfare," *BS*, Sept. 9, 1921; HLM, "Autobiographical Notes, 1925," under the heading "My Father," p. 6, NYPL. August Mencken's stickpin and other items are at MdHS. "West Baltimore Street, As It Was and As It Is," *BS*, October 28, 1906; Beirne, *The Amiable Baltimoreans*, p. 208; Stenerson, *H. L. Mencken: Iconoclast From Baltimore*, p. 39; HLM, "Great Men," 1890, EPFL. Bismarck's mother, Louise Wilhelmine Mencken, from Leipzig, was born February 21, 1790, and married Carl Wilhelm Ferdinand von Bismarck at Schonhausen on July 7, 1806. See: "Menckeniana: Documents, Portraits, Clippings, Pictures and Maps 1650–1938," EPFL; Dr. Conrad Müller, *Bismarck's Mutter und ihre Ahner* (Berlin: Berlag von Martin Warned, 1909).

8. HLM, "The Next Fifty Years," editorial, *American Mercury*, April 1931, pp. 415–16; HLM, *Prejudices: Fifth Series*, pp. 240–43.

9. HLM, *"Happy Days*: Additions . . . ," p. 147, EPFL; *Ten Little Niggers* (New York: 1894), in "H. L. Mencken Music Books," EPFL. The use of this term was so pervasive that it even extended to candy. A "nigger-baby" was black licorice cast in the image of an infant. HLM, "Autobiographical Notes, 1941," EPFL.

10. August Mencken Sr. to L. J. Cornwall, Oct. 29, 1894, Feb. 20, 1895, in "August Mencken & Brothers Letter Book 1894–1895," EPFL. August Mencken, Sr. made it a practice to avoid doing business with anyone whose name "sounded very much like a Jew": Cohen, Rosenberg, or Roswald were "not a good risk." See Oct. 25, 1894, March 30, 1895, ibid.; HLM, "Autobiographical Notes, 1925," p. 182, EPFL.

11. Author interview with Calvin R. Mencken Jr., Nov. 8, 1999. The nephew was Arthur Mencken, his wife, Eva Lillian Behrens, and, as Mencken put it, "a dubious person." When she returned to Baltimore after Arthur's death, "she took to evil courses" and presently married again. Uncle Henry (brother of August Mencken Senior) took the children from her. Lillian eventually committed suicide by swallowing a lethal dose of carbolic acid. HLM, *"Happy Days*: Additions . . . ," p. 19, EPFL; "How I Got That Way as Told to Ruth Crawford by H. L. Mencken," United Press Syndicate, 1926.

12. HLM, *Happy Days*, p. 226; HLM, "Forty Years of Baltimore," *BES*, Oct. 11, 1926; HLM, "School Composition Books: F. Knapp's Institute, Baltimore, 1892," EPFL; George C. Comer, "Growing Up in Baltimore of Gaslights and Cobblestones," *BS Magazine*, May 21, 1978, p. 51.

13. "How the Skyline of Baltimore Has Changed," *BS*, Nov. 29, 1905; Crooks, *Politics and Progress*, pp. 3–5; "Sewer Project Revives Ghost of the Old Herald," *BES*, Dec. 22, 1948; James, *The American Scene*, p. 310.

14. U. R. Long, "A Mindseye View of Baltimore by a Transplanted New Englander," *Baltimore Sunday Herald*, Nov. 5, 1905; "How To Go To A Circus," *Baltimore American*, May 8, 1886; HLM, "School Composition Books F. Knapp's Institute, Baltimore 1892," EPFL; Hollander, *A Guide to the City of Baltimore*, p. 160; HLM, "The Free Lance," *BES*, Jan. 28, 1913; Owen Hatteras (HLM), *Smart Set*, July 1917, p. 62; Janvier, *Baltimore in the Eighties and Nineties*, p. 81; Janvier, *Baltimore Yesterdays*, pp. 105–6; Farrell, *The History of Baltimore's Streetcar*, pp. 59–68.

15. HLM, "School Composition Books F. Knapp's Institute, Baltimore 1892," EPFL; HLM to Raymond S. Tompkins, Aug. 4, 1937, EPFL; *Baltimore: Its History and Its People*, ed. Clayton Coleman Hall, pp. 274–75. H. L. Mencken, "Preface" in Janvier, *Baltimore Yesterdays*, p. viiii.

16. James B. Crooks, "Politics and Reform: The Dimensions of Baltimore Progressivism," *Maryland Historical Magazine*, Fall 1976, p. 424; U. R. Long, "A Mindseye View of Baltimore by a Transplanted New Englander," *Baltimore Sunday Herald*, Nov. 5, 1905. This article was most likely written by Mencken himself, who was fascinated by public health issues. In the piece, writing of his impressions, the author relates this dialogue:

> Turning to a friend I asked where it all came from.
> "Why, those are sewers," he said.
> "Yes," I said, "but where are the manholes? The water seem to be running down the street interminably."
> "Yes, that's right. Surface sewage."
> "Do you mean to say that all your sewage is above ground?" I asked.
> He replied in the affirmative, and my surprise may well be imagined. We have not a town in the North of 5000 inhabitants that has not an excellent sewage system. I could not understand it.
> "But how do people live?" I asked. "I should think that typhoid and malaria would get them by the thousands."
> "Oh," was the careless rejoinder, "We are used to it. We do not know anything else."

Charles C. Euchner, "The Politics of Urban Expansion: Baltimore and the Sewerage Question 1859–1905," *Maryland Historical Magazine*, Fall 1991, pp. 270–91; "Repair the Streets," editorial, *Critic*, Sept. 8, 1888.

17. Bruchey, "The Business Elite in Baltimore 1880–1914," p. 231, EPFL; HLM, "On Radical Professors," *BES*, July 20, 1936.

18. HLM, "On Radical Professors," *BES*, July 20, 1936; "Among the Trades," *Critic*, July 14, 1888; "An Important Meeting," *Critic*, July 28, 1888.

19. HLM, *Happy Days*, p. vii; "How It Turned Out," *BS*, Dec. 20, 1953; HLM to William Manchester, undated, 1947, EPFL; HLM, "Autobiographical Notes, 1925," p. 45, EPFL; Sally McDougall, "Mencken, The Perfect Husband," *New York World*, Aug. 17, 1930; "The Reminiscences of August Mencken," p. 31, COL.

20. James Cain, "Mr. M.," LC; HLM, *Happy Days*, pp. 7, 18; Mencken's baby clothes can be viewed at the MdHS; author interview with Admiral Conrad Abhau, Aug. 22, 1992, and letter, same date, from Admiral Conrad Abhau to the author; author interview with Ruth Goodman Goetz, March 4, 1992; HLM, "*Happy Days*: Additions . . . ," pp. 7, 110, EPFL; Carl Bode interview with Mrs. Hamilton Owens, Feb. 28, 1963, courtesy Gwinn Owens; "The Reminiscences of August Mencken," pp. 34–35, COL; HLM, "Typescripts of Early Fiction: 1889–1903," pp. 5a–6, EPFL.

21. HLM, *"Happy Days*: Additions . . . ," p. 20, EPFL; Bruchey, *The Development of Baltimore Business 1880–1914*, pp. 18–42; 144–60; HLM, *Happy Days*, pp. 234–5; Owen Hatteras (HLM), "Rosemary," *Smart Set*, July 1917, p. 60; Carpenter, *Carp's Washington*, p. 13; "Mencken's Glorious Saloon," *Santa Fe New Mexican*, Jan. 3, 1925.

22. HLM, "Composition Books: 1891–92," EPFL; Mencken's copy of *The Chatterbox* is dated 1887 and is among his childhood books at the HLM Collection, EPFL; HLM, "The Larval Stage of a Bookworm," *New Yorker*, Sept. 23, 1939, p. 28.

23. Ibid.; HLM, "Henry L. Mencken Calls *Times* His Professional 'Alma Mater,' " *Ellicott City Times*, March 17, 1941; HLM, "Autobiographical Notes, 1925," pp. 53–54, EPFL.

24. HLM to Gertrude Mencken, July 28, 1937, EPFL; HLM, "*Happy Days*: Additions . . . ," p. 122, EPFL; "How Christmas Day Was Observed," *BS*, December 26, 1888; Stricker, *Keeping Christmas: An Edwardian Age Memoir* (Owings Mills: Stemmer House, 1981). Preparations for Christmas began immediately after Thanksgiving. Anna Mencken made homemade ornaments. There was also a miniature replica of 1524 Hollins Street with gaily painted effigies of animals from Noah's ark. HLM, *Happy Days*, pp. 11, 106–7, 205; "*Happy Days*: Additions . . . ," p. 122, EPFL; HLM, "Memorials of Gormandizing," *New Yorker*, Aug. 26, 1939, pp. 26–33. Books cited in the text are inscribed "Christmas 1888," and are among Mencken's childhood books, EPFL.

25. HLM, *Happy Days*, pp. 166–67; "How Christmas Day Was Observed," *BS*, Dec. 26, 1888.

26. HLM, *Happy Days*, p. 167; HLM, "Autobiographical Notes, 1941," EPFL; HLM, "The Larval Stage of a Bookworm," *New Yorker*, Sept. 23, 1939, p. 32; Cooke, *The Vintage Mencken*, p. xi.

27. *Chamber's Encyclopaedia*, 1878 ed., is among Mencken's childhood books in the HLM Collection, EPFL. The book was bought and inscribed by August Mencken in 1879; *The Florence Stories: Excursions to the Orkney Islands* (New York: Sheldon & Co., 1868), EPFL. Mencken pasted a note to his own copy, which he purchased in 1941. HLM, *Happy Days*, p. 175; HLM, "The Ordeal of a Philosopher," *New Yorker*, April 11, 1939, p. 21.

28. HLM, *My Life*, p. 17, EPFL; HLM, "Autobiographical Notes, 1925," p. 60, EPFL; *The H. L. Mencken Baby Book*, Howard Markel, M. D., and Frank A. Oski, M. D., eds., pp. 112–13; HLM, "August and Anna Mencken and Their Children: Souvenirs," Vol. I. 1878–1920, pp. 64, 147, EPFL.

29. *Baltimore: Its History and Its People*, Hall, ed., pp. 281–282; HLM, *Happy Days*, pp. 70; 254–56; HLM, "The Ruin of an Artist," *New Yorker*, May 27, 1939, pp. 23–26; HLM, "Autobiographical Notes, 1925," p. 55, EPFL. See HLM, "*Happy Days*, Fair Copy, Corrected with Illustrations, Vol. II, 1940," p. 25, EPFL; Gilbert Sandler, "H. L. Mencken's Boyhood Refuge," *BS Magazine*, June 8, 1980, pp. 9–11; HLM, "August and Anna Margaret Abhau Mencken and Their Family: Photographs 1865–1936," EPFL; HLM to Edgar Lee Masters, Feb. 26, 1943, HRHRC; HLM to Jean Balch, Oct. 25, 1937, EPFL.

30. HLM, "Autobiographical Notes, 1925," p. 56, EPFL; Owen Hatteras (HLM), "Rosemary," *Smart Set*, Oct. 1917, p. 60; Otto Schoenrich to HLM, Feb. 8, 1950, EPFL; HLM, "The Novels That Bloom in the Spring, Tra-la!" *Smart Set*, April 1909, pp. 155–56; ibid., July, 1909, pp. 153–54. The book reviewed was Owen Johnson's *The Eternal Boy: Being the Story of the Prodigious Hickey* (New York: Dodd, Mead, 1909), the best book Mencken said he had read since *Huckleberry Finn*; Griffith, *Boy's Useful Pastimes* pp. 14–15, 32, 153–55, 322–23, EPFL; HLM, *Happy Days*, p. 17; HLM, "Autobiographical Notes, 1941," EPFL; Roderick Ryon, "East-Side Union Halls: Where Craft Workers Met, 1887–1917," *The Baltimore Book*, ed. Elizabeth Fee et al., p. 115.

Chapter 2: The Eternal Boy

1. HLM, *"Heathen Days*: Additions . . . ," pp. 37, 55, EPFL; HLM, "Health Demands Sewers and Schools," *Baltimore Morning Herald*, Jan. 8, 1901; "Minutes of Faculty Meetings of Baltimore Manual Training School, Oct. 18, 1892" p. 17, POLY; G. Norman Anderson, "I Remember . . . When Poly Was on Courtland Street," *BS Magazine*, March 28, 1954, p. 2; Griswold, *Baltimore Polytechnic Institute: The First Century*, pp. 6, 70; "Report of the President," *Poly Register, 1894*, pp. 97–98, POLY; "Boys Who Learn Trades," *BS*, March 6, 1889; HLM, *Heathen Days*, p. 47; "Faculty Minutes June 4, 1896," pp. 33–35, POLY; HLM to Berta Kaessmann and Miss Coplan, May 12, 1936, EPFL; Watson F. Pridell and Albert W. Dowling, "The First Mencken Work the Public Ever Saw," *BS Magazine*, Jan. 24, 1960, pp. 9–11.

2. Rows of index cards from the *BS* Index, in carefully rounded script, attest to "Baltimore Business Trouble," Maryland Collection, EPFL; Olson, *Baltimore*, pp. 228–30; HLM, "The State of the Nation," *BES*, Jan. 4, 1932; " 'Uncle Henry' Mencken Here Celebrating Niece's Graduation—and Talking," *Pittsburgh Sun Telegraph*, June 18, 1933. Mencken is only partially correct. A Citizens Central Relief Committee was organized in 1893, but the problem of coping with the crisis made charities keenly aware of their limitations; much of the population was left destitute. Hirschfeld, *Baltimore 1870–1900: Studies in Social History*, pp. 147–49; Samuel Rezneck, "Unemployment, Unrest, and Relief in the United States During the Depression of 1893–1897," *Journal of Political Economy*, 61; 1953, pp. 324–45.

3. Ginger, *Age of Excess*, p. 164; "August Mencken & Bro. Salesman's Commission Books 1887–1902," pp. 1, 192, EPFL; "August Mencken & Bro. Letterbook 1894–1895," EPFL; "Swept by the Flames," *Baltimore American*, Dec. 3, 1893; "A Mountain of Flame," *BS*, Dec. 3, 1893; "Ravaged by Flames," *Baltimore News*, Dec. 4, 1893; August Mencken to J. V. Eckenrode Harney, Nov. 12, 1894, "August Mencken & Bro. Letter Book: 1894–1895," EPFL; HLM, *Happy Days*, p. viii.

4. "Unable to Tell Why He Became Writer," *Buffalo Times*, Oct. 24, 1926; "Catalogue of Negatives Made by H. L. Mencken From Jan. 1, 1895 to —," in HLM, "School Composition Books, F. Knapp's Institute, Baltimore, 1892," EPFL; "Chemicals in Stock," ibid., EPFL; HLM, *My Life*, pp. 20–23, EPFL.

5. Louis Fabian Bachrach to HLM, April 18, 1943, EPFL; HLM, *"Heathen Days:* Additions . . . ," p. 40, EPFL; "The Reminiscences of August Mencken," p. 45, COL; HLM, *My Life*, p. 26, EPFL; HLM, "The Life of an Athlete," *New Yorker*, June 9, 1939, p. 270; Pat Frayne, "Boxing Best Sport, Golf, None—Mencken," *San Francisco Call*, Nov. 18, 1926 (Mencken recalled, "My brother and I used to fight with gloves, my father used to referee"); HLM, *Thirty-Five Years*, p. 504, EPFL; HLM to Virginia Mencken Jan. 16, 1933, EPFL.

6. The Orioles' combination of ferocity, skill, and trickery won them three championships during the 1890s. Mencken's idol was Henny Reitz, second baseman. The most pugnacious Oriole was third baseman John Joseph McGraw, whose swearing prompted the National League to issue a ruling called "A Measure for the Suppression of Obscene, Indecent and Vulgar Language Upon the Ball Field." McGraw paid little attention to it: if he had to stop cursing, he said, he would have to "abandon the profession entirely." See Bready, *The First 100 Years: Baseball in Baltimore*; Ward, *Baseball: An Illustrated History*; "Sam Trott Discusses the Good Old Days of the National Game," *BS*, Sept. 2, 1906; "Old Time Baseball in Baltimore," Letters, *BES*, July 29, 1954; James Bready, "Play Ball! The Legacy of Nineteenth Century Baltimore Baseball," *Maryland Historical Magazine*, Summer 1992, pp. 127–45; "Champions Welcomed: Thousands Greet Them," *Baltimore American*, Oct. 3, 1894; HLM, *"Happy Days*: Additions . . . ," p. 231, EPFL.

7. "Strike Ordered in the East," "Stern Warning to Strikers," "Labor Leaders Threaten," *NYT*, July 9, 1894; Howard, *First Annual Report of the Bureau of Industrial Statistics of Maryland*, pp. 80–83; 200–204, 210–14; "August Mencken & Bro. Salesman's Commission Books 1887–1902," pp. 1,16, EPFL; HLM, *"Happy Days*: Additions . . . ," p. 248, EPFL; August Mencken to

"Chris," Feb. 11, Feb. 18, 1895 and to William Opdyke, April 10, 1895, "August Mencken & Bro. Letterbook 1894–1895," EPFL. Letters were sent on a daily basis, fifteen or more in one day. Phrases such as "We are very short of money," "We need all the money we can get," "Collections are almost nothing" were a constant refrain; in the worst cases, August threatened to collect payment through a solicitor, "though it would grieve me to do this." See letters dated Oct. 24, 1894; Oct. 25, 1894; Nov. 3, 1894; Nov. 7, 1894; Dec. 24, 1894; March 2, 1895; March 11, 1895. "Baltimore Business Trouble," *BS* Index at the Maryland Room, EPFL; HLM to William Manchester, Aug. 13, 1948, EPFL.

8. *Manual Training School in Baltimore: Preparatory Department, Second Year*, Vol. 2, POLY; "Eight Members of Poly's Smallest Class Celebrate Their Golden Anniversary," *BS*, June 26, 1947; HLM, *My Life*, pp. 22, 27, EPFL; HLM, "Resolved: That City Life Better Than Country Life, Lutheran Church Sunday School, December 8, 1895," in HLM, "Earliest Attempts at Verse and Prose Manuscripts 1895–1901," p. 48, EPFL.

9. "Brother Proud of Mencken's Beer-Drinking, But Cares Little About His Word-Juggling," *Baltimore Post*, Aug. 15, 1932; HLM, "The Ruin of an Artist," *New Yorker*, May 27, 1939, p. 24; Howard B. Bennett to HLM, Dec. 19, 1955, EPFL; *One Hundred Years of Baltimore City College*, p. 187; HLM, *My Life*, pp. 134–35, EPFL; Goldberg, *The Man Mencken*, pp. 87–88; "Entertainments: Polytechnic Institute," *BS*, Dec. 21, 1895; *The Green Bay, Baltimore City College* pp. 24–25; Owen Hatteras (HLM), "Rosemary," *Smart Set*, Oct. 1917, p. 59.

10. HLM, "Memoir of Deceased Pedagogues," *New Yorker*, June 3, 1939, p. 31; "Repetition Generale," *Smart Set*, June 1920, p. 48; Major Owen Hatteras (HLM), "Meditation," *Smart Set*, April 1919, pp. 97–99; W. L. D. Bell (HLM), "A Panorama of Women," *Smart Set*, June 1915, p. 278; HLM, *Ventures Into Verse*, annotated by HLM for Joseph Hergesheimer in 1932, p. 27, HRHRC.

11. "Things Seen and Heard in Good Old Baltimore," *BS*, March 8, 1908; Ziff, *The American 1890s*, p. 165; HLM, "Introduction to Stephen Crane," *Major Conflicts in the Work of Stephen Crane*, Wilson Follett, ed., pp. x–xi; HLM, *Newspaper Days*, pp. 59–60.

12. HLM, *Newspaper Days*, pp. 59–60; "Idyl" was Mencken's first attempt at fiction, written one evening on March 28, 1896. HLM, "Earliest Attempts at Verse and Prose Manuscripts 1895–1901," pp. 37, 38–43, EPFL. There were six home games against New York that summer; see *Baltimore News-American*, May 26, July 1, July 2, Aug. 6–8, 1896.

13. HLM, "Childhood and Schooldays 1880–1896," p. 67, EPFL; David S. Thaler, "H. L. Mencken in the Baltimore Polytechnic Institute," *Baltimore Engineer*, Dec. 1983, p. 4.

14. Ziff, *The American 1890s*, p. 165; Julian Street, "Anecdotes, Memories and Childhood," Princeton/fire; HLM, "Editorial," *American Mercury*, March 1924, p. 248.

15. HLM, "Childhood and Schooldays . . . ," pp. 66–67, EPFL; "Faculty Minutes June 4, 1896," pp. 33–34, POLY; Albert W. Dowling, "H. L. Mencken's Bow as an Orator," *BS*, June 19, 1966; HLM, *My Life*, p. 30, EPFL; Kelly, *Bygone Baltimore*, pp. 127–33; "Ford's Grand Opera House," *BS*, Jan. 26, 1964. HLM learned to operate a typewriter in 1889; his father had an early No. 2 Remington in his office. HLM, "Autobiographical Notes, 1925," p. 201, EPFL. Various stages of the text of Mencken's speech, including the handwritten and typewritten versions, are in HLM, "Souvenirs of Childhood and Schooldays 1880–1896," pp. 55–59, EPFL; HLM, *"Heathen Days*: Additions . . . ," p. 56, EPFL; "Three Rules for Life," *Baltimore American*, June 24, 1896.

Chapter 3: August Mencken and Bro.

1. Janvier, *Baltimore in the Eighties and Nineties*, p. 98; HLM, "The Cobbles: A Ballad of Baltimore, 1897," in HLM, "Earliest Attempts at Verse and Prose Manuscripts 1895–1909," p. 16, EPFL; John S. Spruance Jr., "Mencken, Serene at 60, Foresees Third Term," *Washington Star*, Jan. 28, 1940.

2. HLM, *"Newspaper Days*: Additions . . . ," p. 4, EPFL; author interview with Elise Cheslock, Jan. 21, 1994, who heard the stories from Henry and August Mencken; HLM, *Happy Days*, pp. 248–50.

3. HLM, *"Happy Days*: Additions. . . . ," p. 250, EPFL; "Mencken Calls for 3.6 Beer in 5C Schooners," *Chicago Tribune*, Sept. 27, 1933; HLM, "Autobiographical Notes, 1925," pp. 39–40, EPFL.

4. HLM, "Autobiographical Notes, 1925," p. 47, EPFL; HLM, *"Newspaper Days*: Additions . . . ," p. 4, EPFL; HLM to William Manchester, undated, ca. 1947, EPFL; HLM, "Autobiographical Notes, 1925," p. 81, EPFL; "August Mencken & Bro., Salesmen's Commission Books, 1887–1912," pp. 240–43, EPFL.

5. HLM, *My Life*, p. 32, EPFL; Janvier, *Baltimore Yesterdays*, pp. 138–39; HLM, *"Happy Days*: Additions . . . ," p. 194, EPFL; Sigmund Spaeth, "Coon Songs," *Read 'Em and Weep: The Songs You Forgot to Remember*, pp. 226–27. Another hit, from 1896, was entitled "All Coons Look Alike to Me."

6. HLM, "Introduction," to "August Mencken & Bro., Salesmen's Commission Books, 1887–1902," p. 3, EPFL; HLM, "The Pimlico Road," *BES*, June 22, 1910; HLM, *Thirty-Five Years*, pp. 466–67, EPFL; Fred C. Kelly, "The Great Bicycle Craze," *American Heritage*, Dec. 1956, pp. 69–73; HLM, "Autobiographical Notes, 1941," EPFL; HLM, *"Happy Days*: Additions. . . . ," p. 225, EPFL. The verse on quarrelling sweethearts was written July 1896; HLM, "Earliest Attempts at Verse and Prose Manuscripts, 1895–1901," p. 8, EPFL.

7. Mencken, *"Heathen Days*: Additions. . . . ," p. v, EPFL; "Serenade," written in 1897, in HLM, "Earliest Attempts at Verse and Prose Manuscripts, 1895–1901," p. 14, EPFL; "A Song of Advice," "Till We Meet Again," and "Fidelis ad Urnum," ibid., pp. 17, 24, EPFL; HLM, "The Literary Heavyweight Champion," *Smart Set*, March 1910, p. 158; Wedekind, *The Awakening of Spring*, trans. Francis J. Ziegler, pp. 72–73, 118; HLM, *Happy Days*, p. 187; "Youth Unchanged, Says H. L. Mencken," *Philadelphia Public Ledger*, Dec. 11, 1931; HLM to Edgar Lee Masters, June 2, 1931, HRHRC; HLM to Philip Goodman, Oct. 4, 1918, EPFL.

8. "7:05 PM—What They Were Doing: This Is Hollins Street," *BS*, Aug. 8, 1942. August Mencken Jr. said the cast iron fountain at Union Square was always full of moths; HLM, *Happy Days*, p. 66; HLM, "Autobiographical Notes, 1925," "My Reading," p. 4, NYPL; HLM, "Autobiographical Notes, 1941," EPFL.

9. Shuman, *Steps Into Journalism*, pp. vii–viii, 92–93; HLM, "Autobiographical Notes, 1941," EPFL; HLM to Blanche Knopf, Aug. 4, 1937, HRHRC; HLM, "From a Notebook Begun in 1898 or Thereabouts" in HLM, "Early Newspaper and Magazine Work 1899–1905," pp. 51–59, EPFL; HLM, "Earliest Attempts at Verse and Prose Manuscripts 1895–1901," pp. 26–29, 58, EPFL; HLM, *"Newspaper Days*: Additions . . . ," p. 4, EPFL.

10. HLM, *My Life*, p. 41, EPFL. *Criterion* was not the only magazine with racist undertones. There was a very strong element of anti-Semitism in the illustrations of *M'lle New York*. See Rascoe, "Introduction," *The Smart Set* Anthology, ed. Burton Rascoe and Groff Conklin, pp. xx; Darrell I. Drucker Jr., *The Genteel Rebellion: A Study of Journalistic Impressionism in Terms of Its Audience, 1880 to 1920* (thesis, University of Minnesota, 1956); HLM, *Prejudices: First Series*, p. 129; "A Critic Too Far Ahead of His Time," *Current Literature*, March 1912, pp. 339–40.

11. HLM, "Books for the Hammock and Deck Chair," *Smart* Set, June 1901, p. 153. For more information on Huneker's influence, see Sinclair Lewis, *Diary 1906–1907*, June 11, 1907, YALE; Maxwell Perkins to Joseph Huneker, June 4, 1929, PRIN/fire; Schwab, *James Gibbons Huneker*, pp. 196–97; George Kummer, *Percival Pollard: Precursor of the Twenties* (PhD diss., New York University, September 1946); Pollard, *Their Day in Court*, p. 337; HLM, *"Happy Days*: Additions. . . . ," p. 192, EPFL.

12. Arthur M. Chase to HLM, June 16, 1898, in HLM, "Earliest Attempts at Verse and Prose Manuscripts 1895–1901" pp. 71, 73, 75, EPFL; HLM, "Childhood and Schooldays,

1880–96," p. 81, EPFL; HLM, *My Life*, pp. 38–39, EPFL; "An Alley Case," written Sept. 4, 1898, HLM, "Earliest Attempts at Verse and Prose Manuscripts 1895–1901," p. 79, EPFL.

13. "War Revenue Measure: Beer and Tobacco Will Bear The Heaviest Burdens," *BS*, April 23, 1898; "Foreign Trade Relations," *BS*, April 28, 1898; Willis N. Baer, *The Economic Development of the Cigar Industry in the United States*, p. 138; HLM, "*Newspaper Days*: Additions . . . ," p. 4, EPFL; Mark Twain, *The Complete Travel Books of Mark Twain*, Charles Neider, ed., p. 27; H. L. Mencken, "*Happy Days*: Additions . . . ," p. 221, EPFL.

14. "When the Night Cometh," written at the end of 1898, HLM, "Earliest Attempts at Verse and Prose Manuscripts 1895–1901," p. 27, EPFL; "Weather," *BS*, December 31, 1898; HLM, "*Happy Days*: Additions . . . ," pp. 108, 122. For accompanying me during the re-creation of that uphill, eleven-block trot I am grateful to Vince Fitzpatrick, curator of the HLM Collection at the EPFL, who guided me to various sites in Baltimore. For an account of New Year's Eve celebrations in Mencken's Baltimore, see HLM, "The Free Lance," *BES*, Jan. 1, 1914, and *BS*, Jan 1, 1937.

15. HLM, "*Newspaper Days*: Additions . . . ," p. 1, EPFL; "In and About Town: Almanac for Baltimore on This Day," *BS*, Jan. 2, Jan. 11, 1899; "107 Year History of Union Square," *BS*, Oct. 31, 1954; HLM to William Manchester, Aug. 13, 1948, EPFL; HLM, "*Happy Days*: Additions . . . ," p. vii, EPFL.

16. "Government Weather Report," *BS*, Jan. 13, Jan. 14, 1899; HLM to William Manchester, Aug. 13, 1948, EPFL; August Mencken Obituary, *BS*, Jan. 14, 1899; HLM, "*Newspaper Days*: Additions . . . ," pp. 1, 4, EPFL; HLM to Edgar Lee Masters, Jan. 15, 1940, NYPL; HLM, Diary, Jan. 13, 1946, EPFL.

17. "*Record King David's Lodge No. 68 1891–*," pp. 471, 479. For permission to examine the album I am indebted to Mr. Thomas Butterbaugh, secretary of the King David Lodge, Baltimore, who let me view it on Oct. 4, 1993; funeral notice for August Mencken Sr., *BS*, Jan. 16, 1899, and *Baltimore American*, Jan. 17, 1899. H. L. Mencken's own grave is facing east, toward the rising sun.

18. HLM to Miss Mullen, April 9, 1936, ALA; HLM, "Preface," *Newspaper Days*, p. ix. There has been some confusion as to whether Mencken went to the *Herald* the day after his father's funeral or two weeks later; Mencken gave conflicting versions. Mencken's first written recollection of the event, which he prepared for his biographer Isaac Goldberg in 1925, puts it at two weeks after his father's death, and it is clear to this biographer that this is the more reliable account. Mencken admitted his recollections in *Newspaper Days* contained "occasional stretchers." See HLM, "Autobiographical Notes, 1925," Isaac Goldberg Papers, NYPL/ms.

Chapter 4: Baltimore and Beyond

1. Paul Winchester and Frank D. Webb, *Newspapers and Newspaper Men of Maryland*, pp. 24, 144; "Morning Herald Days Recalled," *Baltimore Press*, April 28, 1932; HLM, "Confidential: To The Literary Editor," *BES*, Oct. 9, 1920; HLM, "*Newspaper Days*: Additions . . . ," p. 154, EPFL; HLM, *Newspaper Days*, pp. 5–6.

2. "To Be Cold All Week," *BS*, Feb. 2, 1899; "Ice in the Streets," *BS*, Feb. 4, 1899; "Tip-Top Sleighing," "Snow a Surprise," *BS*, Feb. 6, 1899; "Still More Snow," *BS*, Feb. 7, 1899; "Zero in Baltimore," "The Cold Snap," "News of the Shipping," *BS*, Feb 10, 1899; "Coldest on Record," "Was Nearly Frozen," "Caught in the Ice," *BS*, Feb. 11, 1899; "Buried in Snow," "Street Railway Troubles," "16.6. Inches for Eight Days," "The Bay Ice-Bound," *BS*, Feb. 13, 1899; "Worst Blizzard Ever Known Here: Business Paralyzed and Travel Suspended While a Fierce Storm Rages 15.5 Inches Snow in a Day," *BS*, Feb. 14, 1899; "Overcome by Cold," "Business at Standstill," "Summary of News," "Railroads Blocked," "All Lines Tied Up," "Trouble of Householders," "The Demand for Aid," "The Storm of Storms," *BS*, Feb. 14, 1899. HLM, *Newspaper Days*, pp. xi, 6; HLM, "Autobiographical Notes 1925," p. 160, EPFL.

By the time Mencken ventured forth, the city was still blanketed with ice. See "Now for a Thaw," "A City, Shrouding Snow," "Frozen Man Found in Home," "Clearing Away the Snow," *BS*, Feb. 15, 1899.

3. HLM, *Newspaper Days*, pp. 6, 9; HLM to Edward Bierce, Sept. 14, 1940, NYPL.

4. HLM, "Reminiscence," *BES*, Jan. 10, 1927; "Scene Along the Waterfront," *Baltimore News*, Aug. 1, 1918; Hall, *Baltimore: Its History and Its People*, Vol. I, pp. 326–29; HLM, "Early News Stories: Baltimore Morning Herald 1899–1901," EPFL; HLM, "Germany's Attitude," *Baltimore Morning Herald*, April 30, 1899.

5. HLM, *Newspaper Days*, pp. v, 11–12, 18–19; HLM, "Days of Innocence: Slaves of Beauty," *New Yorker*, March 1, 1941, pp. 18–20; James M. Barrett, "The Good Old Days," NBC Radio, April 10, 1935, EPFL; HLM to Bernard De Voto, Jan. 2, 1941, HOOV; Julian Street, "When We Were Rather Young," *Saturday Evening Post*, Aug. 30, 1932, pp. 14–15, 43–44, 46.

6. Shepherd, *The America of George Ade 1866–1947*, p. 15; HLM, "The Burden of Humor," *Smart Set*, Feb. 1913, p. 154; Ade, *Fables in Slang*, pp. 115, 151; HLM, "Two Journalists," *American Mercury*, Dec. 1924, pp. 505–7; Mitchell, *Memoirs of an Editor*, pp. 129–372; Ziff, *The American 1890s*, pp. 146–65. Closely examined, *Sun* editorials from 1890 to 1905 anticipate Mencken's syntax and tone. See *Casual Essays of the Sun*, especially pp. 205–65 for its examination of American slang terms; for subjects Mencken used in his own editorials, see pp. 266–341.

7. "Max Ways as H. L. Mencken Knew Him," *BES*, June 5, 1923; HLM, "Health Inspectors Trying to Correct Existing Evils," written for the *Baltimore Morning Herald* July–September 1899 in HLM, "Early News Stories Baltimore Morning Herald 1899–1901," pp. 43–45, EPFL; HLM, "Autobiographical Notes, 1941," EPFL. In 1884, immigrant Jews, mostly from Russia, began arriving in Baltimore. By the time Mencken was visiting their tenements, the city had become an important port of entry for all immigrants entering the U.S., and by 1900, the Russian and Polish immigrants were second in numerical importance to the German-born in Baltimore. "Russo-Polish Hebrews: The Colony of Baltimore," *BS*, Jan. 3, 1889; Hirschfeld, *Baltimore 1870–1900*, pp. 23–25; HLM, *Newspaper Days*, p. 74.

8. HLM, *Newspaper Days*, p. 39; HLM, "*Happy Days*: Additions . . . ," p. 13, EPFL; HLM to William Manchester, Nov. 17, 1948, EPFL; HLM, "On Hanging," *BES*, Nov. 25, 1910; HLM, "Mercy for the Merciless," *BES*, Dec. 25, 1938; HLM, "Pillars of Flame," "Thousands Heard the Story of the Election, News of McKinley Victory," in HLM, "Early News Stories Baltimore Morning Herald 1899–1901," pp. 176, 177; "Democrats Jubilant: The Centre of the City Filled With Shouting Throngs," *BS*, Nov. 8, 1899; "Torchlight Parade," *BS*, November 6, 1899; HLM, *Newspaper Days*, pp. 66, 180–81.

9. HLM, "End of Ninety-Nine: Today Is the First Day of the New Year," *Baltimore Morning Herald*, Jan. 1, 1900; HLM, "*Heathen Days*: Additions . . . ," p. v, EPFL; Lord, *The Good Years*, p. 1; HLM, "*Happy Days*: Additions . . . ," p. 94, EPFL.

Chapter 5: Terse and Terrible Texts

1. HLM, *My Life*, p. 43, EPFL; "The Baltimore Herald," *BES*, Feb. 22, 1937; HLM, "An Overdose of Novels," *Smart Set*, Dec. 1911, p. 152; HLM, "Zola," *Smart Set*, Aug. 1912, p. 154. Mencken hung on to his cherished Kipling volumes for the rest of his life. Unlike some of the volumes at the HLM Collection, each page is cut and worn, a testament to his heavy reading of the volumes. Kipling's *The Seven Seas* was inscribed by Mencken for Arthur Hawks, "Xmas 1902"; shown to the author in her interview with Marshall Wiley Hawks, Aug. 17, 1990; Douglas C. Stenerson, "Mencken's Early Newspaper Experience: The Genesis of a Style," *American Literature*, May 1965, pp. 153–66; "When HLM Was Sweet," *(Norfolk) Virginian Pilot*, June 16, 1926; HLM, "Early Newspaper and Magazine Work 1892–1905," pp. 1–12, 51–61, EPFL.

2. HLM, "10, 700 Deaths Last Year: Statistics of the Health Department Show an Increase Over 1899," *Baltimore Morning Herald*, Jan. 8, 1901; HLM, "Autobiographical Notes, 1925," p. 160, EPFL; Johnston, *Jamaica: The New Riviera, A Pictorial Description*, p. 17; Glenn O. Philips, "Maryland and the Caribbean, 1634–1984, Some Highlights," *Maryland Historical Magazine*, Fall 1988, p. 212; HLM, *Prejudiuces: Fourth Series*, pp. 300–1; HLM to Henry Louis Wilson, Oct. 25, 1911, PRIN/fire; HLM, "At the Edge of the Spanish Main," *Baltimore Morning Herald*, Aug. 26, 1900; HLM to Gertrude Mencken, July 11, 1900, EPFL.

3. HLM to Gertrude Mencken, July 11, 1900, EPFL; HLM, "Seen on the Streets of Kingston," *Baltimore Morning Herald*, Sept. 4, 1900; William George Paul, "*The Shadow of Equality: The Negro in Baltimore 1864–1911*" (PhD diss., University of Wisconsin, 1972), pp. 263–64; Randall Beirne, "The Impact of Black Labor on European Immigration Into Baltimore's Old Town 1790–1910," *Maryland Historical Magazine*, Winter 1988, pp. 331–345; J. D. B. Jarvis [H. L. Mencken], "A Recent Crucifixion in Jamaica," *Pittsburgh Press*, Sept. 16, 1900; HLM, "The Fear of the Savage," "When Magic Met Muscle," from HLM, "Typescripts of Early Fiction," pp. 78–88; 96–114, EPFL; HLM, "Early Newspaper and Magazine Work 1899–1905," pp. 46–48, EPFL; HLM to Jean Allen Balch, Feb. 18, 1936, EPFL; T. L. Roxburgh and Joseph C. Ford, *Handbook of Jamaica 1900* (London: Edward Stanford, 1900), in the H. L. Mencken Collection at the EPFL. The flower can be found on p. 115, leaf on p. 63. Outlines of other plants, now gone, remain on pp. 21 and 48–49; HLM, "Autobiographical Notes, 1925," pp. 160–61, EPFL.

4. Douglas C. Stenerson, "Mencken's Early Newspaper Experience: The Genesis of a Style," *American Literature*, May 1965, pp. 153–66; HLM, "Rhyme and Reason," *Baltimore Morning Herald*, Nov. 4, 1900; Yates, *The American Humorist*, p. 35.

5. HLM, "Autumn Is Here," undated, autumn 1900, from *Baltimore Morning Herald*, HLM, "Early News Stories 1899–1901," p. 172, EPFL; HLM, "Riding For Fun," undated, summer 1900, *Baltimore Morning Herald*, ibid., p. 165, EPFL; HLM, *Newspaper Days*, pp. x, 408; Winchester and Webb, *Newspapers and Newspaper Men of Maryland*, p. 144; HLM, *My Life*, pp. 48–49, EPFL.

6. Judge Oscar Lesser to HLM, May 15, 1937, EPFL; HLM to Betty Hanes July 14, 1939, UNC; HLM, "*Newspaper Days*: Additions . . . ," p. 220, EPFL; HLM, "The Free Lance," *BES*, Oct. 2, 1915.

7. HLM, "*Newspaper Days*: Additions . . . ," p. 307, EPFL; HLM, "The Bend in the Tube," *Red Book*, February 1905, pp. 496–97; HLM, "*Newspaper Days*: Additions . . . ," p. 154, EPFL. A picture of "the preposterous Peard" can be found in *Men of Maryland: A Collection of Portraits of Representative Men in Business and Professional Life in the State of Maryland* (Baltimore: Journalists Club, 1905), p. 56; HLM, "Henry L. Mencken Calls *Times* His Professional Alma Mater," *Ellicott City Times*, March 17, 1941; John S. Spruance Jr., "Mencken, Serene at 60, Foresees Third Term," *Washington Star*, Jan. 28, 1940.

8. HLM, "A Footnote on Journalism, From the View-Point of a Workman in the Ranks," *Optimist*, March 1901, pp. 39–44. As for the "cheerful do-gooders":

> They address themselves, very often, to "the young journalist," and with solemnity and many wise maxims, tell him that his work is as important as the labors of a member of Congress. When he comes to the end of the batch of theories he goes to the cashier's window in the business office of his paper and draws his week's salary—$15. What, in the name of all that is true and beautiful, does he care for the mission of the press? He is but human, like the rest of us, and his own individual future is of more interest to him than the future of such a great, unwieldy, clumsy abstraction as that represented by the world. It requires no philosopher to tell him this. Axioms need not be repeated. He knows that, in the ordinary cause of events, publishers will continue to make profits long after he is dead and forgotten. The problem with which he is doomed to wrestle is the problem as

to whether or not the great engine which moves the world will give him, in the years to come, enough money and glory to compensate him for his services as tender of its fires. (Ibid.)

HLM, *My Life*, pp. 46, 50, EPFL; HLM, "Early Newspaper and Magazine Work 1899–1905," notes dated 1895–1900, pp. 1–12, and pp. 51–61 entitled "Notebook of ideas for stories," EPFL.

　　9. HLM, *Ventures Into Verse* (Baltimore: Marshall, Beek and Gordon, 1903), annotated by H. L. Mencken and given to Joseph Hergesheimer, pp. 28, 45, HRHRC.

Chapter 6: Plays and Players

　　1. HLM, "The Shame of Shorty Ferguson," *Syracuse Evening Herald*, Feb. 27, 1902; HLM, "Baltimore and the Rest of the World," *Baltimore Morning Herald*, Feb. 9, 1902; HLM to Bertha B. Carter, July 24 and Oct. 2, 1942, EPFL; HLM, *Newspaper Days*, pp. 111–12.

　　2. Schwab, *James Gibbons Huneker*, pp. 143–44. The article cited was written by James Huneker in the *New York Sun* for Oct. 18, 1903.

　　3. HLM, *My Life*, pp. 61–62, EPFL; HLM to Dr. A. E. Zucker, Feb. 12, 1941, EPFL; Schwab, *James Gibbons Huneker*, p. 138; HLM, *Newspaper Days*, pp. 120, 122; HLM, "Concerning Hendrik Ibsen's Play, 'Ghosts,' and Its Author," *Baltmore Sunday Herald*, Nov. 2, 1902; HLM, "The Production of Ghosts," *Baltimore Sunday Herald*, Nov. 9, 1902; Mary Shaw, "As To Ibsen and His Play," *Baltimore Sunday Herald*, Nov. 9, 1902.

　　4. HLM, "The Production of 'Ghosts,'" *Baltimore Sunday Herald*, Nov. 9 and 16, 1902; William Faversham, "Baltimore Audiences," *New York Herald*, March 13, 1907; "Ibsen's Morbid and Gruesome Drama," *Baltimore American*, Nov. 12, 1902; "Letters Objecting to Ibsen's Drama," *Baltimore News*, Nov. 13, 1902; "Plays and Players," *Baltimore News*, Nov. 12, 1902; HLM to Dr. A. E. Zucker, Feb. 12, 1941, EPFL; Margaret Georgia Fawcett, "I Remember . . . When Ibsen's Realism Shocked Baltimore," *BS Magazine*, April 7, 1957, p. 2; HLM, *Heathen Days*, p. 66.

　　5. Tom Doerer, "Chasing Copy for Henry L. Mencken No Picnic," *Maryland Delaware Press-News*, May 1966 in "H. L. Mencken Clippings," EPFL; HLM, *Heathen Days*, p. 66; *Baltimore Sunday Herald*, Nov. 30, 1902; HLM to J. T. Belt, Feb. 12, 1940, NYPL; *Guide to the City of Baltimore*, pp. 48–49.

　　6. HLM, *My Life*, pp. 36–37, 74–75, EPFL; Elmer Adler, editor, *Breaking Into Print*, pp. 141, 143–45; Charles Gordon, "Ventures Into Verse," *Menckeniana*, Summer, 1964, p. 7; Betty Adler, *A Census of Ventures Into Verse*, p. 20; HLM to Joseph Hergesheimer in his copy of *Ventures Into Verse*, pp. 3, 14, HRHRC; author interview with Marshall Wiley Hawks, Aug. 17, 1990; Charles Mencken to Gertrude Mencken, July 16, 1903 EPFL; author interview with Arthur Gutman, March 22, 2003; HLM to Fred Munson, March 14, 1932, EPFL.

　　7. Alexander Geddes to August Mencken, June 11, 1937, EPFL; HLM, "Car Riding for Fun: How Baltimoreans Enjoy Themselves in Summer," from HLM, "Early News Stories Baltimore Morning Herald 1899–1901," p. 165; Farrell, *The History of Baltimore Streetcars*, pp. 241–48; author interview with Olga Owens, March 22, 1985; HLM, "*Newspaper Days*: Additions . . . ," p. 293, EPFL; HLM to Edgar Lee Masters, August 11 and 18, 1934, HRHRC.

　　8. HLM, "A Chat with Miss Kline," *Baltimore Morning Herald*, Oct. 3, 1904; HLM, "The Shame of Shorty Ferguson," *Syracuse Evening Herald*, Feb. 27, 1902; "The Belasco Theater," *Los Angeles Examiner*, Nov. 14, 1908; "Virginia Kline," *New York Mirror*, May 14, 1910, and *New Jersey Telegraph*, July 31, 1907; HLM, typewritten note in the poetry section of "Autobiographical Notes, 1925" in the Isaac Goldberg Papers, NYPL/ms; James H. Bready, "Saturday Night Club Plays Last Notes; Donates All Music to Pratt Library," *BES*, Dec. 27,

1950; HLM, "Autobiographies and Sketches of the Vagabonds, First Annual Reunion, New Year's Eve, 1905, Hotel Caswell, Baltimore, Maryland," p. 16, EPFL.

9. HLM to Lynn W. Meekins, Nov. 7, 1933, EPFL; Meekins to HLM, April 27, 1926. See Appendix LVII, The Hatrack Case 1916–1927, Vol. VIII, p. 60, EPFL; HLM, *Newspaper Days*, p. 16 and item cited in *Reader's Digest*, Sept. 1957. When it came to hiring women, Mencken may have recognized that local rival newspapers were well ahead of the *Herald*. See Ross, *Ladies of the Press*, pp. 493–500; Otto Schoenrich to HLM, Dec. 23, 1941, EPFL.

10. HLM, *Newspaper Days*, pp. 167–68; HLM, *My Life*, p. 52, EPFL; HLM, "Autobiographical Notes, 1925," p. 3, NYPL.

11. HLM, *Newspaper Days*, pp. 140–41; HLM, "*Newspaper Days*: Additions . . . ," p. 74, EPFL; HLM, *My Life*, p. 75 1/2, EPFL; Ellery Sedgewick to HLM, Feb. 9, 1904, NYPL.

12. "Weather: Mercury Above Freezing," *BS*, Feb. 6, 1904; Paul Winchester and Frank D. Webb, *Newspapers and Newspaper Men of Maryland*, p. 15; see *Baltimore Morning Herald*, Feb. 7, 1904 and *BS*, Feb. 7–8, 1904; HLM, *Newspaper Days*, p. 276.

Chapter 7: The Great Baltimore Fire

1. HLM, *Newspaper Days*, pp. 276–278; Paul Winchester and Frank D. Webb, *Newspapers and Newspaper Men of Maryland*, p. 15; "When the Big Fire Hit Baltimore," *BS*, Feb. 5, 1928; Harry Lee Hoffman Jr., "I Remember . . . The Sunday of the Fire," *BS Magazine*, Feb. 1, 1976, p. 7; Dr. Robert H. Brotman, "Fleeing the Great Baltimore Fire of 1904," *BS*, Feb. 6, 1966; Williams, *Baltimore Afire*, pp. 11, 17; "The Best Pictures of 1904," *BS Magazine*, Feb. 7. 1954, p.15. Additional photographs can be viewed at the Maryland Room of the EPFL and at MdHS. For a chronology, see Peterson, *The Great Baltimore Fire*, pp. xiv–xv.

2. "32 Years After the Big Fire, City Prepared and Safe," *BES*, Feb. 7, 1936; "Last Night in Baltimore," *New York Evening Post*, Feb. 9, 1904; Olson, *Baltimore*, p. 246; "The Work of Firemen," *Baltimore American*, Feb. 9, 1904; "Cold Wave Here To Add to Fire's Horrors," *Baltimore American*, Feb. 9, 1904. When the fire started, the wind was not blowing a gale, as previously reported; it was not over 30 mph. Aiding the breeze was an artificial wind created by the burning buildings. Hot air was driven upwind, ahead of the fire, which had much to do with the spread of the flames. Author interview with Robert Cobb, battalion chief of the Jersey City, New Jersey Fire Department and contributing editor of *Firehouse Magazine*, July 5, 2002; Ray Allen Willey, "Lessons of the Fire," *Scientific American*, March 12, 1904, p. 218. The Philadelphia firemen discovered the Baltimore firemen were fighting the flames from the side and rear. The fire chief from Philadelphia ordered his men to fight it from the front in order to head off the flames. "Fought Fire from the Front," *BS*, Feb. 9, 1904; "Returning Firemen Criticize Baltimoreans," *Philadelphia Inquirer*, Feb. 9, 1904; Arline Chase, "Hell Loosed in the Streets of Baltimore," *Firehouse Magazine*, Sept. 1981, p. 104; William J. Fryer, "Lessons of the Baltimore Disaster," *American Monthly Review of Reviews*, Dec. 5, 1904, pp. 303–4; "Leveling the Ruins," *BS*, Feb. 9, 1904. In their effort not to place blame, the *Baltimore Herald* questioned whether *any* firefighter could have done more in light of the wind, which blew in every direction. See "Our Firemen All Right," *Baltimore Morning Herald*, Feb. 12, 1904; "To See Ourselves As Others See Us," ibid., Feb. 15, 1904; Peterson, *The Great Baltimore Fire*, pp. 43–44, 51–52, especially pp. 117–27.

3. HLM, "Immense Fire Losses During Present Year," *Baltimore Herald*, March 21, 1901; Olson, *Baltimore*, p. 246. At the time, Baltimore had 35 engines and truck companies, and only one water tower. They were unable to cope with the situation. "35 Years After the Big Fire, City Prepared and Safe," *BES*, Feb. 7, 1936; Williams, *Baltimore Afire*, pp. 8, 11; *Baltimore Sunday Herald*, Feb. 7, 1904; HLM, *Newspaper Days*, pp. 278–79; Benjamin W. Weaver, "Visiting Firemen," *BS Magazine*, Feb. 7, 1954, p. 8; Arline Chase, "Hell Loosed in the Streets of

Baltimore," *Firehouse Magazine*, Sept. 1981, p. 106; "Baltimore's Awful Calamity," *Baltimore American*, Feb. 9, 1904.

4. "Heart of Baltimore Wrecked By Greatest Fire in History," *Baltimore Morning Herald*, Feb. 8, 1904; Yates, *Forged by Fire*, p. 23; HLM to William Manchester, Nov. 17, 1948, EPFL ("The wind was blowing from the west during the great fire, so I was not worried about Hollins Street."); *Baltimore Sunday Herald*, 5 p.m. edition, Feb. 7, 1904; "Fire Chiefs Reminisce on Thirty-Third Anniversary of Biggest Blaze of Their Career Threatened to Wipe Out a City," *Baltimore Evening Sun*, Feb. 7, 1938; "Fought to the Last Ditch," *Baltimore Morning Herald*, Feb. 9, 1904.

5. "Visitors Flock to Town: Reflection of the Fire Seen as Far Away as Westminster," *BS*, Feb. 9, 1904; "Curious Camera," *BS Magazine*, Feb. 7, 1954, p. 19; "Amid Showers of Sparks," *BS*, Feb. 8, 1904; "Last Night in Baltimore," *New York Evening Post*, Feb. 9, 1904. The fire was fought by 1,231 firemen. Men and equipment came from those cities listed in the text, plus Chester, York, Altoona, Harrisburg, and Phoenixville, Pennsylvania; Annapolis, Sparrow's Point, Relay, and St. Denis, Maryland. About 150 were treated for injuries at No. 6 Engine House, which had been turned into a provisional hospital. Someone said it looked like a Civil War field hospital. The firefighters were the heroes of the hour. Local townspeople rushed into the streets with food; others opened up their homes so the men could sleep. "Other Cities Send Help," *BS*, May 3, 1987; "No. 6 Engine House Turned Into Hospital," *Baltimore American*, Feb. 9, 1904; "The Great Baltimore Fire of 1904: Two Neighborhood 'Girls' Remember," *BS Magazine*, Feb. 7, 1979, pp. B-1, B-2; "Our Engines' Quick Start," *New York Evening Post*, Feb. 8, 1904; "Daring Firemen Had No Fear of Death," *Baltimore American*, Feb. 9, 1904.

6. HLM, *Newspaper Days*, p. 280; "Fought to the Last Ditch," *Baltimore Morning Herald*, Feb, 9, 1904; Lynn Meekins to HLM, Feb. 7, 1942, EPFL.

7. "Fought to the Last Ditch," *Baltimore Morning Herald*, Feb. 9, 1904; "Chorus of Praise for the Work of the Herald," *Baltimore Morning Herald*, Feb. 22, 1904; HLM, *Newspaper Days*, pp. 281–283; HLM, "*Newspaper Days*: Additions . . . ," p. 282, EPFL; "The Skyscrapers Were Fireproof," *Baltimore Morning Herald*, Feb. 15, 1904. "Press Club President Recalls Thrills of Great 1904 Fire, 26 Years Ago Today," *Washington Post*, Feb. 7, 1930.

8. "The fire brought the fear and terror of the *pogroms* and mistreatment that they had lived through in Russia back to them," wrote Michael Lipman in a letter to the *Baltimore Sun* years later. "Where shall we go? What shall we do?" wailed a pitiful group of immigrants as they made their way toward Patterson Park, then a haven of safety. This image "seared an impression on me, never to be forgotten." See "1904 Fire Memories" in "Letters to the Editor," *BS*, March 6, 1966; "Pandemonium in East Baltimore," *Baltimore American*, Feb. 9, 1904; "Baltimore's Greatest Calamity," *Afro-American Ledger*, Feb. 13, 1904; "Negroes Frightened" under the heading "Public Awed by the Horror," *Baltimore American*, Feb. 9, 1904. Meanwhile, a crowd of Italians had gathered to pray along the bank of Jones Falls; a statue of Saint Anthony was held up to the sky. The fire eventually did stop—at the bank of Jones Falls. For believers, it was nothing less than a miracle. "Saint Anthony, Fireman," Marie O'Dera, *St. Anthony Messenger*, June 1939; HLM, *Newspaper Days*, p. 283; "Story of Firemen from Old Gotham," *Baltimore Morning Herald*, Feb. 15, 1904.

9. So intense was the concentration of newspapermen to get out their stories that when someone burst into their midst to say their building was on fire, he was met with yells: "Oh, go away!" "Shut up!" "Story of Firemen from Old Gotham," *Baltimore Morning Herald*, Feb. 15, 1904. Many telegraphers stayed on duty at their switchboards, wrapped in wet blankets until they were driven from their posts. Anna Schmidt, "Hot Numbers," *BS Magazine*, Feb. 7, 1954, p. 25; "Telegraph Companies Performed Miracles," *Baltimore Morning Herald*, Feb. 12, 1904; "Telegraphers Were Brave," "How Associated Press Handled the Fire," and "Was a Strenuous Time for Them" gathered in the *Scrapbook of R.E. L. Russell*, EPFL; Charles Gordon, "Ventures

Into Verse," *Menckeniana*, Summer 1964, pp. 6–8; C. Gordon to Mrs. Taylor, Betty Adler Correspondence, HLM Collection, EPFL.

10. "Chorus of Praise for the Work of the Herald," *Baltimore Morning Herald*, Feb. 22, 1904; "Fought to the Last Ditch," *Baltimore Morning Herald*, Feb. 9, 1904; Joseph M. Rogers, "The Baltimore Fire," *American Monthly Review of Reviews*, Dec. 5, 1904, p. 298; "What Witnesses Saw," *New York Evening Post*, Feb. 8, 1904.

11. "Fought to the Last Ditch," *Baltimore Morning Herald*, Feb. 9, 1904; HLM, *"Newspaper Days*: Additions . . . ," p. 284, EPFL. See Harold A. Williams, "HLM and the Great Fire," *Menckeniana*, Summer 1987, pp. 2–8. Whether HLM left from Camden or from Union Station in Baltimore and some other inconsistencies are disputed.

12. "Fought to the Last Ditch," *Baltimore Morning Herald*, Feb. 9, 1904; HLM, *Newspaper Days*, pp. 286–288; "Chorus of Praise for the Work of the Herald," *Baltimore Morning Herald*, Feb. 22, 1904; "Twenty-Four Blocks Burned in Heart of Baltimore," *BS*, Feb. 8, 1904; "Map Showing the Countries Involved in the Russo-Japanese Dispute," ibid.; Frank Kent to HLM, Sept. 9, 1941, EPFL.

13. "One Newspaper Office Left," *New York Sun*, Feb. 9, 1904; HLM, *Newspaper Days*, pp. 287–290; "Evening Sun Spots," *BES*, Feb. 7, 1938; J. Appleton Wilson, "Baltimore Great Fire 1904," *Journal: Nov. 28, 1900–Feb. 20, 1908*, pp. 179–184; pp. 260–63, MdHS; "Devastating Fire Stopped at Last," *BS*, Feb. 9, 1904; Major General Milton A. Reckord, "The Men Who Watched the Watchers," *BS Magazine*, Feb. 7, 1954, p. 11; "Night Amid the Ruins," *BS*, Feb. 15, 1904; "How N. C. Wyeth Sketched the Baltimore Fire," *Baltimore News-American*, Feb. 7, 1974.

14. HLM, *Newspaper Days*, pp. 291–93.

15. The press held a grievance against Brigadier General Riggs, the National Guardsman responsible for the security of the burned district; 2,000 guards patrolled the area for 17 days, denying the press entrance; newsmen complained of being treated roughly. In contrast, young ladies, dressed in their smartest frocks, were free to inspect the devastation, with handsome members of the National Guard gallantly providing escort. Among the fair ones was President Theodore Roosevelt's daughter, Alice, whose stylish blue suit and conspicuous red handbag captivated the crowd. Dean K. Yates, *Forged by Fire*; "Militia Put in Charge, His Word Is the Law," and "General Riggs and His Duty," *BS*, Feb. 10, 1904; "Mighty is Riggs! Overrides Law as Though State of War Existed," *BS*, Feb. 11, 1904; "Retirement of Riggs Is Called," *BS*, Feb. 12, 1904; "Down From His Perch: The Mighty 'Lawrie' Riggs Not So Great After All," *BS*, Feb. 12, 1904; "Militia Issues Drastic Orders," *Baltimore American*, Feb. 10, 1904; "Gen. Riggs Was Not Reprimanded," and editorial, "The Case of General Riggs," *Baltimore Morning Herald*, Feb. 12, 1904; "Baltimore's Great Fire," *Harper's Weekly*, Feb. 13, 1904, p. 258; "Sunday Crowd To Flock to Ruins: The President's Daughter Here," *Baltimore American*, Feb. 14, 1904.

16. "Another Sample of Verse," *BS*, Feb. 18, 1904; "Picture Postcards of the Great Fire," Henry F. Rinn, *BS Magazine*, Feb. 2, 1975, p. 19. The sidewalks around most of the larger buildings, including the *Herald*, were piled with marble, granite, and brownstone, to a depth of 2 to 3 feet. "Lessons of the Fire," *Scientific American*, March 12, 1904, p. 216; HLM, *My Life*, p. 70, EPFL; "Interior of the Herald Building" photograph, MdHS; "Heart of Baltimore Wrecked by Greatest Fire in City's History," *Baltimore Morning Herald*, Feb. 8, 1904; Red Gibson, "Mencken Retrieved It from the Ashes After Fire of 1904," *BS Magazine*, Feb. 15, 1978; HLM, *Newspaper Days*, p. 279; "When the Big Fire Hit Baltimore," *BS*, Feb. 5, 1928; Walter W. Hoopes, "Downtown Baltimore Lay in Ruins," *BS Magazine*, Feb. 6, 1949, p. 2.

17. Ellery Sedgewick to HLM, Feb. 9, 1904, NYPL.

18. HLM, *Newspaper Days*, pp. 277, 294–95; "From a Newsdealer" in "Letters to the Editor," *Baltimore Morning Herald*, Feb. 13, 1904; "Tomorrow's Herald" editorial, *Baltimore Morning Herald*, Feb. 20, 1904; "All Clamored for the Herald" in "Letters to the Editor,"

Baltimore Morning Herald, Feb. 17, 1904; "Tomorrow's Herald" editorial, *Baltimore Morning Herald* Feb. 20, 1904.

19. "Greater Baltimore Begins to Arise from the Ashes," *Baltimore Morning Herald*, Feb. 12, 1904; "To Build a New and Greater Baltimore; Business Men and Financiers Will Meet Today; Not Appalled By Disaster," *BS*, Feb. 10, 1904; "City Recovery from Great Blow Is Rapid," *BS*, Feb. 14, 1904; "First Contract for Rebuilding," *Baltimore Morning Herald*, Feb. 12, 1904; HLM, *Newspaper Days*, pp. 277, 296; E. Haldeman Julius, "Copyboy on a Philadelphia Newspaper," *The World of Haldeman-Julius*, pp. 88–92; Charles Mencken to HLM, Oct. 8, 1941, EPFL; Samuel C. Blythe to HLM, August 6, 1941, NYPL.

20. *Report of the Burnt District Commission to His Honor the Mayor for the Six Months Ending September 11, 1906* (Baltimore, 1906), pp. 1–55, EPFL. Regarding policies that would directly affect the Herald building, see esp. pp. 4, 32–33, 35–36, 38, 47, 48; "To Realign Streets in Burned District: City Officials Decide Upon Straight and Wider Thoroughfares," *BS*, Feb. 13, 1904; "Plan for a New Park," ibid.; Christine Meisner Rosen, "Business, Recovery and Progressive Reform in the Redevelopment of Baltimore After the Great Fire of 1904," *Baltimore History Review*, Summer 1989, pp. 283–328; James B. Crooks, "The Baltimore Fire and Baltimore Reform," *Maryland Historical Magazine*, Spring 1970, pp. 1–17; "The Herald Building" editorial, *Baltimore Morning Herald*, Feb. 13, 1904; "The Skyscrapers Were Fire-Proof," *Baltimore Morning Herald*, Feb. 15, 1904. See the section "Herald in First Class Shape," ibid., and "Lessons of the Fire," *Baltimore Morning Herald*, Feb. 18, 1904. "The saying, 'They builded better than they knew,' was probably never more true," reported the *Baltimore American* in 1904. A sobering fact to consider, when recently many of those old buildings, including a few that survived the 1904 fire, have been torn down. See "Breaking Tackle on Stout Walls," *Baltimore American*, March 2, 1904; Ray Allen Willey, "The Lessons of the Baltimore Fire," *Scientific American*, March 12, 1904, p. 216; Charles C. Euchner, "The Politics of Urban Expansion: Baltimore and the Sewerage Question 1859–1905," *Maryland Historical Magazine*, Fall 1991, p. 286.

21. HLM, "The Free Lance," *BES*, September 2, 1914; HLM, "Aesthetic Diatribe," *BES*, February 7, 1927; "New Herald Plant is Assuming Form," *Baltimore Morning Herald*, Feb. 17, 1904; "Our Baltimore Offices" editorial, *Baltimore Morning Herald*, Feb. 17, 1904.

22. HLM, *My Life*, p. 71, EPFL; Ellery Sedgewick to HLM, March 1, 1904, NYPL.

23. "Story of Firemen from Old Gotham," *Baltimore Morning Herald*, Feb. 15, 1904.

24. There actually *was* some looting, albeit very little. The one life lost in the fire was that of an African American laborer. His charred remains were found at Bailey's Wharf; apparently he had been driven into the water by the approaching flames and drowned. Two firemen later died from pneumonia. Two fire horses were also lost once they returned to Washington. "Guards Accused of Theft," *BS*, Feb. 20, 1904; "One Life Lost in the Fire," *BS*, Feb. 20, 1904; E. Ridgley Simpson, "At 12 I Covered the Great Baltimore Fire of 1904," *BS*, March 8, 1959; Benjamin W. Weaver, deputy chief, Washington Fire Dept., "I Remember . . . Baltimore's Thank You Parade," *BS Magazine*, Jan. 5, 1958, p. 2; Peterson, *The Great Baltimore Fire*, pp. 104–5, 190.

25. "RG 17 Burnt District Commission, 1904–1907. Series 2: Administrative Records 1904–1907," General Correspondence Files, BC; "President's Sympathy," *Baltimore American*, Feb. 9, 1904; "Roosevelt Wires McLane," *BS*, Feb. 9, 1904; "Self-Reliant Baltimore: City Authorities Decide Not To Ask Aid," *New York Evening Post*, Feb. 12, 1904; "Baltimore Brave and Determined: World Admires Our Grit," *Baltimore American*, Feb. 11, 1904.; Paul Winchester and Frank D. Webb, *Newspapers Past and Present*, p. 16; "Heart of Baltimore Wrecked by Greatest Fire in City's History," Baltimore *Morning Herald*, Feb. 8, 1904; "Rushing the News to All the World," *Baltimore Morning Herald*, Feb. 15, 1904.

26. "Winter Resorts: Jamaica," *BS*, Feb. 12, 1904; HLM, *Newspaper Days*, p. 278; HLM, "A Road Map to New Books," *Smart Set*, Jan. 1909, p. 157.

27. Joseph Conrad, "Youth: A Narrative," *The Complete Short Fiction of Joseph Conrad, The Stories*, Vol. 1, Samuel Hynes, ed., pp. 157–58; Janvier, *Baltimore in the Eighties and Nineties*, p. 296; HLM, *Newspaper Days*, pp. 277–78.

Chapter 8: A Man of Ability

1. Elizabeth Banks, "Baltimore's Makeshifts," *Harper's Weekly*, July 2, 1904, p. 1020; Lynn W. Meekins Jr. to HLM, Feb. 7, 1942, EPFL; Walter W. Hoopes, "Downtown Baltimore Lay in Ruins," *BS*, Feb. 6, 1949.

2. HLM to Ellery Sedgewick, Nov. 1, 1941 (courtesy Steven Lauria); HLM, "Theodore Roosevelt Named for President; Charles W. Fairbanks for Vice-President," *Baltimore Morning and Sunday Herald*, June 14, 1904; HLM, "The Free Lance," *BS*, March 4, 1912; "A Tale of 1904," *BS*, July 18, 1910; HLM, *My Life*, p. 159, EPFL.

3. "Planning the Paper," *Baltimore Evening Herald*, Aug. 24, 1905. Evening papers were replaced by television's evening news. At the turn of the century, news was dictated by telephone. At 11:40 a.m. the presses were printing the first edition; at 11:45 newspaper boys were crying headlines on the streets; at noon, the *Herald* staff members could enjoy the next twenty minutes by settling down to five-cent cigars. The first edition, catering to the lunch crowd, contained a sports page and concise news summaries. The *Herald*'s last edition, sold after 3:30 that afternoon, contained longer, more detailed stories for readers to digest in the quiet of their home. Ibid.

4. Advertisement, *Baltimore Evening Herald*, Dec. 10, 1905; "On Sunday Papers," *Baltimore Evening Herald*, Nov. 11, 1905; HLM to Richard Steuart (courtesy Steven Lauria); "About Independent Newspapers," *Baltimore Evening Herald*, Nov. 12, 1905; "More About Newspapers," *Baltimore Evening Herald*, Nov. 19, 1905; HLM, "Clipping Books," vol. 1, p. 40, EPFL.

5. "More About Newspapers," *Baltimore Evening Herald*, Nov. 19, 1905; HLM, *Newspaper Days*, p. 273; Michael Charles Emery, *The American Mass Media and the Coverage of Five Major Foreign Events, 1900–1950: The Russo-Japanese War, Outbreak of World War I, Rise of Stalin, Munich Crisis, Invasion of South Korea* (PhD diss., Univ. of Minnesota, 1968), pp. 1–81.

6. Emery, *The American Mass Media*, pp. 67–76; "Flying Shells Strike Rojestvensky; Five of the Fugitives Elude Togo; Saturday's Big Battle Described; Borodino's End," *Baltimore Evening Herald*, May 30, 1905; HLM, *Newspaper Days*, p. 273.

7. "Flying Shells . . . ," *Baltimore Evening Herald*, May 30, 1905, Last Edition; HLM, *Newspaper Days*, pp. 274–75; "News Hot Off the Wire," *Baltimore Evening Herald*, Dec. 4, 1905; News of the battle was reported by the *NYT*, June 2, 1905; A. Novikoff-Priboy, *Tsushima*, pp. 373–74; "Planning the Paper," *Baltimore Evening Herald*, Aug. 24, 1905; Lynn Meekins Jr. to HLM, Feb. 7, 1942, EPFL.

8. Mark H. Judge, "Should Not the Publishing of False News Be a Misdemeanor?" *Westminster Review*, Dec. 1906, pp. 617–18; John A. Macy, "Factitious Fiction and Fictitious Fact," *Bookman*, March 1906, p. 32; "Discussion and Correspondence: Fakes and the Press," *Science*, March 8, 1907, p. 391; "Black Headlines Here to Stay," *New York Herald*, Nov. 21, 1906.

9. HLM to Joseph Katz, July 25, 1932, EPFL; Alistair Cooke, "Mencken and the English Language," in *On Mencken*, ed. John Dorsey, p. 90; Stenerson, *H. L. Mencken*, p. 111, HLM, *George Bernard Shaw*, p. xvi.

10. HLM, *My Life*, pp. 81, 83–89, EPFL; HLM, *Newspaper Days*, pp. 305–7; HLM, *George Bernard Shaw*, pp. xxvii, xxviii, xxix, 25, 82–83, 99, EPFL; HLM, "Fifteen Years," *Smart Set*, Dec. 1923, pp. 138–144; HLM to George Bernard Shaw, Dec. 3, 1905, HRHRC.

11. "Autobiographies and Sketches of the Vagabonds," First Annual Reunion, New Year's Eve, 1905. Hotel Caswell, Baltimore, Maryland," p. 16, EPFL; "Baltimore Herald Chiefs,"

Editor & Publisher, Feb. 3, 1906, p. 5; "The Herald," *Deutsche-Amerikaner*, Jan. 27, 1906; HLM, *My Life*, pp. 87–88, EPFL; HLM, *Newspaper Days*, p. 305; Ellery Sedgewick to HLM, March 20, 1906, NYPL.

12. HLM, *Newspaper Days*, p. 306; HLM, *My Life*, pp. 87–88, EPFL; "More About Newspapers," *Baltimore Evening Herald*, Nov. 19, 1905; James W. Dove, "Date Books of the *Sunpapers*," Vol. I, June 16, 1906 (courtesy Harold A. Williams). Dove, a pioneer in modern newspaper advertising, worked with Mencken at the *Herald*, then served at the business office of the *Sunpapers* for 44 years, retiring as assistant business manager in 1952. The date books, a valuable compilation of reminiscences and newspaper history, were rescued from the trash bin by Harold A. Williams, who then loaned them to the author. See also "J. W. Dove, Leader in Advertising, Dies," *BS*, Nov. 16, 1954; "Evening Herald Discontinued," *Cecil Whig*, June 23, 1906.

13. Charles Grasty, whom Mencken called a natural showman, proved his audacity after the 1904 fire. Less than sixteen hours after the *News* building burned to the ground, Grasty had purchased a new plant and three new printing presses for $150,000, demonstrating what contemporaries called an "enterprise almost startling to Baltimore, showing a spirit that will contribute greatly to the rehabilitation to the city." See: "First Press Is Here," *Baltimore American*, Feb. 12, 1904; Charles Grasty to Richard Mansfield, June 30, 1906, NYPL/ms.

14. HLM, *Thirty-Five Years*, pp. 11–12, 18, EPFL

15. "Annual Meeting Minutes, July 16, 1906," from "Letters and Documents Relating to the Sunpapers," EPFL; HLM et al., *The Sunpapers of Baltimore*, pp. 111, 268; HLM, *Thirty-Five Years*, pp. 11–18, EPFL; "Minutes of a Special Meeting of the Sunpapers, July 16, 1906" from "Letters and Documents Relating to the Sunpapers," EPFL; "The Whangdoodle Mourneth," *BS*, Sept. 5, 1906.

Chapter 9: A Young Man in a Hurry

1. HLM, *Thirty-Five Years*, pp. 31, 35, EPFL; HLM et al., *The Sunpapers of Baltimore*, p. 256; "Philip Sousa Sounds His Battle Cry Against the Modern Canned Music That Comes in Rolls," *BS*, Aug. 19, 1906; "Origin of Mr. Dooley," *BS*, Dec. 2, 1906; "Picturesque Baltimore: A Series of Drawings by Baltimore Artists," ibid.; "Stories of the Supernatural," ibid.; "The Origin and Meaning of Surnames in Baltimore," *BS*, Dec. 24, 1906; HLM to Edgar Lee Masters, April 13, 1931, HRHRC; *BS*, Dec. 2, 1906.

2. "Right in the City's Heart," *BS*, Nov. 17, 1906; HLM, *Thirty-Five Years*, pp. 22–23; 37, 39, 46, EPFL; Helen Essary, "Dear Washington," *Washington Herald*, Jan. 24, 1940; "Building Now Open for Business," *BS*, Nov. 17, 1906; "A Fine Press Room," *BS*, Nov. 17, 1906; "Auto to Washington: A Guide for Motorists," *BS*, July 28, 1907.

3. Harrison Hale Schaff to Dr. Isaac Goldberg, Aug. 1925, in Goldberg, *The Man Mencken*, p. 373; HLM, "Books About Nietzsche," in *The Philosophy of Friedrich Neitzsche*, pp. 324–325; HLM, *My Life*, p. 90, EPFL; Hoffman et al., *The Little Magazines*, p. 72; letter written in 1923 for George Müller of Munich, publisher of German translation of *In Defense of Women*, in HLM, "Autobiographical Notes, 1941," EPFL.

4. Theodore Dreiser to HLM, March 9, 1908, PENN.

5. Baltimore was a tryout city for shows headed for Broadway. Sarah Bernhardt, Mrs. Patrick Campbell, Anna Held, Julia Marlowe, Alla Nazimova, Minnie Fiske, Richard Mansfield, E. H. Sothern, and many of the luminaries of the stage passed through here, making Mencken's commentary on their acting and the plays a valuable (and hitherto unused) resource to the theater historian. See HLM, "Editorials and Dramatic Reviews Contributed to the Baltimore Sun 1906–1910," EPFL; Beirne, *The Amiable Baltimoreans*, pp. 174–88; "Theaters Look Like New," *BS*, Sept. 16, 1906.

6. HLM, *Thirty-Five Years*, p. 22, EPFL; HLM, "Caesar and Cleopatra," *BS*, Feb. 12, 1907; "Mansfield as Carlos," *BS*, Jan. 10, 1906; "The Test at Ford's," *BS*, Dec. 15, 1908; "The Girl and the Governor," *BS*, circa March 1907, all from HLM, "Editorials and Dramatic Reviews Contributed to the Baltimore Sun 1906–1910," EPFL; "The Reminiscences of Hamilton Owens," p. 230, COL.

7. HLM to Francis Starr, March 4, 1909, HRHRC; HLM, "The Actor," *BES*, July 27, 1910; HLM, "The Play Record," *BES*, June 9, 1910; HLM, "Zangwill's Play Here," *BS*, October 1908 from HLM, "Editorials and Dramatic Reviews Contributed to the Baltimore Sun," circa April 1907, in HLM, "Editorials and Dramatic Reviews Contributed to the Baltimore Sun 1906–1910," p. 44, EPFL; HLM, "Shaw Comedy at Ford's," *BS*, circa Dec. 1906, ibid., p. 30, EPFL.

8. John Caldwell, "The International Dramatic Critiques' Anti-Playwriting Association," *Menckeniana*, Winter 1970, pp. 3–5; "Mr. Mencken's Reception," *Publisher*, Feb. 3, 1906.

9. HLM, "Introduction," *The Player's Ibsen*, p. xxvi; HLM and Holger A. Koppel, Translation of Ibsen's *Hedda Gabler*, original typescript, EPFL; "Translator's Note," "A Doll's House," from *A Player's Ibsen*, pp. xxv, 128, 135, 136; Henrik Ibsen, *A Doll's House*, trans. William Archer, *The Collected Works of Henrik Ibsen*, Vol. VII, pp. 146, 154, 155; HLM, *My Life*, p. 129, EPFL; HLM, "Getting Rid of the Actor," *Smart Set*, Sept. 1913, p. 153.

10. HLM, "Mere Opinion," *Baltimore Evening Herald*, Jan. 14, 1906; HLM, "The New Dramatic Literature," *Smart Set*, Aug. 1911, p. 151.

11. HLM, "At the Sweetair Lyceum" from HLM, "Editorials and Dramatic Reviews Contributed to the Baltimore Sun 1906–1910," p. 37, EPFL; HLM, "On Matchmakers," *BS*, 1907, ibid., p. 51, EPFL.

12. Charles Mencken married Mary Kline on May 8, 1909. HLM, "The Wedding Season," *BES*, May 16, 1910; HLM, "The Martyrs of June," in HLM, "Editorials and Dramatic Reviews Contributed to the Baltimore Sun 1906–1910," p. 42, EPFL; HLM to Edwin Murphy, June 20, 1908, EPFL; HLM to Holger Koppel, c. 1909, 1910, courtesy Steven Lauria.

13. HLM, *My Life*, pp. 95–103, EPFL; "Baltimore Weather," *BS*, Feb. 1–5, 1908; Friedrich Wilhelm Nietzsche, *The Gist of Nietzsche*, ed. Henry L. Mencken (Boston: Luce and Company, 1910); Friedrich Wilhelm Nietzsche, *The Antichrist*, trans. with an introduction by H. L. Mencken (New York: Alfred A. Knopf, 1920); Harrison Hale Schaff to Isaac Goldberg, in Goldberg, *The Man Mencken*, p. 374.

14. Theodore Dreiser to Isaac Goldberg, Aug. 25, 1915, reproduced in Goldberg, *The Man Mencken*, p. 379; HLM, *My Life*, p. 140, EPFL; author interview with Ruth Goodman Goetz, June 13, 1991; Vincent Fitzpatrick, "Mencken and Dreiser: Two Beasts in the Parlor," *Maryland Humanities*, Nov./Dec. 1994, pp. 10–13. See Vincent Fitzpatrick, *Two Beasts in the Parlor: The Dreiser-Mencken Relationship* (PhD diss., State University of New York–Stony Brook, May 1979); HLM, *Thirty-Five Years*, p. 45, EPFL; HLM, *My Life*, pp. 93, 478, EPFL; Mencken told John C. Spruance Jr. that after age 21 he knew what he wanted to do. At this time, he was 28 years old. "Mencken, Serene at 60, Foresees Third Term," *Washington Star*, Jan. 28, 1940.

Chapter 10: Broadening Horizons

1. Dolmetsch, *The Smart Set*, pp. 22–24; HLM, "Some Novels—And a Good One," *Smart Set*, May 1909, p. 154; "Mainly About Novels," *Smart Set*, Dec. 1911, p. 151; HLM, "The Free Lance," *BES*, Dec. 20, 1911; HLM, "Prose Fiction Ad Infinitum," *Smart Set*, Sept. 1912, p. 151; HLM, "The Greatest of American Writers," *Smart Set*, June 1910, p. 157; HLM, "A Stack of Novels," *Smart Set*, March 1911, p. 169; HLM, "The Good, the Bad, and the Best Sellers," *Smart Set*, Nov. 1908, p. 155; HLM, *My Life*, pp. 1081–82, EPFL.

2. HLM, *My Life*, pp. 111, 123, EPFL; HLM, *A Little Book in C Major*, p. 74; HLM, "The Free Lance," *BES*, Dec. 20, 1911; HLM, "A Pestilence of Novels," *Smart Set*, Jan. 1914, p. 153; HLM, "Oyez! Oyez! Ye Who Read Books," *Smart Set*, Dec. 1908, p. 153; Van Wyck Brooks, *The Confident Years*, p. 455; HLM, "Mush for the Multitudes," *Smart Set*, Dec. 1914, pp. 304–10; HLM, "The Literary Olio," *Smart Set*, Feb. 1909, p. 158.

3. "George Jean Nathan Dies at 76; Sharp-Tongued Drama Critic," *BES*, April 8, 1958; Benjamin de Casseres, "The Gorgeous Destroyer," *Jewish Times*, Jan. 6, 1933; James Tully, "The World of Mr. Nathan," *Esquire*, Jan. 1938, p. 42; Isaac Goldberg, "Notes," NYPL/ms; HLM, *My Life*, p. 186, EPFL; Charles Gruenberg, "Nathan Dead at 76; Critic, Wit and Editor," *New York Post*, April 8, 1958.

4. James Cain, "Memo for D. Bode," courtesy Roy Hoopes; Isaac Goldberg, "Musician and Critic of Musicians," *Boston Evening Transcript*, May 23, 1925; GJN, "Self-Revelation," *The World of George Jean Nathan*, ed. Charles Angoff, pp. 10–18; George Jean Nathan, "The Happiest Days of H. L. Mencken," *Esquire*, Oct. 25, 1957, p. 146; "Drama Critic George Jean Nathan Dead at 76," *Long Island Press*, April 8, 1958; Untermeyer, *From Another World*, p. 90; William H. Wright to Kate Wright, Jan. 5, 1913, UVA; "The Prejudiced Palate," *Time*, April 21, 1958, p. 66; "Bosh, Sprinkled with Mystic Cologne," *Milwaukee Journal*, April 16, 1958; HLM to Theodore Dreiser, March 7, 1909, PENN.

5. HLM, *The Artist: A Drama Without Words* (Boston: Luce, 1912); Leonard Keene Hirshberg, *What You Ought to Know About Your Baby* (New York: Butterick Publishing, 1910); HLM to Theodore Dreiser, March 7, 1909; HLM, *Thirty-Five Years*, p. 69, EPFL.

6. HLM, *Thirty-Five Years*, pp. 69, 74–78, EPFL.

7. "A Mencken Item" in "The Four Winds," *Baltimore Houses, Gardens and People*, March 1957, p. 12; HLM, *Thirty-Five Years*, pp. 89–90, EPFL; HLM, "Editorials and Other Articles, Baltimore Evening Sun 1910–1912," EPFL; S. L. Harrison, "Fiscal Mencken: An Accounting," *Menckeniana*, Spring 1995, pp. 1–10.

8. HLM to Rev. Albert Chevalier, Jan. 15, 1943, NYPL; HLM to Willard Wright, circa 1910 (YALE); HLM, *My Life*, p. 159, EPFL; "Men vs. The Man," *Kansas City Star*, April 13, 1910.

9. HLM, *Men Versus the Man*, pp. 110, 112, 115–17.

10. HLM, *Men Versus the Man*, pp. 116–17; Hertzberg, *The Jews in America*, p. 16; W. Ashbie Hawkins, "A Year of Segregation in Baltimore," *Crisis*, Nov. 1911, pp. 27–30; Howard W. Odum, *Social and Mental Traits of the Negro: Research into the Conditions of the Negro Race in Southern Towns; A Study in Race Traits and Prospects* (New York: Columbia University, 1910); Maurice Fishberg, *The Jews: A Study of Race and Environment* (New York: Walter Scott Publishing, 1911); HLM, "A Negro State," *BES*, May 7, 1910; HLM, "The Common Negro," *BES*, Aug. 2, 1910; Hofstadter, *Social Darwinism in American Thought*, pp. 161–67, 170–200, 203; Goldberg, *The Man Mencken*, p. 15; HLM, "On Eugenics," *Chicago Sunday Tribune*, May 15, 1927. At the time of the publication of *Men Versus the Man*, Mencken was upset that the "biological issues have received comparatively little attention." Publisher Henry Holt reminded his author that various statistics had been printed on these issues; he questioned Mencken why he had hesitated to print them to bolster his theories. Mencken replied that doing so would only make his book seem like a number of others. Letters between HLM and Henry Holt, Dec. 27, 1909, PRIN/fire.

11. "Herr Hen, Prodigy," *The Bogus*, Tuesday, April 18, 1911 from "Letters and Documents Relating to the Sunpapers," EPFL; Manchester, *Disturber of the Peace*, p. 58.

Chapter 11: The Bad Boy of Baltimore

1. *Merchants' and Manufacturers' Journal*, Jan. 1912, quoted in "The Free Lance," *BES*, Jan. 26, 1912; "Letters from Our Readers," *BES*, Jan. 26, 1912, Jan. 13, 1913, Oct. 18, 1913,

Dec. 24, 1912. Another letter suggested readers start a fund "with a view to presenting Mr. Mencken a book of synonyms. He has used *flabbergast* and *sapient* until they are frayed." "Complaints Against a Contributor's Vocabulary" in "Letters from Our Readers," BES, March 9, 1912; "Letters from Our Readers," *BES*, Dec. 27, 1912, Feb. 11, 13, 1913; "Readers with Something to Say" in "Letters from Our Readers," *BES*, Aug. 12, 1913; HLM, *Thirty-Five Years*, p. 106, EPFL; Manchester, *Disturber of the Peace*, p. 61.

2. HLM, *Thirty-Five Years*, pp. 105, 146, EPFL. When it came to abuse, Mencken said, "I blush every time I look at a dog. Can you imagine a dog wagging its tail while its master's ears are being cut off? I hope not. Yet men do these things." HLM, "The Free Lance," *BES*, Feb. 13, 1913; "Letters from Our Readers," *BES*, Dec. 27, 1912; "Letters to the Editor," *BES*, Sept. 28, 1913.

3. HLM, *Thirty-Five Years*, pp. 103, 125, EPFL; HLM, "The Free Lance," *BES*, Dec. 13, 1911; Manchester, *Disturber of the Peace*, p. 59; HLM, "The Free Lance," *BES*, Oct. 24, 1912.

4. The use of the press was typically progressive as, throughout the country, it became clear that attempts by public officials and doctors to clean up the cities and suppress the spread of bacteria were insufficient. See Ziporyn, *Disease in the American Popular Press: The Case of Diphtheria, Typhoid Fever and Syphilis 1870–1920*; John Collinson, MD, "The Trend of Tuberculosis Mortality in Baltimore and Eight Other Cities, 1812–1932," *Southern Medical Journal*, Dec. 1934, pp. 992–1002; "Scandalous, Says Dr. Welch of Fever," *BES*, Jan. 17, 1912; HLM, "The Free Lance," *BES*, May 26, 1911, May 31, 1911, June 5, 1911, Nov. 22, 1911, March 28, 1912. Mencken compared Baltimore to Liverpool, Copenhagen, Leipzig, Munich, and Edinburgh. HLM, "The Free Lance," *BES*, Jan. 26 and Feb. 27, 1912, Sept. 10, 18, 1912, June 12, 1911, July 11, 12, 1913. The medical historian would profit from examining Mencken's "Free Lance" columns, especially for the period 1911–1913, in which he discusses infectious diseases and calls for the purification of water, the proper disposition of sewage, the inspection of milk, and other sanitary precautions.

5. HLM, "The Free Lance," *BES*, Jan. 22, 1914; "Letters from Our Readers," *BES*, April 5, 1912; HLM, *Men Versus the Man*, p. 110; HLM, "The Free Lance," *BES*, Oct. 26, 1911, Dec. 7, 1911, Dec. 26, 1911. See especially "The Free Lance," *BES*, April 21, 1915. Mencken proposed that Progressive leaders, composed of all-white, old-stock Baltimoreans, invite African American leader George F. Bragg, whose "prudence, sagacity and good citizenship" Mencken held "in high respect," to be a part of their committee. HLM to Willard Huntington Wright, "Sunday" 1913, NYPL.

6. HLM, *Thirty-Five Years*, pp. 105–6; HLM, "The Free Lance," *BES*, Feb. 26, 1913, Nov. 13, 1911, Sept. 14, 1911, May 8, 1911, Nov. 17, 1911, Jan. 25, 1912.

7. HLM, "The Free Lance," *BES*, November 30, 1912. As he put it: "Why assume so gaily that the average man is intelligent and the average woman a fool?" HLM, "The Free Lance," *BES*, Sept. 21, 1912, Feb. 21, 22, 1912. He emphasized that "to give the vote to the ignorant white woman and not to the ignorant colored woman would be just as bad as to give it to the latter and not to the former." HLM, "The Free Lance," *BES*, Jan. 27, 1912; "Letters from Our Readers," *BES*, Jan. 15, 1913; HLM, "The Free Lance," *BES*, Jan. 15, 1913; HLM, "The Free Lance in Washington," *BES*, March 3, 1913; "Letters to the Editor," "The Inglorious Downfall of a Gladiator," *BES*, Feb. 28, 1913; HLM, "The Free Lance," *BES*, Feb. 20, 1914.

8. Brugger, *Maryland: A Middle Temperament*, pp. 426, 810; and Olson, *Baltimore*, pp. 245–95; H. L. Mencken, "The Free Lance," *BES*, Dec. 30, 1911, Jan. 29, 1912.

9. HLM, "The Free Lance," *BES*, Feb. 15, 1912, March 28, 1912, Nov. 8, 1911, Dec. 15, 1911, Jan. 24, 1912, Jan. 31, 1913. Mencken even offered "a corncob pipe to anyone who will offer one sound excuse for the City Council's existence." HLM, "The Free Lance," *BES*, Nov. 25, 1911.

10. HLM, "The Free Lance," *BES*, June 13, 1912. See Mencken's appeal to smokers in "The Free Lance" for Dec. 22, 1911, aimed at those who, like him, having entered a streetcar,

were forced to throw away their cigars ("a young one, just lit"). Mencken warned: "The day is not far distant when not a single streetcar in Baltimore will admit you. What are you going to do about it? Sit still and suffer—*or raise your yell while it is yet time?* Are we in Russia? No! Are we slaves? NO! But if we don't yell at once we *will* be slaves!" HLM, "The Free Lance," *BES*, Feb. 19, 22, 1913, Sept. 8, 1911. Mencken had given a careful reading of William Osler's *The Principles and Practice of Medicine.*

11. HLM to Harry Leon Wilson, May 27, 1913, PRIN/fire; HLM, "The Free Lance," *BES*, November 7, 1912; "Grand Jury to Inquire: Will Take Up So-Called Social Evil This Week," *BS*, July 7, 1913; "Jury to Ask Mencken: Summons 'Free Lance' to Give His Views on Social Evil in Baltimore," *BS*, July 26, 1913; HLM to Harry Leon Wilson, Dec. 10 [1912], PRIN/fire.

12. "Letters from Our Readers," *BES*, Nov. 21, 25, 29, 1912; "How Segregated Vice Menaces Poor Immigrant," *BES*, Nov. 25, 1912. See "The Free Lance" and accompanying "Letters from Our Readers," *BES*, Nov. 25–29, 1912; H. L. Mencken, "Autobiographical Notes, 1941," EPFL; HLM, "Autobiographical Notes, 1925," p. 96, EPFL. The Maryland antivice campaign was part of a larger political agenda. Pamela Susan Hay, "Vice, Virtue and Women's Wage and Work in Baltimore 1900–1915," *Maryland Historical Magazine*, Fall 1999, pp. 292–308.

13. "Letters to the Editor," *BES*, Jan. 24, 1912; HLM, "The Free Lance," *BES*, Jan. 24, 1912.

14. Buehler Metcalfe, "The Free Lance," *Omaha (Nebraska) World Herald*, Jan. 31, 1932; "The Reminiscences of Hamilton Owens," pp. 38–39, COL; Untermeyer, *From Another World*, p. 190; R. Q., "The Omnivorous Mencken," *BES*, July 18, 1921.

15. HLM, *Thirty-Five* Years, pp. 107, 116, EPFL; Mayor Preston to Leonard Hirshberg, March 14, 1914. Preston Files: "Concerning Charles H. Grasty, Editor of the Baltimore Sun, May 1913–Nov. 1914," BC; HLM, "A Dip into Statecraft," *New Yorker*, Feb. 14, 1942, p. 20; HLM, "The Free Lance," *BES*, January 15, 1913; "A Laurel Reader Is Puzzled by the Free Lance," *BES*, Feb. 3, 1915. "This Favorite Portrait of Mr. Mencken" cartoon was printed alongside the announcement that he was the guest of honor at the Women's City Club. One can only imagine the ladies' reaction when Mencken bounced into view. See also Frederick N. Rasmussen, "Pen, Ink and Mr. Mencken," *Menckeniana*, Winter 1973, pp. 4–8.

Chapter 12: Outside, Looking in

1. HLM, "The Free Lance," *BES*, April 17, 1912.

2. William Huntington Wright to Kate Wright, postcards dated April–May 29, 1913, UVA; HLM et al., *Europe After 8:15*, p. 74; HLM, "The Free Lance," *BES*, Feb. 8, 1913; HLM, *My Life*, p. 263, EPFL; I. A. R. Wylie, *The Germans*, pp. 49, 108, 232, 235, 273, 279, 284, 297–98, 306, 310, 313; HLM, "The Prophet of the Superman," *Smart Set*, March 1912, pp. 156–58; HLM, "Getting Rid of the Actor," *Smart Set*, Sept. 1913, pp. 157–58.

3. HLM, "The Free Lance," *BES*, April 12, 1912; HLM, *Thirty-Five Years*, p. 141, EPFL; HLM, "Newspaper Morals," *Atlantic Monthly*, March 1914, pp. 289–97; HLM, "Getting Rid of the Actor," *Smart Set*, Sept. 1913, p. 158.

4. HLM to Charles L. Swift, Feb. 15, 1911, DICK; HLM, "Autobiographical Notes, 1941," EPFL; HLM to Louis Untermeyer, March 17, 1913, UVA; A. H. McDannald to William Huntington Wright, Oct. 1, 1913, PRIN/fire; Alfred A. Knopf, "H. L. Mencken, A Memoir," in *On Mencken*, ed. John Dorsey, pp. 283–84.

5. William Huntington Wright to Kate Wright, Aug. 15, 1913, UVA; A. H. McDannald to William Huntington Wright, Oct. 1, 1913, PRIN/fire; HLM to William Huntington Wright, Dec. 8, 1913, Aug. 17, 1913, YALE; HLM to Harry Leon Wilson, Feb. 8, 1914,

PRIN/fire; Dolmetsch, *The Smart Set*, pp. 36–40; HLM to Theodore Dreiser, Jan. 11, 1914, PENN.

6. HLM, "The Free Lance," *BES*, April 4, 1914; editorial, *BES*, April 13, 1914; Mayor Preston to Leonard Hirshberg, March 14, 1914, BCAR.

7. HLM, "The Shrine of Mnemosyne," *Prejudices: Fourth Series*, pp. 300–301; HLM, "The Free Lance," *BES*, Oct. 15, 1914; HLM to Louis Untermeyer, May 5, 1914, UVA; HLM to Gertrude Mencken, April 1914, EPFL.

8. Millis, *Road to War: America 1914–1917*, pp. 27–28; HLM, "The Free Lance," *BES*, Aug. 4, 1914; HLM, *Thirty-Five Years*, p. 170, EPFL.

Chapter 13: The Holy Terror

1. HLM to Harry Elmer Barnes, Aug. 19, 1923, WY; "News Brief," *New York Mail*, May 18, 1915.

2. HLM, *Thirty-Five Years*, p. 207, EPFL; Knightley, *The First Casualty*, p. 82. For a further examination how war is packaged and promoted to a gullible public, lending credence to Mencken's observations, see James Duane Squires, *British Propaganda at Home and in the United States from 1914 to 1917* (Cambridge: Harvard University Press, 1935); Harold D. Lasswell, *Propaganda Technique in the World War* (New York: Peter Smith, 1938); M. L. Sanders and Philip M. Taylor, *British Propaganda During the First War, 1914–1918* (London: Macmillan Press, 1982); Stewart Halsey Ross, *Propaganda for War: How the United States Was Conditioned to Fight the Great War of 1914–1918* (London: McFarland 1996). Mencken was not the only Baltimorean expressing his anger at bias in the press. Others, accustomed since childhood to never question the *Sun*'s impartiality, now began writing to the paper; one of them was a priest. See William T. Russell, St. Patrick's Record, "Letters to the Editor," *BS*, Sept. 5, 13, 1914. Russell cited the editorials of Aug. 5, 9, 18, and Sept. 9, 1914, as well as various cartoons for being inflammatory and unfair.

3. HLM, "The Free Lance," *BES*, Oct. 5, 8, Nov. 10, 11, 1914.

4. HLM, "The Free Lance," *BES*, Oct. 5, Nov. 10, 1914; HLM, "The Free Lance," *BES*, Feb. 23, 1915; Ponsonby, *Falsehood in War-Time*, pp. 135–39.

5. "Like Carnival of Light," *BS*, Sept. 7, 1914; "Banner Spirit Thrills City," *BS*, Sept. 8, 1914; "Bryan Heralds Eve of Peace," *BS*, Sept. 13. 1914. Patriotic fervor was so great one reader suggested Baltimore discard the title of "Monumental City" and adopt "The Star-Bangled City" in its place; "Letters to the Editor," *BS*, Sept. 8, 1914; HLM to Theodore Dreiser, Nov. 8, 1914, PENN.

6. HLM to Burton Rascoe, Oct. 22, 1919, PENN; HLM, "The Free Lance," *BES*, Feb. 15, 1915; HLM, *Thirty-Five Years*, p. 175, EPFL.

7. Knightley, *The First Casualty*, pp. 83–84.

8. Telegram to the Associated Press from Roger Lewis (AP), Harvey Hansen (*Chicago Daily News*), Irvin Cobb (*Saturday Evening Post*), James O'Donnell Bennett and John T. M. McCutcheon, *Chicago Tribune*, Sept. 3, 1914; James O'Donnell Bennett letter to the *Chicago Tribune*, Oct. 5, 1914, NEW; Peterson, *Propaganda for War*, pp. 51–70; Ponsonby, *Falsehood in War-Time*, pp. 83–84; 128–34; Knightley, *The First Casualty*, pp. 83–84.

9. HLM, "The Free Lance," *BES*, May 2, 1915, Oct. 8, 1915; "The Cronies of the Free Lance," in "The Evening Sun Forum," *BES*, June 19, 1915; "Who the Deuce is the Free Lance, Anyhow?" in "The Evening Sun Forum," *BES*, June 16, 1915; "Letters to the Editor: English Atrocities," June 30, 1915 and "Letters to the Editor: Anti-German Frees His Mind," Feb. 19, 1915, both *BES*.

10. HLM to Ellery Sedgewick, June 25, 1916, NYPL; "The Free Lance Mystery," and "Another Mourner" in "The Evening Sun Forum," *BES*, March 24, 1915; "Sweet Words,"

"The Evening Sun Forum," *BES*, May 26, 1915; William Trowbridge Larned, "The Mantle of Eugene Field," *Bookman*, March 1915, p. 56; HLM, *Thirty-Five Years*, pp. 183–84, EPFL. When it came to the *Sun* making money, HLM says "the corner was turned at last" toward the end of 1915; ibid., p. 150. HLM et al., *The Sunpapers of Baltimore*, p. 351; HLM, *My Life*, p. 343, EPFL; James Cain, "Mr. M," LC; HLM, "The Free Lance," *BES*, Feb. 17, 1915, Oct. 23, 1915; HLM to Louis Untermeyer, late July, 1917, PRIN/fire.

Chapter 14: Mencken, Nathan, and God

1. HLM to Louis Untermeyer, Aug. 3, 1914, NYPL; to Harry Leon Wilson, Feb. 8, 1914, NYPL; Mencken's contract was to expire in October 1914. HLM to Theodore Dreiser, March 27, 1914, PENN; Dolmetsch, *The Smart Set*, pp. 45, 47.

2. Dolmetsch, *The Smart Set*, p. 75; E. E. Edgar, "Famous Fables," *Washington Star*, May 27, 1959; *Smart Set: A Magazine of Cleverness*, Sept. 1914.

3. "On West 45th Street," *London Express*, Nov. 4, 1923; B. F. Wilson, "I Like Women — But Not Too Young," *Metropolitan Magazine*, Dec. 1923, pp. 36, 101; HLM, "Suggestions To Our Visitors," Appendix XXII, *My Life*, EPFL; George Jean Nathan, "The Happiest Days of H. L. Mencken," *Esquire*, Oct. 25, 1957, p. 147; HLM to Ellery Sedgewick, Aug. 25, 1914, Sept. 1, 1914, PRIN/fire.

4. Dolmetsch, *The Smart Set*, p. 67; HLM, *My Life*, pp. 195–96, EPFL; HLM to GJN, note written on top of a letter from Daisy Anderton to HLM, dated Sept. 3, 1919, CORN; HLM to GJN, undated, CORN; GJN to Franklin Spier, Esq. June 1, 1921, CORN; "Menckeniana," *Kobe Herald*, July 8, 1926; S. N. Behrman, "An Introductory Reminiscence," from Dolmetsch, *The Smart Set: A History and Anthology*, p. xx.

5. HLM, *My Life*, pp. 235, 239, EPFL.

6. Dolmetsch, *The Smart Set*, pp. 82–83; Theodore Dreiser to HLM, April 20, 1915, PENN; HLM, *My Life*, pp. 243, 678, EPFL; HLM, Diary, Feb. 2, 1933, EPFL; Louis Kronenberger, "The *Smart Set's* Palmy Days," *NYT Book Review*, Dec. 9, 1934; HLM to James Joyce, April 20, 1915, CORN; Ezra Pound to James Joyce, Feb. 14, 1914, CORN; HLM, *My Life*, Appendix VI, p. 1, EPFL; HLM, Diary, Feb. 2, 1933, EPFL.

7. Behrman, "An Introductory . . . ," in Dolmetsch, *The Smart Set*, p. xx; HLM, *My Life*, p. 243, EPFL; memos and undated letters are from GJN's papers at Cornell and among Isaac Goldberg's Papers at the NYPL. Cover, *Parisienne*, April and July 1917 issues. The cover for the January 1918 issue featured a French soldier lady wearing a transparent blouse. A Canadian Mountie says: "Yes, mam'selle, it's the only French magazine printed in English." The October 1917 issue featured a typical story, "Confessions of a War Bride," which asked if marriage could be successful "when the woman marries the man through hurt pride." Ads listed books on *Sex Facts Misunderstood*, gypsy fortune-telling, and where to buy contraptions to straighten one's nose. The covers for *Saucy Stories* were less risqué than its sister publication. They featured Gibson girls gazing into crystal balls, which showed them hugging soldiers. William Sanford's "Relief" and "In Practice" are on pp. 26 and 125 of *Saucy Stories*, Jan. 1917; Lew Tennant, "Reveries of An Old Maid" is on p. 42, same issue; John Hamilton, "The Horrible Moment," *Saucy Stories*, Nov. 1920, p. 120. Although Mencken's idea for a magazine for an African American audience created considerable excitement with the Warner Publications circulation manager, that man's ideas were less lofty: the manager recommended perfumed paper "because you know how Negroes like perfume." GJN Papers, CORN, NYPL; "Editorial," *Black Mask*, May 1920. Issues of *Black Mask*, *Parisienne*, and *Saucy Stories* are at UCLA, Special Collections; for a list of HLM's pseudonyms, see Betty Adler and Jane Wilhelm, *The Bibliography of H. L. Mencken*, pp. 348–49.

8. "Sunday May Get $40,000," *BS*, Feb. 17, 1916; "Sunday Greases Hands of Many," *Baltimore American*, March 14, 1916; "Billy Sunday's Sermon This Afternoon," *BES*, March 14,

1916; HLM, *Thirty-Five Years*, pp. 107, 116, EPFL; HLM, "Doctor Seraphicus et Eestaticus," *BES*, March 14, 1916; "Mencken Not a Rival to the Man We All Adore: The Evening Sun Forum," *BES*, May 13, 1916; "Thanks" and "The Tumult Dies": "The Evening Sun Forum," *BES*, May 13, 1916; Howard Kelly to HLM, March 17, 1916; Howard A. Kelly, "Prayer List," section dated March 16–April 30, 1916 in *Diaries January 1916 – February 1921*, JHU/Mason. Others included William H. Welch and William S. Halstead, who were top doctors at Johns Hopkins, and Mayor J. H. Preston of Baltimore.

9. Burton Rascoe to James Branch Cabell, Aug. 17, 1918, UVA.

Chapter 15: Round One!

1. *Bang*, Sept. 25, 1916, pp. 1–2, PENN; HLM to Theodore Dreiser, Nov. 24, 1916, PENN; "A Protest Against the Suppression of Theodore Dreiser's 'The Genius,'" PENN; HLM, *My Life*, pp. 472–73, and Appendix XXV, pp. 17–19, EPFL; HLM to Ernest Boyd, Sept. 6, 1916, NYPL; HLM to Ben Huebsch, March 16, 1918, LC.

2. HLM to William Huntington Wright [1916], YALE; HLM to Theodore Dreiser, Oct. 10 and 18, 1916, PENN.

3. Carl Bode interview with Mrs. Dwight Curtis and Mary Newcomer Moore, July 19, 1965, Carl Bode Papers, EPFL.

4. HLM to Theodore Dreiser, Oct. 10, 1916, PENN; essay among Estelle Bloom's papers in the Dreiser Collection, PENN; HLM to Estelle Bloom, Jan. 23, 1919, NYPL; HLM *In Defense of Women*, pp. 170–72.

5. See Martin, *In Defense of Marion*, pp. xxvii–lii; HLM, "Another Long-Awaited Book," *Chicago Tribune*, Sept. 12, 1926; Marion Bloom to Estelle Bloom, March 20, 1921, NYPL; HLM, *In Defense of Women*, p. 121; HLM to Marion Bloom, June 19, 1917, EPFL; Marion Bloom to Estelle Bloom, August 1, 1916, NYPL; Martin, *In Defense of Marion*, p. 384.

6. Carl Bode interview with Marion Bloom, Aug. 18, 1965, Carl Bode Papers, EPFL; Marion Bloom to Betty Adler, June 27, 1971, EPFL; HLM, *In Defense of Women*, p. 122; Marion Bloom to Betty Adler, Dec. 15, 25, 1968, EPFL; HLM, "The Woman of Tomorrow," *New York Evening Mail*, May 2, 1918; Martin, *In Defense of Marion*, pp. xxxix–xivii.

7. Carl Bode interview with Mrs. Dwight Curtis and Mary Newcomer Moore, July 19, 1965, Carl Bode Papers, EPFL; HLM to Marion Bloom, April 16, 1915, EPFL; HLM to Marion Bloom, 1914 or 1915, EPFL; Marion Bloom to Estelle Bloom, Aug. 2, 1923, June 18, 1927, NYPL; Marion Bloom to Estelle Bloom, Summer 1916, NYPL; Marion Burton, "Silhouettes of Stage and Styles," *Parisienne*, April 1917, p. 126, UCLA; Marianne du Fleur, "My Rival," *Parisienne*, Jan. 1918, p. 88, UCLA.

8. Carl Bode interview with Marion Bloom, Aug. 6, 1965, Carl Bode Papers, EPFL; undated manuscript by Virginia Mencken Morrison, Carl Bode Papers, EPFL.

9. Marion Bloom to H. L. Mencken, Nov. 1916, EPFL; Carl Bode interview with Marion Bloom, Aug. 6, 1965, Carl Bode Papers, EPFL; Martin, *In Defense of Marion*, pp. xi–lii; *Dove Date Books*, Vol. I, 1914, courtesy Harold A. Williams.

10. HLM to Eltinge Warner, undated, CORN; Theodore Dreiser to HLM, Oct. 9, 1916, PENN; GJN, "The Happiest Days of H. L. Mencken," *Esquire*, Oct. 25, 1957, p. 148; HLM, "The Free Lance," *BES*, Aug. 22, 1914, March 19, 1915; HLM to Marion Bloom, March 23, 1915, April 18, 1915, EPFL; HLM, "The Free Lance," *BES*, Sept. 6, 1915; HLM to Herbert Parrish, undated, EPFL; HLM to Isaac Goldberg, Sept. 2, 1931, NYPL/ms.

11. HLM, *My Life*, pp. 255–57; HLM, *Thirty-Five Years*, pp. 187–203, EPFL; Fecher, *Mencken: A Study of His Thought*, pp. 32–34; HLM to Fielding Garrison, Aug. 21, 1919, PRIN/fire; HLM, *My Life*, p. 255, EPFL. See HLM, *The Charlatanry of the Learned*.

12. HLM to Anna Mencken, circa Dec. 1916 and Jan. 2, 1917, in his scrapbook, "Germany, 1917," EPFL; HLM to Marion Bloom, Dec. 28, 1916, EPFL; HLM, *My Life*, p. 334, EPFL.

Chapter 16: Berlin, 1917

1. Oscar King Davis, "Americans out of Germany," *NYT*, Nov. 12, 1917; HLM, "Berlin Diary," pp. 23, 33, EPFL.

2. Ibid., p. 34; Joseph C. Grew, Diary, pp. 80–81, HAR/hou; Papers of Edward M. House, Diary, Dec. 2, 1916, YALE/ Sterling; see Theodore R. Barthold, *Assignment to Berlin: The Embassy of James W. Gerard 1913–1917* (PhD diss., Temple University, April 1981).

3. HLM, "Berlin Diary," pp. 13, 34, EPFL; Grew, Diary, pp. 68, 76–77, HAR/hou; C. Marcus to James Gerard, Feb. 14, 1917, MON. The correspondents who mattered most to Gerard were Carl W. Ackerman, head of the United Press Bureau, and Seymour Conger, chief of the Asssociated Press, because at all times they preserved their "Americanism" and "splendid patriotism." Gerard, *My Four Years in Germany*, pp. 427–28; Oswald Schütte to Edward Price Bell, April 17, 1915, June 28, 1916, and Victor Lawson to Oswald Schütte, Nov. 15, 1916, NEW. For Victor Lawson's most concise statement on a nonpartisan newspaper, see his letter to Edward Price Bell, July 20, 1915 and Charles Dennis to Edward Price Bell, March 19, 1915, NEW. Bell had taken Raymond Swing to task for his anti-English stance. Edward Price Bell to Charles Dennis, Nov. 10, 1914, NEW. Edward Price Bell, "British Deny Sale of Schütte's News," *Chicago Daily News*, Dec. 9, 1916.

4. Kahn, Jr., *The World of Swope*, p. 182; Ritchie, *Faust's Metropolis*, p. 277; "Considers Mencken the Last Man Who Should Be Chosen to Write Impartially of Germany: The Forum," *BES*, Jan. 15, 1917; "The Forum," *BES*, Feb. 3, 1917; "Mencken Is Not Neutral," *BS*, Jan. 21, 1917; "Mr. Mencken's Letters," *BS*, Jan. 20, 1917.

5. HLM, "Reminiscence," *BES*, Nov. 24, 1921; HLM, "Mencken Gives Glimpses of Trench Warfare as Seen on Eastern Front," *BES*, March 12, 1917; HLM, "AN 1941," EPFL; Fussell, *The Great War and Modern Memory*, pp. 76–79.

6. HLM, *Thirty-Five Years*, p. 197, EPFL; HLM, "German Troops Live in Comfort, Free from Fear of Bread Cards," *New York Evening Mail*, March 23, 1917; HLM, "German Occupancy Has Changed Russian Town to Model Community," *New York Evening Mail*, March 21, 1917; C. V. Vignau to H. L. Mencken, Jan. 17, 1920, in scrapbook, "Germany, 1917," EPFL.

7. Gerard, *My Four Years in Germany*, p. 371; Barthold, *Assignment to Berlin*, p. 404.

8. HLM, "Berlin Diary," pp. 4–5, 12, 14, EPFL; "Schulmadchen als Schmeesschippen," Berliner *Tageblatt*, Feb. 3, 1917; "Der Frost in Berlin," *Berliner Tageblatt*, Feb. 5, 1917. The temperature was –22 C. HLM, "Reminiscence," *BES*, June 21, 1937; James Watson Gerard to Mrs. Bowers, Jan. 19, 1917, MON; "The Reminiscences of James Watson Gerard," p. 52, COL.

9. HLM, "Berlin Diary," p. 5, EPFL; HLM, "Ludendorff," *Atlantic*, June 1917, pp. 824–25; HLM, "Berlin Diary," pp. 22, 30, 31, 35–36, 38, EPFL; "U.S. Seizes Interned German Warships," *BS*, Feb. 4, 1917; GJN to August Mencken, Feb. 6, 1917, EPFL; "Mencken and Hapgood Describe Situation in Germany," *BS*, Feb. 4, 1917.

10. Grew, Diary, p. 84, HAR/hou; HLM, "Berlin Diary," p. 60, EPFL; HLM, "Henry Mencken Cables Story of Ticklish Moments in Berlin," *BS*, March 6, 1917.

11. HLM, "Berlin Diary," pp. 55, 57, 77, EPFL; "Die Amerikanischen Journalkisten," *Berliner Tageblatt*, Feb. 6, 1917; "Gerard Sends Word to Egan—Told That Americans Cannot Leave," *NYT*, Feb. 8, 1917; Raymond Swing to Charles Dennis, July 17, 1916, NEW. Predictably, the news caused a stir in the United States, inciting the public to demand that America "should declare war against Germany at noon tomorrow." Ibid. H. L. Mencken, "A Message to Berlin," *NYT*, March 7, 1917; James O'Donnell Bennett, "Berlin Thanks Neutrals Plan to Avoid Action," *Chicago Tribune*, Feb. 8, 1917; Grew, Diary, p. 86, HAR/hou.

12. HLM, "Berlin Diary, "p. 70, EPFL; Carl Ackerman's anti-German stance was not only apparent to Mencken; his own colleagues told him he should not be too intolerant. Carl Ackerman to John F. Ackerman, Jan. 10, 1917, LC; James O'Donnell Bennett, "Erring Reports

Reaching Berlin Cause of Peril: Strained Relations Due in Part to Many Mistakes," *Chicago Tribune*, Feb. 11, 1917; HLM, *Thirty-Five Years*, p. 198, EPFL; HLM, "Ludendorff," *Atlantic*, June 1917, pp. 824–5; HLM, "Berlin Diary," p. 58, EPFL.

13. HLM, "Ludendorff," *Atlantic*, June 1917, pp. 824–25; HLM, "Berlin Diary," p. 87, EPFL; "Die Amerikanischen Journalistes," *Berliner Tageblatt*, Feb. 11, 1917; Barthold, "Assignment to Berlin," p. 414; "Ambassador Pays Cordial Farewell Visit to German Officials," *NYT*, Feb. 10, 1917; Grew, Diary, p. 92, HAR/hou; "Die Ubriefe Gerards," *Lokal Anzeiger*, Feb. 11, 1917; HLM, from a scrap of paper from his original diary, dated "Sunday, February 11," collected in his scrapbook, "Germany, 1917," EPFL.

14. "All Perfectly Safe, Says Mencken," *BS*, Feb. 9, 1917; "Take Me Back to Uncle Sam," *BES*, Feb. 9, 1917; Margaret Lappin, "As I Saw Mencken," p. 179, YALE.

15. HLM, "Berlin Diary," pp. 38, 87–88, 90, 92–94, EPFL; "Can't Find Precedent for Holding Gerard," *NYT*, Feb. 9, 1917.

16. HLM to Ernest Boyd, Feb. 19 [1917], NYPL; HLM, "Reminiscence," *BES*, June 21, 1937; HLM, "Berlin Diary," pp. 134, 138–39, 141, 146, 159, 187, EPFL; "Mr. Gerard en La Coruña," *La Voz de Galicia*, Feb. 27, 1917; "Won't Send Warship to Convey Gerard," *NYT*, Feb. 26, 1917; HLM, *Thirty-Five Years*, p. 200, EPFL.

17. HLM, "Berlin Diary," pp. 173, 187, EPFL; HLM, "Germany 1917," EPFL. HLM, "Days of Innocence: Gore in the Carribbeas," *New Yorker*, Dec. 19, 1942, p. 20; HLM, *Thirty-Five Years*, p. 201, EPFL; *BS*, Feb. 4, 1917; HLM, "Manifest Destiny," *BES*, April 15, 1929; "Latinos More Civilized Than Americans, Believes Mencken While in Havana," *Havana Post*, Jan. 24, 1932; HLM, "Havana Revisted," *BES*, Feb. 1, 1932.

18. HLM to Marion Bloom, March 11, 1917, EPFL; HLM, *In Defense of Women*, p. 54; HLM, "Berlin Diary," p. 175, EPFL; HLM to Marion Bloom, March 15, 1917, EPFL.

19. HLM, "Berlin Diary," pp. 170, 194, 198, 200, EPFL; "Gerard Party Reaches Havana," *NYT*, March 12, 1917; "Gerard Closeted Hours with Lansing—Relieved to End Journey," *NYT*, March 15, 1917; "Mrs. Gerard Arrives, Tired But Happy," *NYT*, March 15, 1917. Herman Oelrichs said stories of spies following Gerard were "the merest rot." Ibid. HLM, *Thirty-Five Years*, p. 202, EPFL; "Envoy Gerard Here to Make His Report," *Washington Evening Star*, November 14, 1917. Gerard arrived to a demonstration that the *NYT* described as "one of the most enthusiastic that New York has given to a public man in years." Gerard traveled throughout the country, giving speeches at Liberty Bond Rallies, becoming one of the most successful fund-raisers during the war. "Gerard Sees Wilson; Starts for New York," *NYT*, March 16, 1917; "James W. Gerard, 84, Dies; Envoy to Germany 1913–17," *NYT*, Sept. 12, 1951; "The Reminiscences of James Watson Gerard," p. 60, COL.

20. Marion L. Bloom, "Kisses," *Smart Set*, Nov. 1917, p. 57.

Chapter 17: The Prevailing Winds

1. Jordan, *The Days of a Man*, pp. 727, 730; Kennedy, *Over Here*, pp. 14–15; HLM to Dreiser, April 9, 1917, PENN.

2. Peterson and Fite, *Opponents of War*, pp. 13–14; Olson, *Baltimore*, pp. 299–300; HLM to Louis Untermeyer, Nov. 22, 1917, UVA; Burns, *The Workshop of Democracy*, p. 440; "Froelicher Hall," *Goucher Quarterly*, Summer 1993, p. 4; The *Sun's* undiluted loyalty to Americanism can be seen in the headlines for that period: "Death of German Language in America," *BS*, April 28, 1918; "German Eliminated From Baltimore City Schools," *BS*, July 18, 1918; "Senate Opposes Teaching of German in Schools," *BS*, June 4, 1918; "Few Poly Students Want German," *BS*, Nov. 1, 1917; "Johns Hopkins Professor Assails Value of German Language," *BS*, Dec. 16, 1917; "German Brewing Company Changed Name to Liberty Brewing Company," *BS*, Dec. 7, 1917; "The German Correspondent Discontinued After Thirty Years of Publication," *BS*, April 29, 1918; "City Council Divided Between Names of Hollins and American," *BS*, May 11,

May 21, 1918; Peterson and Fite, *Opponents of War*, p. 196; Kennedy, *Over Here*, pp. 45–92; HLM, *Minority Report*, p. 186; HLM to Ernest Boyd, July 28, 1918, PRIN/fire; William MacDonald, "The New United States: The Blight of Intolerance," *Nation*, May 3, 1919, pp. 691–92.

3. John Wheeler, President of the J. W. W. Syndicate, to Edward A. Rumley, April 9, 1917, ORE; HLM to Joseph Hergesheimer, March 1917, HRHRC; Kahn, Jr. *The World of Swope*, pp. 183–84; Ellery Sedgewick to HLM, April 11, 1917, and HLM to Ellery Sedgewick, c. April 1917, PRIN/fire; HLM, "Preface" to "Berlin Diary," pp. 1–2, EPFL; HLM, *Thirty-Five Years*, p. 205, EPFL.

4. Mark Sullivan, "Creel–Censor," *Collier's*, Nov. 10, 1917, pp. 13–36; "Newspapers of the Country Are Flooded with Publicity Copy from Washington," *Editor & Publisher*, March 16, 1918, pp. 7–89; Peterson and Fite, *Opponents of War*, pp. 19, 94–96; Zechariah Chafee Jr., "Freedom of Speech," *New Republic*, Nov. 16, 1918, p. 69. Creel's committee issued 6,000 press releases assisting the newspapers' coverage of the war. Mock and Larson, *Words That Won the War*, pp. 122–23; Joseph Creel to A. Bruce Bielaski, Sept. 18, 1918, NA; Richard Berry, "Muzzling the Press," *North American Review*, Nov. 1918, pp. 1–10; HLM to Ernest Boyd , July 23, 1918, PRIN/fire; HLM, *Thirty-Five Years*, pp. 208–9; EPFL.

5. Edward A. Rumley, *Autobiography* (unpublished), ch. 20, "Mail Staff," p. 15, ch. 21, p. 11, ORE; HLM, Preface to "Berlin Diary," pp. 1–2, EPFL; HLM, *Thirty-Five Years*, p. 203, EPFL; HLM, "Heroes of Forensic Battles Royal Make 'Congress Record' Cheapest Book in World," *New York Evening Mail*, Sept. 14, 1917; Burton Rascoe to James Branch Cabell, Aug. 17, 1918, UVA.

6. Scruggs, *The Sage in Harlem*, p. 26; Johnson, *Along This Way*, pp. 305–6; HLM, "Negro Spokesman Arises to Voice His Race's Wrongs," *New York Evening Mail*, Sept. 19, 1917; Schaffer, *America in the Great War*, pp. 75–108.

7. HLM, "A Neglected Anniversary," *New York Evening Mail*, Dec. 28, 1917; HLM, "A Hymn to the Truth," *Chicago Sunday Tribune*, July 25, 1926; HLM to Burton Rascoe, "Critical," p. 2, circa 1918, PENN.

8. Geoffrey T. Helman, "A Very Dignified Pavane," *New Yorker*, Oct. 20, 1948, pp. 45–47; Helman, "Flair is the Word," *New Yorker*, Nov. 27, 1948, pp. 36–52; Helman, "The Pleasures, Prides and Cream," *New Yorker*, Dec. 4, 1948, pp. 40–53.

9. HLM to Burton Rascoe, undated, circa 1918, PENN; HLM to James Branch Cabell, Oct. 29, 1920, UVA. Knopf's nervousness is a running mantra throughout Mencken's letters to his friends. There was reason for Knopf to feel jittery. In 1915 his fledging firm almost toppled when the Society for the Suppression of Vice accused him of publishing pornographic books. Charges were dropped when Knopf agreed to melt down the plates of Stanislaw Przybyszewski's *Homo Sapiens*, one of the prize items on the list. The action saved the firm, but Knopf was embarrassed by the revelation years later. Helman, "The Pleasures, Prides and Cream," *New Yorker*, Dec. 4, 1948, pp. 40–53. H. Epperson to Charles Angoff, Aug. 31, 1963, BU.

10. "A Mencken Item," *Macon, Ga. News*, Aug. 24, 1917; HLM to Dreiser Jan. 30, 1919, PENN; HLM, *Thirty-Five Years*, pp. 205–6, EPFL; HLM to Ernest Boyd, April 20, 1918, PRIN/fire; letter dated July 30, 1918 in "Federal Bureau of Investigation Investigative Case Files 1908–1922, Subject: H. L. Mencken," NA. The sketch is attached to a letter, full of speculation and breathless observations, from a self-styled patriot named D. G. Smart, Aug. 2, 1918, ibid.; James Cain, "Mr. M.," LC.

11. HLM to Ernest Boyd, April 20, 1918, PRIN/fire; William Huntington Wright to Kate Wright, Oct. 11, 1917, UVA; "Sets Trap, Girl Thinks Is Spy," *New York Telegram*, Oct. 5, 1917; "Typists' Charges Against Editor Dropped By U.S.," *New York Evening Journal*, Oct. 6, 1917; HLM to Stanton B. Leeds, June 17, 1918, NYPL; Marion Bloom to Betty Adler, Feb. 14, 1973, EPFL; Marion Bloom to Estelle, July 13, 1926, NYPL; HLM to Ernest Boyd, undated, 1917, PRIN/fire; Martin H. Clark to Isaac Goldberg, Nov. 26, 1925, NYPL/ms.

12. R. J. Lewis Jr., "Speaking of Books," *New York American*, April 9, 1942; "Philip Goodman's Comedy Sensation: The Five O'Clock Girl" playbill, NYPL/pa, MAD; "Just a Good Customer," *Collier's*, March 2, 1929, pp. 18, 46; HLM to Ernest Boyd, April 20, 1918, PRIN/fire; author's interview with Ruth Goodman Goetz, June 13, 1991.

13. HLM, *Damn! A Book of Calumny*, pp. 13–15; letter from E. A. Hogan to the Department of Justice, May 9, 1918, "Federal Bureau of Investigation Investigative Case Files 1908–1922, Subject: H. L. Mencken," NA; HLM to Ernest Boyd, June 29, 1918, PRIN/fire.

14. HLM, *In Defense of Women*, p. 3; HLM, "Apologia pro Sua Vita," *New York Evening Mail*, March 18, 1918; Owen Hatteras (HLM), *Pistols for Two*, p. 22.

15. HLM to Theodore Dreiser, Aug. 20, 1918, PENN; HLM, "Beer and Light Wines Urged as Necessity to Fight Drunkeness," *New York Evening Mail*, June 18, 1917; HLM, "Rattling the Subconscious," *Smart Set*, Sept. 1918, p. 141; Creel to Ochs June 7, 1918, "Friends of Germany Propaganda CPI Files Corr. of Carl Byoir with Government Agencies and Provisions of Committee," NA.

16. "Arrest Rumley: Say Germany Owns the Evening Mail," *NYT*, July 9, 1918; "Statement by Henry L. Stoddard," *New York Evening Mail*, July 9, 1918; "Rumley: In Mail Case, Held in $35,000 Bail," *NYT*, July 10, 1918; "German Stupidity Again," editorial in *NYT*, ibid.; "Dr. Rumley von Der Mail Verbailtet," *New York Staatszeitung*, July 9, 1918; "Proposes Inquiry Into Bribe Fund," *NYT*, July 12, 1918; "Rumley Wanted News Direct from Berlin," *NYT*, August 5, 1918; HLM to Ernest Boyd, July 23, 1919, PRIN/fire; "Records of CPI Executive Division: File: American Alliance for Labor and Democracy," NA. The headlines of *New York Evening Mail* for July 9, 1918, proclaimed it was now being conducted "as a loyal patriotic newspaper" under the direction of Henry L. Stoddard, "whose Americanism is beyond question." HLM, "Autobiographical Notes, 1925," p. 96, EPFL.

17. GJN, "The Happiest Days of H. L. Mencken," *Esquire*, Oct. 25, 1957, pp. 146–50; HLM to Ernest Boyd, Aug. 1, Sept. 4, 1918, PRIN/fire; Dolmetsch, *The Smart Set*, pp. 53–54; HLM, *My Life*, pp. 271–73, 648, EPFL.

18. HLM to Ernest Boyd, Aug. 1, 9, Sept. 4, 1918, PRIN/fire; AAK to Joseph Hergesheimer, Aug. 8, 1917, HRHRC; August Mencken, of Registration Card Order No. 155, did not fight because he was placed in Classification Level V, "Physical Disability as a Claim for Exemption." He had suffered from tuberculosis. Letter to the author from Mr. Gayle P. Peters, Director, National Archives, Southeast Region, April 18, 1995; HLM to C. C. MCulloch Jr., Surgeon General's Library, Aug. 8, 1918, NLM; Fielding Garrison to HLM, Aug. 19, 24, 1918, NLM.

Chapter 18: Over Here

1. "City Hall Bell Rings 100 Times for American Offensive," *Baltimore American*, Sept. 12, 1918; "Today the Day of Days," editorial, *BS*, Sept. 12, 1918; HLM, *Thirty-Five Years*, p. 217; "Casualties of Land Forces," *BS*, Sept. 11, 1918; "Draft Evader Gets 20 Year Sentence," *Philadelphia North American*, July 29, 1918; "Wilson Approves Gregory's Plan of Slacker Round-Ups," *Washington Tribune*, Sept. 12, 1918; "City's Call to Registration," *Baltimore American*, Sept. 12, 1918; Kennedy, *Over Here*, pp. 151–53; Henry Louis Mencken, Registration Card Order No. 2185, Sept. 12, 1918, NA/se, Gayle P. Peters, Director, in letter to author, April 18, 1995. The Selective Service System ceased drafting on Nov. 12, 1918, and Mencken had not been called. Mencken reported to the local draft board at the YMCA; HLM to Theodore Dreiser, Sept. 4, 1918, PENN.

2. Wilbur F. Coyle, "Baltimore in War Time," *BES*, Sept. 12, 1918; "On to Berlin!" editorial, *BES*, Sept. 12, 1918; HLM, "Beer and Light Wines Urged as Necessity to Fight Drunkeness," *New York Evening Mail*, June 18, 1917; HLM, "Anti-Saloon Lobby Has Congress Badly Scared," *Evening Mail*, Aug. 21, 1917; HLM, "Suite Élégiaque," *Smart Set*, Oct. 1918, p. 138; HLM, *My Life*, p. 735, EPFL; HLM to Ernest Boyd, Jan. 18, 1919, NYPL.

3. HLM, *"Happy Days:* Additions . . . ," p. 11, EPFL; HLM, "Autobiographical Notes, 1925," p. 47, EPFL; "Masonry and Brick Work" in *The New Normal Written Arithmatic* (1892), p. 204, among H. L. Mencken's childhood books, EPFL. See especially page 205, stained with brick crumbs; other pages are marked with leaves from the garden. HLM, "Autobiographical Notes, 1941," EPFL; HLM, *Thirty-Five Years,* p. 555, EPFL; HLM, "The Boons of Civilization," *American Mercury,* Jan. 1931, p. 35.

4. HLM, *My Life,* p. 618, EPFL; HLM to Ernest Boyd, Sept. 13, 1918, PRIN/fire; HLM to James Bowcock, March 27, 1947, EPFL; HLM, "Introduction: The Divergent Streams of English," *The American Language* (1919 ed.), pp. vii–x, 1–2; HLM, "Time Will Mold Our Speech," *New York Evening Mail,* Oct. 15, 1917; HLM, "Who Is Honorable?" *New York Evening Mail,* Jan. 26, 1918; Raven McDavid Jr. "Mencken Revisited," *Harvard Educational Review,* Spring 1964, p. 219; HLM to Ernest Boyd, Jan. 8, 1918, PRIN/fire; HLM to Philip Goodman, Oct. 4, 1918, EPFL; HLM to Louis Untermeyer, Oct. 5, 1918, UVA; HLM, "The American Language: Original Typescript 1915–16, Baltimore, 1937," pp. 1–2, EPFL; Schrader, *H. L. Mencken: A Descriptive Bibliography,* pp. 83–98.

5. August Mencken to William Manchester, undated, EPFL; HLM to Estelle Kubitz, Nov. 6, 1918, EPFL; HLM to Ernest Boyd, Oct. 16, Nov. 6, 1918, PRIN/fire; HLM to Burton Rascoe, Oct. 19, 1917, PENN; HLM to Ernest Boyd, Dec. 20, Oct. 8, 1918, PRIN/fire; "Victory Jubilee Wakes Baltimore to Greatest Day," *BES,* Nov. 11, 1918; "Telling Glad News to City's People," *BES,* Nov. 11, 1918; "City Celebrates Greatest of Days in Rioters," *BS,* Nov. 11, 1918; "Goucher Students in Victory March," *BES,* Nov. 11, 1918; "When the Town Went Wild Over Victory," *BES,* Nov. 11, 1918; "The Forum," *BES,* Nov. 11, 1918.

6. HLM, *My Life,* pp. 742–43, EPFL; "The Old Germany Has Gone," *BS,* Nov. 11, 1918; HLM to Ernest Boyd, Sept. 26, 1919, July 16, 1919, PRIN/fire; Herman George Scheffauer to HLM, Sept. 22, 1919, NYPL.

7. HLM, *Notes on Democracy,* p. 27; HLM, *My Life,* p. 481, EPFL; HLM to Fielding Garrison, Aug. 15, 1919, Dec. 26, 1919, PRIN/fire; HLM to Harry Elmer Barnes, Aug. 19, 1923, WY.

8. HLM, *My Life,* p. 757, EPFL; Schrader, *H. L. Mencken: A Descriptive Bibliography,* p. 85; J. R. Hulbert, "The American Language," *Modern Philology,* Sept. 1919, p. 303; Brander Matthews, "Developing the American from the English Language," *NYT,* March 30, 1919, p. 157; Edmund Wilson, "Talking United States," *New Republic,* July 1936, p. 299; Jacques Barzun, "Mencken's America Speaking," *Atlantic,* Jan. 1946, p. 63; HLM, "Off the Grand Banks," *BES,* Sept. 7, 1925; HLM to Fielding Garrison, Oct. 16, 1919, PRIN/fire; HLM to Ernest Boyd, June 6, 1919, PRIN/fire.

9. Unlike Huneker, Pollard championed both European and American authors; Huneker kept his focus across the Atlantic. "A Critic Too Far Ahead of His Time," *Current Literature,* March 1912, pp. 339–40; Burton Rascoe, "A Catnip of Critics," *Shadowland,* Feb. 1923, pp. 35–36; Edmund Wilson, "Mencken Through the Wrong End of the Telescope," *New Yorker,* May 6, 1950, p. 113; "American Critic of Letters and Life," *London New Statesman,* March 27, 1920; James Huneker to HLM, Nov. 5, 1919, *The Intimate Letters of James Gibbons Huneker,* pp. 257–58; HLM, *My Life,* Appendix X, p. 33, EPFL; HLM to Ernest Boyd, July 16, 1919, PRIN/fire; Vincent O'Sullivan, "The American Critic," *London New Witness,* Nov. 28, 1919.

10. Harvey Fergusson, "Bouquets for Mencken," *Nation,* Sept. 12, 1953, pp. 211–12; HLM, *My Life,* pp. 777, 815, EPFL; [untitled] *Philadelphia Press,* Nov. 2, 1919; HLM to August Mencken, c. Nov. 1919, EPFL; HLM to Blanche Knopf, Nov. 21, 1919, EPFL.

11. Gerald Johnson, "Henry L. Mencken [1880–1956]," *Saturday Review of Literature,* Feb. 11, 1956, p. 12; HLM to Fielding Garrison, Nov. 17, 1919, PRIN/fire; HLM to Ellery Sedgewick, Oct. 18 [1919], courtesy Steven Lauria; HLM to Louis Untermeyer, Nov. 25 [1919], UVA; AAK to E. A. Townley Esq., April 6, 1927, EPFL; HLM, "Berlin Diary," p. 2, EPFL; HLM, *Thirty-Five Years,* p. 205.

Chapter 19: The Infernal Feminine

1. Marion Bloom to Betty Adler, Aug. 23, 1970, EPFL; Carl Bode interview with Marion Bloom, Aug. 18, 1965, Carl Bode Papers, EPFL; Marion Bloom to Estelle, March 22, 1920; late June or July 1920, NYPL; HLM to Marion Bloom, Sept. 20, 21, 1918, EPFL; HLM to Marion Bloom, Sept. 21, 1918, EPFL; HLM to Marion Bloom, ca. Sept. 24 and 26, 1918, EPFL; HLM to Ernest Boyd, Sept. 28, 1918, PRIN/fire; HLM to Estelle Bloom, Jan. 9 (1919), NYPL; HLM to Marion Bloom, Sept. 23, 1918, EPFL; HLM to Estelle Bloom, Dec. 29 (1918), NYPL.

2. These descriptions of her experiences are from Marion Bloom's wartime journal. See Martin, *In Defense of Marion*, pp. 83–103; Carl Bode interview with Mrs. Dwight Curtis and Mary Louise Newcomer Moore, July 19, 1965, Carl Bode Papers, EPFL; HLM to Marion Bloom, ca. March 1919, from Martin, *In Defense of Marion*, p. 81; HLM to Ernest Boyd, March 3, 1919, PRIN/fire; HLM to Marion Bloom, ca. March 1919, EPFL; Marion Bloom to Ernest Boyd, Nov. 13, 1918, EPFL.

3. Text of original letter loaned by Marion Bloom to Carl Bode, quoted in Carl Bode interview with Marion Bloom, Aug. 18, 1965, Carl Bode Papers, EPFL; HLM to Marion Bloom, March 24, 1919, EPFL.

4. Carl Bode interview with Mrs. Dwight Curtis and Mary Louise Newcomer Moore, July 19, 1965, Carl Bode Papers, EPFL; Marion Bloom to Betty Adler, July 3, 1966, EPFL; Marion Bloom to Estelle Bloom, "Saturday p.m., circa 1919," NYPL; Marion Bloom to Estelle Bloom, May 13, 1921, NYPL; HLM to Ernest Boyd, December 2, 1918, Aug. 12, 1919, PRIN/fire; Carl Bode interview with Marion Bloom, Aug. 18, 1965, Carl Bode Papers, EPFL. A typical letter showing Marion's belief in Christian Science can be found in her letter to Estelle, Aug. 12, 1919, PENN. HLM to Estelle Bloom, Sept. 10, 1919, NYPL; Martin, *In Defense of Marion*, pp. 123–24; HLM to Estelle Bloom, May 12, 1921, NYPL; HLM to Estelle Bloom, Sept. 16, 1919, NYPL.

5. HLM and GJN, *Heliogabulus, A Buffoonery in Three Acts*, p. 169, EPFL; Marion Bloom to Betty Adler, June 30, 1971, EPFL; Carl Bode interview with Mrs. Dwight Curtis and Mary Louise Newcomer Moore, July 19, 1965, Carl Bode Papers, EPFL; Marion Bloom to Estelle Bloom, Aug. 12, 1919, PENN; HLM to Estelle Bloom, May 12, 1921, NYPL; Marion Bloom to Estelle Bloom, Aug. 1, 1926, NYPL; Marion Bloom to Estelle Bloom, May 7, 1927, NYPL; HLM, *In Defense of Women*, p. 155; HLM to Estelle Bloom, May 28, 1919, NYPL; HLM to Estelle Bloom, May 31 [1919], NYPL; Marion Bloom to Estelle Bloom, Feb. 26, 1920, NYPL.

6. HLM to Estelle Bloom, May 12, 1921, NYPL; HLM, "Répétition Generale," *Smart Set*, March 1920, p. 48; Marion Bloom to Estelle Bloom, March 22, 1920, NYPL; Martin, *In Defense of Marion*, pp. 127–29; Marion Bloom to Estelle Bloom, Jan. 9, 1927, NYPL; Marion Bloom to Estelle Bloom, late June–July 1920, Nov.–Dec. 1919, NYPL; HLM to Marion Bloom, Nov. 4, 1919, EPFL; HLM to Marion Bloom, Dec. 11, 1919, EPFL; Joseph Hergesheimer to James Branch Cabell, Dec. 22, 1919, UVA.

Chapter 20: The Dry Millennium Dawns

1. HLM to Ernest Boyd, Jan. 16, 1920, PRIN/fire; HLM, "Servants of Righteousness," *BES*, May 2, 1921.

2. HLM, "Servants of Righteousness," *BES*, May 2, 1921; Lappin, "As I Saw Mencken," p. 132, YALE; HLM to Dr. W. Horsley Grant, March 16, 1935, EPFL; and James Cain on HLM, collection of Roy Hoopes; HLM, "Autobiographical Notes, 1941," EPFL; HLM to Linn Rudolph Blanchard, Dec. 24, 1943, NYPL. For more information on Mencken and drink, see Johns, *The Ombibulous Mr. Mencken*; HLM to Gerald Johnson, Dec. 28, 1944, collection of Arthur Gutman.

3. HLM to Linn Rudolph Blanchard, Dec. 24, 1943, NYPL; "The Reminiscences of Hamilton Owens," pp. 54–55, COL. Hamilton Owens coined the term "The Maryland Free State"; it is still used today. "Bright, Bustling Baltimore," by R. P. Harriss as told to Neil Grauer, *Baltimore Magazine*, Dec. 1982, pp. 110–11; John C. Schmidt, "The Wet, Wet Years of Prohibition in the Free State," *BS Magazine*, Jan. 14, 1962, pp. 12–14. In Baltimore, a gallon of 185-proof grain alcohol sold for as little as $3, and it would make two gallons or more of gin. Materials to make gin and beer were available in neighborhood stores. The shopkeepers "were the unsung heroes of Prohibition," according to August Mencken. "They helped a lot of people get through without any real damage." Ibid., p. 13; HLM, "The Millennium," *BES*, Jan. 24, 1921; HLM to Philip Goodman, Oct. 21, 1930, EPFL; Louis Schecter to HLM, Aug. 17, 1922, EPFL; HLM, "Sunday Afternoon," *BES*, April 1, 1929; HLM to Philip Goodman, Oct. 5, 1919, Oct. 2, 1921; Dec. 4, 1921; Sept. 5, 1922, EPFL. From 1924–1933, the *American Mercury* devoted 69 articles to drinking, saloons, and Prohibition, with the result that subscribers wrote telling Mencken he had done the subject to death. HLM to Ernest Boyd, Oct. 19 [no year], NYPL/ms. *"The American Mercury* articles on Prohibition 1924–1933," Lawrence Spivak, American Mercury Lists and Notes, LC; HLM, "Overnight Saints," *Delineator*, Oct. 1933, pp. 4, 50.

4. Although the first draft had been written by Harry Black, the content and style of the final version was written by Mencken. Williams, *The Baltimore Sun 1837–1987*, pp. 164–68; "An Editorial Memorandum," Harold A. Williams Collection; author interview with R. P. Harriss, Oct. 24, 1987.

5. HLM, "A Carnival of Buncombe," *BES*, Feb. 9, 1920; Paul Patterson to HLM, Feb. 5, 1920, EPFL; author interviews with Wallace Cohen, Aug. 29, 1993, and Stanley Harrison, Aug. 13, 1990; Fecher, "Preface," *Mencken*, p. xx; Rodgers, ed., *The Impossible H. L. Mencken*, p. xliv; William Zinsser, "That Perlman of Great Price at 65," *NYT Magazine*, Jan. 26, 1969, p. 72; HLM to Marcella DuPont, June 25, 1938, Carl Bode Papers, EPFL; Burton Rascoe, "Mencken, Nathan and Cabell," *American Mercury*, March 1940, pp. 364–65; "The Vintage Mencken: An Interview with Alistair Cooke and Alfred A. Knopf by Clifton Fadiman, 1955," courtesy Jack Sanders; HLM, "The Reporter at Work," *American Mercury*, Aug. 1924, p. 509; Thomas F. Ford, "The Mencken Literary Legend," *Los Angeles Times*, Jan. 3, 1926; "Mencken's Prejudices Didn't Reflect Baltimore," Letters, *NYT*, Dec. 31, 1989; "Mencken Has Gone to Europe; Therefore –," *BES*, Aug. 7, 1922; Emily Clark to Joseph Hergesheimer, April 1923, HRHRC.

6. HLM, "Government by Blackleg," *BES*, Sept. 27, 1920; Perett, *America in the Twenties*, pp. 61–62; F. Scott Fitzgerald, "Echoes of the Jazz Age," in *The Crack-Up*, ed. Edmund Wilson (New York: New Directions, 1956), pp. 13, 21; HLM, "The Bill of Rights," *Chicago Sunday Tribune*, Jan. 17, 1926; Williams, *H. L. Mencken Revisited*, pp. 95, 97; Lewis Gannett, "Books and Things: The Legacy of Sacco and Vanzetti," *New York Herald Tribune*, Oct. 11, 1948. All columns cited by Mencken are in the *BES:* "An Appeal to TNT," Oct. 24, 1921; "Sacco and Vanzetti," April 18, 1927; "A Chance for an Idealist," Aug. 22, 1927; "The Brahmin Takes the Court," Aug. 29, 1927; "The Land of the Free," Jan. 12, 1925; "Slaying the Dragon," Oct. 3, 1921; "Why Not Tell the Truth?" July 10, 1922; "The Invisible Empire," Dec. 4, 1922.

7. Note from James Cain to Carl Bode, undated, collection of Roy Hoopes; HLM, "The Armenian Buncombe," *BES*, May 28, 1920; Arthur O. Lovejoy, "Mr. Mencken and the Armenian Massacres," *BES*, May 31, 1920; "Letters: The Writer Who Asks About Mencken," *BES*, June 7, 1920; "Letters: Shocking to the Friends of America," *BES*, May 31, 1920; "Letters: The Sun Would Regret Very Much to Lose a Subscriber of Fifty Years Standing," *BS*, June 19, 1920; Williams, *The Baltimore Sun 1837–1987*, p. 169. Memo written by Huntington Cairns, dated 1948, LC; "Memo to H. L. Mencken," collection of Harold A. Williams; HLM, *Thirty-Five Years*, p. 293, EPFL; "The Reminiscences of Hamilton Owens," pp. 40–42, COL; Warner, *The Making of a Newspaper*, p. 1; author interview with R. P. Harriss, Oct. 24, 1987; Oswald Garrison Villard, "The Baltimore Suns—A Notable Journalistic Resurrection," *Nation*, April 5,

1922, pp. 390–93; "Its Staff Controls the Baltimore Sun By a Member of Its Editorial Council," *Quill*, Dec. 1925, pp. 3–8; Arthur Link, ed., *The Papers of Woodrow Wilson: The Diary of Josephus Daniels*, vol. 65, p. 231, for entry dated April 27, 1920; James Cain, "Memo to Dr. Bode," collection of Alice Piper.

Chapter 21: Of Politics and Prose

1. Williams, *The Baltimore Sun 1837–1987*, p. 169; HLM, *Thirty-Five Years*, pp. 253–54; HLM to Theodore J. Christensen, May 1, 1939, EPFL.

2. HLM, "Mencken Finds Show Dullest In History," *BES*, June 10, 1920; HLM, "Really Strong Men Lacking at Chicago, Mencken Finds," *BES*, June 8, 1920; [Photograph], *Editor & Publisher*, June 19, 1920, p. 239; HLM, "It's All in Wilson's Hands, Mencken Concludes After Looking Around at Frisco," *BES*, June 29, 1920; HLM, *Thirty-Five Years*, p. 256, EPFL; HLM to August Mencken, June 13, 1920, EPFL.

3. HLM, "It's All in Wilson's Hands . . . ," *BES*, June 29, 1920; "San Francisco Proud of Convention Record, Splendid Achievement, Worthy of Great City; Visitors in Mood of Grateful Wonderment," *San Francisco Chronicle*, July 4, 1920; "California Makes New Friends; Bay City Wins Plaudits of Convention Crowds," *Los Angeles Times*, July 4, 1920; "Architect Explains How He Solved Auditorium Acoustics," *San Francisco Chronicle*, June 27, 1920; AAK, "For Henry, With Love," *Atlantic*, May 1959, p. 54; HLM, "Mencken Says All's Set to Put 'Young William' Over If Wilson Gives the Word," *BES*, July 1, 1920; "Lack of Gouging Happy Shock to Delegates; Hospitality and Weather Win Visitors," *San Francisco Chronicle*, June 27, 1920; HLM, "San Francisco: A Memory," *BES*, July 21, 1920; HLM to Edgar Lee Masters, Feb. 19, 1935, HRHRC; Carl Bode interview with Arthur Krock, June 25, 1963, PRIN/md.

4. HLM, *Thirty-Five Years*, pp. 282–84, EPFL; "Convention at Top Speed Finish Nomination To Music of Bands," *San Francisco Chronicle*, July 1, 1920; "Sing Melodies of Other Days," *Los Angeles Times*, July 1, 1920; HLM, "Bayard vs. Lionheart," *BES*, July 26, 1920; HLM, *Thirty-Five Years*, p. 273, EPFL; HLM to George Sterling, November 23, 1920, HUNT; Theodore Dreiser to George Sterling, Dec. 21, 1920, HUNT.

5. HLM, "Gamalielese," *BES*, March 7, 1921; HLM, "Gamalielese Again," *BES*, Sept. 9 1921.

6. HLM, *My Life*, p. 823, EPFL; Clark, *Innocence Abroad*, p. 105. For a further discussion of Mencken's influence on the Southern literary renaissance, see Fred C. Hobson, Jr., *Serpent in Eden: H.L. Mencken and the South* (Chapel Hill: University of North Carolina Press, 1974).

7. James Branch Cabell to Joseph Hergesheimer, Nov. 4, 1921, UVA; Clark, *Innocence Abroad*, p. 114; Clark, *Ingenue*, pp. 31, 110, 115; Carl Van Vechten, "How I Remember Joseph Hergesheimer," *Yale University Library Gazette*, Jan. 1948, p. 87; HLM, *My Life*, p. 874, EPFL; James Branch Cabell to Burton Rascoe, Dec. 2, 1921, UVA.

8. HLM, *My Life*, pp. 854–55, EPFL; Terence J. Matheson, "H. L. Mencken Reviews Sinclair Lewis' Novels," *Menckeniana*, Fall 1974, pp. 2–7; Grace Hegger to Gene Baker McComasy, Oct. 27, 1920, HRHRC; HLM, "Peasant and Cockney," *BES*, Jan. 3, 1921.

9. Moses Groome, "The Great American Critic," editorial, *BES*, May 26, 1922; Vincent O'Sullivan, "The American Critic," *London New Statesman*, Nov. 28, 1919.

10. HLM to Louise Pound, Nov. 5, 1920, DUKE; HLM to Joseph Hergesheimer, July 19, 1919, PRIN/fire; HLM to Fanny Butcher, Sept. 4, 1920, PRIN/fire; HLM to Louise Pound, Oct. 22, 1920, PRIN/fire; C. Martin Babcock, "Profiles of Noted Linguistics: Henry Louis Mencken," *Word Study*, Dec. 1960, p. 2; Edmund Wilson, "Talking United States," *New Republic*, July 1936, pp. 299–300; HLM to Raven McDavid, Oct. 11, 1946, NEW; HLM to Louise Pound, March 7, 1922, PRIN/fire.

11. Schwab, *James Gibbons Huneker*, pp. 283–84, 288, 294; HLM, *My Life*, p. 880 and Appendix X, EPFL; James Huneker, *Essays by James Huneker*, ed. H. L. Mencken, p. x; HLM,

"James Huneker," *BES*, Feb. 14, 1921; Hamilton Owens, "H. L. Mencken: A Personal Note," in *The Letters of H. L. Mencken*, ed. Guy J. Forgue, p. ix; M. Lincoln Schuster, "Mencken—The Bad Boy of Baltimore," *New York Evening Journal*, Nov. 22, 1922.

Chapter 22: That Man in Baltimore

1. Margaret Lappin, "As I Saw Mencken," pp. 1, 2, 19, YALE; author interview with Ruth Goodman Goetz, March 4, 1992; James Cain, "Memo to Dr. Bode," undated, collection of Roy Hoopes.

2. Margaret Lappin, "As I Saw Mencken," pp. 4, 6, 8, 169–70, YALE; Stacy V. Jones, "Intrepid Herald Staff Man Beards Mencken in His Den, *Washington Herald*, Aug. 28, 1921.

3. Margaret Lappin, "As I Saw Mencken," pp. 29–30, 170, YALE; HLM to Benjamin De Casseres, March 19, 1936, NYPL; William Gaines, "About New York," Associated Press Feature Service, Aug. 9, 1931; Untermeyer, *From Another World*, p. 139; HLM to Blanche Knopf, Sept. 13, 1943, Dec. 13, 1943, EPFL; Julian Boyd to Jim Tully, Aug. 26, 1942, PRIN/fire.

4. Anderson, *Sherwood Anderson's Memoirs*, ed. Roy Lewis White, p. 369; Hecht, *Letters from Bohemia*, p. 72; AAK to Betty Adler, *Menckeniana*, Fall 1970, p. 35; *The New Mencken Letters*, ed. Carl Bode, p. 4; August Mencken to William Feather, Sept. 20, 1961, EPFL; Margaret Lappin, "As I Saw Mencken," pp. 6, 8–9, 29, 130–33, 151, 186-A, YALE.

5. HLM, "New York," *BES*, May 26, 1924; HLM, "Répétition Generale," *Smart Set*, June 1920, pp. 41–42; HLM, *My Life*, p. 872, EPFL; "The Spotlight on Mencken," *BES*, Jan. 27, 1922; Nicholas M. Alter, "A Man and His Dog," *Menckeniana*, Spring 1969, pp. 7–9; HLM to Dr. Nicholas Alter, March 18, 21, 1946, and Dr. Nicholas Alter to HLM, March 19, 1946, NYPL; HLM to August Mencken, Feb. 9, Feb. 10, 1920, April 3, 1920, May 18, May 29, 1920, EPFL; untitled manuscript by Virginia Mencken Morrison, Carl Bode Papers, EPFL; HLM to Sara Haardt, Aug. 14, 1924, Jan. 1, 1925, GOU; Mayfield, *The Constant Circle*, p. 159; Clark, *Ingenue*, p. 56; HLM, "The Comforts of Life," *BES*, July 28, 1930.

6. Julian Boyd to Jim Tully, Aug. 26, 1942 (PRIN/fire); Hamilton Owens, "A Living Biography of H. L. Mencken," *BES*, Jan. 3, 1951; HLM, "Days of Innocence: The Life of Tone," *New Yorker*, Sept. 25, 1943, p. 21.

7. HLM to Burton Rascoe, undated, PENN; HLM to Mrs. Adolph Torovky, Aug. 21, 1945, EPFL; James H. Bready, "Saturday Night Club Plays Last Notes; Donates All Music to Pratt Library," *BES*, Dec. 27, 1950; Louis Cheslock, "Some Personal Memories of HLM," *Menckeniana*, Spring 1974, pp. 3–11; Fecher, *Mencken*, p. 283; Louis Cheslock, "Mencken, the Musician," *Peabody Notes*, Autumn 1954; A. H. McDannald to Julian P. Boyd, Aug. 5, 1942, PRIN/fire; HLM to Louis Cheslock, March 1, 1940, EPFL; Cheslock, "Mencken, the Musician," *BS*, Sept. 8, 1956; author interview with Lawrence Spivak, June 25, 1989; HLM to Paul J. Barker, April 8, 1936, EPFL; A. H. McDannald to Willard Huntington Wright, Dec. 8, 1913, PRIN/fire; Carl Bode interview with Penelope Pearl Pollaczek, Feb. 23, 1965, Carl Bode Papers, EPFL; HLM, "Autobiographical Notes, 1941," EPFL; HLM to Philip Goodman, Sept. 27, 1927, EPFL; author interview with Carolyn Heinmuller, Oct. 22, 1996; author interview with Elise Cheslock, Jan. 21, 1994; AAK, "For Henry, With Love," *Atlantic*, May 1959, p. 52; Mrs. Hazel Ashworth, "I Remember . . . H. L. Mencken and the Saturday Night Club," *BS Magazine*, March 12, 1972, pp. 2, 31; Allan W. Rhynhart to HLM, April 18, 1955, EPFL; Carol Fitzpatrick, "Mencken, Music and the Saturday Night Club, Part II," *Menckeniana*, Winter 1982, p. 14; Mary McKinsey Rideout, "I Remember. . . . Mencken, Beer, Music on a Waterfront Farm," *BS Magazine*, Jan. 25, 1981, p. 21; Barbara Woolcott to HLM, Dec. 24, 1954, EPFL.

8. H. L. Mencken, list of books and music bequeathed to Louis Cheslock, EPFL; Lawrence Gilman, "Notes on the Program," Philharmonic Program of June 30, 1923; Mortimer H. Frank, "Mencken on Music," "Notes on the Program for Carnegie Hall, 14th

Season, 1965–1966," pp. 5–8, 22; HLM, "Franz Joseph Haydn," *BES*, Nov. 23, 1916; Felix Deyo, "Sage of Baltimore Really a Frustrated Musician," *Musical America*, Feb. 1946, pp. 19, 292; James Cain, "Memo to Dr. Bode re: Mencken," undated, courtesy of Alice Piper; George Pullen, "Here's How in Music, According to Mencken," *Nashville Banner*, Sept. 27, 1925; "Negro Music Has Superb Rhythm, Says Mencken," *Pittsburgh Courier*, Dec. 5, 1925; HLM to Isaac Goldberg, March 18, 1927, NYPL/ms; HLM, "Night Club," *BES*, Sept. 3, 1934; AAK, "Reminiscences of Hergesheimer, Van Vechten and Mencken," *Yale University Library Gazette*, April 1950, pp. 157–58.

    9. Fecher, *Mencken*, pp. 282–87; HLM to Carl Van Vechten, June 1, 1925, YALE; HLM to Fanny Butcher, Feb. 20, 1921, PRIN/fire; Louis Cheslock, "Some Personal Memories of H. L. Mencken," *Menckeniana*, pp. 3–11; author interview with Mrs. Arnold Rich, Dec. 2, 1994; Edmund Wilson, "The All-Star Literary Vaudeville," *New Republic*, June 30, 1926, p. 497; HLM, "The Free Lance," *BES*, Oct. 13, 1913; For a collection of Mencken's articles on music, see Louis Cheslock, *Mencken on Music* (New York: Alfred A. Knopf, 1961); for a list of articles, see Adler, *The Mencken Bibliography*, pp. 4, 23–24.

Chapter 23: The Duel of Sex

    1. HLM to Estelle Bloom, June 19, 1920, NYPL; Carl Van Vechten, "How I Remember Joseph Hergesheimer," *Yale University Library Gazette*, Jan. 1948, p. 88; James Cain insisted that Mencken's habit of greeting guests had been picked up from Nathan, who said waiting before putting out hospitality was "nonsense." Undated note from James Cain to Carl Bode, courtesy Alice Piper; HLM to Zoë Akins, April 22, 1921, HUNT; Loos, *A Girl Like I*, p. 147; HLM, *My Life*, pp. 260, 261, 264, 551–52, 680, EPFL; author interview with Ruth Goodman Goetz, June 13, 1991, March 4, 1992; Marion Bloom to Estelle Bloom, March 14, 1921, NYPL; Florenz Ziegfeld said Kay Laurell embodied the perfect type of feminine beauty: blonde, ethereal, and patrician, with a milky complexion and a piquant nose. "If you saw the Follies—you saw Kay." "Miss Kay Laurell," *Town and Country*, June 10, 1918, p. 23; "Kay Laurell," *Detroit News*, March 31, 1918; Delight Evans, "A Sweet Gal," *Photoplay Journal*, Oct. 1919, pp. 44–46, 104, NYPL/pa; Mellow, *Invented Lives*, p. 93.

    2. HLM, "The Lady Politician," *BES*, August 29, 1921; Perrett, *America in the Twenties*, pp. 158–59; HLM, "Some Secrets of Beauty," *New York Evening Mail*, Nov. 23, 1917; HLM to Mrs. Harry S. Smith, Dec. 17, 1921, EPFL; Margaret Lappin, "As I Saw Mencken," p. 11, YALE; HLM, *In Defense of Women*, pp. 184–85.

    3. B. F. Wilson, "H. L. Mencken Says: 'I Like Women—But Not Too Young,'" *Metropolitan Magazine*, Dec. 1923, p. 101; HLM, "Répétition Generale," *Smart Set*, April 1923, p. 33; HLM to Joseph Hergesheimer, April 15, 1921, HRHRC; "Charge Fraud: Hold Woman," *NYT*, Dec. 28, 1923; HLM to George Sterling, Dec. 28, 1923, Feb. 6, 1924, HUNT.

    4. Emily Clark to Joseph Hergesheimer, March 12, 1922, HRHRC; Loos, *A Girl Like I*, pp. 214, 218; HLM, *In Defense of Women*, p. 133; Joseph Hergesheimer, "Mr. Henry L. Mencken," *Borzoi 1925*, p. 105; HLM to Fanny Butcher, undated, ca. 1920–1921, NYPL; HLM to Bee Wilson, Dec. 10, 1925, NYPL; HLM to Dorothy Taylor, Dec. 23, 1923, Sept. 17, 1926, author's collection; Butcher, *Many Lives, One Life*, pp. 403–5; Loos, *A Cast of Thousands*, pp. 74, 251–52; Carl Bode interview with Anita Loos, Oct. 30, 1964, Carl Bode Papers, EPFL.

    5. Ernest Boyd to HLM, Jan. 9, 1924, NYPL; Clark, *Ingenue*, p. 59; B. F. Wilson, "H. L. Mencken Says . . . ," *Metropolitan Magazine*, Dec. 1923, p. 102; Laurel Gray, "Laurel Gray's Love Gossip," *Medford (N.J.) Tribune*, Nov. 20, 1923; HLM and GJN, "Répétition Generale," *Smart Set*, Aug. 1921, pp. 31–40.

    6. B. F. Wilson, "H. L. Mencken Says . . . ," *Metropolitan Magazine*, Dec. 1923, p. 102; HLM, *In Defense of Women*, pp. 207–8; Jerome, *The Secret of Woman*, "Preface" and pp. 143–44; HLM, *My Life*, p. 950, EPFL; "Helen Jerome," *New York Post*, June 22, 1936.

7. Marion Bloom to Estelle Bloom, May 13, 1921, Dec. 16, 1920, NYPL; Marion Bloom to Estelle Bloom, Nov. 8, 1921, NYPL; HLM, "For Better, For Worse," *BES*, July 17, 1922; "Explosion Follows Query to Mencken on Marriage," *BES*, July 24, 1922; "Mencken Desires Wife, Mrs. Schwartz Declares," *BES*, July 20, 1922; "What's The Matter with Mencken, By a Psychoanalyst," *BS*, Aug. 7, 1922; Manchester, *Disturber of the Peace*, p. 138.

8. "The Visit of Mr. Mencken," *English Review*, Aug. 1922; "Mencken," *Outlook*, Aug. 1922; "A Hustler's Day: Bursting an American Myth," *London Telegraph*, Aug. 19, 1922; "Mencken's Views of America," editorial, *Minneapolis Journal*, Sept. 4, 1922; "American Author on America," editorial, *Columbia State*, Aug. 21, 1922; "British Like Mencken—Until He Turns Critic," *Brooklyn Eagle*, Aug. 28, 1922; "London, as USA Critic Sees It," *London Weekly*, Aug. 20, 1922; "London, as a Dream of Fair Women," *Sunday Express*, Aug. 20, 1922; "Mencken in England," *BES*, Sept. 6, 1922; "Mencken," *London Weekly*, Aug. 20, 1922.

9. HLM to August Mencken, Sept. 4, 1922, EPFL; HLM to Marion Bloom, Sept. 4, 1922, EPFL; HLM, *Thirty-Five Years*, pp. 341, 344, 348, EPFL; Ritchie, *Faust's Metropolis*, pp. 322, 324; HLM to August Mencken, Sept. 4, 1922, EPFL; HLM to Paul Patterson, Sept. 9, 1922, EPFL; HLM, "Where Propaganda Ends," *BES*, June 22, 1922; HLM, "Exile at Wieringen Says He Longs for Day When He Can Assist Germany," *BS*, Oct. 11, 1922; Hermann George Scheffauer to H. L. Mencken, Dec. 13, 1922, NYPL; "Again the Man of Memoirs," editorial, *New York Times*, Oct. 12, 1922.

10. "Mencken Sees U.S. War," *New York Call*, Oct. 5, 1922; "Thieves Run New Republics of Europe, Writes H. L. Mencken After Tour There," *Washington Post*, Nov. 12, 1922; Henry Wood to Foreign Minister Herrn von Rosenberg, June 22, 1923, POLIT; HLM to Wood, June 3, 1923, POLIT; HLM, *Thirty-Five Years*, p. 354; Friedrich Schönemann, "Henry Louis Mencken Ein Moderner Amerikanischer Kritic," *Die Neue Zeit*, Jan. 22, 1921; Hermann George Scheffauer to HLM, Oct. 30, 1922, NYPL.

11. HLM to Marion Bloom, Sept. 21, Nov. 2, 1922, EPFL; Marion Bloom to Estelle Bloom, Aug. 2, 1923, NYPL; HLM to Estelle Bloom, Feb. 3, 1923; HLM to Marion Bloom, Nov. 4, 1922, NYPL; Marion Bloom to Estelle Bloom, Aug. 2, 1923, NYPL; Martin, *In Defense of Marion*, pp. 193–94; Marion Bloom to Betty Adler, July 3, 1966, EPFL; HLM to Estelle Bloom, Aug. 10, 1923, EPFL; HLM to Marion Bloom, ca. Aug. 1923, EPFL; HLM to Zoë Akins, May 31 [1923], HUNT.

12. HLM, *Thirty-Five Years*, p. 367, EPFL; Alexander Woolcott on Mencken, *New York Evening Sun*, Feb. 26, 1925; Mayfield, *The Constant Circle*, pp. 2–7; Helen Knipp, "Johnson, Boswell, Mencken and Me," courtesy of Helen Knipp; Sara Haardt to HLM, Aug. 22, 1923, GOU; author interview with Edward Clark, March 16, 1995.

13. Mayfield, *The Constant Circle*, p. 55; Bode, *Mencken*, p. 282; Rodgers, ed., *Mencken & Sara*, p. 13; R. P. Harriss, "Mencken and Sara," *BS*, Feb. 15, 1987; author interview with R. P. Harriss, Oct. 24, 1987; James Cain, "Mr. M," LC; Lella Warren's comment is printed beside Sara Haardt's short story, "King of the Jellies," *College Humor*, Nov. 1928, p. 5; author interviews with Marion Gutman, Jan. 12, 1985, and Mary Ross Flowers, Oct. 10, 1985; Haardt, *Southern Album*, H. L. Mencken, ed., pp. xxii–xxiii; R. P. Harriss to Sara Mayfield, Jan. 25, 1929, ALA/gg; HLM, "Autobiographical Notes, 1925," p. 192, EPFL; Haardt, *The Love Story of an Old Maid*, p. 32.

14. Rodgers, ed., *Mencken & Sara*, pp. 106, 108, 111–13 ; HLM to Sara Haardt, Jan. 15, 1924, GOU; Dr. Marjorie Nicholson to HLM, May 31, 1935, GOU; HLM to Sara Haardt, Jan. 21, 1924, GOU; "The Reminiscences of Marjorie Hope Nicholson," pp. 198, 201–2, COL.

15. Rodgers, ed., *Mencken & Sara*, pp. 3, 10, 120; HLM to Sara Haardt, Feb. 28, 1924, GOU; Sara Haardt to Sara Mayfield, March 5, 1924, ALA/gg; HLM to Sara Haardt, June 8, 1924, GOU; "The Reminiscences of Marjorie Hope Nicholson," pp. 198, 200, COL; HLM to Sara Haardt, April 12, 1924, GOU; "The Three Most Fascinating Men of the United States," *New York News*, April 6, 1924.

Chapter 24: Old Discord and New Alliances

1. AAK, Diary, Oct. 7, 1925, HRHRC; Clark, *Ingenue*, p. 54; author interview with Ruth Goodman Goetz, June 13, 1991, March 4, 1992; Edmund Wilson, "The Aftermath of Mencken," *New Yorker*, May 31, 1969, p. 114; "The Spotlight on Mencken," *BES*, Jan. 27, 1922; HLM to Philip Goodman, Sept. 1, 1932, EPFL; Carl Bode interview with John Owens, Sept. 23, 1964, collection of Harold A. Williams; HLM to Burton Rascoe, "Addendum on Aims," p. 2, ca. 1918, PENN; Herbert M. Simpson, "Three Minus Two: The Rift Between Mencken and Nathan," a paper written for Carl Bode at the University of Maryland, Carl Bode Papers, EPFL; AAK Memoirs, p. 13, HRHRC.

2. Dolmetsch, *The Smart Set*, p. 86; Herbert M. Simpson, "Three Minus Two: The Rift Between Mencken and Nathan," p. 2, EPFL; Hobson, *Mencken: A Life*, p. 242; Rodgers, ed., *Mencken & Sara*, p. 169; HLM, "Notes on Journalism," *Chicago Tribune*, Sept. 19, 1926; HLM, "Fifteen Years," *Smart Set*, Oct. 1923, p. 139; HLM to Max Broedel, July 30, 1923, PRIN/fire.

3. HLM to Morris Fishbein, Aug. 19, 1923, CHI; HLM to Raymond Pearl, Aug. 8, 1923, APS; HLM to Carl Van Doren, Aug. 20, 1923, PRIN/fire; HLM to Sara Haardt, Aug. 24, 1923, GOU; Rumford Press to Alfred Knopf, Inc., Oct. 31, 1923, EPFL; transcript of telephone conversation between Mr. Rossiter and Samuel Knopf, Nov. 2, 1923, EPFL; Delight Evans, " 'With The Horses Running Around,' Said Mr. Mencken; 'And the Band Playing,' Said Mr. Nathan," *New York Telegraph*, Dec. 2, 1923.

4. *American Mercury*, Jan. 1924; Singleton, *H. L. Mencken and the American Mercury Adventure*, pp. 47–48, 181–94. As excellent as this book is, it contains some inaccuracies; it is best examined with August Mencken's notations in hand, which are among his papers at the EPFL; HLM, "Introduction," *Americana: 1925*, pp. v–vi; HLM to Charles Angoff, Jan. 11 [1925], BU; HLM to Aileen Pringle, undated, YALE; HLM, editorial, *American Mercury*, Dec. 1928, pp. 407–10; Fenwick Anderson, "Black Perspectives in Mencken's *Mercury*," *Menckeniana*, Summer 1979, pp. 2–6; "The Reminiscences of George Schuyler," p. 123, COL; Peterson, *Magazines in the Twentieth Century*, pp. 429–34; Delight Evans, " 'With the Horses Running Around,' Said Mr. Mencken, 'And the Band Playing,' said Mr. Nathan," *New York Telegraph*, Dec. 2, 1923; "The Disadvantages of Popularity," *Buffalo Courier*, Feb. 10, 1924; GJN, "The Happiest Days of H. L. Mencken," *Esquire*, Oct. 25, 1927, p. 149.

5. Carl Bode interview with Edith Lustgarten, Oct. 1, 1963, Carl Bode Papers, EPFL; Helen J. Wilcox, "H. L. Mencken: An Intimate Sketch of the Great American Publicist,", *Triad (Sydney) News*, March 1, 1926; Vrest Orton Gardner, "Henry Louis Mencken," *Massachusetts News*, May 8, 1926; Louis Adamic to James Boyd, July 14, 1942, PRIN/fire; HLM, "Memoirs of an Editor," *Vanity Fair*, Feb. 1934, p. 54; HLM to Sara Haardt, June 20, 1924, GOU.

6. AAK Memoirs, p. 13, HRHRC; "George Jean Nathan," *New York Herald Tribune*, May 18, 1952; HLM to Morris Fishbein, Nov. 7, 1924, CHI; HLM, "Breathing Space," *BES*, Aug. 4, 1924; HLM to AAK, Oct. 13, 1924, EPFL; "Convention Notes," *St. Louis Post-Dispatch*, June 10, 1924; HLM "Mencken Found to Flee Before Burton's Oratory; Babbittry Apalls Him," *BES*, June 11, 1924; Rodgers, ed., *The Impossible H. L. Mencken*, p. 260.

7. Rodgers, ed., *The Impossible H. L. Mencken*, pp. 276, 281; HLM to Sara Haardt, July 8, 1924, GOU; "Convention Sidelights," *Roanoke World News*, July 10, 1924; "Such Is Fame," *Elmira Adventurer*, June 28, 1924; HLM, "The Voter's Dilemma," *BES*, Nov. 3, 1924.

8. HLM, *Thirty-Five Years*, p. 407, EPFL; Walter Lippmann, "The Enormously Civilized Minority," *Vanity Fair*, March 1928, pp. 64, 71; HLM to GJN, Oct. 15, 1924, NYPL; GJN to HLM, undated, NYPL; HLM to GJN, Oct. 19, 1924, NYPL; GJN to HLM, "Wednesday," NYPL; Charles Angoff to HLM, Oct. 20, 21, 1924, BU; Norris Osborne to Charles Angoff, Aug. 6, 1924, BU; *New Hampshire Courier* to Charles Angoff, Aug. 2, 1924, BU; Charles Angoff to J. J. Angoff, Nov. 9, 1924, BU; HLM to Charles Angoff, Oct. 31, 1924, BU; "The Reminiscences of Bruce Gould," p. 105, COL.

9. HLM to Charles Angoff, Nov. 28, 1924, BU; Angoff, *The Bitter Spring*, pp. 66, 74, 90, 99–100, 276, 507, 708–9; Charles Angoff to William Manchester, Jan. 27, 1950, BU; HLM to Sara Haardt, Jan. 30, 1925, GOU; Harold V. Ribelow, "A Conversation with Charles Angoff," *The Old Century and the New: Essays in Honor of Charles Angoff*, ed. Alfred Rosa, pp. 41, 53; HLM to Sara Haardt, April 1, 1925, GOU; HLM, "Biography," *Chicago Sunday Tribune*, July 12, 1925; HLM, "James Huneker," *BES*, Feb. 14, 1921; HLM to Isaac Goldberg, March 5, 1925, NYPL/ms; HLM, "Biography and Other Fiction," *Smart Set*, Aug. 1923, p. 138; HLM to Sara Haardt, April 4, 1925, GOU.

10. HLM to Sara Haardt, April 1, 25, 1925, GOU; HLM to GJN, undated, CORN; Carl Bode interview with Huntington Cairns, June 25, 1963, PRIN/md; AAK Memoirs, pp. 37–38, HRHRC; "George Jean Nathan," *New York Herald Tribune*, May 18, 1952; AAK, Diary, Oct. 7, 1925, HRHRC.

11. G. D. Eaton, "Change the American Mercury? Bosh! Its Genius Answer," *New York Telegraph*, April 18, 1925.

12. HLM to Dorothy Taylor, June 9, 1925, author's collection; Singleton, *H. L. Mencken and the American Mercury Adventure*, pp. 156–94.

Chapter 25: The Scopes Trial

1. "Monkey Business," *Nation*, July 31, 1925, p. 118; William Jennings Bryan to Sue K. Hicks, May 29, 1925, LC; HLM, *Thirty-Five Years*, pp. 42, 423, EPFL; "Supreme Court May Get Evolution Case," *Boston Globe*, May 13, 1925.

2. Larson, *Summer for the Gods*, p. 83; "Darrow Says Trial Has Aroused Nation," *Chicago Daily News*, July 8, 1925; HLM, *Thirty-Five Years*, p. 423, EPFL; "Malone Glad Trial Starts Friday," *Chattanooga Times*, July 10, 1925; Stanley L. Harrison, "The Scopes Monkey Trial Revisited: Mencken and the Editorial Art of Edmund Duffy," *Journal of American Culture*, Winter 1994, pp. 55–63.

3. "Last Minute Preparations Proceed, as East Train Brings New Arrivals," *Chattanooga News*, July 9, 1925; "Dayton Hotels Boost Prices to Eight Dollars a Day; Features at Trial," *Knoxville Sentinel*, July 9, 1925; "Airship Will Transport the Sentinel from Knoxville to Scene of Scopes Trial," *Knoxville Sentinel*, July 9, 1925; A. W. Ogden, "Dayton Has Been Designated as the 'Monkey Town' Because of Big Trial," *Knoxville Sentinel*, July 9, 1925; oral history of Quinn Ryan, WGN Radio, UMC/bp; William J. Losh to his wife, July 11, 1925, HOOV. References to the Scopes Trial can be found in Mencken's correspondence at the NYPL and elsewhere, also in HLM, *Heathen Days*, pp. 214–38, and in *A New Dictionary of Quotations*, pp. 165–66. For those who balk at slogging through reels of microfilm, a complete set of Mencken's newspaper reports from the Scopes Trial are in *The Impossible H. L. Mencken*, Rodgers, ed., pp. 560–611.

4. John P. Fort, " 'Local Color' Cry Writers at Dayton," *Chattanooga News*, July 7, 1925; "Table in Drug Store Where Scopes Case Started Object of Interest," *Knoxville Sentinel*, July 9, 1925; "Darrow Turns to Holy Writ; Scopes Scoots," *Chattanooga News*, July 1, 1925; "Bryan in Dayton, Calls Scopes Trial Duel to the Death," *NYT*, July 28, 1925; "Bryan Threatens National Campaign to Bar Evolution," *NYT*, July 8, 1925; HLM, "Mencken Finds Daytonians Full of Sickening Doubts About Value of Publicity," *BES*, July 9, 1925; "Why Make a Monkey Out of Tennessee for Bryan's Sake?" *Chattanooga News*, July 18, 1925; Larson, *Summer for the Gods*, p. 145.

5. HLM, *Thirty-Five Years*, p. 424, EPFL; HLM to Sara Haardt, July 9, 1925, GOU; George F. Milton, "Who's Who in Monkeyville, Tenn.," *New York Herald Tribune Magazine*, July 5, 1925, pp. 1–2; "Mencken Strolls On Main Street," *Chattanooga Times*, July 9, 1925; "Dayton, Keyed Up for Scopes Trial," *NYT*, July 10, 1925; "People About Courthouse During

Trial Look Like Typical Fair Crowd," *Knoxville Sentinel*, July 13, 1925; "Lord, Flesh and Devil Were with Vigor and Vim in Dayton," *New York Herald Tribune*, July 10, 1925; author interview with Eloise Reed, July 18, 1998; HLM, "Mencken Finds Daytonians Full of Sickening Doubts About Value of Publicity," *BES*, July 9, 1925; HLM, *Thirty-Five Years*, pp. 424–25, 432, 434, EPFL; HLM, "Bryan," *BES*, July 27, 1925; John T. Scopes and James Presley, *Center of the Storm*, p. 99; "Dayton Swarming with Evangelists," *BES*, July 10, 1925; "Dayton Disappointed," *Chattanooga Times*, July 11, 1925; HLM, "A Lesson for Pastors," *BES*, January 18, 1926; "Monkeyville Gibberings," *BES*, July 10, 1925; HLM, *Heathen Days*, pp. 228, 231–33, 683; "Dayton Authorities Suppress Skeptics," *NYT*, July 12, 1925; HLM to Sara Haardt, July 8, 1925, GOU.

6. "Cranks and Freaks Flock to Dayton," *NYT*, July 11, 1925; "Scopes Case Causes Greater Demand for Science Reading," *BES*, July 13, 1925; "Evolution Book Sales Boom in Baltimore," *BES*, May 15, 1925; "Dayton to Have College Named for Commoner," *Chattanooga Times*, July 14, 1925; "Bryan Has Won Case Before It Gets Underway," *Chattanooga News*, July 10, 1925; William J. Losh to his wife, July 11, 1925, HOOV; Larson, *Summer for the Gods*, p. 148; Greene, ed., *Star Reporters and 34 of Their Stories*, p. 227; Hays, *Let Freedom Ring*, p. 34; Carl Bode interview with Watson Davis, June 30, 1965, EPFL; "Scopes Jury Chosen with Dramatic Speed," *NYT*, July 14, 1925; "Jury in Scopes Trial All Firm in Bible Belief," *New York Evening Sun*, July 11, 1925; Lindsay Dennison, "Scopes Left Out of First Picture Taken in Court," *New York Evening World*, July 10, 1925. The minister's interminable praying caused Mencken to compare the trial to a religious orgy. Nevertheless, prayer continued throughout the trial. A blessing was given for the newspapermen; a loud Amen! resounded through the room. Darrow said he hoped that the reporters would get the "amen's on the record."

7. "Scopes Jury Firm in Bible Belief," *New York Evening Sun*, July 11, 1925; HLM, "Mencken Likens Trial to a Religious Orgy, with Defendant a Beelzebub," *BES*, July 11, 1925; "A Typical Southern Jury," *Pittsburgh American*, July 17, 1925; "Dayton Disappointed," *Chattanooga Daily Times*, July 12, 1925; HLM, *Thirty-Five Years*, p. 441, EPFL; Warren Allan, "Background of the Scopes Trial at Dayton, Tennessee" (graduate thesis, University of Tennessee, Aug. 1959), p. 81, KNOX. Allen lived in Dayton for six years and interviewed local witnesses to the Scopes Trial. His interviews took place mostly in 1959; many of the men and women are now deceased.

8. Nellie Kenyon, "Mencken's Night Visit to the Holy Rollers," *BS*, Sept. 18, 1977. Nellie Kenyon spoke about her meeting with Mencken for the rest of her life. Martin Ochs, "News Lookout," *Chattanooga News*, Feb. 1, 1956; author interview with John Siegenthaler, Feb. 18, 1997; Henry Hyde, "Man From Monkey" manuscript, UVA; HLM, *Thirty-Five Years*, p. 443, EPFL; HLM, "Yearning Mountaineer's Souls Need Reconversion Nightly, Mencken Finds," *BES*, July 13, 1925; HLM, *Heathen Days*, p. 233; "Holy Rollers Draw Many to Heard Old-Time Religion," *Chattanooga News*, July 15, 1925; Williams, *The Sunpapers of Baltimore 1837–1987*, p. 182; "Crowds Flock to Get the Sentinel by Airplane," *Knoxville Sentinel*, July 14, 1925; "Celebrities and Others Attending the Scopes Trial," *Knoxville Sentinel*, July 10, 1925; Warren Allen, "Background of the Scopes Trial," p. 11; "Dayton Authorities Suppress Skeptics," *NYT*, July 12, 1925; author interviews with Tom Morgan, July 18, 1998, and Kathryn Robinson, Sept. 29, 1998.

9. Darrow, *The Story of My Life*, p. 257; HLM, "Bryan," *BES*, July 27, 1925; Clarence Darrow, draft for his autobiography, from "Speech, Article, and Book File," p. 19, LC; Hays, *Let Freedom Ring*, p. 39; "Malone's Ire Is Stirred by Covert Sneer," *BES*, July 13, 1925; "Darrow Scores Ignorance and Bigotry Seeking to Quash Scopes Indictment," *NYT*, July 14, 1925; Robert T. Small, "Small Sees Friendly Trial Become Furiously Hostile," *BES*, July 24, 1925; HLM, "Darrow's Eloquent Appeal Wasted on Ears That Heed Only Bryan", *BES*, July 14,

1925; "3 Boys Witnesses Against Scopes: Most Excited Persons in Court Room," *New York World*, July 14, 1925; *The World's Most Famous Court Trial: The Tennessee Evolution Case, A Word-for-Word Report* (Dayton: Bryan College, 1990, second edition), p. 87; Larson, *Summer for the Gods*, pp. 164–66; "Lively Clashes in Move to Quash Indictment," *Chattanooga Times*, July 14, 1925; "Dayton's Thirsty Few Hours Last Night," *Knoxville Journal*, July 14, 1925; "Dayton in Fear of One Darrow," *Chattanooga News*, July 16, 1925.

10. "Europe Calls It a Vaudeville Show," *Chattanooga Times*, July 11, 1925; "Europe Is Amazed by the Scopes Case," *NYT*, July 11, 1925; "Moslems Are Amazed by Evolution Case," *BES*, July 10, 1925; "Scopes Case Stirs Berlin," *NYT*, July 19, 1925; " 'Human Monkey' Walks on All Fours in Paris; an Asylum Wanderer Until He Read of Dayton," *NYT*, July 19, 1925; "Dayton Evolution Case Features in Paris Papers; Trial Court Called 'a University of Dispute in the Land of Barnum,' " *BS*, July 13, 1925; "Monkey Case Treated as Joke of the Century by the British Press," *BS*, July 11, 1925; "London Astounded by Dayton Antics," *BES*, July 10, 1925; "Government and Responsibility," *London Times*, July 22, 1925; "Shaw's Comment on Dayton Evolution Trial," *St. Louis Labor*, July 18, 1925; HLM, "Darrow's Eloquent Appeal . . . ," *BES*, July 14, 1925; HLM, "The Sad Case of Tennessee," *Chicago Tribune*, March 13, 1926; Governor Austin Peay to Lehman Johnson, March 27, 1926, "Governor Austin Peay Papers," TSA.

11. "Dayton Disappointed," *Chattanooga Daily Times*, July 11, 1925; "Crowds Have Not Hit Dayton Yet," *Chattanooga News*, July 10, 1925; "Cranks and Freaks Flock to Dayton," *NYT*, July 11, 1925; F. E. Robinson and W. S. Morgan, *Why Dayton of all Places?* (Chattanooga: Andrews Printers, 1925); Warren Allan, "Background of the Scopes Trial," p. 100, KNOX; HLM, "Mencken Finds Daytonians Full of Sickening Doubts . . . ," *BES*, July 9, 1925; "Weird Adventures of 200 Reporters at Tennessee Evolution Trial," *Editor & Publisher*, July 18, 1925, p. 3; Eric Newhouse, "Telegrapher Remembers Mencken as Difficult, Sarcastic and Hard-Digging Reporter at Dayton," *Chattanooga Times*, Nov. 10, 1977; "Dogs Bark, Babes Wail in Dayton Courtroom," UPI Report , July 14, 1925, "Losh scrapbook," HOOV. One newspaperman actually brought in a heavy chair and padlocked it to secure his seat. "Limit Crowd at Trial to Seating Basis," *Knoxville Sentinel*, July 16, 1925; "Sizzling Beef Injects Scents into Tennessee Monkey Trial," *Milwaukee Leader*, July 10, 1925; "Monkeyville Gibberings," *BES*, July 10, 1925; William J. Losh to his wife, July 9, 1925, HOOV; Carl Bode interview with Watson Davis, June 30, 1965, Carl Bode Papers, EPFL; "Dayton Contrasts: Bulletin No. 3," July 18, 1925, KNOX; Haldeman-Julius, *The World of Haldeman-Julius*, pp. 88–92; Greene, *The Era of Wonderful Nonsense*, p. 151.

12. HLM, "Mencken Declares Strictly Fair Trial Is Beyond Ken of Tennessee Fundamentalists," *BES*, July 16, 1925; Robert T. Small, "First Scientific Witness Stuns Judge and Dayton," *BES*, July 16, 1925; "Judge Shatters the Scopes Defense by Barring Testimony of Scientists," *NYT*, July 18, 1925.

13. A. W. Ogden, "Bryan, Leader of Fundamentalists, Champing the Bit, Ready to Go," *Knoxville Sentinel*, July 16, 1925; Jack Lait, "Bryan Evolution Trial May Produce a Number of Chautauqua Lecturers in Opinion of Jack Lait," *Knoxville Sentinel*, July 13, 1925; HLM, "Mencken Declares Strictly Fair Trial Is Beyond Ken of Tennessee Fundamentalists," *BES*, July 16, 1925; Burton W. Folsom, Jr., "The Scopes Trial Reconsidered," *Continuity: A Journal of History*, Fall 1988, p. 104; Bynum Shaw, "Scopes Reviews the Monkey Trial," *Esquire*, Nov. 1970, pp. 86, 88, 90, 94; HLM, "Malone the Victor, Even Though Court Sides with Opponents, Says Mencken," *BES*, July 17, 1925; HLM to Sara Haardt, July 19, 1925, GOU; Scopes, *Center of the Storm*, p. 144; *The World's Most Famous Court Trial*, pp. 181–82; HLM, "Bryan," *BES*, July 17, 1925.

14. Mrs. William Jennings Bryan to her children, July 20, 1925, in "Correspondence of Grace Bryan Hargraves 1924–1934," vol. II, pp. 19, 21, LC; *The World's Most Famous Court Trial*, pp. 187–88; HLM, *Heathen Days*, p. 236; HLM, "Malone the Victor . . . ," *BES*, July 17,

1925; Scopes, *Center of the Storm*, pp. 148, 154–55; Larson, *Summer for the Gods*, p. 179; Hays, *City Lawyer*, p. 157; George F. Milton, "Bested By Malone, Bryan Congratulates Opponent," *BES*, July 17, 1925.

15. Mrs. William Jennings Bryan, letter of July 20, 1925, in "Correspondence of Grace Bryan Hargraves 1924–1934," vol. II, pp. 18–20, LC; Warner Ogden, "Scopes," *Knoxville Sentinel*, July 17, 1960; "Monkey Trial Not a Circulation Maker," *Editor & Publisher*, July 18, 1925, p. 4. The *New York American* described Dayton jurors as "intelligence of the most lowest grade" while *Time* described the population of Dayton ("Bryan's to a moron") as "yowling" a welcome; the *Literary Digest* ran a compilation of jokes, the butt of which were Bryan, fundamentalists, Dayton, and the entire South. See Edward Caudill, "The Roots of Bias: An Empiricist Press and Coverage of the Scopes Trial," *Journalistic Monographs*, July 1989, pp. 1–37; Laurence M. Barnabo and Celeste Michelle Conduit, "Two Stories of the Scopes Trial: Legal and Journalistic Articulations of the Legitimacy of the Science of Religion," in *Popular Trials: Rhetoric, Mass Media and the Law* (Tuscaloosa: University of Alabama Press, 1990), pp. 74–76;"Cranks and Freaks," *NYT*, July 11, 1925; "The Great Trial," *Time*, Aug. 20, 1925.

16. Author interview with Eloise Reed, July 18, 1998; Allen, "Background of the Scopes Trial," p. 92, KNOX; "Unwarranted Ridicule," *Chattanooga Times*, July 19, 1925; A. C. Stribling, "Dayton Tired of False Writings," *Chattanooga News*, July 17, 1925; "Mustard Plaster Mencken," *Bookman*, Dec. 1926, p. 389; sprinkling one's prose with the word *yokel* was the secret in "How To Appear Sophisticated," *Birmingham-Alabama News*, Aug. 29, 1925; "Mr. Mencken's Ancestry," *Chattanooga News*, July 16, 1925; "Mencken Epithets Rouse Dayton's Ire," *NYT*, July 17, 1925. One Dayton boy, a graduate of Harvard, had won a Rhodes Scholarship to Oxford University. "Yokels, Hinds and Booboisie," *Kansas City Times*, July 18, 1925. If Dayton citizens thought Mencken rude ("nothing he saw escaped ridicule," said one), it can also be said that not many understood his humor. Offense was taken when Mencken visited John Scopes's room at W. C. Bailey's house. Mencken, who had compared the entire trial to an inquisition, likened Scopes's room to "a monk's cell." Bailey chafed; he thought Mencken was insulting his home. "One of the most remarkable phases of this remarkable trial," noted the *New York Times*, was the way in which the Dayton populace behaved: "with remarkable constraint and courtesy toward all who have criticized and ridiculed them and their beliefs so unrestrainedly." See Allen, "Background of the Scopes Trial," p. 93, KNOX; "Dayton Hospitable to Critical Guests," *NYT*, July 19, 1925.

17. Scopes, *Center of the Storm*, p. 93; Bynum Shaw, "Scopes Reviews the Monkey Trial," *Esquire*, Nov. 1970, p. 90; HLM, *Thirty-Five Years*, p. 427, EPFL; "Mencken Likes Dayton, But Thinks Trial Nothing But a Joke," *Chattanooga News*, July 9, 1925; "Mencken Pays His Respects to Chattanooga's Police," *Chattanooga News*, July 15, 1925 (the original title was "Law and Freedom, Mencken Discovers, Yield Place to Holy Writ in Rhea County"); A. C. Stribling, "Mencken Unintentionally Praises Dayton, Declares Pastor," *Chattanooga News*, July 15, 1925; C. Carl Knoedler, "As to Mencken" in "Letters to the Editor," *Chattanooga News*, July 15, 1925.

18. Several Methodists suggested they take Mencken "into an alley." A. P. Haggard, chief commissioner of Dayton and one of the town's leading citizens, prevailed on the townspeople to leave Mencken alone. "Mencken Epithets Rouse Dayton's Ire," *NYT*, July 17, 1925; "Mencken Escapes Ride on Rail by Angry Daytonians," *New York World*, July 17, 1925; "H. L. Mencken's Views of Tennessee 'Yokels' Stir Folk at Dayton," *NYT*, July 16, 1925; "Dayton Would Arrest Mencken," *Chattanooga News*, July 18, 1925; "Calls Mencken a Buzzard," *Oklahoma City News*, July 20, 1925; "Darrow Flayed, Mencken Lashed by M. Connell," *Oklahoma City Times*, July 20, 1925.

19. The full story of Mencken's meeting with "the town bravos" can be found in HLM, *Thirty-Five Years*, pp. 428–29, EPFL; HLM to Sara Haardt, July 19, 1925, GOU; Allen, "Background of the Scopes Trial," p. 93, KNOX. In the end, A. P. Haggard persuaded those assembled to go home. In addition, Morgan, the dentist in whose home Mencken was boarding,

sent a message to the committee that the columnist would be protected as long as he stayed under his roof. "Mencken Escapes Ride on Rail by Angry Daytonians," *New York World*, July 17, 1925.

20. "The State Had Won," *Boston Transcript*, July 17, 1925; Carl Bode interview with Watson Davis, June 30, 1965, Carl Bode Papers, EPFL; Charles Potter, "Ten Years After the Monkey Show I'm Going Back to Dayton," *Liberty Magazine*, Sept. 28, 1935, p. 38; HLM, *Thirty-Five Years*, pp. 428, 431, EPFL; HLM to Sara Haardt, July 17, 1925, GOU; HLM, "Battle Now Over, Mencken Sees; Genesis Triumphant," *BES*, July 18, 1925; "Mencken Strolls on Main Street," *Chattanooga News*, July 9, 1925; "Dayton Glad to See Mencken Leave," *Wilmington (Delaware) Star*, July 19, 1925; HLM, *Heathen Days*, p. 216; HLM to George Milton, Aug. 4, 1925, LC; Henry M. Hyde, "Dayton Is Awaiting Verdict and Expects Conviction," *BS*, July 20, 1925.

21. Commentary by Edward J. Larson, "In Search of History: The Monkey Trial," History Channel, A&E Television, 1997; author interview with Eloise Reed, July 18, 1998; Larson, *Summer for the Gods*, pp. 187–88; Paine Knickerbocker, "Play Brings Memories of Real Scopes Trial," *San Francisco Chronicle*, June 20, 1956; "The Memoirs of Grace Bryan Hargreaves," p. 165, LC; *The World's Most Famous Court Trial*, pp. 302–3; Clarence Darrow to HLM, Aug. 15, 1925, NYPL; press copy of an unpublished interview with Bryan, July 27, 1925, William J. Losh Scrapbook, HOOV (most likely the interview was never published because Bryan died soon afterward). "Scopes Declared Guilty by Violating Tennessee Law Against Evolution," *BES*, July 21, 1925; "Weird Adventure of 200 Reporters at Tennessee Evolution Trial," *Editor & Publisher*, July 18, 1925, p. 3.

22. Levine, *Defender of the Faith*, p. 355; "Bryan," *Chicago Tribune*, July 20, 1925; "Science Fought in Many States," *Illinois Miner*, June 13, 1925; "Evolution Battle in West Predicted," *BES*, July 15, 1925; "Evolution Books Upheld," *NYT*, July 25, 1925; HLM, editorial, *American Mercury*, Oct. 1925, p. 160; HLM to O. B. Andrews, July 30, 1925, EPFL; Joseph Wood Krutch, "The Great Monkey Trial," *Commentary*, May 1967, p. 84.

23. Thomas Kelley, M. D., to Grace Bryan Hargraves, June 25, 1931, "Correspondence of Grace Bryan Hargraves 1924–1934," pp. 3–4, 19, LC; author interview with Eloise Reed, July 18, 1998; Scopes, *Center of the Storm*, p. 203; HLM, "A Gladiator of the Law," editorial, *BES*, March 14, 1938; "National Affairs," *Time*, August 10, 1925 in *Time Capsule 1925* (New York: Time-Life Books, 1968), p. 27; "Humor Journals Recalled to Delete Bryan Jokes," *New York Herald Tribune*, July 28, 1925; Larson, *Summer for the Gods*, p. 204; Kazin, *On Native Grounds*, pp. 203–4; HLM, "Bryan," *BES*, July 27, 1925. I am indebted to Jack Sanders, who sent me the two different versions of the obituary that were printed that day; both are from the collection of Holger A. Koppel. Jack Sanders to the author, Feb. 2, 1995.

24. Author interview with Walter Sondheim, June 20, 1994; "A Mencken *Chrestomathy* by Henry L. Mencken," *Houston (Texas) Press*, June 24, 1941; Fitzpatrick, *Gerald W. Johnson*, pp. 75–76; H. L. Mencken to Fielding Garrison, July 27, 1925, NYPL; "Death of Bryan Stirs Mencken's Poison Pen," *Westminster (Maryland) Times*, Aug. 1, 1925; "Barking at the Grave," *Tampa Tribune*, Aug. 8, 1925; "Mencken's Evil Fame," *Nashville Citizen*, Aug. 8, 1925; "Kicking Dead Faces," *Nashville Banner*, Aug. 24, 1925; HLM, *Thirty-Five Years*, p. 432, EPFL; HLM to George Milton, July 27, 1925, Nov. 28, 1925, LC.

Chapter 26: In the Crucible

1. "Two Boswells," *New York Telegraph*, Aug. 31, 1925; Loos, "A Girl Like I," p. 214; HLM, "The German," *BS*, January 24, 1908; author interview with Conrad Abhau, Aug. 22, 1992; Sally MacDougall, "Mencken, The Perfect Husband," *New York World*, Aug. 17, 1930: HLM, "Answers to Correspondents: Mother's Day," *BES*, June 13, 1916.

2. HLM to Sara Haardt, Dec. 17, 1925, GOU; HLM, *Thirty-Five Years*, pp. 468–69, EPFL; HLM to Blanche Knopf, Dec. 12, 1925, EPFL; HLM, "*Happy Days:* Additions . . . ," p. 144, EPFL.

3. HLM, *Thirty-Five Years*, pp. 469–70, EPFL; Riggio, "Introduction," to *Theodore Dreiser: American Diaries, 1902–1926*, pp. 40–41; Helen Dreiser, *My Life with Dreiser*, p. 117; HLM, *Thirty-Five Years*, p. 469, EPFL; HLM to Sara Haardt, Dec. 13, 1925, GOU.

4. HLM, *Thirty-Five Years*, pp. 469–70, EPFL; HLM to Sara Haardt, Dec. 17, 1925, Jan. 2, 1926, GOU; HLM to Sally Bruce, Jan. 12, 1926, EPFL; HLM to Howard Kelly, Dec. 19, 1925, EPFL; HLM to Carl Van Vechten, Jan. 12, 1926, NYPL; "Estate of Mother Is Left in Trust to H. L. Mencken," *BS*, Dec. 18, 1925; Baltimore City Register of Wills: Anna M. Mencken, vol. 154, pp. 121–24, MD.

5. Author interviews with William Muse, Jan. 19, 1994, and Conrad Abhau, Aug. 22, 1992; letter from Conrad Abhau to the author, Aug. 22, 1992; HLM to Sara Haardt, Dec. 16, 1925, GOU.

6. Margaret Lappin, "As I Saw Mencken," p. 23, YALE; HLM, *Thirty-Five Years*, pp. 469–70, EPFL.

7. GJN to Isaac Goldberg, ca. 1925, NYPL/ms; James Cain, "Memo to Dr. Bode," collection of Roy Hoopes; "Mother of H. L. Mencken Dies at Hospital Here," *BS*, Dec. 14, 1925. By odd coincidence, both father and mother had succumbed on the thirteenth, a number that Mencken, always superstitious, would spend his entire life going to outrageous extremes to avoid. He wrote Anna's obituary himself, later pasting the notice into volume 13 of his clipping books—out of sequence, but certainly not out of context, an ironic tribute to the bad luck fate had dealt him. HLM, "Clippings," vol. XIII, EPFL; HLM, "Seven Chapters of an Unnamed and Incomplete Novel," "Typescripts of Early Fiction 1889–1903," p. 10, EPFL.

Chapter 27: Banned in Boston

1. HLM, "U.S. Offers Much Material for Coming Novelists," *New York World*, Aug. 19, 1926; "Mencken Stirs Boston Man to Ban Magazine," *Baltimore American*, March 31, 1926; HLM, *Thirty-Five Years*, p. 471, EPFL; HLM to Oswald Garrison Villard, April 11, 1926, HAR/Hou; James Cain to HLM, April 14, 1926; HLM, Appendix LXII in "The 'Hatrack' Case: The American Mercury vs. The New England Watch and Ward Society, The Postmaster-General of the United States, et al., by H. L. Mencken, 1937," EPFL.

2. "Mencken Returns, Rejoicing in Victory Over Reformers," *BS*, April 10, 1926; Isaac Goldberg, "The Arrest of Mr. Mencken," *Haldeman-Julius Monthly*, June 1926, pp. 77–78; "Harvard No Hugger-Mugger College Says Mencken in Sole Interview–Finds Nothing of Wowser in Thronging Undergraduate Mob but Flouts the Balderdash of Ph.D. Rigmarole," *Harvard Crimson*, April 8, 1926.

3. Margaret Lappin, "As I Saw Mencken," pp. 148–51, YALE.

4. "Chase Is Elated Over U.S. Action Against Mercury," *Atlanta (Georgia) Constitution*, April 10, 1926; Hays, *Let Freedom Ring*, p. 180; "Lewis Feels Sure Book Censor Will Pinch Bible Next," *Pittsburgh Post*, April 13, 1926; Clarence Darrow to HLM, April 12, 1926, in HLM, Appendix LXII in "The 'Hatrack' Case: The American Mercury vs. The New England Watch and Ward Society, The Postmaster General of the United States, et al., by H. L. Mencken, 1937," pp. 57, 60, 66, 100–101, EPFL; "April *Mercury* Ban Stands Despite Appeal of Mencken," *BS*, April 16, 1926; "Censors Job Is Not So Hard," *Cincinnati Post*, April 26, 1926.

5. HLM, "The 'Hatrack' Case . . . ," pp. 76–78, 100–2, EPFL; "Mencken's Case," *Wilmington (Delaware) News*, April 18, 1926; "Public Clamors for Mercury," *Racine (Wisconsin) News*, April 10, 1926; "Hatrack is Golden Literature to Dealer," *Bridgeport, (Conn). Star*, April 10, 1926; "The Menace of Menckenism," *Christian Index*, April 15, 1926; Herbert Asbury,

"The Day Mencken Broke the Law," *American Mercury*, Oct. 1951, p. 168; "Hang Preachers of Farmington, Mencken Urges," *Salt Lake City Telegram*, April 10, 1926.

6. HLM, "Private," Appendix XLIX, Lynn R. Meekins to HLM, April 27, 1926, Appendix LXII, and HLM, "To The Friends of The American Mercury: A Statement by the Editor," April 16, 1926, in Appendix V, all in HLM, "The 'Hatrack" Case . . . ," EPFL; HLM to AAK, April 19, 1926, EPFL; HLM, "The 'Hatrack' Case . . . ," pp. v, 107, EPFL.

7. Hays, *Trial By Prejudice*, p. 8; New England Watch & Ward Society—Minutes of Director's Meetings, HAR/law. According to B. S. Steadwell of the World's Purity Foundation, as of 1930 news clippings indicated that "the law of man against obscene literature and censorship" had been "weakened." Steadwell to Charles Sherman Rodwell of Watch & Ward Society, 1930. See "New England Watch & Ward Society, Box 11, Correspondence 1929–1930," HAR/law; "Pig at Its Trough," *Boston Telegram*, April 27, 1926; HLM, "The 'Hatrack' Case . . . ," pp. 129–30, EPFL.

8. Sinclair Lewis to HLM, April 7, 1926, in Appendix LIV in HLM, "The 'Hatrack' Case . . . ," EPFL; "The Arrest of Mr. Mencken," *Christian Leader*, April 17, 1926; John Drinkwater, "Yankee Chadbands in Their War Paint Again," *London Sunday Express*, April 11, 1926.

Chapter 28: The Great God Mencken

1. Walter Lippmann, reprint from *Saturday Review of Literature*, Dec. 11, 1926, in *H. L. Mencken* (New York: Alfred A. Knopf, 1926), p. 1; HLM, "Sententiae: The Mind of Man," *A Mencken Chrestomathy*, p. 617; "Magazines? Yes, We Read 'Em. But What Kind? Piper Mencken Leads the Way," *Journal of Electrical Workers*, April 1927, p. 173; "The Ultimate Symbol," *San Francisco Chronicle*, July 26, 1925; "University Glee Club at Carnegie Hall," *New York Evening Sun*, Feb. 1, 1927; "H. L. Mencken All Wrong About U.S. Railway Maps, Declares One Mapmaker, Quoting *The Railway Age*," *Topeka State Journal*, Feb. 19, 1927; Manchester, *Disturber of the Peace*, pp. 210–11; "Six Best Sellers," *Baltimore Post*, Dec. 5, 1926; Albert Mordell, "Henry L. Mencken Finds Americans Are Governed by Fear," *Philadelphia Record*, Oct. 18, 1925; "Rare Book Collectors," *New Orleans Times-Picayune*, June 7, 1925; "The Book Hunter," *Publisher's Weekly*, April 4, 1925, p. 125; "First Editions in Demand," *Biblio*, May 1923, p. 462; Carl Van Doren, "Smartness and Light: H. L. Mencken: A Gadfly for Democracy," *Century Magazine*, March 1923, p. 792; "Suggestions for Classroom Study: Charles Swain Thomas, Graduate School of Education, Harvard University," *Independent*, Nov. 27, 1926; "University of Michigan Critic Gets a Beating; Called Faculty 'Asses,' " *Detroit News*, March 2, 1922; "Red Blood in Ann Arbor," *Detroit Saturday Night*, March 4, 1922; Hemingway, *The Sun Also Rises*, p. 42.

2. "McFarlane Brands Literati Who Attack Rotary as Mere Poseurs," *Mobile Register*, March 17, 1925; "The Despised Luncheon Club," *Cincinnati Star*, Jan. 26, 1925; "Mencken Is Called Seer by Moslems," *Oklahoma City Oklahoman*, July 18, 1926; "Dr. Stratton Praying, He Says, For Mencken," *NYT*, Sept. 13, 1926; "Mencken Glad of Pastor's Prayers," *Boston Herald*, Sept. 14, 1926; "Laughter Fills Bible Lecture," *Boston News-Post*, Oct. 16, 1925; "The Forty Against Henry," *Norfolk (Virginia) Pilot*, June 11, 1927; "Mencken Marveled by the Literati of Grub Street," *New York Telegraph*, March 7, 1926; "A National Menace," *Machogee Phoenix*, May 4, 1924; "A Radcliffe Wheeze," *Ashville Citizen*, April 5, 1924; "Row Over Movies: Club Women Tear Mencken Hit," *Columbus Citizen*, Oct. 23, 1925; "Book Gossip: A Professor Reads Mencken," *New York Tribune*, May 30, 1920; "Mencken Wants Suicide Wave Among the College Presidents; Offers to Furnish the Tools," *Trenton (New Jersey) Times*, April 3, 1927.

3. Philip M. Wagner, "Mencken Remembered," *American Scholar*, Spring 1963, p. 258; Warren Wilmer Brown, "A Book for the Day," *Baltimore News*, Jan. 8, 1924; author interview

with Wallace Cohen, Aug. 29, 1993; "The Spread of the Mencken Spirit," *Macon (Georgia) Telegram*, May 27, 1927; Wilson, ed., *The Shock of Recognition*, p. 1156; F. Scott Fitzgerald, "The Baltimore Anti-Christ," *Bookman*, March 1921, p. 79; "Collegiania," *McGill Daily*, Jan. 1926; Clark, *Innocence Abroad*, p. 124; Cabell, *Some of Us*, p. 111; "Mencken," *NYT*, Dec. 4, 1927; Frederick Lewis Allen, "These Disillusioned Highbrows," *Independent*, April 9, 1927, p. 379; also quoted in "Intolerant Menckenites," *Springfield Union*, April 22, 1927; "Mencken to Blame for His Imitators, He Admits It Now," *New Orleans Morning Tribune*, Oct. 22, 1926; Lappin, "As I Saw Mencken," pp. 101–2, YALE; Anderson, *Memoirs*, p. 369; Adamic, *Laughing in the Jungle*, p. 262; Robert F. Nardini, "Mencken and the 'Cult of Smartness,'" *Menckeniana*, Winter 1982, p. 6.

4. "The Nation Honor Roll for 1926," *Nation*, Jan. 5, 1927, p. 4; "Betty in New York," *New Rochelle Star*, March 26, 1927; author interview with Wallace Cohen, Aug. 29, 1993; author interview with Olga Owens, Oct. 24, 1987; author interview with R. P. Harriss, October 24, 1987; Gerald Johnson, "Reconsideration–Mencken," *Menckeniana*, Winter 1975, p. 1; "She's Very Proud of Mencken, She Says," Letters to the Editor, *BES*, Jan. 11, 1927; author interview with Charles Fortenbaugh June 13, 1994.

5. Wright, *Black Boy*, pp. 281, 283–84; Reginald H. Clyne, "Against the Currents," private memoir, 1974, p. 189, courtesy John Clyne; Carl Van Vechten, *Nigger Heaven* (New York: Grossett & Dunlap, 1926), pp. 221–23, 225; Scruggs, *The Sage in Harlem*, p. 27; Adam Clayton Powell, "H. L. Mencken," *Opportunity*, Feb. 1931, p. 39.

6. "Mencken Overseas," *Columbia (South Carolina) Record*, March 6, 1927; Everhart Armstrong, "Mencken and America," *London Nineteenth Century and After*, Jan. 1927; *Independent*, June 13, 1925; "Ein Moderner Americkasher Krititer," *Berlin Das Literarische Echo*, Feb. 15, 1921; Hofmorschall Writing for Kaiser Wilhelm to Professor Harry Barnes, July 27, 1928 and Harry Barnes to HLM, Sept. 24, 1927, NYPL; "The Price of Showmen Among Critics," *Capetown Cape Logic*, Jan. 29, 1927; "Mencken," *El Prevenir* (Cartajena, Columbia), Jan. 29, 1921, *Philadelphia Ledger*, June 16, 1923. See also HLM, "Clippings, Carbons and Souvenirs, Including Music 1893–1938," p. 27, EPFL; *Sydney Triad*, Nov. 10, 1920; "El Universal en los Estados Unidos: Mencken: El Critico Norte Americano," *El Universal*, Feb. 1, 1921; H. L. Mencken, "Hiring a Hall," *New York World*, Oct. 17, 1926; Carl Van Doren, "Smartness and Light: H. L. Mencken: A Gadfly for Democracy," *Century Magazine*, March 1923, p. 795; "A Fellow Writer Talks About the Militant Mencken," *BS*, Feb. 28, 1923; "Calls Mencken an All-American Institution," *Baltimore Sun*, Feb. 25, 1923; "What Besides a Ford?" *New Orleans Times-Picayune*, Feb. 21, 1923.

7. HLM to Hamilton Owens, Jan. 19, 1934, EPFL; HLM to AAK, April 11, 1930, EPFL; "Add a Great Literary Critic to Your Staff," advertisement, *Editor & Publisher*, Oct. 1, 1924; "H. L. Mencken Who Basks in the Evening Sun," advertisement, *Editor & Publisher*, July 8, 1922; "Literary Sandwich Men," *Publisher's Weekly*, May 14, 1921, p. 1422; Margaret Lappin, "As I Saw Mencken," p. 73, YALE; HLM, ed., *Menckeniana: A Schimpflexicon*; "Day By Day With Robert Garland," *Baltimore Post*, Dec. 15, 1926.

8. Joseph Hergesheimer to HLM, June 10, 1926, YALE; HLM to Joseph Hergesheimer, June 10, 1926, HRHRC; Aileen Pringle to Carl Bode, April 3, 1968, Carl Bode Papers, EPFL; "At Aileen Pringle's House," *Macon (Georgia) Telegraph*, Feb. 12, 1928; Aileen Pringle to HLM, Dec. 1927, YALE; Aileen Pringle to Carl Bode, April 3, 1968, Carl Bode Papers, EPFL.

9. De Witt Bodeen, "Aileen Pringle," *Films in Review*, Oct. 1979, pp. 468–69; Stuart Oderman, "Aileen Pringle," *Films in Review*, March 1990, pp. 153, 155–56; Marjory Adams, "Family Background Too Brilliant," *Boston Sunday Globe*, Feb. 28, 1926; Hedda Hopper, "Sirens of the Silents," *Chicago Sunday Tribune*, March 13, 1949; Joseph Hergesheimer to Dorothy Hergesheimer, Dec. 4, 1925, HRHRC; Herbert Howe, "A Lady Surrounded by Men," *Photoplay*, Feb. 1928, p. 66; Katherine Albert, "What Do You Mean—Intellectual?" *Photoplay*, Jan. 1929, p. 57; Liebman, *From Silents to Sound*, p. 243; Carl Van Vechten,

"Hollywood Parties," *Vanity Fair*, June 1927, p. 86; Cal York, "The Girl on the Cover," *Photoplay*, Dec. 1926, p. 1; Aileen Pringle to HLM, Dec. 1927, YALE.

10. HLM to Joseph Hergesheimer, Aug. 24, 1926, HRHRC; Oderman, *Lillian Gish*, pp. 170–71; 206; James Tully to George Jean Nathan, June 21, 1927, CORN; HLM, "Valentino," *BES*, Aug. 30, 1926; GJN to Isaac Goldberg, dated Monday, ca. 1926, Isaac Goldberg Papers, NYPL; "Mencken to Take Rudy's Film Niche," *New Orleans Morning Tribune*, Oct. 21, 1926; HLM, "Original Typescript: Prejudices, Sixth Series, 1927," p. 54, EPFL. The copy paper is dated July 28, 1926, during the time period that Mencken was seeing Aileen.

Chapter 29: A Sentimental Journey

1. HLM, *Thirty-Five Years*, p. 487, EPFL; HLM to Theodore Dreiser, Feb. 5, 1926, PENN; HLM, "New York," *BES*, July 26, 1926; HLM, "Notes of a Baltimorean," *BES*, Aug. 25, 1930; HLM, "Baltimore's Old West," *BES*, Nov. 7, 1927; HLM, "Days of Change," *BES*, July 22, 1929; HLM, "800,000," *BES*, July 21, 1930; HLM, "Midsummer Reflections," *BES*, Aug. 9, 1926; HLM to Gamaliel Bradford, Fall 1919, PRIN/fire; HLM, "AN 1941," EPFL; "Mencken to Take Rudy's Film Niche," *New Orleans Morning Tribune*, Oct. 21, 1926.

2. HLM to Marion Bloom, Dec. 18, 1926, EPFL; Marion Bloom to Estelle Bloom Kubitz, Sept. 13, 1926, NYPL; "Mencken Is Coming," *San Francisco Bulletin*, Oct. 24, 1926; "A Sentimental Journey—American Style," *BES*, Oct. 25, 1926; "H. L. Mencken," *Atlanta Life*, Oct. 24, 1926; "The Reminiscences of Rupert Vance," p. 35, COL; "Mencken Impressed with University," *Greensboro News*, Oct. 17, 1926; Heywood Broun, "It Seems to Me," *New York World*, Nov. 7, 1926; "Mencken to Take Rudy's Film Niche," *New Orleans Morning Tribune*, Oct. 21, 1926.

3. "Mencken of Ironic Mind, Gives Pause," *Los Angeles Times*, Oct. 28, 1926; "The Low-Down on Hollywood by H. L. Mencken," *Photoplay*, April 1929, p. 36; "Mencken and the Movies," *Boston Post*, March 22, 1927. For a vivid description of Hollywood during the 1920s, see the series written by Carl Van Vechten on "Fabulous Hollywood" in *Vanity Fair* for May, June, July, and August, 1927; Richard Merryman provides good atmospherics in *Mank: The Wit, World and Life of Herman Mankiewicz* (New York: William Morrow and Co., 1978). Carl Bode interview with Anita Loos, Oct. 30, 1964, Carl Bode Papers, EPFL; Anita Loos, "A Girl Can't Go On Laughing All the Time: A Personal Souvenir of New York in the Twenties," in *New York, N.Y.: An American Heritage Extra*, ed. David G. Lowe, p. 60; "Something to Write About," *Los Angeles Examiner*, Nov. 4, 1926; Joseph Hergesheimer to Dorothy Hergesheimer, Dec. 4, 1925, HRHRC; HLM to Sara Haardt, Oct. 30, 1926, Nov. 5, 1926, GOU; Carl Van Vechten, "Fabulous Hollywood," *Vanity Fair*, May 1927, p. 54; HLM to Sara Haardt, Nov. 5, 1926, Oct. 30, 1926, GOU; HLM to Bee Wilson, June 11, 1926, NYPL; Carl Van Vechten, "Hollywood Royalty," *Vanity Fair*, July 1927, p. 38, p. 86; "The Low-Down on Hollywood by H. L. Mencken," *Photoplay*, April 1927, pp. 36–37, 118–20; "A Dinner with H. L. M.," *Montgomery Advertiser*, Nov. 11, 1927; "The Uncommon Scold," *Time*, Feb. 6, 1956, p. 38; Frederick James Smith, "What Happens to Your Movie Money," *Photoplay*, Feb. 1927, p. 45; "Mr. Mencken Recommends Movies on Trains," *Dallas News*, Jan. 3, 1927; HLM, "On Movies," *BES*, April 11, 1927.

4. HLM to Bee Wilson, June 11, 1926, NYPL; Kellner, *The Last Dandy*, p. 152; HLM to GJN, March 11, 1927, CORN.

5. "Mr. Mencken Jousts At His Very Own Windmills," *San Francisco Chronicle*, Nov. 16, 1926; HLM, "Sister Aimee," *BES*, Dec. 13, 1926; HLM to Sara Haardt, Nov. 5 and 11, 1926, GOU; "Mencken Visits Movie Lot," *Los Angeles Record*, Nov. 3, 1926; "It's Always Fair Weather," *New York American*, Nov. 27, 1926; "Can This Be Our Own Henry?" *Baltimore Post*,

Nov. 11, 1926; "First Photo of New Film Comic," *Washington News*, Nov. 25, 1926; Tully, *A Dozen and One*, p. 143; Joseph Hergesheimer, "Autobiographical Notes," HRHRC.

6. Joan Miller to Dalton Gross, Oct. 12, 1965, HUNT; "George Sterling, Poet, Takes Own Life, Planned His Death at Bohemian Club," *San Francisco Chronicle*, Nov. 18, 1926; "California's Best Known Author Dies from Poison," *San Francisco Examiner*, Dec. 18, 1926; "George Sterling, Noted Poet, Ends Life by Poison," *New York Herald Tribune*, Nov. 18, 1926; Webster K. Nolan, "Sterling Lauded in Death by H. L. Mencken," *San Francisco Call*, Nov. 18, 1926; HLM to Miss Austin, Dec. 22, 1926, HUNT; HLM to Sara Haardt, Nov. 16, 1926, GOU; "A Good Life, a Good Death, Says Mencken; Last of Free Artists, Critics' Tribute," *San Francisco Chronicle*, Nov. 18, 1926; "San Francisco Author Found Dead in His Bed," *Salinas Index*, Nov. 17, 1926; "Sterling's Swan Song Discovered," *San Francisco Examiner*, Jan. 9, 1927; HLM to Mrs. Liliecrantz, March 5, 1927, HUNT.

7. "Mencken Wants Suicide Wave Among College Presidents; Offer to Furnish the Tools," *New Jersey Trenton Times*, April 3, 1927; Aileen Pringle to HLM, "Saturday," "Today Sunday," "Monday," ca. Nov. 1926, YALE; HLM to Aileen Pringle, Nov. 26, 1926, YALE.

8. HLM to Sara Haardt, Dec. 21, 1926, GOU; Marion Bloom to Estelle Bloom, Jan. 2, 1927, NYPL; HLM to Aileen Pringle, Dec. 24, 1926, YALE; author interview with Ruth Goodman Goetz, June 13, 1991; Blanche Knopf to Aileen Pringle, Nov. 22, 1926, YALE. The engagement announcement originated in *Movieland*. Aileen Pringle enclosed it in her December 18, 1926, letter to HLM, YALE; HLM to Aileen Pringle, Dec. 31, 1926, YALE; "Engagement Called 'Only a Joke,'" *Albany (New York) Knick-Knocks*, Dec. 31, 1926; Aileen Pringle to HLM, Jan. 10, 1927, YALE; "Literature's Naughty Boy Sets Hometown Agog-ing," *New York Tribune*, Dec. 31, 1926; "Mencken to Wed?" *Philadelphia News*, Dec. 3, 1926; "Noted Critic Reported Engaged," *Boston Herald*, Jan. 9, 1926.

Chapter 30: The German Valentino

1. HLM, Diary, Feb. 5, 1942, EPFL. HLM admitted to destroying "purely personal" letters, especially when they came from women. HLM, *My Life*, p. 6, EPFL; Wilson, *The Twenties*, p. 66; HLM to GJN, March 2, ca. 1927, CORN. For more information on Gretchen Hood, see Peter W. Dowell, *Ich Kuss die Hand: The Letters of H. L. Mencken to Gretchen Hood* (Tuscaloosa: University of Alabama Press, 1986); Donald P. Baker, "Oh, So Sincerely, H. L. Mencken. His Letters, Her Life: Miss Gretchen Hood Remembers in the Summer of Her 87th Year," *Washington Post Potomac Magazine*, June 24, 1973, pp. 18–19, 32. As Hood recalled for this article, Mencken "bounded in here, handed over two bottles of rare wines to my mother, which floored her and made her a subject for life. I recall I wore a Delft blue dress . . . which caught his eye at once." She sang German and French songs at the piano. At the train depot, "He kissed me fervently many times and promised to see me soon." "Why They Have Not Married Yet," BS, Nov. 7, 1926; Marion Bloom to Estelle Bloom, Jan. 21, 1927, NYPL; Aileen Pringle to HLM, Dec. 1927, YALE. The undated inscription is from a letter sent to "Mrs. Henry L. Mencken" from "The New May Shoe Salon" but is grouped with the letters from the 1920s in the Aileen Pringle Collection, YALE. Aileen Pringle to HLM, "Friday the 9th," 1928, YALE; Marion Bloom to Estelle Bloom Kubitz, March 15, 1926, NYPL.

2. Mayfield, *The Constant Circle*, pp. 112, 115; "Home Town Folks Here in Baltimore Amazed at the Scandalous Doings of Henry Mencken on His Trip to California," *Baltimore Post*, Nov. 11, 1926; "On Mencken," *Los Angeles Herald*, Jan. 20, 1927; HLM to Dorothy Taylor, Jan. 29, 1927, author's collection; HLM to Betty Hanes, Sept. 26, 1927, UNC; "Mencken to Be Married?" *Dallas News*, Jan. 16, 1927; Marion Bloom to HLM, early July 1928, EPFL; HLM to Joseph Hergesheimer, July 27, 1927, HRHRC; HLM to Dorothy Hergesheimer, Aug. 27, 1927, NYPL.

3. Aileen Pringle to HLM, "Mon. the third, 1927," YALE; Aileen Pringle to HLM, Jan. 5, 1927, YALE; HLM to Blanche Knopf, Jan. 9, 1927, HRHRC; Aileen Pringle to Arthur Krock, dated "Saturday the 18th.," PRIN/md (Aileen copied out this letter and showed it to Mencken, although she left out the section regarding her own suffering).

4. Rodgers, ed., *Mencken & Sara*, pp. 42–45, 283, 300, 304–5; HLM, "Notes in the Margin," *Smart Set*, Nov. 1920, p. 139; "The American Mercury Authors," Lawrence Spivak Papers, LC; "The Reminiscences of Hamilton Owens," pp. 59–60, COL; author interview with Ruth Goodman Goetz, March 4, 1992; HLM to Sara Haardt, Sept. 29, 1927, GOU; Marcella Pierce to the author, July 20, 1987; Sara Haardt to HLM, Nov. 6, 1927, GOU; HLM, "Preface," *Southern Album*, p. xvi; Sara Haardt to HLM, Dec. 6, 1927, GOU. For an analysis of Sara Haardt's writing, see Rodgers, ed., *Mencken & Sara*, pp. 1–69; Henley, ed., *Southern Souvenirs*, pp. 1–45; Sara Haardt's screenplay, "Way Down South," is among her papers at GOU.

5. HLM to Gretchen Hood, Nov. 14, 1927, Oct. 17, 1927, in Dowell, pp. 69–70; HLM to Joseph Hergesheimer, Oct. 28, 1927, Nov. 2, 1927, HRHRC; HLM to Aileen Pringle, Nov. 23, 25, 26, 1927, YALE; HLM to Joseph Hergesheimer, Nov. 25, 1927, HRHRC; HLM to Blanche Knopf, Nov. 17, 1927, HRHRC; Sara Haardt to Sara Mayfield, Dec. 4, 1927, ALA/gg; HLM, "Preface," *Southern Album*, p. xvii; HLM to Sara Haardt, Dec. 23 and 26, 1927, GOU; Aileen Pringle to HLM, Dec. 6, 1927, YALE; Aileen Pringle to HLM, ca. Dec. 1927, YALE; Aileen Pringle to HLM, Feb. 2, 1928, YALE; HLM, "The Low-Down on Hollywood," *Photoplay*, April 1927, pp. 36–37.

6. HLM, "The Holy Estate," *Chicago Sunday Tribune*, Jan. 8, 1928; Aileen Pringle to HLM, Dec. 29, 1927, YALE.

7. HLM, "The Spanish Main," *BES*, January 30, 1928; HLM to Ludwig Lewisohn, March 10, 1928, UVA; HLM, "The Goosegreasers at Work," *BES*, Jan. 23, 1928; Aileen Pringle to HLM, March 8, 1928, YALE; HLM to Aileen Pringle, Jan. 19, 1928, YALE; Aileen Pringle to HLM, ca. Jan. 1928, YALE; Aileen Pringle to HLM, "Monday the 6th," Feb. 1928, YALE: Aileen Pringle to HLM, Feb. 7, 1928; "Monday the 9th," Feb. 1928, Feb. 20, 1928, March 7, 1928, "Friday the 9th," ca. March 1928, "Monday the 13th," 1928, March 20, 1928, YALE; Aileen Pringle to HLM, June 10, 11, and 20, 1928, YALE; HLM to Aileen Pringle (the context of this letter, as well as the typeface from Mencken's typewriter, dates it as 1928), YALE.

8. Marion Bloom to Estelle Bloom, Feb. 6, 1927, NYPL; Estelle Bloom to Marion Bloom, Aug. 30, 1927, PENN; HLM to Marion Bloom, April 14, 1928, EPFL; Marion Bloom to Estelle Bloom, Aug. 1, 1926, NYPL; Carl Bode interview with Marion Bloom, Aug. 18, 1965, Carl Bode Papers, EPFL; HLM to Marion Bloom, June 29, 1928, EPFL; Aileen Pringle to HLM, March 17 and May 11, 1928, YALE; Esther Carples, "Are Actors Unlucky in Love?" *Picture Magazine*, Jan. 1928, p. 107; Gladys Hall, "Confessions of a Movie Star," undated manuscript, pp. 3, 6, AMPAS.

9. Sara Mayfield to Sara Haardt, Sept. 25, 1928, ALA/gg; Sara Haardt to Mary Parmenter, "Monday Morning, 1928," ALA/gg; Sara Haardt to Sara Mayfield, Aug. 10, 1928, ALA/gg; author interview with R. P. Harriss, Oct. 24, 1987; R. P. Harriss as told to Neil Grauer, "Bright, Bustling Baltimore," *Baltimore Magazine*, Dec. 1982, p. 104; Sara Haardt to Sara Mayfield, July 2, 1928, ALA/gg; Jim Tully to GJN, undated, 1928, CORN; HLM to Lillian Gish, Aug. 9, 1928, NYPL; HLM to Carl Van Vechten, May 17, 1928, YALE; HLM to Elizabeth Hanes, Aug. 16, 1928, UNC.

10. Rodgers, ed., *The Impossible H. L. Mencken*, pp. 290–91; see HLM, "Onward, Christian Soldiers!" *BES*, Aug. 24, 1928; HLM, "The Eve of Armageddon," *BES*, Nov. 5, 1928.

11. Mary Parmenter to Sara Mayfield, Oct. 29, 1928, ALA/gg; Sara Powell Haardt Mencken, "Letters, Documents, Souvenirs 1898–1935," pp. 152–53, EPFL; HLM to Sara Mayfield, Nov. 20, 1928, ALA/gg. Marion Bloom wrote in a note attached to the original Nov. 25, 1928, letter that the lunch took place on Nov. 20, 1928, EPFL; Marion Bloom to Betty

Adler, Nov. 3, 1968, EPFL; HLM to Marion Bloom, July 6, 1928, EPFL; Marion Bloom to Betty Adler, July 16, 1971, EPFL; HLM to Marion Bloom, Nov. 25, 1928, EPFL; Carl Bode interview with Mrs. Dwight Curtis and Mary Louise Newcomer, July 19, 1965, Carl Bode Papers, EPFL; Marion Bloom to Estelle Bloom, March 24, 1928, NYPL; see Martin, *In Defense of Marion*, pp. 379–88.

12. HLM to Elizabeth Hanes, Dec. 15, Dec. 18, 1928, UNC; Aileen Pringle to HLM, Dec. 1928, YALE; HLM to Joseph Hergesheimer, Dec. 17, 1928, HRHRC; HLM to Aileen Pringle, Dec. 24, 1928, YALE; HLM to Gretchen Hood, Dec. 24, 1928, in Dowell, *Ich Kuss Die Hand*, p. 127; HLM to Sara Haardt, Dec. 1928, GOU; Sara Haardt to Sara Mayfield, Dec. 30, 1928, ALA/gg.

Chapter 31: The Sea of Matrimony

1. HLM to Philip Goodman, Jan. 17, 1929, EPFL; Sara Haardt to Sara Mayfield, Sept. 15, 1928, ALA/gg; Sally MacDougall, "Mencken, The Perfect Husband," *New York Herald Tribune*, Aug. 17, 1930; *Donnybrook Fair 1921*, Goucher College yearbook, p. 69, GOU; John E. Rosser, "H. L. Mencken: The Bad Boy of Baltimore," *Real America*, Sept. 1933, pp. 22–27; GJN, "The Ultimately Desirable Woman," in *The World of George Jean Nathan*, ed. Charles Angoff, pp. 159, 161; HLM to James Cain, July 25, 1944, NYPL; HLM to Carl Van Vechten, April 11, 1928, YALE; Aileen Pringle to HLM, undated, YALE. Mencken's eyesight had been strained by Aileen's handwriting, which he cursed for being "hieroglyphic"; for Aileen, the typewriter was an "instrument of torture." HLM and Aileen Pringle, Dec. 27, 1926, Jan. 3, 1927, YALE.

2. HLM, "Preface," *Southern Album*, pp. viii, xxi, xxii–xxiii. Sara Haardt's observation was written on an undated scrap of paper, found in "Notes by Sara Haardt 1927–1935," GOU; James Cain, "Mr. M," LC; Rodgers, "Introduction," *Mencken & Sara*, p. 30; Joseph Hergesheimer, "Autobiographical Notes," HRHRC; Mary Parmenter to Sara Mayfield, Oct. 29, 1928, Ala/gg; "The Reminiscences of Hamilton Owens," p. 60, COL; Carl Bode interview with Mrs. Hamilton Owens, May 8, 1963, collection of Gwinn Owens.

3. HLM to Sara Mayfield, June 25, 1929, GOU; HLM to Sara Haardt, June 28, 1929, GOU; Paul De Kruif to Sara Haardt, July 20, 1929, ALA/gg; HLM to Sara Mayfield, July 1, 1929, ALA/gg; Rodgers, ed., *Mencken & Sara*, p. 412; Mayfield, *The Constant Circle*, pp. 126, 137.

4. Margaret Cobb to Sara Mayfield, July 12, 1929, ALA/gg; Rodgers, ed., *Mencken & Sara*, p. 412; HLM to Sara Haardt, Aug. 29, 1929, GOU; HLM to Raymond Pearl, July 16, 1929, APS.

5. Sara Haardt to Marjorie Hope Nicholson, July 1929, ALA/gg; HLM to Sara Haardt, Oct. 28, 1929, GOU; Aileen Pringle to HLM, 1929, YALE; HLM, "Original Typescript of *Treatise on the Gods* 1928–1929," EPFL; Mayfield, *The Constant Circle*, p. 151; Rodgers, ed., *Mencken & Sara*, p. 421; HLM to Sara Haardt, Dec. 27, 1929, GOU; HLM to Sara Haardt, Jan. 10, 1930, GOU; HLM to Aileen Pringle Jan. 30, 1930, YALE.

6. Gertrude Mencken to Sara Haardt, April 26, 1930 in "Sara Powell Haardt Mencken: Letters, Documents and Souvenirs, 1898–1935," p. 176, EPFL; "The Reminiscences of August Mencken," p. 75, COL; Virginia Mencken to HLM, July 31, Aug. 6, 1930, EPFL; Sara Haardt to HLM April 26, April 30, 1930, GOU; HLM to GJN, July 30, 1930, CORN; HLM to Blanche Knopf, July 16, 1930, EPFL; Fielding Garrison to HLM, Aug. 3, 1930; HLM, Appendix XXV, *My Life*, p. 44, EPFL; Joseph Hergesheimer to HLM, July 30, 1930, NYPL; Aileen Pringle to HLM, June 19, 1930, YALE; Rodgers, ed., *Mencken & Sara*, p. 50; "Wise Now, Mencken Says in Telling of His Plans for Marriage," *Fort Dodge (Iowa) Messenger*, Aug. 4, 1930; "Mencken To Be Married," *New York Telegram*, Aug. 13, 1930; Joseph Van Realte, "B. Broadway," *Macon (Georgia) City Globe*, Oct. 30, 1930. Notation by Gretchen Hood in a letter

she received from HLM, Aug. 7, 1930. See Dowell, *Ich Kuss Die Hand*, p. 139. Although Gretchen went to Baltimore often, she never responded to Mencken's subsequent invitations. "I was too completely done in," she explained, "and never able to forgive him, particularly for the heartless way it was done." Donald P. Baker, "Oh, So Sincerely, H. L. Mencken . . . ," *Washington Post Potomac Magazine*, June 24, 1975, p. 35; "Anita Loos Dead at 93; Screenwriter, Novelist," *NYT*, Aug. 19, 1991; Hobson, *Mencken*, p. 326.

7. HLM to Elizabeth Hanes, Aug. 12, 1930, UNC; HLM to Edith Lustgarten, July 28, 1930, NYPL; HLM to Philip Goodman, Aug. 25, 1930, EPFL; HLM to A. H. McDannald, Aug. 6, Aug. 16, 1930, NYPL; HLM to Mrs. Lappin, Aug. 21, 1930, YALE; HLM to Louis Untermeyer Aug. 27, 1930, UVA; "Mencken Blushes," *Memphis Press*, Aug. 22, 1930; Raymond Pearl, Diary, APS; Carl Bode interview with Mrs. Hamilton Owens, Feb. 28, 1963, collection of Gwinn Owens; "Weather," *BS*, Aug. 27, 1930. The outer layer of Mencken's package was of thick brown paper; the German newspapers were within. The postmark is dated Aug. 27, 1930, 8:30 p.m. See Aileen Pringle Papers, Oversize, Folder 134, Box 9, YALE; author interview with Richard Alexander, Dec. 9, 1993; Aileen Pringle to HLM, Nov. 23, 1927, YALE.

8. Carl Bode interview with Hamilton Owens, May 8, 1963, collection of Harold A. Williams; author interview with Olga Owens, March 22, 1985; Cooke, *Six Men*, p. 91; "Wise Now, Mencken Says in Telling His Plans for Marriage," *Fort Dodge (Iowa) Messenger*, Aug. 4, 1930; "H. L. Mencken, Matrimonial Scoffer, Secretly Marries Miss Powell," *Florence (South Carolina) News-Review*, Aug. 28, 1930; HLM, *Thirty-Five Years*, pp. 603, 606–8, EPFL; Edward Clark letters to the author, June 27, 1987, and March 16, 1995; HLM to GJN, Aug. 27, 1930 telegram of 9:08 p.m. and letter dated Aug. 1930, CORN; HLM to Blanche Knopf, Sept. 4, 1930, EPFL; HLM to Paul Patterson, Sept. 1, 1930, collection of Bettina Patterson; HLM to Theodor Hemberger, Sept. 9, 1930, EPFL; Sara Haardt to Mrs. Elsa G. Hayden, dated "Halifax," GOU.

Chapter 32: Variations on a Familiar Theme

1. HLM, "Sabbath Meditation," *American Mercury*, pp. 60–61; HLM to Alfred R. L. Dohme, Dec. 30, 1946, EPFL; HLM, *Minority Report*, p. 140; HLM to Antoinette Felakey, Sept. 14, 1935, GETTY; HLM to Henry W. Chapin, Aug. 23, 1939, NYPL; Arthur Waugh, "Mr. Mencken on Religion: The Amiable Skeptic," *London Daily Telegraph*, June 20, 1930; Louise Casey Rosett, "Mr. Mencken Once More," *Commonweal*, June 5, 1929; Michael Williams, "Mr. Mencken's Bible for Boobs," *Commonweal*, April 2, 1930; "Mr. Mencken, Theologian," *Truth-Seeker*, June 1930, p. 179; "Mr. Mencken Again," *Philadelphia Catholic Herald Times*, Jan. 26, 1929; HLM to Joseph Katz, July 3, 1936, EPFL; HLM to Fielding Garrison, May 15, 1921, NYPL; HLM to Sara Haardt, April 1, 1927, GOU; Fecher, *Mencken*, pp. 89–148.

2. Mary Miller Vass and James L. W. West III, "The Composition and Revision of Mencken's *Treatise on the Gods*," *The Papers of the Bibliographical Society of America*, vol. 77, Fourth Quarter, pp. 447–461; HLM, "Autobiographical Notes, 1941," EPFL; HLM, *Treatise on the Gods*, pp. 345–47.

3. HLM, *My Life*, p. 661, EPFL; "Rabbi Attacks Mencken Views on Religion as Distorted," *BS*, April 7, 1930; "Rabbi Calls Mencken Deluded Anti-Semite," *Toronto Mail*, April 28, 1930; notes by H. L. Mencken, "H. L. Mencken: Various Books," EPFL; AAK to HLM, April 16, 1930, EPFL; HLM to Daniel Sternberg, Sept. 18, 1947, NYPL; HLM to Isaac Goldberg, [n.d.], Isaac Goldberg Papers, NYPL.

4. Joseph Brainin, "Is H. L. Mencken an Anti-Semite?" *Jewish Criterion*, April 1, 1930. All the rest of the quotations and descriptions of Mencken's actions in this chapter are taken from this article.

5. The two men concocted elaborate lists of Americanized WASP first names appended to Jewish surnames. Looking back on it, daughter Ruth Goodman Goetz said, "My father later was embarrassed and ashamed. He felt that it was anti-Semitic." Author interview with Ruth Goodman Goetz, June 13, 1991.

Chapter 33: The Tamed Ogre of Cathedral Street

1. HLM, "The Schooling of a Theologian," *New Yorker*, July 8, 1939, p. 32; James Cain, "Mr. M," LC; HLM to Al Hildebrandt and to Howard Kelly, Jan. 15, 1933, EPFL; HLM to Henry W. Nice, Feb. 12, 1935, to Dr. Wheeler, Aug. 8, 1935, EPFL; author interview with Philip Hamburger, Jan. 3, 1995; author interview with William Abhau, Aug. 22, 1992; HLM to Joseph Hergesheimer, Feb. 18, 1948, HRHRC; Mary Elizabeth Prim, "Married Mr. Mencken Retires to His Victorian Parlor," *Boston Transcript*, Oct. 7, 1933; HLM to Joseph Hergesheimer, Feb. 18, 1948, HRHRC; "The Reminiscences of Hamilton Owens," p. 61, COL; Edwin Alger, "What's Behind the Name," NBC Radio broadcast, March 23, 1931, HRHRC; "Mencken on Beer," *Gastonia (North Carolina) Gazette*, March 3, 1933; Carl Bode interview with Elliott Wheeler and Hamilton and Olga Owens, May 8, 1963, collection of Harold A. Williams.

2. "The Reminiscences of August Mencken," pp. 76–77, COL; Rodgers, ed., *Mencken & Sara*, p. 54; HLM to Richard Steuart, Oct. 21, 1931, EPFL; Ola Elizabeth Winslow, "Bequest of Sara Haardt Mencken, '20," *Goucher Alumnae Quarterly*, Nov. 1935, pp. 24–26; Holly Pomeroy, "Bride Still Finds Mencken Polite," *New York World*, Sept. 17, 1930; Gretta Palmer, "Bachelor Critic Favors Contracts of Two Clauses," *New York Telegram*, July 8, 1930; HLM, "The Fine Art of Conjugal Bliss," *Bohemian Magazine*, Oct. 1909, p. 419; John Carr, "An Interview with James Cain," *Armchair Detective*, Fall 1987, p. 8; John E. Rosser, "H. L. Mencken, The X-Ray Photograph of the Maryland Terror," *Real America*, Sept. 1933, p. 26; HLM to Gertrude Mencken, Aug. 3, 1932, EPFL.

3. HLM to Dr. Elliot Wheeler, Feb. 27, 1936, EPFL; "The Reminiscences of August Mencken," p. 142, COL; August Mencken to Carl Bode, Dec. 18, 1964, Carl Bode Papers, EPFL; HLM to Gertrude Mencken, July 15, 1932, EPFL; untitled manuscript by Virginia Mencken Morrison, pp. 3–4, Carl Bode Papers, EPFL; Mayfield, *The Constant Circle*, p. 177; Howard Kelly, Diary, Jan. 17, 1933, JHU/Mason; HLM, *My Life*, p. 691, and Appendix XXX, p. 26, EPFL; author interview with Dr. Benjamin Baker, Jan. 15, 1994; F. Scott Fitzgerald to Sara Haardt, Oct. 5, 1933, "Sara Haardt Mencken: Letters, Documents and Souvenirs," p. 200, EPFL; "The Reminiscences of Marjorie Hope Nicholson," p. 198, COL; HLM to Philip Goodman, Feb. 23, 1932, EPFL; "Mencken Finds He Was Wrong; Married Life Results in More Freedom; Wife Talks to Bores," *Elgin Courier News*, Oct. 14, 1930; HLM, "The Boons of Civilization," *American Mercury*, Jan. 1931, p. 34; HLM, "Preface," *Southern Album*, pp. xxii–xxiii; HLM to Elizabeth Hanes, Dec. 11, 1930, UNC; AAK to HLM, Nov. 19, 1930, EPFL; Julie Blanshard, "World's Champion Bachelor Turns Out to Be an Ideal Husband," *Washington News*, July 26, 1932; Sara Haardt to AAK, Jan. 25, 1933, EPFL; HLM, Diary, May 31, 1940, EPFL; Lela Mae Stiles, "A Girl's Eye View of New York," *Lexington (Kentucky) Herald*, Jan. 11, 1931; Sara Haardt, *Southern Souvenirs*, ed. Ann Henley, pp. 16–17; Horatio Alger, "What's Behind the Name," NBC Radio broadcast, March 23, 1934, HRHRC; "Mrs. H. L. Mencken, Author, Is Dead," *BES*, June 1, 1935. Mencken gave Sara this sentence to practice: "The corn pone fell on the floor of the Ford." When Sara said it, it became: "*The cawn pawn fell on the flaw of the Fawd.*" These "failures" of pronunciation left Mencken absolutely enchanted. HLM to Elizabeth Hanes, Dec. 11, 1930, UNC.

4. Author interview with Ida Haardt McCulloch, Oct. 1, 1983; author interview with Dr. Benjamin Baker, Jan. 15, 1994; Sara Haardt, "Notebook," GOU; HLM, "Preface," *Southern*

Album, p. xx; Sara Haardt to Mrs. Edgar Lee Masters, Feb. 13, 1934, HRHRC; author interview with William C. Abhau, Aug. 22, 1992; untitled manuscript by Virginia Mencken Morrison, p. 3, Carl Bode Papers, EPFL; Mayfield, *The Constant Circle*, p. 181; Hobson, *Mencken: A Life*, p. 334; Ritchie Watson, Jr., "Sara Haardt Mencken and the Glasgow-Mencken Entente," *Ellen Glasgow Newsletter*, April 1984; Lela Mae Stiles, "A Girl's Eye View of New York," *Lexington (Kentucky) Herald*, Jan. 11, 1931; James Cain, "Mr. M," LC; author interview with Ruth Goodman Goetz, June 13, 1991.

5. Carl Bode interview with Hamilton Owens, May 8, 1963, collection of Harold A. Williams; author interview with Penelope Pearl Russianoff, Jan. 30, 1995. Mencken studied Pearl's *Modes of Research in Genetics, The Biology of Population Growth, The Ancestry of the Long-Lived*, and *The Natural History of Population*. Hours were spent comparing notes on the condition of their sinuses and concocting elaborate jokes to play on one another. Pearl started Margaret Sanger on her career, was the first to state tobacco was injurious to health and that moderate drinkers lived longer than total abstainers. *Alcohol and Longevity* was one of 15 books Pearl wrote during his lifetime; its findings have long been confirmed, but at the time it enraged the advocates of Prohibition. Appropriately, Pearl dedicated it "To My Friends of the Saturday Night Club." Few shared Pearl's self-confidence to question accepted conventions; often he labeled his critics fools. But to Mencken, Pearl was a genius. "Obituary: Raymond Pearl," *Science*, Dec. 27, 1940, pp. 595–97; "Raymond Pearl, 1879–1940," *American Philosophical Society Yearbook 1940*, pp. 431–33, APS; *Dictionary of American Biography*, vol. XXII Supplement, pp. 521–22; "Raymond Pearl, Hopkins Biologist, Dies Suddenly," BS, Nov. 18, 1940; "Raymond Pearl," *Nature*, Feb. 1, 1941, p. 140; HLM, "Raymond Pearl," BS, Nov. 24, 1940; Raymond Pearl, *Alcohol and Longevity* (New York: Alfred A. Knopf, 1926); Raymond Pearl to Major Greenwood, Dec. 7, 1932, APS; H. S. Jennings, "Biographical Memoir of Raymond Pearl," *National Academy of Sciences*, vol. 22, no. 14, 1942, pp. 296–341; Raymond Pearl, "The Reading of Graduate Students," *Scientific Monthly*, July 1925, pp. 34–44; HLM, *Thirty-Five Years*, p. 368, EPFL; HLM, "Mass Breeding, a Vast Study," BS, Feb. 19, 1939; Fee, *Disease and Discovery*, pp. 136–143; Carl Bode interview with Penelope Pearl Russianoff, Feb. 24, 1965, Carl Bode Papers, EPFL. Pearl reserved his enthusiasm for his evenings at the homes of all the other members of the Saturday Night Club; never once does he use the phrase after being at Cathedral Street. Raymond Pearl's "Commonplace Book," May 28, 1932, APS; Carl Bode interview with Mrs. Hamilton Owens, Feb. 28, 1963, collection of Gwinn Owens.

6. HLM, Diary, May 31, 1940, EPFL; author interview with Olga Owens, March 22, 1985; Carl Bode interview with Elliott Wheeler, May 8, 1963, collection of Harold A. Williams. The Duffys lived at 901 Cathedral Street. Author interview with Sara Anne Duffy Chermayeff, March 2, 1992; Carl Bode interview with Hamilton and Olga Owens, May 8, 1963, collection of Harold A. Williams.

7. HLM to "Miss Philips," August 14, 1931, and notation scrawled on the letter cited, author's collection; Sara Haardt, "Solitaire," *Harper's Bazaar*, Aug. 1934, pp. 66–67, 110, 112; HLM, *My Life*, p. 392; HLM, Diary, May 31, 1940; AAK, Diary, May 15, 1931, HRHRC; HLM to Sara Haardt, May 15, 1931, GOU; HLM to Dorothy Hergesheimer, March 20, 1931, HRHRC.

8. Raymond Pearl to Major Greenwood, Nov. 15, 1933, APS; Gertrude Mencken to August Mencken, undated, 1934 and Feb. 8, 1950, EPFL; "Expenses Incurred Regarding Sara's Illness 1930–1935" in file, "H. L. Mencken, Illnesses 1912–1948," EPFL; HLM to Philip Goodman, March 2, April 2, Aug. 26, 1931, EPFL; Sara Haardt to Sara Mayfield, May 27, 1931, ALA/gg; author interview with Mrs. Hamilton Owens, March 22, 1985; HLM, Diary, May 31, 1940; author interview with Philip Hamburger, Jan. 3, 1995; "Says Mencken Is Now Ideal Husband," *Joliet (Illinois) Herald News*, Sept. 1, 1932; "Hergesheimer Offers Bathtub Gin," *NYT*, Sept. 1, 1932.

Chapter 34: Hard Times

1. "The New Mencken," *Madison (Wisconsin) Capital Times*, Oct. 8, 1932; "Fact That Mencken Is 'Ideal Husband' Annoys Dan O'Brian," in "H. L. Mencken Clipping Books," vol. LI, EPFL; HLM to Fulton Oursler, May 7, 1931, GT.

2. "American Mercury Advertising Income 1924–1938," Lawrence Spivak, "American Mercury Financial Papers, Advertising Accounts and Income, American Mercury File 1924–1947," LC; "Profit and Loss Statements 1924–1949," Lawrence Spivak, "Financial Papers, Statements and Account Examinations, American Mercury File 1924–1947," LC; HLM to AAK, memo, Nov. 7, 1931, p. 2, EPFL; AAK, *Memoirs*, HRHRC; AAK to HLM, April 5, 1931, EPFL; AAK, Diary, April 23, 1931, HRHRC; Geoffrey Hellman, "Profiles: Publisher II; Flair Is the Word," *New Yorker*, Nov. 27, 1948, p. 37; HLM, "The Worst American State," *American Mercury*, Sept., Oct., Nov. 1931; "Mr. Mencken 'Condemned' by Arkansas Legislature," *BES*, Feb. 1, 1931; "Arkansas House Sets Mencken on Edge," *Memphis Commercial Appeal*, Feb. 8, 1931.

3. HLM to AAK, Nov. 7, 1931, EPFL; AAK, Diary, Oct. 13, 14, Dec. 18, 1931 (see also entries for Oct. 7 and Dec. 10, 1931), HRHRC; HLM Memo to AAK, Nov. 7, 1931, pp. 1–5, 14, EPFL; Geoffrey Hellman, "Profiles: Publisher II; Flair Is the Word," *New Yorker*, Nov. 27, 1948, p. 48; Blanche Knopf, "Autobiographical Fragment," pp. 6–7, HRHRC; HLM, *Thirty-Five Years*, p. 644, EPFL; HLM to AAK, Aug. 6, Nov. 21, Dec. 1, Dec. 23, 1931, EPFL; AAK to HLM, Dec. 12, 1931, EPFL.

4. AAK, Diary, Oct. 30, Nov. 18, 1931, HRHRC; HLM to GJN, Oct. 22, Nov. 7, 25, 1931, NYPL; Margaret Lappin to Rosalind Lohrfinck, Oct. 27, 1931, YALE; GJN to HLM, "Monday, 3 p.m.," 1931, NYPL; Rosalind Lohrfinck to Margaret Lappin, Oct. 1931, YALE; Sinclair Lewis to GJN, Nov. 8, 1931, CORN; AAK to HLM, Nov. 4, 9, 1931, EPFL; GJN, *The Intimate Notebooks of George Jean Nathan*, p. 121; HLM to AAK, Nov. 7, 1931, EPFL.

5. "Dr. Mencken Retires," *Reading Courier Free Press*, Oct. 14, 1933; "Mr. Mencken on His Own," *NYT*, Oct. 7, 1933; Ted Shane, "Low-Down on the Highbrows: H. L. Mencken Is Dead," *Manhattan Magazine*, Feb. 1, 1933, p. 3; "World Happier as Cynicism Gives Way to Idealism," *Milwaukee Journal*, Jan. 24, 1932; George W. Gray, "Lost Generation," *NYT*, Feb. 5, 1933; H. L. Mencken, "Advice to Young Men," Nov. 29, 1939, EPFL; James Gray, "With Mencken School Jaded, Reviewers Ask 1932 for New Talents to Replace Decadent," *St. Paul Dispatch*, Dec. 31, 1931; Budd Schulberg, "In Memory of F. Scott Fitzgerald: II," *New Republic*, March 3, 1941, p. 312; F. Scott Fitzgerald, "Echoes of the Jazz Age," *Scribner's*, Nov. 1931, pp. 459, 465; AAK, Diary, Dec. 15, 1931, HRHRC.

6. "Prominent Americans Hail Hope of Prosperity in 1931," *New York Evening Post*, Dec. 30, 1930; AAK, Diary, Dec. 15, 1931, HRHRC.

Chapter 35: Happy Days Are Here Again

1. "Sick, Not Drunk, Mencken Says; Satirist Sailing for Health Cruise Resents Being Asked to Sit Down," *Miami (Florida) News*, Jan. 10, 1932; HLM to Philip Goodman, Jan. 2, 1932, EPFL; "H. L. Mencken Sails, Chatting of Beer," *New York Evening Post*, Jan. 17, 1932; HLM to Otto H. Franke, Jan. 11, 1932, EPFL; HLM, "The Caribbean Caravel, Newssheet Aboard S. S. Columbus, North German Lloyd," Jan. 18, 25, 26, 1932, in "HLM: Clippings, Carbons, and Souvenirs Including Music 1893–1938," pp. 66–68, EPFL; HLM, "West Indian Notes," *BES*, Jan. 25, 1932; HLM to Henry Nixdorf, July 15, 1935, EPFL; "Mencken Back, Health Restored on Diet of Beer," *New York Herald Tribune*, Jan. 28, 1932; HLM to Hamilton Owens, Jan. 16, 1932, EPFL.

2. HLM, *Thirty-Five Years*, pp. 644, 646, EPFL; HLM, "What Is Going On in the World," *American Mercury*, March 1932, pp. 257–61; Olson, *Baltimore*, pp. 333–34; "Leave Bridge Tables: Learn to Cook, Mencken Advises Women," *Baltimore Post*, Jan. 13, 1932; HLM to Henry Nixdorf, Oct. 15, 1932, EPFL.

3. HLM to Edith Lustgarten, Nov. 5, 1932, NYPL; Manchester, *Disturber of the Peace*, p. 261; HLM to Virginia Mencken, April 22, 1932, EPFL; HLM to Charles Mencken, Dec. 8, 1932, EPFL; HLM to Frau Anna Mencke, April 9, 1932, EPFL; HLM, "The Hoover Bust," *BES*, Oct. 10, 1932; Leuchtenburg, *Franklin D. Roosevelt and the New Deal*, p. 19; HLM, *Thirty-Five Years*, pp. 647–48, 653–58, EPFL; Rodgers, ed., *The Impossible H. L. Mencken*, p. 313; HLM, Convention Tally Sheet in "HLM: Clippings, Carbons, and Souvenirs, Including Music 1893–1938," p. 21, EPFL; "Convention Sidelights," *Chicago Herald Examiner*, June 15, 1932; "The Reminiscences of Walter Lippmann," p. 162, COL; HLM, "Mencken Finds Both Sides Sour, Thinking Only of Their Losses," *BES*, July 2, 1932; HLM, "Mencken Tells How Magic Word 'Beer' Brought the Cheers," *BES*, Oct. 26, 1932; HLM to Harrison Hale Schaff, July 13, 1932, UVA.

4. HLM, *Thirty-Five Years*, pp. 659–60, 616–17, EPFL.

5. HLM to Louis Untermeyer, Nov. 9, 1932, NYPL; Rodgers, ed., *The Impossible H. L. Mencken*, p. 313.

6. "Press is Bar to Corruption, Says Mencken," *New York Newsday*, Dec. 10, 1932; "Beer Signifies Return of Joy, Mencken Says," *Philadelphia Record*, March 29, 1933.

7. "Jubilee Rings to Greet Beer for 19 States," *Atlanta Journal*, April 7, 1933; John L. Ahlers, "20 Years Ago—Baltimore Quenched Its Thirst With Returning Legal Beer, Found It Good," *Baltimore Sun*, April 7, 1953; Rodgers, ed., *The Impossible H. L. Mencken*, p. 313; James H. Bready, "The Glorious Return of Legal Beer," *BES*, April 3, 1953; "Taxed Beer Is 'Slop,' Says Mencken," *San Francisco News*, March 29, 1933; "Mencken Says Americans Are Too Poor-Spirited and Low Down to Deserve Beer," *Houston Post*, March 29, 1933; "Mencken, High Priest of Brew, Gives Sanction to New Beer," *BS*, April 4, 1933; author interview with Philip Hamburger, Jan. 3, 1995; HLM to Hamilton Owens, April 8, 1933, EPFL; "From Drought to Flood," *London News Chronicle*, April 8, 1933; "Thus Spake Mr. Mencken," *Boston American*, April 7, 1933.

Chapter 36: Maryland, My Maryland

1. Cook, *Eleanor Roosevelt*, p. 177; "Eyewitness to Lynching Tells How Mob Acted," *Baltimore Afro-American*, Dec. 12, 1931; "Salisbury Killer Hanged from Tree at Courthouse," *BS*, Dec. 5, 1931.

2. "A Statement," editorial, *Salisbury Times*, Dec. 5, 1931; Preston, *Newspapers of Maryland's Eastern Shore*, p. 158; HLM, "The Eastern Shore Kultur," *BES*, Dec. 7, 1931; HLM, "Sound and Fury," *BES*, Dec. 14, 1931; Harrison, *The Editorial Art of Edmund Duffy*, pp. i–xxi.

3. "Boycott Baltimore! Is Cry of Business Officials on Shore," *Baltimore Post*, Dec. 11, 1931; "Baltimore's Trade Here is Falling Off," *Easton Star Democrat*, Dec. 18, 1931; "Feud Between Eastern Shore and Baltimore Hurts Business," *Centreville (Maryland) Observer*, Dec. 22, 1931. One of these placards is preserved in volume L of "H. L. Mencken Clippings Books," EPFL; "Baltimore's Center of Commerce Takes Action," *Worcester Democrat*, Dec. 19, 1931; "Baltimore Says, 'Do Not Judge Us By Mencken and the Sun,' " *Snow Hill Democratic Messenger*, Dec. 9, 1931. The letter sent to the *Sun* from Salisbury along with Mencken's prefatory note can be found in the file "Correspondence with Marylanders" for "Williams, Matthew. Negro Lynching at Salisbury, Maryland, Dec. 4, 1931," EPFL; Carl Bode interview with George Schuyler, ca. 1965, Carl Bode Papers, EPFL; Dr. Broadus Mitchell to HLM, Oct. 20, 1933, EPFL; Clarence Mitchell III to the author Feb. 23, 1987; Seldes, *Freedom of the Press*, p. 341;

"1931 Honor Roll of the Nation," *New York Herald Tribune*, Dec. 31, 1931; "Mencken Is on the Warpath Again," *Dayton News*, Feb. 21, 1931.

4. H. Alan Wycherly, "H. L. Mencken and the Eastern Shore, December 1931," *Bulletin of the New York Public Library*, June 1970, p. 390; Cook, *Eleanor Roosevelt*, pp. 176–89, 242–47, 256, 279, 346. For a contemporary discussion of the bill and the investigation of the lynching, see Walter White, "U.S. Department of (White) Justice," *Crisis*, Oct. 1935, pp. 309–10; "Senator's Kill Anti-Lynch Measure," and "Walter White Raises Question of Negro's Participation in Another War," *Pittsburgh Courier*, May 4, 1935; "Memorandum for Mr. Early," from P. L. S. May 10, 1934, in file "Lynching 1933–1935," FDR; "Memorandum for Mr. Early, April 25, 1935." A note on the bottom advises the president not to see White "as he wants to discuss pending legislation"; FDR signed his initials in agreement, FDR; Dr. Broadus Mitchell to HLM, Oct. 20, 1933, EPFL; HLM, "The Costigan-Wagner Bill," *BES*, Jan. 19, 1934. The Anti-Lynching Bill 5.24 & HR 2776, known as the Costigan-Wagner Bill, pointed out that there had been 5,070 lynchings in the United States since 1882. HLM to Henry M. Hyde, Feb. 6, 1934, EPFL; HLM to Walter White, Feb. 6, 1934, LC; "Lane Is Summoned by Senate in Lynch Quiz," *Baltimore News Post*, Feb. 15, 1934; HLM to Elisabeth Gilman, March 8, 1934, EPFL; HLM to Walter White Oct. 4, 1934, Jan. 16, Feb. 16, Sept. 26, 1935, LC; HLM, "Notes on Negro Strategy," *Crisis*, Oct. 1934, p. 304.

5. "Anti-Lynching Bill Hearing Up Next Week," *Afro-American*, Feb. 11, 1934; Arthur Schlesinger Jr., "Letters to the Editor," *New Republic*, Dec. 16, 1957, p. 23. Among those who signed their name to the telegram were Dorothy Parker, AAK, Heywood Broun, W. E. B. Du Bois, Lewis Gannett, GJN, Carl Van Vechten, Arthur Garfield Hays, Joseph Wood Krutch, but it was Mencken who appeared in person. Telegram dated Dec. 4, 1933 to President Franklin D. Roosevelt, FDR; *Punishment for the Crime of Lynching Hearing Before a Subcommittee of the Judiciary, United States Senate, Feb. 14, 1935* (Washington, DC: U.S. Government Printing Office, 1935), p. 24; "Mencken Assails Lynching in State," *BS*, Feb. 15, 1935; HLM, "Statement to Senate Subcommittee Hearing with Costigan-Wagner Anti-Lynching Bill, Feb. 14, 1935," in "H. L. Mencken Miscellaneous Statements and Interviews 1924–1936," p. 163, EPFL; "The Anti-Lynching Law," *Newport News Herald*, Feb. 15, 1935; "Lynching Bill Gains Headstrong Support: Senate Group Likely to Act After Pleas by Mencken, Others," *Washington Post*, Feb. 15, 1935; anonymous letter to H. L. Mencken enclosed in a note to Walter White, undated, ca. 1935, LC; HLM, "The Lynching Psychosis," *BES*, March 28, 1932; HLM, "Notes on Negro Strategy," *Crisis*, Oct. 1934, p. 304.

Chapter 37: The Tune Changes

1. Lipstadt, *Beyond Belief*, pp. 7–10, 15–16, 29, 35–39, 84, 180–86; author interview with R. P. Harriss, Oct. 27, 1987; HLM to Philip Goodman, Feb. 3, 1933, EPFL; Blanche Knopf to HLM, March 24, 1933, EPFL; HLM to Blanche Knopf, March 25, 1933, EPFL; HLM to Edgar Lee Masters, July 18, 1933, HRHRC; Dr. Rathbone Oliver to HLM, Sept. 19, 1933, EPFL; HLM to Philip Goodman, Aug. 11, 1932, May 13, 1933, Ruth Goodman Goetz Collection, NYPL/ms; author interviews with Ruth Goodman Goetz, June 13, 1991, March 4, 1992; "The Reminiscences of August Mencken," pp. 22–23, COL; Ruth Goodman Goetz, "The Faces of Enlightenment," *Menckeniana*, Winter 1988, pp. 3–4; HLM, *Thirty-Five Years*, p. 678; HLM, manuscript on Philip Goodman, dated July 1941, in "HLM: Miscellaneous Writings 1940–41, Clippings and Carbons," p. 5, EPFL.

2. "A request to Mr. Mencken to Discuss Hitlerism," in "Letters," *BES*, July 24, 1933; HLM to Hamilton Owens, July 24, 1931, EPFL; "From Mencken to McGuire," *ADL Bulletin*, May 19, 1957; HLM to Col. Emerson, May 12, 1933, NYPL/ms; HLM to Walther Fischer, June 18, 1933, NYPL; Hawgood, *The Tragedy of German-America*, p. 42.

3. HLM, "The Library," *American Mercury*, Dec. 1933, pp. 506–10; AAK, Diary, Feb. 19, 1932, HRHRC. Alarmed that the American public was not getting the full picture, Cranston some years later translated and published an unexpurgated version of the work. Lipstadt, *Beyond Belief*, pp. 34, 102. HLM dismissed Knopf's concerns to Philip Goodman on June 6, 1933, EPFL. The publisher was touting Wickham Steed's review of *Mein Kampf* in the *London Observer* as model for Mencken to emulate. Mencken dubbed Steed as "the worst fraud of them all." During the First World War, Steed, in his role as foreign editor of the *London Times*, routinely published propaganda as news; this led Mencken to doubt Steed as a trustworthy source in 1933. See the letters from AAK to HLM, Oct. 24, 27, 1933, and from HLM to AAK, Oct. 26, 28, 1933, all, EPFL; Knightley, *The First Casualty*, pp. 91, 121, 141, 146; AAK to HLM, Oct. 27, 1933, EPFL; Hamilton Owens, "H. L. Mencken: A Personal Note," in *The Letters of H. L. Mencken*, Guy J. Forgue, ed., p. xiii.

Chapter 38: The Late Mr. Mencken

1. Fragment written by Clare Boothe Luce, "Lunch Meeting, March 15, 1933" while she was at *Vanity Fair*, LC.

2. Lawrence Spivak, "Circulation Statistics 1924–46 and The American Mercury," LC; Lawrence Spivak, "Financial Papers Advertising Accounts and Income 1924–1947," LC; Lawrence Spivak, "American Mercury Financial Papers: Statement and Account Examination 1924–1932" including "Profit and Loss Statements 1924–1949," LC; AAK to HLM, Nov. 11, 1932, March 2, 1933, EPFL: Singleton, *H. L. Mencken and the American Mercury Adventure*, pp. 218, 223; HLM to Virginia Mencken, Feb. 3, 1933, EPFL; "The Reminiscences of Alfred A. Knopf," p. 57, COL; HLM memo to AAK, Nov. 8, 1932, pp. 2–11, EPFL; Alfred Frankenstein, "The Lively Arts: Mencken a Pioneer in Music Criticism," *San Francisco Chronicle*, Feb. 1, 1956; Blanche Knopf to HLM, June 19, 1933, EPFL; "The Reminiscences of August Mencken," pp. 20–21, COL; AAK to HLM, Nov. 9, 1932, EPFL; HLM, Diary, Jan. 31, 1933, EPFL; Theodore Dreiser to GJN, Oct. 7, 1933, CORN; author interview with William Koshland, Dec. 6, 1994.

3. "Knopf Estate Nets $240,974," *New York Sun*, June 13, 1933; HLM to Henry Hazlitt, June 26, 1933, Henry Hazlitt to HLM, June 19, 1933, Hazlitt to Knopf, April 15, 1933, EPFL; HLM's letter to Edwin Embree, June 21, 1933, is in the HLM-AAK correspondence collection, EPFL.

4. Angoff, *The Bitter Spring*, pp. 378, 689–705, 708; Angoff, *Summer Storm*, pp. 206–7; "America Still in Literary Doldrums, Says Mencken," *BS*, Sept. 8, 1933; Peterson, *Magazines in the Twentieth Century*, pp. 148–49; author interview with William Koshland, Dec. 6, 1994, March 15, 1995; August Mencken to Arthur M. Louis, Dec. 17, 1963, EPFL; author interview with Ruth Goodman Goetz, March 4, 1992; author interviews with Lawrence Spivak, June 25, 1989, and Nancy Angoff Gallin, Nov. 9, 1994; Carl Bode interview with Huntington Cairns, Oct. 3, 1961, PRIN/md; AAK to Huntington Cairns, April 22, 1961, LC; HLM, "Advice to Young Men," May 17, 1939, YALE; Lawrence Spivak, "*The American Mercury* Author Cards," LC; O. H. Epperson to Charles Angoff, Aug. 31, 1963, BU; Carl Bode interview with John Owens, Sept. 23, 1964, collection of Harold A. Williams; HLM to Charles Angoff, March 23, 1926, and undated, ca. 1930s, BU; HLM to Charles Angoff, March 28, 1933, HRHRC; HLM to AAK, Feb. 4, 1942, EPFL; Carl Bode interview with Edith Lustgarten, Oct. 1, 1963, EPFL.

5. Angoff, *Summer Storm*, pp. 75, 80, 560, also pp. 206–7, 264–65; Harold U. Ribalow, "A Conversation with Charles Angoff," *The Old Century and the New: Essays in Honor of Charles Angoff*, ed. Alfred Rosa, pp. 35–68. For August Mencken's notations to Charles Angoff's *H. L. Mencken: A Portrait From Memory*, see Carl Bode's annotated copy among Bode's papers at the EPFL. More information regarding Charles Angoff, other than his own papers at BU, can be found among the AAK papers at HRHRC and letters from various Mencken correspondents to

Julian Boyd at Princeton. HLM to AAK, undated ca. April 1933, March 24, 1933, EPFL. When it came to Angoff, Knopf disagreed with Mencken, see letter of AAK to HLM, April 4, 1933, EPFL. Author interview with Lawrence Spivak, June 25, 1989; author interview with Pat Knopf, Aug. 20, 1995; Charles Angoff to HLM, Oct. 2, 1933, NYPL; Lowell Lemps to Charles Angoff, Dec. 20, 1935, BU.

6. Walter Lippmann to HLM, Oct. 10, 1933, YALE; "The Press: Hazlitt for Mencken," *Time*, Oct. 16, 1933, p. 43; HLM to Isaac Goldberg, Oct. 17, 1933, Isaac Goldberg Papers, NYPL/ms; AAK to HLM, Dec. 13, 1933, EPFL; Henry Hazlitt, "Editorial," in Lawrence Spivak, "American Mercury Subject File," LC; Singleton, *H. L. Mencken and the American Mercury Adventure*, p. 238; AAK, "Memoirs," p. 11A, HRHRC; "Mencken, Tired of Editing, Will Quit Mercury," *New York Herald Tribune*, Oct. 6, 1933; Mary Elizabeth Prim, "Married Mr. Mencken Retires to His Victorian Parlor," *Boston Transcript*, Oct. 7, 1933; R. L. W., "The Ogre of Cathedral Street," *The Teller*, Nov. 16, 1933.

Chapter 39: A Time to Be Wary

1. "Mencken Sees Only Job Pilot by Brain Trust," *New York World Telegram*, April 4, 1934; HLM to Paul Patterson, "At Sea," ca. Feb. 1934, collection of Bettina Patterson; Bishop Francis Kelly to Michael J. Curley, Nov. 3, 1934, ARCH; HLM, "Foreign Parts: Rabat," *New Yorker*, July 21, 1934, pp. 51–52; HLM, "Foreign Parts: Gibraltar," *New Yorker*, June 6, 1934, pp. 71–72; HLM to Virginia Mencken, Jan. 27, 1934, EPFL; HLM to Rosalind Lohrfinck, March 9, 1934, EPFL; author interview with Ida Haardt McCulloch, Oct. 1, 1983.

2. HLM to AAK, March 9, 1934, EPFL; "Mencken Sings Palestine Praise," *Buffalo Jewish Courier*, July 13, 1934; "British Are Using Jews as Suckers in Palestine, Declares Mencken," *Detroit Ledger*, April 28, 1934; HLM, *Heathen Days*, p. 276–77; Philip Rubin, "H. L. Mencken and the Jews," *Congress Weekly*, Feb. 20, 1956, pp. 7–8; HLM, *Thirty-Five Years*, pp. 792–93, EPFL; Sara Haardt to Ellen Glasgow, May 21, 1934, UVA; HLM to Gertrude Mencken, May 7, 1934, EPFL.

3. Sara Haardt, "Southern Souvenirs," p. 3, GOU; HLM to Sara Haardt, Sept. 2, 1934, GOU; HLM, *Thirty-Five Years*, p. 793, EPFL; HLM, Diary, May 31, 1940, EPFL; Walter Winchell column, *New York Mirror*, Oct. 2, 1934; author interview with Dr. Benjamin Baker, March 25, 1994; HLM to Lynn Meekins, Oct. 27, 1934, EPFL.

4. HLM, *Minority Report*, p. 22; HLM, "A Planned Economy," BES, Feb. 5, 1934; HLM to Paul Patterson, Aug. 18, 1933, Carl Bode Papers, EPFL; "Mencken Warns Brain Trust Country May Rise Against It," *BS*, April 28, 1934; Rodgers, ed., *The Impossible H. L. Mencken*, p. liii; Argersinger, *Toward a New Deal in Baltimore*, pp. 205–6; HLM, "Advice to Young Men," Jan. 22, 1940, July 20, 1939, EPFL; "It Takes 3 Reporters and Lots of Copy Paper to Interview H. L. Mencken," *Daytona Beach Journal*, Jan. 15, 1937; HLM, "The Dilemma of Statecraft," BES, Feb. 20, 1933.

5. HLM, "A Time to Be Wary," BES, March 13, 1933.

6. HLM, "HLM: Miscellaneous Speeches, 1913–1938," pp. 45–47, EPFL. Mencken found it difficult to memorize anything, see HLM, "The Schooling of a Theologian," *New Yorker*, July 8, 1939, p. 39. HLM, *Thirty Five Years*, p. 777, EPFL; HLM to Fred Essary, Nov. 27, 1934, EPFL; Fred Essary to HLM, Nov. 29, 1934, EPFL; Stephen T. Early, "Dec. 7, 1934," *Diary 1934-June 1937*, FDR; Carl Bode interview with Arthur Krock, June 25, 1963, PRIN/md; Bode, *Mencken*, pp. 310–11.

7. "FDR Speech, Dec. 8, 1934," FDR; HLM to Jean Balch, Nov. 2, 1934, EPFL; HLM, *Thirty-Five Years*, p. 779–80, EPFL; HLM, "Journalism in America," *Prejudices: Sixth Series*, pp. 9–37; Brayman, *The President Speaks Off-the-Record*, pp. 261–62, reproduces what can be found at the FDR Library; James Cain, "Mr. Mencken and the Multitude," *New York Times Book Review*, April 16, 1950; Harold Ickes, Diary, Dec. 11, 1934, p. 722, LC; Carl Bode interview

with Arthur A. Krock, June 25, 1963, PRIN/md; author interview with Ruth Goodman Goetz, June 13, 1991; Arthur Brisbane to FDR, Dec. 10, 1934, FDR; FDR to Brisbane, Feb. 18, 1934, FDR; Carl Bode interview with John Owens, Sept. 23, 1964, collection of Harold A. Williams; author interview with William Manchester, May 23, 1995; HLM to Alfred Miezychowski, Dec. 26, 1934, PRIN/fire; HLM to Edgar Lee Masters, Dec. 21, 1934, HRHRC; HLM to AAK, Oct. 18, 1934, EPFL; HLM to Isaac Goldberg, Dec. 24, 1934, NYPL/ms.

Chapter 40: A Winter of Horror

1. HLM to Virginia Mencken, Feb. 3, 15, 1935, EPFL; HLM to Ellen Glasgow, March 16, 1935 (UVA); HLM to Blanche Knopf, March 19, 1935, EPFL; HLM to Fulton Oursler, April 1, 1935, GT; HLM, Appendix XXV, *My Life*, p. 46, EPFL; Virginia Mencken to HLM, May 2, 1935, EPFL; Sara Haardt to Elizabeth Hanes, May 2, 1925, UNC; Rodgers, ed., *Mencken & Sara*, p. 515; author interview with Dr. Benjamin Baker, March 25, 1994. Mencken included this 1931 tune ("Das Gibt's nur Einmal" by Werner R. Heymann) at the end of the collection of his correspondence with Sara Haardt. HLM's observation is written on the sheet of music by Heymann. The original phonograph is owned by Barry Cheslock, who inherited HLM's music collection from his father, Louis Cheslock. Author interview with Barry Cheslock, April 14, 1996.

2. "Letters of H. L. Mencken and Sara Haardt," GOU; HLM to Virginia Mencken, April 16, 1935, EPFL; HLM to Jean Balch, April 13, 1935, EPFL; Sara Haardt, "Alabama April," pp. 1–2, GOU; Sara Haardt, "Dear Life," *Southern Album*, pp. 278, 284–86, 289. For notes on the weather, see HLM to Virginius Dabney, April 18, 1935, UVA; HLM to Virginia Mencken, April 16, 1935, EPFL; HLM to Jean Balch, April 28, 1935, EPFL; HLM to Sara Haardt, April 1, 1935, GOU; Sara Haardt to Elizabeth Hanes, May 2, 1935, UNC; HLM to David Weglein, May 14, 1935, EPFL; HLM to Charles Mencken, May 14, 1935, EPFL.; Herbert R. Leggett, real estate agent, to Sara Haardt Mencken, May 14, 1935, GOU; Harriett Jones to Sara Haardt Mencken, May 16, 29, 1935, GOU; Sara Haardt to Katharine Steiner Haxton, Jan. 28, 1935, collection of Katharine Steiner Haxton; author interview with Katherine Steiner Haxton, Oct. 15, 1991; HLM to Virginia Mencken, April 20, May 25, 1935, EPFL: HLM to Benjamin de Casseres, June 4, 1935, NYPL; HLM to Fulton Oursler, May 18, 1935, GT. Mencken's denial of Sara's true condition was also expressed in other letters, e.g., to Ellen Glasgow, March 16, 1935, UVA, and to Holger Koppel, when he stated: "It never occurred to me that my wife's illness might be fatal." HLM to Holger Koppel, June 5, 1935, collection of Steven Lauria.

3. HLM to AAK, May 25, 1935, EPFL; HLM, *Thirty-Five Years*, pp. 793–94, EPFL; author interview with Ida Haardt McCulloch, Oct. 1, 1983; Sara Haardt to Sara Mayfield, "Sunday night," ca. May 1935, ALA/gg; HLM, Diary, May 31, 1940, EPFL; HLM to William Abhau, May 28, 1935, EPFL; HLM to Raymond Pearl, May 29, 1935, APS; HLM to Max Broedel, "Wednesday," May 29, 1935, EPFL; HLM to Elizabeth Hanes, May 30, 1935, UNC; Raymond Pearl, Diary, June 3, 1935, APS; HLM to Pauline Trowbridge, June 7, 1935, HRHRC; HLM to James Branch Cabell, June 10, 1935, UVA; Rodgers, ed., *Mencken and Sara*, p. 515; HLM to Mrs. Jessie Rector, Jan. 6, 1936, EPFL; Theodore Dreiser to HLM, June 4, 1935, GOU; HLM to Hamilton Owens, May 30, 1935, EPFL; HLM to R. P. Harriss, May 30, 1935, EPFL; HLM to Elizabeth Hanes, May 31, 1935, UNC; Hamilton Owens, "A Personal Note," in Forgue, ed., *Letters of H. L. Mencken*, pp. xi–xii.

4. See "Sara Haardt Mencken: Letters and Telegrams After Her Death," GOU. While the hundreds of letters speak eloquently of Sara, they also provide a fine commentary on H. L. Mencken. Among the expressions of sorrow is a telegram from Roy Wilkins representing the NAACP and *Crisis* magazine, and a letter from the Association of the National Negro Press, both dated June 1, 1935. Anita Loos to HLM, Aug. 25, 1935, GOU; HLM to Mrs. Otto Schellhaus, June 5, 1935, EPFL; HLM to Emma Jones, waitress, June 7, 1935, EPFL; Marjorie

Hope Nicholson to HLM, June 7, 1935, GOU; Mrs. Marna Todd to HLM, June 3, 1935, GOU; Jennie H. Cleveland to HLM, June 24, 1935, GOU; HLM to Aileen Pringle, June 4, 1935, YALE.

5. HLM, "Preface," *Southern Album*, p. xiv; author interview with Ida Haardt McCulloch, Oct. 1, 1983; HLM to Hamilton Owens, June 4, 1935, EPFL; HLM to Sara Mayfield, June 5, 1935, ALA/gg; HLM to Ellery Sedgewick, June 7, 1935, PRIN/fire; HLM, Diary, May 31, 1940, EPFL; HLM to Sara Mayfield, June 5, 1935, ALA/gg; HLM to Fred Hanes, June 7, 1935, UNC.

6. "The Frankest Man on Earth Is Here," *London Chroncile*, June 30, 1935; "Mr. Mencken in London," *Manchester Guardian*, June 28, 1935; "Famous U.S. Satirist Arrives in England Trying to Forget the Past," *London Daily Express*, June 29, 1935; Newton Aiken, "Memoirs," Chapter VIII, p. 18, collection of Harold A. Williams.

7. "The Reminiscences of August Mencken," p. 12, COL; HLM, "Prefatory Note to Notes by Sara Haardt 1927–1935," GOU; HLM to Gertrude Mencken, July 27, 1935, EPFL; HLM to Virginia Mencken, July 25, 1935, EPFL; HLM to Dr. Gertrude C. Bussey of Goucher College, Feb. 28, 1936, EPFL; author interview with Sara Anne Duffy Chermayeff, June 14, 1991; HLM to Mary Parmenter, Sept. 25, 1935, EPFL; HLM to Elizabeth Hanes, Aug. 1, 28, Dec. 7, 1935, UNC; HLM to Anne Rector Duffy, Aug. 8, 1935, EPFL; author interview with Ruth Goodman Goetz, June 13, 1991, confirmed by Sara Anne Duffy Chermayeff, June 14, 1991; author interview with Sara Anne Duffy Chermayeff, March 2, 1992; HLM to Mrs. Edmund Duffy, Sept. 17, 1935, EPFL; HLM to Jean Balch, Oct. 17, 1935, EPFL; R. H. Runckles to H. L. Mencken, June 4, 1935, GOU; HLM, "Preface," *Southern Album*, p. xx; Mayfield, *The Constant Circle*, pp. 217–18; HLM, May 31, 1940, EPFL; author interview with Edward Clark, May 14, 1995; HLM to Jean Balch, Aug. 29, 1935, EPFL; HLM to Bee Wilson, Sept. 24, 1935, EPFL; Raymond Pearl, Diary Aug. 31, 1935, APS; HLM to Aileen Pringle, Oct. 22, Sept. 12, 1935, YALE; HLM, Diary, May 31, 1940, EPFL; HLM to Rev. Henri J. Wiesel, Aug. 27, 1935, EPFL; HLM to Mrs. J. H. Mencken, Sept. 14, 1935, EPFL; HLM, "Autobiographical Notes, 1941," EPFL.

8. "Mencken Given Idea of Honors Posterity May Accord to Him," *BS*, Sept. 13, 1935; "H. L. Mencken Honored," *Washington Times*, Sept. 13, 1935; HLM to Miss Coplan, Sept. 14, 1935, to Elliott Wheeler, Sept. 25, 1935, EPFL; HLM to Mrs. Edwin Swift Balch, Sept. 7, 1935, NYPL; author interview with Sara Anne Duffy Chermayeff, March 2, 1992; HLM to Benjamin de Casseres, Sept. 21, 1935, NYPL; HLM to Ezra Pound, Nov. 15, 1934, YALE; HLM to H. L. Davis, Oct. 17, 1935, NYPL; HLM to Gertrude Mencken, Nov. 30, 1935, EPFL; "College Gets Gift of Mrs. Mencken," *BES*, Nov. 1, 1935; Bode, *Mencken*, p. 303; HLM to Miss Mullen, Oct. 19, 1935, ALA; HLM to Dr. Gertrude C. Bussey of Goucher College, Feb. 28, 1936, EPFL; HLM to Sister Miriam, Sept. 15, 1937, GT; HLM to Jean Balch, March 19, 1936, EPFL; HLM to Sara Mayfield, Sept. 10, 1937, ALA/gg.

9. HLM to James Bone, Nov. 19, 1935, NYPL; HLM, *Thirty-Five Years*, pp. 796–97, EPFL; HLM to Elizabeth Hanes, Dec. 7, 1935, UNC; HLM to Frau Anna Mencke, Nov. 14, 1935, EPFL; HLM to Frank Hogan, Nov. 1, 1935, EPFL; James Cain to Elina Cain, Dec. 27, 1935, in Hoopes, *Cain*, p. 273; "The Reminiscences of August Mencken," pp. 12–13, COL; HLM to Virginia Mencken, Nov. 23, 1935, EPFL; HLM to Logan Clendening, Dec. 26, 1935, NYPL; HLM to Mrs. A. D. Emmart, Dec. 27, 1935, EPFL; HLM to Edgar Lee Masters, Dec. 26, 1935, HRHRC.

Chapter 41: Baltimore's Friendly Dragon

1. HLM, "*Happy Days*: Additions . . . ," p. 11, EPFL; HLM to Jean Balch, May 6, June 2, 1936, EPFL; R. P. Thomas to HLM, July 6, 1942, EPFL; HLM to Clarissa Flugel, March 28, 1936, EPFL; HLM to Mrs. Horsey Gannt, March 28, 1936, EPFL; HLM to Elizabeth

Hanes, April 30, 1936, UNC; HLM to Blanche Knopf, March 26, 1936, EPFL; HLM to Charles Mencken, March 28, 1936, EPFL; HLM to Benjamin de Casseres, March 26, 1936, NYPL; HLM to Joe Hergesheimer, March 19, 1936, HRHRC; Carl Bode interview with George Schuyler, ca. 1965, Carl Bode Papers, EPFL.

2. HLM to Dan Henry, March 31, 1936, EPFL; HLM to Charles Mencken, March 7, 1941, EPFL; HLM, *My Life*, p. 766, EPFL; HLM to Charles Abhau, Feb. 29, 1936, EPFL; HLM to Theodore Dreiser, May 25, July 16, 1935, PENN; Fecher, *Mencken: A Study of His Thought*, p. 296; HLM, "Preface to the Fourth Edition," *The American Language*, pp. vii–viii; HLM to James Tully, Sept. 28, 1935, PRIN/fire.

3. St. Clair McKelway, "Mr. Mencken, Mr. Ross," unpublished manuscript, James Thurber Papers, YALE; HLM to William Archer, UVA.

4. HLM to Mr. Warner, Nov. 6, 1936, EPFL; HLM, "Three Years of Dr. Roosevelt," *American Mercury*, March 1936, p. 264.

5. HLM, "Three Years of Dr. Roosevelt," *American Mercury*, March 1936, p. 264; author interview with Lawrence Spivak, June 25, 1989; Blanche Knopf to HLM, Feb. 24, 1936, EPFL; "Ickes Takes Swat at Professional Gadfly—Mencken," *Providence Bulletin*, Feb. 25, 1936; "Baltimore Held Ironclad Spot for First Attack," *New York World Telegram*, April 14, 1936; "U.S. Criticism Duty of Press, Says Mencken," *New York American*, April 25, 1936; HLM, "Speech at the Annual Luncheon of the Associated Press, New York, April 20, 1936," from "HLM: Miscellaneous Speeches 1913–1938," pp. 48–53, EPFL.

6. "Mencken Brings Madstones," *BES*, June 11, 1936; HLM to Charles Mencken, June 30, 1936, EPFL; HLM to Dr. Bertram M. Bernheim, Nov. 25, 1936, EPFL; "Landon Neither Vacuum Nor Kansas Gang's Stooge, Notes Mencken," *BS*, July 26, 1936; "Plain Speech of Plain Man, Says Mencken," *Topeka State Journal*, July 24, 1936; "Mencken Endorses Candidate for First Time—Alf Landon," *Austin Herald*, Sept. 3, 1936; HLM to Jean Balch, Sept. 23, 1936, EPFL; "A Bad Boy Grows Older," *Philadelphia Record*, Feb. 29, 1936; "Fair Enough, by Westbrook Pegler: H. L. Mencken's About-Face Adds for Campaign Hilarity; His Conversion to Landon to Replace That of Al Smith's," *New York Telegram*, Oct. 8, 1936; "Lapdog Writer Exposes Landon, Et. Al.," *Watford City (North Dakota) Farmer*, Aug. 20, 1936; HLM to Virginia Mencken, Sept. 24, 1936, EPFL; HLM to Eric Lageman, Sept. 29, 1937, EPFL; John Abbott Clark, "The Morgue: H. L. Mencken: An Obituary," *American Spectator*, Oct. 1936, p. 12.

7. HLM to Frank Kent, July 3, 1936, EPFL; HLM, *Thirty-Five Years*, pp. 935–36, EPFL; Karl B. Pauly, "Mostly About People: Mencken Is Ace of Reporters," *Columbus State Journal*, Jan. 26, 1938; "Mr. Landon Goes to Church," *New York Sun*, Aug. 24, 1936; Dr. Henry Shilling to Alf Landon, Oct. 17, 1967 in letter from Alfred E. Landon to Betty Adler, June 20, 1967, EPFL; HLM, "Preface," in "Dispatches to the Baltimore Sun from the Republican and Democratic National Conventions, June, 1936," EPFL; HLM to Henry Hyde, Aug. 29, 1936, EPFL; HLM to Kate Coplan, Sept. 12, 1936, EPFL; HLM to AAK, Sept. 16, 1936, EPFL; Duke Shoop, "The Pungent, Cynical Mencken Was a Friendly Man to Meet," *Kansas City Times*, Feb. 4, 1954; D. P. Duncan to Alfred A. Knopf, July 30, 1936, EPFL; HLM to Edgar Lee Masters, Sept. 2, 1936, Masters-Davis Collection, NYPL/ms.

8. Brinkley, *Voices of Protest*, p. 216; HLM, "Rev. Gerald Smith Stars at Townsend Convention in Rabble-Rousing Talk," *BS*, July 16, 1926; HLM, "Roosevelt Competition Takes Edge Off Opening of Coughlin Convention," *BS*, Aug. 15, 1936; letter from Doug Trussel to the author, Feb. 29, 1988; HLM to Edgar Lee Masters, Sept. 2, 1936, Masters-Davis Collection, NYPL.

9. Schlesinger Jr., *The Age of Roosevelt*, pp. 625, 630–31; Williams, *The Baltimore Sun*, pp. 241–42; HLM to Gerald Johnson, Nov. 13, 1936, EPFL.

10. HLM, "The Choice Tomorrow," *BES*, Nov. 2, 1936; Newton Aiken, "Memoirs," ch. X, pp. 3–4, collection of Harold A. Williams; "Part of Throng Watching Election Returns

in Sun Square," *BS*, Nov. 4, 1936; HLM to Bertram Bernheim, Nov. 25, 1936, EPFL; HLM to Virginia Mencken, Oct. 19, 1936, EPFL; HLM to Benjamin de Casseres, Nov. 6, 1936, NYPL; HLM to Philip W. Warner, Nov. 6, 1936, NYPL; HLM to Henry Hyde, Nov. 6, 1936, EPFL.

Chapter 42: Mencken as Boss

1. "The Reminiscences of Edward Bernays," p. 397, COL; Douglas Williams, "The President Sees the Press," *London Daily Telegraph*, Dec. 8, 1934; Winfield, *FDR and the News Media*, pp. 28–29, 33–35; Frank Kent, "The President and Press," May 24, 1934, MdHS; Thomas W. Phelps, "Reporters' Friend: Roosevelt Treats Gentlemen of Press Covering His Activities as Comrades: A Friendly Laugh Helps," *Wall Street Journal*, Sept. 11, 1934; William E. Leuchtenburg, "Why Candidates Still Use FDR as Their Measure," *American Heritage*, Feb. 1988, pp. 36–37; Smith, *Thank You, Mr. President*, pp. 1–29; HLM to Paul Patterson, Jan. 1937, Carl Bode Papers, EPFL; HLM to Paul Ward, May 1, 1939, EPFL.

2. R. P. Harriss, "Mencken as Boss," *BS*, Sept. 4, 1988; R. P. Harriss, Diary, Jan. 24, Feb. 7, March 24, 1938, collection of Margery Harriss; R. P. Harriss to Harold A. Williams, May 26, 1976, collection of Harold Williams; Williams, *The Baltimore Sun 1837–1987*, p. 232; HLM to Hamilton Owens, April 9, 1938, EPFL; author interview with R. P. Harriss, Oct. 24, 1987; HLM, *Thirty-Five Years*, pp. 1024, 1026–27, 1031, EPFL.

3. R. P. Harriss, "Mencken as Boss," *BS*, Sept. 4, 1988; HLM, "Object Lesson," *BES*, Feb. 10, 1938; "Antic Dots," *Time*, Feb. 21, 1938, p. 44; "A Million Dots," *Printer's Ink*, Feb. 17, 1938; "Six Columns of Dots," *Chattanooga News*, Feb. 17, 1938; HLM, "Five Years of the New Deal," *BES*, March 4, 1938; R. P. Harriss, Diary, March 4, 1938, collection of Margery Harriss; author interview with Philip Wagner, Oct. 29, 1989; R. P. Harriss interview with Harold A. Williams, May 26, 1976, collection of Harold Williams; HLM, *Thirty-Five Years*, p. 1024, EPFL.

4. "The Reminiscences of Hamilton Owens," p. 64, COL; Philip A. Wagner, "Mencken Remembered," *American Scholar*, Spring 1963, p. 267; R. P. Harriss, Diary, March 24, 1938, collection of Margery Harriss; R. P. Harriss interviews with Harold A. Williams, May 26, 1976, April 1, 1984, collection of Harold A. Williams; R. P. Harriss, "Life with Mencken," *Gardens, Houses and People*, May 1949, pp. 21–23; "The End of a Yardstick," editorial, *BES*, March 9, 1938; "Man of an Extinct Species," editorial, *BES*, Feb. 22, 1938.

5. R. P. Harriss, Diary, March 8, 1938, collection of Margery Harriss; "The Reds and Fair Play," editorial, *BES*, April 11, 1938; "Note on Human Progress," editorial, *BES*, April 25, 1938; "Who Will Be General?" editorial, *BES*, April 30, 1938; "A Law Against Lynching," editorial, *BES*, May 7, 1938; "A Gladiator of the Law," editorial, *BES*, March 14, 1938; "The Mexican New Deal," editorial, *BES*, April 30, 1938; "Happy Days in Mexico," editorial, *BES*, April 20, 1938; Lipstadt, *Beyond Belief*, p. 87; "Wein Bleibt Wein," editorial, *BES*, March 17, 1938; HLM, *Thirty-Five Years*, pp. 1025–26, EPFL.

6. HLM, *Thirty-Five Years*, pp. 1027, 1031, EPFL; HLM to Hamilton Owens, April 9, 1938, EPFL; R. P. Harriss, Diary, March 24, 1938 collection of Margery Harriss; Philip Wagner, "Mencken Remembered," *American Scholar*, Spring 1963, pp. 267–68; author interview with Elsinor Roman, July 6, 1989; HLM to Sister Miriam, March 23, 1938, GT; Harold A. Williams interview with R. P. Harriss, April 12, 1984, collection of Harold A. Williams; "The Same Mencken," *Canonsburg Notes*, March 16, 1938; Gerald Johnson, "H. L. Mencken [1880–1956]," *Saturday Review of Literature*, Feb. 11, 1956, pp. 12–13.

7. Lipstadt, *Beyond Belief*, p. 89; HLM to Marcella DuPont, Aug. 31, 1938, Carl Bode Papers, EPFL; "H. L. Mencken Medical File," May 16, 1938, May 23, 1938, April 12, 1938, courtesy of Dr. Philip Wagley; HLM to Henry Wood, May 12, 1938, EPFL; HLM to Virginia Mencken, May 16, 1938, EPFL; author interview with Elsinor Roman, July 6, 1989; "The Reminiscences of Hamilton Owens," p. 67, COL; HLM to Sister Miriam, May 6, 1938, GT;

Philip Goodman to HLM, "Wednesday," in "Mencken and Goodman, Later Letters," compiled by Jack Sanders (private printing 1994, collection of Jack Sanders).

Chapter 43: Berlin, 1938

1. "Wetter," *Berliner Tageblatt*, July 7, 1938, June 15, 1938; Ritchie, *Faust's Metropolis*, pp. 407–74. Of particular interest is the chapter "Nazi Berlin—Life Before the Storm"; Hilberg, *The Destruction of the European Jews*, p. 94; HLM to Gertrude Mencken, June 25, June 30, 1938, EPFL; HLM to AAK, July 28, 1938, EPFL; HLM to Elizabeth Hanes, July 1, 1938, UNC; HLM to Louis Cheslock, July 28, 1938, EPFL; HLM to Max Broedel, July 1, 1938, PRIN/fire.

2. HLM to Max Broedel, July 1, 1938, PRIN/fire; Hobson, *Mencken: A Life*, pp. 402–3; HLM to Anne Duffy, July 1, 6, 7, Aug. 10, 1938, collection of Sara Anne Duffy Chermayeff; AAK, "Memoirs," p. 7, HRHRC; Gertrude Mencken to August Mencken, Oct. 20, 1964, EPFL.

3. HLM, *Thirty-Five Years*, pp. 1036–37, 1040, 1047–48, EPFL; HLM to Gertrude Mencken, June 30, 1938, EPFL; HLM to Charles Mencken, Aug. 3, 1938, EPFL; "Neue Hetze Mit Alten Lugen," *Berliner Tageblatt*, July 13, 1938; HLM, "Advice to Young Men," April 6, 1939, EPFL. The negative press Germany received caused one German editorial writer to scoff that the "distortions" had "enlarged our barbarism tenfold." He then posed this chilling question: "What if we for once made one or the other of these lies come true, and really locked up some 60,000 Jews, whose fate the Jewish foreign press is lambasting?" See "Aufklarung uber Ueslerreich," *Berliner Tageblatt*, June 28, 1938.

4. "Goebbels zur Sonnenwende," *Berliner Tageblatt*, June 22, 1938; "Goebbels zur Judenfrage" and "Judenfrage Wird legal Gelost," *Berliner Tageblatt* (evening edition), June 22, 1938; HLM to Max Broedel, July 1, 1938, PRIN/fire.

5. Hilberg, *The Destruction of European Jews*, p. 94; "Jungft 3000 Jüden Engewandert," *Berliner Tageblatt*, July 9, 1938; "Der Judische Grundbesitz," *Berliner Tageblatt Abendausgabe*, July 6, 1938; HLM to Roger Baldwin, July 2, 1938, PRIN/md; "U.S. Aide Sent to Reich for Refugee Data," *BS*, July 16, 1938; HLM, *Thirty-Five Years*, p. 1051, EPFL; Vincent Sheen, "Au Enthalt in Roseheim," *New Republic*, Dec. 7, 1938, from *Reporting World War II*, p. 10; author interview with Lawrence Spivak, June 25, 1989; Manchester, *Disturber of the Peace*, p. 69; HLM to George A. Kubler, May 14, 1936, NYPL.

6. HLM to Max Broedel, July 1, 1938, PRIN/fire; HLM, *Thirty-Five Years*, pp. 1039, 1041–42, 1044, 1050–51, EPFL; Fecher, *Mencken*, p. 35; HLM to August Mencken, July 5, 1939, EPFL; HLM to Raymond Pearl, July 9, 1938, APS; HLM to Gertrude Mencken, July 5, July 9, July 24, 1938, EPFL; HLM to P. E. Cleator, July 29, 1938, NYPL; HLM to Eddie Murphy, Aug. 3, 1938, EPFL; HLM, "Advice to Young Men," Oct. 4, 1938, EPFL; "H. L. Mencken Returns from European Trip," *BS*, July 26, 1938; L. S. B. Shapiro, "Lights and Shadows of Manhattan," *Montreal Gazette*, July 27, 1938; Louis Cheslock, Diary, Nov. 13, 1938, EPFL.

Chapter 44: Polemics and Prejudices

1. Hertzberg, *The Jews in America*, p. 287; HLM, "Help for the Jews," *BES*, Nov. 27, 1938; Lipstadt, *Beyond Belief*, p. 109; "Foreign News: We, the Wanderers," *Time*, Dec. 5, 1938, pp. 18–19; HLM, "Bringing Roosevelt Up to Date," *American Mercury*, March 1939, pp. 257–64. Mencken had been influenced by *The Rape of Palestine*, by British author William B. Ziff, and by *People at Bay*, by Oscar I. Janowsky. The first dealt with British maneuvers in Palestine; the second was a factual examination of the situation of Jews in Eastern Europe. HLM to Jacob M. Moses, Nov. 30, 1938, EPFL; HLM, "Advice to Young Men," May 30, 1939,

EPFL; HLM to Reverend Dr. Morris S. Lazaron, Feb. 27, 1937, EPFL; HLM, *Thirty-Five Years*, p. 331, EPFL; Hobson, *Mencken: A Life*, p. 423.

2. Charles Angoff, "Mencken Twilight," *North American Review*, Winter 1938, pp. 216–39; HLM, "Advice to Young Men," May 17, 1939, EPFL; author interview with Nancy Angoff Gallin, Nov. 9, 1994; Edmund Wilson, "Books: The Aftermath of Mencken," *New Yorker*, May 31, 1969, p. 113; HLM, "Advice to Young Men," March 22, 1939, EPFL; Robert Kanigel, "Did H. L. Mencken Hate the Jews?" reprinted in *Menckeniana*, Spring 1980, pp. 1–7; Ehrlich, *Human Natures*, pp. 294–95; HLM "The Prophet of the Superman," *Smart Set*, March 1912, pp. 156–58, HLM, "Getting Rid of the Actor," *Smart Set*, Sept. 1913, pp. 157–58; HLM, "Advice to Young Men," March 27, 1939, EPFL.

3. HLM, "Advice to Young Men," March 17, 22, 1939, undated entry ca. 1945, Sept. 28, 1939, July 10, 1939, EPFL; author interview with Alistair Cooke, May 19, 1992; HLM, *Thirty-Five Years*, p. 557, EPFL; HLM, "The Murray Case," *BES*, Sept. 23, 1935; "H. L. Mencken Declares Racial Groups Lack Intellectual Life," *Pittsburgh Courier*, Dec. 4, 1926; HLM to Hamilton Owens, April 25, 1926, EPFL; G. E. B. Murphy of the *Afro-American* to HLM, Sept. 24, 1935, EPFL; "Mencken Is on the Warpath Again," *Dayton News*, Feb. 21, 1931; Dowell, "Introduction," *Ich Kuss Die Hand*, pp. 22–23, 100–101; HLM, "The Fruits of Go-Getting," *BES*, June 22, 1925; Cynthia Neverdon-Morton, "Black Housing Patterns in Baltimore City 1885–1953," *Maryland Historian*, Spring/Summer 1985, pp. 25–39; HLM to Blanche Knopf, Jan. 9, 18, ca. 1927, HRHRC; Hamilton Owens to the editor of the *London Times Literary Supplement*, July 28, 1959, EPFL; Carl Bode interview with George Schuyler, ca. 1965, Carl Bode Papers, EPFL; HLM to Jim Tully, April 3, 1939, NYPL; HLM "Autobiographical Notes, 1941," EPFL.

4. AAK, "H. L. Mencken: A Memoir," in *On Mencken*, ed. John Dorsey, p. 292; HLM to Blanche Knopf, March 17, 1939, EPFL; HLM, "Preface to the Days of H. L. Mencken, written April 15, 1947," HLM, "Miscellaneous Typescripts, Carbons and Clipping 1946–48," pp. 41–42, EPFL; Charles Mencken to HLM, Dec. 6, 1939, EPFL; HLM to Charles Mencken, Nov. 29, 1939, EPFL; Helen Essary, "Dear Washington," *Washington Herald*, Jan. 24, 1940; "H. L. Mencken Medical File," July 31, 1939, from author interview with Dr. Philip Wagley, June 8, 1994; HLM, *Thirty-Five Years*, pp. 1157–59, EPFL; HLM to Heinrich Spies, Sept. 29, 1939, NYPL; HLM "Advice to Young Men," Nov. 29, 1939, EPFL; Rodgers, ed., *The Impossible H. L. Mencken*, p. lviii; HLM to Friedrich Schönemann, Nov. 13, 1939, NYPL; Hobson, *Mencken: A Life*, p. 425; HLM to Charles Mencken, Nov. 29, 1939, EPFL; author interview with Sara Anne Duffy Chermayeff, June 14, 1991.

Chapter 45: Triumph of Democracy

1. HLM, "Warming Up the Bugles," *BS*, Dec. 18, 1938; HLM, "On Bogus Neutrality," *BS*, May 16, 1939; HLM, "Advice to Young Men," April 19, 1939, EPFL; HLM, "The Art of Selling War," *BS*, May 9, 1939; Edward T. Folliard, "Editors Told to Save Ire for Dictators," *Washington Post*, April 21, 1939; "Spinach!" *Newsday*, Oct. 7, 1939.

2. R. P. Harriss, Diary, April 14, Sept. 19, 1939, collection of Margery Harriss; "Letters," *BS*, Sept. 12, 1939.

3. HLM, "Farley Talk Described as Only Half a Farewell," *BS*, July 16, 1940; HLM, *Thirty-Five Years*, pp. 1241, 1243, EPFL; Ketchum, *The Borrowed Years*, pp. 457–58, 460, 463; HLM, "Delegates Toe the Mark, Throwing Tradition Out," *BS*, July 18, 1940; HLM to August Mencken, "Friday night," Chicago 1940, EPFL; HLM, "Roosevelt Statement Flabbergasts Delegates," *BS*, July 17, 1940; Goodwin, *No Ordinary Time*, pp. 126, 129, 134; HLM, "Great Name Cheered—Just as Scheduled," *BS*, July 18, 1940; Paul Hodges, "A Voice Answers Its Call—and a Convention Ends," *Cleveland News*, July 19, 1940; HLM, "Triumph of Democracy," *BS*, July 21, 1940.

4. HLM, "Wonder Man," *BS*, June 30, 1940; HLM, "Touring with Willkie," *BS*, Oct. 13, 1940; Ketchum, *The Borrowed Years*, p. 468; HLM, "There He Is!" *BS*, Sept. 15, 1940; Joseph P. McLaughlin, "Mrs. Vanderbilt Steals Show from Willkie in Rhode Island," *Philadelphia Record*, Oct. 1, 1940; HLM, "Coroner's Inquest," *BS*, Nov. 10, 1940; HLM, "Notes on the Campaign," *BS*, Oct. 20, 1940; HLM, "Heil Roosevelt!" *BS*, Sept. 22, 1940; HLM to Elizabeth Hanes, Nov. 6, 1940, UNC; HLM to Friedrich Schönemann, Nov. 6, 1940, NYPL; HLM to Aileen Pringle, Nov. 4, 8, 1940, YALE.

5. HLM, "Raymond Pearl," *BS*, Nov. 24, 1940; HLM, *Thirty-Five Years*, pp. 1279–82, 1292, EPFL; author interview with Alistair Cooke, May 19, 1992.

6. Goodwin, *No Ordinary Time*, p. 210; HLM to George Schuyler, Jan. 20, 1941, YALE.

Chapter 46: The Weapon of Silence

1. HLM, Diary, April 1, July 15, 1945, EPFL. For a further examination, see documents for 1942 in "Letters and Documents Relating to the *Sunpapers*," EPFL.

2. Winfield, *FDR and the News Media*, pp. 163, 172–84; Frank J. Donnor, "Hoover's Legacy," *Nation*, June 1, 1974, pp. 678–79; Kenneth O'Reilly, "A New Deal for the F.B. I.: The Roosevelt Administration, Crime Control and National Security," *Journal of American History*, Dec. 1982, pp. 648–49; Athan G. Theoheris, "The F.B.I.'s Stretching of Presidential Directives 1936–1953," *Political Science Quarterly*, Winter 1976–1977, pp. 649–72; "Federal Bureau for Press Urged," *NYT*, Dec. 29, 1936, FDR; Koop, *Weapon of Silence*, pp. vii, 163, 232. The government scrutiny encompassed 2,000 daily papers; 11,000 weeklies and semi-weeklies; 6,000 technical, scientific and professional publications; 5,000 commercial and financial letters; 16,000 house organs; hundreds of magazines of church, college, and other periodicals, including 900 commercial broadcasting stations. Externally, it monitored mail, land-wire, radio-telegraph, radio-telephone, and all other means of communication between the United States and foreign countries. Byron Price "Memoir," Book 3, Section 2, MAD; HLM, Diary, Aug. 10, 1942, EPFL; Richard W. Steele, "The Great Debate: The Media and the Coming of the War, 1940–1941," *Journal of American History*, June 1984, pp. 69–92; Walter Davenport, "You Can't Say That!" *Collier's*, Feb. 15, 1941, pp. 121–127; David Brown, "Our Propaganda Machine," *Saturday Review of Literature*, March 7, 1942, p. 9; HLM, editorial, *American Mercury*, Dec. 1924, p. 444; HLM to George Stewart, April 17, 1940, EPFL; Malcolm W. Browne, "Reporters at War," *NYT Book Review*, Aug. 27, 1995, p. 27.

3. Koop, *Weapon of Silence*, pp. 207–8; "Weather Report," *BS*, March 30, 1942; HLM to Joseph Katz, March 31, 1942, EPFL; "H. L. Mencken: Photographs of the Mencken House at 1524 Hollins Street, Baltimore, 1939–1942," pp. 87, 90, 91, EPFL; HLM took eleven pictures. The photo of HLM on the frontispiece of *Heathen Days* was taken at this time, on March 30, 1942; HLM, Diary, March 31, 1942, EPFL.

4. HLM, Diary, Sept. 22, 1942, Oct. 1, 1942, EPFL; Winfield, *FDR and the News Media*, pp. 181–82; Elmer Davis to Franklin D. Roosevelt, Aug. 28, 1942, "President's Secretary's File, Subject File: Office of Censorship," FDR; Elmer Davis memo for Stephen Early, Sept. 30, 1942, FDR. Over 250 newspapers wrote editorials on the subject. See ACLU files at PRIN/md and at FDR. "Press Conference #848, Thursday, October 1, 1942, 5:05 p.m. EST," in "Press Conferences" pp. 103–28, FDR; Byron Price Papers, "Notebooks, August–November 1942," pp. 186–201, "Notebook II, August–November 1942, pp. 136–201," "Memoir, Book 3, Section 3," p. 362, "Memoir, Box 5, Folder 1," p. 363, MAD; Richard L. Dunlap, "The Sage at Dusk: An Account of H. L. Mencken's Last Interview," *Menckeniana*, Fall 1970, p. 10.

5. HLM, Diary, Sept. 19, 1942, EPFL; HLM memo to Paul Patterson, Sept. 17, 1942 in HLM, Diary, entry for Sept. 19, 1942, EPFL; memo by N. R. Howard, April 9, 1943, in Byron Price Papers, Notebooks III, February–September 1943, pp. 281–83, MAD; Byron Price

memo to the President, Feb. 28, 1945, FDR; Francis Biddle Papers 1912–1967, "Notebooks: The AP Case," pp. 80–96, Box 2, May 4, 1942, pp. 53–55, FDR; Mary Pat Murphy, "The United States vs. the AP," *Montana Journalism Review*, Spring 1974, pp. 40–46; Fred S. Siebert, "My Experiences with the First Amendment," *Journalism Quarterly*, Summer 1979, pp. 446–50; Zechariah Chafee Jr. and Frederick S. Siebert, "Two Opposing Expressions on Government's Suit to Force the Associated Press to Open Membership to All Applicants," *Chicago Sunday Tribune*, April 18, 1943; HLM, "Journalism in the Republic," *Chicago Sunday Tribune*, June 26, 1927; Robert Lasch, "For a Free Press," *Atlantic Monthly*, July 1944, pp. 39–40.

6. Asbell, *When FDR Died*, pp. 78–85, 178; Bishop, *FDR's Last Year*, pp. 582, 648; Smith, *Thank You, Mr. President*, pp. 175–76; HLM to George Schuyler, June 1, 1945, YALE; George S. Schuyler, "Views and Reviews," *Pittsburgh Courier*, April 25, 1945; Stephen Early to Byron Price, Aug. 31, 1945, "The Papers of Stephen Early, Correspondence #15, Price, Byron," FDR; Stephen Early to Jack Lockhart, Assistant Director, Office of Censorship, Washington, DC, April 26, 1945, FDR; "A Free Press," *Chanute (Kansas) Tribune*, Sept. 14, 1938; Winfield, *FDR and the News Media*, p. 239; Stephen J. Monchak, "H. L. Mencken Rides Again, Rowelling U.S. Newspapers," *Editor & Publisher*, Sept. 10, 1938, pp. 9, 14; Thomas Jefferson to James Currie in 1786, under heading "Free Press," in HLM, *A New Dictionary of Quotations*, p. 965.

Chapter 47: On the Home Front

1. HLM, Diary, Nov. 2, 1944, EPFL; HLM to P.E. Cleator, Aug. 28, 1942, Sept. 2, 1943, NYPL; "Baltimore Blackouts Soon, and City Means Business," *BS*, Jan. 2, 1942; "3-Hour Test Blackout Due Tonight," *BS*, Jan. 3, 1942; "Blackout, An Experience Shared," "Blackout of City Termed 'Perfect,'" *BS*, Feb. 28, 1942.

2. Ward Morehouse, "Report on America," *New York Sun*, June 5, 1946; "Mencken Rival to Bernard Shaw," *Spokesman Review*, Jan. 7, 1946. A letter from an unknown Baltimorean to Stephen Early, ca. May, 1940, asked that the "German iconoclast" be investigated, and that his column on armaments and the New Deal ("The Campaign Opens," *BS*, May 26, 1940) be brought to the attention of "our beloved President." In response, the White House asked Hoover if HLM's expressions were "permitted under the head of free press and free speech" (letter to the Justice Department, May 26, 1940). In a Nov. 24, 1941 letter Hoover wrote that HLM had not been investigated in recent years. One reason may be because, by this time, Hoover and HLM had already exchanged a series of friendly letters. Hoover had been impressed by HLM's article "What to Do with Criminals" (*Liberty*, July 28, 1934) and for his "keen analysis" in his column "Reflections on Homicide" (*BS*, June 4, 1939). HLM, in turn, solicited Hoover's help for the term "G-man" for *The American Language* (HLM to Hoover, Feb. 10, 1944). The entire file is in the FBI records and was obtained from the Criminal Division under the Freedom of Information Act by the author on April 7, 1989. "Mencken Would Go into Debt to Buy Beer for G.I. Readers," *BS*, May 19, 1944; "America Warned to Tighten Belts," *BS*, Feb. 28, 1942; HLM to Virginia Mencken Morrison, June 1, 1943, EPFL; H. K. Fleming, "Autobiography," pp. 30–31, collection of Harold A. Williams; HLM, Diary, Dec. 14, 1945, EPFL; HLM, "Biopsy on Baltimore," *BS*, May 21, 1939; Brugger, *Maryland: A Middle Temperament*, pp. 490–591.

3. "7:15 P.M.—The Life of a City Block," *BS*, May 26, 1942; HLM, Diary, Aug. 15, 1945, Dec. 14, 1945, EPFL; author interview with R. P. Harriss, Oct. 24, 1987; Manchester, *Disturber of the Peace*, p. 293.

4. HLM to Benjamin de Casseres, Oct. 14, 1940, NYPL; "Something About Mencken's New Dictionary of Quotations," memo for *Publisher's Weekly*, April 1, 1942, in "Knopf., Inc. Permanent Title Folders," HRHRC; HLM to AAK, March 31, 1942, EPFL; AAK, *Memoirs 1932–1943*, p. 142, HRHRC; "A New Dictionary of Quotations," promotional memo written by HLM, Jan. 15, 1941, in "Knopf, Inc. Permanent Title Folders," HRHRC.

5. Richardson Wright, "The Heel of the Loaf's Sweetest Bread," *New York Herald TribuneBook Review*, March 7, 1943; Terry Rand, "The Book of the Day," *New York Sun*, Jan. 24, 1940; HLM, "What's Ahead for Books and Authors, Speech Before the American Booksellers Association, 500th Anniversary, 13 May 1940," in "Miscellaneous Writings, 1940–1941, Clippings and Carbons," pp. 54–57, EPFL; "The Philosopher as Philologist," *Christian Science Monitor*, May 29, 1942; HLM, Diary, Oct. 30, 1943, May 9, 1945, EPFL; Ingelhart, *Press Freedoms*, pp. 267, 270; "Esquire Loses Mailing Privileges," *New York City P.M.*, Dec. 31, 1944; "A Public Statement of the Pertinent facts in the Case of Esquire vs. The Postmaster General," *Editor & Publisher*, Jan. 29, 1944, pp. 34–35; HLM to William H. Connelly, Nov. 27, 1939, NYPL; "Testimony of Henry L. Mencken, Esquire Trial, Post Office Department," Oct. 1943, pp. 4, 19–21, JHU/mc; Gilmor et al., *Mass Communication Law*, pp. 648–49; Hixson, *Mass Media and the Constitution*, pp. 233–34; HLM notation to AAK on top of pamphlet, United States Court of Appeals, No. 8899, HRHRC.

Chapter 48: Mencken and the Guild

1. Author interview with Clem Vitek, July 24, 1989; author interview with Grace Darin, July 2, 1989; Baltimore Newspaper Guild, "Contract Between the Baltimore Newspaper Guild and the Baltimore Sunpapers," collection of Clem Vitek; Wagner, *H. L. Mencken*, p. 40; HLM to Samuel Blythe, Nov. 7, 1942, NYPL; HLM, *Thirty-Five Years*, pp. 697, 1205, EPFL; Sam Kuczun, "History of the American Newspaper Guild" (thesis, University of Minnesota, March 1970), pp. 190–91, 225–27; O'Connor, *Heywood Broun*, pp. 178–90; Willard H. Espey, "The Baltimore Sun Goes Down," *Nation*, Feb. 4, 1939, pp. 143–46; R. P. Harriss, Diary, Dec. 19, 1939, collection of Margery Harriss.

2. "Guild Questions and Answers: May 19, 1939," File: Baltimore Guild: 1939–40, Archive of Labor and Urban Affairs, WS; letter from Robert R. Hane of the Baltimore Guild to American Newspaper Guild, Aug. 9, 1940, WS; Julius Goodman Jr. et al., "An Appeal to Reason," p. 8, collection of Ellis T. Baker III; author interview with Ellis T. Baker III, Nov. 13, 1994; Baker, *The Good Times*, p. 131; "Sunlight," Sunpapers Unit Newspaper Guild, 1941, vol. I, n.15, WS; Grace Darin, "Why I Belong," collection of Harold A. Williams; HLM, *Thirty-Five Years*, pp. 1207, 1351, 1534, and transcript of Aug. 7, 1941, meeting between HLM and the Guild, EPFL; author interview with William Manchester, May 23, 1995; author interview with Stanley Harrison, Aug. 13, 1990; Robert R. Hane, Baltimore Newspaper Guild to Officers of the American Newspaper Guild, Aug. 5, 1940, File: Baltimore Guild 1939–1940, Archive of Labor and Urban Affairs, WS; "Sun Employees Join Guild to Boost Pay," *Newspaper Guild Organizer*, April 21, 1941.

3. Author interview with Ellis T. Baker III, Nov. 13, 1994; Baker, *The Good Times*, p. 124; Paul Ward to Bill Ferson, Nov. 24, 1947, File: Newspaper Guild of Baltimore, Maryland, Archive of Labor and Urban Affairs, WS; Julius Goodman Jr. et al., "An Appeal to Reason," collection of Ellis T. Baker III; Julius Goodman Jr. to Ellis Baker III, Dec. 13, 1975, collection of Harold A. Williams; Williams, *The Baltimore Sun 1837–1987*, p. 291.

4. "Hired Men," *Guild Reporter*, Jan. 23, 1948, WS; HLM, "Journalism in America," *Prejudices: Sixth Series*, p. 13; S. L. Harrison, "Fiscal Mencken: An Accounting," *Menckeniana*, Spring 1995, pp. 7–8; HLM, *Thirty-Five Years*, p. 1215, EPFL; Philip A. Wagner, "Mencken Remembered," *American Scholar*, Spring 1963, p. 263. For the Latin terms, see the appendices to HLM, *Thirty-Five Years*, pp. 1318, 1600–03, 1612, EPFL; George Engeman of Baltimore Newspaper Guild to Wilson Bade, American Newspaper Guild, Feb. 8, 1942, Archive of Labor and Urban Affairs, WS.

5. "Sunpapers Battle Mailers: H. L. Mencken Bosses War Against Little Union," *Baltimore Labor Herald*, July 9, 1943; HLM, *Thirty-Five Years*, pp. 1131–32, 1349–51, 1366, 1508, 1592–93, EPFL; author interview with William Manchester, May 23, 1995; "Contract Between

the Baltimore Newspaper Guild and the Baltimore Sunpapers," Sept. 4, 1950 to Sept. 4, 1952, courtesy of Clem Vitek; author interview with Ellis T. Baker III, Nov. 13, 1994.

6. Baker, *The Good Times*, p. 133; John Goodspeed, "Labor War: The Sunpapers Strike of 1965," *Baltimore City Paper*, June 29, 1980; HLM, *"Newspaper Days:* Additions," p. 25; Mary Ann McCardell Daily to the author, July 10, 1989.

7. HLM, *Heathen Days*, p. viii.

Chapter 49: Friends and Relatives

1. HLM to Mrs. Henry Wood, Jan. 27, 1941, EPFL; HLM to James Branch Cabell, Dec. 12, 1944, PRIN/fire; Arthur Davison Ficke, "Notes on Edgar Lee Masters," p. 1, UCLA; Alice Davis to Gerald Sanders, Jan. 14, March 9, 1954, Masters-Davis Collection, NYPL/ms; Alice Davis, "Evenings with Edgar," Nov. 1, 1936, Alice Davis Diary, p. 259, Masters-Davis Collection, NYPL/ms; Roger Butterfield, "Mr. Mencken Sounds Off," *Life*, Aug. 5, 1946, p. 52; HLM to Alice Davis, Dec. 31, 1945, NYPL; HLM, Diary, Dec. 31, 1945, EPFL; Bode, *Mencken*, p. 328; Carl Van Vechten, "How I Remember Joseph Hergesheimer," *Yale University Library Gazette*, Jan. 1948, pp. 87–92; "Mencken On Hergesheimer," *BS*, May 2, 1952; Joseph Hergesheimer, "The Lamentable Trade of Letters," *American Mercury*, March 1932, p. 168; Joseph Hergesheimer to Margaret Lee Morgan, Feb. 16, 1940, HRHRC; AAK to Joseph Hergesheimer, May 23, 1944, HRHRC; Geoffrey Hellman, "Profiles: Publisher III: The Pleasures, Prides and Cream," *New Yorker*, Dec. 4, 1948, p. 42; Stanley Kauffman, "Album of the Knopfs," *American Scholar*, Summer 1987, p. 376; GJN, "The Happiest Days of H. L. Mencken," *Esquire*, Oct. 25, 1957, p. 149; "Blanche Wolf Knopf of Publishing Firm Dies," *NYT*, June 5, 1966; "Mrs. Alfred Knopf," *Current Biography* 1957, pp. 308–10; letters of HLM, AAK, and BK, EPFL and HRHRC; AAK, "Reminiscences of Hergesheimer, Van Vechten and Mencken," *Yale University Library Gazette*, April 1950, pp. 157–64; Blanche Knopf, "Autobiographical Fragment," HRHRC.

2. For book inscriptions by the two men, see the HLM Collection at the EPFL and the GJN Collection at Cornell University; "An Unusual Foursome," *New York Journal American*, Oct. 18, 1943; HLM to GJN, Sept. 26, 1943, CORN; James Tully to GJN, Dec. 23, 1934, CORN; HLM to GJN, Aug. 9, 1937, Nov. 13, 1942, July 3, 1947, NYPL; GJN to HLM, Nov. 12, 14, 1942, Aug. 6, 1937, NYPL; John Mason Brown, "Critics View a Critic," *NYT*, April 13, 1958; "George Jean Nathan's Achievement," *Los Angeles Times*, April 9, 1958; "Drama Critic, George Jean Nathan, Dead at 76," *Long Island Press*, April 8, 1958; "George Jean Nathan Badly Beaten by Two Muggers," *New York Journal American*, Jan. 8, 1943; "Bosh, Sprinkled with Mystic Cologne," *Milwaukee Journal*, April 6, 1958; author interview with Al Hirschfeld, Oct. 8, 1999; Huntington Cairns to August Mencken, Aug. 10, 1939, EPFL; Earl Wilson, "Two on the Aisle: George Jean Nathan, the Critic, Is Fond as Usual of Hollywood," *New York Post*, July 24, 1943; Elsa Maxwell, "Elsa Maxwell's Party Line: Bachelor of the Arts," *New York Post*, March 4, 1943; Letter from GJN to HLM, where he coyly hints "if you like Chinese girls, I have discovered two lulus," GJN to HLM, Dec. 10, 1941, NYPL; GJN to HLM, Dec. 23, 1941, Nov. 23, 1943, Oct. 29, 1947, all NYPL. The letter telling Mencken to "avoid Toy" is dated "Tuesday," but is most likely from 1942, NYPL.

3. GJN to HLM, March 14, 1942, NYPL. Aileen Pringle's 1944 marriage to James Cain lasted less than two years. Put off by his excessive drinking, she divorced Cain on grounds of extreme cruelty, later explaining that the writer was "moody, melancholy, and grim. Instead of building castles in the air he built dungeons." She told Cain the only reason he had married her "was to show Mencken you could do something he couldn't." For his part, however, Cain could never forget Aileen. He sent her three dozen roses for her birthday every year until his death. See "James Cain Weds Aileen Pringle," *Los Angeles Times*, Aug. 13, 1944; "Third Wife of James M. Cain Asks Divorce," *Los Angeles Times*, June 4, 1946; "Aileen Pringle Divorces James Cain,

Author," *NYT*, Sept. 5, 1946; letter to Roy Hoopes from Aileen Pringle, Sept. 18, 1978, collection of Roy Hoopes; author interview with Ruth Goodman Goetz, March 4, 1992; HLM to GJN, March 9, 1942, NYPL.

4. Virginia Alvarez to HLM, Aug. 4, 17, 1942, NYPL; HLM to Virginia Alvarez, Aug. 4, 6, 1942, NYPL; Clare Leighton, "Cynical Fantasy," *Menckeniana*, Fall 1970, pp. 1–3; Joseph Katz to HLM, May 14, 1944, EPFL; Clare Leighton to Ellen Glasgow, May 3, 1940, UVA; Lappin, "I Remember Mencken," p. 13, YALE; "The Reminiscences of August Mencken," p. 50, COL; author interview with Ellen M. Hawks, July 26, 1999; Carl Bode interview with Mrs. Hamilton Owens, Feb. 28, 1963, collection of Gwinn Owens; HLM, Diary, May 30, 1945, EPFL; Julian Lee Rayford, "Fourteen Years to H. L. Mencken," *Amateur Book Collector*, Dec. 1955, p. 2; author interview with William Manchester, May 23, 1995; author interview with Dr. Philip Wagley, June 8, 1994.

5. Virginia Mencken to HLM, March 14, 1931, EPFL; HLM, "Radio Programs," *BES*, June 29, 1931; August Mencken to Gertrude Mencken, June 4, 1950, EPFL; August Mencken Diary, June 8, 1950, EPFL; Gertrude Mencken to August Mencken, Sept. 13, 1953, EPFL; "The Reminiscences of August Mencken," p. 36, COL; letters between Henry and Gertrude Mencken, HLM Collection, EPFL; author interview with Elise Cheslock, Jan. 21, 1994; author interview with William Manchester, May 23, 1995; Margaret Lappin, "I Remember Mencken," p. 172, YALE; Louis Cheslock, "The Happy Days of August Mencken," *BS*, Feb. 18, 1968; author interview with Johnson and Charles Fortenbaugh, June 13, 1994; author interviews with Dr. Philip Wagley, June 8, 1994, with Admiral Conrad Abhau, Aug. 22, 1992.

6. Sara Anne Duffy to HLM, undated, EPFL; Bettina Patterson to HLM, Dec. 28, 1947, EPFL; Julian P. Boyd to August Mencken, June 22, 1964, EPFL; author interview with Sara Anne Duffy Chermayeff, June 14, 1991; HLM to Virginia Mencken, Jan. 20, 1947, EPFL.

7. HLM to Benjamin De Casseres, Dec. 11, 1939, NYPL; Richard Hart, "The Mencken Industry," *Menckeniana*, Winter 1974, p. 4; "Memorandum re: Henry L. Mencken Collection in the Enoch Pratt Free Library, Feb. 21, 1945," "EPFL Correspondence," EPFL. A locked enclosure at the north end of the third stack level was known as "the Mencken Alcove" but employees called it "the Mencken Cage," since the old lion spent so much time in it. Author interview with Sara Siebert, ca. 1993; HLM to Stuart Olivier, May 14, 1936, EPFL; AAK, Diary, March 14, 1945, HRHRC; Kate Coplan to Emerson Greenaway, Dec. 5, 1950, PRIN/fire; "File System," *New York Post*, March 27, 1940; HLM to Elliott Wheeler, Jan. 10, 1938, EPFL; Edwin Castagna, "Long Warm Friendship: HLM-EPFL" (Baltimore: Enoch Pratt Free Library, 1964), pp. 1–9, EPFL.

8. HLM, "*The American Language:* Supplement I, H. L. Mencken Galley Proofs 1945," EPFL; Marcella Miller DuPont, "Heroic Days and Hours with Henry Mencken," *Menckeniana*, Summer 1966, p. 7; HLM, *A New Dictionary of Quotations*, p. 107.

Chapter 50: The Man Who Hates Everything

1. HLM to Alexander H. McDannald, Aug. 5, 1946, EPFL; HLM, Diary, Jan. 29, 1945, May 26, 1946, EPFL; AAK, Diary, March 14, 1945, HRHRC.

2. HLM, Diary, Jan. 29, 1945, EPFL; Sommerville, *World War II Day by Day*, pp. 278–311; "Belsen: Where 60,000 Were Starving," Metrogravure section, *BS*, May 6, 1945; Lipstadt, *Beyond Belief*, pp. 240–78; Lee McCardell, "McCardell Visits Scene of Nazi Mass Murder," *BS*, April 7, 1945; R. P. Harriss, Diary, May 2, 1945, collection of Margery Harriss; Louis M. Cheslock, Diary, October 16, 1943, EPFL; AAK, Diary, June 21, 1943, HRHRC; Carl Bode interview with John Owens and Mrs. Semmes, Sept. 23, 1964, collection of Harold A. Williams; Cooke, *Six Men*, p. 99; author interviews with Alistair Cooke, April 15, May 19, 1992; author interview with Elise Cheslock, Jan. 21, 1994; Hobson, *Mencken: A Life*, p. 477.

3. HLM to Dr. F. E. Chidester, Feb. 14, 1947, NYPL; Ritchie, *Faust's Metropolis*, pp. 604–73; Hobson, *Mencken: A Life*, p. 490; Georg Kartzke to HLM, June 21, 1946, NYPL; HLM to Dieter Spielberg, May 8, 1947, courtesy Dieter Spielberg; HLM to Georg Kartzke, May 5, 1947, NYPL; Julie Hassenkaup [Otto Julius Merkel's sister] to HLM, April 28, 1947, EPFL; Otto Julius Merkel to HLM, Aug. 30, 1947, NYPL.

4. HLM to the Supreme Commander for the Allied Powers, April 12, 1948, NYPL; HLM to Georg Kartzke, May 3, 1948, NYPL; HLM to Otto Julius Merkel, July 17, 1948, NYPL. Mencken also mailed books to Japan; see Sobel Arakawa from Nagoya, Japan, to HLM, March 6, 1947, NYPL and HLM to Paul Patterson, April 30, 1948, collection of Bettina Patterson; HLM to Paul Patterson, Jan. 3, 1947, DART; author interview with Janet Proctor, Feb. 24, 1995.

5. HLM to Otto Julius Merkel, March 14, 1947, NYPL; "Truman Talk Believed Help to United Nations," *BS*, March 4, 1947; HLM to Heinrich Spies, March 1947, NYPL; HLM, "Answers Written June 22–23 to Questions Sent to Me by Roger Butterfield for the Foregoing Interview in *Life*, August 5, 1946," in "Miscellaneous Typescripts, Carbons, Clippings 1946–1948," pp. 11–28, EPFL; Roger Butterfield, "Mr. Mencken Sounds Off," *Life*, Aug. 8, 1946, p. 62; "Report on the August 8th Issue," *Life* Interoffice Circular, Sept. 6, 1946, HLM, "Clippings," vol. LXXXIX, EPFL.

6. Edgar Kemler to Joseph Hergesheimer, Feb. 20, 1947, HRHRC; Joseph Hergesheimer, "Autobiographical Notes," Feb. 1947, HRHRC; HLM to Joseph Hergesheimer, Feb. 20, 1947, HRHRC; "Mencken Biographer," *Houston (Texas) Post*, Feb. 4, 1951; William Manchester, "Memorandum for Harper & Brothers, April 10, 1950," pp. 5–6, JFK; William Manchester, "Interview with H. L. Mencken, June 2, 1947 at the Maryland Club, Baltimore, Maryland," JFK; Manchester, "Introduction," *Disturber of the Peace* (1986 edition), pp. xv, xix; author interview with William Manchester, May 23, 1995.

7. HLM to Thomas Cullen, March 25, 1947, EPFL; Ward Morehouse, "Quiet Chat," *New York Sun Digest*, July 1946, p. 13; HLM, Diary, Nov. 23, 1946, EPFL; Howard B. Bishop of the Human Engineering Foundation to HLM, Oct. 28, 1947, NYPL; HLM, "Preface for the Days of H. L. Mencken," written April 15, 1947, "Miscellaneous Typescripts, Carbons and Clippings 1946–1948," pp. 41–42, EPFL; HLM, Diary, Aug. 29, 1946, EPFL; "Mencken Sues Owner of Dog," *BS*, Feb. 9, 1946; Mencken's entries for Feb. 1, 5, 7, 8, 1946, in "Fortenbaugh" file under "Correspondence with Marylanders," EPFL; Leon Asner, "Henry Mencken, as a Painter of a Turtle," *BS Magazine*, p. 37. A *Sun* photographer took a picture of the pup, peering forlornly from behind the lace curtains of the Fortenbaugh residence at 1526 Hollins Street. The picture broke everyone's heart—including Mencken's. "Dogs," he growled, "have no right to be so confoundingly appealing." It did not convince him to drop the lawsuit, however. Charles Fortenbaugh reasoned "Harry must be working on a new book and wants the publicity." Louis Sobol, "New York Calvacade," *New York Journal American*, March 12, 1946; "Skippy, Mencken's Foe, Finds Some New Friends," *BES*, Dec. 31, 1946; author interview with Johnson Fortenbaugh, June 13, 1994; "H. L. Mencken, *The American Language* Supplement II Original Typescript 1945–1947, Fair Copy June 28, 1947, Revision, p. 2," EPFL; HLM to Ralph A. Beals, Dec. 5, 1947, EPFL.

8. HLM, Diary, July 22, 1946, July 31, 1947, EPFL; HLM to Alan C. Woods, Aug. 5, 7, 1947, EPFL; HLM, "*Happy Days:* Additions . . . ," p. 231, EPFL.

Chapter 51: The Great Upset of 1948

1. Manchester, *Disturber of the Peace*, pp. 307–8; Maclean Patterson to HLM, March 26, April 12, 1948, collection of Bettina Patterson; HLM to Maclean Patterson, March 27, April 14, 1948, collection of Bettina Patterson; "People Who Read and Write," *NYT*, April 5, 1948; Ken

Clark, "Mencken's Seven Keys to Our Lingo," *PM*, April 4, 1948, p. 14; Jean and Robert Boardman, "About People," *New York Herald Tribune*, March 26, 1948; Paul Patterson to Maclean Patterson, March 29, 1948, collection of Bettina Patterson; HLM to Joseph Hergesheimer, June 4, 1948, HRHRC.

2. HLM, "Television Lamps Stir Up 2-Way Use for Beer," *BS*, June 21, 1948; Stanley Cloud and Lynne Olson, *The Murrow Boys*, p. 285; "The T.V. Cable Tripped Neither Mencken Nor Classic Beer Coverage," *Buffalo News*, May 12, 1972; "Henry L. Mencken Interviewed by Donald Howe Kirkley Sr., June 30, 1948," issued by Caedmon Records as "H. L. Mencken Speaks," LC; HLM, "Letters to the Editor: The Booboisie Again," *Fortune*, April 1947, p. 29; HLM to Joseph Hergesheimer, Aug. 10, 1948, HRHRC; HLM, Diary, Sept. 17, 1947, EPFL; author interview with William Manchester, May 23, 1995.

3. "Sunpapers press release, Oct. 27, 1947," HLM, "Letters and Documents Pertaining to the Sunpapers," EPFL; Friedrich, *City of Nets*, p. 343; Carroll Hebbel, "Pioneer TV: You Wanna Catch the Collegians or the Test Pattern?" *BS Magazine*, Oct. 30, 1977, pp. 34–36; HLM, "Postscripts to the American Language: Video Verbiage," *New Yorker*, Dec. 11, 1948, pp. 102–5; HLM, "Video Glossary," *Hollywood Citizen News*, Sept. 16, 1949; HLM to Neil Swanson, Aug. 6, 1948, EPFL; "Convention Notes," *Montgomery Advertiser*, June 22, 1948; "Henry L. Mencken Interviewed by Donald Howe Kirkley Sr., June 30, 1948" issued by Caedmon Records as "H. L. Mencken Speaks," LC; HLM, Diary, Sept. 15, 1947, Feb. 14, June 26, 1948, EPFL; HLM to William Abell, Feb. 18, 1948, gift of William Abell to author; "1948: Live . . . From Philadelphia . . . It's the National Conventions," *NYT Magazine*, April 17, 1988, p. 37; "20 Million May See Televised Convention," *Philadelphia Inquirer*, June 19, 1948; "Air-Conditioning Awful," *Philadelphia Inquirer*, June 22, 1948; Reuven Frank, "The National Convention in 1948," *NYT Magazine*, May 15, 1988, p. 12; HLM, "Television Lamps Stir Up 2-Way Use for Beer," *BS*, June 21, 1948; "Philadelphia," *Fitchburg (Mass.) Sentinel*, June 22, 1948; D. W. Brogan, "Greatest Show on Earth," *London Spectator*, July 30, 1948; HLM to Gertrude Mencken, June 26, 1948, EPFL; HLM to P.E. Cleator, June 26, 1948, NYPL; author interview with Bradford Jacobs, Sept. 15, 1989.

4. Manchester, *The Glory and the Dream*, p. 453; HLM to P.E. Cleator, June 26, 1948, NYPL; HLM to Herr. Prof. Otto Julius Merkel, Nov. 15, 1948, NYPL; Cooke, *Six Men*, p. 103; author interview with Chalmers Roberts, Aug. 10, 2000; author interview with Anthony Lewis, Feb. 26, 1998; "Convention Notes," *Waterville (Mass.) Sentinel*, July 16, 1948; "The Uncommon Scold," *Time*, Feb. 6, 1956, p. 38; author interview with Bradford Jacobs, Sept. 15, 1989; Bradford Jacobs, "The Great Man Enlivens a Convention," *BES*, Dec. 13, 1989; author interview with Grace Darin, July 2, 1989; author interview with Ellis Baker III, Nov. 13, 1994; author interview with Stanley Harrison, Aug. 13, 1990; HLM, "Sudden Flap of Wings Would Be No Surprise," *BS*, July 24, 1948; Bascom M. Timmons, "In Washington," *Wichita Falls Record News*, July 31, 1948; Cooke, *Six Men*, pp. 103, 105, 107; Cooke, "The Last Happy Days of H. L. Mencken," *Atlantic*, May 1956, pp. 33–38; author interview with Murray Kempton, Feb. 20, 1995.

5. Bascom N. Timmons, "In Washington," *Wichita Falls Record News*, July 31, 1948; Dewey L. Fleming, "Wallace Silent on Guru Puzzle," *BS*, July 24, 1948; Cooke, *Six Men*, pp. 107–8; Culver, *American Dreamer*, pp. 482–84; Westbrook Pegler, "Today: Guru Letter Mystery," *Philadelphia Inquirer*, July 24, 1948; George Dixon, "Convention Notes," *Crookston (Minn.) Times*, July 27, 1948.

6. HLM, "Sudden Flap of Wings Would Be No Surprise," *BS*, July 24, 1948; author interview with Bradford Jacobs, Sept. 15, 1989; Cooke, *Six Men*, p. 109; "Mencken Escapes Move to Censure," *BS*, July 26, 1948; William E. Bohn, "Close Up of H. L. Mencken, An American Iconoclast," *New Leader*, Sept. 11, 1948; "Mencken Baiting Resolution Rejected and Target Is Sorry," *Chicago Tribune*, July 26, 1948; Lewis Nordyke, "Random Thoughts," *Texas News*, July 14, 1948.

7. Richard Dunlap, "The Sage at Dusk," *Menckeniana*, Fall 1970, p. 10; HLM to Henry Hyde, Oct. 7, 1948, EPFL; HLM, "Truman's Election: Mencken Says Country Jolly Well Deserves It," *BS*, Nov. 7, 1948; author interview with Donald Patterson, June 18, 1991; HLM to GJN, Nov. 8, 1948, NYPL; HLM to C. Willis, Nov. 8, 1948, EPFL; HLM, Diary, June 26, 1948, EPFL.

8. HLM, Diary, Oct. 9, Nov. 5, 1948, EPFL; "Mencken Says Truman Won Although It Was Impossible," Associated Press, Nov. 4, 1948, EPFL; AAK, Diary, April 19, 26, 1948, Nov. 27, 1948, HRHRC; Louis Cheslock, Diary, Nov. 20, 1948, EPFL; HLM to Charles Mencken, Nov. 17, 1948, EPFL; Blanche Knopf to GJN, Nov. 10, 1948, CORN.

9. HLM, "My Current Reading," *Saturday Review of Literature*, May 22, 1948, p. 14; "Mr. Mencken Again," *Newsweek*, April 5, 1948, pp. 89–91;George A. Ranson, "Causerie— They Know Not," *Toledo (Ohio) Times*, Oct. 24, 1948; "Maxwell Geismer Analyzes Mencken-Lewis-Cather Era: John Chamberlain Reviews 'The Last of the Provincials,'" *Chicago Tribune*, Dec. 14, 1947; Charles Poore, "Literary History of the United States," *NYT Book Review*, Dec. 18, 1948; "What SRL Reviewers Are Giving For Christmas," *Saturday Review of Literature*, Dec. 4, 1948, p. 14; James Daniel Scripps, "Whatever Happened To . . . H. L. Mencken?" Scripps-Howard Newspapers, March 12, 1948; "Argosy Book Store Pamphlet, New York 1948," EPFL; Siegfried Weisberger to Rosalind Lohrfinck, Aug. 4, 1948, PENN; "Henry L. Mencken Interviewed by Donald Howe Kirkley, Sr. June 30, 1948," issued by Caedmon Records as "H. L. Mencken Speaks," LC; William E. Bohn, "Close Up of H. L. Mencken, An American Iconoclast," *New Leader*, Sept. 11, 1948; Richard L. Dunlap, "The Sage at Dusk," *Menckeniana*, Fall, 1970, pp. 7–8; Hal Boyle, "Correspondent's Notebook: Portrait of a Happy Man," *Philadelphia Bulletin*, July 30, 1947; HLM to Jacob Blanck, Jan. 19, 1948, NYPL; HLM, "Mencken Meditated on Red Hunt," *BS*, Aug. 8, 1948; HLM, "Communism," *BES*, July 14, 1930; Henry Shapiro, "Soviet Writer Claims Strength to Other Countries," *Paterson (New Jersey) News*, Nov. 6, 1948; HLM, "H. L. Mencken Calls Tennis Order Silly, Nefarious," *BES*, Nov. 9, 1948; "On an Author: H. L. Mencken," *New York Herald Tribune*, July 3, 1949.

10. Louis Cheslock, Diary, Nov. 24, Dec. 6, 1948, EPFL; "The Reminiscences of August Mencken," p. 80, COL; author interview with Dr. Benjamin Baker, March 25, 1994; "H. L. Mencken, Famed Writer, in Hospital," *Oregon Gazette Times*, Dec. 1, 1948; Benjamin Baker to Joseph Hergesheimer, Nov. 29, 1948, HRHRC; AAK to August Mencken, Dec. 7, 1948, EPFL; AAK, Diary, Nov. 26, 27, 1948, HRHRC.

Chapter 52: The Last Days

1. "The Reminiscences of August Mencken," pp. 47–48, 68, 83–87, COL; Hamilton Owens to Paul Patterson, Dec. 28, 1948, collection of Gwinn Owens; "Memo August Mencken Made at Baker's Office, ca. Dec. 1948," "Record of HLM's Health After the Stroke of November 1948," EPFL. August's account differs from that of one of his physicians. In the last two decades research has provided new understandings of aphasia that have led to advances in diagnosis and treatment. Current research has also enlarged our understanding of the neural basis of language, a factor apparently not lost on Mencken. According to August, his brother was eager to get started on a book that would be an account of his illness as he had experienced it, with a parallel account by doctors that would enable others to know "just exactly what was going on." August Mencken to AAK, July 15, 1950, EPFL. Antonio R. Damasio, MD, "Aphasia," *New England Journal of Medicine* 1992, 536(8):531–39; author interview with Dr. Philip Wagley, June 8, 1994; August Mencken memo, April 10, 12, 1949, EPFL; note August made on Louis Cheslock letter to HLM, March 9, 1954, EPFL; August Mencken to Charles Mencken, July 3, 1950, EPFL; Louis Cheslock, "The Happy Days of August Mencken," *BS*, Feb. 18, 1968; August Mencken to AAK, Dec. 23, 1954; August Mencken memo, "Tests Given HLM by Dice," given sometime during June 1949; William G. Hardy, director, Hearing and

Speech Center, Johns Hopkins Hospital, to August Mencken, Aug. 29, 1949, EPFL; August Mencken memo, May 24, 1949, EPFL; Gertrude Mencken to August Mencken, Aug. 29, 1949, EPFL; HLM to Ben Hecht, Jan. 17, 1949, NEW; HLM to AAK, Jan. 17, 1949, EPFL. Mencken said he hoped within three to five years he would be able to "produce a masterpiece." Rosalind Lohrfinck to AAK, May 24, 1949, YALE; Dr. Benjamin Baker, too, was optimistic; he thought he could start to read in a few weeks. Rosalind Lohrfinck, "Notes on Mencken," Feb. 24, 1949, YALE; HLM to AAK, Jan. 24, 1949, EPFL; Rosalind Lohrfinck to AAK, Feb. 7, 1949, EPFL; Richard L. Dunlap, "The Sage at Dusk," *Menckeniana*, Fall 1970, p. 7; Siegfried Weisberger to Joe Katz, May 2, 1949, EPFL; Siegfried Weisberger to Rosalind Lohrfinck, May 7, 1949, PENN.

2. "The Reminiscences of August Mencken," p. 98, COL; Rosalind Lohrfinck, "Notes on Mencken," March 28, April 1, 8, 25, 27, 1949, May 13, 1949, June 23, 24, 27, 28, 1949, Oct. 29, 1949, March 10, 1952, YALE; Rosalind Lohrfinck to GJN, March 15, 1949, CORN; August Mencken to AAK, May 26, 1952, EPFL; "Letters Pertaining to *The American Language* Received by H. L. Mencken After He Became Ill in 1949," EPFL. Most of the letters are dated between 1949 and 1951. According to August, after 1951 the letters were considerably fewer, only two or three a day. "The Reminiscences of August Mencken," p. 31, COL; August Mencken to Joe Katz, Jan. 6, 1954, EPFL; James Farrell, "Personal Memories of H. L. Mencken," manuscript, PENN; James Farrell to AAK, Nov. 22, 1950, HRHRC.

3. August Mencken to AAK, May 25, 30, June 14, 1949, EPFL; HLM note, dated April 14, 1949, from "Notes and Interpretations by Margaret Lappin," note 19, YALE; "The Week's Best Sellers," *St. Louis Globe Democrat*, July 17, 1949; Rosalind Lohrfinck, "Notes on H. L. Mencken," April 29, June 2, 24, 1949, YALE; Rosalind Lohrfinck to Elizabeth Hanes, Dec. 21, 1949, UNC.

4. "Mencken Fools Doctors Again," *Oklahoma City Times*, March 20, 1951; William Manchester, "Marburg Notations," Feb. 27, 1951, JFK; Arthur J. Gutman, editor, "Guttmacher/ Mencken," *Menckeniana*, Winter 1979, p. 10; James H. Bready, "Saturday Night Club Plays Last Note: Donates All Music to Pratt Library," BES, Dec. 27, 1950; "The Man Who Wouldn't Die," *Charlotte (North Carolina) News*, March 31, 1951; "Mencken Laughs at Death Again," *New York Post Home News*, March 20, 1951; "August Mencken Diary of HLM's Hospitalization," Dec. 3, 1950; Dec. 4, 1950; Jan. 16, 1951; Jan. 24, 1951 (August wrote this date as 1851 by mistake), EPFL; author interview with Dr. Philip Wagley, June 8, 1994; "Mencken Quits Hospital, But Says I'll Be Back," *Austin American*, March 21, 1951; "Mencken, Leaving Hospital for Home Says 'I'll Be Back,'" *Richmond Times-Dispatch*, March 21, 1951; "Mencken Leaves Hospital," BES, March 21, 1951.

5. Rosalind Lohrfinck, "Notes on Mencken," May 28, 1952, YALE; Margaret Lappin, "As I Saw Mencken," p. 132, YALE; "The Reminiscences of August Mencken," p. 72, COL; Dr. Philip Wagley to August Mencken, and his notations Aug. 30, 1954, EPFL; HLM, *Newspaper Days*, p. 306; Joseph Conrad, *Youth: A Narrative*, in *The Complete Short Fiction of Joseph Conrad*, vol. 1, ed. Samuel Hynes, pp. 157–58; author interview with William Manchester, May 23, 1995.

6. Author interview with Jesse Glasgow, Jan. 30, 1992; Margaret Lappin, "As I Saw Mencken," p. 132, YALE; author interview with William Abell, Aug. 17, 1991; Rosalind Lohrfinck "Notes on H. L. Mencken", March 29, 1949, YALE.

7. "$300,000 Estate Left by Mencken," *NYT*, Feb. 15, 1956. August Mencken explained to John T. Kenny of Mercantile Safe and Deposit Co., the largesse accorded to the EPFL was due, in part, to Mencken's being "much dissatisfied with the treatment, other than medical, he received at Johns Hopkins Hospital." August Mencken to John T. Kenny, Sept. 5, 1954, EPFL; R. P. Harriss, Diary, Nov. 13, 1949, collection of Margery Harriss; Rosalind Lohrfinck to Siegfried Weisberger, Sept. 12, 1955, PENN; Raven J. McDavid, "The Impact of Mencken on American Linguistics," *Menckeniana*, Spring, 1966, p. 3; August Mencken to John T. Kenney, Mercantile Safe and Deposit Co., Sept. 12, 1955, EPFL. Marion Bloom once observed of

Mencken, "He's always been a fighter when it comes to protecting the home. His own, I mean." For those currently trying to save the H. L. Mencken House in Baltimore—take heed! Marion Bloom to Estelle Bloom, Sept. 25, 1927, NYPL. "Good-By, Sun Square," *BES*, Dec. 23, 1950; "This Edition of the Sun is Last Printed at Baltimore and Charles Streets," *BS*, Dec. 14, 1950; "The Fifties," HLM, "Clippings Books," vol. CIX; EPFL; "Sewer Project Revives Ghost of the Old Herald," *BES*, Dec. 22, 1948; AAK to August Mencken, Feb. 2, 1954, EPFL; August Mencken to AAK, Feb. 18, 1954, EPFL; Rosalind Lohrfinck to Gertrude Mencken, April 26, 1954, EPFL; Gertrude Mencken to August Mencken, June 18, 1952, EPFL; Siegfried Weisberger to HLM, Sept. 19, 1954; Rosalind Lorhfinck to Siegfried Weisberger, Aug. 16, Sept. 4, Sept. 21, 1954, PENN.

8. August Mencken to AAK, May 12, 1951, EPFL; Charles Mencken to August Mencken, April 10, 1951, EPFL; Robert Allen Durr, "The Last Days of H. L. Mencken," *Yale Review*, Autumn 1958, pp. 63–65; Louis Cheslock, Diary, Sept. 6, 1953, EPFL; August Mencken to Louis Cheslock, June 23, 1953, EPFL; Lois Gentry Macks, "I Remember . . . Three Years as a Nurse for H. L. Mencken," *BS Magazine*, Nov. 30, 1980, p. 49; author interview with Martin Asner, June 28, 1994; H. Allen Smith, "The Most Unforgettable Character I've Met," pp. 11–13 of the original manuscript before it was edited by *Reader's Digest*, Dec. 1958 edition, Carl Bode Papers, EPFL.

9. Charles Mencken to August Mencken, March 30, 1953, EPFL; August Mencken to AAK, Dec. 16, 1951, EPFL; August Mencken to Gertrude Mencken, June 3, 1955, EPFL; author interview with William Manchester, May 23, 1995. Rosalind Lohrfinck apparently consulted *What's Happening in Hollywood*, a monthly newsletter of current pictures, trends, and publications, in order to choose films that would distract and entertain Mencken. See Rosalind Lohrfinck note, dated Jan. 26, 1970, "After Death." Interpreted by Margaret Lappin, YALE. Also Bob Thomas, "Movie World: Mencken, Now a Movie Fan, But He Still Dislikes 'Em," *Providence Bulletin*, May 12, 1949; Lois Gentry Macks, "I Remember . . . Three Years as a Nurse for H. L. Mencken," *BS Magazine*, Nov. 30, 1980, p. 46; Rosalind Lohrfinck, "Notes on Mencken," June 3, 1949, YALE; author interview with Alistair Cooke, May 19, 1992; Louis Cheslock, Diary, June 26, 1951, EPFL. Cheslock maintained Mencken's eyesight was better than he proclaimed, because "the octave jumps are accurate, as is the entire fragment he plays." One night, when Mencken played the wrong note, the dissonance disgusted him. "Damn it," he exclaimed, stomping his foot, "I'll never touch the keys again!" True to his word, he never did. Ibid. May 1, Aug. 8, 1951, EPFL; author interview with Elise Cheslock, April 14, 1996; "Cheslock Recording," Oct. 30, 1951, EPFL and courtesy of Jack Sanders; Bob McHugh, "Mighty Mencken, in Moderation," *Shreveport (Louisiana) Times*, July 10, 1955. Various projects were suggested—even buying a toy printing press—but Mencken rejected them all. When Mencken broached the possibility of putting together another *Days* volume of eight stories, this time it was Knopf who advised against it; Mencken was the first to agree. See AAK to August Mencken, Oct. 15, 1952, EPFL; HLM to AAK, Oct. 20, 1952, EPFL; August Mencken to AAK, June 26, 1955, EPFL. The treatment HLM received at Johns Hopkins was confirmed by Louis Cheslock. While the Mencken brothers were fond of Dr. Philip Wagley and thought well of his skills, according to Dr. William Muse, they were "disheartened by the cold attitude of Hopkins." Louis Cheslock, Diary, entries for years 1949–1956, EPFL; author interview with William Muse, Jan. 19, 1994.

10. "The Reminiscences of August Mencken," pp. 93, 97–98, COL; August Mencken to Gertrude Mencken, June 14, 1954, EPFL; August Mencken to Philip Wagley, April 29 and May 10, 1954, EPFL; August Mencken to Gertrude Mencken, Aug. 27, 1950, June 14, 1954, EPFL; H. J. Tauginbaugh, Knowles and Tauginbaugh Opticians to August Mencken, Nov. 28, 1956; see also Gertrude Mencken to August Mencken, May 7, 1954, EPFL; August Mencken to Philip Wagley, May 24 and July 29, 1954, EPFL; Dr. William Muse said the lens was not strong enough—author interview with William Muse, Jan. 19, 1994; Edgar Kemler, "The Bright

Twilight of H. L. Mencken," *NYT*, Sept. 12, 1955; Robert Allen Durr, "The Last Days of H. L. Mencken," *Yale Review*, Autumn 1958, p. 72; James Bready, "The Man in the Backyard," *New York Post*, Sept. 18, 1955; August Mencken to Charles Mencken, Sept. 24, 1955, EPFL; August Mencken to AAK, Sept. 25, 1955, EPFL; AAK, *Memoirs*, p. 390, HRHRC; William Manchester, "H. L. Mencken at Seventy-Five: America's Sam Johnson," *Saturday Review of Literature*, Sept. 10, 1955, pp. 11–13; Joseph Miller, "A Mellow H. L. Mencken Marks His 75th," *Boulder (Colorado) Bulletin*, Sept. 12, 1955; "Inherit the Wind, Play Based on Scopes Trial, Praised," *BES*, April 1, 1955; "The Reminiscences of August Mencken," pp. 109–10, COL; L. K. Bradish, "The Sick Sage of Baltimore, H. L. Mencken," *Melbourne Age*, May 21, 1955; Bob McHugh, "Mighty Mencken, in Moderation," *Shreveport (Louisiana) Times*, July 10, 1955; R. P. Harriss, "H. L. Mencken at Seventy-Five," *Baltimore Gardens, Houses and People*, Aug. 1955, pp. 12–13; William Manchester, "Mencken, 73, Mellows, Does Not Dislike Ike," *BS*, Jan. 11, 1954; Manchester, *The Glory and the Dream*, pp. 576, 581; "In Mencken's Baltimore," *Des Moines Tribune*, Sept. 16, 1955; "The Vintage Mencken: Clifton Fadiman in conversation with Alfred A. Knopf and Alistair Cooke upon the publication of Cooke's *The Vintage Mencken* in 1955," courtesy of Jack Sanders.

11. August Mencken to AAK, Nov. 19, 1955, EPFL; HLM, *Minority Report*, p. v; author interview with William Koshland, Dec. 6, 1994; HLM to AAK, Jan. 10, 1956, EPFL; Robert McHugh, "I've Had Fun; Now I'm Ready for Heaven—Mencken," *Detroit Free Press*, Jan. 30, 1956.

12. "H. L. Mencken, Author, Dies at 75," *BS*, Jan. 29, 1956; Louis Cheslock, Diary, Jan. 28, 1956, EPFL; author interview with Elise Cheslock, Jan. 21, 1994; "H. L. Mencken, Dead," *Mobile Register*, Jan. 30, 1956; August Mencken to Charles Mencken, "Instructions for Harry's Care," Oct. 1951, EPFL; "The Week in Radio," *BS*, Jan. 22, 1956. The Philadelphia Orchestra, conducted by Eugene Ormandy, played Mozart's Symphony no. 40 in G Minor and Symphony in C by Bizet. See also "Radio Programs," *BS*, Jan. 28, 1956. The *Sun* made a typographical error in listing the Mozart Symphony as no. 4 instead of 40 (no. 4 in G minor does not exist— see Solomon, "Index of Compositions," *Mozart*, pp. 614–24). HLM, "On Hearing Mozart," *Damn! A Book of Calumny*, p. 118. According to his doctors, HLM died sometime between the hours of four and five in the morning. Lee McCardell, "Private Funeral Is Planned for H. L. Mencken," *BES*, Jan. 30, 1956.

Epilogue: The Passing of an Era

1. *BS*, Jan. 29, 1956; author interview with Grace Darin, July 2, 1989; author interview with Clem Vitek, July 24, 1989; Jan. 30, 1992. HLM's instructions were written on June 1, 1943, collection of Bettina Patterson; August Mencken to Penny Molstead, Feb. 4, 1956, EPFL; "Old Friends Will Join in Mencken Farewell," *BS*, Jan. 3, 1956; Louis Cheslock, Diary [n.d.], EPFL; R. P. Harriss, "H. L. Mencken at Seventy-Five," *Houses, Gardens and People*, Sept. 12, 1955, pp. 12–13; "Mencken Service Will Be Private," *NYT*, Jan. 31, 1956; author interviews with Elise Cheslock, Jan. 21, 1994, April 14, 1996; Robert McHugh, "Mencken's Funeral Just as He Wished," *NYT*, Feb. 1, 1956; "Our Rites May Have Proved Mencken's Adage Correct," *Washington Times Herald*, Feb. 1, 1956; "The Reminiscences of August Mencken," p. 39, COL; author interview with William Abell, Aug. 17, 1991; author interview with Gwinn Owens, Jan. 13, 2002; AAK, Diary, Jan. 31, 1956, HRHRC; James Cain to Arthur Krock, Feb. 1, 1956, PRIN/md; Rosalind Lohrfinck, Diary, Jan. 31, Feb. 6, 1956, YALE.

2. AAK, Diary, Jan. 31, 1956, HRHRC; AAK, *Memoirs*, p. 2, HRHRC.

3. "Letters," *BES*, Feb. 6, 1956; Gerald Johnson, "Henry L. Mencken (1880–1956)," *Saturday Review of Literature*, Feb. 11, 1956, p. 12; author interview with Elise Cheslock, Jan. 21, 1994; author interview with Barry Cheslock, April 14, 1996; "Nathan Upset By Death of Pal," *NYT*, Jan. 29, 1956; Aileen Pringle to August Mencken, Jan. 30, 1956, EPFL; "Federal Bureau

of Investigation Investigative Case Files," NA; author interview with Neil McNeill, Aug. 2, 2000; HLM, "Epitaph," *A Mencken Chrestomathy*, p. 627.

4. Rosalind Lohrfinck to Perry Molstead, Feb. 2, 1956, NYPL; Rodgers, *Mencken & Sara*, p. 537; August Mencken to AAK, July 30, 1956, EPFL; "Mencken's Brother Dies in Pittsburgh," *BES*, April 9, 1956; "August Mencken Dead," *BS*, May 21, 1967; "Plane Crash Kills Young Executive," *Lancaster New Era*, Nov. 14, 1974.

5. William Manchester, "Marburg Notes," Feb. 27, 1951, JFK; author interview with Alistair Cooke, May 2, 1992; HLM, "Off the Grand Banks," *BES*, Sept. 7, 1925; James Cain, "Notes for Dr. Bode," courtesy of Roy Hoopes; HLM, "Autobiographical Notes, 1941," EPFL; HLM, "Mark Twain's Americanism," *New York Evening Mail*, Nov. 1, 1917; HLM, "Mark Twain on Himself," *American Mercury*, Dec. 1924, pp. 507–8; "Mencken a Problem," *NYT*, March 1, 1956; "Senate Joint Resolution #22, Feb. 20, 1956 and Approved by the Governor March 26, 1956," EPFL; "For the Associated Press for Use in My Obituary, Nov. 20, 1940," in "H. L. Mencken: Miscellaneous Writings 1940–1941, Clippings and Carbons, Including Contributions to the Baltimore Sun, 1942," p. 82, EPFL; James Cain, "Mr. Mencken and the Multitudes," *NYT Book Review*, April 16, 1950.

When it comes to Charles Angoff's *H. L. Mencken: A Portrait from Memory*, a careful perusal of Angoff's papers at BU disputes the claim that he kept a notebook during the years he worked for Mencken. What remains in the collection are a series of drafts giving various versions of the same stories and conversations, not all of which were in *Portrait*. The allegation of Mencken's anti-Semitism, however, first raised in *Portrait*, surfaced again upon the 1989 publication of *The Diary of H. L. Mencken*, edited by Charles Fecher. For just a sampling of the discussion that ensued, see Doris Grumbach, "Mencken: Just Plain Antisemitism," *Washington Post*, Jan. 12, 1989; Martin Walker, "The Sage and the Rage," *Manchester Guardian*, Nov. 12, 1989; Jonathan Yardley, "Still Disturbing the Peace," *Washington Post Book World*, Dec. 10, 1989; Russell Baker, "Prejudices Without the Mask," *NYT*, Dec. 13, 1989; "Diary Confirms Mencken Was an Anti-Semite," *Baltimore Jewish Times*, Dec. 15, 1989; "Letters," *NYT Book Review*, Feb. 4, 1990; Jonathan Clark, "Look Back in Naivety," *London Evening Standard*, Feb. 15, 1990; Richard Lingeman, "Prejudices: Last Series," *Nation*, Feb. 19, 1990; "Letters," *New York Review of Books*, March 15, 1990; John Kenneth Galbraith, "Viva Mencken!" *New York Review of Books*, June 28, 1990.

BIBLIOGRAPHY

Author's Interviews

William S. Abell – Admiral William and Harriet Abhau – Mrs. Leon Adler – Richard Alexander – Michael Asner – Benjamin Baker – Ellis Baker III – James Bready – Sara Anne Duffy Chermayeff – Elise Cheslock – Barry Cheslock – Edward C. Clark – Robert Cobb – Wallace Cohen – Alistair Cooke – Grace Darin – Dudley Digges – Mary Ross Flowers – Charles Fortenbaugh – Johnson Fortenbaugh – Donald Fritz – Nancy Angoff Gallin – Lillian Gish – Jesse Glasgow – Ruth Goodman Goetz – Dorothy Granger – Emerson Greenaway – Arthur Gutman – Marion Gutman – Mabel Haardt – Louis P. Hamburger Jr. – Philip Hamburger – Stanley Harrison – Clarinda Harriss – Robin Preston Harriss – Margery Harriss – Richard Hart – Ellen M. Hawks – Marshall Wiley Hawks – Wells Hawks – Katharine Steiner Haxton – Carolyn and Dwight Heinmuller – Dallett Hemphill – Al Hirschfeld – Bradford Jacobs – Murray Kempton – Helen F. Knipp – Patrick Knopf – William Koshland – Anthony Lewis – William Manchester – Philippa Haardt McClellan – Ida Haardt McCulloch – Neil McNeil – Calvin R. Mencken Jr. – Clarence Mitchell III – Tom Morgan – William T. Muse – Gwinn Owens – James Owens – Olga Owens – Bettina Patterson – Donald Patterson – Mrs. Maclean Patterson – John Pentz – Alice Piper – Janet Proctor – William E. Pyne – Eloise Reed – Mrs. Arnold Rich – Chalmers Roberts – Elsinor Roman – Penelope Pearl Russianoff – Frieda Schellhase – Albert Sehlstedt Jr. – Sara Siebert – John Siegenthaler – Walter Sondheim – Lawrence Spivak – Clem Vitek – Philip Wagley – Philip Wagner – Isabel Yates

Oral History Transcripts

At the Oral History Research Office, Columbia University: Edward L. Bernays – Virginius Dabney – Felix Frankfurter – James Watson Gerard – Bruce Gould – Ben Huebesch – Edith Kean – Alfred A. Knopf – Arthur Krock – Walter Lippmann – Mrs. Edgar Lee Masters – August

Mencken – Marjorie Hope Nicholson – Broadus Mitchell – Hamilton Owens – George Schuyler – Benjamin Stolberg – Rupert B. Vance – Carl Van Vechten
   Carl Bode Interviews are at the H. L. Mencken Collection, Enoch Pratt Free Library, unless otherwise noted: Marion Bloom – Arthur Krock and Huntington Cairns (Princeton) – Mrs. Dwight Curtis and Mary Louise Newcomer Moore – Watson Davis – Anita Loos – Ruth Lustgarten – Penelope Pearl – Mrs. Edgar Lee Masters – Hamilton and Olga Owens and Elliott Wheeler (courtesy of Harold A. Williams) – Hamilton and Olga Owens (courtesy of Gwinn Owens) – John Owens and Mrs. Semmes (courtesy of Harold A. Williams) – George Schuyler
   At the Broadcast Pioneers Library, University of Maryland: Quinn Ryan, WGN-Radio

Library and Manuscript Collections

ALA   State of Alabama Department of Archives and History
             (Grover C. Hall; Henry Louis Mencken)
ALA/gg   Amelia Gayle Gorgas Library at the University of Alabama
             (Sara Mayfield Collection)
AMPAS   Margaret Herrick Library, Academy of Motion Picture Arts and Sciences
             Foundation
             (Gladys Hall; Hedda Hopper)
APS   American Philosophical Society Library
             (Raymond Pearl)
ARCH   Archdiocese of Baltimore Archives
             (Archbishop Kelley)
BCAR   Baltimore City Archives
             (Mayor James Preston)
BU   Mugar Library, Boston University
             (Charles Angoff; Herbert Bayard Swope)
CHI   University of Chicago Library
             (Morris Fishbein)
COL   Oral History Collection at Columbia University
             (see Oral History Transcripts)
CORN   Carl A. Kroch Library, Cornell University Library
             (James Joyce; George Jean Nathan)
DICK   Archives and Special Collections, Dickinson College
             (Charles L. Swift)
EPFL   Enoch Pratt Free Library
             (H. L. Mencken Collection)
FDR   Franklin D. Roosevelt Library at Hyde Park
             (FDR Papers: Personal and Official Files; President's Secretary's Files; Francis
             Biddle; Stephen T. Early)
GETTY   Musselman Library, Gettysburg College
             (Antoinette Feleky)
GOU   Julia Rogers Library, Goucher College
             (Sara Haardt Mencken Collection)
GT   Special Collections Division, Georgetown University
             (Ernest and Madeleine Boyd; Henry Hazlitt; Sister Miriam; Fulton Oursler;
             William White; Franklin B. Williams)
HAR/arc Harvard University Archives
             (Minutes of Faculty of Arts and Sciences, 1926; Samuel Eliot Morison Papers)

HAR/hou   The Houghton Library, Harvard University
     (Joseph Grew; David Houston; Alan Seeger; Oswald Garrison Villard)
HAR/law   Harvard Law School Library
     (Felix Frankfurter; Papers of the New England Watch & Ward Society)
HOOV   Hoover Institution Archives, Stanford University
     (Stephen Miles Bouton; William J. Losh)
HRHRC   Harry Ransom Humanities Research Center, University of Texas at Austin
     (Joseph Hergesheimer; Alfred A. Knopf Collection; Sinclair Lewis; Edgar Lee
     Masters; Christopher Morley; Ezra Pound; V. S. Pritchett; George Bernard
     Shaw; Francis Starr; Hugh Walpole)
HUNT   Huntington Library
     (Zoë Akins; George Sterling)
JFK   John Fitzgerald Kennedy Library
     (William Manchester)
JHU/mc   Alan Mason Chesney Medical Archives, Johns Hopkins Medical Institutions
     (Howard Kelly)
JHU/me   Milton S. Eisenhower Library, Johns Hopkins University
     (John C. French; Elizabeth Gilman)
KNOX   Special Collections, University of Tennessee at Knoxville
     (Judge Sue Hicks; Nellie Kenyon)
LC   Manuscript Division, Library of Congress
     (Carl Ackerman; Daniel Carter Beard; William Jennings Bryan; James Branch
     Cabell; James M. Cain; Huntington Cairns; Lewis Chase; Raymond Clapper;
     Clarence Darrow; Felix Frankfurter; Benjamin Huebsch; Burton Kline; Joseph
     Wood Krutch; Clare Boothe Luce; George Middleton; George Fort Milton;
     Merrill Moore; NAACP Records; Theodore Roosevelt Jr.; Raymond Swing;
     Lawrence E. Spivak; T. Swann; Irita Van Doren; William Allen White)
MAD   State Historical Society of Wisconsin at Madison
     (Ruth Goodman Goetz; Byron Price)
MD   Maryland State Archives
     (Baltimore City Register of Wills)
MaHS   Massachusetts Historical Society
     (Henry Cabot Lodge; Ellery Sedgewick)
MdHS   Manuscripts Division, Maryland Historical Society
     (HLM personal items; Frank R. Kent)
MON   Mansfield Library, University of Montana
     (James Watson Gerard)
NA   National Archives
     (Correspondence of Carl Byoir with Government Agencies and Division of the
     Committee; General Correspondence of George Creel; Department of Justice;
     Council of National Defense; Committee on Public Information)
NA/se   National Archives, Southeast Region
     (World War I Draft Records for H. L. Mencken and August Mencken)
NEW   Newberry Library, Chicago
     (Sherwood Anderson; Edward Price Bell; James O'Donnell Bennett; Ben Hecht;
     Victor Lawson; Paul Mowrer; Oswald F. Shütte; Raymond Swing)
NYPL   New York Public Library
     (H. L. Mencken letters, bequeathed to the library by HLM)

NYPL/ms Rare Books and Manuscripts Division, New York Public Library
(H. L. Mencken Papers and Additions; Ruth Goodman Goetz; Isaac Goldberg; Richard Mansfield; Masters-Davis Collection; Carl Van Vechten)

NYPL/pa Billy Rose Theatre Collection, Performing Arts Research Center, New York Public Library
(Ruth Goodman Goetz; Aileen Pringle; Robinson-Locke Collection)

NYPL/sc Schomburg Center for Research in Black Culture, New York Public Library
(George Schuyler)

NLM History of Medicine Division, National Library of Medicine
(Fielding Garrison)

ORE Special Collections, Library, University of Oregon
(Edward A. Rumley Papers)

PENN Annenberg Rare Book and Manuscript Library, University of Pennsylvania
(Theodore Dreiser; James T. Farrell; Burton Rascoe; Friedrich Weisberger)

POLIT Politisches Archiv Auswartigen, AMTS, Germany
(Henry Wood and H. L. Mencken Correspondence to German Officials)

POLY Archives of Polytechnic High School in Baltimore, Maryland
(School Archives)

PRIN/fire Firestone Library, Princeton University
(Louis Adamic; Julian Boyd; F. Scott and Zelda Fitzgerald; H. L. Mencken; Charles Scribner's Sons; Julian Street; Allen Tate)

PRIN/md Seeley G. Mudd Manuscript Library, Princeton University
(ACLU; Arthur Krock)

TSA Tennessee State Archives, Nashville
(Governor Austin Peay)

UCLA Young Research Library, University of California at Los Angeles
(Popular Literature & Printed Materials: *Saucy Stories, Parisienne*)

UMBC Albin O. Kuhn Library and Gallery, University of Maryland Baltimore County
(Philip Wagner)

UMC/bp Broadcast Pioneers Library, University of Maryland at College Park
(Oral History with Quinn Ryan)

UMC/md Maryland Room of McKeldin Library, University of Maryland at College Park
(Tobacco Workers International and Cigar Makers International Union of America)

UNC Southern Historical Collection, Wilson Library, University of North Carolina at Chapel Hill
(Correspondence of H. L. Mencken with Elizabeth and Frederic Hanes)

UVA Special Collections, Alderman Library, University of Virginia
(Emily Clark Balch; Barrett Collection; James Branch Cabell; Ellen Glasgow; Henry Hyde; Mencken-Untermeyer Collection; Southern Writers Convention; Willard Huntington Wright)

WS Archives of Labor and Urban Affairs, Wayne State University
(Papers of the Baltimore and Newspaper Guild)

WY American Heritage Center, University of Wyoming
(Harry Elmer Barnes; Edward A. Rumley)

YALE Beinecke Rare Book and Manuscript Library, Yale University
(Arthur Davison Ficke; James Weldon Johnson; Margaret Lappin & Rosalind Lohrfinck; Sinclair Lewis; Aileen Pringle; Carl Van Vechten; William Huntington Wright)

Private Collections

William S. Abell – Ellis T. Baker III – Sara Anne Duffy Chermayeff – Arthur J. Gutman – Robin P. and Margery Harriss – Katharine Steiner Haxton – Roy Hoopes – R. P. Lasco – Steven Lauria – Gwinn Owens – Bettina Patterson – Alice Piper – Jack R. Sanders – Richard J. Schrader – Dieter Spielberg – George H. Thompson – Dr. Philip Wagley – Charles Wallen Jr. – Harold A. Williams – Mrs. J. Hofmann Wilson

Audio-Visual and Sound Recordings

"In Search of History: The Monkey Trial," History Channel, A & E Television, 1997.
Henry L. Mencken interviewed by Donald Howe Kirkley Sr., June 30, 1948, Library of Congress.
Henry L. Mencken: Recordings collected by Dr. Louis Cheslock; Recordings made by Barry Cheslock at the Cheslock Home, October 30, 1951; Enoch Pratt Free Library, 1999.
The Vintage Mencken: Clifton Fadiman in conversation with Alfred A. Knopf and Alistair Cooke upon the publication of Cooke's *The Vintage Mencken*, 1955, collection of Jack R. Sanders.
Eric F. Goldman interviews Alfred Knopf on the occasion of the Fiftieth Anniversary of Alfred A. Knopf, Inc., 1965, collection of Jack R. Sanders.

Books

Adamic, Louis. *Laughing in the Jungle*. New York: Harper & Row, 1932.
Ade, George. *Fables in Slang*. New York: Grosset & Dunlap, 1897.
Adler, Betty. *A Census of Ventures Into Verse*. Baltimore: Enoch Pratt Free Library, 1972.
———. *H.L.M. The Mencken Bibliography*. With the assistance of Jane Wilhelm. Baltimore: Johns Hopkins Press, 1961.
Adler, Elmer, ed. *Breaking Into Print: Being a Compilation of Papers Wherein Each of a Select Group of Authors Tells of the Difficulties of Authorship and How Such Trials are Met, Together with Biographical Notes and Comment*. New York: Simon & Schuster, 1938.
Allen, Frederick Lewis. *Only Yesterday: An Informal History of the 1920s*. New York: Harper & Row, 1931.
Anderson, Sherwood. *Sherwood Anderson's Memoirs: A Critical Edition*. Ed. Ray Lewis White. Chapel Hill: University of North Carolina Press, 1969.
Angoff, Charles. *The Bitter Spring*. New York: Thomas Yoseloff, 1961.
———. *H. L. Mencken: A Portrait from Memory*. New York: Thomas Yoseloff, 1956.
———. *The Old Century and the New: Essays in Honor of Charles Angoff*. Ed. W. Alfred Rosa. Rutherford: Association University Presses, 1978.
———. *Summer Storm*. New York: Thomas Yoseloff, 1963.
Argesinger, Jo Anne. *Toward a New Deal in Baltimore: People and Government in the Great Depression*. Chapel Hill: University of North Carolina Press, 1998.
Asbell, Bernard. *When FDR Died*. New York: Holt, Rinehart & Winston, 1961.
Baer, Willis N. *The Economic Development of the Cigar Industry in the United States*. Lancaster, Pa.: 1933.
Baker, Russell. *The Good Times*. New York: William Morrow, 1989.
Beirne, Francis F. *The Amiable Baltimoreans*. New York: E. P. Dutton, 1951.
Bishop, Jim. *FDR's Last Year*. New York: William Morrow, 1974.
Black, George. *The Good Neighbor: How the United States Wrote the History of Central America and the Caribbean*. New York: Pantheon Books, 1988.

Bode, Carl. *The Editor, the Bluenose, and the Prostitute: H. L. Mencken's History of the "Hatrack" Case*. Boulder: Roberts Rinehart, 1988.

———. *Mencken*. Carbondale: Southern Illinois University Press, 1969.

———, ed. *The New Mencken Letters*. New York: Dial Press, 1977.

Boller, Paul F. *Presidential Campaigns*. New York: Oxford University Press, 1984.

Bordman, Gerald. *American Theater: A Chronicle of Comedy and Drama, 1869–1914*. New York: Oxford University Press, 1994.

Boyd, Ernest. *H. L. Mencken*. New York: McBride Press, 1925.

Brayman, Harold. *The President Speaks Off the Record: Historic Evenings with America's Leaders, the Press, and Other Men of Power at Washington's Exclusive Gridiron Club*. Princeton: Dow Jones Books, 1976.

Bready, James H. *The First 100 Years: Baseball in Baltimore*. Baltimore: Johns Hopkins University Press, 1998.

Brinkley, Alan. *The End of Reform: New Deal Liberalism in Recession and War*. New York: Alfred A. Knopf, 1995.

———. *Voices of Protest: Huey Long, Father Coughlin and the Great Depression*. New York: Vintage Books, 1982.

Brooks, Van Wyck. *The Confident Years, 1895–1925*. New York: E. P. Dutton, 1952.

Brugger, Robert J. *Maryland: A Middle Temperament, 1634–1980*. Baltimore: Johns Hopkins University Press, 1988.

Burns, James MacGregor. *The Workshop of Democracy: From the Emancipation to the Era of the New Deal*. New York: Vintage Books, 1985.

Butcher, Fanny. *Many Lives, One Life*. New York: Harper & Row, 1972.

Calcott, George H. *Maryland and America: 1940–1980*. Baltimore: Johns Hopkins Press, 1985.

Cashman, Sean Dennis. *America in the Twenties and Thirties: The Olympian Age of Franklin Delano Roosevelt*. New York: New York University Press, 1989.

Clark, Emily. *Ingenue Among the Lions: The Letters of Emily Clark to Joseph Hergesheimer*. Ed. Gerald Langford. Austin: The University of Texas Press, 1965.

———. *Innocence Abroad*. New York: Alfred A. Knopf, 1931.

Cloud, Stanley, and Lynne Olson. *The Murrow Boys: Pioneers on the Front Lines of Broadcast Journalism*. New York: Houghton Mifflin, 1996.

Conrad, Joseph. *Youth*. San Francisco: Chandler Publishing, first published 1902.

Cook, Blanche Wiesen. *Eleanor Roosevelt: 1933–1939*. New York: Viking Press, 1999.

Cooke, Alistair. *Six Men*. New York: Alfred A. Knopf, 1977.

———. *The Vintage Mencken*. New York: Vintage Books, 1955.

Cooke, Robert Grier, ed. *Casual Essays of the Sun: Editorial Articles on Many Subjects, Clothed with the Philosophy of the Bright Side of Things*. New York: Robert Grier Cooke, 1905.

Craig, Gordon A. *The Germans*. New York: Penguin Books, 1983.

Crane, Stephen. *Major Conflicts in the Works of Stephen Crane*. With an introduction by H. L. Mencken, ed. Wilson Follett. New York: Alfred A. Knopf, 1925–1926.

Crooks, James B. *Politics and Progress: The Rise of Urban Progressivism in Baltimore 1895–1911*. Baton Rouge: Louisiana State University Press, 1968.

Culver, John C., and John Hyde. *American Dreamer: The Life and Times of Henry Wallace*. New York: W. W. Norton, 2000.

Daniel, Clifton, ed. *Chronicle of the Twentieth Century*. New York: Chronicle Publications, 1987.

Daniels, Josephus. *The Diary of Josephus Daniels*. Ed. Arthur Link. Princeton: Princeton University Press, 1981.

Darrow, Clarence. *The Story of My Life*. New York: Charles Scribner's Sons, 1932.

Dolmetsch, Carl R. *The Smart Set: A History and Anthology.* With an Introductory Reminiscence by S. N. Behrman. New York: Dial Press, 1966.

Dorsey, John, ed. *On Mencken.* New York: Alfred A. Knopf, 1980.

Douglas, Ann. *Terrible Honesty: Mongrel Manhattan in the 1920s.* New York: Farrar, Straus & Giroux, 1995.

Dowell, Peter W. *Ich Kuss Die Hand: The Letters of H. L. Mencken to Gretchen Hood.* Tuscaloosa: University of Alabama Press, 1986.

Dreiser, Theodore. *American Diaries, 1901–1926,* ed. Thomas P. Riggio. Philadelphia: University of Pennsylvania Press, 1983.

Ehrlich, Paul R. *Human Natures: Genes, Cultures and the Human Prospect.* International Press: Clearwater Books, 2000.

Farrell, James T. *Reflections at Fifty and Other Essays.* New York: Vanguard Press, 1954.

Farrell, Michael R. *A History of Baltimore Streetcars.* Sykesville, Md.: Greenberg Publishing, 1992.

Fecher, Charles A. *Mencken: A Study of His Thought.* New York: Alfred A. Knopf, 1978.

Fee, Elizabeth, Linda Shopes, and Linda Zeidman, eds. *The Baltimore Book: New Views of Local History.* Philadelphia: Temple University Press, 1991.

Fitzpatrick, Vincent. *Gerald W. Johnson: From Southern Liberal to National Conscience.* Baton Rouge: Louisiana State University Press, 2002.

———. *H. L. Mencken.* New York: Continuum, 1989.

———. *H.L.M. The Mencken Bibliography: A Ten-Year Supplement, 1961–1971.* Baltimore: Enoch Pratt Free Library, 1971.

———. *H.L.M. The Mencken Bibliography: A Second Ten-Year Supplement, 1971–1981.* Baltimore: Enoch Pratt Free Library, 1981.

Forgue, Guy J., ed. *Letters of H. L. Mencken.* New York: Alfred A. Knopf, 1961.

Freeman, Joshua, American Social History Project, et al. *Who Built America? Working People and the Nation's Economy, Politics, Culture and Society. Volume II: From the Gilded Age to the Present.* New York: Pantheon Books, 1992.

Gerard, James Watson. *My Four Years in Germany.* New York: G. H. Doran, 1917.

Gilbert, Martin. *The First World War: A Complete History.* New York: Henry Holt, 1994.

———. *A History of the Twentieth Century, Volume I (1900–1933)* and *Volume II (1933–1951).* New York: William Morrow, 1997, 1998.

Gilmor, Donald M., Jerome A. Barron, Todd F. Simon, and Herbert A. Terry. *Mass Communication Law: Cases and Comment.* New York: West Publishing, 1950.

Ginger, Ray. *Age of Excess: The United States from 1877 to 1914.* New York: Macmillan, 1965.

Goldberg, Isaac. *The Man Mencken: A Biographical and Critical Survey.* New York: Simon & Schuster, 1925.

Goodwin, Doris Kearns. *No Ordinary Time: Franklin and Eleanor Roosevelt: The Home Front in World War II.* New York: Simon & Schuster, 1994.

Gordon, Sarah. *Hitler, Germans, and the "Jewish Question."* Princeton: Princeton University Press, 1984.

Grant, Roger H. *Self-help in the 1890s Depression.* Ames: Iowa State University Press, 1983.

Greene, Lawrence. *The Era of Wonderful Nonsense: A Casebook of the Twenties.* New York: Bobbs-Merrill, 1939.

Greene, Ward, ed. *Star Reporters and 34 of Their Stories.* New York: Random House, 1948.

Griffith, Robert. *A Boy's Useful Pastimes and Profitable Amusement for Spare Hours.* New York: A. L. Burt, 1888.

Griswold, Howell M. *Baltimore Polytechnic Institute: The First Century.* Baltimore: NPS Inc., Centennial Committee, 1984.

Haardt, Sara. *The Love Story of an Old Maid.* Girard, Kansas: Haldeman-Julius, 1927.

———. *Southern Album*. Edited and with a preface by H. L. Mencken. New York: Doubleday & Doran, 1936.

———. *Southern Souvenirs: Selected Stories and Essays of Sara Haardt*. Ed. Ann Henley. Tuscaloosa: University of Alabama Press, 1999.

Hall, Clayton Coleman, ed. *Baltimore: Its History and Its People*. New York: Lewis Historical Publishing, 1912.

Harrison, Stanley. *The Editorial Art of Edmund Duffy*. Madison: Fairleigh Dickinson University Press, 1998.

Hawgood, John A. *The Tragedy of German-America: The Germans in the United States of America During the Nineteenth Century—and After*. New York: G. P. Putnam's Sons, 1940.

Hays, Arthur Garfield. *City Lawyer: The Autobiography of a Law Practice*. New York: Simon & Schuster, 1942.

———. *Let Freedom Ring*. New York: Liveright Publishing, 1937.

———. *Trial by Prejudice*. New York: Covici Friede Publishers, 1933.

Hertzberg, Arthur. *The Jews in America: Four Centuries of an Uneasy Encounter*. New York: Simon & Schuster, 1989.

Hilberg, Paul. *The Destruction of the European Jews*. New York: Holmes and Meier, 1971.

Hirschfeld, Charles. *Baltimore, 1870–1900: Studies in Social History*. Baltimore: Johns Hopkins University Press, 1941.

Hixson, Richard F. *Mass Media and the Constitution: An Encyclopaedia of Supreme Court Decisions*. New York: Garland Publishing, 1989.

Hobson, Fred. *Mencken: A Life*. New York: Random House, 1994.

———. *Serpent in Eden: H. L. Mencken and the South*. Chapel Hill: University of North Carolina Press, 1974.

Hoffman, Charles. *The Depression in the Nineties*. Westport: Greenwood Publishing, 1970.

Hofstadter, Richard. *The Age of Reform: From Bryan to F.D.R.* New York: Vintage Books, 1955.

———. *Social Darwinism in American Thought*. Boston: Beacon Press, 1944, 1992.

Hollander, J. H. *A Guide to the City of Baltimore*. Baltimore: John Murphy, 1893.

Hoopes, Roy. *Cain: The Biography of James M. Cain*. New York: Holt, Rinehart & Winston, 1982.

Huneker, James. *Essays by James Huneker*. Selected with introduction by H. L. Mencken. New York: Simon & Schuster, 1929.

———. *The Intimate Letters of James Gibbons Huneker*. Collected by Josephine Huneker with foreword by Benjamin de Casseres. New York: Liveright Publishing, 1936.

Ibsen, Henrik. *The Collected Works of Henrik Ibsen in Thirteen Volumes*. With an introduction by William Acher, vol. VII. New York: Charles Scribner's Sons, 1907.

Ickes, Harold L. *The Secret Diary of Harold L. Ickes: The First Thousand Days*. New York: Simon & Schuster, 1953.

Ingelhart, Louis Edward. *Press Freedoms: A Descriptive Calendar of Concepts, Interpretations, Events and Court Actions from 4000 BC to the Present*. New York: Greenwood Press, 1987.

Jackson, Kenneth T. *The Encyclopaedia of New York City*. New Haven: Yale University Press and New York Historical Society, 1995.

James, Henry. *The American Scene*. New York: Charles Scribner's Sons, 1906, 1946 edition.

Janvier, Meredith. *Baltimore in the Eighties and Nineties*. Baltimore: H. G. Roebuck & Son, 1933.

———. *Baltimore Yesterdays*. Baltimore: H. G. Roebuck & Son, 1937.

Jerome, Helen. *The Secret of Woman*. New York: Boni and Liveright, 1923.

Johns, Bud. *The Ombibulous Mr. Mencken*. San Francisco: Synergistic Press, 1968.

Johnson, Gerald W., Frank R. Kent, H. L. Mencken, and Hamilton Owens. *The Sunpapers of Baltimore*. New York: Alfred A. Knopf, 1937.

Johnson, James Weldon. *Along This Way: The Autobiography of James Weldon Johnson*. New York: Viking Press, 1933.

Johnson, Owen. *The Eternal Boy: Being the Story of the Prodigious Hickey*. New York: Dodd, Mead, 1909.

Johnston, Jason, MD. *Jamaica: The New Riviera, a Pictorial Description*. London: Caswell & Co., 1903.

Jordan, David Starr. *The Days of a Man: Being Memories of a Naturalist, Teacher and Minor Prophet of Democracy 1900–1921*. New York: World Book Company, 1922.

Julius, E. Haldeman. *The World of Haldeman-Julius.* Compiled with an introduction by Albert Mordell, foreword by Harry Golden, and profile by Sue Haldeman-Julius, 1960.

Kahn, E. J., Jr. *The World of Swope*. New York: Simon & Schuster, 1965.

Kazin, Alfred. *On Native Grounds: An Interpretation of Modern American Prose Literature*. New York: Reynal & Hitchcock, 1942.

Keller, Morton. *Regulating a New Society: Public Policy and Social Change in America 1900–1933*. Cambridge: Harvard University Press, 1994.

Kellner, Bruce. *The Last Dandy: Ralph Barton, American Artist, 1891–1931*. Columbia: University of Missouri Press, 1991.

Kelly, Jacques. *Bygone Baltimore: A Historical Portrait*. Norfolk Beach: Donning Company, 1982.

Kemler, Edgar. *The Irreverent Mr. Mencken*. Boston: Little, Brown, 1950.

Kennedy, David M. *Over Here: The First World War and American Society*. New York: Oxford University Press, 1980.

Ketchum, Richard M. *The Borrowed Years, 1938–1941: America on the Way to War*. New York: Doubleday-Anchor, 1989.

Knightley, Philip. *The First Casualty: From Crimea to Vietnam: The War Correspondent as Hero, Propagandist and Myth Maker*. New York, London: Harcourt, Brace & Jovanovich, 1975.

Koop, Theodore F. *Weapon of Silence*. Chicago: University of Chicago Press, 1946.

Krock, Arthur. *Memoirs: Sixty Years on the Firing Line*. New York: Funk & Wagnalls, 1968.

Larson, Edward J. *Summer for the Gods*. New York: Basic Books, 1997.

Leuchtenburg, William E. *Franklin D. Roosevelt and the New Deal, 1932–1940*. New York: Harper & Row, 1963.

Levine, Lawrence W. *Defender of the Faith: William Jennings Bryan: The Last Decade, 1915–1925*. Cambridge: Harvard University Press, 1987.

Liebman, Roy. *From Silents to Sound: A Biographical Encyclopaedia of Performers Who Made the Transition*. Jefferson, N.C: Mayfair, 1988.

Link, Arthur S. *Woodrow Wilson and the Progressive Era, 1910–1917*. New York: Harper & Row, 1954.

Lipstadt, Deborah E. *Beyond Belief: The American Press and the Coming of the Holocaust, 1933–1945*. New York: Free Press, 1986.

Loos, Anita. *A Cast of Thousands*. New York: Grosset & Dunlap, 1977.

———. *A Girl Like I*. New York: Viking Press, 1966.

Lord, Walter. *The Good Years: From 1900 to the First World War*. New York: Harper & Brothers, 1960.

Manchester, William. *Disturber of the Peace: The Life of H. L. Mencken*. Amherst: University of Massachusetts Press, 1986.

———. *The Glory and the Dream: A Narrative History of America, 1932–1972*. New York: Bantam Books, 1990.

Markel, Howard, M. D., and Frank A. Oski, M. D., *The H. L. Mencken Baby Book: Comprising the Contents of H. L. Mencken's What You Ought To Know About Your Baby, with Commentaries*. Philadelphia: Hanley & Belfus, 1990.

Martin, Edward R. *In Defense of Marion: The Love of Marion Bloom and H. L. Mencken*. Athens: University of Georgia Press, 1996.

Masters, Hilary. *Last Stands: Notes from Memory*. Boston: David R. Godine, 1982.

Mayfield, Sara. *The Constant Circle: H. L. Mencken and His Friends*. New York: Delacorte Press, 1968.

Mellow, James R. *Invented Lives: F. Scott and Zelda Fitzgerald*. Boston: Houghton Mifflin, 1984.

Mencken, H. L. *The American Credo: A Contribution Toward the Interpretation of the National Mind*. New York: Alfred A. Knopf, 1920.

———. *The American Language: An Inquiry Into the Development of English in the United States*. New York: Alfred Knopf, 1919. Revised editions published in 1921, 1923, and 1936; *Supplements I* and *II* published in 1945 and 1948. An abridged version of the fourth edition and two supplements, edited by Raven I. McDavid Jr., was published by Knopf in 1963.

———. *A Book of Prefaces*. New York: Alfred A. Knopf, 1917.

———. *The Charlatanry of the Learned*. New York: Alfred A. Knopf, 1937.

———. *Christmas Story*. New York: Alfred A. Knopf, 1946.

———. *Damn! A Book of Calumny*. New York: Philip Goodman, 1918.

———. *The Days of H. L. Mencken: Happy Days, Newspaper Days, Heathen Days*. New York: Alfred A. Knopf, 1947.

———. *Europe After 8:15*. Written in collaboration with George Jean Nathan and Willard Huntington Wright. New York: Lane, 1914.

———. *George Bernard Shaw: His Plays*. Boston: John W. Luce, 1905.

———. *H. L. Mencken on Music: A Selection of His Writings on Music Together with an Account of H. L. Mencken's Musical Life and a History of the Saturday Night Club*. Selected by Louis Cheslock. New York: Alfred A. Knopf, 1961.

———. *Happy Days, 1880–1892*. New York: Alfred A. Knopf, 1940.

———. *Heathen Days, 1890–1936*. New York: Alfred A. Knopf, 1943.

———. *In Defense of Women*. New York: Philip Goodman, 1918.

———. *Making a President: A Footnote to the Saga of Democracy*. New York: Alfred A. Knopf, 1932.

———. *Men Versus the Man: A Correspondence Between Rives La Monte, Socialist, and H. L. Mencken, Individualist*. New York: Henry Holt, 1910.

———. *A Mencken Chrestomathy*. New York: Alfred A. Knopf, 1949.

———. *Minority Report: H. L. Mencken's Notebooks*. New York: Alfred A. Knopf, 1956.

———. *A New Dictionary of Quotations on Historical Principles from Ancient and Modern Sources*. New York: Alfred A. Knopf, 1942.

———. *Newspaper Days, 1899–1906*. New York: Alfred A. Knopf, 1941.

———. *Notes on Democracy*. New York: Alfred A. Knopf, 1926.

———. *The Philosophy of Friedrich Nietzsche*. Boston: John W. Luce, 1907.

———. *Pistols for Two*. Signed by Owen Hatteras; written by H. L. Mencken in collaboration with George Jean Nathan. New York: Alfred A. Knopf, 1917.

———. *Prejudices*. There are six series. All were published in New York by Alfred A. Knopf in 1919, 1920, 1922, 1924, 1926, 1927.

———. *Treatise on the Gods*. New York: Alfred A. Knopf, 1930, 1946.

———. *Treatise on the Right and Wrong*. New York: Alfred A. Knopf, 1934.

———. *Ventures Into Verse*. Baltimore: Marshall, Beek & Gordon, 1903.

———, ed. *Menckeniana: A Schimpflexion*. New York: Alfred A. Knopf, 1928.

Merryman, Richard. *Mank: The Wit, World and Life of Herman Mankiewicz*. New York: William Morrow, 1978.

Millis, Walter. *Road to War: America, 1914–1917*. Boston: Houghton-Mifflin, 1935.

Mitchell, Edward P. *Memoirs of an Editor*. New York: Charles Scribner's Sons, 1924.

Mock, James R., and Frederick Larson. *Words That Won the War: The Story of the Committee of Public Information, 1917–1919*. Princeton: Princeton University Press, 1939.

Mott, Frank Luther. *American Journalism, A History: 1690–1960*. New York: Macmillan, 1962.

Nabers, Charles Haddon. *Mediterranean Memories*. Greenville, S.C.: Keys Publishing, 1934.

Nathan, George Jean. *The Intimate Notebooks of George Jean Nathan*. New York: Alfred A. Knopf, 1932.

———. *The World of George Jean Nathan: Essays, Reviews and Commentary*. Ed. Charles Angoff. New York: Alfred A. Knopf, 1952.

Nolte, William. *H. L. Mencken, Literary Critic*. Middletown, Conn.: Wesleyan University Press, 1966.

O'Connor, Richard. *Heywood Broun: A Biography*. New York: G. P. Putnam's Sons, 1975.

Oderman, Stuart. *Lillian Gish: A Life on Stage and Screen*. Jefferson: McFarland, 2000.

Olson, Sherry H. *Baltimore: The Building of an American City*. Baltimore: Johns Hopkins University Press, 1980.

Perrett, Geoffrey. *America in the Twenties*. New York: Simon & Schuster, 1982.

Peterson, H. C. *Propaganda for War: The Campaign Against American Neutrality, 1914–1917*. Norman: University of Oklahoma Press, 1939.

Peterson, H. C., and Gilbert C. Fite. *Opponents of War, 1917–1918*. Madison: University of Wisconsin Press, 1957.

Peterson, Peter P. *The Great Baltimore Fire*. Baltimore: Maryland Historical Society, 2004.

Peterson, Theodore. *Magazines in the Twentieth Century*. Chicago: University of Illinois Press, 1972.

Pollard, Percival. *Their Day in Court*. New York: Neale Publishing, 1909.

Ponsonby, Arthur. *Falsehood in War-Time*. Torrance, Cal.: Institute for Historical Review, 1980 reprint of the 1928 edition.

Preston, Dickson J. *Newspapers of Maryland's Eastern Shore*. Queenstown: Queen Anne's Press & Tidewater Publishers, 1986.

Priboy-Novikoff, A. *Thushima*. Translated from Russian by Eden and Cedar Paul. New York: Alfred A. Knopf, 1937.

Rampersad, Arnold. *The Art and Imagination of W.E.B. Du Bois*. Cambridge: Harvard University Press, 1976.

Rascoe, Burton, and Groff Conklin, eds. *The Smart Set Anthology*. New York: Reynal & Hitchcock, 1934.

Rhea County Historical Society. *The World's Most Famous Court Trial: Tennessee Evolution Case*. Dayton: Bryan College, 1990.

Riggio, Thomas P., ed. *Dreiser-Mencken Letters: The Correspondence of Theodore Dreiser and H. L. Mencken*, vols. 1–2. Philadelphia: University of Pennsylvania Press, 1986.

Ritchie, Alexandra. *Faust's Metropolis: A History of Berlin*. New York: Carroll & Graff, 1998.

Robinson, F. E., and W. S. Morgan. *Why Dayton of All Places?* Chattanooga: Andrews Printers, 1925.

Rodgers, Marion Elizabeth., ed. *The Impossible H. L. Mencken: A Selection of His Best Newspaper Stories*. New York: Doubleday-Anchor, 1991.

———. *Mencken & Sara: A Life In Letters: The Private Correspondence of H. L. Mencken and Sara Haardt*. New York: McGraw-Hill, 1987.

Ross, Isabel. *Ladies of the Press: The Story of Women in Journalism*. New York: Harper & Brothers, 1936.

Roxnurgh, T. L., and Joseph C. Ford. *Handbook of Jamaica 1900*. London: Edward Stanford, 1900.

Schaffer, Ronald. *America in the Great War: The Rise of the War Welfare State*. New York: Oxford University Press, 1991.

Schieber, Clara Eve. *American Sentiment Toward Germany, 1870–1914*. Boston: Cornhill Publishing, 1923.

Schlesinger, Arthur M., Jr. *The Age of Roosevelt: The Politics of Upheaval*. Boston: Houghton Mifflin & Co., 1960.

Schrader, Richard J. *H. L. Mencken: A Descriptive Bibliography*. With the assistance of George H. Thompson and Jack R. Sanders. Pittsburgh: University of Pittsburgh Press, 1998.

Scruggs, Charles. *The Sage in Harlem: H. L. Mencken and the Black Writers of the 1920s*. Baltimore: Johns Hopkins University Press, 1984.

Schwab, Arnold T. *James Gibbons Huneker: Critic of the Seven Arts*. Stanford: Stanford University Press, 1963.

Scopes, John T., and James Presley. *Center of the Storm: Memoirs of John T. Scopes*. New York: Holt, Rinehart & Winston, 1967.

Seldes, George. *Freedom of the Press*. New York: Bobbs-Merrill, 1935.

Shepherd, Jean. *The America of George Ade, 1866–1947*. New York: G. P. Putnam's Sons, 1960.

Shuman, Edwin Llewellyn. *Steps into Journalism: Helps and Hints for Young Writers*. Evanston, Ill.: Correspondence School of Journalism, 1894.

Singleton, M. K. *H. L. Mencken and the American Mercury Adventure*. Durham: Duke University Press, 1962.

Smith, Merriam A. *Thank You, Mr. President: A White House Notebook*. New York: Harper, 1946.

Sloan, William David. *American Journalism History*. New York: Greenwood Press, 1989.

Smith, Richard Norton. *The Colonel: The Life and Legend of Robert R. McCormick*. Boston: Houghton Mifflin, 1997.

Sommerville, Donald. *World War II Day By Day*. Greenwich: Dorset Press, 1989.

Spaeth, Sigmund. *Read 'Em and Weep: The Song You Forgot to Remember*. New York: Doubleday & Page, 1926.

Stenerson, Douglas C. *H. L. Mencken: Iconoclast from Baltimore*. Chicago: University of Chicago Press, 1971.

————, ed. *Critical Essays on H. L. Mencken*. Boston: G. K. Hall, 1987.

Stricker, William F. *Keeping Christmas: An Edwardian Age Memoir*. Owings Mills, 1981.

Sullivan, Mark. *Our Times: The United States, 1900–1925*. Vols. I, III, VI. New York: Charles Scribner's Sons, 1927, 1930, 1937.

Tully, Grace. *F.D.R., My Boss*. New York: Charles Scribner's Sons, 1949.

Tully, James. *A Dozen and One*. New York: Murray & Gee, 1943.

Twain, Mark. *The Complete Travel Books of Mark Twain*. Ed. Charles Neider. New York: Doubleday, 1967.

Untermeyer, Louis. *From Another World*. New York: Harcourt, Brace, 1939.

Villard, Oswald Garrison. *Fighting Years: Memoirs of a Liberal Editor*. New York: Harcourt, Brace, 1939.

Wagner, Philip. *H. L. Mencken*. Minneapolis: University of Minnesota Press, 1966.

Walsh, Richard. *Maryland: A History, 1632–1974*. Baltimore: Maryland Historical Society, 1974.

Ward, Geoffrey. *Baseball: An Illustrated History*. New York: Alfred A. Knopf, 1994.

Warner, Henry Edward. *The Making of a Newspaper: A Description of the Baltimore Sun Building*. Baltimore: A. S. Abell, 1924.

White, Gerald T. *The United States and the Problem of Recovery after 1893*. University of Alabama Press, 1982.

Williams, Harold A. *Baltimore Afire*. Baltimore: Schneidereith & Sons, 1979 (1954).

————. *The Baltimore Sun, 1837–1987*. Baltimore: Johns Hopkins University Press, 1987.

Williams, W. H. A. *H.L. Mencken Revisited*. Boston: Twayne Publishers, 1998.

Wilson, Edmund, *The Shores of Light: A Literary Chronicle of the 1920s and 1930s*. New York: Farrar, Straus & Giroux, 1975.

———. *The Twenties: From Notebooks and Diaries of the Period.* Edited with introduction by Leon Edel. New York: Farrar, Straus & Giroux, 1975.

———, ed. *The Shock of Recognition: The Development of Literature in the United States Recorded by the Men Who Made It.* New York: Farrar, Straus & Giroux, 1955.

Winchester, Paul, and Frank D. Webb. *Newspapers and Newspaper Men of Maryland.* Baltimore: Frank I. Sibley, 1905.

Winfield, Betty Houchin. *FDR and the News Media.* Chicago: University of Chicago Press, 1990.

Witcover, Jules. *Sabotage at Black Tom: Imperial Germany's Secret War in America, 1914–1917.* Chapel Hill: Algonquin Books, 1989.

Yates, Dean K. *Forged by Fire: Maryland's National Guard at the Great Baltimore Fire of 1904.* Westminster, Md.: Family Line Publications, 1992.

Yates, Norris W. *The American Humorist: Conscience of the Twentieth Century.* New York: Citadel Press, 1965.

Zelizer, Barbara. *Remembering to Forget: Holocaust Memory Through the Camera's Eye.* Chicago: University of Chicago Press, 1998.

Ziff, Larzer. *The American 1890s: Life and Times of a Lost Generation.* New York: Viking Press, 1966.

Ziporyn, Terra. *Disease in the American Popular Press: The Case of Diphtheria, Typhoid Fever and Syphilis, 1870–1920.* New York: Greenwood Press, 1988.

Magazines and Journals

Amateur Book Collector – American Heritage – American Mercury – American Monthly Review of Reviews – American Scholar – American Spectator – Armchair Detective – Atlantic – Baltimore City Paper – Baltimore Engineer – Baltimore History Review – Baltimore Magazine – Baltimore Sun Magazine – Bang – Bookman – Bulletin of the New York Public Library – Century – Cigar Aficionado – College Humor – Collier's – Commentary – Continuity: A Journal of History – Crisis – Criterion – Delineator – Editor & Publisher – English Review – Esquire – Films in Review – Firehouse Magazine – Gardens, Houses and People – Ellen Glasgow Newsletter – Goucher Alumnae Quarterly – Haldeman-Julius Monthly – Harper's Bazaar – Harper's Weekly – Jewish Criterion – Jewish Times – Journal of American History – Journal of Electrical Workers – Journalism Quarterly – Journalistic Monographs – Liberty Magazine – Life – Look – Manhattan Magazine – Maryland Historical Magazine – Maryland Humanities – Menckeniana – Metropolitan Magazine – M'lle New York – Montana Journalism Review – Movieland – Musical America – Nation – New England Journal of Medicine – Newsweek – New Republic – New York Herald Tribune Magazine – New York Times Magazine – New York Sun Digest – New Yorker – North American Review – Optimist – Outlook – PM Magazine – Papers of the Bibliographic Society of America – Parisienne – Photographic Journal – Photoplay – Picture Magazine – Political Science Quarterly – Printer's Ink – Reader's Digest – Real America – Rhetoric, Mass Media and the Law – Saturday Evening Post – Saturday Review of Literature – Saucy Stories – Science – Scientific American – Scribner's Magazine – Smart Set – Time – Town and Country – Yale Review – Yale University Library Gazette – Westminster Review – Vanity Fair

Newspapers

Albany Knick-Knocks – Der Arbeiter (Berlin) – Atlanta Constitution – Atlanta Journal – Atlanta Life – Austin Herald – Baltimore Afro-American – Baltimore American – Baltimore City Paper – Baltimore Evening Herald – Baltimore Evening Sun – Baltimore Morning Herald – Baltimore News – Baltimore Sun – Baltimore Sunday Sun – Berliner Tageblatt – Boston

Evening Globe – Boston Globe – Boston Herald – Boston News-Post – Boston Telegram – Boston Transcript – Boston Traveler – Bridgeport Star – Brooklyn Eagle – Buffalo News – Capetown Cape Logic – Cecil Whig – Chestertown Enterprise – Chattanooga Daily Times – Chattanooga News – Chicago Herald Examiner – Chicago Tribune – Christian Index – Cincinnati Post – Colorado Bulletin – Columbia Record – Columbus State Journal – Courier Free Press – Critic – Crisis – Cumberland News – Delaware Press News – Des Moines Tribune – Democratic Messenger – Deutsche Amerikaner – Detroit Free Press – Elgin Courier News – Fitchburg Sentinel – Fort Dodge Messenger – Gastonia Gazette – Harvard Crimson – Hollywood Citizen News – Jefferson City Staff-News – Jewish Criterion – Jewish Times – Kansas City Times – Knoxville Journal – Knoxville Sentinel – Das Literarische Echo (Berlin) – Lexington Herald – London Daily Express – London Daily Mail – London Evening Standard – London Independent – London New Witness – London News Chronicle – London Spectator – London Sunday Express – London Telegraph – London Times – London Weekly – Long Island Press – Los Angeles Examiner – Los Angeles Herald Express – Los Angeles Times – Macon City Messenger – Macon Telegraph – Manchester Guardian – Massachusetts Transcript – Milwaukee Journal – Milwaukee Leader – Montgomery Advertiser – Montreal Gazette – Nashville Banner – Nashville Citizen – Die Neau Zeit – New Bedford Times – New Britain Editor – New Haven Ledger – New Leader – New Orleans Item Tribune – New Orleans Morning Tribune – New Orleans Times Picayune – Newport News – New York Evening Journal – New York Evening Mail-Herald – New York Evening Post – New York Evening Sun – New York Evening World – New York Herald Tribune – New York Journal American – New York Leader Republican – New York Post – New York Post Home News – New York Telegram – New York Telegraph – New York Times – New York World – Norfolk Pilot – Ohio Inquirer – Oklahoma City News – Oklahoma City Times – Omaha World Herald – Oregon Gazette Times – Paterson News – Peoria Journal – Philadelphia Inquirer – Philadelphia North American – Philadelphia Record – Philadelphia Sentinel – Pittsburgh Courier – El Prevenir (Cartagena, Columbia) – Providence Bulletin – Racine News – Salinas Index – Salisbury Times – Salt Lake City Telegram – San Francisco Bulletin – San Francisco Chronicle – San Francisco Examiner – Shreveport Times – South Manchester Herald – Springfield Republican – Springfield Union – St. Louis Labor – Sydney Triad – Tampa Tribune – Teller – Toledo Times – Topeka State Journal – Trenton Times – El Universal (Caracas, Venezuela) – La Voz de Galicia (Spain) – Washington Herald – Washington Post – Washington Times – Washington Star – Watford City Farmer – Westminster Times – Wichita Falls Record-News – Wilmington Star – Worcester Democrat

INDEX